The Reception of Aristotle's *Poetics* in the Italian Renaissance and Beyond

Bloomsbury Studies in the Aristotelian Tradition

General Editor:
Marco Sgarbi, Università Ca' Foscari, Italy

Editorial Board:
Klaus Corcilius *(University of California, Berkeley, USA)*; Daniel Garber *(Princeton University, USA)*; Oliver Leaman *(University of Kentucky, USA)*; Anna Marmodoro *(University of Oxford, UK)*; Craig Martin *(Oakland University, USA)*; Carlo Natali *(Università Ca' Foscari, Italy)*; Riccardo Pozzo *(Consiglio Nazionale delle Ricerche, Rome, Italy)*; Renée Raphael *(University of California, Irvine, USA)*; Victor M. Salas *(Sacred Heart Major Seminary, USA)*; Leen Spruit *(Radboud University Nijmegen, The Netherlands)*.
Aristotle's influence throughout the history of philosophical thought has been immense and in recent years the study of Aristotelian philosophy has enjoyed a revival. However, Aristotelianism remains an incredibly polysemous concept, encapsulating many, often conflicting, definitions. *Bloomsbury Studies in the Aristotelian Tradition* responds to this need to define Aristotelianism and give rise to a clear characterization.
Investigating the influence and reception of Aristotle's thought from classical antiquity to contemporary philosophy from a wide range of perspectives, this series aims to reconstruct how philosophers have become acquainted with the tradition. The books in this series go beyond simply ascertaining that there are Aristotelian doctrines within the works of various thinkers in the history of philosophy, but seek to understand how they have received and elaborated Aristotle's thought, developing concepts into ideas that have become independent of him.
Bloomsbury Studies in the Aristotelian Tradition promotes new approaches to Aristotelian philosophy and its history. Giving special attention to the use of interdisciplinary methods and insights, books in this series will appeal to scholars working in the fields of philosophy, history and cultural studies.

Available Titles:
Elijah Del Medigo and Paduan Aristotelianism, Michael Engel
Phantasia in Aristotle's Ethics, edited by Jakob Leth Fink
Pontano's Virtues, Matthias Roick
The Aftermath of Syllogism, edited by Marco Sgarbi, Matteo Cosci
A Political Philosophy of Conservatism, by Ferenc Hörcher

The Reception of Aristotle's *Poetics* in the Italian Renaissance and Beyond

New Directions in Criticism

Edited by Bryan Brazeau

BLOOMSBURY ACADEMIC
LONDON • NEW YORK • OXFORD • NEW DELHI • SYDNEY

BLOOMSBURY ACADEMIC
Bloomsbury Publishing Plc
50 Bedford Square, London, WC1B 3DP, UK
1385 Broadway, New York, NY 10018, USA
29 Earlsfort Terrace, Dublin 2, Ireland

BLOOMSBURY, BLOOMSBURY ACADEMIC and the Diana logo are trademarks
of Bloomsbury Publishing Plc

First published in Great Britain 2020
This paperback edition published in 2021

Copyright © Bryan Brazeau and Contributors, 2020

Bryan Brazeau has asserted his right under the Copyright, Designs and Patents Act, 1988,
to be identified as Editor of this work.

For legal purposes the Acknowledgements on p. xi constitute an extension
of this copyright page.

Cover image: *Montaigne and Tasso*, 1821, by Fleury Francois Richard (1777-1852)
© DEA PICTURE LIBRARY / Getty Images

All rights reserved. No part of this publication may be reproduced or transmitted
in any form or by any means, electronic or mechanical, including photocopying,
recording, or any information storage or retrieval system, without prior permission
in writing from the publishers.

Bloomsbury Publishing Plc does not have any control over, or responsibility for, any
third-party websites referred to or in this book. All internet addresses given in this
book were correct at the time of going to press. The author and publisher regret any
inconvenience caused if addresses have changed or sites have ceased to exist, but can
accept no responsibility for any such changes.

A catalogue record for this book is available from the British Library.

A catalog record for this book is available from the Library of Congress.

ISBN: HB: 978-1-3500-7893-2
PB: 978-1-3502-5143-4
ePDF: 978-1-3500-7894-9
eBook: 978-1-3500-7895-6

Series: Bloomsbury Studies in the Aristotelian Tradition

Typeset by Deanta Global Publishing Services, Chennai, India

To find out more about our authors and books visit www.bloomsbury.com
and sign up for our newsletters.

Contents

List of figures — vii
List of contributors — viii
Acknowledgements — xi

1 Introduction
   Bryan Brazeau — 1

Part I Mapping the field and retracing boundaries

2 A scholar-collector in mid-century Chicago: The books of Bernard Weinberg
   Eufemia Baldassarre, Paul F. Gehl and Lia Markey — 19

3 Sound Aristotelians and how they read
   Micha Lazarus — 38

4 Inventing a Renaissance: Modernity, allegory and the history of literary theory
   Vladimir Brljak — 60

Part II Case studies: Critical quarrels and readings

5 Shedding light on the readings of Aristotle's *Poetics* developed within the Alterati of Florence (1569–*c.* 1630): From manuscript studies to the social and political history of aesthetics
   Déborah Blocker — 97

6 Quarrelling over Dante: Revisiting Weinberg on the first phase of the quarrel and on Sperone Speroni's second *Discorso sopra Dante*
   Simon Gilson — 133

7 Poetics in practice: How Orazio Lombardelli read his Homer
   Sarah Van der Laan — 157

Part III New theoretical frontiers

8 Epic (in)hospitality: The case of Tasso
   Jane Tylus — 181

9 Soul to squeeze: Emotional history and early modern readings of
   Aristotle's *Poetics*
   Bryan Brazeau 201
10 Critical *imitatio*: Renaissance literary theory and its postmodern avatars
   Ayesha Ramachandran 227

Appendix
   Early modern books in the library of Bernard Weinberg
   Eufemia Baldassarre, Paul Gehl and Lia Markey 251

Index 287

Figures

2.1	Bernard Weinberg in his office, *c.* 1970, Courtesy Special Collections Research Center, University of Chicago Library	20
2.2	Examples of bookplates and accession numbers in Weinberg's books, Courtesy Special Collections Research Center, University of Chicago Library and the Newberry Library	24
2.3	Letter from Bernard Weinberg to John Tedeschi, dated 22 September 1969, Courtesy the Newberry Library	33
3.1	Cambridge, Trinity College, Wren Library, Adv.c.17.3, p. 95	49
5.1	*Aristotelis Poetica Petro Victorio Interprete*, ed. by G.-B. Strozzi, Florence, Giunti, 1617, title page, BNCF Magl. 5.9.119	99
5.2	*Aristotelis Stagiritae Poetica Petro Victorio Interpetre* [*sic*], collectively annotated manuscript, Florence, 1573–1617, BNCF Magl. VII, 1199, fols. 1^{ver}-2^{rec}	102
5.3	*Aristotelis Stagiritae Poetica Petro Victorio Interpetre*, BNCF Magl. VII, 1199, fols. 2^{ver}-3^{rec}	103
5.4	*Aristotelis Stagiritae Poetica Petro Victorio Interpetre*, BNCF Magl. VII, 1199, title page	104
5.5	*Aristotelis Stagiritae Poetica Petro Victorio Interpetre*, BNCF Magl. VII, 1199, fol. 6^{ver}, on which the hand at the top of the page is that of F. Sassetti, while the hand directly below it is that of G.-B. Strozzi	108
5.6	*Aristotelis Stagiritae Poetica Petro Victorio Interpetre*, BNCF Magl. VII, 1199, fol. 80^{rec}	110
8.1	*Landscape with Erminia in Discourse with the Old Man and his Sons* (oil on canvas), Claude Lorrain (Claude Gellée) (1600–82) / By kind permission of the Earl of Leicester and the Trustees of the Holkham Estate / Bridgeman Images	182

Contributors

Eufemia Baldassarre is a graduate student of Italian in the Department of Romance Languages and Literatures at the University of Chicago. She is a native of Italy, where she received a BA in Foreign Languages and Literatures and an MA in Translation from the University of Turin. In 2016, she received an MA in Italian Language and Literature at the University of Pittsburgh. Her interests focus on Renaissance studies including questions of patronage, the epistolary genre and the importance of space in the construction of early modern identities.

Paul F. Gehl is Curator Emeritus at the Newberry Library in Chicago. He is an historian of education and printing, with a particular interest in early modern Italy. His *Humanism for Sale: Making and Marketing Books in Italy 1450-1650* is an online publication: http://www.humanismforsale.org/text.

Lia Markey is Director of the Center for Renaissance Studies at the Newberry Library in Chicago. She is the author of *Imagining the Americas in Medici Florence* and the co-editor of the forthcoming *Italy and the New World, 1492–1750*. She specializes in artistic and cultural exchange between Italy and the Americas, Medici patronage, prints and drawings and the history of collecting. Markey has held fellowships at Kunsthistorisches Institut in Florence, the Folger Library, the Warburg Institute, Harvard's Villa I Tatti and the Metropolitan Museum of Art, and she has taught at Princeton University and the University of Pennsylvania.

Micha Lazarus is a research fellow at Trinity College, Cambridge, where he works on the reception of classical poetics in Renaissance England. He was educated at Oxford, the Hebrew University and UC Berkeley. He is writing a book for OUP entitled *Aristotle's Poetics in Renaissance England*. Since 2016, he has co-piloted a project entitled *Poetics before Modernity: Literary Theory in the West from Antiquity to 1700*, which has so far produced a seminar series (2016–17), a collected volume (under consideration) and an early career conference (December 2017). He has also written on Greek learning and literacy in the sixteenth century; the reception of Longinus, Philip Sidney and Aldus Manutius; and the literary history of Centaurs.

Vladimir Brljak is Assistant Professor in Early Modern Literature in the Department of English Studies at Durham University. He works mainly on English literary and intellectual history, 1500–1700, with wider interests in the history of poetics and hermeneutics in the Western tradition. His current projects include *The Allegorical Heresy*, a monograph consolidating his doctoral and postdoctoral research on allegory in sixteenth- and seventeenth-century English literature and poetics, as well as several edited and co-edited collections. Together with Micha Lazarus, he convenes *Poetics before Modernity*, a collaborative cross-disciplinary project aimed at rethinking the history of early European literary theory.

Déborah Blocker is Professor of French at UC Berkeley, and affiliated faculty in Italian Studies. She studies the social and political history of early modern aesthetics. Her first book (*Instituer un 'art': politiques du théâtre dans la France du premier XVIIe siècle*, 2009) examined the processes through which early modern French theatre was institutionalized into an art. From 2008 to 2016, she researched the understandings of art developed in Medici Florence, through a micro-historical study of the Accademia degli Alterati (1569-*c*. 1625). In 2010–11, her archival work was supported by a Florence J. Gould Fellowship at the Villa I Tatti, Florence. Her second book, *Le Principe de plaisir: savoirs, esthétique et politique dans la Florence des Médicis (XVIe-XVIIe siècles)*, will be published in 2020 with Les Belles-Lettres in Paris.

Simon Gilson is Agnelli-Serena Professor of Italian at the University of Oxford and Fellow of Magdalen College. He is the author of *Dante and Renaissance Florence* (Cambridge: Cambridge University Press, 2005) and *Reading Dante in Renaissance Italy: Florence, Venice and the 'Divine Poet'* (Cambridge: Cambridge University Press, 2018).

Sarah Van der Laan is Associate Professor of Comparative Literature at Indiana University. Her first book, *The Choice of Odysseus: Homeric Ethics in Renaissance Epic* (forthcoming), explores the creative reception of Homer's *Odyssey* in Renaissance epic and opera from Petrarch to Milton. She has published articles on Renaissance epic and Homeric reception, and in journals including *PMLA*, *The Seventeenth Century*, *MLN* and *Milton Studies*. Her current projects include books on the emergence of epic as a space for cross-confessional dialogue in the sixteenth and seventeenth centuries, and on the transformation of Ovidian lament into an active form of female heroism in Renaissance epic, lyric, madrigal and opera.

Jane Tylus is Andrew Downey Orrick Professor of Italian and Comparative Literature at Yale University. She previously taught at NYU in Italian Studies and Comparative Literature. Her recent books include *Siena, City of Secrets* (Chicago, 2015); *Early Modern Cultures of Translation* (co-edited with Karen Newman; Philadelphia, 2015); and translations of the complete poetry of Gaspara Stampa and Lucrezia Tornabuoni de'Medici. She has been General Editor for the journal *I Tatti Studies in the Italian Renaissance* since 2013, and currently sits on the advisory committee for *PMLA*.

Bryan Brazeau is Senior Teaching Fellow in Liberal Arts in the School for Cross-Faculty Studies at the University of Warwick. His work focuses on early modern Italian and Neo-Latin epic and poetics. He has published on Dante, Torquato Tasso, Jacopo Sannazaro, the first English translation of Ariosto's *Orlando Furioso*, on the early modern reception of Aristotle's concept of *hamartia*, and on the Italian surrealist artist

Giorgio de Chirico in edited collections and in journals such as *The Italianist*, *MLN*, *History of European Ideas* and *Renaissance and Reformation*. He is currently working on his first monograph, which focuses on Torquato Tasso and Christian Epic.

Ayesha Ramachandran is Associate Professor of Comparative Literature and an affiliate of the Programs in Renaissance Studies and the History of Science and Medicine. Her prizewinning first book, *The Worldmakers* (University of Chicago Press, 2015), provides a cultural and intellectual history of 'the world', showing how it emerged as a cultural keyword in early modernity. She has also published on Spenser, Lucretius, Tasso, Petrarch, Montaigne, on postcolonial drama, and on the histories of religious fundamentalism and cosmopolitanism in various journals and volumes including *NLH*, *Spenser Studies*, *MLN*, *Forum Italicum* and *Anglistik*. Her new book manuscript in progress is tentatively entitled *Lyric Thinking*.

Acknowledgements

Research leading to this publication was funded by the European Research Council under the European Union's Seventh Framework Programme (FP/2007–2013)/ERC Starting Grant 2013 – 335949 ('Aristotle in the Italian Vernacular: Rethinking Renaissance and Early-Modern Intellectual History' PI: Marco Sgarbi). Additional support was provided by the University of Warwick's Humanities Research Centre (Transatlantic Fellowship), Warwick's Humanities Research Fund, the Warwick Centre for the Study of the Renaissance, the Bibliographical Society and the Newberry Library in Chicago. Special thanks are due to David Lines, Simon Gilson, Marco Sgarbi, Ingrid De Smet, Daniel Javitch, Jane Tylus, and Lia Markey who encouraged and supported this venture throughout. For image permissions, I am grateful to the Special Collections Research Centre at the University of Chicago Library, to the Newberry Library, to the Biblioteca Nazionale Centrale in Florence, to the Earl of Leicester and the Trustees of the Holkham Estate, to Bridgeman Images, and to the Master and Fellows of Trinity College, Cambridge. Finally, this publication would not have been possible without the continued support of Becky Holland, Helen Saunders, Jade Grogan, Sophie Campbell, and Andrew Wardell at Bloomsbury, and the diligent work of Leela Ulaganathan at Deanta Global.

Introduction

Bryan Brazeau

A crucial feature of intellectual culture in early modern Italy was the reception of classical texts of literary criticism such as Horace's *Ars Poetica*, Longinus' *On the Sublime* and, most importantly, Aristotle's *Poetics*. The *Poetics* quickly became a central text for literary criticism in the period after its translations into Latin by Alessandro de' Pazzi in 1536 and into the vernacular by Bernardo Segni in 1549, along with the publication of the first large commentary by Francesco Robortello in 1548.[1] These works – along with many other translations, commentaries and treatises – provided poets with precepts for their compositions, ideas of genre and a means to justify literary experimentation.[2] Many of the interpretive debates and quarrels surrounding these texts occurred on the printed page in various translations, commentaries, polemic treatises, and published lectures.[3] Yet, a significant challenge is posed to scholarship by the diverse heterogeneity of these texts; by their frequent syncretism in combining Aristotelian, Neoplatonic and Horatian positions; and by their combination of rhetorical, literary critical, ethical, and political thought. These texts also often engaged with contemporary cultural developments such as the Protestant Reformation and the Catholic Counter-Reformation, along with responding to the emergence of experimental literary forms such as the publication of Ludovico Ariosto's *Orlando Furioso*, Sperone Speroni's *Canace* or Battista Guarini's *Pastor Fido*. To attempt to

---

[1] Alessandro Pazzi de' Medici, *Aristotelis Poetica, per Alexandrum Paccium ... in latinum conuersa* (Venice: in aedibus haeredum Aldi, et Andrae Asulani soceri, 1536); Bernardo Segni, *Rettorica e Poetica d'Aristotile tradotte di greco in lingua vulgare fiorentina* (Florence: Lorenzo Torrentino, 1549); Francesco Robortello, *In librum Aristotelis de arte poetica explicationes* (1548; repr., Munich: Wilhelm Fink Verlag, 1968). On Segni's translation, see Simone Bionda, 'Un "traduttor dei traduttori"? Bernardo Segni dalla *Retorica* alla *Poetica*', in *Aristotele fatto volgare: tradizione aristotelica e cultura volgare nel Rinascimento*, ed. David A. Lines and Eugenio Refini (Pisa: Edizioni ETS, 2014), 77–97; and idem., 'La *Poetica* di Aristotele volgarizzata: Bernardo Segni e le sue fonti', *Aevum* 75, no. 3 (2001): 679–94. For a rich reappraisal of Robortello's perspective on the *Poetics* that challenges the reductive simplifications of earlier accounts and contextualizes the *Explicationes* within his broader intellectual career, see Marco Sgarbi's chapter on 'Poetics', in *Francesco Robortello (1516-1567): Architectural Genius of the Humanities* (Abingdon: Routledge, 2019).
[2] See Daniel Javitch, 'The Emergence of Poetic Genre Theory in the Sixteenth Century', *Modern Language Quarterly* 59, no. 2 (1998): 139–69.
[3] For a succinct and clear summary of the reception of the *Poetics* and surrounding debates, see Daniel Javitch, 'The Assimilation of Aristotle's *Poetics* in Sixteenth-Century Italy', in *The Cambridge History of Literary Criticism: Volume 3, The Renaissance*, ed. Glyn P. Norton (Cambridge: Cambridge University Press, 1999), 53–65. On the passage from commentaries on the *Poetics* to new arts of poetry in their own right between 1500 and 1640, see Enrica Zanin, 'Les commentaires modernes de la *Poétique* d'Aristote', *Études littéraires* 43, no. 2 (2012): 55–83.

explore these texts is to enter into a knotty and complex intellectual forest with forking pathways, occasional clearings, surprising encounters and frequent dead ends.

Bernard Weinberg's seminal two-volume *A History of Literary Criticism in the Italian Renaissance* (1961), along with his four-volume *Trattati di poetica e retorica del Cinquecento* (1970–74) cleared a now well-worn path through these materials, consolidating and circumscribing the study of poetics in early modern Italy.[4] As Weinberg noted in the preface to *A History*, his ambitious and monumental project was nothing short of rewriting the history of literary criticism in the Italian Renaissance in order to revise earlier accounts by Ciro Trabalza (1915) and Joel Elias Spingarn (1899). 'Their methods', Weinberg writes, 'were those of the literary historians of an earlier generation [… who] tended rather to summarize texts than to analyse them, rather to disrupt texts (by isolating terms and passages) than to discover their structures, rather to construct chronologies than to write histories'.[5] His approach, instead, would be that of an intellectual historian who would craft a narrative history around the 'main intellectual traditions of the century as they relate to literary criticism'.[6] Weinberg's account traces how Aristotle's *Poetics* came to be 'distorted' through a Horatian lens in order to assimilate the text to a purportedly well-established tradition of rhetorically inflected literary criticism.[7] Indeed, subsequent scholarship on the reception of Aristotle's *Poetics* in early modern Italy has often emphasized how the text was received within particular interpretive frameworks – read within a tradition that considered poetry from a rhetorical perspective influenced primarily by Horace's *Ars Poetica*, but also by Cicero, Quintilian and Aristotle's own *Rhetoric*. Indeed, a number of early Cinquecento literary theorists saw Horace's *Ars Poetica* as a translation and re-appropriation of the *Poetics*.[8] Baxter Hathaway, in *The Age of Criticism*, published one year after Weinberg's *A History*, notes similar tendencies to assimilate and 'distort' Aristotle's text on the part of critics with Platonic and Neoplatonic tendencies, who either wished to make Aristotle's *Poetics* agree with Plato's condemnation of poetry in books II and III of the *Republic* or interpreted Aristotle's assertion in the *Poetics* of a social role for poetry as a direct response to Plato.[9] The rhetorical approach via

---

[4] Bernard Weinberg, *A History of Literary Criticism in the Italian Renaissance*, 2 vols. (Chicago: University of Chicago Press, 1961); idem., *Trattati di poetica e retorica del Cinquecento*, 4 vols. (Bari: Laterza, 1970–74).

[5] Weinberg, *A History of Literary Criticism*, I:vii.

[6] Ibid., I:viii.

[7] Ibid., I:71–249.

[8] Adelheid Conte, 'La rinascita della poetica nel cinquecento Italiano', in *La Poetica di Aristotele e la sua storia: atti della giornata internazionale di studio organizzata dal seminario di greco in memoria di Viviana Cessi (Pavia, 22 Febbraio 2002)*, ed. Diego Lanza and Viviana Cessi (Pisa: ETS, 2002), 45–58, p. 51. Weinberg notes that many of the early treatises on 'Arts of Poetry' in the first half of the cinquecento, such as Marco Girolamo Vida's *De arte poetica* (1527), Gian Giorgio Trissino's *La poetica I-IV* (1529), and Bernardino Daniello's *La poetica* (1536), all demonstrate strong rhetorical and Horatian inflections in their emphases on rhetorical devices and on the poet's role in teaching men to live well (2.715-730). Indeed, the first book of Vida's treatise concerns the training of the poet and models this education on Cicero and Quintilian's advice to the young orator (Weinberg, 2.715).

[9] Hathaway claims that Robortello's approach to the *Poetics* was to effect a reconciliation between Platonic and Aristotelian positions on poetry. See Baxter Hathaway, *The Age of Criticism: The Late Renaissance in Italy* (Ithaca, NY: Cornell University Press, 1962), 214–20.

Horatian criticism led to an increased interest in the poet's audience, not only in terms of poetry's aim as 'dulce et utile' but also in terms of the Ciceronian triad of the aims of the orator to 'delectare, probare, movere'.[10] Such a focus on audience was responsible, in part, for the increasing importance of verisimilitude and of the 'three unities' in Aristotelian-influenced poetic treatises of the period, despite the fact that neither had a strong basis in the original text of the *Poetics*. Neoplatonic discussions of poetry saw the *Poetics* not only as a response to Plato, justifying the role of poetry, but also as a text that confirmed their allegorical interpretations of poetry and its concomitant civic role.[11] In both cases, the *Poetics* was purportedly viewed as a text that confirmed pre-existing ideas about poetry and how it should be composed.

Weinberg and Hathaway's accounts, however, leave out a number of other interpretive and cultural frameworks that equally shaped the reception of the *Poetics* in early modern Italy and Europe. First, the terms of Weinberg's study focus it nearly exclusively on the Cinquecento, with only occasional forays into certain texts from the Quattrocento and nearly no texts after 1600. His account – no doubt indirectly influenced by the views of Italian philosopher Benedetto Croce who negatively associated the cultural production of the Counter-Reformation with the authoritarian environment of Italian fascism – often ignores the impact of the religious culture of the Catholic Counter-Reformation on poetic treatises – with the exception of those 'ultra-Catholic' theorists who imposed the conclusions of the Council of Trent 'which tended to place stringent limitations on the practice and use of poetry'.[12] Yet, as a number of recent studies have demonstrated, the Italian Counter-Reformation was a period that was rich in poetic theorization and a wide diversity of poetic practice, much of which has only been seriously discussed by scholarship over the past two decades.[13] Another key interpretive framework that Weinberg's study does not adequately address is the firmly established tradition of Aristotelian thought both in Latin and in the vernacular. Despite the frequent use of this latter framework by many sixteenth-century critics who explained Aristotle's text by glossing difficult passages in the *Poetics* with other works in the Aristotelian canon, such as the *Politics,* the *Nicomachean Ethics* and *On the Soul*,

---

[10] The citation is from section 49 of Cicero's *Brutus*; cited in Conte, 'La rinascita della poetica', 49.
[11] For an overview of Neoplatonic poetics and their relation to Florentine humanism, see Craig Kallendorf, 'From Virgil to Vida: The Poeta Theologus in Italian Renaissance Commentary', *Journal of the History of Ideas* 56, no. 1 (January 1995): 41–62, doi:10.2307/2710006. For how this approach to poetic theory influenced Angelo Poliziano in the late fifteenth century (one of the first humanists to lecture on Aristotle's *Poetics* in 1480), see Peter Godman, *From Poliziano to Machiavelli: Florentine Humanism in the High Renaissance* (Princeton, NJ: Princeton University Press, 1998), 52–75, and idem., 'Poliziano's Poetics and Literary History', *Interpres* 13 (1993): 110–209.
[12] See, for example, Benedetto Croce, *Storia del'Età Barocca in Italia* (Bari: Laterza, 1957), x; Weinberg, *A History of Literary Criticism*, I:297.
[13] See Virginia Cox, *The Prodigious Muse: Women's Writing in Counter-Reformation Italy* (Baltimore: Johns Hopkins University Press, 2011); Marco Faini, 'La poetica dell'epica sacra tra Cinque e Seicento in Italia', *The Italianist* 35, no. 1 (2015): 27–60; Idem., 'Le "sacrosante muse di Giordano," la riflessione sul poema sacro nella prima metà del Cinquecento', in *Autorità, modelli e antimodelli nella cultura artistica e letteraria tra riforma e controriforma*, ed. Antonio Corsaro, Harald Hendrix and Paolo Procaccioli (Rome: Vecchiarelli Editore, 2007), 243–65. Mario Chiesa, 'Poemi Biblici fra Quattro e Cinquecento', *Giornale storico della letteratura italiana* 179, no. 585 (1° trimestre, 2002): 161–92; Erika Milburn, *Luigi Tansillo and Lyric Poetry in Sixteenth-Century Naples* (Leeds: Modern Humanities Research Association, 2003).

scholarship has neglected to explore in depth how this tradition shaped the reception of the *Poetics*. While the *Poetics* does not seem to have been part of the standard Aristotelian university curriculum prior to 1550, there were notable exceptions, such as Poliziano's 1480 lectures at the University of Florence and Lombardi and Maggi's 1543 lectures in Ferrara.[14] As Paul Grendler has discussed, the *Poetics* only entered the lecture hall in the latter half of the sixteenth century, coinciding with an expansion of the curriculum that also emphasized greater knowledge of ancient Greek, and texts from Latin and Greek orators along with Aristotle's own *Rhetoric*.[15] Complex or confusing passages of the *Poetics* were often glossed over in commentaries with reference to Aristotle's other works, suggesting that the *Poetics* were read not only from a rhetorical perspective but also as a series of precepts for poetic composition that reflected the Stagirite's positions in his other works. Though this practice speaks primarily to the importance of Aristotelian philosophy in early modern intellectual culture and university education, it is worth noting that the medieval Arabic tradition of the *Poetics*, notably exemplified by the commentaries of Avicenna (Ibn-Sīnā) and Averroes (Ibn-Rushd), considered the text as part of the Aristotelian system, often placing it as the first work in the *Organon*.[16]

The use of this interpretive framework as one of the critical lenses through which the *Poetics* were received in sixteenth-century Italy has important implications. Critics such as Torquato Tasso began to refer not only to other Aristotelian texts but also to their commentary traditions – for example, citing Thomas Aquinas's commentary on the *Politics* to explain the applicability of Aristotelian catharsis in epic;[17] others, such as Giason Denores, would attempt to combine Aristotle's ideas on poetry with his discussion of three different kinds of government in the *Politics* – attempting to show which genres were most appropriate for cultivating citizens living under each kind of government.[18] Thus, the set of pre-existing ideas into which the *Poetics* was received in sixteenth-century Italy was not solely limited to rhetorical criticism and Platonic philosophy, it also included a wide-ranging and rich tradition of Aristotelian thought, which was at that very moment being increasingly translated, commented, domesticated and discussed in the vernacular. Such uses of the Aristotelian canon by

---

[14] For an overview of educational curricula in fifteenth- and sixteenth-century Italy, see David A. Lines, *Aristotle's Ethics in the Italian Renaissance (1300-1600): The Universities and the Problem of Moral Education* (Leiden and Boston: Brill, 2002); Paul F. Grendler, *The Universities of the Italian Renaissance* (Baltimore and London: Johns Hopkins University Press, 2002); Robert Black, *Humanism and Education in Medieval and Renaissance Italy: Tradition and Innovation in Latin Schools from the Twelfth to the Fifteenth Century* (Cambridge: Cambridge University Press, 2001).

[15] Grendler, *The Universities of the Italian Renaissance*, 239–41.

[16] Ismail M. Dahiyat, *Avicenna's Commentary on the Poetics of Aristotle: A Critical Study with an Annotated Translation of the Text* (Leiden: Brill, 1974), 61–3. See also Arbogast Schmitt, 'La *Poetica* di Aristotele e la sua reinterpretazione nella teoria poetica del secondo cinquecento', in *La Poetica di Aristotele e la sua storia: atti della giornata internazionale di studio organizzata dal seminario di Greco in memoria di Viviana Cessi (Pavia, 22 febbraio 2002)*, ed. Viviana Cessi and Diego Lanza (Pisa: ETS, 2002), 32–3.

[17] Torquato Tasso, *Giudizio sovra la Gerusalemme da lui medesima riformata*, ed. Claudio Gigante (Rome: Salerno, 2000), 172.

[18] Giason Denores, *Discorso intorno a que' principii, cause et accrescimenti che la comedia, la tragedia et il poema eroico ricevono dalla filosofia morale e civile e da' governatori delle republiche…[1586]*, in *Trattati di poetica e retorica del Cinquecento*, ed. Bernard Weinberg (Bari: Laterza, 1972), 3:373–419.

Tasso and Denores to explain the *Poetics* were not idiosyncratic, but rather emerged from a tradition of similar use by sixteenth-century translators and commentators of the *Poetics*. The diversity and complexity of vernacular Aristotelianism in Renaissance Italy has only recently been explored in significant depth thanks to two research projects: the 2010–13 AHRC-funded 'Vernacular Aristotelianism in Renaissance Italy' at the University of Warwick and the Warburg Institute (led by David Lines, Simon Gilson, and Jill Kraye) and the 2014–19 ERC-funded 'Aristotle in the Italian Vernacular' at the University of Ca' Foscari (PI Marco Sgarbi), with a team at the University of Warwick led by David Lines.[19]

Weinberg's achievement was nothing short of monumental, and it remains foundational for the study of early modern poetics in Italy and beyond. Yet, the imposing breadth and archival depth of his study frequently appears to have sealed off the study of early modern poetics for anglophone scholarship, presenting it as a closed field to which few new observations may be added. While Weinberg certainly did not miss the forest for the trees, the pathways he cleared through these materials have frequently become a substitute for examination of the individual texts themselves, leaving large areas of these materials underexplored. Moreover, Weinberg's work remains a product of its time and was shaped by his activity as a major collector of early modern books. As the chapter and detailed bibliographical appendix by Baldassarre, Gehl and Markey in this volume make clear, *A History* was produced in a particular environment in postwar Chicago where Weinberg drew on existing academic strengths at the University of Chicago and greatly benefitted from the collecting activity of Hans Baron, who was both a research fellow and bibliographer at the Newberry library. At the same time, this work was also a product of the particular ideological assumptions of the Chicago School as the essays by Micha Lazarus and Vladimir Brljak in this volume demonstrate. Thus, in a sense, this volume can be seen to examine two moments in the Aristotelian tradition; the reception of Aristotle's *Poetics* in early modern Italy and the critical examination of this reception by Weinberg and the Neo-Aristotelian Chicago School, who employed Aristotle in order to reply to the ideological assumptions of the New Criticism.

Just as Weinberg deemed it important to revisit standard accounts of the history of literary criticism in the early 1960s, so too do the essays in this volume seek to go *hors-piste* by interrogating, revisiting and opening up Weinberg's account nearly sixty

---

[19] Key publications emerging from these projects are: *Vernacular Aristotelianism in Renaissance Italy*, ed. Luca Bianchi, Simon Gilson and Jill Kraye (London: The Warburg Institute, 2016); David A. Lines, 'Beyond Latin in Renaissance Philosophy: A Plea for New Critical Perspectives', *Intellectual History Review* 25, no. 4 (2015): 373–89; *Venezia e Aristotele (ca. 1450–ca. 1600): greco, latino e italiano / Venice and Aristotle (c. 1450–c. 1600): From Greek and Latin to the Vernacular*, exhibition catalogue (Venice, Sale Monumentali della Biblioteca Nazionale Marciana, 21 April–19 May 2016), ed. Alessio Cotugno and David A. Lines (Venice: Marcianum Press, 2016); *Aristotele fatto volgare: Tradizione aristotelica e cultura volgare nel Rinascimento*, ed. David A. Lines and Eugenio Refini (Pisa: Edizioni ETS, 2014); Marco Sgarbi, 'What Does a Renaissance Aristotelian Look Like? From Petrarch to Galilei', *HOPOS. The Journal of the International Society for the History of Philosophy of Science* 7 (2017): 226–45; *I generi dell'aristotelismo volgare nel Rinascimento*, ed. Marco Sgarbi (Padua: CLEUP, 2018); and *'In Other Words': Translating Philosophy in the Fifteenth and Sixteenth Centuries*, special issue of *Rivista di storia della filosofia*, ed. David A. Lines and Anna Laura Puliafito 74, no.2 (2019).

years after its publication. Rather than writing a new monographic history of literary criticism, the studies collected in this volume aim to open a space for dialogue that will provoke new thoughts on the reception of Aristotle's *Poetics* in sixteenth-century Italy, in mid-twentieth-century Chicago and indeed in our own critical moment. In doing so, they hope to open up new potential pathways for research and to creatively reshape existing horizons of criticism and reception. These essays bring together scholars from a variety of backgrounds on both sides of the Atlantic who have endeavoured to present new perspectives, new sources and new ways of framing the myriad literary-critical materials produced in late Renaissance Italy. These studies are not simply meant to challenge or question Weinberg's invaluable contribution to scholarship, but rather to use his work as that of a foundational interlocutor, placing it for the first time within its own historical context. These works aim to re-open the questions raised in his study, and to return to the early printed books and manuscripts of literary criticism in the period – asking how we might approach these in light of new theoretical developments and fresh critical perspectives in the study of early modern literature, philosophy and culture. As such, the chapters are split into three parts: 'Mapping the field and retracing boundaries', 'Case studies: Critical quarrels and readings' and 'New theoretical frontiers'.

The contributions in this volume function as a coherent and structured sequence that gradually discloses three central arguments that underpin the collection as a whole; first, that a more nuanced understanding of the ways in which the *Poetics* has been read may be gained through a careful study of the work's reception that goes beyond the influential narratives of Weinberg, Butcher and Spingarn. Second, that material culture, intellectual history and literary criticism can be productively combined to generate new insights; indeed, the contributions in this volume gesture towards a more nuanced understanding of material culture that builds on the relationship between books as objects, broader critical frameworks and the interpretive agency of individual readers. This focus on material culture and books as objects returns throughout the contributions in the volume, which demonstrate that such contextualization is not at odds with literary criticism, but rather can engage with criticism in a productive manner that sheds new light not only on the reception of the *Poetics*, or on the commentators, translators and readers of Aristotle's text in early modern Italy, but indeed on our own scholarly methods and assumptions. Thus, the third argument that is gradually unveiled throughout the sequence of these essays is that the ways in which the *Poetics* has been understood not only reveal unique methodological approaches and practices of adaptation but indeed have also been fundamental for the definition of literary trends in modern criticism that continue to influence our current work as scholars and critics.

The chapters in the first part focus on a re-evaluation of Weinberg's contribution, its ideological assumptions and those of twentieth-century studies of early modern literary criticism more broadly. The first chapter in the volume, by Eufemia Baldassarre, Paul Gehl and Lia Markey, provides a rich contextualization of Bernard Weinberg's life and activity, and his role in calling attention to early modern Aristotelian poetics and their continuing value to modern criticism, emphasizing the experimental and pedagogical nature of his approach to literary history. Baldassarre, Gehl and Markey not only provide a clear intellectual biography of Weinberg but also underline his role in the Chicago School of Criticism and, most importantly, his activity as a collector in mid-twentieth-century Chicago with a detailed discussion of his activity as a book collector of primary materials for *A History* and French literary-critical materials; the chapter is complemented by a detailed bibliography – Appendix – which brings together for the first time 684 early modern books in Weinberg's collection that were used to support his teaching and research at the University of Chicago. The chapter underlines how Weinberg's *A History* and four-volume *Trattati di poetica e retorica del Cinquecento* would have been impossible to produce if not for the rich collections that existed in mid-century Chicago and his collegial relationship with Hans Baron at the Newberry Library. The discussion that Baldassarre, Gehl and Markey provide opens the volume with an inspiring start as it demonstrates how Weinberg integrated teaching and research throughout his career, and how he succeeded in publishing a field-defining work that was enhanced by his book collecting.

Micha Lazarus' chapter delves into the critical stakes of how the *Poetics* was read by the Chicago School, examining how their ideological investment in the stability and conceptual unity of Aristotle's meaning in the *Poetics*, on the one hand, led to a 'legitimate point of methodological departure', yet, on the other hand, also crystallized an influential methodological view that framed the 2,000-year fragmented history of the text as a history of error and deviation. While Baldassarre, Gehl and Markey detail the material conditions and bibliographical contexts of Weinberg's analysis, Lazarus contextualizes Weinberg's account as a particular episode in the reception history of the *Poetics*, as a 'synthesis of a particular kind of reading at a particular time'. The essay provides a concise synthesis of the reception history of the *Poetics* and the text's complex relationship with Aristotle's *Rhetoric*, beginning with our oldest manuscript exemplar from the mid-tenth century – which re-emerged after the fall of Constantinople – through to the reception of the text on both sides of the Atlantic in the late nineteenth and twentieth centuries. As Lazarus demonstrates, sententious readings of tragedy as a source from which to draw maxims – a practice that Weinberg and his colleagues in the Chicago School vociferously opposed – are already present in Aristotle's own writing and cannot simply be viewed as a later distortion imposed by his Renaissance commentators. The chapter concludes with engaging reflections on our own critical moment, reminding us that 'criticism and its society must be treated as symbiotic', enjoining us to reflect on the effect that new forms of communication today might have on the fragmentation, commonplacing and even moral readings of literary texts, and the types of criticism that will emerge in future.

Vladimir Brljak builds on the concerns in Lazarus' chapter, asking the broad and difficult question of how we consider the periodization of sixteenth- and seventeenth-century poetics in attempts to pinpoint the moment in which European poetics became 'modern', with values such as 'aesthetic autonomy', 'willing suspension of disbelief' and a hostility towards allegory that many would recognize today. Brljak demonstrates, through careful attention to the history of poetic theory, how Joel Spingarn and George Saintsbury had created and consolidated the canonical conception of 'Renaissance' literary criticism as the origin of poetic modernity, founded with the dissemination of Aristotle's *Poetics*, with its 'progress … measurable in degrees of its supposed hostility to allegory'. This pattern, Brljak demonstrates, is not solely limited to English literary criticism, but would also go on to inform Weinberg's *A History* and the Chicago School. Indeed, Brljak shows how Weinberg's incidental treatment of allegory omits allegorical poetics from a large number of early modern Italian sources and paints a misleading picture whereby allegory was not considered an important poetic position in the period. Weinberg, as Brljak shows, is guided by a Burkhardtian view whereby the Renaissance is seen as the teleological starting point of modernity. As such, the consignment of allegory to a 'medieval' poetics is shown to not only be a misleading representation of the role of allegory in early modern poetics but indeed also replicates the traditional model that aestheticists such as Spingarn and Saintsbury put forward in their own histories. Such a model is also shown to influence later accounts of poetics prior to 1500 and allegorical poetics after 1500. Thus, Brljak underlines how, despite many rich attempts to author a history of Renaissance poetics by scholars from multiple national traditions and across several generations, such a task is a quixotic undertaking 'because of a conceptual impasse at the very heart of that subject'. Our own concepts of periodization and of the Burckhardtian thesis that underlies the Renaissance as the teleological origin point of the modern world are continually confounded by the existing evidence, of which allegory is a chief example. Brljak concludes by asking, like Lazarus, how we might move 'in new directions', considering our own critical moment and the ideological assumptions that lead us to reproduce or challenge existing accounts.

The second part in the volume expands out from Weinberg's history, containing chapters that each focus on an in-depth case study related to sixteenth-century poetics and reading practices. Each of these essays demonstrate how much remains to be studied and reconsidered in the field of early modern Italian poetics, underlining that Weinberg's account – despite its erudition and imposing depth of scholarship – is far from the last word on the matter. Déborah Blocker's chapter considers a particular literary society in late sixteenth- and early seventeenth-century Florence, asking how perspectives from book history and manuscript circulation studies might contribute to the study of how this group read Aristotle's *Poetics*. Blocker's methodological chapter reflects on the work that was needed to contextualize a little-known, collectively annotated manuscript of Aristotle's *Poetics* (dated 1573), which she found by chance in the *sala manoscritti* of the Biblioteca Nazionale di Firenze in the summer of 2008, and which she identifies as a group production of the academy of the Alterati in Florence (1569–*c.* 1630). In this chapter, Blocker reflexively analyses the various research procedures by which she managed to solve a number of the manuscript's most engaging mysteries, the reasons for which she felt compelled to examine such a manuscript, and the epistemological benefits she reaped from doing so. In the course of these considerations, Blocker shows how the history of books and of manuscript circulation can serve as fertile ground for the development of innovative forms of intellectual and more generally cultural history. In particular, she stresses how these book-historical approaches can support the inclusion of social, institutional and political perspectives that traditional histories of ideas and/or literature – often based on modern editions of canonical texts – too often tend to ignore. Thus, Blocker shows how our understanding of the history of the circulation of the *Poetics*, and of the development of early modern aesthetics more generally, could be radically transformed by the inclusion of these social, institutional, and political realities, which the history of the book and of manuscript circulation can help document. The essay is richly complemented by a number of photographs of the manuscript and a careful analysis of the hands therein, providing a helpful field guide for future scholars.

Building on the role of considering such geographical and ideological contexts in literary criticism, Simon Gilson's chapter re-evaluates Weinberg's account of the Dante quarrel in light of recent contributions that demonstrate how the quarrel was not simply about the appreciation of Dante (or lack thereof) but indeed also involved key philosophical and critical issues in the period such as theory of the imagination and the purposes of fiction. Gilson begins by reframing the three authors Weinberg discusses in the 'opening phases of the quarrel' – namely, Pietro Bembo, Bernardino Tomitano and Carlo Lenzoni – placing a new emphasis on their ideological frameworks and institutional/geographical contexts. As he demonstrates, through attention to the regional nature of responses to the quarrel, we can begin to trace an intensive dialogue of creative exchanges between positions held by Florentine and Paduan intellectuals. He then delves into a detailed case study of Sperone Speroni's second *Discoro sopra Dante*, paying careful attention to the argumentative and interpretive strategies used by Speroni. Gilson shows how this work is a major critical contribution to the Dante quarrel that has been undervalued due to Weinberg's emphasis on the rediscovery of Aristotle's *Poetics* and concomitant devaluation of other modes of criticism. The key contribution of Speroni's second *Discorso*, Gilson demonstrates, lies in its ability to step aside from the intricate arguments within the Dante quarrel and to evaluate Dante's poem on its own merits, with a particular emphasis on language, narrative strategy and characterization. This case study demonstrates how a new evaluation of such texts can lead us to reconsider them on their own terms, placing new emphasis on their originality, critical acumen, and institutional contexts.

Sarah Van der Laan's chapter builds on the theme of how sixteenth-century reading practices influenced poetic thought. As she notes, major studies of Renaissance poetics – such as Weinberg's – do not take into account how early modern readers read and engaged with their texts, and rarely discuss the role of annotations. New perspectives from the history of reading as a discipline can offer insight allowing us to combine the history of poetics with the history of reading. Van der Laan provides an engaging case study that examines how the Sienese academician, Orazio Lombardelli, read and engaged with Homer's *Odyssey* based on a particular 1549 translation held in the British Library with copious annotations. Such reading practices, she demonstrates, have profound implications on Lombardelli's poetic judgements in theory and in practice – particularly his reliance upon the *Odyssey* to make sense of Torquato Tasso's *Gerusalemme liberata*. This reconstruction also provides invaluable insight into the climate of reading in which Tasso constructed his revisions of Homer, revealing that a range of different reading practices could coexist in close proximity in a single reader's encounters with the *Odyssey*. As such, the chapter suggests how we might use marginalia and sets of reader annotations to glean particular theoretical positions that are not expressed elsewhere in a poetic treatise or commentary. Ultimately, this contribution indicates a new path for scholarship on sixteenth-century poetics, suggesting how we might read poetic theory not only through larger institutional or geographical contexts but indeed also through intimate textual and bibliographical micro-contexts.

The final part in the volume explores ways in which contemporary theoretical positions may be placed in productive dialogue with Renaissance poetics. Jane Tylus' chapter focuses on Torquato Tasso, continuing many of the themes raised in Van der Laan's contribution, and further developing Gilson's call for a renewed focus on literary style. Combining aspects of contemporary translation theory with the study of early modern poetics and rhetoric, Tylus engages with questions about one of the most important transitions of the Renaissance: the emergence of Europe's vernaculars. She shows how Tasso represented an interesting counter-example to attempts in the period to define this vernacular, challenging norms that sought to canonize Tuscan as Italy's official language. Tasso, an itinerant and pilgrim himself, sought a home for what he would call his 'foreign' or pilgrim style, embedding within his poem foreign and exotic words – Latinisms, dialect, neologisms – thereby asking readers of his radically new Christian epic to ensure both for his pilgrim characters and his pilgrim words the hospitality associated with actual 'Christian' pilgrims on earth. As such, Tylus' chapter proposes a new aesthetic of *pellegrinità* in Tasso's style and in his creation of a new literary form that calls attention to its own foreignness, and thus a unique sense of the marvellous. In other words, Tylus asks, how does Tasso create a meaningful relationship between the offer of *ospitalità* to the pilgrim and the force of novelty inherent in the presence of the stranger himself? Tylus' chapter thus proposes an interdisciplinary method for integrating translation theory, stylistic criticism and rhetorical analysis in the study of Tasso's poetic theory and practice from the *Gerusalemme Liberata* to the revised *Gerusalemme Conquistata*.

Following on in the vein of combining literary criticism with other methodologies, my chapter interrogates possible intersections between the history of emotions and early modern literary criticism. Using notions such as 'emotional community' and 'emotives', the chapter explores the kinds of readings that emerge if we read early modern poetic theory not simply as an abstract debate, but rather as an attempt to describe contemporary reactions to new genres, texts and performances. Rather than assuming that such texts were imposing a prescriptivist methodology on poetic production, my chapter asks whether the new emphasis on psychology and spectator reactions in the poetic theories of Lodovico Castelvetro, Torquato Tasso and Giason Denores might be read as symptomatic of a broader shift in emotional norms during the period. In order to approach Castelvetro, however, I examine why such an author has frequently been ignored and cast aside in anglophone scholarship, finding that Weinberg's analysis of Castelvetro's poetics continues to cast a large shadow on reception. Building on Tylus' discussion of meraviglia in Tasso's writings, my chapter calls attention to the links between Tasso's conception of the marvellous and Castelvetro's use of the same concept as part of his theory of oblique pleasure. Ultimately, my chapter seeks to create a dialogue between depictions of the emotions in poetic theory and the conceptual tools used by historians of the emotions, indicating potential new avenues for future research.

Finally, Ayesha Ramachandran closes the volume with an chapter that draws on many themes throughout the collection: such as the heterogeneity of Renaissance literary criticism, the continued presence of multifaceted allegorical poetics, and an exhortation to move beyond the frequent and reductive characterizations of Renaissance literary criticism as simply Neo-Aristotelian. Instead, Ramachandran argues, we ought to consider the continuing significance of such criticism as a still-relevant repository of theoretical methods and conceptual experiments that resonate with contemporary critical concerns. Moving beyond traditional classifications that tend to group early modern critical exegeses according to their classical philosophical or rhetorical frameworks, Ramachandran asks what points of contact we can discern between twenty-first-century literary-critical trends and the intellectual foci of Renaissance literary critics. Rather than embrace the Burckhardtian thesis that Brljak shows is often at the heart of histories of literary criticism such as those of Spingarn and Weinberg, Ramachandran carves a pathway for transhistorical dialogue: reading Renaissance commentators as they read their classical predecessors in order to make sense of contemporary concerns and to help shape future debates. She focuses on a number of key areas, showing, for example, how the origins of the contemporary debate between New Historicists and New Formalists may be found throughout Renaissance criticism, with its twin focus on rhetoric and poetics, along with historical difference, thus building on calls for a renewed stylistic criticism found in Lazarus', Gilson's and Tylus' chapters. A return to such humanist criticism, she argues, 'is thus an invitation to write a revisionist history of criticism: one that imagines the claims of form and history as profoundly interlinked'. More broadly, Ramachandran's claim that literary criticism might offer the intellectual tools to make sense of a shifting world, both in the Renaissance and today, emphasizes how engagement with such texts involves the participation in a 'new literary humanism' that opens up critical conversations across various times and places. Just as early modern critics used Aristotle's *Poetics* and other classical literary-critical texts to explore and develop solutions that met their own needs – what Daniel Javitch refers to as a 'progressive classicism' – so, too, does Ramachandran's chapter, and indeed all of the chapters in this volume, invite us to think about how we might use early modern literary critics as key interlocutors to speak to our own critical moment and to address contemporary theoretical debates.[20]

The series of nine chapters in this volume develops as a sequence whereby the first three (Baldassarre, Gehl and Markey; Lazarus; and Brljak) serve to map out the field by reconstructing the material, cultural and intellectual conditions that led to the production of Weinberg's monumental work. Such contextualization is crucial not only in understanding the debt that scholars in this field owe to Weinberg but also how his influential narrative continues to shape much of the writing on the reception of Aristotle's *Poetics* and early modern literary criticism today. Moreover, these chapters encourage us as scholars and critics to interrogate our own methodologies and assumptions – recognizing that our own work is also shaped by a careful balance between interpretive agency and our material, social and cultural conditions. The following three chapters (Blocker, Gilson, and Van der Laan) move beyond Weinberg's work, challenging, integrating and updating his account with insights from the study of social history, institutional contexts, and reading practices. Finally, the last three

[20] Javitch, 'The Emergence of Poetic Genre Theory', 169.

chapters (Tylus, Brazeau, and Ramachandran) reassess the centrality of Aristotle's *Poetics*, making the work part of a wider system that not only contributes to modern literary criticism through many forms of interpretation but indeed may also be placed in productive dialogue with contemporary theoretical concerns, new methodologies and emerging forms of criticism.

A common thread that emerges in several of the essays in this volume is that the interpretive literary-critical frameworks that obtained in early modern Italy cannot simply be explained with reference to translations, commentaries, and paraphrases of the *Poetics*. The contributions by Gilson, Van der Laan and myself underline the importance of how Dante's *Commedia*, Tasso's *Gerusalemme Liberata*, Homer's *Odyssey*, Sophocles' *Oedipus Rex* and other literary works were debated, annotated, and performed on stage. Attention to these modes of engagement can reveal key insights about the interpretive frameworks with which individuals approached these texts in practice and, in turn, shine a new light on how the *Poetics* were understood. Several essays also highlight the crucial role of manuscript studies and book history for studying how the *Poetics* was read – among the small group of Alterati in early modern Pisa and Florence (Blocker), by S. H. Butcher in late-nineteenth-century Cambridge, Oxford and Edinburgh (Brljak), and by Weinberg in mid-twentieth-century Chicago (Baldassarre, Gehl and Markey). Finally, several chapters underline the ongoing generative nature of Aristotle's *Poetics* for literary theory, stylistic criticism, and contentious scholarly debates – such as the origin of 'literary modernity' (Brljak), sixteenth-century debates around the role of the Italian vernacular and Tasso's defiant development of stylistic *pellegrinità* (Tylus), along with the transhistorical tension between historicist and formalist approaches to literary texts (Ramachandran). It would, of course, be impossible within an edited volume to exhaustively discuss every way in which we might re-evaluate and reconsider the reception of Aristotle's *Poetics*. As such, the methodological variety and the range of different research questions addressed in these chapters demonstrates the broader programmatic aim of this volume: to pave the way for fresh explorations and new ways of looking at the field by going beyond traditional reception narratives and scholarly assumptions. Indeed, if this collection succeeds in revisiting the field while also opening up new pathways of research, it is in virtue of the juxtaposition of different productive approaches contained herein.

The contributions in this volume grow out of a symposium entitled 'Contexts of Early Modern Literary Criticism in Italy and Beyond', which was held at the Newberry Library in Chicago on 9–10 March 2017. The original aim of this gathering was to re-evaluate early modern literary criticism in light of development of book history and manuscript studies as part of the Newberry's Centre for Renaissance Studies' History of the Book seminar series. Yet, it quickly became apparent that book history was only one of many perspectives from which early modern literary-critical texts might be reconsidered. Other recent approaches such as the study of academies in Renaissance Italy; the social, political and economic dynamics of early modern literary debates; the history of emotions; translation theory; genre theory; and questions of transnational and global approaches also suggested themselves as relevant to the study of early modern Italian literary criticism. As such, this volume also aims to create productive dialogue between disciplines and traditions of scholarship. It is hoped that these future avenues of analysis will not only occur on the printed page and at academic conferences but indeed also in the archives, the lecture hall and the seminar classroom, bringing in not only other researchers as interlocutors but also passionate archivists, bibliographers and students at all levels as we seek to explore what early modern literary criticism and Aristotle's *Poetics* in particular means to us today. As a caveat before we begin this conversation, we might echo Weinberg's own methodological call *ad fontes* for his readers at the end of the first section on *Poetic Theory* in his history:

> All such efforts at summary and generalization are helpful only to the extent to which one also reads the texts – many of the texts, most of the texts, all of the texts. It is only the reading of the texts that gives – and this is true for any intellectual endeavour – the properly rewarding insights into literary theory in the Italian Renaissance.[21]

Bibliography

Bianchi, Luca, Simon Gilson and Jill Kraye, eds. *Vernacular Aristotelianism in Renaissance Italy*. London: The Warburg Institute, 2016.

Bionda, Simone. 'La *Poetica* di Aristotele volgarizzata: Bernardo Segni e le sue fonti'. *Aevum* 75, no. 3 (2001): 679–94.

Bionda, Simone. 'Un "traduttor dei traduttori"? Bernardo Segni dalla *Retorica* alla *Poetica*'. In *Aristotele fatto volgare: tradizione aristotelica e cultura volgare nel Rinascimento*, edited by David A. Lines and Eugenio Refini, 77–97. Pisa: Edizioni ETS, 2014.

Black, Robert. *Humanism and Education in Medieval and Renaissance Italy: Tradition and Innovation in Latin Schools from the Twelfth to the Fifteenth Century*. Cambridge: Cambridge University Press, 2001.

Chiesa, Mario. 'Poemi Biblici fra Quattro e Cinquecento'. *Giornale storico della letteratura italiana* 179, no. 585 (1° trimestre, 2002): 161–92.

Conte, Adelheid. 'La rinascita della poetica nel cinquecento Italiano'. In *La poetica di Aristotele e la sua storia: atti della giornata internazionale di studio organizzata dal seminario di greco in memoria di Viviana Cessi (Pavia, 22 Febbraio 2002)*, edited by Diego Lanza and Viviana Cessi, 45–58. Pisa: ETS, 2002.

Cotugno, Alessio and David A. Lines, eds. *Venezia e Aristotele (ca. 1450-ca. 1600): greco, latino e italiano / Venice and Aristotle (c. 1450-c. 1600): From Greek and Latin to the Vernacular*, exhibition catalogue (Venice, Sale Monumentali della Biblioteca Nazionale Marciana, 21 April–19 May 2016). Venice: Marcianum Press, 2016.

Cox, Virginia. *The Prodigious Muse: Women's Writing in Counter-Reformation Italy*. Baltimore: Johns Hopkins University Press, 2011.

Croce, Benedetto. *Storia del' Età Barocca in Italia*. Bari: Laterza, 1957.

Dahiyat, Ismail M. *Avicenna's Commentary on the Poetics of Aristotle: A Critical Study with an Annotated Translation of the Text*. Leiden: Brill, 1974.

---

[21] Weinberg, *A History of Literary Criticism*, 2:813.

Denores, Giason. *Discorso intorno a que' principii, cause et accrescimenti che la comedia, la tragedia et il poema eroico ricevono dalla filosofia morale e civile e da' governatori delle republiche…[1586]*. In *Trattati di poetica e retorica del Cinquecento*, edited by Bernard Weinberg, 4 vols., 3:373–419. Bari: Laterza, 1970–74.
Faini, Marco. 'La poetica dell'epica sacra tra Cinque e Seicento in Italia'. *The Italianist* 35, no. 1 (2015): 27–60.
Faini, Marco. 'Le "sacrosante muse di Giordano," la riflessione sul poema sacro nella prima metà del Cinquecento'. In *Autorità, modelli e antimodelli nella cultura artistica e letteraria tra riforma e controriforma*, edited by Antonio Corsaro, Harald Hendrix and Paolo Procaccioli, 243–65. Rome: Vecchiarelli Editore, 2007.
Godman, Peter. *From Poliziano to Machiavelli: Florentine Humanism in the High Renaissance*. Princeton, NJ: Princeton University Press, 1998.
Godman, Peter. 'Poliziano's Poetics and Literary History'. *Interpres* 13 (1993): 110–209.
Grendler, Paul F. *The Universities of the Italian Renaissance*. Baltimore and London: Johns Hopkins University Press, 2002.
Hathaway, Baxter. *The Age of Criticism: The Late Renaissance in Italy*. Ithaca, NY: Cornell University Press, 1961.
Javitch, Daniel. 'The Assimilation of Aristotle's *Poetics* in Sixteenth-Century Italy'. In *The Cambridge History of Literary Criticism: Volume 3, The Renaissance*, edited by Glyn P. Norton, 53–65. Cambridge: Cambridge University Press, 1999.
Javitch, Daniel. 'The Emergence of Poetic Genre Theory in the Sixteenth Century'. *Modern Language Quarterly* 59, no. 2 (1998): 139–69.
Kallendorf, Craig. 'From Virgil to Vida: The Poeta Theologus in Italian Renaissance Commentary'. *Journal of the History of Ideas* 56, no. 1 (1995): 41–62, doi:10.2307/2710006.
Lines, David A. *Aristotle's Ethics in the Italian Renaissance (1300–1600): The Universities and the Problem of Moral Education*. Leiden and Boston: Brill, 2002.
Lines, David A. 'Beyond Latin in Renaissance Philosophy: A Plea for New Critical Perspectives'. *Intellectual History Review* 25, no. 4 (2015): 373–89.
Lines, David A. and Anna Laura Puliafito, eds. *'In Other Words': Translating Philosophy in the Fifteenth and Sixteenth Centuries*. Special issue of *Rivista di storia della filosofia* 74, no.2 (2019).
Lines, David A. and Eugenio Refini, eds. *Aristotele fatto volgare: Tradizione aristotelica e cultura volgare nel Rinascimento*. Pisa: Edizioni ETS, 2014.
Milburn, Erika. *Luigi Tansillo and Lyric Poetry in Sixteenth-Century Naples*. Leeds: Modern Humanities Research Association, 2003.
Pazzi de' Medici, Alessandro. *Aristotelis Poetica, per Alexandrum Paccium … in latinum conuersa*. Venice: in aedibus haeredum Aldi, et Andrae Asulani soceri, 1536.
Robortello, Francesco. *In librum Aristotelis de arte poetica explicationes*. 1548; repr., Munich: Wilhelm Fink Verlag, 1968.
Schmitt, Arbogast. 'La *Poetica* di Aristotele e la sua reinterpretazione nella teoria poetica del secondo cinquecento'. In *La Poetica di Aristotele e la sua storia: atti della giornata internazionale di studio organizzata dal seminario di Greco in memoria di Viviana Cessi (Pavia, 22 febbraio 2002)*, edited by Viviana Cessi and Diego Lanza, 31–44. Pisa: ETS, 2002.
Segni, Bernardo. *Rettorica e Poetica d'Aristotile tradotte di greco in lingua vulgare fiorentina*. Florence: Lorenzo Torrentino, 1549.
Sgarbi, Marco. *Francesco Robortello (1516–1567): Architectural Genius of the Humanities*. Abingdon: Routledge, 2019.

Sgarbi, Marco, ed. *I generi dell'aristotelismo volgare nel Rinascimento*. Padua: CLEUP, 2018.

Sgarbi, Marco, ed. 'What Does a Renaissance Aristotelian Look Like? From Petrarch to Galilei'. *HOPOS. The Journal of the International Society for the History of Philosophy of Science* 7 (2017): 226-45.

Tasso, Torquato. *Giudizio sovra la Gerusalemme da lui medesima riformata*. Edited by Claudio Gigante. Rome: Salerno, 2000.

Weinberg, Bernard. *A History of Literary Criticism in the Italian Renaissance*, 2 vols. Chicago: University of Chicago Press, 1961.

Weinberg, Bernard. *Trattati di poetica e retorica del Cinquecento*, 4 vols. Bari: Laterza, 1970-74.

Zanin, Enrica. 'Les commentaires modernes de la *Poétique* d'Aristote'. *Études littéraires* 43, no. 2 (2012): 55-83.

Part I

Mapping the field and retracing boundaries

2

A scholar-collector in mid-century Chicago

The books of Bernard Weinberg

Eufemia Baldassarre, Paul F. Gehl and Lia Markey

Bernard Weinberg (Figure 2.1) (1909–73) laid the ground for and directly or indirectly inspired many of the chapters included in the present volume. In this contribution, we would like to reconstruct an aspect of his career that is rarely considered, namely, his collecting of early modern books. He did so both for his own scholarship and teaching and also (together with other Renaissance specialists) in the service of a broader Chicago scholarly community. For Weinberg, this larger mission – to create Chicago collections for Renaissance studies – was clearly a passion as strong as his own personal urge to collect. Weinberg's books, then, must be understood in the context of both Renaissance specializations in outstanding academic departments at the University of Chicago and the remarkable collecting impulse of historian Hans Baron (1900–86), who held the title of bibliographer and research fellow at the private, independent Newberry Library.[1]

A Chicago life and the Chicago School

A Chicago native, Weinberg completed both his PhB (1930) and his PhD (1936) at the University of Chicago,[2] earning a diploma between his Chicago degrees from the Sorbonne at the University of Paris (1931). Collectively, for research, he spent many years in France and Italy, especially in Florence. He taught at Washington University in St. Louis from 1937 to 1949 (with a stint in the Army Air Corps during the war years) and at Northwestern University from 1949 to 1955. In 1955, he returned to the University of Chicago where he went on to serve as chairman of the Department of Romance Languages and Literatures for some nine years, effectively transforming

---

[1] We are grateful to Déborah Blocker, Bryan Brazeau, Paolo Cherchi, Mary Kennedy, Claire Ptaschinski and Eugenio Refini for their assistance with the research and writing of this chapter. We also wish to thank Catherine Uecker and the staff of the University of Chicago Library as well as Alan Leopold and the staff of the Newberry Library.

[2] His dissertation was published as *French Realism: The Critical Reaction, 1830-1870* (New York and London: Modern Language Association of America and Oxford University Press, 1937).

Figure 2.1 Bernard Weinberg in his office, *c.* 1970, Courtesy Special Collections Research Center, University of Chicago Library.

the department into a world-renowned centre for Romance studies. Weinberg held fellowships from the Guggenheim Foundation (1945 and 1955), the Fulbright Foundation (1951–2) and the Institute for Advanced Study (1956–7), and he taught as visiting professor at the University of Iowa (1965), the University of Minnesota (1966) and the Scuola Normale Superiore di Pisa (1970). He was a prolific scholar. A pamphlet printed on the occasion of an 'Exhibition of Italian and French Books of the Renaissance from the Bequest of Bernard Weinberg' (February 1974), written by his colleague Peter Dembowski, lists some eighty essays and books written between 1935 and 1972.[3] While he is best known for his two-volume *A History of Literary Criticism in the Italian Renaissance*,[4] he published on topics as wide-ranging as Mallarmé's *Le tombeau d'Edgar Poe*, the art of Jean Racine and the writing of Rabelais.

Weinberg was deeply committed to the insights offered by classical philology and analytical bibliography, but he was also among the first generation of American New Critics for whom literary texts had lives of their own, anchored in history, but not finally determined by it. Weinberg is usually listed among the founding members of the group of New Critics called the Chicago School of Criticism, often also known (alas dismissively and with scant understanding of their real philosophy) as Neo-

---

[3] Peter F. Dembowski, *Bernard Weinberg, 1909-1973, A Tribute and a Bibliography* (Chicago: University of Chicago Library and Department of Romance Languages and Literature, 1974), unpaginated.

[4] Bernard Weinberg, *A History of Literary Criticism in the Italian Renaissance* (Chicago: University of Chicago Press, 1961).

Aristotelians.[5] Certainly, the chapters in this volume demonstrate that Aristotelian poetics have continuing value to modern criticism. But it is not necessary to take sides in the mid-twentieth-century version of that debate to see that Weinberg's principal contribution to the Chicago School was as an historian of critical thought. He called his *History* (modestly but also tendentiously) 'an experiment in the writing of intellectual history'. This claim was likely occasioned by the ideal history of criticism described by the movement's founder R. S. Crane (1886–1967), whom Weinberg came to know in his undergraduate years. In *Critics and Criticism* (1952), an anthology often called the Chicago School's manifesto, Crane proposed creating a useful history of literary criticism:[6]

> What is needed is a history of critical writings that describes [the] methodology [of writers on criticism] ... [and their] successive efforts to cope with perennial problems of the literary arts ... stated in universal terms, independently of the shifting particulars of the discourses in which they function. And a history of criticism of this sort ... can be made to serve a number of important purposes in the education of critics beyond the mere satisfaction of their historical curiosity. ... Such a history is the pluralistic philosophy of criticism teaching by example.

It is clear from this passage and other writings of the Chicago School that Weinberg and his colleagues were working within the long tradition of the history of ideas (not social or cultural history in a more recent sense). They had absorbed and continued to value the philological achievements of earlier generations of literary scholars, but they believed (with other New Critics) in the importance of close readings of literature with an eye towards contemporary aesthetic values. They applied this modernist idea of close reading to texts about texts as well as to the canonical creative products that occupied most New Critics because they felt this task of valourizing the critical literature of the past – this useful history – was essential to modern criticism. By editing and translating critical texts, compiling careful case studies and eventually synthesizing a broad study of Aristotelianism in the Italian Renaissance, Weinberg intended to

---

[5] See the useful summary in Louis Groarke, 'Following in the Footsteps of Aristotle: The Chicago School, the Gluestick, and the Razor', *Journal of Speculative Philosophy*, no. 6 (1992): 190–205, esp. 191–5. Also useful: Tom Kindt, *The Implied Author, Concept and Controversy* (Berlin: Walter de Gruyter, 2006), 22–46; George Kimball Plochmann, *Richard McKeon, a Study* (Chicago: University of Chicago Press, 1990), 21–2; Wayne C. Booth, 'Between Two Generations: The Heritage of the Chicago School', *Profession* (1982): 19–26.

[6] See R. S. Crane, ed., *Critics and Criticism, Ancient and Modern* (Chicago: University of Chicago Press, 1952), 11–12, where he cites Weinberg's introduction to *Critical Prefaces of the French Renaissance* (Evanston: Northwestern University Press, 1950) as a statement of the historical goals of the school. In earlier statements of principles, Crane argued for the value of literary criticism as a supplement and corrective to the history of ideas; see his 'History versus Criticism in the Study of Literature', *English Journal* 24 (1935): 645–67 and 'Interpretation of Texts and the History of Ideas', *College English* 2 (1941): 755–65. It is significant that both these pieces appeared in journals devoted to the teaching of English, for the Chicago critics felt strongly that literary history was useful for teaching. They typically demurred at the suggestion that they were a school, preferring to call themselves 'a group of friends who came to know one another at the University of Chicago' (*Critics and Criticism*, 1); in a later, abridged edition, they rejected the notion of manifesto too: *Critics and Criticism, Essays in Method* (Chicago: University of Chicago Press, 1957), iii–v.

create just such a useful history.[7] This was his role along with Richard McKeon (1900–85) and Elder Olson (1909–92) in the historical essays offered in *Critics and Criticism*; and it is the lasting contribution of *A History of Literary Criticism* and Weinberg's edition in four volumes of some fifty-nine *Trattati di poetica e retorica del Cinquecento* (1970–4).[8] It is notable in this regard that Weinberg, Olson and McKeon all curated influential editions and anthologies of critical texts (ancient, medieval and early modern) both in original languages and in translation.[9] This work was fundamental to their notion of teaching by historical example, providing primary source material for students of various moments in the history of criticism.[10] As we shall see, these principles also informed Bernard Weinberg's collecting of early modern books.

Sources of this study

Clearly, Weinberg considered Chicago, the University and the so-called Chicago School his intellectual home. No surprise then that he eventually donated the primary sources assembled for his research to Chicago collections. Weinberg gifted many early modern books related to his *History* (1961) to the University of Chicago in 1963. Over the years, he made individual gifts as well, both books from his own collection and money to buy books, sometimes in honour of colleagues. His will stipulated that his remaining books be given to the University, and that they should pass on books they did not want (presumed to be duplicates) to the Newberry Library. If neither the University nor the Newberry Library had use for a given volume, it was to be sold to benefit acquisitions at the University. This process was completed in 1973–4.[11]

The sources for Bernard Weinberg's personal library allow us to characterize its contents in general terms, but they are incomplete and somewhat problematic when we try to assemble a full inventory of individual titles and assess their varying importance to him. Valuable additional clues can be found in the annotated bibliography of *A History of Literary Criticism* and in the rich notes to his *Trattati di poetica e retorica del Cinquecento*, where he gives considerable discursive information about his reading of sources. Moreover, we have bibliographical specifics on the books in his 1963 gift and 1973 bequest, which together represent an impressive collection of 684 early modern titles. But this was certainly not the entirety of his library, and

---

[7] See the spirited explication of proper literary historiography in Bernard Weinberg, 'Scholarship and the Southern Renaissance, a Victory for History', *Modern Language Quarterly* 26 (1965): 184–202.
[8] Bernard Weinberg, ed., *Trattati di poetica e retorica del Cinquecento* (Bari: G. Laterza, 1970–1974). All four volumes have been digitized by the Biblioteca Europea di Informazione Culturale (BEIC) and are now open access and fully searchable: https://www.beic.it/it/articoli/scrittori-ditalia.
[9] In addition to Weinberg's *Trattati* and *Critical Prefaces*, see Olson's *Aristotle's Poetics and English Literature* (Chicago: University of Chicago Press, 1965) and McKeon's *Selections from Medieval Philosophers* (New York: Scribner's, 1929), *Basic Works of Aristotle* (New York: Random House, 1941), and his collaboration with Blanche Boyer on Peter Abelard, *Sic et Non, a Critical Edition* (Chicago: University of Chicago Press, 1976).
[10] Our thanks to Déborah Blocker for thoughtful advice on the Chicago critics; she remarks on Weinberg's role in her chapter in this volume. Simon Gilson's and Micha Lazarus's chapters also respond to Weinberg's scholarship.
[11] Dembowski, *Bernard Weinberg*.

perhaps not even all of his early modern books. Weinberg does not seem to have used a personal bookplate, and his name or recognizable notes appear only rarely in the books. For the ordinary scholarly books Weinberg owned, we remain entirely in the dark, but most of the early modern books can be tracked. A rapid list was assembled by Weinberg for his 1963 gift (sixty-seven titles).[12] A second, careful inventory made for the bequest distinguishes between books retained by the University of Chicago (516 titles), those which duplicated University holdings and were consequently donated to the Newberry Library (forty-seven titles) and those duplicated at both institutions that the University intended to sell (thirty-four titles).[13] It is altogether harder to get a sense of the books Weinberg may have donated singly before his death to either institution, or others he may have owned and disposed of by sale or trade. Both libraries inserted bookplates or accession marks (Figure 2.2) in the volumes they received from Weinberg acknowledging his gift; but until recently, these provenance marks were not traced in the library catalogues. To verify that a given volume in either library came from Weinberg, it was necessary to examine the books individually. A list of the early modern books we are certain Weinberg owned is included in the Appendix, which also indicates which titles can be found presently at the University of Chicago or at the Newberry.

However unwieldy the sources, a close reading of the online catalogues of the two libraries against the notes to Weinberg's *History* and *Trattati*, the 1963 gift list and the post-mortem inventory reveals some interesting facts about the state of Renaissance collections in Chicago in the middle decades of the twentieth century. In particular, it tells us what resources were already available to Weinberg at local institutions, how he collected with those resources in mind, and the ways his intellectual interests and personal collecting influenced the work of the librarians who were simultaneously building larger and broader Renaissance collections.

Early in his career, Weinberg spent a great deal of research time in European libraries, and he continued to visit Italy and France throughout his life; but as his own library and the institutional collections in Chicago grew, he could find more and more of the books he needed in town. For understanding how Weinberg's collecting intersected with that of Chicago institutions and how this might have affected his study habits, it is the third part of the post-mortem inventory that yields the most certain information. These are books he owned that were already at both the University Library and the Newberry Library by the time of his death. In most cases, we can be fairly sure that neither institution's present copies were gifted by Weinberg, since he still had these personal copies at home in 1973. Presumably, he used these

---

[12] Special Collections Research Center, The University of Chicago Library, collection file: Weinberg, Bernard, 'List of Books: Literary Criticism in the Italian Renaissance', typescript, (1963); cf. University Archives, Office of the University Librarian, Annual Reports, 1961–62, 3, which remarks a gift of seventy volumes.

[13] Special Collections Research Center, The University of Chicago Library, collection file 'Weinberg, Bernard' contains SFH [Sidney F. Huttner], "The Bernard Weinberg Bequest, Permanent File Copy," typescript dated 2/19/74. Our thanks to Mr Huttner for communicating his thoughts about this inventory to us by email, and to the staff of the Special Collections Research Center for their many courtesies. Upon analysis (see Appendix 1) the actual total of titles we can document is 684.

Figure 2.2 Examples of bookplates and accession numbers in Weinberg's books, Courtesy Special Collections Research Center, University of Chicago Library and the Newberry Library.

volumes at home and intended to continue using them right up to the time of his unexpected death.

The list reflects his larger library closely; it is predictably strong on Aristotle and Renaissance texts on rhetoric and poetics, but it also includes other classical authors, neo-Latin oratory and poetry, Italian and French poetry and philosophy, and works by authors of the Enlightenment. Weinberg might have acquired some of these books early in his career, before the two great early modern collections in Chicago were fully developed (and in the expectation that he might end up permanently teaching elsewhere).¹⁴ Other books he may have simply wanted to have on hand at home even though he could have consulted institutional copies. In this last regard, it is probably worth reminding ourselves that during Weinberg's lifetime, it was difficult to know what books were in any given American library. A scholar had to examine card catalogues on site or ask a staff member by phone to search for a title. The great, multivolume *National Union Catalog, Pre-1956 Imprints* provided substantial help as it appeared between 1968 and 1981, but it was still highly incomplete in 1973, and was in any case retrospective and did not represent the actual state of rapidly growing institutional collections like those in Chicago.

We know Weinberg spent considerable research time at libraries in Chicago, Florence, Rome and Paris, but it is also clear that he had assembled a rich personal library of early modern books, something that was within reach of a scholarly booklover in the 1950s when prices were still low and the dollar strong.¹⁵ An examination of the Weinberg books now at the University and the Newberry demonstrates that he did not worry very much about condition. There are no modern collectors' bindings and few early bindings of any pretension. Instead, he bought unlovely copies in modest vellum covers that were down-market even in their own day, and he sometimes acquired early miscellaneous volumes (*Sammelbände*) that evidenced the way literary texts were collected and used in the sixteenth and seventeenth centuries. It is safe to say that he was collecting for the texts above all and was only secondarily interested in these books as physical objects. The remarkable number of editions of Aristotle and Voltaire, to cite just two examples, demonstrate that for some authors, he felt the need to have some texts in different versions. In a few cases, we can see that he deliberately assembled multiple editions of a single text when the printing history seemed telling to him (as in the cases of Bouhours and Helvétius described below), and even multiple copies of the same edition when there were interesting variants (e.g. works by Minturno and Ruscelli).¹⁶

The case of Piero Vettori

A few case studies will illustrate what we can and cannot know about Weinberg's library. We might take as typical the works of Piero Vettori (1499–1585), one of the most important humanist philologists of the sixteenth century and an honorary member of the *Accademia degli Alterati*, a late-sixteenth-century Florentine literary academy that was a subject of Weinberg's research in the 1950s and is the topic of Déborah Blocker's chapter in this volume.¹⁷ Vettori edited, commented upon and published

---

[14] The 1961–62 annual report of the University Librarian, cited earlier, indicates that many books in the 1963 gift 'were extremely scarce and had been acquired by [Weinberg] over a period of more than twenty years'. If this is accurate, he must have been collecting since the early 1940s at least.
[15] Anthony Rota, *The Changing Face of Antiquarian Bookselling 1950-2000 A.D.* (Charlottesville: Book Arts Press, 1995), 5–7, 20–2.
[16] See notes on specific copies in Appendix.
[17] See Bernard Weinberg, 'The Accademia degli Alterati and Literary Taste from 1570 to 1600', *Italica* 31, no. 4 (1954): 207–14; Bernard Weinberg, 'Argomenti di discussione letteraria nell'Accademia

textual emendations for a variety of classical authors including Aristotle, Aeschylus, Euripides, Cicero, Sallust, Demetrius of Phaleron and Varro. Weinberg did not donate any copies of Vettori's works to the University in 1963, but eleven titles are found in the Weinberg bequest (appearing in all three parts of the inventory). Weinberg considered Vettori's commentary on Aristotle's *Poetics* one of three 'great commentaries' of the period, and he devoted six full pages of his *History* to it.[18] The 1560 first edition appears in the bibliography, but this book was never in his personal library as nearly as we can tell. The Newberry acquired it only in 1956, and the University of Chicago does not own it even today. Weinberg presumably used the Newberry copy late in the work on his 1961 *History*, but he had studied the relevant manuscripts at the Vatican, and he could have used the printed first edition there, in the libraries of Florence or at the Bibliothèque Nationale.

The cardinal importance of Vettori's Aristotle to Weinberg is attested by the fact that, although the 1573 reprint of it was available both at the Newberry and the University, Weinberg also owned two personal copies. We may surmise that Weinberg used this reprint edition (and another reprint of 1579 that he also still owned in 1973) for his intensive study of the commentary, but that for his *History*, he wanted to cite the first edition. He had a collegial relationship with Hans Baron, the bibliographer for European books at the Newberry from 1949 to 1966, and Weinberg was serving on a book-advisory committee at the time the Newberry purchased the first edition, so he may well have influenced that purchase directly.[19]

The bibliography to Weinberg's *History* includes only one other title by Vettori, a collection of his letters and orations published in 1586. This volume is in the Newberry too, purchased in 1955. It appears in the third section of the bequest, so it was in the University of Chicago collection by 1973, but that copy was not Weinberg's. Since the bequest copy was sold, we have no clues as to whether he owned it before he published the *History* or acquired it afterwards. We do know that Weinberg collected Vettori's works more widely than the *History* might seem to indicate, since his bequest included five volumes to the University of Chicago that centre on the great philologist's text critical work on Cicero and three more miscellaneous works given to the Newberry. Here again, the contrast is instructive. In 1973, the University already owned the three works that went to the Newberry: Vettori's commentary on Demetrius of Phaleron, a compendium of his text critical work and a charming short book in praise of olive growing.[20] The first two relate at least tangentially to Weinberg's *History* and to his

---

degli Alterati (1570-1600)', *Giornale storico della letteratura italiana* 131, no. 394 (1954): 175–94. Also, see Weinberg's 'Chapter Sixteen. The Quarrel over Dante' in his *History*, 819–76, particularly 837–47. For more on the Alterati see Déborah Blocker's forthcoming book, *Le Principe de plaisir: savoirs, esthétique et politique dans la Florence des Médicis (XVIe-XVIIesiècles)* (Paris: Les Belles Lettres, 2020).

[18] Weinberg, *History*, 461–6.
[19] Weinberg served on the Trustees Book Committee as a 'non-trustee member', i.e. a subject expert, from at least 1955 to 1959; Newberry Library Archives (hereafter NLA) 03/05/02 box 4 folder 169. His name does not occur on the record for the purchase of the first edition Vettori commentary; it was ordered by Baron from advance proofs of Martin Breslauer's catalogue 83, *Fine Books* (London, 1956).
[20] See Appendix: Vettori 1574, 1582 and 1594.

work on the *Alterati*. But as far as we can tell, the University's present copies never belonged to Weinberg, and he still owned copies of these books at the time of his death. We know from other sources that Hans Baron considered collecting classical philology in depth to be the work of the university libraries and not the Newberry, so it is perhaps understandable that he had not actively gone after the first two of these titles while the University had done so.[21] The work on the cultivation of olives, *Trattato di Piero Vettori delle lodi, et della coltiuatione degl'vliui* (1574), is a thoroughgoing humanist exercise, combining Vettori's personal experience managing his own olive groves with a careful account of the classical sources. It might already have been in the University Library because of its significance for agricultural history, while Baron might have considered it a literary trifle, another reason for which he would not have sought it out.[22] It would, however, have been as appropriate in a literary collection as in one on the history of science, so there is no surprise that it was already at the University and was gladly accepted as a gift to the Newberry in 1973 (some seven years after Baron's retirement).

History and the *History of Literary Criticism*

Weinberg's book acquisitions clearly intersected with his research for *A History of Literary Criticism*, suggesting that his most active period of collecting was in the 1950s. For example, three editions of translations of Aristotle's *Poetics* and *Rhetoric* by Alessandro Piccolomini (1508–78) feature prominently in the *History*, and three other titles by this author were in the Weinberg bequest. Piccolomini was a prolific philosopher, natural scientist and poet who held a number of important clerical positions in Bologna, Siena and Rome. He maintained a lifelong relationship with the Sienese Accademia degli Intronati and wrote extensively on ethics, natural history, mathematics and astronomy. The Newberry owned eighteen editions of Piccolomini's works before 1949 and Hans Baron added twenty-one more, to create a very thoroughgoing collection of Piccolomini's literary and philosophical output. The University of Chicago has forty early editions and is particularly strong for his work in the sciences. While it is clear that the two institutional libraries collected systematically in different directions over the years, it is hard to discern a substantial direct influence by Weinberg on either collection except that the Aristotle translations now at the University were his copies, donated in 1963.[23] These translations are just the sort of works we would expect a Chicago School critic to value; they contribute directly to a history of critical ideas in the Renaissance. But a generalist university librarian with a limited budget for early modern books might consider them only marginally

---

[21] Paul F. Gehl, 'A Scholar-Librarian Collects: Hans Baron at the Newberry Library', in *Lux librorum: Essays on Books and History for Christian Coppens*, ed. Goran Proot et al. (Mechelen: Flanders Book Historical Society, 2018), 197–213, p. 207. The University meanwhile emphasized acquisitions in Renaissance science and classical studies; see University of Chicago Library, University Archives, Library, Office of the Director, Annual Reports, 1961–62, 3.
[22] For this aspect of his acquisitions philosophy, see Gehl, 'A Scholar-Librarian Collects', 200.
[23] See Appendix, editions of Aristotle dated 1565, 1572 and 1575.

important (compared with Piccolomini's more original contributions) unless prompted by a faculty member to acquire them. Given these realities, it is interesting that three similar translations by Piccolomini were acquired by the Newberry in just the years when Weinberg served on the library's book committee and when he would surely have been in regular contact with Baron.[24]

Another author important to Weinberg was Battista Guarini (1538–1612). Guarini's *Pastor fido* was a major locus of literary discussion in the last years of the sixteenth century and into the seventeenth. Not surprisingly, the debates surrounding this work figure prominently in Weinberg's *History*,[25] and seven titles by Guarini (including three editions of the *Pastor fido*) appear in the post-mortem inventory. One late-eighteenth-century edition of the *Pastor fido* was earmarked to be sold and the remainder were retained by the University. In his *History*, Weinberg cited the 1601 collected poetry for the *Pastor fido*, but he could have consulted three earlier editions now at the University, as well as the University's copy of the 1588 edition of *Il Verrato*, cited in the *History*. The 1593 edition of the *Pastor fido* in the post-mortem inventory probably served for the *History* too, but Weinberg clearly held onto it for at-home reference even though he could have consulted the first edition at the Newberry or the second at the University of Chicago. *A History of Literary Criticism* also makes clear that Weinberg studied Guarini manuscripts at the Vatican. Given the strength of his own library, it is possible that Weinberg never had to consult editions of Guarini at the Newberry, though Hans Baron was busy in the 1950s on this author too, doubling the number of editions in the library and adding most of the early, critical responses to the *Pastor fido*. The case of the *Pastor fido* may, however, give us some idea of the nature of Weinberg's collecting as it related to the University Library. He gave the University many books that he had used for his *History* in 1963, but he did not donate any of his Guarini holdings at that time, just as he did not gift any of his Vettori titles then. In addition to the five titles by Guarini he still had in 1973 that the University lacked, he also still owned three of the important immediate responses to the *Pastor fido*, those by Paolo Beni (1552–1625), by Faustino Summo (d. 1611) and by Giovanni Pietro Malacreta (fl. *c.* 1600).

Occasionally, Weinberg's use of specific early modern books can be pinpointed fairly precisely. He published an article on the *Dialogo contra i poeti* of Francesco Berni (1497–1535) in 1949 and refers to it in *A History of Literary Criticism*. The very rare 1526 original edition of this work is not to be found in any Chicago library. Weinberg describes that edition in the bibliography of his *History*, indicating that he had studied the copy at the Bibliothèque Nationale, but he also notes that his citations in text are to the 1537 edition. For lack of access to the first edition while preparing the *History*, then, he probably used the later one at the Newberry after Hans Baron purchased it in 1956.[26]

---

[24] The Newberry accession records indicate that they were selected individually by Hans Baron from the stock of booksellers Arnaldo Nanni (Bologna), Bernard Rosenthal (New York) and University Place Bookshop (New York).
[25] Weinberg, *History*, 1074–110.
[26] Ibid., 1117; Bernard Weinberg, 'Une édition du "Dialogo contra i poeti" de Berni', *Bulletin du Bibliophile et du Bibliothécaire* (January 1949): 33–4.

French interests

A rather different pattern emerges if we look at authors prominent in the post-mortem inventory but not cited in any form in *A History of Literary Criticism in the Italian Renaissance*. Many of these are authors of the French classical age and Enlightenment. Dominique de Bouhours (1628–1702) is one example. He was a Jesuit writer on language and literature, author of works on church history and devotional subjects and an influential exponent of French literary classicism. Weinberg did not collect his works in any systematic way, but the post-mortem inventory includes four volumes left to the University. One of these, the 1671 edition of *Les Entretiens d'Ariste et d'Eugène*, contains notes that may be in Weinberg's hand as well as two dealer's descriptions of the book.[27] By contrast, Hans Baron added no fewer than twelve titles by Bouhours to the Newberry collection between 1949 and 1964. There is no evidence that Weinberg and Baron ever discussed this author, but the case clearly represents a shared opinion that Bouhours was important. Baron wanted a thorough collection consisting of multiple editions of the Jesuit's major works and copies of minor ones as well. Weinberg could afford to collect more spottily even though the University of Chicago Library never set out to have a major collection of this author because he knew the Newberry was rich in editions he or his students might want to consult occasionally.

The *philosophe* Claude Adrien Helvétius (1715–71) also appears prominently in the post-mortem inventory of Weinberg's library – six editions in eleven volumes, all of which went to the University of Chicago. There are three early 'London' editions (all now considered false imprints) of the posthumously published poem, *Le bonheur*, plus an Italian translation of it; a two-volume Amsterdam edition of the notorious *De l'esprit*; and the *Oeuvres complettes* in five volumes (1792–7). We do not know when Weinberg acquired these books, but we do know something about the Helvétius holdings of institutional collections in Chicago. When he arrived back in Chicago in 1949, Weinberg would have found the *Oeuvres complettes* at the Newberry, but not at the University of Chicago nor at Northwestern University, where he was just then starting to teach. In the 1950s, Hans Baron acquired six other Helvétius titles for the Newberry, presumably in recognition that the editions published in the author's lifetime were significant for understanding the influential philosopher's career. Although the University did not have the *Oeuvres complettes* until his death, Weinberg would likely have found the major philosophical treatises there in earlier editions. Helvétius' *De l'esprit* was one of the most controversial works of the Enlightenment, condemned by the Sorbonne for Epicureanism, atheism and immorality; but while Weinberg contented himself with a single edition of *De l'esprit* (one of twenty-six eighteenth-century editions known), he chose to buy three early editions of *Le bonheur* in French as well as the Italian translation printed in Lausanne. This last is the only true rarity in any of the Chicago collections of Helvétius; it is the only copy recorded in North

---

[27] Pasted in is a clipping identified in manuscript as being from a 1957 catalogue of the Rome dealer Rappaport, priced at Lit. 35,000; the same hand identifies a slip laid in as a clipping from Lucien Dorbon catalogue no. 650 (1961), item 147, priced at $40.00. As noted here, Weinberg apparently read Dorbon catalogues for the Newberry in the 1950s; Rappaport tickets appear in several volumes from the Weinberg bequest.

America as of this writing. Although he never seems to have published on Helvétius, the fact that he had so many early editions of Le bonheur suggests that Weinberg at one time intended to work on this unusual, poetic account of philosophic materialism. It is the only substantial work of Helvétius in poetic form and the only one of his poems to have had significant influence, though it is relatively little studied even today.[28] It is impossible to know for sure, but the poem's essential benevolence and optimism, concerned as it is with service to the common good, may have particularly appealed to Weinberg.

Chicago collections

Another index of the richness (and limitations) of Chicago libraries for philological work on the Renaissance in Weinberg's day may be found by comparing the online catalogues of the Newberry and the University to his last major work, the important four-volume anthology of *Trattati di poetica e retorica del Cinquecento* published in the Laterza series *Scrittori d'Italia*. Three volumes appeared during his lifetime and a fourth one appeared posthumously; he was responsible for planning the entire series and he did virtually all of the editorial work. The set contains sixty annotated texts edited from eleven manuscript sources and forty printed ones. Of the latter, some twelve are not even now found in Chicago. But an amazing number of the editions needed for work on the *Trattati* were in fact available to Weinberg in town before the first volume of the set appeared. Five were or had been in his private collection. He gave two of them to the University in 1963. Three others were included in his bequest, two to the University and one to the Newberry. Another twenty-three printed sources were at the Newberry and twenty at the University; about a dozen of these were to be found at both institutions. In total, nearly half of the primary sources for the *Trattati* – and fully 70 per cent of the printed sources – were in Chicago. Perhaps more than the individual purchases we can document, these numbers testify to the remarkably active collecting of Renaissance literature in mid-century Chicago.

The statistics also point to an important general tendency in American collecting of Renaissance books at mid-century – a privileging of printed sources. This was a logical and indeed necessary consequence of the market, which overwhelmingly consisted of printed books and not manuscripts. But it also reflects a general tendency of American literary scholars in the period to content themselves with tracing the contents of and relationships between texts as published in their author's lifetimes. True, Weinberg actively sought out manuscripts by authors who had not published their ideas and studied them in the European libraries where they were preserved; but for the history of critical ideas that he was writing, the influential published works were primary. We might contrast this New Critical bias towards (perhaps we should just

---

[28] David Smith, *Bibliography of the Writings of Helvétius* (Ferney-Voltaire: Centre international d'étude du XVIIIe siècle, 2001), 244–88; idem, 'Le chef-d'œuvre impossible: Genèse, publication et réception du Bonheur d'Helvétius', in *Être matérialiste à l'âge des Lumières: Hommage offert à Roland Desné* (Paris: Presses Universitaires de France, 1999), 135–46.

call it complacency with) published sources to the post-war mania among American historians of early modern Italy for studies based largely on original archival digging. One pioneer of this documentary school (concerned especially with Florentine history) was Weinberg's younger colleague at the University of Chicago, Eric W. Cochrane (1928–85).[29]

Himself an avid collector, the charismatic Weinberg clearly influenced other scholars and collectors in Chicago. In some cases, we have surmised that he directly prompted purchases by Hans Baron for the Newberry Library. The striking numbers of sources used for the *History* and the *Trattati* that were acquired by the Newberry in the 1950s and the 1960s attest to his influence. We can document at least one specific case, though it concerns a French Renaissance author not an Italian one. Early in 1954, the Paris dealer Lucien Dorbon offered a 1593 edition of the collected works of the important poet Philippe Desportes (1546–1606).[30] Desportes appeared prominently in Weinberg's introduction to an anthology of French Renaissance poetry in translation that appeared exactly in 1954.[31] Dorbon was asking the modest price of 7,000 francs, equivalent to $21.65. At the period, both the University of Chicago Library and that of Northwestern University (where Weinberg was still teaching) had very limited funds for rare-book purchases and probably would not have prioritized this volume, while the Newberry was buying Renaissance books aggressively on behalf of the Chicago scholarly public. A note by Baron on the dealer's catalogue reads: 'Recommended by Professor Bernard Weinberg. Seconded by HB. I suppose we should have the first French edition.' This note represents Baron's conclusion (and even more clearly Weinberg's ability to convincingly state his own judgement) that the publication history of this author was important for studying his career. The Newberry had in fact purchased a different collected edition some years earlier, and Baron bought still others in 1954 and in 1956. The author was obviously of interest to both Weinberg and Baron. Another work by Desportes, a 1623 edition of his translation of the psalms plus other prayers and meditations, appears in the inventory of the Weinberg bequest among the books to be added to the University collection. In 1967, the Newberry had acquired this work too (in a 1624 edition) on the recommendation of Baron, who had by that time retired. Thus, Philippe Desportes offers a good example of the cooperative

---

[29] Cochrane's first book, *Tradition and Enlightenment in the Tuscan Academies, 1690-1800* (Chicago: University of Chicago Press, 1961) was published the same year Weinberg's *History* appeared from the same press; Cochrane's influential *Florence in the Forgotten Centuries, 1527-1800* (Chicago: University of Chicago Press, 1973) appeared in the year of Weinberg's death. Cochrane served on the board of trustees of the Newberry from 1964 until his death in 1985, a period that roughly coincided with the curatorial tenure of Hans Baron's successor, John Tedeschi, mentioned here. Collaborations between individual professors at the University and the Newberry continued, though the close collection-building cooperation between Weinberg and Baron seems to have been unique, at least in the area of European literature.

[30] Philippe Desportes, *Les oeuvres de Philippes Des Portes: reueües, corrigees & de beaucoup augmentees outre les precedentes impressions* (Lyons, Rigaud, 1593). It is item no. 726 in catalogue no. 614 of Lucien Dorbon, *Livres anciennes e modernes* (Paris, February 1954).

[31] H. Peyre, P. A. Wadsworth and F. G. Hoffherr, eds, *French Poetry of the Renaissance* (New York: Harper, 1954) includes notes and an introduction by Weinberg. It was later revised and reprinted with Weinberg as editor: *French Poetry of the Renaissance* (Carbondale: Southern Illinois University Press, 1964).

relationships among Renaissance scholars across Weinberg's career as well as his personal ability to influence purchases of rare books.

On another occasion, also after Hans Baron's retirement, Weinberg played a major role in an important Newberry acquisition, an assemblage of documents known locally as the Strozzi manuscripts since they derive from the archives of that Florentine family.[32] Composed of thirty-two robust volumes of documents dating from the sixteenth through eighteenth centuries, the materials include numerous poems and writings by Giovanni Battista Strozzi (1551–1634), one of the ringleaders of the *Alterati* whom Weinberg had studied. Professor Aldo Scaglione (1925–2013) of the University of North Carolina called the attention of the Newberry staff to the archive, which was on offer from the Florentine dealer Luigi Gozzini & Figli. There was some debate internally at the library about this purchase, even though the asking price was a mere $4,200, particularly since it was unclear exactly what the archive contained. By good fortune, Weinberg was in Florence that summer, so his opinion was solicited. A letter from Weinberg dated 22 September 1969 to curator John Tedeschi (Figure 2.3) describes his experience examining the collection on the Gozzini premises and strongly recommends the purchase of the documents 'not only because of the unpublished texts and of the original drafts, but also from the point of view of the making and writing of manuscripts in the sixteenth and seventeenth centuries'.[33] This last remark suggests that by the late 1960s, Weinberg had become interested in the documentary, artefactual value of manuscript sources for training students. In this case, Weinberg's longstanding interest in unpublished texts was intertwined with the Newberry's growing collection of primary, especially manuscript sources for the study of the Italian Renaissance, something Tedeschi, an historian trained in archival research, was promoting. Weinberg's comment, perhaps a reflection of Tedeschi's interests, was forward-looking too, since some ten years later, the Newberry added instructional programmes for paleography and archival/manuscript studies to its offerings.

The chronology of Weinberg's career offers some further insights into the development of the three early modern collections in Chicago. The years when Weinberg was teaching at Northwestern University (1949–55) coincided with Hans Baron's first years as bibliographer at the Newberry. Weinberg later jokingly referred to this period as his time of exile from the University of Chicago.[34] But that circumstance probably worked to the benefit of the Newberry, which is located almost equidistant from the two great Chicago-area universities, right on the public transit lines that connect them. So this period would also have been one when Weinberg could most conveniently and frequently use the Newberry. We do not in fact have extensive evidence for the personal relationships between Weinberg, Hans Baron and the head of the Newberry Library, Stanley Pargellis.[35] But many of the Newberry's purchases of

---

[32] The collection is Newberry Library, Case MS 6A 11.
[33] Newberry Library, Special Collections Administrative Files.
[34] Dembowski, *Bernard Weinberg*.
[35] There are a few letters in the Stanley Pargellis Papers at the Newberry (NLA 03/05/02 box 4, folder 169) that make it clear that Pargellis and Weinberg were on a first name basis but that Weinberg and Baron followed the more formal University of Chicago usage of calling each other 'Mr'.

> THE UNIVERSITY OF CHICAGO
> CHICAGO · ILLINOIS 60637
> DEPARTMENT OF ROMANCE LANGUAGES AND
> LITERATURES
>
> September 22, 1969
>
> Dear John,
>
>   I was pleased to have a look, as you asked me to do, at the Strozzi family manuscripts in Gonnelli's shop in Florence. It is an extraordinarily rich collection, containing many poems of both the elder and the younger Strozzi, of contemporary poets such as Francesco Grazzini, several unpublished plays, commentaries on several works of Aristotle, short prose treatises by both of the Strozzis, historical writings and letters. Many of these are autograph, and according to Fortuna (who studied the MSS and made the list) many of the works of the Strozzis are unpublished.
>
>   This collection would be an extremely valuable addition to the Italian Renaissance materials now available at the Newberry and at this University. It would be useful to the scholarly community not only because of the unpublished texts and of the original drafts, but also from the point of view of the making and writing of manuscripts in the sixteenth and seventeenth centuries. I hope that it will be possible to buy it for the Newberry.
>
>   Cordially,
>
>   Bernard Weinberg

Figure 2.3 Letter from Bernard Weinberg to John Tedeschi, dated 22 September 1969, Courtesy the Newberry Library.

books pertinent to *A History of Literary Criticism* were made in exactly these years. It was Baron who made those choices from catalogues or from lists of Renaissance books offered privately by dealers. Both Baron and Weinberg were deeply interested in the literary aspects of humanism, so it is easy to conclude that they found common ground in a passion for collecting both major and minor texts. They shared an appreciation of French classical and Enlightenment achievements as well, an enthusiasm that is clear in Weinberg's publications, but is not a well-known aspect of Baron's thought. Both Baron and Weinberg were educated in an intellectual history or history-of-ideas tradition; they conceived of the ideal research library as a repository of as many historically useful texts as it was possible to assemble.

Weinberg's recognition that the Newberry was collecting actively in these fields no doubt contributed to his willingness to serve on the Trustees Book Committee that oversaw Newberry purchases on a twice-monthly schedule. In this role, he reviewed lists of books on offer and made suggestions about authors to collect. In one case in 1956–7, he polled his colleagues at the University of Chicago to compile a list of French, Spanish and Latin American authors that the Newberry should consider for its Martin Collection of contemporary fine press poetry. His service on this committee continued until at least 1959, well after he had moved from Northwestern to the University of Chicago.[36]

Meanwhile, as the University of Chicago Library's budgets for rare books increased gradually across the 1950s and the 1960s, Weinberg became more and more active in collection development there too. He was able to influence rare-book collecting at the University of Chicago through his own gifts, and as a member of faculty committees that advised the University Library on purchases and helped prepare for the creation of a new central facility, what is now the Joseph Regenstein Library.[37] The University Librarian's annual reports begin to mention sustained attention to rare-book acquisitions in 1961, with special emphasis on certain fields of Renaissance studies.[38] As in the Newberry case, there are few documents to evidence Weinberg's personal relationships, especially with Robert Rosenthal, head of the University Library's Special Collections Department (organized in 1952). But the two men knew each other well. In a 1971 letter to Weinberg, Rosenthal acknowledged the 'support you have given to the Library for the acquisition of French and Italian books', and added, 'We've come a long way in the last decade with your moral as well as tangible support.'[39]

Given Weinberg's collegial nature and his passion for collecting, then, it is certain that the two men discussed collecting and probable that Weinberg shared his knowledge of European book dealers with Rosenthal. They collaborated on the Weinberg gift in 1963, and around 1971, Weinberg donated to a book fund in honour of Herman H. Fussler (1911–84), the director of the Library who retired in that year.[40] Moreover, Rosenthal knew about Weinberg's plans to leave his remaining books to the University and would have considered that fact in his own purchases of rare books. After Weinberg's death, Rosenthal had the use of the memorial fund created by the sale of duplicates. When, in 1975, the Department of Special Collections mounted an exhibit of 100 notable new acquisitions, three books from Weinberg's bequest and five purchased on the new fund were included.[41] In a variety of ways, Bernard

---

[36] Stanley Pargellis Papers, NLA 03/05/02 box 4, folder 169.
[37] Dembowski, *Bernard Weinberg*.
[38] University Archives, Office of the University Librarian, Annual Reports, 1949–2017. Weinberg's 1963 gift is recorded as part of an ongoing programme of early modern acquisitions.
[39] Special Collections Research Center, The University of Chicago Library, collection file: Weinberg, letter of 26 November 1971.
[40] As evidenced by the bookplate in a copy of Salvino Salvini, *Fasti consolari* (Florence: Tartini and Franchi, 1717).
[41] *One Hundred Books and Manuscripts Recently Acquired by the University of Chicago Library: A Catalogue of an Exhibition Held at the Joseph Regenstein Library, Spring 1975*, Chicago, 1975.

Weinberg made important contributions to the development of the University's rare-book collection.[42]

In this chapter, we have attempted a case study that describes the city-wide research context of a single private collection of Renaissance books. In fact, many American faculty members and hundreds of American research libraries in the period were collecting early modern books in enormous numbers.[43] Studies of American institutional book collecting are in their infancy, so it is hard to say how unusual the Chicago collecting community around the middle of the twentieth century really was. Even the single example we offer presents problems of evidence and interpretation, but we hope to have provided a good general picture of Weinberg's and Chicago's rare-book world. Although it is impossible to recreate his personal library completely, it is clear that Weinberg was collecting early modern books with the existing and growing collections of the University and the Newberry in mind, at least from the time he returned to Chicago in 1949.[44] We may imagine that his collecting began in his student years in Chicago, and it continued through his many years of study in Europe and teaching in St. Louis, perhaps also during his wartime service. His devotion to Chicago and especially to the University of Chicago never failed.[45] The collegial Chicago library world was an immediate and conditioning factor in his maturity as a collector, just as the Chicago School of Criticism was the essential context for his most important scholarly achievements. His great project for *A History of Literary Criticism in the Italian Renaissance* matured when he returned to Chicago, so the 1950s and the 1960s were the years when his need for early modern editions of Italian texts was most critical. It was his great fortune to find a welcoming community at the Newberry and a kindred collecting spirit in Hans Baron as well as in the University community that came in his years of teaching there to recognize the importance of collecting early modern books systematically. Moreover, because of his collegial advice, his many gifts of books and his long-planned bequest, it is fair to say that he was not only a Chicago collector but also a collector *for* Chicago.

---

[42] The other great book collector of the Chicago School was Richard McKeon, whose contributions to the University of Chicago's collections (some 15,000 volumes purchased in 1986) were prodigious but remain unstudied. We have not attempted to assess his role, if any, in Weinberg's collecting.

[43] We need look no farther than the University of Illinois at Urbana-Champaign for stellar examples. Professor Harris F. Fletcher (1892–1979) was the driving force behind that university's collecting of English texts of the age of Milton while Professor T. W. Baldwin (1890-1984) promoted collecting of earlier English literature; see Valerie Hotchkiss, *English Print from Caxton to Shakespeare to Milton* (Urbana: University of Illinois Press, 2008).

[44] Weinberg was also a collector of early modern art. Dembowski, *Bernard Weinberg*, writes that '[Weinberg] bequeathed his own collection of art to The Art Institute of Chicago'. Unfortunately, few records exist recording this bequest. One seventeenth-century drawing by an unknown artist of a mythological figure is catalogued in the Art Institute's collection as a gift of the Estate of Bernard Weinberg, 1973.151.

[45] Peter F. Dembowski, *Memoirs Red and White* (Notre Dame: University of Notre Dame Press, 2015), 176–8.

Bibliography

Booth, Wayne C. 'Between Two Generations: The Heritage of the Chicago School'. *Profession* (1982): 19–26.

Boyer, Blanche and Richard McKeon. *Sic et Non, a Critical Edition*. Chicago: University of Chicago Press, 1976.

Cochrane, Eric. *Florence in the Forgotten Centuries*, 1527–1800. Chicago: University of Chicago Press, 1973.

Cochrane, Eric. *Tradition and Enlightenment in the Tuscan Academies, 1690–1800*. Chicago: University of Chicago Press, 1961.

Crane, R. S., ed. *Critics and Criticism, Ancient and Modern*. Chicago: University of Chicago Press, 1952.

Crane, R. S., ed. *Critics and Criticism, Essays in Method*. Chicago: University of Chicago Press, 1957.

Crane, R. S., ed. 'History versus Criticism in the Study of Literature'. *English Journal* 24 (1935): 645–67.

Crane, R. S., ed. 'Interpretation of Texts and the History of Ideas'. *College English* 2 (1941): 755–65.

Dembowski, Peter F. *Bernard Weinberg, 1909–1973, A Tribute and a Bibliography*. Chicago: University of Chicago Library and Department of Romance Languages and Literature, 1974.

Desportes, Philippes. *Les oeuvres de Philippes Des Portes: reueües, corrigees & de beaucoup augmentees outre les precedentes impressions*. Lyons, Rigaud, 1593.

Dorbon, Lucien. *Livres anciennes e modernes*, Paris, February 1954.

Gehl, Paul F. 'A Scholar-Librarian Collects: Hans Baron at the Newberry Library'. In *Lux Librorum: Essays on Books and History for Christian Coppens*, edited by Goran Proot et al., 197–213. Mechelen: Flanders Book Historical Society, 2018.

Groarke, Louis. 'Following in the Footsteps of Aristotle: The Chicago School, the Gluestick, and the Razor'. *Journal of Speculative Philosophy*, no. 6 (1992): 190–205.

Kindt, Tom. *The Implied Author, Concept and Controversy*. Berlin: Walter de Gruyter, 2006.

McKeon, Richard. *Basic Works of Aristotle*. New York: Random House, 1941.

McKeon, Richard. *Selections from Medieval Philosophers*. New York: Scribner's, 1929.

Olson, Elder. *Aristotle's Poetics and English Literature*. Chicago: University of Chicago Press, 1965.

Peyre, H., P. A. Wadsworth and F. G. Hoffherr, eds. *French Poetry of the Renaissance*. New York: Harper, 1954.

Plochmann, George Kimball. *Richard McKeon, a Study*. Chicago: University of Chicago Press, 1990.

Rota, Anthony. *The Changing Face of Antiquarian Bookselling 1950–2000 A.D.* Charlottesville: Book Arts Press, 1995.

Salvini, Salvino. *Fasti consolari*. Florence: Tartini and Franchi, 1717.

Smith, David. *Bibliography of the Writings of Helvétius*. Ferney-Voltaire: Centre international d'étude du XVIIIe siècle, 2001.

Smith, David. 'Le chef-d'œuvre impossible: Genèse, publication et réception du Bonheur d'Helvétius'. In *Être matérialiste à l'âge des Lumières: Hommage offert à Roland Desné*, edited by Béatrice Fink et Gerhardt Stenger, 135–46. Paris: Presses Universitaires de France, 1999.

Weinberg, Bernard. 'The Accademia degli Alterati and Literary Taste from 1570 to 1600'. *Italica* 31, no. 4 (1954): 207–14.

Weinberg, Bernard. 'Argomenti di discussione letteraria nell'Accademia degli Alterati (1570-1600)'. *Giornale storico della letteratura italiana* 131, no. 394 (1954): 175–94.

Weinberg, Bernard. *Critical Prefaces of the French Renaissance*. Evanston: Northwestern University Press, 1950.

Weinberg, Bernard, ed. *French Poetry of the Renaissance*. Carbondale: Southern Illinois University Press, 1964.

Weinberg, Bernard. *French Realism: The Critical Reaction*, 1830–1870. New York and London: Modern Language Association of America and Oxford University Press, 1937.

Weinberg, Bernard. *A History of Literary Criticism in the Italian Renaissance*. Chicago: University of Chicago Press, 1961.

Weinberg, Bernard. 'Scholarship and the Southern Renaissance, a Victory for History'. *Modern Language Quarterly* 26 (1965): 184–202.

Weinberg, Bernard, ed. *Trattati di poetica e retorica del Cinquecento*. Bari: G. Laterza, 1970–1974.

Weinberg, Bernard. 'Une édition du 'Dialogo contra i poeti' de *Berni*'. *Bulletin du Bibliophile et du Bibliothécaire* (January 1949): 33–4.

3

Sound Aristotelians and how they read

Micha Lazarus

The Chicago School made the most thoroughgoing attempt at Aristotelian revival since the seventeenth-century *Académie française*, and like the *Académie*, its critical writings began in polemic.[1] Ronald Crane articulated its principles by way of defence against gathering criticism in his introduction to *Critics and Criticism: Ancient and Modern* (1952), 'a selection from the writings on critical theory and method of a group of friends who came to know one another at the University of Chicago in the middle thirties' which became in effect the School's manifesto.[2] On the docket were the charges that 'they were concerned with criticism alone' rather than other branches of the humanities, such as 'linguistics (in the broad sense of the word), the analysis of ideas ... and history'; that they were partisans of an exclusively Aristotelian criticism, 'an extreme form of aesthetic atomism', at the expense of historical, rhetorical, ethical and philological approaches, to name but a few; and that even their Aristotelianism was in fact a 'pseudo-Aristotelian formalism which defines all poetry, on *a priori* grounds, as imitation and its end as pleasure'.[3] Yet Crane's answer to these charges was not to deny their truth, but rather to double-down on their justification. The Chicago School was concerned with all the humanities, but criticism alone, founded on sufficiently 'systematic' principles, could serve as the architectonic art to unite all their forms in the face of 'guild prejudices', 'the perennial jealousies of rhetoricians and philosophers, grammarians and rhetoricians, historians and critics'.[4] Partisans of Aristotelian criticism they were indeed, even in the face of 'the necessary relativity of all critical utterances', because Aristotle's *Poetics* alone provided a blueprint of the inductive method, 'principles of formulation and proof', which manifest 'in universal terms independently of the shifting particulars of the discourses in which they function'.[5] This Aristotelian criticism was 'comprehensive', 'systematic' and comparable to scientific method; it operated according to Aristotelian *differentia*, considering

[1] Michael Moriarty, 'French Criticism in the Seventeenth Century', in *The Cambridge History of Literary Criticism, III: The Renaissance*, ed. Glyn Norton (Cambridge: Cambridge University Press, 1999), 555–65, gives a concise overview.
[2] Ronald S. Crane, introduction to *Critics and Criticism: Ancient and Modern*, ed. Ronald S. Crane (Chicago: University of Chicago Press, 1952), 1–24, p. 1.
[3] Ibid.
[4] Ibid., 3.
[5] Ibid., 8–11.

'what a poet does *distinctively as a poet*' as opposed to as a psychologist or moralist; it considered poems (in the broad sense embracing prose fiction and drama) as 'concrete artistic wholes' and analysed 'the internal causes of poems, viewed as artistic products, in analytical separation from the activities that produced them'.[6] The *Poetics* itself was limited, certainly, since its sole surviving part discusses only mimetic poetry, and of that only tragedy and epic. Yet the Chicago School adhered not to any particular doctrine of Aristotle's, but to his *method*:

> The important thing in Aristotle for the present essayists … is not so much the statements of doctrine and history contained in the *Poetics* itself as the method through which these statements are derived and validated in the arguments of the treatise when it is read in the light of the methodological principles stated explicitly in its author's other works or inferable from them. The Aristotle they have thus reconstructed is not, it will easily be seen, the Aristotle of the Renaissance and neoclassical commentators or any of the more recent Aristotles of such interpreters as Butcher, Bywater, Murray, Lane Cooper, or Francis Fergusson. It may not, indeed, except in a general way, be Aristotle at all! They think it is; but, whether Aristotle's or not, the poetic method which they credit to him can be described in universal terms in such a manner as to remove it effectually from the circumstances of its historical origin and make it accessible, once its nature is clarified and its potentialities further developed, as a method for common use today.[7]

In the face of accusations that the Chicago School maintained an exclusive focus on 'criticism' and a doctrinal Neo-Aristotelianism, Crane upped the ante, justifying criticism's place at the heart of the modern humanities and Aristotle's at the heart of criticism, 'inseparable from the much larger problem of how the humanities in general might be brought to play a more influential role in the culture and action of the contemporary world'.[8]

As long as its focus was the contemporary world, Crane's argument may be considered as successful as its results. Perhaps Aristotelian poetics really can be the font of cultural renewal; less interesting texts have been proposed, and indeed equally bombastic claims been made for the fructuous powers of the *Poetics*.[9] But for the *history* of criticism, a method based on Aristotle's *Poetics* was uniquely maladapted. Crane hailed the Chicago School's adherence to Aristotle as merely pragmatic, 'much like a modern physicist's preference for Einsteinian over Newtonian concepts', purporting to deflect dogmatism into the disinterested march of scientific dialectic.[10] Yet seven years after Hiroshima,

---

[6] Ibid., 13–14, p. 22.
[7] Ibid., 17.
[8] Ibid., 2.
[9] For example, the preface to *Aristotle's Art of Poetry* (London: Daniel Browne and William Turner, 1705), sig. [b7^{r-v}]: tragedy having been three times lost to history, poets 'need only keep to these Rules, which will teach them what they are ignorant of, and the fourth time restore *Tragedy* to its first Lustre and Brightness.'
[10] Crane, *Critics and Criticism*, 13.

preference for Newtonian physics was hardly a real option. Parallel appeals to the hard sciences from the seventeenth to the twentieth centuries, comparing the *Poetics* to 'the *Elements* of Euclid', indicate Crane's true drift: that the *Poetics* was to be seen as natural law, anchoring the epistemology of the humanities at the start of a decade in which the work of Thomas Kuhn would unsettle the claims of the natural sciences themselves to objectivity.[11] Still more troubling is the 'reconstructed' Aristotle that Crane promised. In practice, the Chicago *Poetics* owed more to Crane's list of interpreters, Butcher in particular, than he acknowledges, as we will shortly see. But as Crane makes clear, their 'strong temperamental affinity' for Aristotle led the Chicago School to assess the 2,000-year interpretive history of the *Poetics* by the standards of a single reading of the work current in mid-twentieth-century Chicago. If the *Poetics* was an instrument to unify the humanities across the boundaries of the ancient *trivium*, 'the perennial jealousies of rhetoricians and philosophers, grammarians and rhetoricians', what was one to make of historical readings of the *Poetics* that braced against those boundaries? If the *Poetics* was taken to stand for conceptual unity in the face of fragmentation, how to treat historical practices of commentary and commonplacing that understood the *Poetics*, indeed Aristotelian method itself, as their model? How, in short, if they were ideologically invested in the essential stability of Aristotle's meaning, could the Chicago School account for its actual historical variance as their own Aristotelian method demanded – methodically, dispassionately and inductively? An essentialized *Poetics* could provide a legitimate point of methodological departure for the analysis of a wide range of literary and historical materials, but its own history could only ever be a history of error.

Unsound Aristotelians

Bernard Weinberg's work of this time, synthesized at last into his monumental *History of Literary Criticism in the Italian Renaissance* (1961) and dedicated to Crane, Richard McKeon and Elder Olson, was a product of this tension, profoundly ill at ease with how the *Poetics* actually looked in the Renaissance and, again like *Critics and Criticism*, owing more to a series of early-twentieth-century scholarly commonplaces than it readily acknowledged.[12] His two contributions in *Critics and Criticism*, chapters on Robortello and on Castelvetro, are early case studies of the ways in which the Chicago method conditioned Weinberg's historical account, but a clearer statement of his methodology at this time appeared in an essay published the following year in *Comparative Literature* entitled 'From Aristotle to Pseudo-Aristotle'. For Weinberg, the passage from true to false Aristotelianism plotted a course from an understanding of the *Poetics* as an argument for the aesthetic autonomy of its objects to one that

---

[11] Joseph Warton, *An Essay on the Writings and Genius of Pope* (London, 1756), 170; Gotthold Ephraim Lessing, *Hamburgische Dramaturgie*, 2 vols. ([Leipzig], 1769), II:396 (parts 101–4, 19 April 1768); Lane Cooper, *The Poetics of Aristotle: Its Meaning and Influence* (London: George G. Harrap, 1923), ix.

[12] Bernard Weinberg, *A History of Literary Criticism in the Italian Renaissance* (Chicago: University of Chicago Press, 1961).

increasingly emphasizes poetry's subordination to the demands of its audiences. From Robortello to Castelvetro, Corneille and Boileau, the *Poetics* is assimilated to Horace and his Roman, rhetorical model of poetics that works by instructing the audience, through pleasure, to their own 'moral betterment'. It is in Robortello's commentary (1548) that we see a 'general movement away from the poem and towards the demands or the expectations of the audience'; by Castelvetro's (1570), 'aesthetic preoccupations have disappeared, and their place has been taken by rhetorical and physical concerns of the lowest order'.[13] Weinberg's opprobrium is unmistakable. These are not simply variant readings of Aristotle, but erroneous episodes in a lamentable history of critical decline, charted against the fixed point of the *Poetics*:

> Let us state the contrast briefly thus: Aristotle's *Poetics* is a work which concentrates its attention on the poem itself and asks primarily this question: By what means can a poem of a given kind be made as beautiful as possible, so that it will produce the proper artistic effect?[14]

There is little recognition here that Robortello's or Castelvetro's *Poetics* was no more or less a fixed point for them than Weinberg's was for him, little recognition that the Chicago School itself was equally vulnerable to the charge of trying to '"modernize" Aristotle, to adapt him to their own times and their own peoples, in a manner scarcely authorized by the Aristotelean text' – even though that was Crane's central claim in the group's own manifesto! On the contrary: though Renaissance critics 'thought of themselves as Aristotelians and of their theories as going back to the authority of Aristotle', Weinberg observes, 'never did they realize that their ideas would be completely unacceptable to a sound Aristotelean'.[15] Thus, in his more detailed contributions to the School's 1952 collection, Weinberg found of Robortello that 'the fundamental conceptions of the *Poetics* escape him'; 'unfortunately', he comments, 'this will be the procedure for all of Robortello's successors', such as Castelvetro, whom he finds promulgating 'an essentially un-Aristotelian system of poetics, one which was even farther removed from the presuppositions of the original text than had been the theory contained in the commentary of Robortello'.[16]

Eliding the differences between 'un-Aristotelian', 'unacceptable to a sound Aristotelean' and 'the authority of Aristotle', it is clear that Weinberg's and his colleagues' 'strong temperamental affinity' for Aristotle amounted to a kind of hieratic order – which in turn casts their messianic hopes for the *Poetics* and fervid inquisitions into aesthetic heresy in a revealing light. It is unclear why a historian, especially one aspiring to the 'inductive' method that Crane so proudly claimed,

---

[13] Bernard Weinberg, 'From Aristotle to Pseudo-Aristotle', *Comparative Literature* 5 (1953): 97–104, pp. 100–1.
[14] Ibid., 98.
[15] Ibid., 103–4.
[16] Bernard Weinberg, 'Robortello on the *Poetics*', in *Critics and Criticism: Ancient and Modern*, ed. Ronald S. Crane (Chicago: University of Chicago Press, 1952), 319–48, p. 346; 'Castelvetro's Theory of the Poetics', in *Critics and Criticism: Ancient and Modern*, ed. Ronald S. Crane (Chicago: University of Chicago Press, 1952), 349–71, p. 371.

should imagine that he knew more about how to be a sixteenth-century Aristotelian than a sixteenth-century Aristotelian. Indeed, Weinberg's sense of the limits of the inductive method emerge in a review from this period of Marvin Herrick's *Comic Theory in the Sixteenth Century* (1950). Herrick is perhaps best known for his 1946 book *The Fusion of Horatian and Aristotelian Literary Criticism*, still widely cited in the field, which argued that between the 1530s and the 1550s, 'Aristotelian and Horatian features in Renaissance critical theory were almost inextricably mingled', as Horace was read in effect as a follower of and commentator on Aristotle.[17] Stressing the blending of poetics and rhetoric, Aristotle and Horace, working on similar primary sources, Weinberg might be expected to have been largely in sympathy with Herrick. Yet he takes issue with 'certain matters of method' in Herrick's work, insisting that 'what Mr. Herrick calls "fusion" is really "confusion"' – that 'the addition of disparate terms to a critical tradition, far from enriching it, tends to invalidate its whole basis of procedure'.[18] He complains that Herrick makes *sense* of these 'confused' jumbles rather than maintaining 'a more objective and philosophical attitude towards his materials, and devot[ing] to the central issues time and space which have been spent on matters which must be regarded, I fear, as extraneous'. For Weinberg these 'extraneous' matters enter through Herrick's tendency to assume 'the role of a Renaissance commentator' when he seeks in Terentian comedy 'examples of the kinds of practice which the Renaissance commentators might have sought there'. Weinberg's critique of Robortello and Castelvetro a year later for providing 'no philosophical reading of the text' is thus prefigured here in his demand for a 'more objective and more philosophical attitude' in Herrick.[19] In short, Weinberg finds Herrick's method *too* inductive, too willing to judge Renaissance commentaries on their own merits, and too ready to surrender the essence of the text to the historical accidents of its transmission and interpretation.

If my only purpose here were to carp at Weinberg's methods almost seventy years after the fact – even if those methods do still underpin large parts of the discipline – I would deserve the same criticism I am levelling at him. None of us is truly conscious of the currents of our historical moment, not Robortello, not Weinberg, not I, and all one can hope for from future scholars is the grace of forbearance. Weinberg's *History* is a work of titanic accomplishment, possessing a sheer weight of learning and utility that has given it the extraordinary quality of outliving its own methods. Besides, I would hardly be the first to outline such a critique.[20] What interests me is rather that Weinberg's account of the *Poetics* is not quite a work of history or of reception, but something more symptomatic – a synthesis of a particular kind of reading at a particular time meriting, as such, an episode of its own in the long history of criticism.

---

[17] Marvin T. Herrick, *The Fusion of Horatian and Aristotelian Literary Criticism, 1531-1555* (Urbana: University of Illinois Press, 1946), 1.
[18] Bernard Weinberg, 'Review of Herrick, *Comic Theory in the Sixteenth Century*', *Modern Philology* 48, no. 4 (1951): 271–3.
[19] Ibid.
[20] I cite the objections of Stephen Halliwell, Brian Vickers and Daniel Javitch, below.

The Peripatetic *Poetics*: Athens, Constantinople, Venice

To enshrine their *Poetics*, Weinberg and his colleagues, as we have seen, had to anathematize several defining aspects of the Renaissance *Poetics*. Because the *Poetics* was both the engine of their criticism and itself a theory of reading poetry, however, many of their criticisms equally enshrine their opposition not only to Renaissance modes of reading Aristotle but also of reading poetry in general. When Weinberg criticizes interpretations of the *Poetics* as overly 'rhetorical', that is, he is also articulating his opposition to modes of reading *poetry* as rhetorical or for rhetorical effects, and his distaste for poetry that is itself overly ornate and/or didactic. But from its earliest surviving traces, Aristotle's *Poetics* was always intimate with rhetoric – not necessarily rhetoric in the broad sense of didactic persuasion at which Weinberg and his twentieth-century colleagues wrinkled their noses, but rhetoric as one aspect of a training in the language arts, the classical *trivium*.

Our oldest manuscript exemplar of the *Poetics* is Paris, Bibliothèque Nationale, MS grec 1741. We can trace its provenance only from the mid-sixteenth century, when it emerged in Florence, but stemmatic reconstruction and a reference in a letter written by Cardinal Bessarion between 1457 and 1468 shows it must have been around for at least a century by then, which dates its re-emergence (as might be expected) around the fall of Constantinople.[21] The mid-tenth-century Greek hand in which it is written places it amid the large-scale project of bibliographic curation commanded by Constantine Porphyrogenitus. At this time, the standard Byzantine rhetorical syllabus consisted of Aphthonius's *Progymnasmata*, or elementary exercises, followed by Hermogenes's *Rhetoric* and its accompanying commentaries. Rhetorical works outside this corpus – including the *Poetics* and *Rhetoric* – had been marginalized almost to extinction.[22] Whether for practical reference or cultural preservation, the Paris manuscript was assembled as an anthology of this 'anti-*corpus*': it pointedly excludes the standard syllabus, preserving Aristotle's *Poetics* and *Rhetoric* alongside works by Dionysius of Halicarnassus (including *On Composition* and 'Dionysius' *Art of Rhetoric*), 'Demetrius' (*On Style*), Menander (*On Epideictic*), Ps.-Aristides (*Art of Rhetoric*), Apsines (*Art of Rhetoric, On Figured Problems*), Alexander (*On Figures*), Minucianus/Nicagoras (*On Arguments*), Phoibammon (*On Figures*) and a couple

---

[21] The standard work on the manuscripts of the *Poetics* remains Edgar Lobel, *The Greek Manuscripts of Aristotle's Poetics* (London: Oxford University Press, 1933), which discusses Bessarion's letter (6-7), on which see also Aubrey Diller, 'Notes on the History of Some Manuscripts of Aristotle', in *Studia Codicologica*, ed. Kurt Treu (Berlin: Akademie-Verlag, 1977), 147–50, p. 148. Subsequent manuscript discoveries are accounted for in Aristotle, *Poetics: Editio Maior of the Greek Text with Historical Introductions and Philological Commentaries*, ed. Leonardo Tarán and Dimitri Gutas (Leiden and Boston: Brill, 2012); see also Richard Janko's further observations on the textual transmission in his review of that edition, *Classical Philology* 108, no. 3 (July 2013): 252–7, and Tarán's response, 'The Text of Aristotle's Poetics in the Codex Parisinus Graecus 2038', *Mnemosyne* 69, no. 5 (2016): 785–98.

[22] The standard syllabus is described by George A. Kennedy, *Greek Rhetoric under Christian Emperors* (Princeton: Princeton University Press, 1983), 52–132; for further outliers, see Thomas Conley, 'Notes on the Byzantine Reception of the Peripatetic Tradition in Rhetoric', in *Peripatetic Rhetoric after Aristotle*, ed. William W. Fortenbaugh and David C. Mirhady (New Brunswick and London: Transaction Publishers, 1994), 217–42.

of shorter texts.[23] Having travelled together in ancient lists of Aristotle's works, the *Rhetoric* and *Poetics* in this collection at least were understood to be inseparable partners within the broad genre of Greek rhetoric.[24] When the *editio princeps* of the two texts in Greek emerged from the Aldine Press in 1508, therefore, it was in a volume entitled *Rhetores graeci* ('The Greek Rhetoricians') which consciously reunited nearly the entire contents of Paris 1741, the minor *corpus* of Greek linguistics, with the standard curriculum of Hermogenes and Aphthonius, a printing project apparently preserving the entire Greek rhetorical *corpus* in a new age of Greek diaspora, just as Paris 1741 had preserved the 'anti-corpus' more than five centuries before.[25] But perhaps the most remarkable fact is that the Paris manuscript, despite its almost perfect parallel in the *Rhetores graeci*, was not Aldus's immediate copy text. Similarity between the two volumes is due not to a common material source, but to their shared conceptual unity as a disciplinary corpus. The preservation of Aristotle's *Poetics* in a tenth-century Byzantine manuscript and its dissemination in a Venetian book at the turn of the sixteenth century, that is, was in both cases a function of its identity as a work of Greek rhetoric.

Nor was the relationship without rationale in Aristotle's own works. *On Interpretation* refers to both the *Poetics* and the *Rhetoric* as those treatises which deal with significant statements unconcerned with truth or falsity, and the majority of Aristotle's own references to the *Poetics* appear in the *Rhetoric*, just as the *Poetics* points the reader to the *Rhetoric* for more detail on διάνοια (*dianoia*, 'thought').[26] Professorships of 'rhetoric and poetry' were founded throughout the sixteenth century at Italian universities, and the *Poetics* and *Rhetoric* were often brought into the classroom even when not on the formal curriculum.[27] These are just a few prominent examples; similar stories could be told about the relationship of the *Poetics* to grammar and to logic, and indeed about the long intimacy of rhetoric and poetry itself – 'an affinity in the wordish consideration', as Sir Philip Sidney put it – whether through epideictic genres, a training in narrative and dramatic techniques from elementary *progymnasmata* to full declamations, or simply what George Kennedy has called *letteraturizzazione*, the gravitation towards written

---

[23] Hugo Rabe, 'Rhetoren-Corpora', *Rheinisches Museum für Philologie* 67 (1912): 321–57; Dieter Harlfinger and Diether Reinsch, 'Die Aristotelica des Parisinus Gr. 1741. Zur Überlieferung von Poetik, Rhetorik, Physiognomonik, De signis, De ventorum situ', *Philologus* 114, no. 1 (1970): 28–50, whence 'Anti-Corpus' (32); Thomas M. Conley, 'Aristotle's Rhetoric in Byzantium', *Rhetorica* 8, no. 1 (1990): 29–44.

[24] Paul Moraux, *Les listes anciennes des ouvrages d'Aristote* (Louvain: Éditions universitaires de Louvain, 1951).

[25] For full contents see Harlfinger and Reinsch, 'Die Aristotelica des Parisinus Gr. 1741'; Paul Naiditch et al., *The Aldine Press: Catalogue of the Ahmanson-Murphy Collection* (Berkeley, Los Angeles and London: University of California Press, 2001), nos. 99 and 104. Similarities between the two collections are tabulated in Henri Omont, ed., *La Poétique d'Aristote: manuscrit 1741 fonds grec de la bibliothèque nationale* (Paris: Ernest Leroux, 1891). I am preparing work on the *Rhetores graeci* as a project of diasporic cultural preservation by post-Byzantine Greeks.

[26] As Weinberg, of course, recognized: *History*, 753–4, 804. References at *On Interpretation* 4 (17a5); *Rhetoric* 1.11 (1372a1), 3.1 (1404a39), 3.2 (1404b7, 1405a5), 3.18 (1419b5); *Poetics* 19 (1456a35).

[27] Paul F. Grendler, *The Universities of the Italian Renaissance* (Baltimore and London: Johns Hopkins University Press, 2002), 214–47.

form typical of all rhetorical genres.[28] The *Poetics* had a life independent of the *trivium*, to be sure, and the *trivium* independent of the *Poetics*, but their fruitful and intentional coexistence was hardly a Renaissance innovation.[29] For Weinberg to declare them irreconcilable in the face of more than 2,000 years of historical fact, dating back to Aristotle himself, or to cast upon their partnership the shadow of error, reveals his own reading as the exception and not the rule.

Similarly, when Weinberg rails at the 'habits of fragmentation and methodological anarchy' of Renaissance critics that dismembered this 'closely constructed and tightly argued document' for the purposes of explication, he is demanding that Aristotle's text be treated as a 'concrete artistic whole' no less than a poem; that just as Aristotle treated poetic works as '*synola*', so his own work on poetics must be understood through synthesis, through 'philosophical reading of the text'.[30] Weinberg's remarks on these habits of fragmentation in his essay 'From Aristotle to Pseudo-Aristotle' are striking:

> For those who use this method all statements in all texts are of an equal value. Since each one is in a sense torn from its context, it loses its status as a first principle, or as an intermediary statement, or as the final conclusion of a long process of deductive reasoning. The structure of a given document disappears; the form of the forest is lost and only isolated trees remain for contemplation.[31]

However valid in its own right, such an objection swims entirely against the current of Renaissance practice. Fragmentation was far from a sign of 'methodological insouciance', but a crucial stage in the long history of comprehending this difficult and telegraphic text. Indeed inasmuch as we can reconstruct what Crane called Aristotle's 'poetic method', philological practices of fragmentation and commentary originated in the line-by-line exegesis by which Aristotle and his disciples fixed the text of Homer, later to be sharpened by the Alexandrian librarians into the toolkit of classicists today.[32] Both Aristotle's method and the history of his own texts demonstrate that holistic and fragmentary critical practices pulled under the same yoke.

---

[28] Sir Philip Sidney, 'A Defence of Poetry', in *Miscellaneous Prose of Sir Philip Sidney*, ed. Katherine Duncan-Jones and J. A. Van Dorsten (Oxford: Clarendon Press, 1973), 59–121, p. 119; for a range of similar formulae see John M. McManamon, *Funeral Oratory and the Cultural Ideals of Italian Humanism* (Chapel Hill: University of North Carolina Press, 1989), 135. Epideictic: Jeffrey Walker, *Rhetoric and Poetics in Antiquity* (New York and Oxford: Oxford University Press, 2000). Progymnasmata and declamation: D. A. Russell, *Greek Declamation* (Cambridge: Cambridge University Press, 1983); Kennedy, *Greek Rhetoric*, 54–73; George A. Kennedy, *Progymnasmata: Greek Textbooks of Prose Composition and Rhetoric* (Leiden: Brill, 2003). *Letteraturizzazione*: Kennedy, *Greek Rhetoric*, 18–19, and 'The Classical Tradition in Rhetoric', in *Byzantium and the Classical Tradition*, ed. Margaret Mullett and Roger Scott (Birmingham: Centre for Byzantine Studies, University of Birmingham, 1981), 20–34, pp. 22–3.

[29] Compare, e.g. Weinberg, *History*, 805: 'The criteria evolved by Renaissance theorists ... take on, progressively, more of a rhetorical than of a poetic cast.'

[30] '*Synola*' is from Crane, *Critics and Criticism*, 17.

[31] Weinberg, 'From Aristotle to Pseudo-Aristotle', 99; cf. his chapter on 'The Methodology of the Theorists', *History*, 38–70.

[32] James Turner, *Philology: The Forgotten Origins of the Modern Humanities* (Princeton and Oxford: Princeton University Press, 2014), 11.

The drive to excerpt and consider 'in a sense torn from its context' needs to be situated, moreover, in 'the broader perspectives of noetic history', as Walter Ong put it, among the central pillars of literature's relationship to culture.[33] In his short discourse on education entitled *De ratione studii* (1511), Erasmus declares that the best teacher 'should have at the ready some commonplace book of systems and topics, so that wherever something noteworthy occurs he may write it down in the appropriate column', and points the reader to his vast manual of commonplacing, *De copia*, for advice on how to go about this.[34] After mastering linguistic basics, students should then be 'trained in topics', which involved the extraction from literature and history of maxims and anecdotes that would constitute the basic tissue of any new composition; the teacher, 'well versed in the best authorities, will compile a small widely chosen anthology of this sort and will present such selections, or will even adapt them to a form suitable to boys' abilities'.[35] Such adaptation in Erasmus's own practice involved sometimes the accommodation of pagan mores to Christian principles (by which Virgil's second eclogue might be explained as a study of friendship), and sometimes the adaptation of situated utterances into general moral principles. Tanya Pollard points out, for example, that Erasmus's Latin translation of Euripides broadens Odysseus's counsel to Hecuba – 'Know your strength, and the nature of your troubles' – into sententious form, 'One thing is certainly known, that even in the midst of trouble, each man knows in himself those things which are necessary to know'; numerous further examples stud his great commonplace collections, *De copia* and the *Adagia*.[36]

Set off by marginal quotation marks, these sententious readings methodologically mirror in tragedy itself the commentary fragmentation of the *Poetics*.[37] Yet it was again by orthodox Aristotelian authority that such dismemberment and decontextualization took place. As every Renaissance Aristotelian knew, the standard Latin translation of Aristotle's διάνοια, one of his six parts of tragedy that we have already encountered in cross references to the *Rhetoric*, was '*sententia*', 'thought' in the sense of 'a thought' as much as a broad art of 'discourse'; Aristotle's own definition stipulates that the term

---

[33] Walter J. Ong, 'Commonplace Rhapsody: Ravisius Textor, Zwinger and Shakespeare', in *Classical Influences on European Culture A.D. 1500-1700*, ed. R. R. Bolgar (Cambridge: Cambridge University Press, 1976), 91–126, p. 92.
[34] Desiderius Erasmus, *De ratione studii*, trans. Brian McGregor, in Erasmus, *Literary and Education Writings, 2: De copia; De ratione studii*, ed. Craig R. Thompson, Collected Works of Erasmus 24 (Toronto, Buffalo and London: University of Toronto Press, 1978), 672.
[35] Ibid., 676–8.
[36] Tanya Pollard, 'Greek Playbooks and Dramatic Forms in Early Modern England', in *Formal Matters: Reading the Materials of English Renaissance Literature*, ed. Allison Deutermann and András Kiséry (Manchester: Manchester University Press, 2013), 99–123, p. 102.
[37] On commonplacing in general and quotation marks in particular: G. K. Hunter, 'The Marking of Sententiae in Elizabethan Printed Plays, Poems, and Romances', *The Library* s5, VI, no. 3-4 (1951): 171–88; Zachary Lesser et al., 'The First Literary Hamlet and the Commonplacing of Professional Plays', *Shakespeare Quarterly* 59, no. 4 (2008): 371–420; Peter Mack, 'Rhetoric, Ethics and Reading in the Renaissance', *Renaissance Studies* 19, no. 1 (2005): 1–21; Ann Moss, *Printed Commonplace-Books and the Structuring of Renaissance Thought* (Oxford: Clarendon Press, 1996); William H. Sherman, *Used Books: Marking Readers in Renaissance England* (Philadelphia: University of Pennsylvania Press, 2008).

describes how we 'prove that something is or is not, *or state a general maxim*'.[38] If one of the six constituent elements of tragedy was *sententia*, an authentic and important mode of reading tragedy was for *sententiae* – for nuggets of wisdom which applied beyond the limits of their dramatic circumstances. Weinberg opposed such reading vociferously, feeling with his Chicago colleagues that the *Poetics* and Aristotelian method in general warranted the treatment of tragedy and other poetry as 'concrete aesthetic wholes'. Yet it is Aristotle himself who distils Greek poetry into *sententiae* to argue that memories, even of nasty experiences, are pleasant, by reference to Euripides's (lost) *Andromeda*, 'Truly it is pleasant to remember toil after one has escaped it', and explains through the *Iliad* that anger is 'far sweeter than dripping honey'; that change is natural, through Euripides's *Orestes*, 'Change in all things is sweet'; and that there is a notion of natural justice through Sophocles's *Antigone*, 'Neither today nor yesterday, but from all eternity, these statutes live and no man knoweth whence they came.'[39]

These are just a very few examples of Aristotle participating in precisely the same reading practices of fragmentation and redeployment as his Renaissance followers, who in following him, exhibited an understanding of his method that was not just reasonable, but correct. Theoretical justification as well as many more examples might be drawn from his discussion in the *Rhetoric* of γνῶμαι (*gnomai*, 'maxims'), in the course of which he draws on fragments of several plays by Euripides, shows how they deal not in 'particulars' but in 'universals' (καθόλου), and observes that one of their uses is to make speeches 'ethical' because they make the speaker's choice (προαίρεσις) clear. The terms and phenomena addressed here are plainly continuous with passages in the *Poetics* on character and the universality of poetry.[40] Through his own discussion and application of διάνοια, Aristotle makes clear that the fragmentary, sententious approach to texts was if anything the standard mode of reading and composing literary texts in his time and before. Much of the Greek literature that we know of today has only survived through the assiduous commonplacing of ancient sources. Instruction in poetry from the earliest practices of the Sophists utilized gnomic anthologies, and later education in the language arts – the context in which the *Poetics* was transmitted, received and read – mandated exercises in γνῶμαι (maxims) and χρεῖαι (anecdotes).[41] Given the ubiquity of these modes of reading, there is every reason to imagine that the dramatists themselves wrote with such practices in mind, and that our own aversion to reading for *sententiae* misconstrues their works.[42] Such aversion may be defensible in a critic, but not in an historian – and Weinberg does understand himself to be writing

---

[38] *Poetics* 6 (1450b12-13), italics mine; for the Renaissance view see, for example, Francesco Robortello, *In librum Aristotelis de arte poetica explicationes* (Florence: Laurentius Torrentinus, 1548), 223: 'Sententia: quam Aristoteles caeterique omnes Rhetores Graeci διάνοιαν vocant' ('*Sententia*: which Aristotle and all the rest of the Greek rhetors call *dianoia*').

[39] Aristotle, *Rhetoric*, trans. J. H. Freese (Cambridge, MA: Harvard University Press, 1926), 1:11–13 (1370b–3b).

[40] Ibid., 2:21 (1394a19–95b20); cf. *Poetics* 6 (1450b8–11), 9 (1451b5–10).

[41] Teresa Morgan, *Literate Education in the Hellenistic and Roman Worlds* (Cambridge: Cambridge University Press, 1998), 120-51; John Barns, 'A New Gnomologium: with Some Remarks on Gnomic Anthologies', *Classical Quarterly* 44, no. 3-4; n.s. 1, nos. 1–2 (1950-1951): 126-37; 1–19.

[42] William Slater, 'Gnomology and Criticism', *Greek, Roman, and Byzantine Studies* 41 (2001): 99-121. I am most grateful to Vaios Liapis for this as well as the preceding references.

as an 'historian' among historians, classifies his work as 'an experiment in the writing of intellectual history', and deploys throughout the systematizing, disinterested tone of the Chicago School.[43] Again, Weinberg's objection to 'fragmentation', whether of Aristotle or of the texts Aristotle treats, marks out his own mode of reading as the historical exception to a much longer tradition.

Modern *Poetics*: Edinburgh, Chicago

These brief remarks suggest some of the forms Aristotle's *Poetics* took outside Chicago. Yet the Chicago School's own eager citation of the belief that the *Poetics* stood for the core principles of aesthetic autonomy itself amounts to a kind of didactic commonplacing, since, for all Crane's deflections, it did derive from an identifiable source. Published in 1895, S. H. Butcher's *Aristotle's Theory of Poetry and Fine Art* had gathered enormous influence over the intervening years not only as a critical edition, translation and commentary in its own right but also through its capillary diffusion through intermediary accounts of historical criticism. Butcher was in no doubt as to what Aristotle really meant, holding that 'the general views of Aristotle on Poetry and Art are not affected by the minor difficulties with which the *Poetics* abounds'.[44] Aristotle was, quite simply, 'the first who attempted to separate the theory of aesthetics from that of morals'; the ethical elements of the *Poetics*, notably his discussions of character, are merely vestiges of 'the earlier influence'; and his critical judgements on poetry 'rest on aesthetic and logical grounds, they take no direct account of ethical aims or tendencies'.[45]

How this position hardened in the early years of Butcher's influence can be traced through his own personal copies of the first three editions of *Aristotle's Theory of Poetry and Fine Art*, extensively marked up for revision, now in the library of Trinity College, Cambridge.[46] Butcher's translation of *Poetics* 25 (1461a4–9), for example, appears in the first edition as follows:

περὶ δὲ τοῦ καλῶς ἢ μὴ καλῶς εἰ εἴρηταί τινι ἢ πέπρακται, οὐ μόνον σκεπτέον εἰς αὐτὸ τὸ πεπραγμένον ἢ εἰρημένον βλέποντα, εἰ σπουδαῖον ἢ φαῦλον...

Again, in examining whether what has been said or done by some one is right or wrong, we must not look merely to the particular speech or action, and ask whether it is in itself good or bad.[47]

---

[43] Weinberg, *History*, vii–x.
[44] S. H. Butcher, *Aristotle's Theory of Poetry and Fine Art* (London and New York: Macmillan, 1895), vii–viii (preface).
[45] Ibid., 209, 221.
[46] Cambridge, Trinity College, Wren Library, Adv.c.17.3-7 comprise five editions of the *Poetics* owned and annotated by S. H. Butcher: two copies of his own first edition (1895, Adv.c.17.3-4), one of the second (Adv.c.17.5), and the editions of Franciscus Ritter (Cologne: I. E. Renard, 1839) and Johannes Vahlen (Berlin: Francis Vahlen, 1874). All were donated on 6 February 1911, two months after Samuel's death at the end of 1910, by his brother John George Butcher, once a Trinity student.
[47] Butcher, *Aristotle's Theory of Poetry and Fine Art*, 94–5.

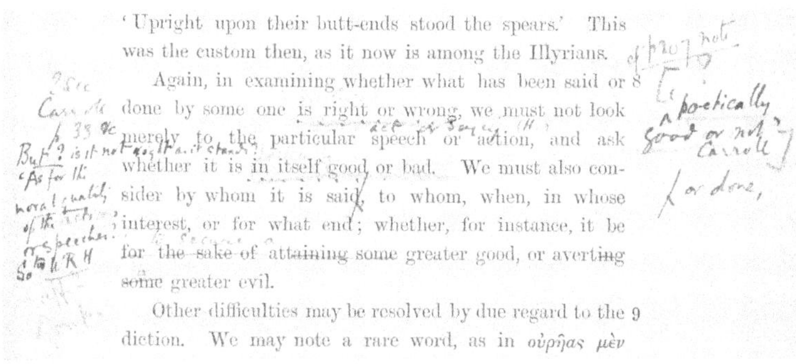

Figure 3.1 Cambridge, Trinity College, Wren Library, Adv.c.17.3, p. 95.

'Right or wrong' (καλῶς ἢ μὴ καλῶς) and 'in itself good or bad' (σπουδαῖον ἢ φαῦλον) here identify, naturally, ethical qualities – qualities corresponding to shared social expectations independent of the poem. Yet in preparation for the second edition, Butcher replaces 'right or wrong' with 'poetically good or not', and he alters 'in itself good or bad' to 'poetically good or bad', attributing both readings to 'Carroll' (Figure 3.1).[48] So urgent were these corrections that they could not wait until 1898 for the second edition to go to press: a leaf of printed addenda to the first edition identifies 'Carroll' as Mitchell Carroll, who earned a doctorate in 1893 from Johns Hopkins for his work on *Poetics* 25, itself guided by the aestheticizing tendencies of Butcher's first edition.[49] A blue pencil note against the addendum here nevertheless reads '(?doubtful)', suggesting that although Butcher updated the official text, he may not yet have been wholly convinced of this reading.

Another example is Butcher's translation of 'βλαβερὰ' (harmful) in *Poetics* 25 (1461b23), which at first he took to mean that one kind of bad poetry was 'morally hurtful'. Again, manuscript comments in the margin replace the ethical reading with an aesthetic one – now he sees such bad poetry 'as violating artistic principles' – and an interlinear note supplies Carroll's own translation of the following lines, 'contrary to artistic correctness'.[50] The exegetical essays then fell in line: an entire paragraph of the first edition, explaining that 'the charge that a poem is morally hurtful is evidently a grave one in the eyes of Aristotle', is struck through and excised from subsequent printed editions, a note pointing to 'Carroll's expl.' inscribed in the margin.[51] With or without Carroll, however, Butcher was more than willing to expunge moral criteria from his rendering on his own. Dense annotations in his working copy of Vahlen's 1874 edition of the *Poetics*, representing his understanding of the text over many years, are content to gloss 'σπουδαῖον ἢ φαῦλον' in the first passage with '(? moral use = καλῶς ἢ μὴ above)' and to take 'βλαβερὰ' in the second in the sense of 'immoral tendency'; but though he declared in the first edition that Aristotle's focus

---

[48] Wren Library, Adv.c.17.3, 95.
[49] Ibid., 2; see Mitchell Carroll, *Aristotle's Poetics, C. XXV, in the Light of the Homeric Scholia* (Baltimore: John Murphy & Co., 1895), 33ff.
[50] Ibid., 101; cf. Carroll, *Aristotle's Poetics, C. XXV, in the Light of the Homeric Scholia*, 21–3.
[51] Ibid., 210.

here was 'moral character', a note on the flyleaves of Butcher's Vahlen reads 'Βελτίων not moral sense: but higher [artistic sense]', already registering resistance to the ethical terms in which Aristotle demands that the characters of tragedy be 'better' than us.[52] Buoyed by its good reception at home and abroad, across three editions in just seven years, Butcher aestheticized his *Poetics* at the expense of morality.

Institutional history ensured that Butcher's aestheticized Aristotle was fed directly into the critical mainstream. Butcher had been a fellow of Trinity College, Cambridge and University College, Oxford, but when his Aristotle came out in 1895, he had been professor of Greek at Edinburgh for thirteen years. At Edinburgh, his colleagues included George Saintsbury, chair of Rhetoric and English Literature since 1895 and author of the great late-Victorian *summa*, the three volumes of *A History of Criticism and Literary Taste in Europe* (1900–4). Saintsbury was a forceful synthesizer in the Victorian vein, and despite 'occasionally differing, on the purely critical side' – his Aristotle is 'doubly and triply ethical' – nonetheless recommended Butcher as a crucial resource for those 'who do not care to "grapple with whole libraries"'.[53] Another of Butcher's colleagues at Edinburgh was G. Gregory Smith, lecturer in English since 1892, who had a still more lasting influence on the field of Renaissance criticism, at least, as editor and compiler of *Elizabethan Critical Essays* in two volumes.[54] Smith further reinforced the movement by citing Butcher generously and declaring that 'no venturer in this subject dare reckon without the learned author of the *History of Criticism*, or the American scholar who broke fresh ground in the remarkable volume on *Literary Criticism in the Renaissance*', the former Saintsbury and the latter Joel Spingarn, whom we will meet in a moment.[55] Though Butcher's influence spread beyond English literature alone, its centrality to anglophone scholarship is inseparable from its absorption into the history of English literary criticism, a burgeoning field shaped by these pioneer works in 1890s Scotland. Only in 1893 was Aberdeen's Professorship of English Language and Literature separated from that of Logic; in 1895, David Nichol Smith – Gregory Smith's younger brother – became Edinburgh's first graduate with First Class Honours in English. An aesthetically fundamentalist *Poetics*, distanced from the roots of the English school in stylistics and composition, offered the Edinburgh set classical warrant and critical rigour for a nascent discipline squeezed between, on one front, the coalface of philology and classics, and on the other, 'pink sunsets' – as the new English studies were then known at Oxford.[56]

---

[52] Wren Library, Adv.c.17.7, 66, 72, second rear endpaper; for 'moral character' see the 1st edn (1895), 240.
[53] George Saintsbury, *A History of Criticism and Literary Taste in Europe from the Earliest Texts to the Present Day*, 3 vols. (Edinburgh and London: Blackwood, 1900–1904), I:38n1, 31n2.
[54] G. Gregory Smith, ed., *Elizabethan Critical Essays*, 2 vols. (Oxford: Clarendon Press, 1904); its forthcoming publication was advertised in the second (Renaissance) volume of Saintsbury's *History of Criticism* in 1902 (II:144n1).
[55] Smith, *Elizabethan Critical Essays*, I:viii.
[56] Brian Doyle, *English and Englishness*, new edn (London and New York: Routledge, 1989), 3; on Scotland in particular, see Robert Irvine, 'English Literary Studies: Origins and Nature', in *The Edinburgh Introduction to Studying English Literature*, ed. Dermot Cavanagh (Edinburgh: Edinburgh University Press, 2010), 16–24.

Meanwhile, Butcher was popularized across the Atlantic through the work of Joel Spingarn. Spingarn was a remarkable figure, a public-schooled, first-generation Jewish immigrant to America, enthusiastic botanist (he amassed the world's largest clematis collection), and lifelong campaigner for the rights of African Americans, serving from 1914 successively as chairman, treasurer and president of the then just-founded NAACP.[57] When at twenty-four years of age, newly appointed as professor of Comparative Literature at Columbia, he published his PhD thesis as *A History of Literary Criticism in the Renaissance* (1899), it decisively reshaped the field as a comparative one, placing 'Aristotelian canons, as restated by the Italians' at the root of critical developments in France and England as well. Ancient and medieval literature, in Spingarn's telling, had been judged according to 'unaesthetic' categories, 'the criteria of reality and morality', to which the answer came 'only with the recovery of Aristotle's *Poetics*'; Butcher is again widely cited for this transformative aesthetic reading of the *Poetics*, and Spingarn is as certain as Butcher was of what Aristotle 'really meant'.[58] Fracastoro makes the cut, and Castelvetro, too, is found mostly in accord with 'the true Aristotelian conception'. But others among Spingarn's Italian, French and English critics are 'of course entirely un-Aristotelian' in their understanding of poetic justice and their distinctions between tragedy and comedy.[59] Though ostensibly a history of interpretation, Spingarn's *History*, like Weinberg's *History* some decades later, has a very fixed sense of what Aristotle's 'aesthetic' treatise 'really meant'; much of the time it differs from what Renaissance Italians thought Aristotle 'really meant', which raises questions about the extent to which Spingarn's work should be thought of as a history of interpretation at all, rather than as a new work of literary criticism whose materials happen to be historical. This new criticism owed much to the Italian philosopher Benedetto Croce (another influence Crane was at pains to disavow), who wrote the preface to the Italian second edition of the *History* in 1905, and in turn was mediated for American audiences through a lecture given by Spingarn at Columbia in March 1910 entitled 'The New Criticism'. In this lecture, Spingarn rejects prior critical paradigms in favour of Croce's principle of the autonomy of the expressive work of art, the principle that 'every poet re-expresses the universe in his own way, and every poem is a new and independent expression'.[60] To the extent that such a principle is a 'modern' invention, it is clear that Butcher and Spingarn spoke through Aristotle rather than about him, locating in the *Poetics* ancient authority for a programme of aesthetic renewal.

Through the dual routes of Smith's account of English criticism and Spingarn's account of the continent's, Butcher's *Poetics* became enshrined in the historical study

---

[57] Two biographies exist: Marshall Van Deusen, *J. E. Spingarn* (New York: Twayne Publishers, 1971), and B. Joyce Ross, *J. E. Spingarn and the Rise of the NAACP, 1911-1939* (New York: Atheneum, 1972), which gives more attention to his activism, which he shared with his Harvard professor George Woodberry. The Spingarn Medal, for example, offered from March 1913, served as 'a reminder that America was not solely a country of, by, and for Anglo Saxons' (Ross, *J. E. Spingarn and the Rise of the NAACP, 1911-1939*, 28).

[58] I quote from the second edition: J. E. Spingarn, *A History of Literary Criticism in the Renaissance*, 2nd edn (New York: Columbia University Press, 1908), 3–4, 15–18, 33.

[59] Ibid., 33, 44, 52.

[60] J. E. Spingarn, *The New Criticism: A Lecture Delivered at Columbia University, March 9, 1910* (New York: Columbia University Press, 1911), 24.

of criticism. L. S. Friedland's authorities in his seminal article on 'The Dramatic Unities in England' (1911) are Spingarn and Butcher, and consequently, 'the true lesson of Aristotle's example was lost' on his Renaissance critics; portions of J. E. Sandys's magisterial *History of Classical Scholarship* (1903–8) surveying the *Poetics* are closely cribbed from Spingarn, as is the overview of Renaissance Aristotelianism in Wimsatt and Brooks's *Literary Criticism: A Short History* (1957).[61] Though Butcher ventured no opinion on the historical reception of the *Poetics*, therefore, he nevertheless defined, during the first formative decades of the field, the nature of the object that was received. His edition of the *Poetics* provided the elucidation necessary, James Hutton admiringly remarked in 1982, 'to recommend it to modern ways of thinking'.[62] Thus among Weinberg's immediate precursors, it was Butcher's Aristotle that co-ordinated teleological accounts of critical history. We have seen Spingarn anticipate Weinberg in levelling the charge of 'un-Aristotelian' theory at Renaissance interpreters of the *Poetics*; in Lane Cooper's *The Poetics of Aristotle* (1923) we are introduced to Castelvetro, 'who understands Aristotle almost as well as we do'; with Marvin Herrick, Cooper's doctoral student at Cornell, the thesis took shape that the *Poetics* was 'fused' with Horace's *Ars poetica*, which Weinberg preferred to think of as 'confusion' since 'rhetoric and poetic are immiscible arts'; and in Weinberg's own *History* it is Butcher who sponsors the claim that a moral reading of the *Poetics* 'for a modern Aristotelian ... would be considered incorrect'.[63]

History as criticism, criticism as history

Even at the height of Butcher's influence, in the years preceding Weinberg's and the Chicago School's entry into the field in the early 1950s, it was recognized that a dogmatically 'aesthetic' *Poetics* posed serious methodological problems for the history of criticism. An essay 'On the Relation of Horace to Aristotle in Literary Criticism' in 1947 by Allan Gilbert and H. L. Snuggs, ostensibly a review of Herrick's *Fusion* and now largely forgotten, stands out as a powerful refutation both of Butcher and of the inverted history of Aristotle's reception that had grown up around his reading of the *Poetics*.[64] Beginning again from the earliest primary sources, Snuggs and Gilbert point out that the Renaissance belief that Horace was a follower of Aristotle is prima facie quite sensible, and that in fact 'Horace may have derived such a theory from writers whom he supposed to be followers of Aristotle'; 'Renaissance students who

---

[61] L. S. Friedland, 'The Dramatic Unities in England', *The Journal of English and Germanic Philology* 10 (1911): 56–89, 280–99, 453–67, 64; J. E. Sandys, *A History of Classical Scholarship*, 3 vols. (Cambridge: University Press, 1903-1908), II:133–5, 188; William K. Wimsatt and Cleanth Brooks, *Literary Criticism: A Short History* (New York: Knopf, 1957), 156.

[62] *Aristotle's Poetics*, trans. James Hutton (New York: Norton, 1982), 33; of course, one might instead say that Butcher contributed to modern ways of thinking that by 1982 had rendered his elucidation of the *Poetics* necessary.

[63] Spingarn, *History*, 52, 64; Cooper, *The Poetics of Aristotle*, 112; Herrick, *Fusion*; Weinberg, Review of Herrick, 271; Weinberg, *History*, 799.

[64] Allan H. Gilbert and H. L. Snuggs, 'On the Relation of Horace to Aristotle in Literary Criticism', *The Journal of English and Germanic Philology* 46 (1947): 233–47.

found Horace like Aristotle would not feel uncomfortable in the company of modern scholars'.[65] Given this stemma of influence, 'no reconciliation of Horace and Aristotle was needed', since the two had never truly been disseevered.[66] Just as the association of the *Poetics* with the *trivium* was no Renaissance invention but a long-attested historical fact of its reception, so the ethical didactic reading of the *Poetics* supposedly effected by its Renaissance association with Horace had been present in the texts and its reception all along: 'The *Poetics* has enough of a didactic tinge to permit the men of the Renaissance to see there all the didactic theory they had themselves acquired from Roman and mediaeval thought.'[67] Herrick's 'fusion' hypothesis presupposes that the two works were meaningfully distinct in the first place; on the contrary, Snuggs and Gilbert insist, even if the 'non-didactic theory of poetry is obviously not a new invention', it only became truly influential around the end of the nineteenth century.[68] The authors trace this influence to Croce's *Aesthetic* in Italy (1900) and Bosanquet's *History of Aesthetic* in England (1892), but above all, from their vantage point in the American academy, to Butcher's volume of 1895:

> Butcher is apparently responsible for the spread in English-speaking countries of an aesthetic interpretation of the *Poetics*. In America, indeed, Aristotle has been until recently, or even still is, the thinker Butcher presents in his essays; even students who have turned to the original text have tended to read it through Butcher's spectacles. This is not a new phenomenon in Aristotelian studies.[69]

Snuggs and Gilbert, in short, recognized that the standard model of the Renaissance reception of Aristotle's *Poetics* – misunderstood; 'hopelessly adulterated with Horatian maxims'; distorted by the gravitational pull of grammar, rhetoric or logic; fragmented into lexical smithereens, or justifying the fragmentation of its poetic objects into ethical smithereens – was itself anachronistic, the result of a teleological model of critical history culminating in an uniquely twentieth-century *Poetics*.[70] It is not difficult to see among their targets the lineaments of Weinberg's work, which began appearing just a few years later and proved so influential as to overshadow their short review essay. Yet their lasting insight was of the need to historicize Butcher's, Herrick's and, by extension, Weinberg's *Poetics*, to understand them as not superordinate to but constitutive of the history of criticism, as subject to historical contingency as the criticism they surveyed. Snuggs and Gilbert recognized that in the modern period no less than the Renaissance, the meaning of the *Poetics* tends not to generate, but to be generated by, critical doctrine.

This insight resurfaced sporadically over the following decades. Stephen Halliwell, in his classic study of Aristotle's *Poetics*, noted that 'despite reactions against the critical stance of the Chicago school, their interpretation of Aristotle has, I believe, done much

---

[65] Ibid., 233–4.
[66] Ibid., 240.
[67] Ibid.
[68] Ibid., 246.
[69] Ibid., 246–7.
[70] The quotation is from Marvin Herrick, *The Poetics of Aristotle in England* (New Haven: Yale University Press), 34.

to spread the dominant modern belief that the *Poetics* embodies a clean separation of poetic and ethical standards'.[71] Brian Vickers, not given to leniency in demonstrating that 'the major commentaries on the *Poetics* in the Italian sixteenth century are all basically rhetorical', nonetheless scrupled that 'Weinberg's antithesis between Horace and Aristotle is too extreme', and at the turn of the century, Daniel Javitch observed that 'because of the influence of Weinberg's *History of Literary Criticism in the Italian Renaissance*, the so-called distortion of Aristotle's theory to make it fit mainstream ethico-rhetorical poetics has been taken to be the most characteristic feature of its reception in the late Renaissance'.[72] In fact, by this time several tenets of the Chicago model had been independently challenged in their respective fields. Jeffrey Walker's powerful *Rhetoric and Poetics in Antiquity* reframed his two subjects as natural companions, marking a turn in rhetorical studies towards the wider Greek *corpus* with epideictic rhetoric (rather than the forensic persuasion that seemed so distasteful to previous decades) at its centre. Charles Schmitt's ground breaking work on Renaissance Aristotelianism inaugurated a rich and vibrant field of scholarship, dismissing the biases inherited from humanist polemics against scholastic pedantry.[73] Halliwell's studies of the *Poetics*, in turn, reintroduced a text more complex than the monolithic defence of aesthetic autonomy familiar for much of the twentieth century, and the history of scholarship championed by Anthony Grafton revitalized interest in the detailed work of Renaissance commentary.[74]

Yet if this brief historiographical sketch has a moral it is that criticism and its society must be treated as symbiotic; neither the principled arguments of historians of criticism nor several decades of detailed scholarship in contiguous fields would have sufficed to overturn Weinberg's synthesis if it still satisfied the demands of the field. Whatever complex of needs the Chicago School arose to answer, it is clear that the academy today has chosen rather different modes of reading. Fashion has turned again to asking ethical and political questions of our curricular texts: whether a work represents approved maxims about gender or race, for example, and if not, whether it should be curricular or even read at all; whether the ingredients of an author's identity statistically represent the social constitution of her time, or the constitution of a society anticipated and furthered by that representation. Essays both pupillary and professional in cultural studies as well as in literature (to the extent that literary scholarship now considers itself a form of cultural studies) amount to variations

---

[71] Stephen Halliwell, *Aristotle's Poetics* (London: Duckworth, 1986), 317.
[72] Brian Vickers, 'Rhetoric and Poetics', in *The Cambridge History of Renaissance Philosophy*, ed. Charles B. Schmitt et al. (Cambridge: Cambridge University Press, 1988), 715–45, p. 720; Daniel Javitch, 'The Assimilation of Aristotle's *Poetics* in Sixteenth-Century Italy', in *The Cambridge History of Literary Criticism, III: The Renaissance*, ed. Glyn Norton (Cambridge: Cambridge University Press, 1999), 53–65, p. 58.
[73] Among Schmitt's many works *Aristotle and the Renaissance* (Cambridge, MA: Harvard University Press, 1983), remains the classic study; for extensive bibliography in this field see Dmitri Levitin, *Ancient Wisdom in the Age of the New Science* (Cambridge: Cambridge University Press, 2015).
[74] In addition to works already cited see Stephen Halliwell, 'Epilogue: The *Poetics* and its Interpreters', in *Essays on Aristotle's Poetics*, ed. Amélie Rorty (Princeton: Princeton University Press, 1992), 409–24, p. 420. For an early, pertinent example of Grafton's work, see 'Renaissance Readers and Ancient Texts: Comments on Some Commentaries', *Renaissance Quarterly* 38, no. 4 (1985): 615–49, in addition to his many books.

upon *gnomai* or *chreiai*: ritualized debates *in utramque partem* of moral maxims and examples, rewarded less for ingenuity of argument than for their virtuous reproduction of normative moral positions. Through social media, email signatures and online profiles, literary and cultural texts are fragmented, commonplaced, stripped of context, creatively misquoted and adapted into universal maxims or applied as though they were. And university literature departments, especially in the United States, again are deputed to provide classes in written composition, the training in the language arts from which the *Poetics* did so much to release them in 1890s Edinburgh. Emphasis on correct writing and on effective writing tailored to target audiences and pragmatic ends reproduces the disciplinary boundaries of grammar and rhetoric, and the most common defence of a humanities degree, that it provides a training in 'critical thinking' independent of any specific content is not, I think, far from the claims of Aristotelian logic in the Renaissance university. The ADE (Associated Departments of English) Bulletin for 2018 reflects that following the financial crisis of 2008, 'student attitudes toward the curriculum are overwhelmingly presentist'; across the sector, 'the curricular structure that conveys literary history is being progressively abandoned'; consideration is given once more, under pressure of falling registration and the renewed necessity of justifying the utility of a humanities degree, to the taxonomy of writing courses and the boundaries between composition and rhetoric.[75] 'The perennial jealousies of rhetoricians and philosophers, grammarians and rhetoricians, historians and critics' have returned with new names, but the same old guild prejudices. As I write almost seven decades after the publication of *Critics and Criticism*, it seems that poetics is once again re-entering the *organon*; that we are witnessing not just the resurgence of reading for morality, but nothing less than the return of the *trivium*.[76]

From this perspective, it would be churlish to join the Chicago School in holding Renaissance critics to be misguidedly ethical, rhetorical or scholastic. On the contrary, the historiographical legacy of the Chicago Aristotle was radically to constrain the scope of the Renaissance *Poetics* and misrepresent its interpreters. Yet the particular shape and necessity of that misrepresentation has its roots in the early development of our modern literary disciplines, tracking the rise of a professional class of literary scholars in need of methodological justification for their fields. In the long view, the belief in aesthetic autonomy championed through the twentieth century seems itself to be an aberration in the much longer history of the place of poetry in civilized society. Attempting to write a study of didactic literature in Weinberg's wake, O. B.

---

[75] Kent Cartwright, 'The Changing English Major and the Fate of Literary History', *ADE Bulletin* 155 (2018): 20–4; Eric Detweiler, 'Toward Pedagogical Turnings', *ADE Bulletin* 155 (2018): 52–60; James Seitz, 'Inventing the Writing Program: How to Name What We Do When, However Old, It's New', *ADE Bulletin* 155 (2018): 42–6. I am grateful to Michael Schoenfeldt for pointing me towards these pieces and for discussion on the topic.

[76] An explicit call to return to the *trivium* was made in Robert Scholes's 2004 presidential address to the Modern Languages Association, 'The Humanities in a Posthumanist World', *PMLA* 120, no. 3 (2005): 724–33, and his subsequent correspondence with James D. Hoff and Harold Fromm, 'Rebuilding the Humanities', *PMLA* 121, no. 1 (2006): 296–8. The popular press has followed: see Martin Robinson, *Trivium 21c: Preparing Young People for the Future with Lessons from the Past* (Carmarthen: Independent Thinking Press, 2013); John Michell et al., *Trivium: The Classical Liberal Arts of Grammar, Logic, & Rhetoric* (New York: Bloomsbury, 2016).

Hardison observed in 1962 that 'whenever a theory of poetry becomes widespread, a commentary on the *Poetics* appears that makes Aristotle a proponent of the theory and, in turn, helps to transform it from speculation into dogma'.[77] What reading of the *Poetics* will emerge to authorize this reactionary moment remains to be seen.

Bibliography

Aristotle. *Aristotle's Art of Poetry. Translated from the Original Greek, According to Mr. Theodore Goulston's Edition. Together, with Mr. D'acier's Notes*. Translated from the French. London: Dan. Browne and Will. Turner, 1705.

Aristotle. *Aristotle's Poetics*. Translated by James Hutton. New York: Norton, 1982.

Aristotle. *Poetics: Editio Maior of the Greek Text with Historical Introductions and Philological Commentaries*, edited by Leonardo Tarán and Dimitri Gutas Leiden. Boston: Brill, 2012.

Aristotle. *Rhetoric*. Translated by J. H. Freese. Cambridge, MA and London: Harvard University Press, 1926.

Barns, John. 'A New Gnomologium: With Some Remarks on Gnomic Anthologies'. *Classical Quarterly* 44, nos. 3–4 (1950): 126–37; n.s. 1, nos. 1–2 (1951): 1–19.

Butcher, S. H. *Aristotle's Theory of Poetry and Fine Art: With a Critical Text and Translation of the Poetics*, 3rd edn. London: Macmillan, 1902.

Cartwright, Kent. 'The Changing English Major and the Fate of Literary History'. *ADE Bulletin* 155 (2018): 20–4.

Conley, Thomas. 'Aristotle's Rhetoric in Byzantium'. *Rhetorica* 8, no. 1 (1990): 29–44.

Conley, Thomas. 'Notes on the Byzantine Reception of the Peripatetic Tradition in Rhetoric'. In *Peripatetic Rhetoric after Aristotle*, edited by William W. Fortenbaugh and David C. Mirhady, 217–42. New Brunswick and London: Transaction Publishers, 1994.

Cooper, Lane. *The Poetics of Aristotle: Its Meaning and Influence*. London: George G. Harrap, 1923.

Crane, Ronald S., ed. *Critics and Criticism: Ancient and Modern*. Chicago: University of Chicago Press, 1952.

Detweiler, Eric. 'Toward Pedagogical Turnings'. *ADE Bulletin* 155 (2018): 52–60.

Diller, Aubrey. 'Notes on the History of Some Manuscripts of Aristotle'. In *Studia Codicologica*, edited by Kurt Treu, 147–50. Berlin: Akademie-Verlag, 1977.

Doyle, Brian. *English and Englishness*, New edn. London and New York: Routledge, 2003.

Erasmus, Desiderius. *Literary and Education Writings, 2: De Copia; De Ratione Studii*. Translated by Betty I. Knott and Brian McGregor. *Collected Works of Erasmus*, vol. 24, edited by Craig R. Thompson. Toronto, Buffalo and London: University of Toronto Press, 1978.

Friedland, L. S. 'The Dramatic Unities in England'. *The Journal of English and Germanic Philology* 10 (1911): 56–89, 280–99, 453–67.

Gilbert, Allan H. and H. L. Snuggs. 'On the Relation of Horace to Aristotle in Literary Criticism'. *The Journal of English and Germanic Philology* 46 (1947): 233–47.

Grafton, Anthony. 'Renaissance Readers and Ancient Texts: Comments on Some Commentaries'. *Renaissance Quarterly* 38, no. 4 (1985): 615–49.

---

[77] O. B. Hardison, *The Enduring Monument: A Study of the Idea of Praise in Renaissance Literary Theory and Practice* (Chapel Hill: University of North Carolina Press, 1962), x.

Gregory Smith, G., ed. *Elizabethan Critical Essays*, 2 vols. Oxford: Clarendon Press, 1904.
Grendler, Paul F. *The Universities of the Italian Renaissance*. Baltimore and London: Johns Hopkins University Press, 2002.
Halliwell, Stephen. *Aristotle's Poetics*. London: Duckworth, 1986.
Halliwell, Stephen. 'Epilogue: The *Poetics* and Its Interpreters'. In *Essays on Aristotle's Poetics*, edited by Amélie Rorty, 409–24. Princeton: Princeton University Press, 1992.
Hardison, O. B. *The Enduring Monument: A Study of the Idea of Praise in Renaissance Literary Theory and Practice*. Chapel Hill: University of North Carolina Press, 1962.
Harlfinger, Dieter and Diether Reinsch. 'Die Aristotelica Des Parisinus Gr. 1741. Zur Überlieferung Von Poetik, Rhetorik, Physiognomonik, De Signis, De Ventorum Situ'. *Philologus* 114, no. 1 (1970): 28–50.
Herrick, Marvin T. *The Fusion of Horatian and Aristotelian Literary Criticism, 1531–1555*. Urbana: University of Illinois Press, 1946.
Herrick, Marvin T. *The Poetics of Aristotle in England*. New Haven; London: Yale University Press; Oxford University Press, 1930.
Hunter, G. K. 'The Marking of Sententiae in Elizabethan Printed Plays, Poems, and Romances'. *The Library* s5-VI, nos. 3–4 (1951): 171–88.
Irvine, Robert. 'English Literary Studies: Origins and Nature'. In *The Edinburgh Introduction to Studying English Literature*, edited by Dermot Cavanagh, 16–24. Edinburgh: Edinburgh University Press, 2010.
Janko, Richard. Review of Aristotle, *Poetics: Editio Maior of the Greek Text with Historical Introductions and Philological Commentaries*, edited by Leonardo Tarán and Dimitri Gutas. *Classical Philology* 108, no. 3 (2013): 252–57.
Javitch, Daniel. 'The Assimilation of Aristotle's Poetics in Sixteenth-Century Italy'. In *The Cambridge History of Literary Criticism, Iii: The Renaissance*, edited by Glyn P. Norton, 53–65. Cambridge: Cambridge University Press, 1999.
Kennedy, George A. 'The Classical Tradition in Rhetoric'. In *Byzantium and the Classical Tradition*, edited by Margaret Mullett and Roger Scott, 20–34. Birmingham: Centre for Byzantine Studies, University of Birmingham, 1981.
Kennedy, George A. *Greek Rhetoric under Christian Emperors*. Princeton: Princeton University Press, 1983.
Kennedy, George A. *Progymnasmata: Greek Textbooks of Prose Composition and Rhetoric*. Leiden: Brill, 2003.
Lesser, Zachary, Peter Stallybrass and G. K. Hunter. 'The First Literary Hamlet and the Commonplacing of Professional Plays'. *Shakespeare Quarterly* 59, no. 4 (2008): 371–420.
Lessing, Gotthold Ephraim. *Hamburgische Dramaturgie*, 2 vols. [Leipzig]: J. Dodsley, 1769.
Levitin, Dmitri. *Ancient Wisdom in the Age of the New Science*. Cambridge: Cambridge University Press, 2015.
Lobel, Edgar. *The Greek Manuscripts of Aristotle's Poetics*. London: Oxford University Press, 1933.
Mack, Peter. 'Rhetoric, Ethics and Reading in the Renaissance'. *Renaissance Studies* 19, no. 1 (2005): 1–21.
Michell, John et al., *Trivium: The Classical Liberal Arts of Grammar, Logic, & Rhetoric*. New York: Bloomsbury, 2016.
Morgan, Teresa. *Literate Education in the Hellenistic and Roman Worlds*. Cambridge: Cambridge University Press, 1998.

Moriarty, Michael. 'French Criticism in the Seventeenth Century'. In *The Cambridge History of Literary Criticism, III: The Renaissance*, edited by Glyn Norton, 555–65. Cambridge: Cambridge University Press, 1999.

Moss, Ann. *Printed Commonplace-Books and the Structuring of Renaissance Thought*. Oxford: Clarendon Press, 1996.

Naiditch, Paul, Nicholas Barker and Sue A. Kaplan. *The Aldine Press: Catalogue of the Ahmanson-Murphy Collection*. Berkeley, Los Angeles and London: University of California Press, 2001.

Omont, Henri, ed. *La Poétique D'aristote: Manuscrit 1741 Fonds Grec De La Bibliothèque Nationale*. Paris: Ernest Leroux, 1891.

Ong, Walter J. 'Commonplace Rhapsody: Ravisius Textor, Zwinger and Shakespeare'. In *Classical Influences on European Culture, A.D. 1500–1700*, edited by R. R. Bolgar, 91–126. Cambridge: Cambridge University Press, 1976.

Pollard, Tanya. 'Greek Playbooks and Dramatic Forms in Early Modern England'. In *Formal Matters: Reading the Materials of English Renaissance Literature*, edited by Allison Deutermann and András Kiséry, 99–123. Manchester: Manchester University Press, 2013.

Rabe, Hugo. 'Rhetoren-Corpora'. *Rheinisches Museum für Philologie* 67 (1912): 321–57.

Robinson, Martin, *Trivium 21c: Preparing Young People for the Future with Lessons from the Past*. Carmarthen: Independent Thinking Press, 2013.

Robortello, Francesco. *In Librum Aristotelis De Arte Poetica Explicationes*. Florence: Laurentius Torrentinus, 1548.

Ross, B. Joyce. *J. E. Spingarn and the Rise of the NAACP, 1911–1939*. New York: Atheneum, 1972.

Russell, D. A. *Greek Declamation*. Cambridge: Cambridge University Press, 1983.

Saintsbury, George. *A History of Criticism and Literary Taste in Europe from the Earliest Texts to the Present Day*, 3 vols. Edinburgh and London: Blackwood, 1900–1904.

Sandys, John Edwin. *A History of Classical Scholarship*, 3 vols. Cambridge: University Press, 1903–1908.

Schmitt, Charles B. *Aristotle and the Renaissance*. Cambridge, MA: Harvard University Press, 1983.

Scholes, Robert, 'Presidential Address 2004: The Humanities in a Posthumanist World'. *PMLA* 120, no. 3 (2005): 724–33.

Scholes, Robert, James D. Hoff and Harold Fromm, 'Rebuilding the Humanities'. *PMLA* 121, no. 1 (2006): 296–8.

Seitz, James. 'Inventing the Writing Program: How to Name What We Do When, However Old, It's New'. *ADE Bulletin* 155 (2018): 42–6.

Sherman, William H. *Used Books: Marking Readers in Renaissance England*. Philadelphia, PA: University of Pennsylvania Press, 2008.

Sidney, Sir Philip. *Miscellaneous Prose of Sir Philip Sidney*. Edited by Katherine Duncan-Jones and J. A. Van Dorsten. Oxford: Clarendon Press, 1973.

Slater, William. 'Gnomology and Criticism'. *Greek, Roman, and Byzantine Studies* 41 (2001): 99–121.

Spingarn, Joel Elias. *A History of Literary Criticism in the Renaissance*, 2nd edn. New York: Columbia University Press, 1908.

Spingarn, Joel Elias. *The New Criticism: A Lecture Delivered at Columbia University*, 9 March, 1910. New York: Columbia University Press, 1911.

Tarán, Leonardo, 'The Text of Aristotle's Poetics in the Codex Parisinus Graecus 2038'. *Mnemosyne* 69, no. 5 (2016): 785–98.

Turner, James, *Philology: The Forgotten Origins of the Modern Humanities*. Princeton and Oxford: Princeton University Press, 2014.

Van Deusen, Marshall. *J. E. Spingarn*. New York: Twayne Publishers, 1971.

Vickers, Brian. 'Rhetoric and Poetics'. In *The Cambridge History of Renaissance Philosophy*, edited by Charles B. Schmitt, Quentin Skinner, Eckhard Kessler and Jill Kraye, 715–45. Cambridge: Cambridge University Press, 1988.

Walker, Jeffrey. *Rhetoric and Poetics in Antiquity*. New York and Oxford: Oxford University Press, 2000.

Warton, Joseph. *An Essay on the Writings and Genius of Pope*. London: M. Cooper, 1756.

Weinberg, Bernard. 'Castelvetro's Theory of the *Poetics*'. In *Critics and Criticism: Ancient and Modern*, edited by Ronald S. Crane, 349–71. Chicago: University of Chicago Press, 1952.

Weinberg, Bernard. 'From Aristotle to Pseudo-Aristotle'. *Comparative Literature* 5 (1953): 97–104.

Weinberg, Bernard. *A History of Literary Criticism in the Italian Renaissance*, 2 vols. Chicago: University of Chicago Press, 1961.

Weinberg, Bernard. 'Review: Herrick, *Comic Theory in the Sixteenth Century*'. *Modern Philology* 48, no. 4 (1951): 271–3.

Weinberg, Bernard. 'Robortello on the *Poetics*'. In *Critics and Criticism: Ancient and Modern*, edited by Ronald S. Crane, 319–48. Chicago: University of Chicago Press, 1952.

Wimsatt, William K. and Cleanth Brooks. *Literary Criticism: A Short History*. New York: Knopf, 1957.

4

Inventing a Renaissance

Modernity, allegory and the history of literary theory

Vladimir Brljak

I

When did European poetics emerge into modernity? When did the answers of Western thinkers to those perennial questions of what literature is, what purpose it serves and to which sphere of human endeavour it belongs begin to assume forms similar to our own? When did such categories as pleasure, emotion or expression rise to the foreground of poetic theory? When did the notions now routinely designated by such phrases as 'aesthetic autonomy', 'free play of imagination', or 'willing suspension of disbelief' receive their earliest literary-theoretical articulations? When was 'imaginative' literature, as we still say when we want to make the distinction unambiguously clear, first recognized as a form of art, distinct from such neighbouring domains as philosophy and rhetoric, or the more amorphous category of 'letters'? Locating and elucidating this watershed is of self-evident importance to historians of poetics and literary criticism, but is also of considerable significance in other corners of literary studies and beyond, in the history of aesthetics and indeed the humanities at large, being a vital element in our understanding of the wide and complex range of phenomena falling under the rubric of 'modernity'. It is therefore no surprise that the question has exercised numerous scholars in a variety of disciplines and subdisciplinary specializations, and that they have, collectively, provided us with a fairly conclusive answer: namely, the modern understanding of art in general, and of imaginative literature in particular, emerges in or around the eighteenth century – certainly not much earlier than 1700 and not much later than 1800.

Of course, as soon as a claim of this magnitude is made, a litany of caveats is in order. Details continue to be debated. Attempts to further narrow the date have been inconclusive. In the 1900s, George Saintsbury placed the divide at 'the meeting

---

A draft of this chapter was discussed in the Workshop in Poetics at Stanford University in April 2018; I am thankful to Roland Greene, Nicholas Jenkins, and Melih Levi for organizing, Radhika Koul for responding and everyone else who contributed to the conversation on that occasion.

of the seventeenth and eighteenth centuries, or a little later, or much later, as the genius of different countries and persons would have it'.[1] In the 1950s, scholars who, in spite of major differences in emphasis, assigned a decisive importance to the advent of Romanticism, inclined to the early decades of the nineteenth century.[2] In the 1970s, the philologically oriented research of René Wellek, centring on the changing meanings of *literature* and other associated terms, pointed to a mid-eighteenth-century date.[3] In the 1990s, Richard Terry argued that 'the elementary idea of literature' – 'the category or "space" of literature' as distinct from non-literature, apart from any further 'definitional theories that might happen to get mapped on to' – is detectable behind certain usages of such terms as *belles lettres* or *polite learning*, along with the older *poetry* and *poesy*, perhaps already by the 1700s.[4] Still more recently, Paul Guyer – in a history of general aesthetics, but on the basis of examples specifically from the literary sphere – argues for a similarly early date of *c*. 1709–20, with 'grumblings' already in the later seventeenth century.[5] In part, this oscillation is due to problems intrinsic to theorizing specifically poetic rather than broadly aesthetic modernity: theorizing the least 'pure' of the arts, whose medium is most 'contaminated' by non-artistic usage. In part, it also has to do with the fact that much of this scholarship does not adequately draw the key distinction between poetics or literary theory and the much wider category of literary criticism, and then also between explicit and implicit poetics: actual instances of literary-theoretical reflection as opposed to reconstructions based on literary and literary-critical practice, which, however valuable in their own right, should not be confused with, or substituted for, the former.

Taking a step back, however, it is clear that these variations all fall comfortably within the bounds of a 'long' eighteenth century, refining rather than supplanting the received view. It is, of course, possible to relativize this by altering the scale on which the problem is viewed. We can zoom out to a point where such a notion of modernity begins to seem arbitrarily limited or zoom in until everything before the later twentieth century becomes ancient. Any idea of literature, let alone any sustained reflection on this idea, can be legitimately described as modern if viewed against the millennia of oral tradition that preceded it. At the other end of the spectrum, we will find books like M. A. R. Habib's *Modern Literary Criticism and Theory: A History*, opening with a two-page summary of 'formative' developments from classical

---

[1] George Saintsbury, *A History of Criticism and Literary Taste in Europe from the Earliest Texts to the Present Day*, 3 vols. (Edinburgh: Blackwood, 1900–04), 3:10.
[2] M. H. Abrams, *The Mirror and the Lamp: Romantic Theory and the Critical Tradition* (New York: Oxford University Press, 1953); Raymond Williams, *Culture and Society, 1780–1950* (London: Chatto, 1958).
[3] 'The Attack on Literature', *The American Scholar* 42 (1972–73): 27–42; 'Literature and Its Cognates', in *Dictionary of the History of Ideas: Studies of Selected Pivotal Ideas*, ed. Philip P. Wiener, 5 vols. (New York: Scribner, 1973–74), 2:81–9; 'What Is Literature?', in *What Is Literature?*, ed. Paul Hernadi (Bloomington: Indiana University Press, 1978), 16–23.
[4] 'The Eighteenth-Century Invention of English Literature: A Truism Revisited', *Journal for Eighteenth-Century Studies* 19 (1996): 47–62, p. 47.
[5] Paul Guyer, *A History of Modern Aesthetics*, 3 vols. (Cambridge: Cambridge University Press, 2014), 1:6–8.

antiquity to AD 1900.[6] Between these extremes, other potential watersheds come into view, each with its own set of ancients and moderns, and among them we look for the scale most appropriate to the problem at hand. Acknowledging that any scale is ultimately relative, collective efforts of several generations of scholars strongly indicate that the perspective adopted by the advocates of the consensus view, as well as its most compelling challengers, is adequately suited to the subject of inquiry. We largely agree, in other words, that modern occidental poetics emerges at some point between 1500 and 1800. We disagree on when precisely within this window it emerges, but comparison and contrast with pre-1500 and post-1800 periods shows that we are at least looking in the right place.

Relating to this problem of scale is that of dynamic. Could it be that poetic modernity had already been won and lost long before this time, and that we are not dealing with a historically delimited phenomenon but with one potentially arising in any, or at least more than one, historical period? Did not Aristotle argue that 'correct standards in poetry are not identical with those in politics or in any other particular art', a statement recently described as 'the most explicit claim for poetic autonomy in antiquity'?[7] Yet Aristotle's views, if perhaps not unique, were by all accounts exceptional: they do not seem to have exercised much influence until the rediscovery of the *Poetics* at the end of the fifteenth century, and even then they continued to be conflated with doctrines now recognized as un- and even anti-Aristotelian for centuries to come. Fast-forwarding to the seventeenth century, we find Francis Bacon repeating and surpassing Aristotle's achievement: breaking with the traditional definitions and classifications, aligning his 'poesy' with the positively re-evaluated faculty of the imagination, and elevating it to the top of his tree of knowledge, on equal terms with history and philosophy.[8] Yet the earliest reception of Bacon's work was as abortive as that of the *Poetics* appears to have been: no new school of Baconian literary theory arose, and even those critics who respond to his publications betray fundamental misunderstandings of his views. Thus we return to the question of scale: yes, isolated instances of poetic (proto)modernity have occurred before AD 1700, but only from this time onward have such views met with any level of widespread acceptance.

At the same time, the fact that it took us millennia to catch up with Aristotle, and centuries to catch up with Bacon, raises the question of whether we might again depart from this trajectory. Only a generation ago it was evidently very easy to believe that precisely this was happening or had indeed already happened. Notions of postmodernity and postmodernism arose, accompanied by expressions of post-aesthetic and post-literary sentiments of varied emphasis and complexity. 'Significantly in recent years', Raymond Williams could write by 1976, '*literature* and *literary*, though they still have

---

[6] M. A. R. Habib, *Modern Literary Criticism and Theory: A History* (Oxford: Blackwell, 2008), 3–4.
[7] Aristotle, *The 'Poetics' of Aristotle: Translation and Commentary*, ed. and trans. Stephen Halliwell (Chapel Hill: The University of North Carolina Press, 1987), 61 (1460b); Andrew Ford, 'Literary Criticism and the Poet's Autonomy', in *A Companion to Ancient Aesthetics*, ed. Penelope Murray and Pierre Destrée (Chichester: Blackwell, 2015), 143–57, p. 147.
[8] Francis Bacon, *The Twoo Bookes … Of the proficience and aduancement of Learning, diuine and humane …* (London: [Purfoot and Creede] for Tomes, 1605), Ee1v–3v; *Opera … , tomvs primvs: Qui continet De Dignitate & Augmentis Scientiarum Libros IX …* (London: Haviland, 1623), P2r–S1r.

effective currency in post-C18 senses, have been increasingly challenged, on what is conventionally their own ground, by concepts of *writing* and *communication* which seek to recover the most active and general senses which the extreme specialization has seemed to exclude'.⁹ Alternatively, the modern notion could still be accepted, indeed with renewed fervour and in its most radical form, provided the underlying historical framework was manipulated into ideologically acceptable configurations. '"Literature"', wrote Michel Foucault, 'as it was constituted and so designated on the threshold of the modern age, manifests, at a time when it was least expected, the reappearance, of the living being of language.'¹⁰ Elsewhere, this being had been wiped out by the Enlightenment,

> And yet, throughout the nineteenth century, and right up to our own day – from Hölderlin to Mallarmé and on to Antonin Artaud – literature achieved autonomous existence, and separated itself from all other language with a deep scission, only by forming a sort of 'counter-discourse', and by finding its way back from the representative or signifying function of language to this raw being that had been forgotten since the sixteenth century.

Here, in a textbook instance of the 'antimodernist' manoeuvre, as diagnosed in Jürgen Habermas's classic essay, the modern idea of literature is fully embraced as long as it is construed as a reappearance rather than an appearance – as long as it is not acknowledged as an actual product of a fallen modernity but as an anomalous survival from a prelapsarian premodernity, and at the same time an intimation of a paradisiacal postmodernity just beyond reach, to be inaugurated by some cataclysmic event 'of which we can at the moment do no more than sense the possibility'.¹¹ Others still lost their way entirely. Adrian Marino might be replying to Foucault when he writes that 'the notion accredited in contemporary (particularly French) criticism – that the idea of literature in its "present-day sense" (What sense may that be? Can "literature" be limited to one sense in our day and age?) only emerged in the nineteenth century – is completely mistaken'.¹² But a history of an idea that cannot be limited simply cannot be written: all notions are equally correct and equally mistaken, and we are left with infinite accumulation of data without a grounding hypothesis around which this data could meaningfully organize – with, precisely, a *Biography* (rather than a history) *of 'The Idea of Literature'* (in scare quotes).

Today, however, as these enthusiasms are subsiding, it is clear that the eighteenth-century consensus still holds. This includes, and has always included, most comprehensive histories of literary criticism. Saintsbury received the consensus fully

---

⁹ Raymond Williams, *Keywords: A Vocabulary of Culture and Society* (London: Fontana, 1976), 154.
¹⁰ Michel Foucault, *The Order of Things: An Archaeology of the Human Sciences*, trans. Alan Sheridan (1970; repr. London: Routledge, 2002), 48.
¹¹ Jürgen Habermas, 'Modernity: An Unfinished Project', trans. Nicholas Walker, in *Habermas and the Unfinished Project of Modernity: Critical Essays on 'The Philosophical Discourse of Modernity'*, ed. Maurizio Passerin d'Entreves and Seyla Benhabib (Cambridge, MA: The MIT Press, 1997), 38–58, p. 43; Foucault, *Order*, 442.
¹² Adrian Marino, *The Biography of 'The Idea of Literature': From Antiquity to the Baroque*, trans. Virgil Stanciu and Charles M. Carlton (Albany: State University of New York Press, 1996), xi.

formed from still earlier scholars, of whom more below (pp. 65–71), and although harder to identify due to the dispersal of the argument over multiple volumes, the same overall perspective continues to govern the work of J. W. H. Atkins.[13] Wellek too found 'the middle of the 18th century … a meaningful place to start' his *History of Modern Criticism*, 'as then the neoclassical system of doctrines, established since the Renaissance, begins to disintegrate', whereas 'to describe the changes within that system between 1500 and 1750 seems to me largely an antiquarian task, unrelated to the problems of our day'.[14] By this time, the influence of the more radical currents of twentieth-century literary theory is making itself felt, yet the consensus still stands. The case of the Wimsatt-Brooks *Short History* is instructive: even here, in a programmatically ahistorical history of the subject, occasional slips of the New Critics' periodizing unconscious show that the received view still underwrites the narrative. The book's central premise is that of 'the continuity and real community of human experience through the ages' – including 'continuity and intelligibility in the history of literary argument', where 'Plato has a bearing on Croce and Freud, and vice versa' – yet its summary still divides into the ancient and medieval, Renaissance and neoclassical and Romantic to contemporary periods.[15] More recently, comparable statements of qualified acceptance are found in the comprehensive accounts by Richard Harland, M. A. R. Habib, Gary Day and, notionally at least, Pelagia Goulimari, as well as non-comprehensive studies, reference works and anthologies too numerous to be systematically surveyed here.[16]

There is, however – to bring the litany to a close and proceed to the main subject of the present study – one field of literary and intellectual history where the eighteenth-century consensus does not hold: Renaissance studies, and specifically, the study of Renaissance poetics and literary criticism. Unlike most of their colleagues in literary studies and beyond, scholars in this field, beginning with Joel Elias Spingarn and his 1899 *History of Literary Criticism in the Renaissance*, have argued that poetic modernity arises already in the Renaissance period, usually dated to between the fourteenth and sixteenth century in the precocious case of Italy, with variable amounts of 'delay' in other, especially northern, European countries. This, moreover, is not just any claim

---

[13] See J. W. H. Atkins, *Literary Criticism in Antiquity: A Sketch of Its Development*, 2 vols. (Cambridge: Cambridge University Press, 1934); *English Literary Criticism: The Medieval Phase* (Cambridge: Cambridge University Press, 1943); *English Literary Criticism: The Renascence* (London: Methuen, 1943); and esp. *English Literary Criticism: 17th and 18th Centuries* (London: Methuen, 1951), v. The earlier series of studies by Baldwin is unfinished and therefore inconclusive in this respect: see Charles Sears Baldwin, *Ancient Rhetoric and Poetic, Interpreted from Representative Works* (New York: Macmillan, 1924); *Medieval Rhetoric and Poetic (to 1400), Interpreted from Representative Works* (New York: Macmillan, 1928); *Renaissance Literary Theory and Practice: Classicism in the Rhetoric and Poetic of Italy, France, and England 1400–1600*, ed. Donald Lemen Clark (New York: Columbia University Press, 1939).
[14] René Wellek, *A History of Modern Criticism*, 8 vols. (London: Cape, 1955–86 [vols. 1–6]; New Haven: Yale University Press, 1991–92 [vols. 7–8]), 1:v.
[15] William K. Wimsatt Jr. and Cleanth Brooks, *Literary Criticism: A Short History* (New York: Knopf, 1957), vii–ix, 723–31.
[16] Richard Harland, *Literary Theory from Plato to Barthes: An Introductory History* (Basingstoke: Macmillan, 1999), 1–2, 30, 37, 48, 55, 244–6; M. A. R. Habib, *A History of Literary Criticism: From Plato to the Present* (Malden, MA: Blackwell, 2005), 357; Gary Day, *Literary Criticism: A New History* (Edinburgh: Edinburgh University Press, 2008), 157; Pelagia Goulimari, *Literary Criticism and Theory: From Plato to Postcolonialism* (Abingdon: Routledge, 2015), 102.

or even one of the major claims in this field, but its central, defining hypothesis, which Spingarn's book was specifically written to uphold, and which his successors have continued to reproduce to this day. And yet, although this thesis radically contradicts the eighteenth-century consensus, scholarship on both sides has almost entirely failed to address this discrepancy. Neither have historians of Renaissance poetics openly contested the consensus, nor have their views been challenged by its adherents. For the most part, each faction has simply continued to reproduce its narrative, and the limited interaction between period-specializations within literary studies, and between literary studies and other disciplines with overlapping interests, has enabled these narratives to cohabit the relevant institutional spaces without being submitted to genuine critical scrutiny.

The ensuing pages seek to disturb this undeclared peace by surveying the scholarship on Renaissance poetics and literary criticism – mostly anglophone, and mostly concerned with the English corpus, but with considerable implications for other national traditions – and by focussing on one issue in particular, namely, the systematic suppression of allegorical poetics in this scholarship. This emphasis on allegory will perhaps strike some readers as arbitrary, but allegory is not one problem among others. The current model of the history of Renaissance literary criticism was forged precisely at the moment when the radically anti-allegorical impulse in post-Romantic aesthetics intersected with the Burckhardtian account of the Renaissance as the origin of Western modernity, giving rise to a powerful historiographical narrative in which allegory, understood as the epitome of poetic and aesthetic premodernity, is relegated to the redefined and repositioned Middle Ages, and is evacuated from a correspondingly redefined and repositioned Renaissance. Although now generally discarded in contemporary allegory studies, this decline-of-allegory narrative continues to exert an influence in other domains, and in the historiography of Renaissance poetics and literary criticism this influence has been particularly strong. In structuring their accounts of the history of Renaissance literary criticism as Burckhardtian decline-of-allegory narratives, Spingarn and his successors have seriously impaired our understanding of the subject, while also rendering their research incompatible with parallel work elsewhere in literary studies and beyond. This is an unproductive state of affairs, it needs to end, and the present study hopes to contribute to this cause.

II

As a distinct development within the broader purview of English literary history, interest in the history of literary criticism emerges in the later seventeenth century. This in itself presents major evidence in favour of the eighteenth-century consensus, as it reflects the institutionalization of literary-critical practice underway at this time, which in turn reflects the emergent stages of a modern notion of imaginative literature, separable from such neighbouring domains as philosophy, rhetoric, or 'letters'.[17]

---

[17] Cf. Michael Gavin, *The Invention of English Criticism, 1560–1760* (Cambridge: Cambridge University Press, 2015), 2, ascribing the heterogeneity of 1650–1760 English criticism precisely to

Initially, this interest is confined to the post-Restoration period, and knowledge of pre-Restoration materials is perfunctory at best. 'Till of late years', Thomas Rymer writes in 1674, '*England* was as free from Criticks, as it is from *Wolves*', with the single exception of Ben Jonson, who 'had all the Critical learning to himself'.[18] The beginnings of modern criticism are related to the revival of classical learning, but the idea of the Renaissance as a period in its history, in anything like its now-familiar form, is non-existent. In 1711, Alexander Pope's *Essay on Criticism* posits a three-part scheme comprising classical antiquity, the '*second* Deluge' of the Middle Ages, and the restoration of classical criticism, of which Girolamo Vida is the earliest named Italian representative, while in 'the *Northern World*', this third period is delayed by well over a century – until Boileau in France and Wentworth Dillon in England.[19] To Pope, then, the critical Middle Ages lasted essentially until the Restoration, and in this he is representative of the period's opinion in general: when they 'looked back on the fifteenth through the seventeenth centuries', eighteenth-century English authors 'saw not continuity but a break', and 'by marking the *terminus ad quem* of the previous age', they 'marked the *terminus ad quo* of their own'.[20]

By the latter part of the century, this three-part scheme is evolving into a four-part one. Samuel Johnson identifies John Dryden as 'the father of English criticism' and his essay *Of Dramatick Poesie* as 'the first regular and valuable treatise on the art of writing' in the language, but also mentions that 'two *Arts of English Poetry* were written in the days of Elizabeth by Webb and Puttenham … and a few hints had been given by Jonson and Cowley'.[21] This remains broadly Pope's scheme, but 'the days of Elizabeth' have now appeared on the horizon, and although still medieval, they are no longer entirely void of interest. Also, with the grouping of Ben Jonson with Abraham Cowley rather than with William Webbe and George Puttenham, a fourth period has emerged – an early modern interim between the premodernity of the Elizabethans and the full modernity of Dryden. Around this time, Joseph Warton authors what would seem to be the first separate publication in England strictly concerned with the subject: an edition of Philip Sidney's *Defence of Poesie* together with the relevant extracts from Jonson's *Discoveries*. Warton explicitly acknowledges the novelty of such a work: 'The Public has paid, of late, so much attention to our *old Poets*, that it has been imagined a perusal of some of our *old Critics* also may be found equally agreeable', Sidney and Jonson being 'the two earliest in our language that deserve much attention'.[22] Commentary is limited to a single paragraph, of interest mostly for its historical significance, but

---

the fact that '"literature" had not yet consolidated into a unitary object of inquiry'.
[18] 'The Preface of the Translator', in *Reflections on Aristotle's Treatise of Poesie* … , by René Rapin, trans. Thomas Rymer (London: Herringman, 1674), A3r–b2v, sig. A3v.
[19] Alexander Pope, *An Essay on Criticism* (London: Lewis, 1711), E5v–F1v.
[20] Jack Lynch, *The Age of Elizabeth in the Age of Johnson* (Cambridge: Cambridge University Press, 2003), vi.
[21] Samuel Johnson, *The Lives of the Most Eminent English Poets; with Critical Observations on Their Works*, ed. Roger Lonsdale, 4 vols. (Oxford: Clarendon, 2006), 1:118–19.
[22] Philip Sidney and Ben Jonson, *Sir Philip Sydney's Defence of Poetry. And, Observations on Poetry and Eloquence, from the Discoveries of Ben Jonson*, ed. Joseph Warton (London: J., Robinson, and Walter, 1787), a2r.

not devoid of insight either.[23] The edition is also illustrative of the bibliographical bias that shaped the formative work on the subject, influencing all subsequent scholarship. In England, topics belonging to the sphere of literary criticism are almost invariably raised sporadically, in the most heterogeneous array of works, until the 1570s. This largely remains so even after this date, but beginning with George Gascoigne's *Notes* of 1575, English criticism becomes bibliographically visible in the form of vernacular essays and treatises specifically devoted to the subject. Consequently, once an interest in the subject appears, it is inevitably such works that first receive notice, especially those by major figures like Sidney and Jonson.

The effect of this bibliographical bias is evident in the earliest accounts of the subject, beginning, it would seem, with the two-page excursus in Edmond Malone's 1800 life of Dryden.[24] Besides those of Gascoigne, Sidney, Puttenham, Webbe and Jonson, Malone mentions the works of Thomas Campion, Samuel Daniel and Edmund Bolton: all separate publications or at least separate items within larger works. Commentary is again minimal and no fine historical distinctions are drawn, but it is worth noting, in the light of later developments, that Malone fails to mention any publications on the subject between Bolton's *Hypercritica* and Dryden's *Of Dramatick Poesie*. This is not a deliberate omission – had Malone been aware of any such publications, these would have been included[25] – yet it inadvertently creates the impression of the Gascoigne-to-Bolton stretch as a coherent, delimited unit in the history of the subject. Seven years later, a longer account appears, this time as a separate chapter, in a work by the miscellaneous writer and translator William Beloe.[26] Apparently unfamiliar with Malone's passage, Beloe notes that the suggestion for compiling such an account came from the antiquary George Chalmers, who also supplied him with most of the materials and whose 'communications were so ample and so satisfactory, that little has been left ... except to methodize and arrange them'. The list includes all the works mentioned by Malone except Gascoigne and Jonson, but adds the treatises of James VI/I and John Harington. Like Malone, Beloe can find no comparable works between Bolton and Dryden, and although he uses no literary-historical terms whatsoever, nor excludes the possibility that there is relevant pre-Restoration material yet to be recovered, the resulting impression of 'a long interval of time before we come to any treatise on the subject of English Poetry' perpetuates the tendency already seen with Malone.

Beloe's list may have been the blueprint for the first anthology of early English criticism, the *Ancient Critical Essays* of Joseph Haslewood: except for three

---

[23] Cf. Micha Lazarus, 'Sidney's Greek Poetics', *Studies in Philology* 112 (2015): 504–36, p. 506.
[24] John Dryden, *The Critical and Miscellaneous Prose Works* ... , ed. Edmond Malone, 3 vols. (London: Baldwin for Cadell and Davies, 1800), 1.1:58–60.
[25] This is also shown by the insertion, in Malone's own interleaved copy of his work, of a sentence on the 'few critical strictures found' in Davenant's and Hobbes' essays occasioned by Davenant's *Gondibert*: see Bodleian Library, Mal. E. 61; William Davenant and Thomas Hobbes, *A Discourse upon Gondibert ... With an Answer to it ...* (Paris: Guillemot, 1650). On the *c.* 1621 composition of Bolton's *Hypercritica*, see Thomas H. Blackburn, 'The Date and Evolution of Edmund Bolton's *Hypercritica*', *Studies in Philology* 63 (1966): 196–202 – Malone and other early scholars date it to the 1610s.
[26] *Anecdotes of Literature and Scarce Books*, 6 vols. (London: for Rivington, 1807–12), 1:229–38.

additions – Gascoigne, Francis Meres and the *Letters* on versification exchanged by Edmund Spenser and Gabriel Harvey – Haslewood's selection is simply Beloe's list in anthologized form. Beloe's caveats, however, have been forgotten, and Haslewood is reading new implications into this corpus. 'Although few in number', he writes, 'such a body of early criticism as these tracts collectively present … is not any where to be found. Independent of rarity, intrinsic value may justly entitle this volume, although a humble reprint, to range with those of the Elizabethan æra.'[27] This is no longer simple antiquarianism. What began as a self-confessedly random assemblage, with Malone listing such works as he was aware of at the time, or Beloe's antiquarian friends supplying him with such titles as happened to be available to them, has now become a 'body' of work, an 'Elizabethan' body of work and an Elizabethan body of work of 'intrinsic' rather than merely historical value. Haslewood further notes that he is unable to find any relevant publications prior to Gascoigne except such 'notices upon the poets scattered through the works of Ascham, Eliot, Wilson, and others', indicative of 'the imperfect state of criticism of that age'.[28] Finally, he explains that his original intention was 'to have printed uniformly all the Essays upon Poetry to the time of Dryden', but that he was defeated by the difficulty of the task. Like Beloe, he does not claim that the pre-Gascoigne or post-Bolton decades are void of interest – elsewhere he had, for example, already printed extracts from Henry Reynolds's *Mythomystes*[29] – but by failing to add material from these decades, he further strengthens the impression inadvertently created by his predecessors.

After lists, chapters, extracts, editions and, now, anthologies, the next milestone in the field's development is a sustained history of the subject. Such a work was envisioned at least as early as 1737, when Elizabeth Cooper announced that the sequel to her *Muses Library* would include 'some Account of the Progress of Criticism in *England*; from Sir *Philip Sidney*, the Art of *English* Poesy (written by Mr. *Puttenham*, a Gentleman Pensioner to Queen *Elizabeth*:) Sir *John Harrington*, Ben *Johnson*, &c'.[30] Unfortunately, the work never materialized nor did, some decades later, Samuel Johnson's plan for a 'History of Criticism, as it relates to judging of authours, from Aristotle to the present age. An account of the rise and improvements of the art; of the different opinions of authours; ancient and modern'.[31] Midway through the nineteenth century, John Wilson's *Specimens of the British Critics* – originally published serially in *Blackwood's Edinburgh Magazine* under the pseudonym 'Christopher North' – would seem to constitute the first book-length study in the language, although one still far short of a genuine history. Even in conception, the rambling essays collected under this title are but 'an irregular history of Criticism in this island', and in execution they are much less, limited in coverage to Dryden and Pope and concerned largely with critical rather

---

[27] Joseph Haslewood, *Ancient Critical Essays upon English Poets and Poesy*, 2 vols. (London: Triphook, 1811–15), 2:xxii.
[28] Ibid.
[29] See H[enry] R[eynolds], *Mythomystes* … , in *The British Bibliographer*, ed. Egerton Brydges and Joseph Haslewood, 4 vols. (London: Triphook, 1810–14), 4:373–9.
[30] Elizabeth Cooper, *The Muses Library; Or a Series of English Poetry, from the Saxons, to the Reign of King Charles II* (London: Wilcox et al., 1737), xvi.
[31] Joseph Boswell, *The Life of Samuel Johnson* … , 2 vols. (London: Baldwin for Dilly, 1791), 2:557n3.

than metacritical inquiry.³² *Blackwood's* readers are invited 'to take a look along with us at the choice critics of other days, waked by our potent voice from the long-gathering dust', but 'other days' means 'one longish stride backwards of some hundred and fifty years or so', beyond which lies 'the darkness of antiquity'.³³ The four-period scheme is retained but the early modern stretch is extended up to Pope. The Elizabethan epoch remains the last of the premodern rather than the first of the modern ages: 'With Elizabeth the splendor of the feudal and chivalrous ages for England finally sets. A world expires, and ere long a new world rises.'³⁴ This is the neoclassical world of Jonson, Dryden and Pope – a world closer to but not quite yet Wilson's – and the final divide, between this early modernity and modernity proper, comes with Joseph Addison's essays on the *Pleasures of the Imagination* of 1712.³⁵

Another development to be noted at this point is the anomalous growth of interest in Sidney's *Defence*. Although most of the Elizabethan essays and treatises were printed by Haslewood, and several received separate editions later in the century, the *Defence* is a special case in that it has remained widely available from its original publication to the present day.³⁶ Other factors contributing to this unique status included its superior stylistic quality, Sidney's literary and biographical significance, and the fact that, taken out of context, some of its passages – notably the famous description of the poet who refuses to accept the 'brazen' world of nature, replacing it with the 'golden' world of poetic creation – could be construed as Romantic ahead of their time.³⁷ All this conspires to make Sidney the first literary critic of his age to be seen as modern, and to the extent to which they engage in such judgements, his Victorian editors are unanimous in this verdict. Arber emphasizes 'Sidney's use of the word Poet and its modern acceptation'; Flügel portrays him as England's 'earliest and most significant *aesthete* (in the Schillerian sense)'; to Cook, the treatise presents 'a link between the soundest theory of ancient times and the romantic production of the modern era'; and for Shuckburgh, most of it is 'as applicable now as when Sidney penned' it.³⁸ But even if Sidney is modern, his age emphatically is not. To be modern, Sidney must be ahead of his time, a harbinger of a later epoch rather than a representative of his own.

The commentary of Sidney's early editors also anticipates a related development, soon to assume a major role: the suppression of allegory. Allegory, it is still worth

---

³² John Wilson, *Specimens of the British Critics* (Philadelphia: Carey and Hart, 1846), 57.
³³ Ibid., 15.
³⁴ Ibid., 112.
³⁵ Ibid., 95, 157.
³⁶ After the initial editions of 1595, the *Defence* was included in the 1598 expanded edition of the *Arcadia* (twenty-three printings between 1599 and 1674), while the eighteenth century could consult in the collected edition of John Henley (single reprint in Dublin in 1739), as well as a separate edition of a bare text printed in Glasgow, followed by Warton's, and at least six more in the nineteenth century. For references, see *Sir Philip Sidney World Bibliography*, ed. Donald Stump et al., http://bibs.slu.edu/sidney.
³⁷ Philip Sidney, 'An Apology for Poetry' (or 'The Defence of Poesy'), ed. Geoffrey Shepherd, 3rd edn, rev. R. W. Maslen (Manchester: Manchester University Press, 2000), 84–5.
³⁸ Philip Sidney, *Apologie for Poetrie*, ed. Edward Arber (Birmingham: 34 Wheeleys Road, 1868), 8; *Sir Philip Sidney's Astrophel and Stella und Defence of Poesie* ... , ed. Ewald Flügel (Halle: Niemeyer, 1889), xlix: 'der früheste und bedeutendste *Ästhetiker* (im Schiller'schen Sinne)'; '*The Defense of Poesy*' ... , ed. Albert S. Cook (Boston: Ginn, 1890), v; *An Apologie for Poetrie*, ed. Evelyn S. Shuckburgh (Cambridge: Cambridge University Press, 1891), xxxi.

emphasizing, is an essential element in Sidney's poetics, and in this the *Defence* is entirely typical of the poetic theory of its day.[39] By the nineteenth century, however, allegory is widely considered as an outdated aesthetic and hermeneutic doctrine, if not the very debasement and antithesis of art. This anti-allegorical sentiment begins to emerge already in the seventeenth century, grows in the course of the eighteenth century and eventually receives articulate theoretical expression in the Romantic and post-Romantic aesthetics of the nineteenth and early twentieth centuries. Along the way, modern anti-allegorism also acquires a historical dimension and a former 'age of allegory' emerges in literary history. This age of allegory is effectively identified with the Middle Ages, but not as we now know them: it begins in the earliest stages of English literary history, culminates in Spenser's *Faerie Queene* and only then enters a phase of decline, lingering well into the eighteenth century.[40] There is thus both a growing hostility to allegory and a recognition that a taste for allegorical literature and art was now a thing of the past, yet one looks in vain for any statement that would separate the Renaissance, as currently understood, from this past. None of this poses any problem for historians of literary criticism as long as they do not go looking for modernity before the Restoration, yet once Sidney is made an exception to this rule, his endorsement of the doctrine increasingly understood as the very antithesis of this modernity becomes a substantial concern. At this stage, however, dealing with a single treatise rather than an entire corpus, and a single author rather than an entire age, the solution is simple: the relevant passages are simply omitted from discussion and either unaccompanied by annotation or annotated in a way that fails to acknowledge any implications for Sidney's poetic theory.

All of these developments – the emergence of the Elizabethan corpus, the dating of critical modernity to the post-Restoration period, the growing and increasingly historicized hostility towards allegory and the anomalous proto-modern role attributed to Sidney's *Defence*, premised on the suppression of the allegorical element in the treatise – come together in what is to my knowledge the first formal and comprehensive history of English literary criticism, and also the first doctoral dissertation by a woman published by Yale University: Laura Johnson Wylie's 1894 *Studies in the Evolution of English Criticism*.[41] Wylie's treatment of the 1500–1660 period synthesizes the tendencies delineated above (pp. 56–70), with three important innovations. First, it is one of the earliest instances of the term *Renaissance* being employed in this context, although Wylie's is still the older, pre-Burckhardtian notion of the revival of classical learning, with an admixture of Matthew Arnold's 'movement', rather than a

---

[39] See Sidney, 'Apology', 82, 92, 97, 103, 106, 116; cf. Kenneth Borris, *Allegory and Epic in English Renaissance Literature: Heroic Form in Sidney, Spenser, and Milton* (Cambridge: Cambridge University Press, 2000), 110–14.

[40] E.g., Thomas Warton, *Observations on the Faerie Queene of Spenser* (London: Dodsley and Fletcher, 1754), Gg2r–Hh4r; Wilson, *Specimens*, 160–4. For a fuller account, see Vladimir Brljak, 'The Age of Allegory', *Studies in Philology* 114 (2017): 697–719.

[41] Laura Johnson Wylie, *Studies in the Evolution of English Criticism* ... (Boston: Ginn, 1894). On Wylie, see Suzanne Bordelon, *A Feminist Legacy: The Rhetoric and Pedagogy of Gertrude Buck* (Carbondale: Southern Illinois University Press, 2007), *passim*.

comprehensive period in cultural, literary or literary-critical history.[42] Jonson is 'the great Classic dramatist of the English Renaissance' not because, but despite the fact that 'he wrote under the very shadow of the Elizabethan literature', and while the rise of English criticism is attributed to the prevalence of 'Renaissance' tendencies, this moment is dated to the post-Restoration period.[43] Second, Wylie revises the transitional four-part periodization into its now-familiar, three-part shape, where the seventeenth century is dismembered between a 'long' Elizabethan period and a 'long' eighteenth century. Third, and most importantly, by her day any differences between Pope and Addison, or between them and Dryden at one end and Johnson at the other, paled in comparison to the sum difference between their age and the age, now clearly discernible, of Wordsworth and Coleridge. The latter alone is modern. 'Between the new criticism' of the Romantics 'and the great thinkers of the eighteenth century' lies 'a complete break', 'an impassable chasm of interest and sympathy'.[44] Of any modernity to be found in still earlier periods there can obviously be no discussion whatsoever, except of course for Sidney's *Defence*, which is afforded its now-customary transhistorical role – it is 'the poetry rather than the art or theory of criticism', in which 'Sidney had spoken to the fine spirits of all ages' – but only on the condition that its appeals to allegory and other signal premodern doctrines are entirely suppressed.[45]

III

The contrast between the diffusely essayistic mid-century manner of Wilson and the focused and methodical exposition of Wylie's and other late-century works is striking.[46] With these publications, the history of literary criticism fully emerges as a specialized field within general literary history. In other respects, however, these books were dated almost on publication, for by this time a new narrative of poetic and aesthetic modernity, retaining and indeed intensifying the hostility towards allegory, while fundamentally altering the underlying historiographical framework, had already emerged on the continent and was just about to make its full impact in the Anglo-American sphere. 'The Middle Ages were essentially the ages of allegory', wrote Jacob Burckhardt with axiomatic clarity in his *Civilization of the Renaissance in Italy*, the book which consolidated and popularized, if it did not entirely invent, a new understanding of the Renaissance as a comprehensive period in European cultural history, and one no longer standing at the end of the premodern but at the beginning of the modern

---

[42] See Wylie, *Studies*, 1, 4, 59, 67. Cf. Matthew Arnold, *Culture and Anarchy: An Essay in Political and Social Criticism* (London: Smith, Elder, 1869), 159–66.
[43] Wylie, *Studies*, 1–2, 4, 13–14.
[44] Ibid., 110–12.
[45] Ibid., 13.
[46] A similarly focused approach, although limited to the theory of versification, appears already in Felix E. Schelling, *Poetic and Verse Criticism of the Reign of Elizabeth* (Philadelphia: University of Pennsylvania Press, 1891). Close on the heels of Wylie's book followed the 1896 anthology by Vaughan, where the exact same scheme is adopted: see *English Literary Criticism*, ed. C. E. Vaughan (London: Blackie, 1896), esp. xii–xiii, xix–xxvi, xxvi–xxvii, lxv.

phase of that history – the Renaissance as 'the leader of the modern ages'.[47] Here again, allegory was not one problem among many. Burckhardt had to find a way to reconcile his paradigmatically Romantic distaste for allegorical art with the paradigmatically anti-Romantic thesis of his book, and the virtually inevitable solution, once these parameters were in place, was to quarantine allegory to the new, foreshortened Middle Ages. If the Middle Ages were the age of the collective, the age in which 'man was conscious of himself … only through some general category', then it was only natural for that age to express itself in the art of universals, just as it was natural for the new age of the individual to express itself in the art of particulars.[48] Accordingly, any presence of allegory in the Renaissance is now to be explained as a residuum of the Middle Ages rather than a genuine aspect of the period.

What we now know as Renaissance literary criticism came into being when the earlier work on the subject was reconfigured in terms of the Burckhardtian paradigm, a feat performed almost singlehandedly by Joel Elias Spingarn in his 1899 *History of Literary Criticism in the Renaissance*, effectively his doctoral dissertation from Columbia University's newly formed Department of Comparative Literature.[49] By this date, all the elements were there, waiting to be integrated into a coherent narrative by this young and passionately idealist scholar, who would later in his life pursue progressive political causes with the same commitment with which he, between twenty-one and twenty-four years of age, pursued his quest for the 'birth of modern criticism'.[50] This, rather than any intrinsic interest in the period, was the driving impulse behind the *History* and indeed all of Spingarn's scholarly work. The Renaissance, according to the newest Burckhardtian coordinates, was where the origins of Spingarn's own aesthetic modernity were supposed to lie, and from where they were yet to be excavated. This was a fully conscious, explicitly stated, and methodically executed agenda:

> The influence of the Italian Renaissance in the development of modern science, philosophy, art, and creative literature has been for a long time the subject of much study. It has been my more modest task to trace the indebtedness of the modern

---

[47] Jacob Burckhardt, *The Civilization of the Renaissance in Italy*, trans. S. G. C. Middlemore (1878; repr. London: Phaidon, 1995), 262, 364.

[48] Ibid., 87.

[49] Joel Elias Spingarn, *A History of Literary Criticism in the Renaissance, with Special Reference to the Influence of Italy in the Formation and Development of Modern Classicism* (New York: Columbia University Press, 1899), vii–viii. One major precursor is Karl Borinski, *Die Poetik der Renaissance und der Anfänge der literarischen Kritik in Deutschland* (Berlin: Weidmann, 1886). Spingarn knew the book and would have found there a precedent for some key elements in his *History*, notably the adoption of the term *Renaissance* and the idea of a balance between classicist and anti-classicist impulses. What he did not find there, however, was the Burckhardtian configuration of the allegory-modernity nexus. For Borinski, allegory is not an anomaly – an anti-aesthetic aberration of the Christian Middle Ages – but, 'so to speak, the aesthetic Ur-Idea of mankind', continually present since antiquity onwards; see Borinski, *Poetik*, 65 ('sozusagen die ästhetische Uridee der Menschheit'), and cf. his *Die Antike in Poetik und Kunsttheorie von Ausgang des Klassischen Altertums bis auf Goethe under Wilhelm von Humboldt*, ed. Richard Newald (vol. 2), 2 vols. (Lepizig: Dieterich, 1914–24), 1:21–8. On Spingarn, see Marshall Van Deusen, *J. E. Spingarn* (New York: Twayne, 1971) and B. Joyce Ross, *J. E. Spingarn and the Rise of the NAACP, 1911–1939* (New York: Atheneum, 1972).

[50] Spingarn, *History*, vi–vii.

world to Italy in the domain of literary criticism; and I trust that I have shown the Renaissance influence to be as great in this as in the other realms of study.[51]

With Spingarn, the suppression of allegory, originally patented for the modernizing of Sidney's *Defence*, is reconfigured in Burckhardtian parameters and pursued on a grand scale. If the Middle Ages regarded poetry as a vassal of philosophy and theology, allegory is the very means by which this vassalage was exacted: 'While perhaps justifying poetry from the standpoint of ethics and divinity, [allegory] gives it no place as an independent art; thus considered, poetry becomes merely a popularized form of theology.'[52] Accordingly, allegory becomes the litmus test of poetic premodernity and the progress of poetic theory becomes measurable in degrees of its abandonment of the doctrine. Yet however coherent in theory, the decline-of-allegory narrative was bound to fail in practice, for as any objective inquiry must concede, allegorical poetics is virtually omnipresent in the very materials onto which this narrative was to be mapped. Consequently, Spingarn's and most subsequent accounts cannot proceed very far before running into major conceptual and chronological obstacles. A cultural historian like Burckhardt could afford to be highly selective in his treatment of the period's literary and literary-critical output, and could thus get away with greatly under-representing the extent to which it is informed by allegory. A literary historian like John Addington Symonds already finds 'the allegorical heresy' much more widespread, but can still evade it by appealing to the supposedly orthodox literary practice of the age.[53] Although 'the contemporary theory of æsthetics demanded allegory', Dante the poet knows better than Dante the critic, for 'no metaphysical sophistication, no allegory, no scholastic mysticism, can … cloud a poet's vision'.[54] Boccaccio 'repeated current theories about … the dignity of allegory', but he had little influence on Boccaccio, whose work 'showed how little he had appropriated these ideas'.[55] No such loophole is open to the historian of poetics, however, and immediately after describing allegory as the quintessential reflection of the medieval hostility towards imaginative literature, Spingarn must concede that the doctrine not only was central to the poetical views of the early humanists but that it 'did indeed continue throughout the Renaissance', and that 'this theory of poetic art, one of the commonplaces of the age, may be described as the great legacy of the Middle Ages to Renaissance criticism'.[56]

Thus Spingarn finds himself torn between two irreconcilable variables, seeking to affirm modernity for Renaissance criticism in terms fundamentally incompatible with the doctrine of allegory, while at the same time acknowledging that this doctrine was 'almost universally accepted by Renaissance writers'.[57] But how can this be? How can Renaissance poetics stay modern while almost universally accepting a doctrine defined as the very essence of poetical premodernity? The answer, of course, is that it

---

[51] Ibid., vi.
[52] Ibid., 8.
[53] John Addington Symonds, *Renaissance in Italy: Italian Literature*, 2 vols. (London: Smith, Elder, 1881), 1:81.
[54] Ibid., 1:54.
[55] Ibid., 1:81–7.
[56] Spingarn, *History*, 9, 261–2.
[57] Ibid., 263.

cannot – not without major concessions in one's understanding of what, and especially when, the Renaissance was. Ultimately, relegating allegory to the Middle Ages means that its presence in post-medieval poetics needs to be suppressed and negotiated by a whole arsenal of evasive manoeuvres, some combination of which is encountered in most subsequent treatments of the subject: suppression and exclusion of texts or parts of texts – the original and still the most efficient tactic – but now also conceptual and/ or temporal displacement (in order to make it free of allegory, the 'Renaissance' is redefined and/or chronologically repositioned), understatement ('Renaissance' critics do appeal to allegory, but this is an inessential and increasingly irrelevant element in their arguments), and relativization ('Renaissance' critics appeal to allegory but they do not really mean it, or the allegory to which they appeal is not the same kind as that of the Middle Ages, or their theoretical statements are found to be contradicted by their own literary practice, and so on).

The final piece in this puzzle was Aristotle's *Poetics* and here the influence of S. H. Butcher's 1895 study of the treatise, published just as Spingarn was beginning his graduate studies, played a key role.[58] Butcher broke with the 'Pseudo-Aristotelian', moralist-neoclassicist interpretations that had dominated the work's reception since its rediscovery at the end of the fifteenth century, recovering from it an essentially modern theory of poetry, resonant with the proto-Romantic position of Bacon and the fully Romantic positions of Goethe and Coleridge.[59] This included explicit repudiation of the moralized Pseudo-Aristotle in general and of individual Pseudo-Aristotelian doctrines in particular, such as the conflation of Aristotle's notion of the poetic universal with allegory: a major weapon in the Pseudo-Aristotelian's arsenal, encountered at least as late as the 1670s.[60] To Butcher's Aristotle, as to Butcher himself and many post-Romantic thinkers of his day, the end of poetry and the fine arts is 'pleasure', or, more precisely, 'aesthetic enjoyment proper', namely, such as 'proceeds from an emotional rather than from an intellectual source'.[61] Consequently, poetry and allegory are mutually exclusive categories: Aristotle's poetic universal 'does not imply that a general idea shall be embodied in a particular example – that is the method of allegory rather than that of poetry – but that the particular case shall be generalized by artistic treatment', and 'it is in the main the same thought which runs through Aristotle, Goethe, and Coleridge'.[62]

Construed in Butcher's terms, the recovered *Poetics* seemed to offer an ideal example of the Renaissance narrative. Salvaged from the darkness of the Middle Ages, this all but extinguished torch of poetic modernity is now finally passed from classical antiquity to its modern rebirth. This is the final premise, with which everything falls

---

[58] S. H. Butcher, *Aristotle's Theory of Poetry and Fine Art with a Critical Text and a Translation of the Poetics* (London: Macmillan, 1895). Spingarn's acknowledgements in *History*, vii–viii, indicate that he was corresponding with Butcher already during his doctoral studies.

[59] Butcher, *Theory*, 174, 181–4; cf. Weinberg, 'From Aristotle to Pseudo-Aristotle', *Comparative Literature* 5 (1953): 97–104.

[60] See, e.g., René Le Bossu's *Treatise*, in *Monsieur Bossv's Treatise of the Epick Poem* ... (London: for Bennet, 1695), B2v: 'In the *Epopea*, according to *Aristotle*, let the Names be what they will, yet the *Persons* and the *Actions* are *Feign'd, Allegorical, and Vniversal*; not *Historical* and *Singular*.'

[61] Butcher, *Theory*, 189.

[62] Ibid., 181–4.

into place. With the recovered *Poetics*, it becomes possible to defend literature– the 'justification of imaginative literature' being the 'first' and 'fundamental' goal of Renaissance criticism – on aesthetic rather than moral grounds, and thus without recourse to allegory.[63] There is a price to be paid here, but Spingarn is willing to pay it. The high criteria of aesthetic modernity announced in the book's opening sentences must give way to the more modest cause of neoclassicist 'rationalism', and the critical Renaissance must be postponed to the recovery and dissemination of the *Poetics*. And even then, the *Poetics* can only lay 'the foundation of modern criticism', which cannot reach maturity until it replaces the rule of an authority, even if that authority is Aristotle, with the rule of 'reason'.[64] Here Spingarn's account can finally link up with the larger Burckhardtian narrative, for this rationalist classicism can now be presented as a facet of that same 'liberation of human reason' which resulted in 'the growth of the sciences and arts, and in the reaction against mediæval sacerdotalism and dogma'.[65] The final touch comes with the claim that Renaissance criticism contains 'the germs of romantic as well as classical criticism', and the integration of this 'romantic' element – essentially amounting to poetry's freedom to venture beyond the bounds of probability and verisimilitude, but ignoring, as originally with Sidney, its allegorical corollary[66] – into the ultimate ideal of 'imaginative reason'. Thus, 'according as the reason or the imagination predominates in Renaissance literature, there results neo-classicism or romanticism, while the most perfect art finds a reconciliation of both elements in the imaginative reason'.[67] It is in this sense, and this sense only, that Spingarn can at long last declare that 'the theory of poetry, as enunciated by the Italians of the sixteenth century, has not diminished in value, but has continued to pervade the finer minds of men from that time to this'.[68]

In the end, then, we do get a nominally Renaissance poetics, and one superficially purged of allegory, but at what cost? Spingarn must sacrifice not only Petrarch and Boccaccio but also the entire Quattrocento and even the first half of the Cinquecento. In his own words, the earliest Italian editions of the *Poetics* – Giorgio Valla's Latin translation of 1498 and the 1508 Greek text in the Aldine *Rhetores Graeci* – had 'scarcely any immediate influence on literary criticism'.[69] Thus Renaissance criticism must be postponed until Alessandro de' Pazzi's Latin translation of 1536, for only 'from this time, the influence of the Aristotelian canons becomes manifest in critical literature'.[70] But again, this is only the foundation, and there remains the final step of replacing the authority of Aristotle with the authority of reason. Spingarn cites the appeal in a

---

[63] Spingarn, *History*, 3.
[64] Ibid., 145.
[65] Ibid., 147.
[66] See, e.g., Borris, *Allegory*, 35–6. This is another position that retains currency well into the seventeenth century: see Edward Phillips, *Theatrum Poetarum, or A Compleat Collection of the Poets ... Together with a Prefatory Discourse of the Poets and Poetry in Generall* (London: Smith, 1675), **6r, requiring 'proper Allegorie' in a heroic poem, 'for what ever is pertinently said by way of *Allegorie* is Morally though not Historically true'.
[67] Spingarn, *History*, 155.
[68] Ibid., 148.
[69] Ibid., 17.
[70] Ibid.

1587 work by Jason Denores to 'reason and Aristotle's *Poetics*, which is indeed founded on naught save reason', and adds: 'This is as far as Italian criticism ever went. It was the function of neo-classicism in France, as will be seen, to show that such a phrase as "reason *and* Aristotle" is a contradiction in itself, that the Aristotelian canons and reason are ultimately reducible to the same thing.'[71] The process is completed by Boileau, whose strictures against the use of Christian themes are taken to be the culmination of that 'combined effect of humanism, essentially pagan, and rationalism, essentially sceptical', that produced the 'irreligious character of neo-classic art'.[72] The year is 1674. The real agenda of Spingarn's book – elimination of allegory by any means necessary – has argued its nominal subject, Renaissance literary criticism, out of existence.

The French and English chapters then repeat this pattern with some minor variations. The narrative stumbles when Spingarn is unable to find any Aristotelian influence on French criticism before the final third of the sixteenth century and fully formed neoclassicist doctrine before the beginning of the seventeenth – 'excepting, of course, Scaliger', an Italian, and even then 'it was not until the very end of the century that he held the dictatorial position afterward accorded to him'.[73] 'There was, one might almost say, little critical theorizing in the French Renaissance.'[74] To be sure, there was plenty of critical allegorizing, as exemplified by a generous extract from Ronsard, but that is of no use.[75] Still, what is one to conclude – that French Renaissance criticism does not begin until some decades after the Pléiade, or worse yet, until the seventeenth century? The only solution is to relax the Aristotelian criterion to the point of meaninglessness and present the beginning of French Renaissance criticism as the singlehanded achievement of Joachim du Bellay's *Defence and Illustration of the French Language* – 'In no other country of Europe is the transition from the Middle Ages to the Renaissance so clearly marked as it is in France by this single book' – even though the *Defense* meets the Aristotelian criterion only in the most superficial manner, by virtue of containing the earliest French reference to the *Poetics*, a reference which, as Spingarn himself notes, shows 'no evidence whatsoever' of direct acquaintance with Aristotle's treatise, 'of whose contents [du Bellay] knew little or nothing'.[76] Elsewhere, we read on the same page that the *Defence* marks the beginning of 'modern criticism in France' and that it is 'not in any true sense a work of literary criticism at all'.[77]

The situation with England was different in that it required neither this ironically un-Aristotelian intervention of a deus ex machina, nor such messy amputations as that of the pre-Pazzi period in the case of Italy. Here the analogous result could be achieved almost effortlessly, for the English dynastic periodization, with its long-established notion of the reign of Elizabeth I as a national golden age, was uniquely suited to the purpose. A novel and foreign concept in anglophone literary history of the later nineteenth century, Burckhardt's Renaissance was quickly assimilated to what seemed its obvious

---

[71] Ibid., 151.
[72] Ibid. 154.
[73] Ibid., 184–9.
[74] Ibid.
[75] Ibid., 193.
[76] Ibid., 171, 184.
[77] Ibid., 177.

native analogue.⁷⁸ In the history of literary criticism, the impetus for this assimilation was exceptionally strong. In other domains, the usual Renaissance criteria – classical learning, art and literature drawing on classical models, the printing press, geographical exploration and volatile social circumstances comparable to those to which Burckhardt attributed to the emergence of individualism among the Italian elites – were all present by the early sixteenth century, some of them considerably earlier. Yet when one looked for English Renaissance poetics and literary criticism, there seemed to be very little of it until the 1570s, whereas from that point on, right on cue, Haslewood's *Essays* were there for the taking. All Spingarn had to do was to conflate, in the opening sentence of his English chapter, 'Elizabethan' with 'English Renaissance' criticism, and there it was, stretching from Gascoigne to Bolton, and easily expandable forward, to Milton, and backward, to the relevant passages in 'early Tudor' documents. The starring role is again Pseudo-Sidney's: he is England's first Aristotelian, hence England's first anti-allegorist, hence England's first critical modern. In his analysis of the *Defence*, Spingarn predictably fails to cite any of its multiple appeals to allegory, acknowledging them only later on, in a summary statement of the decline narrative: the allegorical element is 'minimized' in Sidney's treatise and its 'death-knell' is rung by Bacon, who is thereby 'foreshadowing the development of classicism, for from the time of Ben Jonson the allegorical mode of interpreting poetry ceased to have any effect on literary criticism'.⁷⁹ This flatly contradicts Spingarn's own earlier claim, quoted above, that allegory persisted 'throughout the Renaissance' and was 'one of the commonplaces of the age', but this contradiction must be suffered if there is to be such a thing as English Renaissance poetics, or at least one which conforms to the Burckhardtian notion of the period.

Three years later, Spingarn's account was effectively reaffirmed in the second volume of Saintsbury's *History*, an episode which calls for some comment since, unlike Spingarn, Saintsbury was no Burckhardtian. On the contrary, in his view, medieval achievements in literary practice take 'equal rank as a whole with those of classical and those of modern times', while it is classicism, seen as one unbroken development stretching from the early sixteenth to the late eighteenth century, that takes on the role of the middle age, the degenerative interlude between two healthy and productive literary epochs.⁸⁰ Accordingly, Saintsbury's overall framework is still that of Wylie and Vaughan: 'Modern Criticism' comes only after the 'end of Eighteenth-Century Orthodoxy'. Furthermore, Saintsbury's criticism of Spingarn's work – both explicit, of Spingarn's negative assessment of the Middle Ages, and implicit, addressing 'our newest Neo-Classics'⁸¹ – leads to the first and unfortunately still the only genuine polemic on the subject. The title of Spingarn's response, 'The Origins of Modern Criticism', precisely identifies the issue at stake. Predictably, he finds Saintsbury's views 'aggressively romantic', yet what the exchange ultimately shows is that their differences

---

⁷⁸ John Hale, *England and the Italian Renaissance: The Growth of Interest in Its History and Art*, 4th edn (Malden, MA: Blackwell, 2005), 110, quotes Symonds's diary entry of 5 April 1866 – 'the English Renaissance, the Elizabethan Age' – as the earliest instance of this rebranding.
⁷⁹ Spingarn, *History*, 177.
⁸⁰ Saintsbury, *A History of Criticism and Literary Taste in Europe from the Earliest Texts to the Present Day*, 1:469.
⁸¹ Ibid., 2:7–8, 2:35.

were really a matter of perspective and emphasis rather than truly incompatible conceptions of aesthetic modernity.[82] Now if not before, Spingarn must have finally seen his 'modern classicism' for what it really was: a fragile and ultimately untenable compromise between the same principles of modern aesthetics shared by his adversary, the Burckhardtian theory of the Renaissance, and the sobering reality of the materials onto which these principles and this theory were to be projected. Although Spingarn tries to save face by presenting himself as the greater scholar, meticulously cataloguing minor errors and oversights in Saintsbury's treatment of the period, his article is quite explicitly a statement of capitulation with regard to the principal issue at stake: 'Imitation, theory, law; wit, reason, taste – each in its turn became a guiding principle of criticism, until with the romantic movement all were superseded by the concept of the creative imagination.'[83]

That Spingarn realized the significance of this concession is clear from the fact that he included a revised version of this article as a new conclusion to the 1905 Italian translation of his *History*, and then also the 1908 revised edition and all subsequent impressions of the original. Indeed, he made the point still more emphatic by adding another sentence to the one just quoted, and making the resulting passage the very last words of the book:

> Imitation, theory, law; wit, reason, taste – each in its turn became a guiding principle of criticism, until with the romantic movement all were superseded by the concept of the creative imagination. The first three represent, as it were, the stages through which Renaissance poetics passed in the process of complete codification; the last three represent the stages of its decline and death.[84]

Spingarn continued to repudiate his original thesis in his later work. 'The Greeks', he writes in the important 1910 lecture on 'The New Criticism',

> conceived of Literature, not as an inevitable expression of creative power, but as a reasoned 'imitation' or re-shaping of the materials of life … . The Romans conceived of Literature as a noble art, intended (though under the guise of pleasure) to inspire men with high ideals of life. The classicists of the sixteenth and seventeenth centuries accepted this view in the main … . The eighteenth century complicated the course of Criticism by the introduction of vague and novel criteria, such as 'imagination', 'sentiment', and 'taste'. But with the Romantic Movement there developed the new idea which coordinates all Criticism in the nineteenth century.[85]

---

[82] Spingarn, 'The Origins of Modern Criticism', *Modern Philology* 1 (1904): 477–96, p. 482.
[83] Spingarn, 'Origins', 496. See also his review of Saintsbury's *History*: 'Saintsbury's History of Criticism', *The Nation*, 15 January 1903.
[84] Joel Elias Spingarn, *A History of Literary Criticism in the Renaissance*, 2nd edn (New York: Columbia University Press, 1908), 330; cf. *La critica letteraria nel Rinascimento: Saggio sulle origini dello spirito classico nella letteratura moderna*, trans. Antonio Fusco (Bari: Gius, 1905), 328.
[85] Joel Elias Spingarn, *The New Criticism: A Lecture Delivered at Columbia University, March 9, 1910* (New York: Columbia University Press, 1911), 10–11.

By this point, the quest for origins, back on course after its Burckhardtian detour, was almost complete. In 1908–9 appeared Spingarn's edition of the *Critical Essays of the Seventeenth Century*, followed by one of the critical writings of William Temple – although already printed in the *Essays*, these merit a separate edition as the statements of England's first proto-Romantic.[86] Two notes from the late 1900s show him searching for the origin of the notion of 'art for art's sake'.[87] Finally, between 1909 and *c*. 1912–3, Spingarn edited the *Literary Essays* of Goethe, whose ideas he elsewhere describes as the 'the guiding star ... of all modern criticism'.[88] With this, the scholarly output of the man for whom the Renaissance was only a means to an end – and who did not publish a word on the subject after the 1899 *History*, except for the polemic occasioned by the book, and revisions prompted by that polemic – had run its course. Spingarn's work now turns to essayistic and critical writing, and while this turn certainly has to do with his infamous dismissal from Columbia in March 1911, a more considered impression is that the latter was an effect rather than a cause – that the 'New Criticism' lecture is the real turning point, that Spingarn was essentially done with academia by this date regardless of the events that followed, and that these were perhaps little more than the inevitable institutional reflex of key intellectual positions he had adopted by this date.[89] Yet the damage was done: the final sentences of the revised editions of the *History* were hardly sufficient to negate the argument explicitly announced at its beginning and systematically pursued over the intervening 330 pages.

Turning back to Spingarn's adversary, we find that, for all his aggressive Romanticism, Saintsbury's chapters on the Renaissance amount to a faithful replica of Spingarn's *History*, including his treatment of allegory. This is surprising at first, as Saintsbury's treatment of ancient and medieval criticism contains multiple and

---

[86] Joel Elias Spingarn, *Critical Essays of the Seventeenth Century*, 3 vols. (Oxford: Clarendon, 1908–09); *Sir William Temple's Essays on Ancient & Modern Learning and On Poetry* (Oxford: Clarendon, 1909), iv–v.

[87] Joel Elias Spingarn, 'Art for Art's Sake: A Query', *Modern Language Notes* 22 (1907): 263; 'L'Art pour l'Art', *Modern Language Notes* 25 (1910): 95.

[88] Joel Elias Spingarn, *Goethe's Literary Essays* (New York: Harcourt, 1921), 291; *New Criticism*, 16–17.

[89] For example, Spingarn's categorical dismissal of moral criticism – 'We have done with all moral judgement of Literature' – correlates with his conduct in the case of the classicist Henry Thurston Peck, fired from Columbia later that year over a moral issue, a breach of promise in marriage. Spingarn initiated a resolution whereby the Faculty of Philosophy undertook 'to place on record its sense of [Peck's] academic services', to be strictly distinguished, as he later clarified, from his 'personal or non-academic conduct'. Whether or not this played a part in Spingarn's own firing – as he plausibly affirmed and the administration less plausibly denied – his initiative is telling. Details in his correspondence with Butler – the unconcealed sarcasm of Butler's 'hope' that Spingarn will continue his career 'as a productive scholar in the field of literary criticism in which you have already made so substantial a beginning', or Spingarn's own mention of 'differences of literary and scholarly ideals between my colleagues and myself' – suggest that the lecture had a still more direct relation to the whole affair. It is further indicative that Spingarn 'never sought another teaching position, although he undoubtedly could have secured a professorship at any number of first-rate institutions. In fact, after an initial period of bitterness he expressed a relief at having been freed from the narrow confines of the university ... . Nor did time bring regret; in 1936, he held a cocktail party to celebrate the twenty-fifth anniversary of his departure from the university'. See Spingarn, *New Criticism*, 26; Nicholas Murray Butler and J. E. Spingarn, *A Question of Academic Freedom, Being the Official Correspondence between Nicholas Murray Butler ... and J. E. Spingarn ... During the Academic Year 1910–1911 with Other Documents* (New York: for Distribution among the Alumni, 1911), 16, 18; Ross, *Spingarn*, 9.

emphatic expressions of his deep distaste for allegorical poetics, and also states explicitly that the ancient '*sacra fames* … for Allegory … was not in the least checked by the Renaissance, though the sauce of what it glutted itself on was somewhat altered'.[90] If so, why do allegory's appearances suddenly become much sparser in Saintsbury's second, Renaissance-neoclassical volume – where he glosses over its presence even in some cases where Spingarn had actually acknowledged it[91] – to then disappear altogether with the onset of modern criticism in the third? There is, however, a logic behind this, and if fact Spingarn's problem – how to erase allegory from that historical period in which one wishes to locate the origin of one's own critical modernity – is also Saintsbury's problem, yet Spingarn's solution is unavailable. Instead of a chronological, Saintsbury must therefore opt for a conceptual adjustment: a definition of literary criticism as concerned chiefly with the 'form' rather than the 'matter' of literature, and the resulting conviction that allegory 'has only to do with literary criticism in the sense that it is, and always has been, a very great degrader thereof, inclining it to be busy with matter instead of form'.[92] This is a crucial gambit, setting up one of the work's central arguments, namely, that medieval literary theory is next to non-existent and that the Middle Ages' success in literary practice is directly consequent on their lack of interest in theorizing this practice, whereas the post-1500 explosion of neoclassicist theory strangled the literary production of that epoch. Ironically, it is thus precisely Saintsbury's Romantic medievalism that saves the modernity of his Renaissance. If medieval literature is an outburst of natural genius unbridled by critical constraints, this can only be if allegory is excluded from the definition of criticism, yet the same principle must then be maintained in the rest of the book, and consequently, although Saintsbury nominally acknowledges allegory's persistence beyond the Middle Ages, and categorically denies modernity to Renaissance criticism, his account of the 1500–1700 period contains nothing that would contradict Spingarn's account.

IV

By the early 1900s, Spingarn had thus created, and Spingarn and Saintsbury had between them consolidated, the canonical and still dominant conception of English Renaissance literary criticism. Chronologically, it extends from Gascoigne's *Notes* to the Restoration, plus some overflow on each side, to catch some of the pre-Gascoigne material in the earlier sixteenth century, and the relevant statements of Milton and Hobbes in the later seventeenth century. Teleologically, it represents the beginning of English poetical and literary-critical modernity, whose progress is measurable in degrees of its supposed hostility to allegory, which is not a genuine expression of the period's poetic and aesthetic sensibilities but an atavism inherited from the Middle Ages. Any exceptions can now only prove the rule, as when Spingarn prints Reynolds's

---

[90] Spingarn, *History*, 1:448.
[91] See Saintsbury, *History*, 8, 9–10, 30, 34, 193, 261, 267, 176; cf. Saintsbury, *History*, 1:456, 2:42–46, 2:66, 2:119–26, 2:148–51, 2:170–6.
[92] Saintsbury, *History*, 1:11.

heavily pro-allegorical *Mythomystes*, but only to distinguish 'this perverse work' from the straight neoclassicist path trod by Sidney, Jonson and Dryden.⁹³

Most subsequent studies offer variations on this basic pattern, including Bernard Weinberg's widely influential *History of Literary Criticism in the Italian Renaissance*, additionally interesting here for being a deliberate 'experiment in writing intellectual history' according to the doctrines of the so-called Chicago Aristotelianism, especially R. S. Crane's ideas about 'history … without a thesis'.⁹⁴ If anywhere, then, it is here that we might hope for an account that will not be trying to fit the materials to any preconceived historiographical scheme, and indeed Weinberg assures his readers that his approach is determined exclusively 'by the nature of the materials' in question.⁹⁵ In practice, however, it is easy to see that the book is governed by two powerful, interrelated and rigorously executed theses. The first is stated openly in the preface, where Weinberg explains that his method of discerning 'the main intellectual traditions of the century as they related to literary criticism' will be 'to distinguish and identify them as developments and continuations of three great critical positions of the classical past: those of Plato, Aristotle, and Horace'.⁹⁶ In this, Weinberg is closely following his sources, however unwilling he may be to acknowledge them. In the preface, he briefly mentions only three predecessors – Spingarn, Ciro Trabalza and Marvin T. Herrick – and later adds that his study contains 'virtually no secondary bibliography', for he has 'chosen to discuss works themselves rather than the interpretation of those works by others'.⁹⁷ He has, however, certainly read his Saintsbury, who is particularly explicit on this point ('the main texts and patterns of the critics of the Italian Renaissance were three – the *Ars Poetica* of Horace, the *Poetics* of Aristotle and the various Platonic places dealing with poetry'), and who is himself summarizing the more discursive exposition of the same idea in Spingarn's *History*.⁹⁸

The consequences for the book's treatment of allegory are obvious: when encountered, it is not to be treated as a 'great critical position' but as an auxiliary concern at most – if not simply as a 'failure' or an 'inconsistency'⁹⁹ – and it is no surprise to find it omitted from Weinberg's discussions of a number of important and even major texts. This 'misleadingly incidental' treatment of allegory has already been criticized

---

⁹³ *Essays*, 1:xxi.
⁹⁴ Bernard Weinberg, *A History of Literary Criticism in the Italian Renaissance*, 1 vol. in 2 (Chicago: The University of Chicago Press, 1961), vii–viii; R. S. Crane, *The Idea of the Humanities, and Other Essays Critical and Historical*, 2 vols. (Chicago: The University of Chicago Press, 1967), 2:174. Cf. René Wellek, 'Reply to Bernard Weinberg's Review of My *History of Modern Criticism*', *Journal of the History of Ideas* 30 (1969): 281–2. For representative Spingarnian studies until Weinberg, see Guy Andrew Thompson, *Elizabethan Criticism of Poetry …* (Menasha: The Collegiate Press, 1914); Elizabeth J. Sweeting, *Early Tudor Criticism: Linguistic and Literary* (1940; repr. New York: Russell, 1964); Atkins, *Renascence*. The older paradigm retains some currency into the early decades of the twentieth century, expiring with such publications as James Routh's *Rise of Classical English Criticism: A History of the Canons of English Literary Taste and Rhetorical Doctrines, from the Beginning of English Criticism to the Death of Dryden* (New Orleans: Tulane University Press, 1915).
⁹⁵ Weinberg, *History*, ix.
⁹⁶ Ibid., viii.
⁹⁷ Ibid., vii, x.
⁹⁸ Saintsbury, *History*, 2:213; Spingarn, *History*, 18–23.
⁹⁹ Weinberg, *History*, viii.

by Kenneth Borris, and further examination amply confirms his judgement.[100] Of the nearly two hundred authors discussed in Weinberg's study, only about a quarter are noted to endorse the doctrine, whether in general or in relation to a particular genre or work. The figure is suspiciously low, and even the most cursory review reveals that in addition to those of Viperano and Fornari, mentioned by Borris, Weinberg omits allegory from his accounts of the works of Badius, Parrasio, Fracastoro, Minturno, Segni and Capriano. Of the thirteen works classified as the 'new arts of poetry' – 'general treatises that attempt to present a total conception of the art rather than to discuss an individual point or to elucidate some phase of ancient doctrine'[101] – nine embrace allegory to at least some degree. Nor is there any discernible pattern of decline. Commenting on a 1586 work by Lorenzo Pariguolo, Weinberg notes that this critic's appeal to allegory 'repeats one of the essential arguments in the early defenses of poetry', and thus 'returns to the traditions of the beginning of the century'.[102] Yet Weinberg's intuition of allegory as 'early' is disproved by his own index – even without additions, the works listed in the entry for *allegory* are evenly distributed throughout the century.

The second of Weinberg's theses is the classic Burckhardtian one: mapping a teleology of modernity onto the medieval-Renaissance divide. Unlike the first, however, it is never openly stated, for it is precisely such histories with theses that a Chicago-Aristotelian seeks to avoid, yet is betrayed by slips scattered among Weinberg's indefatigable analyses – slips that predictably have to do with allegory. Thus we read that the defence of poetry by the Horatian critics partly 'consists in the allegorical interpretation of poetry, where again both a renewed Platonism and a continued medievalism enter into the sum of "Horatian" ideas', and that the 'old medieval justification by allegory still serves as an auxiliary to the discussion of the utilitarian ends of poetry'.[103] This identification of allegory with the Middle Ages – a thesis by any, let alone Chicago-Aristotelian, standards – is matched by an equally revealing comment on the prominence of allegorical poetics in the 1564 commentary on Horace's *Ars poetica* by Francesco Filippi Pedemonte, said to demonstrate that this critic's 'whole conception of the ends of poetry is unaffected by his study and his citation of Aristotle'.[104] This is the reason, precisely as it was with Spingarn, for pushing the emergence of 'Renaissance' criticism not only to the Cinquecento but specifically to Pazzi's translation of 1536.[105] Ultimately, the conviction that history can be written without a thesis leads the historian only into unconsciously adopting the most conventional of theses, and once set into action Weinberg's experiment unerringly reproduces Spingarn's scheme. A history of Renaissance criticism might be what the

---

[100] Borris, *Allegory*, 260n11–12, 264n29.
[101] Weinberg, *History*, 715.
[102] Ibid., 621.
[103] Ibid., 109, 198. Here of course Weinberg ignores Horace's allegorical or at least rationalist interpretation of the legends of Orpheus and Amphion, through which – along with the general Pseudo-Horatian chorus of *dulce et utile* – the *Ars poetica* connects to the allegorical tradition, and on which sixteenth- and seventeenth-century critics draw with an almost formulaic consistency: allegory must be a medieval rather than a classical doctrine.
[104] Ibid., 115.
[105] Ibid., 367.

title promises, yet when the question of periodization is tackled directly, Weinberg can speak of the Renaissance only without the capital 'R', or in quotation marks, or as disintegrated into phases:

> I have given to the term 'Renaissance' a highly restricted meaning: I have limited it to the sixteenth century, except for those few cases in which I have found it necessary to trace a movement back into the Quattrocento. Here again, the decision was determined by the nature of the materials. The Cinquecento was the century of major development and full realization, both in poetic theory and in practical criticism; the Quattrocento, for all its overwhelming importance in other phases of the Renaissance, provided only a minor impetus in the domain of literary criticism, and the Seicento did little more than repeat and reorder the ideas of the preceding century. By 1600, the renaissance in criticism had run its full course.[106]

The only escape route is the one paved by Spingarn: pushing the 'Renaissance' forward to the assimilation of the *Poetics*, relegating allegory to the thereby extended 'Middle Ages', and suppressing and relativizing its presence in the resulting corpus. Finally, in Weinberg's edition of the Italian *Trattati*, the term is dropped entirely, along with any attempt at historical contextualization, with a thesis or without: the operative term is now simply the 'Cinquecento' and conspicuously absent is a foreword, afterword or any other kind of comprehensive editorial paratext.[107]

Of Weinberg's influence there is no better example than Concetta Carestia Greenfield's *Humanist and Scholastic Poetics, 1250–1500*, surveying the work of fifteen Italian critics of the stated period. Attention to such scholars as Paul Oskar Kristeller, Ernst Robert Curtius, and Jean Seznec makes Greenfield's the first major study to operate on the premise of continuity rather than rupture between medieval and post-medieval tradition, which has numerous important repercussions, particularly in the role assigned to allegory. Thus she criticizes 'the nineteenth-century prejudice that allegory was a medieval invention rejected by humanists, who turned to a nonallegorical antiquity' as well as the views of 'Late Crocean aestheticians like Spingarn', who 'have read the humanist emphasis on "form" as an emphasis on beauty and pleasure for its own sake', a position which 'does not find support in humanist poetics'.[108] On the contrary, while scriptural allegorism is essential to both scholastic and humanist modes of thought, secular allegorism is a specifically humanist cause and indeed the 'central issue' in the humanist-scholastic debate.[109] Accordingly, the received configuration of the allegory-modernity nexus is turned on its head. It is scholasticism, emerging with the recovery of the Aristotelian corpus, that presents a novelty in the intellectual landscape, while humanism retains 'the general scheme of medieval culture against the contemporary attempt of the scholastic culture to supersede it'; it is scholasticism, in accordance with Aquinas' dictum that 'in no science invented by humans … can be

---

[106] Ibid., ix.
[107] Bernard Weinberg, *Trattati di poetica e retorica del Cinquecento*, 4 vols. (Bari: Laterza, 1970–74).
[108] Concetta Carestia Greenfield, *Humanist and Scholastic Poetics, 1250–1500* (Lewisburg: Bucknell University Press, 1981), 32.
[109] Ibid., 28.

found anything but the literal sense', that dismisses secular allegorism, while humanism champions it.[110]

All this would seem to hack right at the root of Spingarnian orthodoxy, but there is another major influence on Greenfield's thesis which pulls in the opposite direction, namely, that of the two imposing tomes of Weinberg's *History*, and ultimately it is this influence that shapes the book's overall conceptual and historical framework.[111] Not even Kristeller, who contributes a foreword to Greenfield's book, can withstand it. Greenfield frequently cites Kristeller's *Renaissance Thought*, where the Renaissance is defined as 'that period of Western European history which extends approximately from 1300 to 1600, without any preconceptions as to the characteristics or merits of that period, or of those periods preceding and following it'.[112] The obvious objections to the latter portion of this statement can be passed over here – what is important is that Kristeller, like most other scholars, sees the Renaissance as lasting roughly from the fourteenth through the sixteenth century, and accordingly, in his foreword, he designates the period covered in Greenfield's book as that of 'the later Middle Ages and the early Renaissance'.[113] In Greenfield's own preface, however, we meet with a crucially different formulation: 'While the history of literary criticism in the Renaissance has been written several times, practically no work has been devoted to humanist poetics, that is, to the development of a theory of poetry from Petrarch to Pontano'.[114]

This is no slip. The distinction between 'humanist' and 'Renaissance' is consistently maintained throughout the book, since defining its subject as 'Renaissance' or even 'early Renaissance' would mean open conflict with Weinberg and the whole canonical conception of the subject. It would raise some very awkward questions, not least that of the fate of allegory in the post-1500 period. How did an issue that had been of 'central' importance for two and a half centuries become irrelevant virtually overnight? It would make one think twice about Weinberg's dismissal of the Quattrocento as having 'provided only a minor impetus in the domain of literary criticism', and consequently of his whole conception of 'Renaissance' criticism.[115] Does it make more sense to find Italian Renaissance criticism practised in the period to which that term customarily applies, or to make it begin almost at the point at which the Italian Renaissance, as commonly understood, ends? There would also be implications for other national traditions. Does it make sense to begin the history of English Renaissance criticism in the 1570s, more than a century after the earliest stirrings of English humanism, and

---

[110] Ibid., 20, 51.
[111] A trivial but striking indicator of the depth of this influence is found in Greenfield's preface, where what she evidently thinks of as her own sentences turn out to be almost verbatim reproductions of Weinberg's. See Greenfield, *Poetics*, 12–13: 'I have not followed any author through his career or any concept through the century'; 'What I have said about each text does not represent the totality of its contents'; 'I present them [the translations included in the study] with the usual modesty of the translator'. Cf. Weinberg, *History*, viii– x: 'I have not sought to follow any author through his career or any term and concept through the century'; 'what I have said about any individual text is not intended to represent the totality of its contents'; 'I present these translations with the usual reservations of the translator'.
[112] Paul Oskar Kristeller, *Renaissance Thought*, rev. edn (New York: Harper, 1961), 3–4.
[113] Greenfield, *Poetics*, 9.
[114] Ibid., 11.
[115] Weinberg, *History*, ix.

many decades after Erasmus and Colet? By dropping the curtain at 1500 and excising a word from her vocabulary, Greenfield avoids such questions, but thereby also forfeits the chance to make a more significant intervention into the canonical account of the subject.

While the achievements of either Weinberg's *History* or Greenfield's *Poetics* are not to be disputed, the latter should serve as a warning against uncritical reception of the former. A more recent example of such reception is the introduction to the *Renaissance* volume in *The Cambridge History of Literary Criticism*, in which Glyn P. Norton, in true Weinbergian fashion, fails to mention a single one of his numerous predecessors until the last paragraph, where, in 'One final coda', he showers praise on Weinberg: 'The luminosity of his scholarship has not dimmed over the years and, as this volume attests, continues to invigorate critical dialogue and bring us back to fundamental theoretical issues about great writing.'[116] And yet, while Weinberg's influence on Norton is certainly clear – Renaissance criticism breathes an 'air of modernity', the chaste marriage of Philology and Protestantism ends the depraved *ménage à quatre* of medieval exegesis, and so on[117] – his volume attests no such thing. Already in the second chapter, Michel Jeanneret's on 'Renaissance Exegesis', we read that 'allegorical reading was particularly active in Italy, where (there being no gap between the Middle Ages and the Renaissance) it continued well into the sixteenth century'.[118] Norton promotes Erasmus to a 'chief' position among his imaginary Renaissance anti-allegorists, yet Jeanneret's chapter, as well as Marjorie O'Rourke Boyle's, remind us that Erasmus was in fact a fervent advocate of both scriptural and non-scriptural allegorism.[119] Norton fails to mention the heresy even in relation to the Neoplatonists, a connection which multiple chapters go on to discuss, including Michael J. B. Allen's, emphasizing allegory as 'the new key to the validity of poetry in the Platonic republic'.[120] Furthermore, even as this mutiny unfolds between the covers of his volume, Norton's views are also contradicted by neighbouring titles in the series, whose editors broadly accept the consensus view, consigning the so-called 'Renaissance' to the premodern phase of literary thought.[121]

The same patterns and tensions punctuate the major anthologies of the corpus. To G. Gregory Smith, Spingarn's 'modern classicism', oxymoronic as most would have found it already in 1899, was wholly obsolete, but even as he sets a new tone by noting 'the modern dislike of the classical elements in the essays', he retains the rest of Spingarn's scheme, including the decline-of-allegory narrative.[122] Fast-forwarding to Brian Vickers's *English Renaissance Literary Criticism*, expressly intended to replace Smith's *Essays* as the standard reference work on the subject, we find not merely continuity but radicalization, with Vickers's antipathy towards allegory, combined with his sympathy

---

[116] *The Cambridge History of Literary Criticism: The Renaissance*, ed. Glyn P. Norton (Cambridge: Cambridge University Press, 1999), 21.
[117] Ibid., 4, 8.
[118] Ibid., 37.
[119] Ibid., 4, 40, 48–9.
[120] Ibid., 37, 67, 91–2, 153, 162, 204, 439.
[121] *The Cambridge History of Literary Criticism: The Eighteenth Century*, ed. H. B. Nisbet and Claude Rawson (Cambridge: Cambridge University Press, 1997), 7; *The Cambridge History of Literary Criticism: Romanticism*, ed. Marshall Brown (Cambridge: Cambridge University Press, 2000), 1.
[122] G. Gregory Smith, *Elizabethan Critical Essays*, 2 vols. (Oxford: Clarendon, 1904), 1:xii, 1:xxiv–xxv.

for rhetoric, and his quixotic insistence that the culture of Renaissance England was 'a truly homogeneous culture, in which theory and practice interlocked', resulting in a particularly thorough campaign of anti-allegorical whitewashing.[123] There is thus room in the 672 pages of Vickers's collection for thirty-six items, including a host of minor documents, many of which represent literary criticism only in the broadest sense of that term, but not for even the briefest extract from Thomas Lodge's reply to Stephen Gosson's *Schoole of Abuse*, Reynolds's *Mythomystes*, or Kenelm Digby's *Observations on the ... Faery Queen*, to mention only three very important works – the first defence of poetry in the English language, the chief English specimen of Neoplatonic poetics, and one of the earliest sustained and self-contained close readings of a piece of English literature – respectively printed by Smith, Spingarn and Tayler, and all heavily allegorical in approach.[124] In a programmatically 'comprehensive' anthology, these are glaring, patently intentional omissions, explicable only in terms of the wider agenda outlined above.[125]

V

Given the critical thrust of these analyses, it is perhaps now worth emphasizing what should be obvious enough, namely, that the works discussed above do not represent the whole of the scholarship on the subject, which includes numerous valuable contributions by several generations of scholars. The focus has been almost exclusively on the major histories and anthologies, attempting a comprehensive account of the subject, and even from these there is much to be learned regardless of the biases that I have tried to bring to light. Spingarn and his successors went to work under the influence of the established historical conception of the Renaissance, expecting to find an analogous state of affairs in their chosen field of study. When they could not find it

---

[123] See Brian Vickers, *Appropriating Shakespeare: Contemporary Critical Quarrels* (New Haven: Yale University Press, 1993), 372–416; *In Defence of Rhetoric* (Oxford: Clarendon, 1998); *English Renaissance Literary Criticism* (Oxford: Clarendon, 1999), vii.

[124] See *Essays*, ed. Smith; *Essays*, ed. Spingarn; *Literary Criticism in Seventeenth-Century England*, ed. Edward W. Tayler (New York: Knopf, 1967).

[125] Appeals to allegory are also omitted from Vickers's extracts from the works of Wilson and Puttenham, as are the examples of allegorical meanings in Harington's *Apologie*. Harington's view – distinguishing between a literal and allegorical sense, and subdividing the latter into moral, philosophical and religious – is designated as 'medieval', in contrast to that of 'Renaissance scholars (notably Erasmus)', who 'rejected this scheme, usually preserving only the moral sense'. Ironically, one of the sources for such 'medieval' schemes most influential with Harington and his contemporaries was precisely Erasmus's *De copia*, where four senses are distinguished – 'historical' (i.e. rationalist or euhemerist), 'theological', 'physical', and 'moral' – with the proviso that 'quite often there is a mixture of more than one type'. The sole mention of allegory in Vickers's introduction follows directly on a nod back to Spingarn: 'In the Middle Ages, ... only those works of literature were valued that had an explicitly moral and educational function, or could be given one retrospectively by allegorical interpretation.' In this same passage, Vickers goes on to write that 'two outstanding early humanists confronted medieval enmity with well argued defences, Giovanni Boccaccio in *De genealogia deorum* ... , and Coluccio Salutati in *De laboribus Herculis*' – as if these were not themselves allegorical in approach. See Vickers, *Criticism*, 47, 309n11; Desiderius Erasmus, *Literary and Educational Writings*, ed. Craig R. Thompson et al., 7 vols. in 4 (Toronto: University of Toronto Press, 1978–89), 1:610–13.

in the period as commonly understood – fourteenth through sixteenth century in Italy, with variable amounts of 'transalpine delay' – they were forced to resort to measures which distorted the notion almost beyond recognition. But this is, emphatically, not to say that all these scholars were simply in the wrong. In fact, their collective failure to produce a coherent account of the subject is a rather conclusive success, proving that they did not blindly impose their premises on their materials, and that they did not simply bow to the logic of general cultural history when this logic threatened to obscure specifically literary-historical developments. It is not for lack of able pens that a viable history of Renaissance poetics has not yet been written, but because of a conceptual impasse at the very heart of that subject. A viable history of Renaissance poetics has not yet been because it cannot be written, since the very concept of the Renaissance – as first formulated in reference to the spheres of classical learning and the fine arts, and subsequently expanded into a whole-scale cultural epoch said to represent the emergence of Western modernity – was formed without taking into account a substantial portion of the literary and literary-critical materials produced in the period it is supposed to cover. Therefore, these materials will remain a foreign body in any study that does not run away from the evidence, and will keep returning to haunt anyone who, unconvinced by the present analysis, decides to take another swing at the same impossible task.

Allegory, as I have tried to show, is the chief among these revenants. Historians stage rushed funerals of this arch-nemesis of modern aesthetics, but from its uneasy grave, allegory is still pulling the strings. Suppressed as an increasingly irrelevant medieval atavism, it revenges itself by making this suppression the true burden – spoken or unspoken, conscious or unconscious – of the canonical accounts of the subject. It is allegory that drove Spingarn to delay Renaissance criticism to the dissemination of Aristotle's *Poetics*, and it is allegory that has made Spingarn's successors retain his framework, even after it was conclusively repudiated by Spingarn himself. It is allegory that has led these Burckhardtians to postpone their Renaissances almost to the point where Burckhardt's ends, envelop them in scare quotes, dissect them into phases and refine them out of existence. Consequently, the way forward consists largely in acknowledging the integral place of allegorical poetics in the period's literary thought, which will inevitably result in a major revision of its place in the broader historical framework. Another imperative is a more rigorous distinction between poetics and literary criticism. It is clear that the 1570s introduce a more institutionalized and self-conscious stage in English literary criticism, a phenomenon certainly worthy of the ample attention it has received. Yet it is precisely this unprecedented richness of the period's overall critical output that has impoverished our understanding of its developments, or lack thereof, in poetic theory proper. However commendable in themselves, the efforts of historians and editors to encompass the totality of the period's critical activity have tended to obscure the situation with the narrower but decisive question of theoretical fundamentals, even as their claims for the emergence of poetic modernity in this period have been based, as they must, precisely on arguments relating to these fundamentals. To advance on the present state of the field, future work must carefully disentangle the familiar accounts of the consolidation of a national literary tradition, the rise of the vernacular, the development of prosody, the introduction of continental influences, the institutionalization of the critic and any number of other subjects, however important in their own right, from its account of the period's elementary literary theory – if only so they can then be re-entangled in more coherent and insightful ways.

In doing so, historians of 1500–1700 poetics would be making a vital contribution not only to their own field but also to the wider, cross-disciplinary attempt to understand the history of Western poetic and aesthetic thought, and especially the key question of the transition from the premodern to the modern stage of that history. At present, work on this question is paralysed by at least four irreconcilable tendencies: the eighteenth-century consensus, which remains the dominant but by no means universally accepted position; the scholarship in the Burckhardt-Spingarn-Weinberg tradition, dating the watershed to the Renaissance period; the tendency, emerging in the early twentieth century, to redraw the line at a significantly later date, around 1900 or even 1960;[126] and the never-sleeping lure of ahistoricism, bent on flattening such narratives into 'traditions', 'conversations' and the like.[127] Each of the four positions contradicts the other three. At some point, between roughly 1500 and 1950, there either occurred or did not occur a major watershed in Western literary theory, and if it did occur – which eliminates the fourth position – then it matters greatly whether it occurred in the sixteenth, eighteenth or twentieth century, as these dates obviously entail very different and ultimately irreconcilable explanations of the phenomenon.

But there is, at the bottom of all this, a still more pressing question – that of where one locates one's own poetic and aesthetic self in this history. In an appendix to his edition of Goethe, Spingarn recalls how its manuscript, 'virtually completed' by 1912–13, came to be

> mislaid among some old papers, and when it was recovered the European War was at its height. Never again, it then seemed, could I regard my work with the same disinterested temper in which it was begun, for what was recovered was no longer a manuscript but a ghost, no longer a book but a strange spirit returned from an all too irrecoverable past. When I re-read these words from the lips of the one who had spent his life 'with spirits god-like mild', and related them to our new and altered world, I understood once more how man forever fashions history to his own meaning, and how it has not life except such as is given to it by his creative mind.[128]

Surely Spingarn eventually came to see how the same was true of his *History*, the star-crossed *juvenilium* which he effectively disowned within five years of its publication, but which has nevertheless continued to shape the scholarship on the subject.

---

[126] For an early example, see Richard Green Moulton, *The Modern Study of Literature: An Introduction to Literary Theory and Interpretation* (Chicago: The University of Chicago Press, 1915).

[127] Most recently in James Seaton's *Literary Criticism from Plato to Postmodernism: The Humanistic Alternative* (New York: Cambridge University Press, 2014), 1–2, where the history of literary theory is 'a continuing conversation among three traditions', namely the 'Platonic', 'Neoplatonic', and 'Aristotelian or humanistic'.

[128] Goethe, *Essays*, 291.

Yet if Spingarn fashioned the history of 1500–1700 literary thought to his own meaning, at least he did so because he felt passionately about this meaning – about those paradigmatically modern and anti-allegorical 'Newer Ideals of Criticism' he championed in the 1910 lecture – and at least these same ideals eventually led him to doubt and ultimately discard his original thesis. The question for us, then, is, what ideals of our own, or absence thereof, drive us to reproduce his account? If we continue to fashion history to our own meanings, and there are no histories without theses, what are our meanings and our theses? To move in new directions, as this collection invites us to do – which is to say, away from Weinberg, which effectively means away from Spingarn and consequently, as always, away from Burckhardt – the field must meaningfully engage with this fundamental question and must be ready to follow wherever such engagement may take it, regardless of the institutional resistance it is certain to encounter in its path.

Bibliography

Abrams, M. H. *The Mirror and the Lamp: Romantic Theory and the Critical Tradition*. New York: Oxford University Press, 1953.

Aristotle. *The 'Poetics' of Aristotle: Translation and Commentary*. Edited and translated by Stephen Halliwell. Chapel Hill: The University of North Carolina Press, 1987.

Arnold, Matthew. *Culture and Anarchy: An Essay in Political and Social Criticism*. London: Smith, Elder, 1869.

Atkins, J. W. H. *English Literary Criticism: 17th and 18th Centuries*. London: Methuen, 1951.

Atkins, J. W. H. *English Literary Criticism: The Medieval Phase*. Cambridge: Cambridge University Press, 1943.

Atkins, J. W. H. *English Literary Criticism: The Renascence*. London: Methuen, 1943.

Atkins, J. W. H. *Literary Criticism in Antiquity: A Sketch of Its Development*, 2 vols. Cambridge: Cambridge University Press, 1934.

Bacon, Francis. *Opera … , tomvs primvs: Qui continet De Dignitate & Augmentis Scientiarum Libros IX …* . London: Haviland, 1623.

Bacon, Francis. *The Twoo Bookes … Of the Proficience and Aduancement of Learning, Diuine and Humane …* . London: [Purfoot and Creede] for Tomes, 1605.

Baldwin, Charles Sears. *Ancient Rhetoric and Poetic, Interpreted from Representative Works*. New York: Macmillan, 1924.

Baldwin, Charles Sears. *Medieval Rhetoric and Poetic (to 1400), Interpreted from Representative Works*. New York: Macmillan, 1928.

Baldwin, Charles Sears. *Renaissance Literary Theory and Practice: Classicism in the Rhetoric and Poetic of Italy, France, and England 1400–1600*. Edited by Donald Lemen Clark. New York: Columbia University Press, 1939.

Beloe, William. *Anecdotes of Literature and Scarce Books*. 6 vols. London: for Rivington, 1807–12.

Blackburn, Thomas H. 'The Date and Evolution of Edmund Bolton's *Hypercritica*'. *Studies in Philology* 63 (1966): 196–202.

Bordelon, Suzanne. *A Feminist Legacy: The Rhetoric and Pedagogy of Gertrude Buck*. Carbondale: Southern Illinois University Press, 2007.

Borinski, Karl. *Die Antike in Poetik und Kunsttheorie von Ausgang des Klassischen Altertums bis auf Goethe under Wilhelm von Humboldt*. Edited by Richard Newald (vol. 2), 2 vols. Lepizig: Dieterich, 1914–24.

Borinski, Karl. *Die Poetik der Renaissance und der Anfänge der literarischen Kritik in Deutschland*. Berlin: Weidmann, 1886.

Borris, Kenneth. *Allegory and Epic in English Renaissance Literature: Heroic Form in Sidney, Spenser, and Milton*. Cambridge: Cambridge University Press, 2000.

Boswell, Joseph. *The Life of Samuel Johnson …* , 2 vols. London: Baldwin for Dilly, 1791.

Brljak, Vladimir. 'The Age of Allegory'. *Studies in Philology* 114 (2017): 697–719.

Brown, Marshall, ed. *The Cambridge History of Literary Criticism: Romanticism*. Cambridge: Cambridge University Press, 2000.

Burckhardt, Jacob. *The Civilization of the Renaissance in Italy*. Translated by S. G. C. Middlemore. 1878; repr. London: Phaidon, 1995.

Butcher, S. H. *Aristotle's Theory of Poetry and Fine Art with a Critical Text and a Translation of the Poetics*. London: Macmillan, 1895.

Butler, Nicholas Murray and J. E. Spingarn. *A Question of Academic Freedom, Being the Official Correspondence between Nicholas Murray Butler … and J. E. Spingarn … During the Academic Year 1910-1911 with Other Documents*. New York: for Distribution among the Alumni, 1911.

Cooper, Elizabeth. *The Muses Library; Or a Series of English Poetry, from the Saxons, to the Reign of King Charles II …* . London: Wilcox et al., 1737.

Crane, R. S. *The Idea of the Humanities, and Other Essays Critical and Historical*, 2 vols. Chicago: The University of Chicago Press, 1967.

Davenant, William and Thomas Hobbes. *A Discourse upon Gondibert … With an Answer to it …* . Paris: Guillemot, 1650.

Day, Gary. *Literary Criticism: A New History*. Edinburgh: Edinburgh University Press, 2008.

Dryden, John. *The Critical and Miscellaneous Prose Works …* . Edited by Edmond Malone, 3 vols. London: Baldwin for Cadell and Davies, 1800.

Erasmus, Desiderius. *Literary and Educational Writings*. Edited by Craig R. Thompson et al., 7 vols in 4. Toronto: University of Toronto Press, 1978–89.

Ford, Andrew. 'Literary Criticism and the Poet's Autonomy'. In *A Companion to Ancient Aesthetics*, edited by Penelope Murray and Pierre Destrée, 143–57. Chichester: Blackwell, 2015.

Foucault, Michel. *The Order of Things: An Archaeology of the Human Sciences*. Translated by Alan Sheridan. 1970; repr. London: Routledge, 2002.

Gavin, Michael. *The Invention of English Criticism, 1560-1760*. Cambridge: Cambridge University Press, 2015.

Goethe, Johann Wolfgang (von). *Goethe's Literary Essays*. Edited by Joel Elias Spingarn. New York: Harcourt, 1921.

Goulimari, Pelagia. *Literary Criticism and Theory: From Plato to Postcolonialism*. Abingdon: Routledge, 2015.

Greenfield, Concetta Carestia. *Humanist and Scholastic Poetics, 1250-1500*. Lewisburg: Bucknell University Press, 1981.

Guyer, Paul. *A History of Modern Aesthetics*, 3 vols. Cambridge: Cambridge University Press, 2014.

Habermas, Jürgen. 'Modernity: An Unfinished Project'. Translated by Nicholas Walker. In *Habermas and the Unfinished Project of Modernity: Critical Essays on 'The Philosophical Discourse of Modernity'*, edited by Maurizio Passerin d'Entreves and Seyla Benhabib, 38–58. Cambridge, MA: The MIT Press, 1997.

Habib, M. A. R. *A History of Literary Criticism: From Plato to the Present*. Malden, MA: Blackwell, 2005.
Habib, M. A. R. *Modern Literary Criticism and Theory: A History*. Oxford: Blackwell, 2008.
Hale, John. *England and the Italian Renaissance: The Growth of Interest in Its History and Art*, 4th edn. Malden, MA: Blackwell, 2005.
Harland, Richard. *Literary Theory from Plato to Barthes: An Introductory History*. Basingstoke: Macmillan, 1999.
Haslewood, Joseph, ed. *Ancient Critical Essays upon English Poets and Poesy*, 2 vols. London: Triphook, 1811–15.
Johnson, Samuel. *The Lives of the Most Eminent English Poets; with Critical Observations on Their Works*. Edited by Roger Lonsdale, 4 vols. Oxford: Clarendon, 2006.
Kristeller, Paul Oskar. *Renaissance Thought*, Rev. edn. New York: Harper, 1961.
Lazarus, Micha. 'Sidney's Greek Poetics'. *Studies in Philology* 112 (2015): 504–36.
Le Bossu, René. '*Treatise of the Epick Poem* … '. In *Monsieur Bossu's Treatise of the Epick Poem … To which are Added, An Essay upon Satyr, by Monsieur D'Acier; and A Treatise upon Pastorals, by Monsieur Fontanelle*, by René Le Bossu, André Dacier and Bernard Le Bovier de Fontenelle. Translated by W. J. London: for Bennet, 1695.
Lynch, Jack. *The Age of Elizabeth in the Age of Johnson*. Cambridge: Cambridge University Press, 2003.
Marino, Adrian. *The Biography of 'The Idea of Literature': From Antiquity to the Baroque*. Translated by Virgil Stanciu and Charles M. Carlton. Albany: State University of New York Press, 1996.
Moulton, Richard Green. *The Modern Study of Literature: An Introduction to Literary Theory and Interpretation*. Chicago: The University of Chicago Press, 1915.
Nisbet, H. B. and Claude Rawson, eds. *The Cambridge History of Literary Criticism: The Eighteenth Century*. Cambridge: Cambridge University Press, 1997.
Norton, Glyn P., ed. *The Cambridge History of Literary Criticism: The Renaissance*. Cambridge: Cambridge University Press, 1999.
Phillips, Edward. *Theatrum Poetarum, or A Compleat Collection of the Poets … Together with a Prefatory Discourse of the Poets and Poetry in Generall*. London: Smith, 1675.
Pope, Alexander. *An Essay on Criticism*. London: Lewis, 1711.
R[eynolds], H[enry]. *Mythomystes* … . In *The British Bibliographer*, edited by Egerton Brydges and Joseph Haslewood, 4 vols., 4:373–79. London: Triphook, 1810–14.
Ross, B. Joyce. *J. E. Spingarn and the Rise of the NAACP, 1911–1939*. New York: Atheneum, 1972.
Routh, James. *The Rise of Classical English Criticism: A History of the Canons of English Literary Taste and Rhetorical Doctrines, from the Beginning of English Criticism to the Death of Dryden*. New Orleans: Tulane University Press, 1915.
Rymer, Thomas. 'The Preface of the Translator'. In *Reflections on Aristotle's Treatise of Poesie …* , by René Rapin. Translated by Thomas Rymer, A3r–b2v. London: Herringman, 1674.
Saintsbury, George. *A History of Criticism and Literary Taste in Europe from the Earliest Texts to the Present Day*, 3 vols. Edinburgh: Blackwood, 1900–04.
Schelling, Felix E. *Poetic and Verse Criticism of the Reign of Elizabeth*. Philadelphia: University of Pennsylvania Press, 1891.
Seaton, James. *Literary Criticism from Plato to Postmodernism: The Humanistic Alternative*. New York: Cambridge University Press, 2014.
Sidney, Philip. *Apologie for Poetrie*. Edited by Edward Arber. Birmingham: 34 Wheeleys Road, 1868.

Sidney, Philip. *An Apologie for Poetrie*. Edited by Evelyn S. Shuckburgh. Cambridge: Cambridge University Press, 1891.
Sidney, Philip. *'An Apology for Poetry' (or 'The Defence of Poesy')*. Edited by Geoffrey Shepherd, 3rd edn, Rev. R. W. Maslen. Manchester: Manchester University Press, 2000.
Sidney, Philip. *'The Defense of Poesy', Otherwise Known as 'An Apology for Poetry.'* Edited by Albert S. Cook. Boston: Ginn, 1890.
Sidney, Philip. *Sir Philip Sidney's Astrophel and Stella und Defence of Poesie nach den ältesten Ausgaben mit einer Einleituweng über Sidney's Leben und Werke herausgegeben*. Edited by Ewald Flügel. Halle: Niemeyer, 1889.
Sidney, Philip and Ben Jonson. *Sir Philip Sydney's Defence of Poetry. And, Observations on Poetry and Eloquence, from the Discoveries of Ben Jonson*. Edited by Joseph Warton. London: J., Robinson, and Walter, 1787.
Smith, G. Gregory, ed. *Elizabethan Critical Essays*, 2 vols. Oxford: Clarendon, 1904.
Spingarn, Joel Elias. 'Art for Art's Sake: A Query'. *Modern Language Notes* 22 (1907): 263.
Spingarn, Joel Elias, ed. *Critical Essays of the Seventeenth Century*, 3 vols. Oxford: Clarendon, 1908–09.
Spingarn, Joel Elias. *A History of Literary Criticism in the Renaissance, with Special Reference to the Influence of Italy in the Formation and Development of Modern Classicism*. New York: Columbia University Press, 1899.
Spingarn, Joel Elias. *A History of Literary Criticism in the Renaissance*, 2nd edn. New York: Columbia University Press, 1908.
Spingarn, Joel Elias. *La critica letteraria nel Rinascimento: Saggio sulle origini dello spirito classico nella letteratura moderna*. Translated by Antonio Fusco. Bari: Gius, 1905.
Spingarn, Joel Elias. 'L'Art pour l'Art'. *Modern Language Notes* 25 (1910): 95.
Spingarn, Joel Elias. *The New Criticism: A Lecture Delivered at Columbia University, March 9, 1910*. New York: Columbia University Press, 1911.
Spingarn, Joel Elias. 'The Origins of Modern Criticism'. *Modern Philology* 1 (1904): 477–96.
Spingarn, Joel Elias. 'Saintsbury's History of Criticism'. *The Nation*, 15 January 1903.
Stump, Donald, C. Stuart Hunter and Jerome S. Dees, eds. *Sir Philip Sidney World Bibliography*. http://bibs.slu.edu/sidney.
Sweeting, Elizabeth J. *Early Tudor Criticism: Linguistic and Literary*. 1940; repr. New York: Russell, 1964.
Symonds, John Addington. *Renaissance in Italy: Italian Literature*, 2 vols. London: Smith, Elder, 1881.
Tayler, Edward W., ed. *Literary Criticism in Seventeenth-Century England*. New York: Knopf, 1967.
Temple, William. *Sir William Temple's Essays on Ancient & Modern Learning and On Poetry*. Edited by Joel Elias Spingarn. Oxford: Clarendon, 1909.
Terry, Richard. 'The Eighteenth-Century Invention of English Literature: A Truism Revisited'. *Journal for Eighteenth-Century Studies* 19 (1996): 47–62.
Thompson, Guy Andrew. *Elizabethan Criticism of Poetry …* . Menasha: The Collegiate Press, 1914.
Van Deusen, Marshall. *J. E. Spingarn*. New York: Twayne, 1971.
Vaughan, C. E., ed. *English Literary Criticism*. London: Blackie, 1896.
Vickers, Brian. *Appropriating Shakespeare: Contemporary Critical Quarrels*. New Haven: Yale University Press, 1993.
Vickers, Brian. *In Defence of Rhetoric*. Oxford: Clarendon, 1998.
Vickers, Brian, ed. *English Renaissance Literary Criticism*. Oxford: Clarendon, 1999.

Warton, Thomas. *Observations on the Faerie Queene of Spenser*. London: Dodsley and Fletcher, 1754.
Weinberg, Bernard. 'From Aristotle to Pseudo-Aristotle'. *Comparative Literature* 5 (1953): 97–104.
Weinberg, Bernard. *A History of Literary Criticism in the Italian Renaissance*. 1 vol. in 2. Chicago: The University of Chicago Press, 1961.
Weinberg, Bernard, ed. *Trattati di poetica e retorica del Cinquecento*, 4 vols. Bari: Laterza, 1970–74.
Wellek, René. 'The Attack on Literature'. *The American Scholar* 42 (1972–73): 27–42.
Wellek, René. *A History of Modern Criticism*, 8 vols. London: Cape, 1955–86 (vols. 1–6); New Haven: Yale University Press, 1991–92 (vols. 7–8).
Wellek, René. 'Literature and Its Cognates'. In *Dictionary of the History of Ideas: Studies of Selected Pivotal Ideas*, edited by Philip P. Wiener, 5 vols., 2:81–8. New York: Scribner, 1973–74.
Wellek, René. 'Reply to Bernard Weinberg's Review of My *History of Modern Criticism*'. *Journal of the History of Ideas* 30 (1969): 281–2.
Wellek, René. 'What Is Literature?' In *What Is Literature?*, edited by Paul Hernadi, 16–23. Bloomington: Indiana University Press, 1978.
Wiener, Philip P., ed. *Dictionary of the History of Ideas: Studies of Selected Pivotal Ideas*. 5 vols. New York: Scribner, 1973–74.
Williams, Raymond. *Culture and Society, 1780–1950*. London: Chatto, 1958.
Williams, Raymond. *Keywords: A Vocabulary of Culture and Society*. London: Fontana, 1976.
Wilson, John. *Specimens of the British Critics*. Philadelphia: Carey and Hart, 1846.
Wimsatt, William K., Jr. and Cleanth Brooks. *Literary Criticism: A Short History*. New York: Knopf, 1957.
Wylie, Laura Johnson. *Studies in the Evolution of English Criticism* …. Boston: Ginn, 1894.

Part II

Case studies: Critical quarrels and readings

5

Shedding light on the readings of Aristotle's *Poetics* developed within the Alterati of Florence (1569–c. 1630)

From manuscript studies to the social and political history of aesthetics*

Déborah Blocker

On a hot spring day of June 2008, I landed in Florence, having travelled for almost twenty-four hours, from Berkeley, California. I had come all this way to a town I had not visited since my adolescence with the hope of discovering new or at least understudied sources for the elaboration of a comparative history of early modern European aesthetics, which I had been working towards since the early 2000s. My plan for finding such sources was fairly simple but, because of how little I knew about the town, it felt uncertain.

I had mainly conducted research, until then, in the field of early modern French literature, with a focus on the social and political history of literary practices and institutions, and a special interest in both theatre and aesthetics. Yet, while finishing my first book (*Instituer un « art » : politiques du théâtre dans la France du premier XVIIᵉ siècle*, Paris: Honoré Champion, 2009), I had begun to develop my enquiries into the social and political history of early modern conceptions of art in comparative directions. It had become obvious to me, while working on seventeenth-century French poetics and theatre, that many of the aesthetic concepts which had allowed for the rise of new understandings of the arts we now designate as the 'fine arts' came out of

---

* This chapter contains twenty-four images of archival materials, printed or manuscript, of which six (numbered 5.1 to 5.6) are published in this printed volume. The other images provided, referred to as E-Figures and numbered as E-Figure 1 to E-Figure 18, can be viewed – alongside this essay and images 5.1 to 5.6 – on the eScholarship repository, using this permanent URL : https://escholarship.org/uc/item/9133m8k5 or, alternatively, this Digital Object Identifier (DOI) : 10.25350/B51590. To avoid any confusion, references to figures 5.1 to 5.6 are in roman, while references to E-Figures 1 to 18 have been highlighted in bold. Please also note that, in what follows, all manuscript transcriptions are diplomatic transcriptions. The aim has been to make the annotations studied accessible to the reader in a form that is as close as possible to their original language and syntax. To enhance readability, abbreviated words have been spelled out and punctuation has occasionnally been modernized for clarity. All other editorial interventions have been signaled by brackets ([…]).

the intense intellectual activity that the rediscovery of Aristotle's *Poetics* had generated in Italy between 1530 and 1600. I thus harboured a strong curiosity for this specific historical moment, first investigated by Bernard Weinberg in his two-volume *History of Literary Criticism in the Italian Renaissance* (Chicago: Chicago University Press, 1961). I had in particular developed a desire to gain direct access to the sources that documented these developments, hoping that they could yield information about the social, economic, cultural, political and intellectual contexts in which these evolutions took place. These contexts were something to which Bernard Weinberg's extremely broad and erudite investigation into 'literary criticism' in the Italian Renaissance had, in my mind, paid too little attention. This major figure of the Chicago School of literary scholarship had chosen to focus rather on the reconstitution of aesthetic doctrines in isolation, according to the protocols of intellectual history. I was however convinced that any deeper understanding of how and why such theories had than been elaborated demanded both a wider and more precise historical perspective – that is, one that examined not only the history of ideas but also the social, economic and institutional settings in which these ideas were produced, as well as the kinds of relationships the individuals who produced them entertained with political power.

Yet, when searching the internet catalogues of Florentine libraries, in attempts to locate from afar materials that might furnish me with means to unlock this more comprehensive historical perspective, I worried: if I had no precise idea of what material I might be looking for, how could I possibly find sources of use to me? I had not yet experienced that the uncertainty generated by the lack of a preconceived understanding of what exactly is being searched for creates a form of open-endedness, in which objects that fall into none of the existing historiographical paradigms become more susceptible of attracting your attention. As a result, I clung to devising strategies for mastering the unknown. Among the many leads I could have chosen, I decided my best bet was to investigate the activities of the humanist Piero Vettori (1499–1585) who taught Greek at the *Studio Fiorentino* for over forty years, with the aim of researching the aesthetic writings of his numerous students, if they could be located. I was, in particular, hoping to trace how Vettori's hedonistic understanding of Aristotle's *Poetics* (as reflected in his 1560 and 1573 commentaries of the work) had been appropriated among the young patricians he had trained and mentored, during their adolescence, over so many decades. In this chapter, I reflect on the unexpected materials this initial research led me to unearth and on how I went about making sense of them, trying to highlight in what ways the open-endedness of my enquiry proved methodologically fruitful with respect to the history of early modern poetics and aesthetics.

On my first morning in Florentine libraries, I promptly registered as a new reader at the Biblioteca Nazionale Centrale di Firenze (BNCF) and made my way up to the reading rooms. There, I searched the catalogues to identify books printed not only by Vettori but also by his entourage. I already knew many of the books in the catalogue, but there was, however, one book, under Vettori's own name, that I had never seen in any other collection. Furthermore, the contents of the book seemed to be exactly what I was looking for, as its title defined it as a rendering Vettori's Latin translation of the *Poetics*. Indeed, the book – which had originally been a part of the *fondo Magliabechiano*, as its shelf mark (BNCF Magl. 5.9.119) testified – was listed under the title of *Aristotelis Poetica Petro Victorio Interprete*. I ordered it and was soon handed a small booklet in-8°, printed in Florence in 1617 by the Giunti press (Figure 5.1). The booklet's general appearance was shabby (poor printing, low quality paper, modest format, etc.). Yet, its binding, which was unstitched down the middle from what could only have been too much wear and tear, indicated that it had been well used, thereby suggesting a finding of some social and/or cultural importance.

The contents of the book were intriguing. The booklet included a dedication letter in Latin, in which a Florentine patrician I subsequently identified as Giovan Battista Strozzi Il Giovane (1551–1634) presented his young nephew of the same name, also known as the *Marchese di Forano* (1597–1636), with the printed booklet (**E-Figure 1**). This Latin dedication was elegantly written and sophisticated in its arguments. It was also structured like a *quaestio* developed in a university setting (with *pro* and *contra* positions being expressed, followed by a synthesis) – but its subject was not strictly a scholarly one. Rather, the dedication (effectively an academic *discorso* in disguise, as I was soon to understand) asked enticingly whether it was more pleasurable to teach or to learn. Two thirds into his *pro et contra* argument, Giovan Battista Strozzi Il Giovane, attempting the reconciliation of opposing opinions that would have been expected of him, affirmed that it was always best to teach and to learn all at once, wherever this delicate balance could be achieved. He then proceeded to give examples of moments when himself had experienced such a fulfilling experience, first by recalling the times during which, fifty years prior, he had listened to Piero Vettori elucidate Aristotle's *Poetics* (presumably during lessons offered at the *Studio Fiorentino*), also reminding his readers of how he himself had discussed the text of the *Poetics* in front of an academy

Figure 5.1 *Aristotelis Poetica Petro Victorio Interprete*, ed. by G.-B. Strozzi, Florence, Giunti, 1617, title page, BNCF Magl. 5.9.119.

he designated as the academy of the Alterati (in other words the academy of the Altered Ones), twenty years later:

> But of what little importance it is to us to know whether it delights us more to learn or to teach, if it is certain that both give us an extraordinary amount of pleasure. What is certain is that I can testify to the pleasure experienced in both cases, most dear Giovan Battista. Often, I found it pleasing to learn many things, but I found greater pleasure in hearing, fifty years ago, Piero Vettori – the brightest luminary of his times, and of knowledge – as he explained with great erudition the *Poetics* of Aristotle. Then, twenty years later, I had the pleasure to see the academy of the Alterati put me in charge of presenting the same book in front of it; among the auditors sitting in the first rows, to whom I was proud to have brought intellectual assistance, was Filippo Strozzi, a man much sought after for his integrity and your father, whom I now would like to see serve as an example for you in your family.[1]

The dedication then went on to describe the Alterati's arduous labour on the text of the *Poetics*, as translated by Piero Vettori, even seeming to allude between the lines to the existence of a systematically interfoliated and collectively annotated manuscript, as well as to its role as a reference tool in Giovan Battista Strozzi's entourage:

> But Nature highlights excellence in difficulty only and Aristotle has not revealed the oracles of wisdom to those whom read his writings with their eyes closed. Must I tell you about all the evenings we spent working on the book? Even the little I have understood demanded long nightly working sessions. How could I describe the study of this little book? I am not unhappy to have often used my quill. It is befitting to an eminent Preceptor to transcribe words and to add to each folio of the text other blank pages on which I could transcribe – as I would on a blank board – my thoughts as well as those of others, found with a zeal that was anything but ordinary, so that, if the need to help my friends arose, I would have ready-made teachings on poetics on which to draw from on the spot, as if from a reserve. Today, with the intention of doing what can be profitable to you, to your entourage and to your friends, who come and join me when I discuss the *Poetics*, I have taken the trouble of having Aristotle's book printed and it is the translation given by Vettori which I chose among all the others. Indeed, I do not know it if it is possible that the majesty and concision of Aristotle's Greek owes more to a translator than to Vettori. I have given up on lengthy commentaries and have inserted only briefly

---

[1] Giovan Battista Strozzi, *Aristotelis Poetica Petro Victorio Interprete* (Florence: Giunti, 1617), dedication (no pagination):

> […] Sed nostra parvi referat, in discendo nè an in docendo potior sit oblectatio, dum constet utrumque plurimùm delectare. Utriusque ego certè me tibi testem voluptatis exhibeo (Ioannes Baptista dilectissime). Sæpe non pauca suaviter didici: suavius autem cum quinquaginta ab hinc annos Petrum Victorium suæ aetatis ac literarum lumen clarissimum, Aristotelis Poeticam artem doctissimè explanantem audirem. Præteræ post viginti elapsos annos, magnam cœpi iucunditatem cum munus obirem mihi ab Academis Alteratis eumdem librum exponendi delatum, ubi inter primarios auditores quibus me aliquam ingenii operam præstitisse gaudeo, Philippus Stroza vir integerrimis moribus Pater tuus frequentissimus adherat, quem hac in re tibi propositum velim domesticæ imitationis exemplum. […]

remarks in the margins, out of fear that the weight of the volume might overwhelm the readers; as a consequence (in the same way Alexander did with the Homer's *Iliad*, we are told), you now have this small booklet of modest weight in your hands – may it nourish your mind and thoroughly delight you.[2]

Having reached that point in the dedication, I was fascinated by the seemingly unimpressive booklet I had been handed three hours prior. In particular, the prospect of possibly finding the manuscript that seemed to be alluded to in its dedication galvanized my curiosity. I asked for the small printed *libretto* be placed *in deposito* (on hold) and headed over the *sala manoscritti*. Assuming that the said manuscript, if it still existed, would probably also have entered the collections of the BNCF via the Magliabechi collections, in which the printed *libretto* itself had been housed, I asked the curator on duty where I might find the catalogue of the Magliabechiani manuscripts. She pointed me to a handwritten index of this *fondo*, in which I found nothing referenced under the name of the Alterati or under that of Giovan Battista Strozzi. However, when I checked under Aristotle, I suddenly spotted an *Aristotelis Poëtica cum notis Petro Victorio Interprete* (BNCF Magl. VII, 1199). I filled out the appropriate paperwork to order the book in all haste, ardently hoping that what whatever would soon come out of the BNCF's collections would indeed turn out to be a manuscript of Piero Vettori's Latin translation of Aristotle's *Poetics* collectively annotated by a Florentine sodality calling themselves the academy of the Altered Ones.

The manuscript appeared shortly thereafter, just as a major thunderstorm began to break. All the windows of the *sala* were immediately shut tight and hail soon started to fall heartily into the Arno, right in front of the Palazzo Torrigiani, which, I was to realize only several months later, had earlier belonged to Tommaso del Nero, one of the seven men who had founded the Alterati in the year 1569. As such, his sumptuous home had originally served as the academicians' primary meeting place.[3] That day, however, I marvelled only at the shimmering white veils that the late spring hail, descending from

---

[2] Strozzi, *Aristotelis Poetica Petro Victorio Interprete*:

> […]. Sed quæ præclara sunt, Natura ipsa difficultate commendat, nec sapientiæ oracula detegit iis Aristoteles qui conniventibus oculis, eius scripta percurrunt. Decet ne nostras tibi recensere vigilias? Quæ ego quantulacumque percæpi, magnis constant lucubrationibus. Quid dicam de huiusce libelli studio? Non me pinguit manum calamo sæpius admovere: præstantissimi Præceptoris verba excribere: singulis quibusque excripti textus membranis pura paginas inserere, in quas tum aliorum, tum meas interdum sententias non vulgari studio quæsitas velut in album referrem, ut si quandò amicorum utilitas id postularet, parata haberem quæ velut e penu depromerem poetica documenta. Nunc tuæ, affinium, amicorumque tuorum me de Poetice differentem convenientium commoditati inserviens, Aristotelis librum hunc imprimendum curavi, eamque quam Victorius versionem fecerat, ex omnibus apprimè elegi; non enim scio an alii latino interpreti Græca Aristotelis maiestas & brevitas magis debeat quam Victoriæ. Omissa sunt longiora commentaria, brevesque tantum notulæ margini adscriptæ, ne degravet legentes, voluminis sarcina, utque (quod Alexander de Homeri Iliade fecisse scribitur) vos hunc tenui mole libellum, in manu, in mente, & in deliciis habeatis. […]

[3] This is the palace now located at 5 Piazza de' Mozzi, on which see Leonardo Ginori Lisci, *I Palazzi di Firenze nella storia e nell'arte*, 2 vols. (Florence: Giunti, G. Barbèra, 1972), 2:675–82, which explains that Tommaso del Nero was the architect of a large part of the façade, as well as the man who redecorated the grand *salone* of the *piano nobile*, where the Alterati originally met. Tommaso

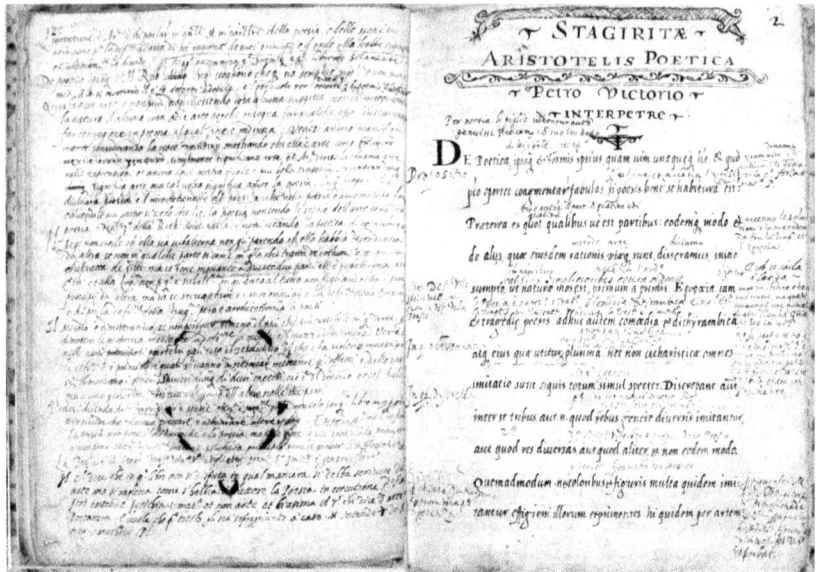

Figure 5.2 *Aristotelis Stagiritae Poetica Petro Victorio Interpetre* [*sic*], collectively annotated manuscript, Florence, 1573–1617, BNCF Magl. VII, 1199, fols. 1^{ver}-2^{rec}.

the heavens, created over the river. Soon the skies dried up, and the windows of the *sala* were reopened, letting in much cooler air. The elegant façades of the Oltrarno palazzi were once again clearly visible in the crisp white light that the storm had carried in with it. Suddenly, I remembered the manuscript I had been handed.

Unfortunately, because of a tight early-twentieth-century rebinding, the manuscript was a little difficult to open. Once I had become aware of the Alterati's collective taste for secrecy and the restricted manuscript circulation of their works, this characteristic would retrospectively strike me as befitting for a volume the use of which had always been exclusively restricted to the members of this secluded academy. But for now, I proceeded to position the codex – which was a little under of size of an in-4º – on one of the elegant wooden reading stands provided in the *sala manoscritti*. On folios 1^{ver}–2^{rec}, at the opening of the manuscript, I discovered a bewildering textual device, displaying simultaneously yet alternatively text and commentary, the latter being in a variety of hands (Figure 5.2). The codex did indeed contain a transcription of Piero Vettori's Latin translation of Aristotle's *Poetics*, as it appeared in the commentary of the text that the Florentine Hellenist published in 1560 and 1573. Vettori's translation of the *Poetics* (**E-Figure 2**) was edited in *particelle*: in it, brief passages of the Greek text are followed by a Latin translation and extensive commentary in the same tongue (**E-Figure 3**). But in the manuscript I was looking at, the fragmented Latin text had been copied out of the Vettori commentary into a continuous text by a scribe, with the aim of creating a text

del Nero (known in the academy as Il Sconcio) had dedicated this room to the Alterati with the inscription: « *Erigitur ab Alteratis Academia/Scribendi Dicendique Studio Creata/A. MDLXVIII* ».

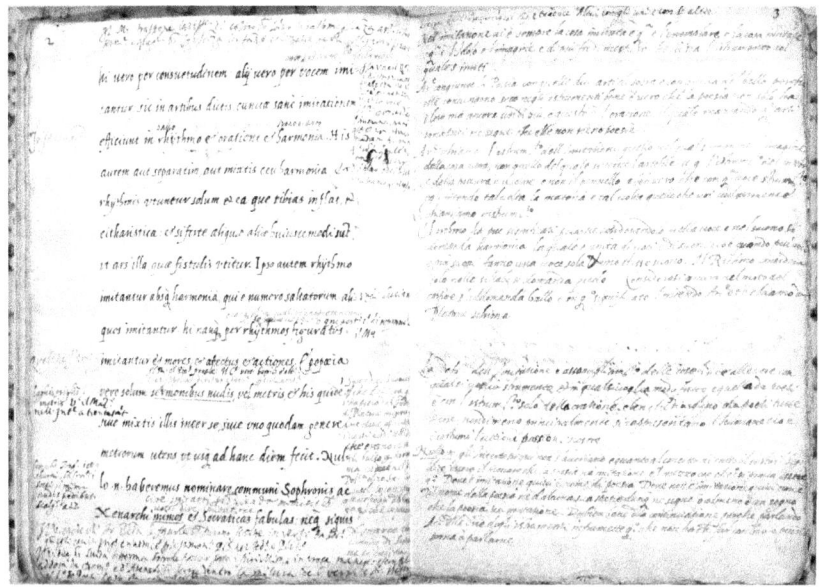

Figure 5.3 *Aristotelis Stagiritae Poetica Petro Victorio Interpetre*, BNCF Magl. VII, 1199, fols. 2^{ver}-3^{rec}.

easier to follow for the owner of the manuscript, while making it possible for him to add personal annotations. As folios 2^{ver}–3^{rec} (Figure 5.3) illustrate, these annotations mostly tackled certain propositions that the annotators had underlined in the text. When I looked at the manuscript's quire structure more carefully, it also appeared to have been created to alternate one folio of Vettori's translation with one folio of annotations. In two instances (quires i and iv), interfoliation had also occurred – that is, one or two additional folios had been inserted into the quire, so as to make room for additional comments, just like Strozzi's dedication had suggested. The pages of transcribed text also contained annotations, some of which indicated divisions in the text. For instance, on folio 17^{rec} (**E-Figure 4**), a marginal annotation on the bottom left located Aristotle's definition of tragedy. Other annotations provided brief linguistic or philosophic clarifications of the Latin translation, as shown on the detail of folio 2^{rec} (**E-Figure 5**).

The manuscript bore the date of 1573 on its title page (Figure 5.4), which I assumed indicated both when the Latin translation of the *Poetics* was transcribed, and when the annotation process had begun. The annotators who laboured on the text were, however, not identified in the manuscript, on which I could spot no other name then that of Vettori, plus a number of abbreviations designating other contemporary commentators of the *Poetics* (Robortello, Maggi, Castelvetro, etc.) whose views were also discussed in the annotations. From the index of the Magliabechi collections that had led me to the codex, it was clear its compilers had themselves not been able to identify the authors of the manuscript – or it would not have been indexed and catalogued solely under Aristotle. Furthermore, from the title page added in 1679 by Luigi di Carlo Strozzi (**E-Figure 6**), it seemed that among the early cataloguers of

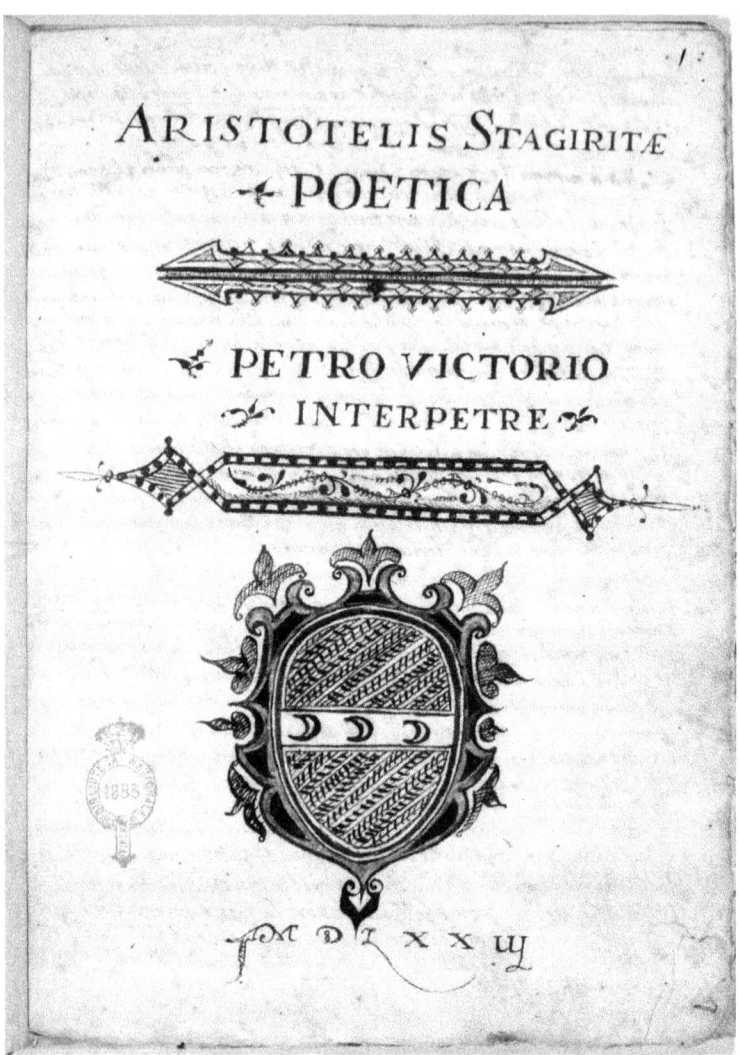

Figure 5.4 *Aristotelis Stagiritae Poetica Petro Victorio Interpetre*, BNCF Magl. VII, 1199, title page.

the Strozzi papers, in which the small manuscript volume had originally been held (as manuscript n° 805), neither Carlo Strozzi nor his son Luigi had known precisely who the authors of the codex were. I looked at the booklet from every angle, with the hope of finding some obvious indication that it had indeed belonged to the academy to which the author of the dedication of the printed volume I had earlier consulted had alluded in writing to his nephew – but could find none. Had the makers of such a complex textual object wanted to remain anonymous? If so, to what end?

My perplexity ended up attracting the attention of one of the BNCF's curators, Piero Scapecchi, then head of the *sala manoscritti*. 'What have you found there?', he asked kindly, as he walked by me on his way to the reserves. 'I am not quite sure', I answered, explaining that, in the booklet, I could find no explicit indication of who had copiously annotated this transcription of Vettori's translation of the *Poetics*. Scapecchi picked up the book and leafed through it, soon returning to the title page (Figure 5.4). 'True', he said, 'the annotators do not seem to have identified themselves.' 'But, look', he added, pointing to the elegant coat of arms that had been carefully drawn on the original title page, 'here are the arms of the Strozzi – namely, three crescents in reverse in a band. This book belonged to a distinguished and most probably wealthy member of the Strozzi family, that much we know for sure.' I smiled and thanked him, then mentioned the book I had found earlier in the rare-book section, in which a Giovan Battista Strozzi dedicated what appeared to be a printed version of Vettori's translation of the *Poetics* to a nephew of the same name, while omitting however to reproduce the extensive annotations present in the manuscript. I added that the dedication seemed to indicate that the manuscript had been collectively annotated among the *Accademia degli Alterati*. 'Really, the Alterati? And Giovan Battista Strozzi had a private edition made from this manuscript, for use among his friends, his family and members of the academy?', he said, intrigued. 'It looks like you have stumbled on something well worth looking into. We are closing in a few minutes, but tomorrow, if you show me that piece of printed matter, we can have a look at it together and compare it with this manuscript.' I accepted his offer, picked up my things, had the manuscript placed *in deposito* at the bank and proceeded to walk down the great internal marble staircase of the BNCF, past the stern bust of Antonio Magliabechi, who himself seemed to be wondering what I could possibly have found, by chance, in the library he had once headed.[4]

Nine years later, I know what I had found that day. But understanding the nature of this peculiar manuscript, in a way with which I could be satisfied, took examining thousands of pages of other manuscript materials. The effort also involved writing a 450-page book on the Alterati of Florence, scheduled to appear in French with Les Belles Lettres in Paris in 2020, under the title *Le Principe de plaisir: savoirs, esthétique et politique dans la Florence des Médicis (XVIe-XVIIe siècles)*. In the next sections, I describe the work that was needed to contextualize the material object I found that day in the *sala manoscritti* of the BNCF, and explain why this research calls our understanding of early modern poetics into question, possibly even pointing to the need to reframe the history of early modern aesthetics more generally. I begin with reflexively analysing the various research procedures by which I managed to solve many (but surely not all) of the manuscript's mysteries. I then go on to explain how this painstaking enquiry helped me reconsider some of the larger questions I harboured about the history of early modern aesthetics, while allowing also me to frame a number of follow-up enquiries.

In all three of the next sections, I strive to point out how rare books and manuscripts can serve as fertile grounds for the development of innovative forms of intellectual and, more generally, cultural history, by allowing us to move back and forth from

[4] On Antonio Magliabechi, see Caroline Callard, 'Diogène au service des princes: Antonio Magliabechi à la cour de Toscane (1633-1714)', *Histoire Economie Société* XIX (2000): 85–103 and Jean Boutier, Maria Pia Paoli and Corrado Viola, eds, *Antonio Magliabechi nell'Europa dei saperi*, 2 vols. (Pisa: Edizioni della Normale, 2017), which includes an edition of the life of Magliabechi by Anton Francesco Marmi.

a restricted set of material objects to a larger group of historical questions. In the process, existing paradigms can come into question or be reformulated. In this respect, this essay owes much to the current renewal of philological investigations, in which book history and manuscript studies are mobilized to generate new understandings of the history of culture, thereby constantly oscillating – in the tradition of the research protocols set forth by nineteenth-century German philologists, such as August Boeckh – from small-scale material objects to large-scale cultural interrogations.[5] My own approach pays particular attention to how book-historical approaches (be they based on rare books or on manuscripts) can support the inclusion of social, institutional and political perspectives that traditional histories of ideas – which are often based on modern editions of canonical texts – tend to ignore. I focus specifically in what follows on highlighting the ways in which our understanding of the history of the circulation of the *Poetics*, and of the development of early modern aesthetics more generally, can be enhanced and even transformed by the inclusion of these social, institutional and political perspectives, which the history of the book and of manuscript circulation can help document.

* * *

The Alterati's collective commentary of the *Poetics* had immediately appeared to me as a piece of meaningful evidence – even though its specific intellectual and/or cultural meanings were initially an enigma. The fact that this document did not belong to the known tradition of Italian Renaissance treatises on the *Poetics*, as documented by Bernard Weinberg,[6] made it more appealing to me rather than less because it gave me hope that the information to be found in it might allow one to tell the story of Renaissance poetics somewhat differently. But before any intellectual or cultural meaningfulness could be inferred, the creation, purpose and uses of the manuscript needed to be clarified.

---

[5] On August Boeckh's understanding of philology, conceived as a meta-knowledge of all things known, see August Boeckh, *On Interpretation & Criticism*, trans. and ed. John Paul Pritchard (Norman: University of Oklahoma Press, 1968). On the tension between 'hyperconcentration' and 'hyperdiffusion', which was built in to most philological enterprises developed in nineteenth-century Germany, see Constanze Güthenke, '"Enthusiasm Dwells Only in Specialization": Classical Philology and Disciplinarity in Nineteenth Century Germany', in *World Philology*, ed. Sheldon Pollock, Benjamin A. Ellman and Ku-ming Kevin Change (Harvard: Harvard University Press, 2015), ch. 12, 264–84. On innovative ways to elaborate cultural and intellectual history using books and manuscripts, see Dinah Ribard and Nicolas Schapira, 'L'Histoire par le livre, XVIe-XXe siècle', *Revue de Synthèse* 128, no. 1–2, 6th series (2007): 19–25.

[6] Bernard Weinberg had, however, written two seminal articles on the Alterati, as I soon discovered. See: 'The *Accademia degli Alterati* and Literary Taste from 1570 to 1600', *Italica* 31, no. 4 (1954): 207–14 and 'Argomenti di discussione letteraria nell'Accademia degli Alterati (1570-1600)', *Giornale Storico della Letteratura Italiana* 131 (1954): 175–94. Weinberg also published several *discorsi* by Alterati members in his *Trattati di poetica e retorica del Cinquecento*, 4 vols. (Bari, Laterza, 1970-1974), v. 3 (Francesco Bonciani, 'Lezione sopra il comporre delle novelle', 137–74; Giulio del Bene, 'Due discorsi', 175–204 and Lorenzo Giacomini, 'De la purgazione de la tragedia', 345–74 and 'Del furor poetico', 421–54) and vol. 4 (Giovan Battista Strozzi, (comma instead of semicolon) 'Dell'unità della favola', 333–44). Weinberg held the production of modern editions of important orations to be more important than the careful study of the materiality and circulation of the manuscripts by which they have been transmitted to us.

My progressive elucidation of the BNCF Magl. VII, 1199 manuscript began with an investigation of its authors, and particularly of Giovan Battista Strozzi Il Giovane, who, as the coat of arms on the title page of codex testifies, was the primary owner of the text. This involved researching the *Accademia degli Alterati* in all of the existing secondary literature, which turned out to provide only partial overviews of this institution's activities.[7] From it, I did however manage to extract extensive references to much of the Alterati's surviving manuscript works, which comprise at least seventeen known codices of academic origin, many of which are in in-folio format and contain over 300–400 folios (or 600–800 pages) of manuscript materials (letters, *discorsi*, *abozzi*, poems, dialogues, detailed registries of daily academic activity, etc.). I realized later, however, that the Alterati's written productions were in fact even more plentiful than that, with the obvious and clearly identified materials preserved in the Florentine archives under their name often being less revealing than the materials they had originally hidden from sight or circulated discreetly, if not in secrecy – such precisely as the BNCF Magl. VII, 1199.

At first, the items contained in these previously documented codices seemed both fascinating and discouraging to me. How could I ever manage to situate these texts with respect to one another – and, more importantly, would I ever be able to reassemble the pieces of this gigantic textual puzzle to make some sort of greater picture appear? But this profusion of manuscript materials also proved a boon as I tried to identify the various hands which appeared on BNCF Magl. VII, 1199, because it not only provided me with the names of most of the members of the academy but also put a good number of samples of the hands of the most active Alterati members at my disposal. Thanks to such comparisons, I was able to identify Giovan Battista Strozzi's handwriting in the manuscript, where most of the indexical headings added in the transcription are in fact his, as well as a substantial amount of the explanatory notes. It appears for instance on folio 6^{ver} (Figure 5.5) where Strozzi's hand is the one which penned in the annotation starting with 'Delle Parodie non ci è molto notitia …' However, the principal annotator, in terms of both the number and the sophistication of the remarks provided, turned out to be another of the distinguished members of the academy, Filippo Sassetti, whose

---

[7] In 2008, the existing bibliography was as follows. Two early modern accounts of the academy were published in the eighteenth century: Salvino Salvini (1667-1751), *Fasti consolari dell'Accademia Fiorentina* (Florence: Gio. Gaetano Tartini and Santi Franchi, 1717), 202–8 and Domenico Maria Manni (1690-1788), *Memorie della famosa Accademia fiorentina degli Alterati* (Florence: G.-B. Stecchi, 1748), 25 p. Modern studies of the sodality included the two above-mentioned articles by Bernard Weinberg; Claude Palisca, 'The Alterati of Florence, Pioneers in the Theory of Dramatic Music' (1968), in *Studies in the History of Italian Music and Music Theory* (Oxford: Clarendon Press, 1994), 408–31; Eric Cochrane, *Florence in the Forgotten Centuries, 1527-1800* (Chicago: The University of Chicago Press, 1973), 93–161; Michel Plaisance, *L'Accademia e il suo Principe: cultura e politica a Firenze al tempo di Cosimo I e di Francesco de' Medici. L'Académie et le Prince: Culture et politique à Florence au temps de Côme Ier et de François de Médicis* (Manziana (Rome): Vecchiarelli, 2004), 393–406; Anna Siekiera, 'Il volgare nell'Accademia degli Alterati', in *Italia linguistica: discorsi di scritto e di parlato, nuovi studi di linguistica italiana per Giovanni Nencioni*, ed. Marco Biffi, Omar Calabrese and Luciana Salibra (Siena: Protagon, 2005), 87–112; Gaspare de Caro, *Euridice. Momenti dell'umanesimo civile fiorentino* (Bologna: Ut Orpheus, 2006), 73–116 and Henk van Veen, 'The Accademia degli Alterati and Civic Virtue', in *The Reach of the Republic of Letters: Literary and Learned Societies in Late Medieval and Early Modern Europe*, ed. Arian van Dixhoorn and Susie Speakman Sutch, 2 vols. (London and Boston: Brill, 2008), t. 2, 285–308.

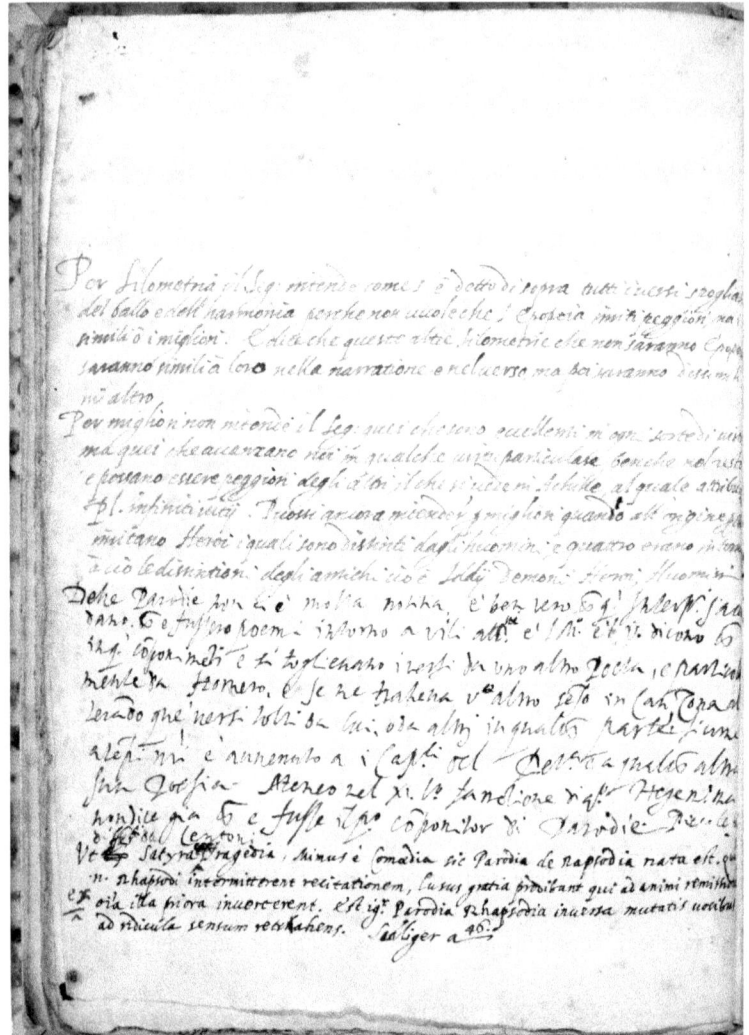

Figure 5.5 *Aristotelis Stagiritae Poetica Petro Victorio Interpetre*, BNCF Magl. VII, 1199, fol. 6ᵛᵉʳ, on which the hand at the top of the page is that of F. Sassetti, while the hand directly below it is that of G.-B. Strozzi.

handwriting is also widely represented in Florentine archives and easily recognizable on the manuscript. On folio 6ᵛᵉʳ (Figure 5.5), it appears directly above Strozzi's hand, in the annotations beginning with 'Per Silometria, il Seg. intende …'[8]

Sassetti's correspondence, which Vanni Bramanti edited in 1970, also provided me with external evidence that he and Strozzi had originally worked on the manuscript

---

[8] For further details on these identifications, please see the codicological description furnished in Annex 1.

together while studying at the University in Pisa. While a letter to another Alterati member, Lorenzo Giacomini, dated 2 December 1573, mentions that Strozzi and Sassetti were living and studying together in Pisa the year the commentary of the manuscript was begun, a second letter, dated 3 December 1575, shows a precise exchange between Sassetti and Strozzi concerning an annotation (*postilla*) to add to what is most probably the manuscript text of Vettori's translation.[9] This second letter also gives us quite a bit of information about the spirit in which the Alterati laboured over the text. But for the moment, suffice it to point out that this exchange both confirms that Sassetti and Strozzi were the primary annotators of the manuscript and suggests that the bulk of their initial annotations were penned between 1573 and 1575. This last hypothesis is also confirmed by the fact that when printed commentaries of the *Poetics* are cited, none of the ones referred to postdate 1575–6.[10] However, I found at least four other hands on the manuscript, some of which are clearly later additions, as they fill the spaces left blank by Sassetti and Strozzi. One of these hands is probably the hand of the prominent Alterati member mentioned earlier, that is, that of Lorenzo Giacomini, whose profusely annotated edition of Annibale Caro's translation of Aristotle's *Rhetoric* is preserved at the University Library in Pisa, thereby documenting his hand, and his familiarity with such annotative processes.[11] For instance, on folio 80^{rec} (Figure 5.6), the last annotation to be added to the page, which starts with 'La maraviglia non par sempre dilettevole …', appears to be in his hand. Furthermore, the date of the book printed by Strozzi – the dedication of which indicates that the manuscript served as a reference and study tool in the academy for several decades – suggest that the manuscript may have been annotated, albeit sporadically, up until 1617, when Strozzi dedicated the private edition he had had made to his nephew. The manuscript could even have been worked on up to the death of the *marchese* of Forano, in 1636, since it is unclear when the Alterati ceased to meet regularly, although they do not appear to have been very active after 1610 or so.

* * *

After having identified the main contributors to the manuscript, I realized everything this document might allow me to historicize, that is, not only what the Alterati, as students of Vettori, had read into the *Poetics* of Aristotle but also how, as members of a learned Florentine academy, they had laboured upon such a text in collaboration. The interplay of annotations in the margins of Vettori's translation seemed to document not only the trains of thought and major poetic/aesthetic concepts of interest within the academy but also the specific forms that intellectual exchanges took among them, that is, what they actually did, as a collective, with Aristotle's *Poetics*, both orally and in writing. In other words, the manuscript provided a window into the Alterati's scholarly

---

[9] Filippo Sassetti, *Lettere da vari paesi, 1570-1588*, ed. Vanni Bramanti (Milan: Longanesi & Co., 1970): 120–2 and 171–6.
[10] See Annex 2, which details the books the Alterati quote in the manuscript, as well as the ones which they left out.
[11] BUP Ms. 551 and 552 are two volumes of Aristotle's *Rhetoric* (Venice: A la Salamandra, 1570) translated into Tuscan by Annibale Caro, with extensive annotations by Lorenzo Giacomini. I thank Anna Siekiera for having brought these two volumes to my attention.

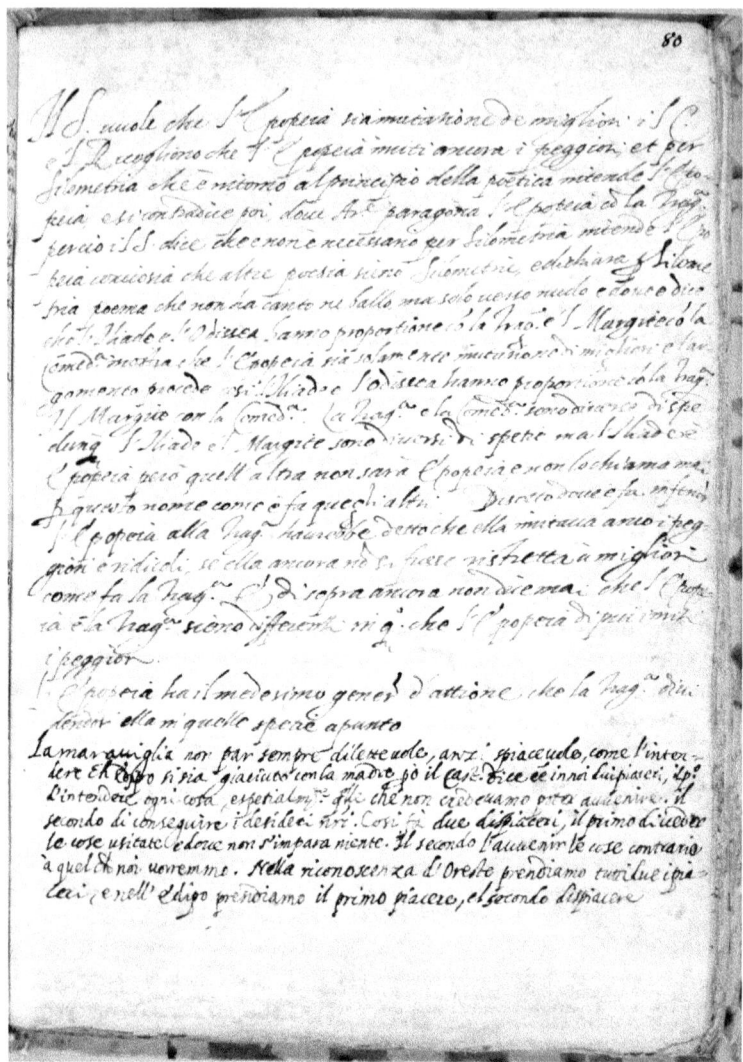

Figure 5.6 *Aristotelis Stagiritae Poetica Petro Victorio Interpetre*, BNCF Magl. VII, 1199, fol. 80[rec].

practices, both when they crafted the manuscript and when they subsequently used it, in the context of their academy. The present section details these practices and uses.

The manuscript was initially a product of the student culture that surrounded the *Studio Pisano*, the University of Pisa, one of Italy's oldest universities, which the Medici had reopened to students in 1543 after a long closure. There, the sons of Tuscany's upper classes could follow *lectiones*, but they also frequently studied on their own or with other students, outside of lectures, most notably because very few of them actually needed to receive a degree. Indeed, many of them would not enter a particular profession in which the three main sciences taught at the University (law, medicine and theology) might be of use to them. Rather, most Florentine patricians, such as Giovan Battista Strozzi Il Giovane, would restrict themselves to the duty of fructifying their inherited wealth. As such, they mainly came to Pisa to get a smattering of philosophy and to share in the boisterous student culture that existed there. Given these circumstances, Strozzi's choice to spend time analysing and interpreting the *Poetics* while in Pisa may have been triggered simply by the fact that, at the time, no professor at the University covered this material, which Strozzi, who was a member of the Alterati since 1570, would have understood as central to his literary interests. In the dedication to his nephew, which Strozzi placed at the opening of the printed book, Strozzi also claims that he heard Piero Vettori explain the *Poetics* in Florence around 1567, when he was sixteen ('I found it pleasing to learn many things, but I found greater pleasure in hearing, fifty years ago, Piero Vettori – the brightest luminary of his times, and of knowledge – as he explained with great erudition the *Poetics* of Aristotle)'.[12] It is difficult to determine exactly in what precise circumstances Strozzi followed such lectures – these lessons may have taken place in the *Studio*, or at Vettori's home – but it is not impossible that Sassetti might have heard them too, as his correspondence testifies to the fact that he was one of Vettori's most dedicated students and sustained intellectual exchanges with him until the very last years of his life.[13]

It is possible that Strozzi and Sassetti, by choosing to work collaboratively on Vettori's translation of the *Poetics* in 1573, were attempting to reconstruct, in Pisa, the kind of intellectual labour and excitement they had shared while studying with Vettori in Florence, as adolescents. Their approach to the text, as it is reflected in the manuscript, appears to confirm this, as it seems very similar to the kind of approach they would found have in an introductory lecture on the *Poetics*. They followed the text line by line, first elucidating Aristotle's vocabulary (the *verba*), as well as the historical references that appear in his text (the *res*), then attempting to reconstruct his reasoning in passages where it appears unclear. When striving to determine Aristotle's line of thought, they also often draw on the logical skills provided by their scholarly education. Sassetti in particular underlines the syllogistic nature of Aristotle's thought wherever he can, for instance on folio 21[rec] (**E-Figure 7**) which glosses *Poetics*, 1450a 15–20 and attempts to demonstrate through a syllogism that plot (*favola*) is the end of tragedy.[14] He also frequently draws charts to illustrate the many distinctions he understands Aristotle to be making, such as on folio 12[rec] (**E-Figure 8**), where a distinction between Homer

---

[12] Latin text quoted in footnote 1.
[13] See Sassetti's letters to Vettori, in Sassetti, *Lettere da vari paesi, 1570-1588*: letters 16, 19, 22, 23, 25, 26, 35, 37, 41, 50 and 103.
[14] Filippo Sassetti's *postilla*, BNCF Magl. VII, 1199, fol. 21[rec] can be transcribed as follows:

> La Tragedia ha per fine il rappresentarci la felicità e l'infelicità. Ma la felicità e l'infelicità consiste nell'attione, dunque il suo fine è l'attione, ma l'attione non è altro che la favola, dunque la favola è il fine, ma il fine è principale dunque la favola è principale. Che la favola e non il costume sia fine si prova per mezzo della felicità, e che il costume non sia fine si prova per mezzo dell'habito, perciòche il costume è habito, l'habito non è fine, dunque il costume non è fine. E che la favola e 'l costume non sieno il medesimo ne segue perchè se il costume non è fine e la favola è fine necessariamente la favola non sarà costume. C[astelvetro] riduce in sillogismi tutto questo discorso.

and all other poets allows Sassetti to account for the existence of various poetic genres. Occasionally, Sassetti and Strozzi spend more energy on a specific problem that the linear commentary has brought to light – such is the case in the long annotation that Sassetti devotes to the question of the goal (*fine*) of tragedy at the very end of the commentary, on folio 92^{ver} (**E-Figure 9**).[15] This note does not bear an immediate relationship to the text transcribed in the surrounding pages. Rather, it brings together several passages of the text and strives to reconcile Aristotle with himself when various affirmations throughout the *Poetics* seem at odds. But such attempts at synthesis are rare.

Initially, Strozzi and Sassetti mostly combed through the text together in a linear manner, summarizing the contents of their discussions on the page as they went along. On folio 8^{rec} (**E-Figure 10**) appears a very interesting example of their close collaboration: Sassetti begins a remark on the question of whether the poet who speaks in his own name can be deemed an imitator, but he interrupts himself in the middle of a phrase. Strozzi picks up where he left off, only to interrupt himself as well. Finally, Sassetti's hand completes the remark.[16] Furthermore, the 1575 Sassetti

---

[15] Filippo Sassetti's lengthy *postilla*, BNCF Magl. VII, 1199, fol. 92^{rec} can be transcribed as follows:

> Pare che Aristotile voglia la Tragedia e l'Epopeia havere un fine medesimo cioè il muoverci a speranza e a terrore e mediante questi affetti purgarci dagli affetti contrarii e per conseguente il piacere, il quale è congiunto con questi due fini e dice Aristotile se la Tragedia adunque Avanza la Epopeia: in tutto quello et che io ho detto et oltre à quello artis opere cioè nel piacere e non in [uno] spiacere, ma nel suo proprio, cioè quello che nasce dalla misericordia e terrore e dal purgarcene, <u>manifestum – s – est – quod melior</u> etc. E che ella più consegua il suo fine si può dire perchè ella mette davanti agli occhi sì come ei ci ha monstrato di sopra dove e provò che ella era più evidente e più dilettevole.

> Il fine della Tragedia è stato diversamente mostrato da Aristotile et il fine similmente dell'Epopeia perciò che egli fa che l'una e l'altra habbia il medesimo : e pare che quattro d[e]va[no] esser i fini cioè la favola e l'attione, l'eccitar misericordia e terrore, il purgar delle passione & ultimamente un certo piacere. Quanto à che la favola sia fine si prova perchè la Tragedia è un tutto composto di più parti fra le quali una ve ne ha che è il fondamento e l'esser d'essa, e si chiama fine della Tragedia perche è fine di tutte le parti di lei, essendo l'altre ordinate e servendo à essa ò sieno qualitative ò sieno quantitative sì come il corpo serve all'anima la quale è fine. Perciò poco dopo la definitione disse Aristotile la favola essere fine. E nella definitione accennò la purgatione di certi affetti esser fine. E in un altro luogo mostra il terrore e con il terror intende anco la misericordia esser fine della Tragedia e dell'a Epopeia ma questi duoi sono fini perchè e' sono operatione della Tragedia il che apparirà dicendo che ogni cosa che ha la sua virtù e faculta è ordinata à qualche operatione et è in lei l'operatione e sì come nell' huomo l'anima è fine in un modo, così la favola nelle tragedia, e si come in un altro l'operar virtuoso dell'anima è fine cosi l'operatione della Tragedia e da questo si cava che ella habbia dua altri fini cioè l'eccitare gli affetti et il purgare, etc. Ci dobbiamo ricordare che alcune operationi lasciano qualche opera dopo di loro e alcune no. Hora in quelle che lasciano qualcosa il fine è non solamente far quelle operationi ma ancora l'opera stessa, come del pittore, il dipigner è fine, e la pittura ancora, la quale è molto più da essere apprezzata. Cosi se la Tragedia ha per fine l'eccitare gli affetti e purgare, che sono suoi fini come sue operationi è necessario che gli affetti eccitati e la purgatione sieno ancor essi fini essendo che e' restano in noi e rimangono quando e' non è più l'operatione della Tragedia; pero altro è il muovere gli affetti, altro è gli affetti mossi, e il medesimo aviene della purgatione ch'e è usata in noi e del purgare.

[16] See BNCF Magl. VII, 1199, fol. 8^{rec}. I have distinguished each author according to his handwriting:

> [Sassetti] Questo luogo dove Aristotile mostra il Modo dell'Imitare è variamente esposto perciòche sono alcuni, che volendo che solo si trovi imitatione in quei poemi ne' quali il poeta non parla in propria persona espongono eundem & non se immutamtem che

letter mentioned earlier testifies to the continuation of such collaborative work from afar, once Sassetti had returned to Florence, while Strozzi remained in Pisa. Having been asked for a note on the passage beginning with 'Nullo non haberemus', Sassetti produces in his letter four pages of linear commentary of the said passage, which he then asks Strozzi – provided he approves of the reading proposed – to summarize into a *postilla* and insert into the manuscript, which, as this letter testifies, had remained in Strozzi's possession in Pisa.[17] However, in the manuscript, the *postilla* is actually in Sassetti's hand, suggesting that Strozzi may actually have waited for Sassetti's return (Figure 5.3). Thus, both internal and external evidence suggests that the manuscript was initially the product of a collaborative extra-curricular student exercise, which probably involved note-taking only in as much as it was necessary to keep a trace of the conclusions which had emerged from the oral (or, when needed, epistolary) intellectual exchanges of Sassetti and Strozzi. Many other examples of collaboration appear on the manuscript, in a variety of different hands, some contemporaneous and some not, as is for instance visible on fol. 38^{ver} (**E-Figure 11**), where four different hands added comments over several years, if not decades. This suggests that intense collaboration in the annotative process remained a dominant feature of the use of the manuscript when it was subsequently mobilized among the Alterati.

However, over time, and as the academy of the Alterati developed, the manuscript seems also to have been endowed with other functions. This is particularly visible in the way scholarly references to the work of other commentators of Aristotle's *Poetics* appear in the annotations. Initially, the annotators took into account only the books published by Maggi, Robortello, Segni and Vettori, which constitute the first few scholarly publications published on the *Poetics*, as they all appeared between 1548 and 1560 – as in Sassetti's initial comments, in which he cites 'Mag^o', 'Seg', 'Vi' and 'Rob'. (Figure 5.2).[18] But, as time went by, other references are frequently inserted, which point to later contributions on the *Poetics*. Among these, one finds Castelvetro's commentary on the *Poetics*, published in 1570, or Piccolomini's remarks on the same book, first published in 1575. For example, the last annotation to be penned into the first folio of the manuscript also includes references to 'C^o' and 'P^i' in (Figure 5.2). On the bottom of folio 6^{ver} (Figure 5.5) a comment clearly penned in after the manuscript was first annotated adds a reference to Scaliger's treatise on poetics, published in 1561, with a precise page reference. A similar evolution is visible on folio 10^{rec} (**E-Figure 12**),

> il poeta diventi [Strozzi] uno altro e da principio del Poema fino al fine parli sempre in persona di questo stesso, nel quale e' sè trasformato, sì come fa Ovidio nelle [e]pistole e Licofrone nella Cassandra e allegano Ilacio [?] suo interprete. A me par' egli che e sia meglio far la divisione in questa maniera. Che il Poeta ò parli sempre in persona propria come è il Mureto di Virgilio e quasi tutte le poesie liric[h] e [Sassetti] ò parli sempre in persona d'altri come fa la Tragedia e la Comedia e ci comprenderei di più que' poemi che in favore d'altri hò di sopra allegati, ò parli tal volta in persona sua propria e tal volta in persona d'altri come fa l'Epopeia, e così divide Platone nel 3º della Republica questi tre modi, il perchè manifestamente si vede, che usando qui Aristotile le medesime parole che usa quivi Platone a questo proposito, che e'gli habbia tolti da lui. […].

---

[17] Sassetti, *Lettere da vari paesi, 1570-1588*, 171–6.
[18] See Annex 2, listing which contemporary commentaries on the *Poetics* are mentioned by the Alterati and which are not.

where, at the end of the annotation located at the top of the folio, an unfavourable note about Piccolomini's text was inserted: 'P¹ s'avviluppa per voler salvare la sua prosa.'[19] These additions signal that, in the decades after it was first annotated, the status of manuscript evolved somewhat. Originally produced in the framework of an extra-curricular student exercise, it later became a study tool and even a reference book for the Alterati. In it, members of the academy could familiarize themselves with the original work of two of the earliest and most respected members of the academy. But by perusing the references to all the most famous contemporary commentators of the *Poetics*, which had been inserted progressively by those who had used the manuscript over the years, they could also use the manuscript to explore, study and compare the main printed interpretations of Aristotle's text available to them.

This is precisely how Strozzi described the elaboration and subsequent use of the manuscript, when he dedicated the printed version of the transcription to his nephew:

> How could I describe the study of this little book? I am not unhappy to have often used my quill. It is befitting to an eminent Preceptor to transcribe words and to add to each folio of the text other blank pages on which I could transcribe – as I would on a blank board – my thoughts as well as those of others, found with a zeal that was anything but ordinary, so that, if the need to help my friends arose, I would have ready-made teachings on poetics on which to draw from on the spot, as if from a reserve.[20]

Strozzi depicts himself not only adding his remarks or those of his friends to the blank pages that had been inserted into the transcription but also penning in the excellent words of the best masters on the topic, so that should his academic colleagues ever require help understanding the *Poetics*, he could take the manuscript out of his stock of victuals (or 'goodies': 'ex penu') and present them with it. Thus, in the later years of the academy, the manuscript effectively became the central repository for the institution's collective knowledge on the topic of Aristotle's *Poetics*. It is for this reason that, in 1617, at a moment when the academy was in decline, Strozzi had its printed counterpart made by the Giunti presses, before presenting it to his nephew. As the end of the printed dedication indicates, Strozzi expresses the hope that the *marchese* and his own group of adolescent friends would, upon working on the manuscript, go on to take up poetics and poetry, and even embrace academic endeavours, just as he and the *marchese*'s father, Filippo Strozzi, had done – thereby not only cultivating the reputation of this branch of the Strozzi family but also enhancing that of Florence itself. The manuscript was even so important to Giovan Battista Strozzi that, shortly before his death, he distributed all the remaining printed copies of the booklet he had printed in 1617 to younger members of the Strozzi family, in an effort to publicize, disseminate and perpetuate the work of the academy to which he had devoted so much of his life. This we know from Strozzi's will, dated 1631, in which he donated remaining copies of

---

[19] This snappy notation is probably best translated as 'Piccolomini ties himself into knots as he attempts to salvage his argument'.
[20] Latin text quoted in footnote 2.

the book to several young family members or friends.[21] His gesture suggests that the printed booklet, just as much as the annotated manuscript itself, had by then become, in his eyes, an emblem of the academy's collaborative learning practices as well as a testimony to the scope and sophistication of its intellectual endeavours.

As a material object, manuscript Magl. VII, 1199 thus allows for the reconstruction of many of the practices that shaped it as well as for a good understanding of the way it was subsequently used within the academy. We can, for instance, be sure that while in the academy's library, the manuscript was consulted for many of the intellectual enterprises to which the academicians devoted their energies, whether collectively or individually. For instance, when, in August 1575, Filippo Sassetti and Antonio degli Albizzi prepared a polemic response to Alessandro Piccolomini's *Annotationi* on the *Poetics* (Venice: Giovanni Guarisco, 1575), which was then circulated in manuscript under the academy's name, they most probably used it as a source.[22] In the same way, when Sassetti attempted to produce a full commentary of the *Poetics* in the vulgar tongue, the first folios of which are now preserved in BRF Ricc. 1539, folios 81[rec] to 126[ver], he drew quite heavily on the work he had originally done with Strozzi. **E-Figure 13** shows the first page of this manuscript (folio 81[rec]) in Filippo Sassetti's hand. The commentary was left unfinished.

However, while reconstructing what the Alterati were doing with the manuscript was well within my reach, what they were thinking, individually or collectively, while labouring over Aristotle's *Poetics*, seemed to be far less easy to make out, though some of the Alterati's fragmented annotations did point to a specific perspective on the text of the *Poetics*. In the next section, I describe the interpretations that the Alterati's annotations suggested, while reflecting on why thoughts might be less accessible than practices in such a manuscript. In the final part of this essay, I discuss how book history and in particular manuscript studies can be used not only to recover the social, institutional and political contexts in which rare books and codices where produced but also to piece together the representations, values and ideas of those who produced them. In particular, understanding the collective musings of such a group of thinkers as the Alterati from their manuscript (and printed) productions often requires using the book-historical or manuscript sources to move beyond these very sources, into the social, institutional and political configurations, and representations, which these materials can however be used to document with some precision. Such enterprises are labour intensive and time-consuming. But the return on investment can be high.

---

[21] ASF Notarile Moderno 9323, n° 42, fols 90[ver] to 95[ver], in particular fol. 94[rec]: 'A figliuoli del Senatore Signor Amerigo Strozzi et del Senatore Giovanni Dini trinepoti d'esso Signor Testatore, et a ciascuno d'essi una Poetica d'Aristotile dedicata da esso al sopradetto Signor Giovanni Battista Strozzi loro Zio'. Immediately afterward on the same folio: 'Al Signor Giovanni Battista di Lorenzo Strozzi, una Poetica d'Aristotile simile'. Finally, fol. 94[ver]: 'Al Signor Francesco Rovai, La Difesa di Dante in dua tomi di Jacopo Mazzoni, una Poetica d'Aristotile fatta stampare da esso Signor Testatore, ragionamento d'Agnolo Segni appartenente a Poetica'.

[22] The text appears in BNCF Magl. IX, 125, fols 229[rec]-238[ver] under the title of *Discorso degli'Accademici Alterati sopra le Annotationi della Poetica di Messer Alessandro Piccolomini All'Illustrissima Signora Leonora di Toledo di Medici nella detta Accademia chiamata l'Ardente*. Other versions of the text are collected, under different titles, in BRF Ricc. 2435, fols 127[rec]-134[ver] and BNCF Magl. IX, 124, fols 153[rec]-158[rec]. See also BNCF Postillati 15, which contains an edition of Piccolomini's remarks on the *Poetics* entirely annotated by Filippo Sassetti.

For the elucidation of these configurations makes it possible to understand how the intellectual positions of a set of individuals relate to a social and political world view, thereby providing us with a much deeper grasp of not only how these ideas originally came into existence but also to what specific ends they were mobilized by groups and individuals alike.

* * *

The first element that makes it difficult to extract thoughts from the notes that were inserted in the manuscript is a direct consequence of the oral and occasionally written exchanges in which the annotations were originally produced. In particular, many of Sassetti and Strozzi's annotations bear the stylistic traces of their verbal interactions, as they discussed Vettori's translation: their syntax is often chaotic, their phrases lack punctuation and, even in the lengthier annotations, they tend to transcribe oral exchanges in the form of notes (*appunti*) rather than search for elegant formulations. But even greater difficulties arise because of the fragmentary, discontinuous and generally allusive nature of the entire annotation process. This is a general feature of *marginalia*, but it is worth underscoring that this characteristic persists even when a text is extensively and meticulously annotated. Abundant and attentive annotations are not necessarily clearer than elliptic or scarcer ones, and things obviously get far more complicated when more than one hand is involved. Folio 45^{ver} (numbered 44) furnishes a good example of the difficulties one encounters when trying make sense of the abbreviated comments of several annotators. In a marginal remark at the top of the page, Sassetti comments upon an element of Vettori's translation which begins with the words, 'De constitutione quidem igitur rerum & quales quasdam esse oportet fabulas, dictum est satis'. In this passage, Aristotle appears to abandon the subject of the plot (*favola*) and prepares to go on to the topic of *mores*. Sassetti enters a brief note (**E-Figure 14**), which can be transcribed as follows: 'Qui lascia Aristotile la favola alla bellezza e perfettione della quale ha assegnate piu conditioni delle quali ne soggiunera di sotto dall' altre come che e non vi debbe essere Macchine. Ma vedi il Castelvetro che le riduce a otto bellezze e ve ne lascia molte altre.'[23] In his annotation, Sassetti underlines that Aristotle abandons the topic of *favola*, although he has already suggested many conditions necessary to ensure its beauty and perfection, and will add more conditions further on in his text, such as the necessity to avoid machinery on stage. He then refers the reader to Castelvetro, who, according to him, reduces all of these beauties to a list of eight and leaves no room for others.[24] The literal meaning of the note is obvious enough, but the author's intention (if indeed he harboured a specific

[23] BNCF Magl.,VII, 1199 bears three foliations, two of them complete. See the codicological description in Annex 1 for details. On this folio (numbered 44 on the top left), the numbering is on the *verso* of the folio and refers to page 44 of Vettori's translation. Under the other foliation, it would be fol. 45^{ver}.

[24] Castelvetro's comments on this section of the *Poetics* can be found in Lodovico Castelvetro, *Poetica d'Aristotele vulgarizzata, et sposta* (Vienna: Gaspar Stainhofer, 1570), 167–77. However, in this part of his commentary, there is no mention of eight beauties specific to tragedy. Sassetti is likely mentionning these beauties from memory and importing them from another part of the commentary.

intention) in making such a remark is not. Is he trying to stress that Aristotle's text is disorderly and has thus confused commentators? Or is he underlining the importance of *favola* and the beauties Aristotle associates with it in his philosophical reasoning? And does he approve of Castelvetro's reduction of the beauties of tragedy to eight or not? Obviously, an author's intentions are never transparent, and continuous texts can be even more difficult to make out than fragmentary notes in this respect. But the discontinuous quality of annotative remarks poses specific challenges. In particular, these fragmentary texts require that the reader accepts that he is dealing with the elaboration of thoughts rather than with a finished product and that he keep in mind that works-in-progress are probably best deciphered for what they are – that is, without attempting to artificially fill in the blanks that their mode of composition has created.

Provided careful attention is paid to its fragmentary form, the collectively annotated transcription found in BNCF Magl. VII, 1199 can actually tell us a great deal about the interests and curiosities of some of the Alterati as they pored over the *Poetics*. But in order to bring this information to the surface, the interpreter will do best to approach these annotations as if they were giving him access to the annotators' workshop, rather than with the idea that they are offering him a polished commentary on the *Poetics*. This can be done by focussing on how, in the experimental intellectual *locus* the manuscript provided for the group, certain concepts emerge, are tested and begin to be articulated to one another. From this perspective, a number of key terms recur in the marginalia, and, in the places where the annotation is especially lavish and extensive, several problems or questions have clearly attracted the annotators' attention more than others. For instance, reading the manuscript with an eye for the concepts that the Alterati pondered at length repeatedly brings to the fore the annotators' interest in the idea of action, their fascination for the concept of plot or *favola*, their perplexity in front of the notion of tragic purgation (otherwise known as *catharsis*) and, above all, their attraction to the concept of pleasure, which some of them are tempted to declare the true end of dramatic activity. Paying attention to these traces of intellectual elaboration also allows one to get a sense of how these concepts are put into relation with one another. By bringing together a few of the passages, the main preoccupations of the Alterati become discernible and some of the voices of their most active members can be heard with greater clarity.

On folio 21[rec] (**E-Figure 7**), which we considered earlier as an example of syllogistic reasoning, Sassetti glosses Aristotle's reflections on the importance of action in the crafting of a tragedy (1450a 1–30).[25] At first sight, Sassetti appears to have attempted to summarize Aristotle's thinking, but a closer look at the annotation seems to indicate that he was also particularly interested in establishing the primacy of the *favola* (μῦθος) over the *costumi* (τά ἤθη). Indeed, Sassetti insists that tragedy's main goal (*fine*) is the plot (i.e. the fact of providing the imitation of an action) rather than the *mores* of the characters (i.e. the fact of providing an imitation of their habits and moral traits). The last lines of the note even suggest that he holds the latter (*mores*) to be entirely distinct from the *plot* ('la favola non è costume', that is, 'the plot is not the habits') and, as such, somewhat unessential to the creation of an effective tragedy. Sassetti is not misreading

---

[25] This annotation is transcribed earlier, in footnote 15.

Aristotle's text here, but he is certainly tweaking it so as to make morality appear a secondary preoccupation when crafting plays, while placing plot and action at the centre of the art of tragedy. However, this note, because of its allusiveness, would not in itself suffice to document such a bias, which can only be ascertained by articulating this remark to a number of other annotations Sassetti pens into the manuscript. Among these is the one he produces about the passage where Aristotle declares that in order for tragic poems to produce the pleasure that is proper to them, they must be composed of a single, whole and complete action (1459a 15–20). On folio 74^{rec} (**E-Figure 15**), Sassetti rephrases this assertion in a way that indicates that, here too, he is interested in stressing the importance of action in the creation of tragic pleasure and in distinguishing this pleasure from the question of morality.[26] In particular, in this remark, Sassetti underlines that the pleasure that arises from the adequate type of tragic action is the pleasure of the play's own beauty, not that which arises from the purgation of the passions. He also stresses that poetry and history are different because history does not aim at the beauty (*bellezza*) that poetry hopes to attain when imitating truth. The distinction between the beauty of the plot and the effect of the purgation of the passions is not part of Aristotle's text per se. Rather it is something that Sassetti is reading into it, and it is a telling interpretation, given that, since the mid-sixteenth century, the clause in which Aristotle defines tragedy as an action which provokes a type of catharsis (1449b 23–29) had played such a central role in those readings of the *Poetics* which had attempted to attribute to tragedy a moral aim. By stressing the importance of action and the specific beauty it generates, Sassetti is clearly trying to distance himself from such moralizing interpretations. In their place, he is interested in defining a poetics of tragedy based on pleasure rather than ethics or moral utility.

However, establishing pleasure as the central goal of tragedy in Aristotle's treaty is not easily accomplished, and Sassetti can often be seen struggling with the tensions of Aristotle's text on this issue, for instance on folio 92^{ver}, also previously mentioned (**E-Figure 9**).[27] In this substantial remark, Sassetti lists four goals for tragedy, designating 'un certo piacere' ('a certain kind of pleasure') as the last or *ultimate* one, after having enumerated among these four goals 'plot and action', the excitement of pity and terror and the purgation of the passions. If, in the annotation, 'ultimately' (*ultimamente*) refers not only to the place of 'pleasure' in the enumeration but also to its importance (or status) within it, the phrase ('e pare che quattro d[e]va[no] esser i fini cioè la favola e l'attione, l'eccitar misericordia e terrore, il purgare delle passione & *ultimamente* un certo piacere') could mean that tragedy's *ultimate* goal is a 'un certo piacer'. Yet the adverb *ultimamente* could also have the opposite meaning. Indeed, the first edition

---

[26] BNCF Magl. VII, 1199, fol. 74^{rec}:

Mostra [Aristotile] perchè conto l'attione per esser bella debba havere l'unità con l'esempio delle cose naturali belle, le quali hanno unità e integrità le quali dua cose fanno la bellezza dalla quale nasce il piacere; però è da avvertire che egli [Aristotile] intende qui il piacere della sua propria bellezza e non quello che nasce dalla purgatione. Se uno dirà che all'historia ancora fa di mestierie questa bellezza, gli risponderemo esser vero che ell' è una e intiera ma non ricerca la bellezza della poesia che consiste [i]n'imitare, ma verità.

[27] This annotation is transcribed above, in footnote 15.

of the *Vocabolario degli accademici della Crusca* (1612) defines *ultimamente* as 'in ultimo, alla fine, nell'ultimo luogo. Lat. *postremò, ultimo*'. This could make 'pleasure' the last (and thus least important) item on Sassetti's list, or it could make 'pleasure' the ultimate and even all-encompassing goal of tragedy. Both meanings appear possible in this remark and, though the second seems more coherent with things Sassetti has said elsewhere in his annotations, it is difficult to be sure of what he meant specifically here. This is especially true since, in the following remarks of this *postilla*, Sassetti's thoughts meander quite a bit, as if he were unsure of which goal should (or even could) be declared most central to tragedy. In particular, in his attempt to synthesize his understanding of what Aristotle might have been saying regarding the central goals of tragedy, Sassetti mentions the pleasure to be found in the purgation of the passions, as well as Aristotle's claim that plot is the central goal of tragedy. It is fair to suppose that both of these elements relate to his interest in tragic pleasure. However, towards the end of his remark, Sassetti insistently investigates the moral effects of tragedy, as well as of epics, stressing that if the rousing of affects and the resulting 'purgation' are the main takeaways of spectators, then one would also need to suppose that the said stirring of the passions and ensuing purgation are the (primary) goals of tragedy.

To a reader looking for a clear and definitive interpretation of the *Poetics*, Sassetti's hesitations may come as a disappointment, especially as they pop up on the last page of the manuscript, seeming to indicate that a central problem in the *Poetics* was in fact left unsolved amid the Alterati. But it is probably more useful to view these hesitations as telling traces of the initial interpretative struggles with which some of the Alterati wrestled when trying to establish a poetics centred on pleasure and beauty, rather than on utility and morality. Indeed, such hesitations can be seen in many other instances throughout the annotations. For while it is clear that Sassetti and most of the other annotators of the manuscript have a particular interest for the intricacies of tragic action and the pleasures they create, as the concentration of their remarks on topics such as reversal, recognition, and wonder (*meraviglia*) indicates, most of them also attempt to articulate pleasure and utility. From this point of view, some of the annotations on folios 82^{ver} to 84^{rec} are revealing. They show how Sassetti and one of the other main annotators of the manuscript – who is most probably Lorenzo Giacomini – work both to distinguish poetic goals from political ones and to pinpoint how tragic pleasure and the wonder it produces can serve moral ends. In the first annotation (**E-Figure 16**), Sassetti stresses that, according to Aristotle, poetry and politics concur, as both aim at making the body politic happy (*felice*).[28] He is thus trying once again to find a middle ground between poetry's own means and ends, and the moral and political necessities of the body politic. Yet in the following annotation (**E-Figure 17**), in response to Sassetti's

---

[28] BNCF Magl. VII, 1199, fol. 82^{ver}:

> […] [Sassetti] Hora è da sapere che di queste due poesie in fino sono duoi, un prossimo, et uno ultimo, il prossimo eccita misericordia e terrore, l'ultimo il purgare. I mez[z]i loro sono le cose terribili e compassionevoli. Hora la rettitudine dell'arte poetica consiste nel conseguire questo fine mediante questi mezzi. Aristotile fece mentione dell'arte Politica perche ella concorre con la Poetica: in trattare attioni humane & il suo fine è il fare tutta la citta felice et i suoi mezzi sono le buone leggi, però la sua rettitudine consisterà in conseguire questo fine mediante i suoi mezzi.

remark, the Alterati member whom I believe is Lorenzo Giacomini seems to stress solely the importance of pleasure, insisting that tragic poetry must delight by the novelty of the events it stages.[29] Finally, in the very last quotation, taken from folio 84rec (**E-Figure 18**), the same annotator, directly adding a note to a remark previously penned in by Sassetti, designates wonder (*meraviglia*) as tragedy's main goal, which is not a common reading among sixteenth-century glossators of the *Poetics*. Yet in the very next clause, the same hand stresses that it is precisely because poetry delights that it generates good *costumi* in its spectators, as 'it is not unbefitting that one end [pleasure] concurs to the other [utility]'.[30] Once again, the pleasure that appears to be promoted here is one that is not at odds with utility, with the Alterati ultimately appearing as particularly curious, in this exchange as well as in Sassetti's previously analysed remark, of the ways in which both and utility could work in association in tragic spectacle. If this complex stance was 'hedonism', it was a nuanced and sophisticated form of 'hedonism', one which was in fact equally preoccupied with morality – or perhaps more accurately a 'hedonism' centrally concerned with something one could call an *ethics of pleasure*.

* * *

When I first deciphered the Alterati's collectively annotated manuscript of Aristotle's *Poetics*, I was both very much intrigued by what appeared to me as the Alterati's hedonistic aesthetics and quite frustrated that my minute examination of the codex did not furnish me with a clearer and a better articulated understanding of the Alterati's overarching reading of Aristotle's *Poetics*. The manuscript certainly manifested how the Alterati, as a group, had laboured together on the *Poetics*. It also documented the specificity of their training, the creativity of their speculations and, more generally, the originality of their intellectual activity. Yet, not only were their annotations elusive and their ideas hard to pinpoint but the manuscript which contained them also told me little, at least at first, about the specific reasons for which the members of this academy might be upholding such a convoluted hedonistic understanding of poetry. Why would the ethics of pleasure which seemed such a central element of their annotations in BNCF Magl. VII, 1199 be important to them as a collective? What could such a position signify in late Renaissance Florence, when compared to other (possibly) competing aesthetic viewpoints? And what social and/or political stakes

---

[29] BNCF Magl. VII, 1199, fol. 83rec: '[Giacomini] Ma la dirittura della Poetica consiste in rassomigliar con parole harmonizzate una attione humana possibile ad avvenire, dillettevole per la novità dello accidente'.

[30] BNCF Magl. VII, 1199, fol 84rec:

[Sassetti] Si quæ adversus, ipsam artem: qui coniunge l'impossibile e'l peccar in un arte e dice così se il poeta fa cose impossibili e pecca ancora in qualche arte egli ha peccato, ma non dimeno ha fatto bene perché e' l'ha fatto per conseguire il suo fine, e se bene ha tolto mezzi non buoni è da salvarlo perchè cosi l'ha conseguito maggiormente. [Giacomini] Il M[aggi] pon per fine della Poesia homines virtutibus exornare, ma non è inconveniente che un fine riguardi l'altro, come nella medicina la sanità è il fine, e questo per potere operare, così la maraviglia è il fine della Poesia, e questa per poter in altrui genrar buon costumi.

might have been associated with defining and selectively circulating such a standpoint for the Florentine patricians who populated this secretive academy?

I was also aware that the Alterati's collectively annotated manuscript did not provide me with what theoreticians of literature and aesthetics would, in today's world, consider to be a full-blown set of aesthetic 'theories'. Many historians of early modern poetics have strived to articulate fully developed theories of poetics when their sources do not furnish them with such totalizing perspectives. This was something that Bernard Weinberg was prone to do in his *History of Literary Criticism in the Italian Renaissance*, where he wove texts of many different natures and purposes (treatises, letters, academic discourses, polemical attacks, *abbozzi*, *appunti*, *libri postillati* or annotated books, etc.) into an all-encompassing history of poetic and aesthetic ideas, mostly without investigating the reasons for which each text was originally circulated, and often contextualizing each of them only in terms of how the ideas set forth within in it might enter into dialogue (whether intentionally or unintentionally) with the other texts assembled in his *corpus*. In doing so, Weinberg and those who followed in his footsteps conformed to the main understanding of 'theory' accepted in mid-twentieth-century literary discourse, particularly as practised by the Chicago School – that is one in which normativity, completeness and coherence (or non-contradiction) are believed to be central features of proper theoretical enunciations. However, Renaissance scholars did not necessarily adhere to such an understanding of theory. Nor did they believe that learned discourses on the arts needed to be isolated from moral or political considerations to be true to the essence of these very arts, which is a representation to which Weinberg, as a central figure of New Criticism, also seems to have generally adhered.[31] In fact, many probably did not even believe in the existence of the types of discourses we now understand to be 'theory': early modern representations of science or knowledge were quite different from those we now harbour and made much more room for craft and experimentation then we normally tend to do.[32] In particular, Renaissance thought on poetics did not carry with it a strict binary distinction between theory and practice, as is suggested by Weinberg's category of 'practical criticism'. The Chicago School critic devotes the second volume of his book (in which he deals with major literary polemics) to this form of 'practice', after having dealt with 'poetic theory' in the first volume.

With these considerations in mind, I concluded that it would be best to hold the elusiveness, incompleteness and even what I perceived, at times, to be the opacity of the Alterati's reflections on poetry, theatre and the arts – both in BNCF Magl. VII, 1199 and in their other writings, such as their academic *discorsi*, which I had been investigating in parallel – as characteristics worth exploring in and of themselves.[33] I

---

[31] On the Chicago School, Neo-Aristotelianism and Bernard Weinberg's approach to the history of poetics, see Ravindra Nath Shrivastava, *Literary Criticism in Theory and Practice* (New Delhi: Atlantic Publishers and Distributors, 2004), especially 77–102, as well as Eufemia Baldassarre, Paul F. Gehl and Lia Markey's article on 'A Scholar-Collector in Mid-Century Chicago: The Books of Bernard Weinberg', in this volume.

[32] See Pamela H. Smith, Amy R. W. Meyers and Harold J. Cook, *Ways of Making and Knowing: the Material Culture of Empirical Knowledge* (Ann Arbor: The University of Michigan Press, 2014).

[33] On aesthetic knowledge as 'elusive', see the work of Ulrike Schneider and her research group ('Theorie und Ästhetik elusiven Wissens in der Frühen Neuzeit: Transfer und Institutionalisierung',

also came to think of them as traces of an understanding of poetics and poetry that considered them more as a craft, to be dealt with via an unending trial and error process, than as a definite and stable body of knowledge. Finally, I decided to take the main social practice that the Alterati's collectively annotated manuscript offered to me as evidence – that is, the Alterati's secretiveness (as producers of anonymous manuscripts and printed matter apparently designed for internal use only) and their elliptical evasiveness (when expressing their thoughts and the principles which founded them) – as my point of departure into the investigation of the ethos and, more generally, the social and political positioning of their academy.

From this last point of view, two material characteristics of the manuscript and its printed companion clearly demanded further investigation. First, the existence of such luxury objects as a carefully calligraphed manuscript and a printed booklet made for private use by one of the most famous printers in Florence begged the question of the wealth, social status and possible political clout of the academicians who had annotated the manuscript. Second, the intensive collaborative work displayed on the manuscript, as well as the forms of academic discursiveness that found themselves replicated in the dedication of the printed booklet, seemed to require that the values, social practices, institutional habits and even political viewpoints of these men be investigated. For what could be their goal in privileging parity, collaboration and *pro et contra* discursive exchanges when discussing Aristotle in their academy – as subjects of the Medicean regime, which had precisely worked so hard to detach Florence's institutions and social structures from the oligarchic ideals and practices of the former Republic, even while appearing to preserve them? These questions led me to momentarily abandon the Florentine libraries whose holdings are centred on belles-lettres – such as the Biblioteca Nazionale Centrale, the Biblioteca Riccardiana and the Biblioteca Medicea Laurenziana, where most Alterati manuscripts are now held – to make my way to the Florence's central archival institution, the Archivio di Stato di Firenze. There I looked for genealogical records, official and domestic correspondence, and family papers for the most prominent members of the academy. I also carefully scrutinized some of their tax records, the number and importance of the civil offices they held in Florence's urban governance, and even the contents of their wills, with the goal of gaining a detailed understanding of their social, institutional and political positioning, both individually and as a group.

The results of this investigation, in which Strozzi, Sassetti and Giacomini – the major annotators of the transcription of Vettori's translation of the *Poetics* – were given pride of place, form the material of my forthcoming book. They are somewhat surprising, not only with respect to what we thought we knew about the Florentine patriciate in late Renaissance Florence but also with regard to Florence's academic culture more generally, and even in view of our current understanding of the history of early modern aesthetics. On the one hand, these findings invite a revaluation of Florentine academic culture in the late sixteenth century and of the place of the Alterati within it. On the

SFB 980, group Episteme in Bewegung, project B05), as reflected, for instance, in Ulrike Schneider, 'Vom Wissen um *gratia*. Strategien der Diskursivierung elusiven Wissens in der Frühen Neuzeit', in Anne Eusterschulte and Ulrike Schneider, *Gratia. Mediale und diskursive Konzeptualisierungen ästhetischer Erfahrung in der Vormoderne* (Wiesbaden: Harrassowitz, 2018), 89–105.

other hand, they suggest that our understanding of the social and political history of early modern aesthetics needs some reconfiguring.

The question of the place of the Alterati in Florence's academic culture can serve as a good point of entry into the many mysteries of this elitist institution. The Alterati have sometimes been described as a pro-Medicean academy.[34] However, my research shows that this private academy was in fact initially created to rival and contest the intellectual legitimacy of the academy the Medici had taken over since 1547: the Accademia Fiorentina. Moreover, the Alterati's academy initially constituted a secretive space of cultural resistance, which, contrary to the Academia Fiorentina, brought together nothing but members of the Florentine patriciate, stemming quasi-exclusively not only from wealthy and well-established patrician households but also from lineages that had fought, in one way or another, to uphold the late Florentine Republic before 1537. In Cosimo I's Florence, these men and their families were silently kept out of both civil charges and courtly positions because of their prior political commitments. To counter the forms of social marginalization that could result from such a situation, they developed the academy they founded in 1569 both as a space for discreet political contestation and as a locus that could help facilitate a form of (individual and/or collective) social reintegration. In the unlikely middle ground that the academy offered, the patrician members of this institution both worked through their residual political resentment and developed the intellectual and social skills they needed to find a new place for themselves within the Medici regime. For the most part, they were successful in both their intellectual and their social endeavours. Indeed, having proven their literary capacities and leadership abilities within the setting of an academy, many moved on to occupy positions of consequence as cultural intermediaries (diplomatic envoys on special missions, preceptors of a Medici offspring, orchestrators of elaborate *divertimenti*, etc.) at the Medici court, after 1600.

The role of intellectual activity among these academicians is also telling. For collectively developing philosophical, rhetorical and literary skills among themselves was absolutely essential to their progressive social integration, which was based first and foremost on the belief – sometimes actively mobilized and spread in their social entourage – that the Alterati mastered a variety of important 'arts' (to be understood here mainly in the terms of the French call 'savoir faire'). It is possible to reconstitute how the Alterati acquired the skills they needed to make themselves desirable to the Medici princes by carefully examining the activities in which they engaged in their academy, when they met twice a week to exchange *pro* and *contra* orations, have improvised discussions and evaluate each other's poetry. These collaborative exchanges, through which the ideals and practices of the academy were elaborated and refined, can be studied across their printed and manuscript works (which contain no complete or finalized treatises, but include countless academic discourses, as well as letters, polemical interventions, *abbozzi*, *appunti*, annotated poems and *libri postillati*) whose mode of circulation and conservation in early modern Florence is of great interest. Indeed, the Alterati privileged manuscript circulation of their works over publication in printed form. Scribal diffusion allowed these academicians to circulate

---

[34] See in particular, Cochrane, *Florence in the Forgotten Centuries*, 93–161 and Plaisance, *L'Académie et le Prince*, 363–404.

their academic *discorsi* in forms that preserved a link to the orality of their academic exchanges. Manuscript publication was also somewhat easier to control. It allowed the Alterati to keep their debates accessible only to a handful of people, while also generating widespread curiosity for them in Florence.

By studying a number of collective manuscripts and/or projects the Alterati developed together, I was also able to reconstitute how collective understandings of literary issues and, in some cases, common intellectual horizons were worked out among these academicians on a variety of subjects. In this respect, it soon became clear that the academy generally valued *dissensus* over consensus. For this reason, in order to discern the Alterati's collective voice, it is of crucial importance to pay attention to the structural role of discussion among them. Indeed, parity, debate and the expression of judgement in the academy constituted ways for these academicians to re-enact, within the seclusion of their academy, the Republican *mores* that they could no longer fully and openly mobilize in Florence's civic life. This means that the format of their collaborative exchanges – of which BNCF Magl. VII, 1199 constitutes a striking written incarnation – is, in and of itself, a social and political statement. For in them, all voices theoretically bore equal weight and no position of enunciation was ever *a priori* privileged, not even that of their regent (or chair). Interestingly enough, this oligarchic institution, with its corresponding parity-oriented statutes, by-laws and debate practices, simultaneously developed a distinctive relationship to literature and the arts, defined by a specific kind of shared, and even socialized, intellectual pleasure.

To begin with, the Alterati centrally defined their academy as an institutional *locus* in which learning, art and artistic practices could be elaborated into worthy activities for men of their status. Within this *locus*, the various ways in which they practised and discussed art helped them refashion themselves to exercise new kinds of social functions. In particular, these academicians valourized art and knowledge by transferring onto these practices and discourses the values that had defined their families as patricians for centuries, in Florence's civic culture. These values, which the Alterati transferred from late Florentine Republican civic life to the realm of art and aesthetics, as elaborated in the academy, oppose academic leisure to servile political service (in the Medicean bureaucracy or at court), while extolling nobility, freedom, parity and judgement in the pursuit of art and knowledge. But first and foremost, these values claim a form of pleasure that the Alterati envisage as the central principle bringing together the members of their sodality, often asserting it as the basis for all their gatherings and activities. This pleasure is defined by Giovan Battista Strozzi – in notes he prepared late in life, with the aim of assisting with the writing of a history of the academy – as a 'praiseworthy pleasure' ('*lodevole diletto*'). Such a concept not only aimed to distinguish intellectual pleasures from purely sensuous ones but also tied the pleasure of common activities of learning, conducted in parity and reciprocity, with the civic notoriety and reputation to be collectively gained in these pursuits.[35] In

---

[35] In a series of *appunti* contained in BNCF Magl. IX, 124, Giovan Battista Strozzi highlights this notion of 'praiseworthy pleasure', defining it as central to the academy's ethos and practices. See in particular fol. 74bis: 'Noi però comprendo tutti diremo che l'Accademia è adunanza d'amici [con] leggi proprie, desiderosi mediante l'esercitarsi nelle scienze e nell'arti [non] senza lodevole diletto, di migliorar vicendevolmente se stessi et essere [ad] altri di giovamento cagione'. On fol. 78[ver],

claiming these values in the context of academic life, the Alterati were attempting to create a new social identity for themselves as Florentine patricians, one in which art, the practices by which it is made to exist, and the laudable pleasures it generates were mobilized to uphold their threatened primacy in Florentine society, as members of the patriciate, without subjecting them to any form of professionalization.

The ways in which the Alterati understood the sophisticated hedonistic relationship they established with the arts is probably best captured through an analysis of how these views are expounded, in allegorical fashion, in a court opera to which a few Alterati members contributed heavily: Ottavio Rinuccini's and Jacopo Peri's *Euridice*, created at the Medici court in October 1600, during the celebration of the in absentia marriage of Maria de' Medici and Henry IV of France. This opera makes clear that the Alterati's conceptions of pleasure and of its importance in social and even political life were linked both to materialism and Neoplatonism, while also owing a great deal to Torquato Tasso. A pragmatic and contextualized analysis of the *libretto* also suggests that, in this work, the Alterati – of which Ottavio Rinuccini was a central member – were both producing an allegorical representation of their understanding of the role of pleasure in art (as well as in love and life) and indirectly staging their own social position within the court, in which they aspired to become insiders, even though they often continued to claim for themselves the status of outsiders. With the production of this *divertimento*, the Alterati, by asserting pleasure as their ethos and art as their central skill, did not just distinguish themselves, thanks to their academy, from Florentine court practices. They simultaneously publicized an ethical as well as intellectual set of competences from which to lobby the Medici regarding their reintegration into the social and political economy of the court.

This *praiseworthy pleasure* – which not only is at the heart of the intellectual dynamic of BNCF Magl. VII, 1199 but also forms the basis of the Alterati's overarching ethical, social and aesthetic understanding – begs to be put into comparative perspective. For in early modern Europe, it was in fact not rare for aristocratic writers or groups of writers operating under an authoritarian regime to claim for themselves a space of freedom and distinction by (re)fashioning themselves socially and culturally via a hedonistic aesthetic. Sir Philip Sidney and his entourage are a case in point, but so is the circle of Mme de Rambouillet in France, and, later in the seventeenth century, the group of authors surrounding Mlle de Scudéry and her 'tender friend' Paul Pellisson. These groups (and others) have in common with the Alterati the fact that they created a social identity for themselves around a hedonistic aesthetics of social distinction, in

---

Giovan Battista Strozzi further glosses the previous definition, underscoring the link between praiseworthiness and reputation:

Non senza lodevole diletto: Ecco lo stimolo, ecco l'incitatione ch'e ha possanza di movere ogn'uno ad operare. A lui attribuirono tanto alcuni, che affermarono in lui consister la stessa felicità. E veramente egl' è un suo conseguente, e una proprietà che mai non si disgiunge da lei. Noi l'habbiamo congiunto con lodevole per distinguerlo da['] piaceri inimici di virtù, la qual del ben oprar dilettandosi e con la contemplatione più in alto surgendo, i sensuali diletti disprezza, ò solamente quant' è di necessità ci se ne vale. Nelle Accademie l'insegnar, l'imparare, il sentirsi liberar da ignoranza, il vedere che nelle scienze s'acquista, e che ne risulta gran lode, è dilettevole sì che niente più.

I thank Dr Francesco Martelli, the curator of the Medicean collections at the *Archivio di Stato* in Florence, for his help in the transcription of these two notes.

a gesture that was just as much about voicing freedom and opposition to monarchical power, as it was a form of courtship destined to ingratiate them with the very power they were simultaneously distancing themselves from. In this respect, the pragmatic tension between courtship and defiance, which manifested itself in the European circulations of this politics of praiseworthy aesthetic pleasure, seems to have played a crucial role, historically, in the definition of early modern understandings of art.

Even more interestingly, a very similar kind of tension was at work during the rise of aesthetics as an academic discipline in late-eighteenth- and early-nineteenth-century Prussia. For, strikingly enough, the 'autonomy' of art, as it was defined by Immanuel Kant and Karl Philip Moritz, at the turn of the eighteenth and the nineteenth centuries, was defined though an antagonistic relationship with absolutism, which nonetheless mimicked authoritarian control in the extraordinary powers it attributed to art.[36] In this respect, it is clear that modern aesthetics have a social and political history that goes back far beyond the 1780s – the moment that is generally considered to have witnessed the birth of modern aesthetics – and that this history cannot not be recaptured solely in intellectual terms, but rather calls for a structural investigation of how certain kinds of social groups related to power via the theorization and practice of learning and/or the arts. Understanding how these structural tensions played out in early modern Europe is not only important for recovering why and how early modern understandings of poetry and more generally art developed and spread but also central in view of developing a contextualized understanding of what was actually at stake in the aesthetics articulated within German idealism, which in more ways than one reproduced pre-existing structural tensions between poetry, art and power, while attempting to reconfigure or even supersede them. Such a historicized perspective would be especially important to develop because the aesthetics defined in nineteenth-century Prussia tended to claim for itself a form of a-historicity, which, in today's world, has often led to its essentialization as a doctrine.

My study of the social and political underpinnings of the Alterati's understanding of poetry and the pleasures it provides is a step towards elaborating a *longue durée* understanding of the rise of modern-day aesthetics. It also attempts to develop an understanding of aesthetics that does not shy away from material, social, institutional and/or political realities, but rather makes them the central terrain of its investigation. For such an enterprise, manuscripts such as the BNCF Magl. VII, 1199 constitute invaluable documents in that they make it possible to articulate the history of ideas with social, institutional and political history. Thanks to them, existing paradigms can be questioned and reframed, provided one tracks the meaning of singular documents without losing sight of the larger frameworks in which they might fit. In this way, the very materiality of a document, when analysed in micro-historical terms, can serve as a way to bridge the gap between intellectual history and its social and political contexts, shedding new light on the history of poetics and aesthetics alike.

[36] See Jonathan M. Hess, *Reconstituting the Body Politic: Enlightenment, Public Culture and the Invention of Aesthetic Autonomy* (Detroit: Wayne State University Press, 1999), in particular 155–79. On page 175, Hess writes : 'Autonomous art may indeed be conceived of as a negation of 'the dominant idea of utility' embodied by the absolutist body politic and its economy of bodily pleasure, but ultimately it too turns against its creators, perpetuating in its functionings the working of the dominant political order it aspired to oppose.'

ANNEX 1

Codicological description of BNCF Magl. VII, 1199[37]

SHELF MARK: Florence: Bibilioteca Nazionale Centrale di Firenze, MS. Magl. VII, 1199, *olim* Strozzi 4°, 805.

SHORT TITLE, PLACE AND DATE: *Aristotelis Stagiritae Poetica cum notis Petro Victorio Interprete*, Pisa and Florence, 1573[–1617].

DESCRIPTION OF CONTENTS: Titled *Aristotelis Stagiritae Poetica Petro Victorio Interpetre* [sic] on fol. 1. This title page imitates that of a printed book. Collectively annotated transcription of Piero Vettori's Latin translation of Aristotle's *Poetics* (taken from *Petri Victorii Commentarii in primum librum Aristotelis de Arte poetarum [...]*, Florence, Giunti, 1560), with extended glosses in Italian by Giovan Battista Strozzi, Filippo Sassetti et al., produced and circulated within the *Accademia degli Alterati* (Florence and Pisa, 1569-ca 1625).

NUMBER OF LEAVES: [i]+ vii + 93 + viii + [i] (one flyleaf added in the front with s. xx binding, and one in the back).

FOLIATION: Folios 1–93 of text and commentary. One continuous and exact s. xvi foliation numbering, on the *recto* of all the fol. from the title page (numbered fol. 1). One other previous continuous s. xvi foliation numbering only the fol. of Vettori's Latin translation of the *Poetics* and appearing both on the *recto* and the *verso* of each fol. of his text. The numbers of this previous foliation which appear on the *recto* of the fol. of Vettori's translation were crossed out when the second foliation, covering both text and commentary, was added. Current fol. 3, 7 and 9 also bear numbering (2, 3 and 4) appearing to signal a third attempt to foliate the manuscript. But this last foliation is not continuous.

MATERIAL: Paper. Watermark visible on flyleaves (fol. vi in front and fol. ii in back): heart with a M inside, surmounted by a cross similar to Briquet, vol. 3, 4269 and 4273. No watermarks on the folios of the manuscript per se.

DIMENSIONS OF PAGE: 210 x 150 mm.

DIMENSIONS OF WRITTEN TEXT: 170 × 110 mm. 15 lines per page in the transcription. Annotations in the transcription appear in the margins, both left and right of the text, as well as above the first line and under the last one. In the pages bearing exclusively annotations, the dimensions of the written text vary widely. In

---

[37] I am loosely following the template proposed by N. R. Ker, *Medieval Manuscripts in British Libraries*, 5 vols. (Oxford: Clarendon Press, 1969–2002), vii–xiii.

some folios the whole page is utilized. In others, just a small portion of it is used. The annotations usually stretch out over the whole width of the page, leaving room vertically for other possible additions. Some pages have also been left blank.

RULING: Light dry ruling in the transcription.

QUIRING: i^6 (including one bi-folio added at the end of the quire as fol. 6), ii-iii^4, iv^8 (including two bi-folios added in the middle of the quire as fol. 19 and 20), v-xxiii^4 (last folio is blank).

SCRIPTS: Italic calligraphic script used for the Latin transcription. Annotations are in current hands, some with calligraphic efforts, others writing more hastily.

MARGINALIA: The manuscript was structured to alternate one fol. of transcribed text with one fol. of commentary (from selected *lemmata*), which means that the annotations were thought of as central part of the manuscript. This alternate structure is respected except from fol. 4 to 7, where an extra fol. of commentary appears (fol. 6), and from fols. 17 to 23 where 2 fols. of text are followed by 3 fols. of commentary then 2 fols. of text. These disruptions to the structure appear to signal that folios were added to allow for more commentary. The pages of transcribed text also contain annotations (some indicate divisions in the text, some provide brief linguistic or philosophic clarification of the Latin translation). At least six different annotators can be isolated. The two dominant hands are that of Giovan Battista Strozzi Il Giovane (1551–1634) and that of Filippo Sassetti (1540–1588), both of whom were prominent members of the *Accademia degli Alterati*. But the hand of Lorenzo Giacomini (1552–1598) also seems present. Sassetti's hand is the one that appears with the greatest frequency, though the manuscript belonged to Strozzi, who also annotated it widely. The following manuscripts, among many others, allow for the identification of these three hands by comparison: (1) for Giovan Battista Strozzi, Florence: Bibliotheca Medicea Laurenziana, Ashburnham 558, vol. 1, 2nd part, fol. 48^{ver} (where Strozzi's hand appear as he identifies himself by his academic name and initials) and Florence: Biblioteca Nazionale Centrale di Firenze, Ginori Conti 27, cc. 19, doc. 3, fol. 4; doc. 8, fol. 1 and doc. 10 in its entirety ; (2) for Filippo Sassetti: Florence: Biblioteca Nazionale Centrale di Firenze, Postillati 15, as well as Florence: Bibliotheca Riccardiana, Ricc. 1539 and Ricc. 2438bis, III; (3) for Lorenzo Giacomini: Bibliotheca Universitaria di Pisa, Mss 551 and 552. The hand which is most likely that of Lorenzo Giacomini, intervenes principally towards the end of the manuscript, fols. 73, 74, 75^{rec}, 77, 78^{ver}, 79^{rec}, 80^{rec}, 81^{ver}, 83^{rec}, 84^{rec}, 85^{ver}, 86^{rec}, 92^{ver}. Three other hands can be isolated: one appears on fols. 8^{rec}, 9^{ver}, 10^{ver}, 11^{rec}, 13^{rec}, 19^{ver}, 44^{ver}, 54^{rec}, another one on fol. 12^{rec} and yet another hand is visible on fol. 13^{rec}.

BINDING: Modern binding (s. xx). Earlier and possibly original white skin binding preserved in manuscript section of the Bibilioteca Nazionale Centrale di Firenze. No provenance marks on the previous binding.

HISTORY AND PROVENANCE: The manuscript is anonymous, but the title page bears the coat of arms of the Strozzi (a shield in the shape of a roundel with a bar containing three crescents on a background of diagonal hatching designed to represent gold). A printed book also allows for a better understanding of the status of the manuscript: Florence: Bibilioteca Nazionale Centrale di Firenze, *Aristotelis Poetica Petro Victorio Interprete*, Florence, Giunti, 1617, Magl. 5.9.119 (possibly the only surviving copy). It contains the transcription of Vettori's translation, but without the *Alterati* annotations (except for some of the brief divisions that the manuscript suggests for the reading of the text). The dedication letter, addressed by Giovan Battista Strozzi to his nephew, Giovan Battista Strozzi, *marchese* of Forano (1597–1636), discreetly alludes to the manuscript, hinting that it served as a reference book within the academy, while encouraging the younger Strozzi and his entourage to use it to study the text and pursue academic endeavours. This book and the coat arms clearly indicate that the manuscript belonged to Giovan Battista Strozzi. The letters of Filippo Sassetti, which show consistent interest in Aristotle's *Poetics*, also point to the existence of the manuscript and suggest in what conditions it was originally produced. See Filippo Sassetti, *Lettere da vari paesi*, 1570–1588, Vanni Bramanti (ed.), Milan, Longanesi & C°, 1970, letter 32, dated 2 December 1573, p. 120 (which mentions that Strozzi and Sassetti were living and studying together in Pisa the year the commentary of the manuscript was begun) and letter 45, dated 3 December 1575, p. 171 (which shows a precise exchange between Sassetti and Strozzi concerning an annotation to add to this commented manuscript of the *Poetics*). It is likely that both the manuscript and the printed book (for which we have no indication of provenance) entered the manuscript collections of Carlo Strozzi (1587–1670) after the death of the *marchese* of Forano. The manuscript bears a secondary title page with the Strozzi shelf mark and this note: 'Di Luigi del Senatore Carlo di Tommaso Strozzi. 1679', signalling that it was catalogued by Luigi Strozzi, Carlo's son. In 1786, many of the elements of the Strozzi collections which concerned belles-lettres (including presumably this manuscript and the printed book meant to accompany it) entered the grand duke's *Libreria Magliabechiana*, while most of what partook to the history of Florence was sent to the *Archivio di Stato*, where this material now forms the *Carte Strozziane*.[38]

---

[38] On the history of the constitution of the Strozzi archive and their current dispersion in Florentine repositories, see Cesare Guasti, *Le Carte Strozziane del R. Archivio di Stato: Inventario*, serie prima, 2 vols. (Florence: Tipographia Galileiana, 1884–1891), 1:V–XXXIX.

ANNEX 2

The Alterati's readings in and around the *Poetics*[39]

A) Works mentioned in BNCF Magl. VII, 1199 (in chronological order):

Robortello, Francesco. *In librum Aristotelis De Arte poetica explicationes. Qui ab eodem authore ex manuscriptis libris, multis in locis emendatus fuit, ut iam difficillimus, ac obscurissimus liber a nullo antedeclaratus facile ab omnibus possit intelligi*. Florence: Lorenzo Torrentino, 1548.

Maggi, Vicenzo and Lombardi, Bartholomeo. *In Aristotelis Librum De Poetica communes explantiones ; Madii vero in eundem librum propriæ annotationes, eiusdem de Ridiculis ; et in Horatii librum De arte Poetica interpretatio. In fronte præterea operis apposita est Lombardi in Aristotelis Poeticam præfatio*, Venice: Vincenzo Valgrisi, 1550.

Segni, Bernardo. *Rettorica et Poetica d'Aristotele tradotte di greco in lingua vulgare Fiorentina*. Florence: Lorenzo Torrentino, 1549, republished in Venice in 1551.

Vettori, Pietro. *Petri Victorii Commentarii in primum librum Aristotelis de Arte poetarum [...]*. Florence: Sons of Bernardo Giunti, 1560, reprinted in 1573.

Scaliger, Julius Cesar, *Poetices libri septem [...] ad Sylvium Filium*, Lyon?: Vincent Antoine, 1561.

Castelvetro, Lodovico. *Poetica d'Aristotele vulgarizzata, et sposta*. Vienna: Gaspar Stainhofer, 1570.

Piccolomini, Alessandro. *Il libro della Poetica d'Aristotele tradotto di greca in lingua volgare*. Siena: Luca Bonetti, 1572.

Piccolomini, Alessandro. *Annotationi nel libro del Poetica d'Aristotile con la traduttione del medesimo libro, in lingua volgare*. Venice: Giovanni Guarisco, 1575.

Castelvetro, Ludovico. *Poetica d'Aristotele vulgarizzata e sposta, riveduta & ammendata secondo l'originale, & la mente dell'autore. Aggiuntovi nella fine un racconto delle cose piu notabili, che nella spositione si contengono*. Basel: Peter Perna and Piero de Sedaonis, 1576.

B) Works not mentioned in BNCF Magl. VII, 1199 (in chronological order):

Segni, Agnolo. *Ragionamento fiorentino sopra le cose pertinenti alla poetica: dove in quattro lezzioni lette da lui nell'Accademia fiorentina si tratta dell'imitazione poetica, della favola, della purgazione procedente dalla poesia*. Florence: Giorgio Marescotti, 1581.

Riccoboni, Antonio. *Poetica Aristotelis latine conversa, Eiusdem Riccoboni Paraphrasis in Poeticam Aristotelis, Eiusdem Ars Comica ex Aristotele*. Padova: Paulo Meieto, 1587.

---

[39] These works are alluded to in the BNCF Magl. VII, 1199 through the first letters of the author's last name (for instance: Rob., P.V. or V^i., Mag^o., Scal., Pic.). It is not always possible to distinguish Bernardo Segni from Agnolo Segni (possibly both referred to as Seg.), but most references appear to be to Bernardo Segni, given that Agnolo Segni did not publish a selection of his 1573 lectures on the *Poetics* until 1581 and they did not constitute a linear commentary of the text.

Riccoboni, Antonio. *Compendium Artis poeticæ Aristotelis ad usum conficiendorum poematum ab Antonio Riccobono ordinatum, & quisdam Scholiis explanatu*. Padova: Lorenzo Pasquato, 1591.

Patrizi, Francesco. *Della Poetica. La Deca Istoriale, Nella quale, con dilettevole antica novità, oltre à Poeti, e lor poemi innumerabili, che vi si contano: si fan palesi, tutte le cose compagne, e seguaci dell'antiche poesie. E con maravigliosa varietà, e notizia di cose, maraviglioso piacere, ed utile, si pone avanti à Leggitori. E si gittano i veri fondamenti all'arte del poetare alla Serenissima Madama Lucrezia da Este duchessa d'Urbino*. Ferrare: Vittorio Baldini,1586.

Heinsius, Daniel. *Q. Horatii Flacci Opera Omnia cum Notis Danielis Heinsii, accedit Horatii ad Pisones epistola, Aristotelis de poetica libellus; ordini suo nunc demum ab eodem restitute*. Leiden: Franciscus Raphelengius,1610.

Beni, Paulo. *Pauli Beni Eugubini in Aristotelis Poeticam Commentarii*. Padova: Francesco Bolzetta, 1613.

Work Cited

Manuscripts

Biblioteca Nazionale Centrale, Florence:
BNCF Magl. VII, 1199: Aristotelis Stagiritae Poetica cum notis Petro Victorio.
BNCF Magl. IX, 124: Accademia degli Alterati. Imprese, Motti e Nome degli Accademici.
BNCF Magl. IX, 125: Varia.
BNCF Postillati 15: *Annotationi di Alessandro Piccolomini nel libro de la Poetica d'Aristotele, con la traductione del medesimo libro, in lingua volgare* (Venice: Giovanni Guarisco, 1575), with annotations by Filippo Sassetti.
Archivio di Stato, Florence:
ASF Notarile Moderno 9323.

Primary printed sources

Manni, Domenico Maria. *Memorie della famosa Accademia fiorentina degli Alterati*. Florence: G.-B. Stecchi, 1748.
Piccolomini, Alessandro. *Annotationi nel libro del Poetica d'Aristotile con la traduttione del medesimo libro*, in lingua *volgare*. Venise: Giovanni Guarisco, 1575.
Salvini, Salvino. *Fasti consolari dell'Accademia Fiorentina*. Florence: Gio. Gaetano Tartini and Santi Franchi, 1717.
Sassetti, Filippo. *Lettere da vari paesi, 1570–1588*. Edited by Vanni Bramanti. Milan: Longanesi & C°, 1970.
[Strozzi, Giovan Battista]. *Aristotelis Poetica Petro Victorio Interprete*. Florence: Giunti, 1617. BNCF Magl. 5.9.119 appears to be the only surviving copy of this book, which was printed for private use.
Vettori, Pietro. *Petri Victorii Commentarii in primum librum Aristotelis de Arte poetarum [...]*. Florence: Sons of Bernardo Giunti, 1560; reprinted in1573.

Secondary sources

Blocker, Déborah. *Instituer un « art »: politiques du théâtre dans la France du premier XVIIe siècle*. Paris: Honoré Champion, 2009.
Boeckh, August. *On Interpretation & Criticism*. Translated and edited by John Paul Pritchard. Norman: University of Oklahoma Press, 1968.
Cochrane, Eric. *Florence in the Forgotten Centuries, 1527–1800*. Chicago: The University of Chicago Press, 1973.
De Caro, Gaspare. *Euridice. Momenti dell'umanesimo civile fiorentino*. Bologna: Ut Orpheus, 2006.
Guasti, Cesare. *Le Carte Strozziane del R. Archivio di Stato: Inventario, serie prima*, 2 vols. Florence: Tipographia Galileiana, 1884–1891.
Güthenke, Constanze. '"Enthusiasm Dwells Only in Specialization": Classical Philology and Disciplinarity in Nineteenth Century Germany'. In *World Philology*, edited by Sheldon Pollock, Benjamin A. Ellman and Ku-ming Kevin Change, ch. 12, 264–84. Cambridge, MA: Harvard University Press, 2015.
Hess, Jonathan M. *Reconstituting the Body Politic: Enlightenment, Public Culture and the Invention of Aesthetic Autonomy*. Detroit: Wayne State University Press, 1999.
Palisca, Claude, 'The Alterati of Florence, Pioneers in the Theory of Dramatic Music (1968)'. In Claude Palisca, *Studies in the History of Italian Music and Music Theory*, 408–43. Oxford: Clarendon Press, 1994.
Plaisance, Michel, *L'Accademia e il suo Principe: cultura e politica a Firenze al tempo di Cosimo I e di Francesco de' Medici. L'Académie et le Prince: Culture et politique à Florence au temps de Côme Ier et de François de Médicis*. Manziana: Vecchiarelli, 2004.
Ribard, Dinah and Nicolas Schapira, 'L'Histoire par le livre, XVIe-XXe siècle'. *Revue de Synthèse* 128, no. 1–2, 6th series (2007): 19–25.
Siekiera, Anna, 'Il volgare nell'Accademia degli Alterati'. In *Italia linguistica: discorsi di scritto e di parlato, nuovi studi di linguistica italiana per Giovanni Nencioni*, edited by Marco Bifi, Omar Calabrese and Luciana Salibra, 87–112. Siena: Protagon, 2005.
Smith, Pamela H., Amy R. W. Meyers and Harold J. Cook. *Ways of Making and Knowing: The Material Culture of Empirical Knowledge*. Ann Arbor: University of Michigan Press, 2014.
Shrivastava, Ravindra Nath. *Literary Criticism in Theory and Practice*. New Delhi: Atlantic Publishers and Distributors, 2004.
Ulrike Schneider, 'Vom Wissen um *gratia*. Strategien der Diskursivierung elusiven Wissens in der Frühen Neuzeit'. In *Gratia. Mediale und diskursive Konzeptualisierungen ästhetischer Erfahrung in der Vormoderne*, edited by Anne Eusterschulte and Ulrike Schneider, 89–105. Wiesbaden: Harrassowitz, 2018.
van Veen, Henk, 'The Accademia degli Alterati and Civic Virtue'. In *The Reach of the Republic of Letters: Literary and Learned Societies in Late Medieval and Early Modern Europe*, edited by Arian van Dixhoorn and Susie Speakman Sutch, 2 vols., t. 2, 285–308. London and Boston: Brill, 2008.
Weinberg, Bernard. 'The *Accademia degli Alterati* and Literary Taste from 1570 to 1600'. *Italica* 31, no. 4 (1954): 207–14.
Weinberg, Bernard. 'Argomenti di discussione letteraria nell'Accademia degli Alterati (1570-1600)'. *Giornale Storico della Letteratura Italiana* 131 (1954): 175–94.
Weinberg, Bernard. *History of Literary Criticism in the Italian Renaissance*, 2 vols. Chicago: Chicago University Press, 1961.

6

Quarrelling over Dante

Revisiting Weinberg on the first phase of the quarrel and on Sperone Speroni's second *Discorso sopra Dante**

Simon Gilson

The two lengthy chapters that Bernard Weinberg dedicated to 'The Quarrel over Dante' in Part 2 of his *A History of Literary Criticism in the Italian Renaissance* (2:819–76; 2:876–911) remain the fundamental contribution to the debates animating criticism of Dante and his poem in the final third of the sixteenth century. Many things are remarkable about these chapters of which I will signal two.

The first thing to note is the deep historical perspective offered by Weinberg in assembling a rich array of sixteenth-century Italian judgements and discussions about Dante. This depth of view is an outgrowth of the painstaking scholarly work he undertook, both in libraries and in archives, scouring multiple print editions and numerous manuscripts. Weinberg's own annotated bibliography to *A History* (2:1113–58) is testament to such work, and so is his later three-volume set of Latin and vernacular editions of some fifty-nine sixteenth-century texts on poetics and rhetoric. Building upon such work, Weinberg demonstrates throughout both chapters an admirable power of historical synthesis in providing a chronologically ordered and reasoned account of the quarrel. Though he does recognize an earlier phase of controversy *c*. 1525–72, Weinberg identifies the quarrel proper as beginning with Ridolfo Castravilla's polemical manuscript tract, *Il discorso contro Dante* (1572), which, in utilizing categories drawn from Aristotle's *Poetics*, attempted to deny any poetic status to Dante's *Commedia*. In his first chapter, he works through the writings of some twenty different authors, and discusses several anonymous manuscripts and other brief

---

* A version of this essay was presented to the Oxford Dante Society on 6 November 2019, and I am grateful for the many helpful comments and questions raised by colleagues on that occasion. I am also grateful to Alessio Cotugno for his advice and encouragement at early stages of the research, and to both Alessio and David Lines for their comments on an earlier draft. See *Trattati di poetica e retorica nel Cinquecento*, ed. Bernard Weinberg, 3 vols. (Bari: Laterza, 1970–74); for a balanced critical estimate of these editions, see Conor Fahy's review in *Modern Language Review* 72, no. 4 (1977): 968.

mentions of Dante. He proceeds in strict chronological order, beginning with Pietro Bembo's strictures against Dante (1525) and discussing several authors in the opening phase up to 1572. After assessing Castravilla's treatise, Weinberg then considers the first print defence of Dante mounted by the Cesenese Jacopo Mazzoni and moves onto discussions in the Florentine Accademia degli Alterati. He subsequently passes from Vincenzo Borghini's interventions in Florence to further attacks on Dante by the Sienese academician and polemicist Bellisario Bulgarini, before assessing both the later defences and attacks by figures based in Florence, Bologna and Padua such as Orazio Capponi, Girolamo Zoppio, Alessandro Cariero and Sperone Speroni. Weinberg's second chapter picks up the account with Mazzoni's later and monumental print, *Della difesa di Dante* of 1587, and then assesses the contributions of at least another fifteen figures, again in strict chronological sequence up to 1600. This chapter also includes some analysis of references made to the Dante quarrel in other literary controversies, helpfully illustrating the interwoven nature of such polemics in the period.

The second – and perhaps still more significant – thing to signal about Weinberg's treatment of the Dante quarrel is the directness with which he stakes out his own methodological positions. He formulates most explicitly his approach at the opening of the first essay, noting that his concern lies *not* with the history of the quarrel – understood as the circumstances of the debates, personalities and related facts and dates influencing the documents – but rather with the history of critical ideas. Weinberg does not decry the value of historicist work on the debates and personalities, and he does incorporate a very small amount of such external material when necessary to his discussion. However, his commitment remains unflinching to a history of critical ideas and to their relation more broadly to the history of sixteenth-century critical theory.[1] These methodological principles undergird, of course, the very structure and organization of *A History*, and attest – as is also well known – to Weinberg's affiliations, personal, professional and theoretical, with the so-called Chicago School of Neo-Aristotelianism.[2]

In spite of its seminal and pioneering character, its depth of perspective and its formidable qualities of synthesis and analysis, *A History* presents various limitations, both methodological and contextual. Several major gaps to what one might call Weinberg's non-historicist mode of writing literary history have begun to be filled in recent work on the Dante quarrel. In the last twenty years in particular, a body of work has offered a more richly contextualized and documented sense of the areas in

---

[1] Bernard Weinberg, *A History of Literary Criticism in the Italian Renaissance* (Chicago: University of Chicago Press, 1961), 2:819: 'I wish to write, rather than a history of the literary quarrels, the history of critical ideas involved in them … . I wish … to seek an answer to this central question: To what extent is the history of the ideas in each quarrel related to the history of critical theory in general?'.

[2] The most important work (in effect a manifesto of their programme) is R. S. Crane, *Critics and Criticism: Ancients and Moderns* (Chicago, IL: University of Chicago Press, 1952), reprinted with revised preface in 1957. Weinberg mentions Elder Olson at *A History* 2:352. A resonance with the driving concerns of the Chicago School is evident in Weinberg's interests in structures and literary wholes, in generalizing to the literary problem itself, in Aristotle and in his relative lack of interest in extrinsic matters. On the Chicago School, there is an extensive literature; for some preliminary orientation, see at least Vincent B. Leitch, *American Literary Criticism since the 1930s* (Abingdon: Routledge, 2010).

which Weinberg was least interested – the nature of the debates, their geographical and institutional settings, and the personalities involved. This work has treated Bulgarini and Mazzoni above all, although it has also encompassed figures such as the still enigmatic Castravilla, Borghini, Speroni and even some individuals not directly mentioned by Weinberg in relation to the Dante quarrel such as Torquato Tasso.[3] While this recent

---

[3] The following is only an indicative list of contributions made since Weinberg. For overviews, see Giuliana Angiolillo, *Tra 'l vero e lo 'ntelletto. Vecchi e nuovi studi su Dante* (Naples: Liguori, 1987), 9-30 and on Giovanni Degli Albizzi, see 31-57; Salvatore Battaglia, 'Processo a Dante nel Cinquecento', *Filologia & Letteratura* 13 (1967): 1-23; reprinted in his *Esemplarità e antagonismo nel pensiero di Dante*, 2 vols. (Naples: Liguori, 1967), 2:52-72; Aldo Vallone, *L'interpretazione di Dante nel Cinquecento. Studi e ricerche* (Florence: Olschki, 1969), 59-170. More recent overviews (though in monographs concerned primarily with other issues) include Davide Dalmas, *Dante e la crisi religiosa del Cinquecento italiano: da Trifon Gabriele a Lodovico Castelvetro* (Rome: Vecchiarelli, 2005), 150-1; Simon Gilson, *Reading Dante in Renaissance Italy: Florence, Venice and the 'Divine Poet'* (Cambridge: Cambridge University Press, 2018), 136-9. Though dated in parts there is still much value in the overview of the quarrel provided by Michel Barbi, *Dante nel Cinquecento* (Pisa: Nistri, 1890), 37-56 (a work which is cited by Weinberg). For a treatment that has a valuable focus on the earlier seventeenth century, see also Marco Arnaudo, *Dante barocco. L'influenza della 'Divina commedia' su letteratura e cultura del Seicento italiano* (Ravenna: Longo, 2013), 15-57: also on the seventeenth century (which is entirely neglected by Weinberg given his chronological limits), see Umberto Cosmo, 'Le polemiche letterarie, la Crusca e Dante sullo scorcio del Cinque e durante il Seicento', in his *Con Dante attraverso il Seicento* (Bari: Laterza, 1946), 1-91. For informed recent work on Castravilla and/or reactions to him, see at least Paolo Procaccioli, 'Castelvetro vs Dante: uno scenario per il Castravilla', in *Lodovico Castelvetro. Letterati e grammatici nella crisi religiosa del Cinquecento*, ed. Massimo Firpo and Guido Mongini (Florence: Olschki, 2008), 207-49; Erminia Ardissino, 'Appunti di critica dantesca: la risposta di Vincenzio Borghini al *Discorso* del Castravilla', *Giornale storico della letteratura italiana* 180 (2003): 56-85. On Jacopo Mazzoni, see at least Saverio Bellini, 'Iacopo Mazzoni, Galileo e le bugie dei poeti', in *Studi di letteratura italiana per Vitilio Masiello*, ed. Pasquale Guaragnella and Marco Santagata (Bari: Laterza, 2006), 695-719; Davide Dalmas, s.v., 'Mazzoni, Jacopo', in *Dizionario Biografico degli Italiani* (Rome: Istituto della Enciclopedia Italiana, 2009), 72:709-14; Claudio Gigante, *Esperienze di filologia cinquecentesca. Salviati, Mazzoni, Trissino, Costo, il Bargeo, Tasso* (Rome: Salerno, 2003), 9-45; Claudio Scarpati, *Dire la verità al principe. Ricerche sulla letteratura del Rinascimento* (Milan: Vita e Pensiero, 1987), 231-69. On the theory of the imagination in Mazzoni's Dante criticism (as well as the essays by Scarpati noted above), see now Guido Giglioni, 'The Matter of Imagination: The Renaissance Debate over Icastic and Fantastic Imagination', *Camenae* 8 (2010): 1-21, esp. at 5-10; Claudio Moreschini, 'Idolo, fantasia e poesia da Ficino a Mazzoni', *Bruniana & Campanelliana* 22, no. 1 (2016): 47-60. A critical edition of the first two books of Mazzoni's work is also now available; see *Della Difesa della Commedia di Dante: libro primo*, ed. Claudio Moreschini and Luigia Businarolo (Cesena: Società di Studi Romagnoli, 2017); and *Della Difesa della Commedia di Dante: libro secondo*, ed. Sara Petri, Claudio Moreschini and Luigia Businarolo (Cesena: Società di Studi Romagnoli, 2018). For Bulgarini (author of seven printed works on the quarrel, 1583-1616), useful documentation, including related manuscript notes and correspondence is available in Daniele Danese, *Cento anni di libri: La biblioteca di Bellisario Bulgarini e della sua famiglia, 1560-1660* (Pisa: Pacini, 2014), esp. 16-17, 37-43, 665-6, 771, 1018; Margherita Quaglino, 'Gli scritti danteschi di Bellisario Bulgarini: Vicende redazionali e cronologia', *Rivista di Studi Danteschi* 10, no. 2 (2010): 275-317; eadem, '"Pur anco questa lingua viva, e verzica", Bellisario Bulgarini e la questione della lingua a Siena tra la fine del Cinquecento e l'inizio del Seicento* (Florence: Accademia della Crusca, 2011), esp. 80-2, 89-91, 126-34, 166-8, 176-80. For Tasso's annotations on Mazzoni's *Difesa* (Biblioteca Ginori Conti 0213), see Guido Baldassarri, 'Notizie di postillati tassiani. 1. Varia', *Studi Tassiani* 47 (1999): 117-28 and the edition of these annotations and further commentary in Emilio Russo, 'Il rifiuto della sofistica nelle postille tassiane a Jacopo Mazzoni', *La Cultura. Rivista trimestrale di filosofia letteratura e storia* 38, no. 2 (2000): 279-318. On Speroni, see Stefano Jossa, 'La verità della *Commedia*: I *Discorsi sopra Dante* di Sperone Speroni', *Rivista di Studi Danteschi* 1, no. 2 (2001): 221-41. For the role of the Dante debate and illustrations, see Michael Brunner, *Die Illustrierung von Dantes 'Divina Commedia' in der Zeit der Dante-Debatte (1570-1600)* (München: Deutscher Kunstverlag, 1999).

work has tended to focus on individual personalities, a number of lively contributions have also begun to show how the quarrel was concerned with more than estimates of Dante, and involved major philosophical and critical issues of the period, from the theory of the imagination to a probing of the very nature and purposes of fiction.[4]

Rather than attempting to synthesize this work, I believe it may be more productive instead to highlight two overarching tendencies in Weinberg's treatment of the quarrel. In doing so, my purpose is not to be unsympathetic to his essays: it is rather to help us to understand better his own contribution and its limits, and to provide us with a framing context for this chapter. Perhaps the most significant and explicit tendency is the way Weinberg's critical stance leads him to pivot his discussions, with a markedly teleological inflection, upon Aristotle's *Poetics*. For Weinberg, the ways that this text was assimilated from the 1540s onwards represented what he calls the 'signal event' in the history of sixteenth-century literary theory.[5] As a result, the *Poetics* comes to be taken, implicitly and explicitly, as both the ultimate catalyst for, and the principal yardstick against which to measure, literary criticism in the Cinquecento. Allied to the pivotal, almost causal, position that Weinberg assigns to the *Poetics* is a further tendency. This concerns the way in which he understates, demotes or even elides the legacy of a variety of cultural phenomena that continued to have considerable bearing on the critical enterprise such as the continuing impact of fifteenth-century humanism, other forms of criticism (such as the tradition of Dante commentary), the place and status of rhetoric and poetics, and the *questione della lingua*.

Beginning with some earlier reviewers, critics have, of course, long recognized these issues in Weinberg's account.[6] One of the more important revisionist critiques has come from Daniel Javitch, who has highlighted how, with regard to genre theory, a range of other literary and cultural needs, driven by poets and writers themselves, helped to promote genre-specific approaches from the mid-Cinquecento onwards.[7] In other words, Javitch shows that Aristotle's *Poetics* was neither the sole nor the primary driver of interest in genre theory. Another example comes from Martha Feldman's work on the Italian madrigal in the Venetian environment. Feldman has illustrated the centrality of rhetorical concerns, even after the middle of the Cinquecento, in critical, literary and musical contexts. In this regard, she has noted how Weinberg's account notably downplays such preoccupations.[8] A still more recent and related strand of

---

[4] See the contributions by Giglioni, Jossa and Moreschini mentioned in the previous note.
[5] Weinberg, *History*, 1:349.
[6] An especially valuable early review is that by Cecil Grayson in *Romance Philology* 17, no. 2 (1963): 490–6. Several minor points in Weinberg's account require updating and/or correction; for example, it is most unlikely that Girolamo Benivieni is the author of the defence of Dante found in the Marucelliana manuscript (A. 137; mentioned at 821), and a matter of dispute whether Vincenzo Borghini penned the two works (*Difesa di Dante come cattolico*; *Introduzione al poema di Dante per l'allegoria*) mentioned at 849–51.
[7] See Daniel Javitch, 'The Emergence of Poetic Genre-Theory in the Sixteenth Century', *Modern Language Quarterly* 59, no. 2 (1998): 139–69. In his work on Ariosto's reception, Javitch also notes how Weinberg's presentation of the Tasso–Ariosto quarrel may lead to an underestimation of the continued status of Ariosto; see Daniel Javitch, *Proclaiming a Classic: The Canonization of Orlando Furioso* (Princeton, NJ: Princeton University Press, 1991), 5.
[8] Martha Feldman, *City Culture and the Madrigal* (Berkeley, Los Angeles and Oxford: University of California Press, 1995), 145 and 154.

work, based in part in reception studies, has focused on the complex nature of the recovery of the *Poetics*. This work has begun to show how, in the first decades of the Cinquecento, a range of other texts on poetics, grammar and rhetoric helped to prepare the ground for the later assimilation of the *Poetics*.[9]

In what follows, and in the light of these framing comments, we will now reflect upon some issues raised by the Dante quarrel as presented by Weinberg. We will do this in a circumscribed way in two main sections, by offering supplementary notes to several of the texts presented by Weinberg. First, we will re-examine three authors included by Weinberg in what he calls the 'opening phases of the quarrel', reading them with a stronger emphasis on their intricate dialogue with one another and on questions related to geographical and institutional setting and ideological framework.[10] In the following section, we will then offer a case study of one text in the quarrel itself – Sperone Speroni's second *Discorso sopra Dante* – whose value, I believe, Weinberg notably underestimated, in large part because of the character of his own theoretical and methodological assumptions.

The first phase of the quarrel: Bembo's *Prose*, Tomitano's *Ragionamenti* and Lenzoni's *Difesa*

As we have noted, Weinberg recognizes – and judiciously so – an earlier phase to quarrelling over Dante, one which he traces back to Pietro Bembo's own judgements on Dante in the *Prose della volgar lingua* (1525). In little more than half a page, he signals the major passage in which Bembo criticizes Dante (Book 2, Chapter 5) for the *Commedia*'s mixed and uneven linguistic and stylistic choices, and its miscellaneous assemblage of learning. The passage is the one in which Bembo famously compares Dante's poem to a beautiful and spacious field of wheat blighted by tares and weeds. Weinberg does not mention the comparison, but instead quotes and comments upon the passages that precede it. He argues that the Venetian humanist's discussion here incorporates classical notions of the three styles, and observes how Bembo regards the presence of philosophy in the *Commedia* as problematic. Both points are judicious. Revealingly, however, Weinberg prefaces his discussion with a comment about Bembo having written 'at a time when linguistic considerations were more urgent than literary ones' (2:820).

Inevitably, such a brief account cannot do justice to the complex and nuanced judgements on Dante elaborated in the *Prose* (which is, I would argue, as much concerned with literary and stylistic matters as it is with linguistic ones), nor to the influence of Bembo on later discussions regarding Dante's status as a model. Weinberg notes en passant threads of continuing Bembian influence, both in the earlier and later

---

[9] See Kristine Louise Haugen, 'The Birth of Tragedy in the Cinquecento: Humanism and Literary History', *Journal for the History of Ideas* 72, no. 3 (2011): 351–70; Rolf Lohse, 'The Early Reception of Aristotelian *Poetics*', *Horizonte* N.S. 2 (2016): 38–58, available online at http://horizonte-zeitschrift.de/de/aktuelle-ausgabe/ (accessed 10 September 2018).

[10] Weinberg, *History*, 2:873.

phases of the quarrel. However, he provides no real discussion nor documentation of the extensive and multifaceted reception of Bembo's overall critical judgements on Dante, especially before the 1572 quarrel proper. In fact, Bembo's discussions of Dante's style and his linguistic decorum – including his choice of low vocabulary, his tendency to linguistic mixing, his use of similes and his handling of grammar – helped to drive dialogue over Dante's value, and remained a key feature in later discussions. In this way, Bembo acted as a kind of *fil rouge* across the first half of the century and in later discussions, including those concerned with the quarrel proper. The positions adopted on Bembo, in fact, range from passionate support for Bembo's 'giuditioni' ('critical judgements') to vehement opposition, with many other forms of accommodation, nuance and even satire registered between these poles. Many of the later figures mentioned by Weinberg, including Niccolò Liburnio, Giovan Battista Gelli, Pierfrancesco Giambullari, Carlo Lenzoni, Bernardino Daniello, Lodovico Castelvetro, Vincenzo Borghini, Sperone Speroni and Benedetto Varchi, are intricately involved in opposing, restating or re-accommodating Bembo's judgements on Dante. Bembo is, in short, a constant point of reference in discussion of Dante from the late 1520s onwards, often in pronounced dialogical form, and often by means of extended comparisons between Dante and Petrarch.[11]

A text that receives even briefer notice from Weinberg, though one intimately connected to Bembo's judgement on Dante, is Bernardino Tomitano's *Ragionamenti*. Weinberg mentions only the 1545 print (there is also an expanded 1546 print version) and restricts himself to Tomitano's criticism of Dante's indiscriminate use of language and philosophy, as it is voiced in the *Ragionamenti* by the main character, Sperone Speroni. A major figure at the University of Padua, Tomitano taught logic (1539–63), and lectured extensively on Aristotle. At the same time, he had strong interests in the vernacular, and was both a close disciple of Bembo and Speroni, and an important figure in one of the most influential early Italian Academies, the Paduan Accademia degli Infiammati (1540–5).[12] Members of this Academy included Speroni, as well as Varchi and Alessandro Piccolomini – all three of whom had major roles in structuring its objects and methods of study. The Academy was especially notable for its programme of vernacular learning and its cultivation of philosophical interests in

[11] For documentation, see Gilson, *Reading Dante*, ad. ind. but esp. 26–34, 36, 38–41, 145, 235n, 322n.
[12] On the Infiammati, see at least Francesco Bruni, 'Sperone Speroni e l'Accademia degli Infiammati', *Filologia & Letteratura* 13 (1967): 24–71; Florindo Cerreta, 'An Account of the Early Life of the Accademia degli Infiammati in the Letters of Alessandro Piccolomini', *Romanic Review* 48 (1957): 249–64; Antonio Daniele, 'Sperone Speroni, Bernardino Tomitano e l'Accademia degli Infiammati di Padova', *Filologia veneta* 2 (1989): 1–55; Richard S. Samuels, 'Benedetto Varchi, the "Accademia degli Infiammati," and the Origins of the Italian Academic Movement', *Renaissance Quarterly* 29, no. 4 (1976): 599–633; Valerio Vianello, *Il letterato, l'Accademia, il libro: contributi sulla cultura veneta del Cinquecento* (Padua: Antenore, 1988). See now Annalisa Andreoni, *La 'via della dottrina'. Le lezioni accademiche di Benedetto Varchi* (Pisa: Edizioni ETS, 2012), 43–63; Salvatore Lo Re, *Politica e cultura nella Firenze cosimiana. Studi su Benedetto Varchi* (Rome: Vecchiarelli, 2008), 192–252; Franco Tomasi, 'Le letture di poesia e il petrarchismo nell'*Accademia degli Infiammati*', in *Il Petrarchismo. Un modello di poesia per l'Europa*, ed. Loredana Chines, Floriana Calitti and Roberto Gigliucci, 2 vols. (Rome: Bulzoni, 2007), 1:229–50. See also Jean-Louis Fournel, *Les dialogues de Sperone Speroni. Liberté de la parole et règles de l'écriture* (Marburg: Hitzeroth, 1990). Most recently, Roberta Giubilini, 'Reassessing the Role of the *Accademia degli Infiammati* in the Evolution of Early Modern Logic', *Bruniana & Campanelliana* 21, no. 1 (2015): 219–24.

the vernacular. Weinberg naturally recognizes, in Part 1 of his *History*, that this was the Academy in which some of the earliest and most powerful theoretical interest in the *Poetics* arose. And yet, his later discussion of Tomitano in the Dante quarrel makes no mention of the Academy, even though the *Ragionamenti* is set there, and Speroni is chosen as speaker at the very moment when he became its *principe* and reformed its programme of study. The brief account Weinberg offers of the *Ragionamenti* also means that he cannot give the treatise its due as one of the first treatises on oratory in prose, nor consider its extensive use of Cicero and Aristotle, and the ways in which it mediates Speroni's critique of Latin humanism and his promotion of vernacular learning.[13] There is also no mention in *A History* of the fact that Tomitano revised his own work in a further print dialogue of 1570, which not only offered an enriched extended discussion of vernacular oratory but also, and more significantly for our purposes, excised the very passages in which the character Speroni had previously criticized Dante, a point to which we shall return.[14]

The text to which Weinberg pays most attention (2:823-26) in the early phase of the quarrel is Carlo Lenzoni's *Difesa di Dante*, a remarkable and hybrid work, composed by both Lenzoni and after his death by Pierfrancesco Giambullari. Weinberg is judicious in selecting and discussing this text; and several other recent critics have recognized the *Difesa* as a major contribution to discussions about Dante's value in the first half of the Cinquecento.[15] Weinberg's own focus lies primarily with Aristotelian precepts, and with Lenzoni's and Giambullari's precocious and important use of the *Poetics* in

[13] On Speroni there has been significant revitalized interest in recent years, see at least Alessio Cotugno, 'Dalla traduzione alla'imitazione. Sperone Speroni fra Erasmo, Bembo e Pomponazzi', *Lingua e stile* 2 (2017): 199–239 and now idem, *La scienza della parola: Retorica e linguistica di Sperone Speroni* (Bologna: Il Mulino, 2018); Teodoro Kantinis, *Sperone Speroni and the Debate over Sophistry in the Italian Renaissance* (Leiden: Brill, 2017); Simona Oberto, 'What Happens to Aristotle in Practice? Sperone Speroni's *Canace* before the Background of the Accademia degli Infiammati and Elevati', *Horizonte* N.S. 2 (2016), available online at http://horizonte-zeitschrift. de/de/aktuelle-ausgabe (accessed 10 September 2018); Elena Panciera, *l'officina di Speroni. Trasmissione del sapere e vita contemplativa*, unpublished doctoral thesis, Université Paris 8, (2012), available online at http://octaviana.fr/document/181110210 (accessed 19 September 2018); eadem, 'Alle radici dell'Accademia degli Infiammati di Padova: i Discorsi del modo di studiare di Sperone Speroni', *Cahiers du Celece* 6 (2013), available online at http://cahierscelec.ish-lyon.cnrs.fr/nod e/64 (accessed 19 September 2018); Jean-Louis Fournel, 'Le travail de la critique dans les écrits sur Virgile de Sperone Speroni', in *Les commentaires et la naissance de la critique littéraire. France/Italie (XIVe–XVe siècles)*, ed. Gisèle Mathieu-Castellani and Michel Plaisance (Paris: Aux Amateurs de Livres, 1990), 235–43. The monographs by Fournel and Vianello remain seminal, as do the essays by Bruni, 'Sperone Speroni' and Daniele, 'Sperone Speroni'.
[14] On Tomitano, see the biographical and bibliographical details in Maria Rosa Davi, *Bernardino Tomitano, Filosofo, medico e letterato (1515-1576). Profilo biografico e critico* (Trieste: Lint, 1995). The most important work is by Maria Teresa Girardi, see her *Il sapere e le lettere in Bernardino Tomitano* (Rome: Vita e Pensiero, 1995), esp. 39, 46–52; eadem, 'Il ruolo delle *humanae letterae* nella riflessione di Bernardino Tomitano', *Philosohical Readings* 8, no. 2 (2016): 79–82. See also Francesco Bruni, '*Fiorentinità e Florentinitas*: Una scheda per il lessico intellettuale cinquecentesco', *Lingua e stile* 39 (2004): 48–55.
[15] Judith Bryce, *Cosimo Bartoli (1503-72): The Career of a Florentine Polymath* (Geneva: Droz, 1983), 212–27; Margaret Daly Davis, 'Carlo Lenzoni's *In difesa della lingua fiorentina e Dante* and the Literary and Artistic World of the Florentine Academy', in *Cosimo Bartoli (1503-1572). Atti del Convegno internazionale, Mantova 18-19 novembre, Firenze, 20 novembre 2001*, ed. Francesco Paolo Fiore and Daniela Lamberini (Florence: Olschki, 2011), 261–82; Valentina Martino, 'La *Difesa della lingua fiorentina e di Dante, con le regole da far bella et numerosa la prosa* di Carlo Lenzoni', *Giornale storico della letteratura italiana* 189 (2012): 23–69. See now Gilson, *Reading Dante*, 132–6.

defining the genre of Dante's poem. Weinberg does mention some of the linguistic concerns in the dialogue, but he pays less attention to these matters than is justified by their place in the overall defence. What also remains absent in Weinberg is any sense of the dialectical and regional nature of the response, the polemical charge and seriousness with which the views of Bembo and Tomitano are rebutted, and the sheer range of arguments and *auctoritates* used to buttress the defence of Dante. Notable, too, is the way his defence takes place not only at the level of style but also at that of content; indeed, the linguistic and stylistic features of Dante's poem are defended with equal vigour and charge to the defence of his interest in all fields of knowledge. In other words, the dialogue between the Florentine positions staked out in the text and Paduan ones is revealing of the intense and creative exchanges between the two centres. Bembo remains an explicit target of the *Difesa*'s polemic, too. It seems, moreover, highly likely that it was further discussions between these groupings, and Lenzoni/Giambullari's critique of Tomitano's positions, which led to modifications on the overall view of Dante expressed in the 1570 print.

Sperone Speroni and his second *Discorso sopra Dante*

Weinberg mentions the Paduan polymath and academician Sperone Speroni (1500-88) at several points in *A History*, and pays most attention to his tragedy the *Canace* and his own defences of it. As regards Speroni's interventions in the Dante quarrel, Weinberg notes that he composed two late works – both remained in manuscript – written in defence of Dante, and suggests a dating of c. 1585.[16] Concentrating on the second defence, Weinberg writes that Speroni's contribution was 'retrograde and old-fashioned' (2:868) and that it did 'not enter the current of discussion, remaining unpublished until the eighteenth century'. Weinberg recognizes some critical merit to Speroni's work, in particular its treatment of the question of unity. However, he concludes that 'it had, indeed, little to offer to that current, since most of its commonplaces were completely familiar' (2:869).

Almost all these points and judgements are either inaccurate or problematic. The aim of what follows is not a minute rebuttal of these points as such; rather, the intention is to study Speroni's second defence of Dante in more depth, both on its own terms and in relation to the quarrel. In so doing, we suggest how very different judgements to Weinberg's might be made. Indeed, we will argue that Speroni's work is a major, if neglected, critical contribution, one combining a deep knowledge of Dante's poem and considerable critical acumen in its approach to reading and interpreting the *Commedia*. At the risk of belabouring the point, the case study helps to reveal how Weinberg's tendency to privilege Aristotle's *Poetics* and to devalue linguistic

See also Mario Pozzi, *Discussioni linguistiche del Cinquecento* (Turin: UTET, 1988), 339–44 for an introduction and his partial modern edition with useful notes is found at 347–429.

[16] The first defence (see following note) is a close reading of the first two cantos of *Inferno*: there is no real mention of the quarrel as such within this work, though there is an extended close reading of the cantos in relation to the journey, Dante's predicament and own vices, and the role of Mary, Lucia and Beatrice.

and stylistic modes of criticism can lead to or reinforce neglect of works that might have considerable interest, not only to students of the quarrel but also perhaps for contemporary readers and critics of Dante.

Let us begin with some errors of fact, namely, the question of circulation and the supposed lack of influence on the quarrel. It is true that the two works of defence, which both bear signs of being incomplete, were only printed in 1740.[17] However, Speroni's 'discourses' did have some circulation, as is demonstrated by the fact that Jacopo Mazzoni refers to his 'bellisima apologia' in his 1587 print *Difesa*.[18] Still more notable is the fact that Belissario Bulgarini, one of the key protagonists in the quarrel, wrote an entire treatise, the *Antidiscorso* of 1616, targeting this very work. The way Weinberg restricts the quarrel to the rigid confines of the sixteenth century means that the *Antidiscorso* finds no place in his account. In this polemical tract, Bulgarini vehemently opposed Speroni's arguments in the second defence, quoting many of its sections at length in order to reassert his own positions against Dante. Bulgarini even questioned, as the full title of the work shows, its Speronian paternity. We also know that he possessed a manuscript copy of Speroni's defence, which he heavily annotated; further work, both on the print and this manuscript, as well as Speroni's autograph manuscripts housed the Biblioteca Capitolare of Padua, may assist a better assessment of the textual state of the *Discorsi sopra Dante*.[19] Among the texts examined in Weinberg's *A History*, Alessandro Cariero's *Apologia* of 1583 also draws heavily upon Speroni's views in his second *Discorso*, or at the very least on earlier or contemporary

[17] The works were first printed by Laste and Forcellini in 1740; see 'Sopra Dante discorso primo' and 'Sopra Dante discorso secondo', in *Opere di M. Sperone Sperone degli Alvarotti*, ed. Natale dalle Laste and Marco Forcellini (Venice: Domenico Occhi, 1740), 5:497–504, 5:504–19; a later edition is *Apologia di Dante scritta intorno al 1575 dal Padovano Sperone Speroni* (Padua: Libreria Sacchetto Editrice, 1865). Quotations in the text and notes are from the dalle Laste and Forcellini print. The dating is certainly after 1583, the year of print publication of Bulgarini's *Considerazioni* but the text may well be an immediate response to that work, given that in the 1583 print *Apologia* by Alessandro Cariero (with dedicatory letter of 30 November; see notes 21–2), we find close use of Speroni's ideas. Mariella Magliani lists the *Apologia* (the 'discorso secondo') among Speroni's *Opere a stampa*; see *Sperone Speroni* (Padua: Editoriale Programma, 1989), 307, and there is a record of autograph copies in Bellinati's 'Catalogo dei manoscritti', in *Sperone Speroni*, 323–58, at 347 (referring to Biblioteca capitolare di Padova, XII/1, fols. 8–16 and fols. 18–32). See also Giulia Grata, 'Sperone Speroni', in *Autografi dei letterati italiani. Il Cinquecento* II (Rome: Salerno, 2013), 327–43. Further information can be found in Silvio Bernardinello, *Catologo dei codici della Biblioteca capitolare di Padova* (Padua: Istituto per la Storia Ecclesiastica Padovana, 2007). On the second *Discorso*, see the important study by Jossa, 'La verità', and the comments in Daniele, 'Sperone Speroni'. Daniele (pp. 20–1) notes adroitly that 'la critica speroniana a Dante dà rilievo a punti sostanziali di invenzione narrativa e di lingua, non convenzionali e nuovi nella tradizione esegetica del Cinquecento' ('Speroni's critical writing on Dante pays attention to important points regarding the poet's narrative and linguistic inventiveness in new and unconventional ways when compared with the sixteenth-century exegetical tradition', 21).

[18] Jacopo Mazzoni, *Della difesa della Comedia distinta in sette libri nella quale si risponde alle oppositioni fatte al discorso di m. Jacopo Mazzoni e si tratta pienamente dell'arte poetica…parte prima* (Cesena: Raverij, 1587), 728 (with reference to Dante's Virgilian imitation). Other undeclared dependencies on Speroni in Mazzoni may well be worth investigating further.

[19] See Bulgarini, *Antidiscorso. Ragioni di Bellisario Bulgarini Sanese, L'Aperto Accademico Intronato, in Risposta al primo Discorso sopra Dante scritta a penna, sotto finto nome di M. Speron Speroni* (Siena: Bonetti, 1616); for the death of Speroni 7; for its being a likely forgery, full or partial, fashioned by Alessandro Cariero; see 11–12, 63. On Bulgarini's earlier manuscript annotations to Speroni's *Apologia*, see Biblioteca comunale di Siena, ms. H.VII.19, signalled in Girardi, *Il sapere*, n. 194, 133.

oral discussions. In particular, Cariero records explicitly, in his *Apologia*, Speroni's views on Dante's intention to celebrate Beatrice in accordance with the promise made at the end of the *Vita nova*, and signals his disagreement with Lenzoni on this point. Cariero provides the same quotation from the *Vita nova* that Speroni makes in the second *Discorso*, and he copies its account of how Dante's prosimetrum influenced other writers.[20] Cariero also makes several further references that are indebted to Speroni when he defends Dante, including comments on the poet's Virgilian imitation, on the rhetorical power of Francesca da Rimini's tale, and on the excellence of his comparisons and language.[21] In all these ways, then, Speroni is a more notable figure in the quarrel (and not just in the Paduan milieu) than Weinberg's account might at first lead us to believe.

Speroni's decision to write in defence of Dante in the early 1580s might appear surprising given that, as we saw earlier, Tomitano, in the *Ragionamenti*, expressed negative views on Dante through the voice of Speroni's character. Some scholars have argued that Speroni's views developed over time, and became more positive to Dante.[22] There are, after all, some derogatory comments regarding Dante's use of language in Speroni's early *Dialogo delle lingue* (1535).[23] However, we must recall that the criticisms are voiced within the dialogue by the character of Pietro Bembo. Moreover, the available evidence, both external and internal, suggests that Speroni held passionately sympathetic views of Dante, most probably throughout his career. We find, for example, praise of Speroni as a stout defender of Dante in Lenzoni's *Difesa* (1556). As Maria Teresa Girardi has argued, Speroni's own pro-Dantean views most probably influenced Tomitano's revision of the passages on Dante in the later version of his own vernacular dialogue on oratory.[24] In a similar vein, a suggestive comment by Varchi also relates Speroni's profound admiration for Dante in the period covering the late 1530s and very early 1540s.[25] As for evidence provided by other Speronian works,

---

[20] See Alessandro Cariero, *Apologia di Mons. Alessandro Cariero padovano contra le imputazioni del Sig. B. Bulgarini sanese. Palinodia del medesimo Cariero nella quale si dimostra l'eccellenza del poema di Dante* (Padua: Paolo Meietti, 1583), fols. 11r–12v.

[21] Other references to Speroni in Cariero are: *Apologia* fol. 15r (on journey motif as providing unity); fol. 17v (on Dante's comparisons); fols. 18r-20v (on imitation and surpassing of Virgil); fols. 23r-24r (on Francesca da Rimini's tale), fols. 30v-31r and 32v (on Dante's language and comparison with Lucretius). The debts are more extensive than often appreciated.

[22] See e.g. Amelia Fanto, *Sperone Speroni (1500-1588). Saggio sulla vita e sulle opera* (Padua: Fratelli Drucker, 1909), 51–2, 137–8.

[23] See Sperone Speroni, *Dialogo delle lingue*, ed. Antonio Sorella (Padua: Libreria dell'Università Editrice, 1999), 169: 'che la lingua di Dante sente bene, & spesso più del Lombardo, che del toschano; & ove è toschano; è piu tosto thoscano di contado, che di città' ('for Dante's language smacks of Lombard and often more of this vernacular than of Tuscan; and when it is Tuscan, his language is a Tuscan of the countryside not the city').

[24] See Girardi, *Il sapere*, 156–60 (and for the quotation from Lenzoni's *Difesa* see the following note).

[25] See Carlo Lenzoni, *In difesa della lingua fiorentina, et di Dante. Con le regole da far bella et numerosa la prosa* (Florence: Torrentino, 1556), 59: 'il dottissimo e eccellentissimo Padovano M. Sperone, il qual oltra le onoratissime qualità sue, per aver già a viso aperto difeso Dante contro colui che l'ha tanto morso, merta che tutti gli amatori dello onesto lo lodino grandemente, i toscani senza fine lo ringrazino, e sopra tutti gli altri gli restino obligatissimi i fiorentini' ('the most learned and excellent Paduan, Mr. Speroni, who, in addition to his most honourable qualities, and for having openly defended Dante against those who would so savage him, deserves that all lovers of honourable things praise him greatly, that Tuscans give him infinite thanks, and that Florentines remain most

Speroni's deploys the *De vulgari eloquentia* and expresses strong approval of Dante in his own defence and lessons (1550 and 1558) on the *Canace*. There are also diffuse echoes of Dantean language across his production that call for closer evaluation, but indicate nonetheless how thoroughly he was steeped in the poet's language.[26] One of Speroni's late letters (1581), moreover, indicates his ongoing interest in Dante, his tendency to pair Dante with Virgil and his continuing reflections upon Bembo's own negative judgements of the *Commedia*.[27] And there are several laudatory evaluations of Dante as poet in Speroni's own late *Dialogo della istoria* (*c.* 1585–7), some with parallels to the comments made in the second 'discorso' on Dante.[28]

Let us now outline the character and content of the second defence. As regards its structure, the opening section (5:504a–8b) take the form of a series of carefully articulated observations on Dante's aim in composing the *Commedia*, its novelty, its imitative concerns, its self-reflexive qualities, its title and the role of the guides. The following section then delivers a lavish eulogy of Dante by means of what Speroni calls 'laudi' ('praises'; 5:508b–10b). Here, he treats some aspects of Dante's life and political career, as well the genesis of the poem and its title, but he concentrates above all on questions of language, style and artistry. The remaining section of the defence turns more directly to a rebuttal of the charges, or 'biasimi', made in the quarrel by Bulgarini (5:510b–19b) and others. The final pages have a more note-like and disjointed quality with what seem like isolated comments and the assemblage of references to specific authorities (esp. 5:518b–19b).

Having clarified these main subdivisions, we can now turn to the main argumentative and interpretative strategies utilized in the work. Speroni makes clear at the outset that he desires to defend Dante from the calumnies of those who criticize the *Commedia* ('defender Dante dalle calunnie di chi biasima la sua Commedia' [5:504a]), but before he does so, he thinks it proper to explore the poem's aim ('intenzion': ibid). He asserts with heavy irony that had the Sienese academician considered

---

obliged to him above all others'). For Varchi, see *L'Hercolano*, ed. Antonio Sorella, 2 vols. (Pescara: Libreria dell'Università, 1995), 2:975: 'mi pare ricordarmi che M. Sperone, quando io era in Padova, fosse nella medesima sentenza ... egli non si poteva saziare di celebrarlo, e di ammirarlo' ('I recall when I was in Padua that Speroni had the same view ... and he would never have enough of celebrating and admiring Dante').

[26] See Sperone Speroni, *Canace e scritti in sua difesa*, ed. Christina Roaf (Bologna: Commissione per i testi di lingua, 1982), esp. 192, 195–6: 'nostro Dante, il quale con tanto studio e sì bella arte distingue i vizi e acremente fa castigarli dalla giustizia di Dio ... autorità di tanto uomo...il divino Alighieri' ('our Dante, who, with such study and such adorned artistry, differentiates the vices and makes divine justice castigate them harshly ... the authority of such a man ... the divine Alighieri') and 262–3, 265–6 on his use of the *De vulgari eloquentia*.

[27] Speroni's late letter (19 May 1581 to Felice Paciotto) suggests a supportive stance given the pairing with Virgil, see *Lettere Familiari*, ed. Maria Rosa Loi and Mario Pozzi, 2 vols. (Alessandria: Edizioni dell'Orso, 1993–94), 2:229 (letter CCLXXI): 'Vediamo un poco, se il nostro Dante, il qual fu sommo Virgiliano, come egli dice, è degno d'esser letto, come fu già altra volta; o se è nulla, siccome il Bembo soleva dirmi ...' ('Let's see then if our Dante, who was a supreme Virgilian, as he says, is worthy of being read as he once was; or if instead he amounts to nothing, as Bembo used to say to me').

[28] See Speroni, *Dialogo della Istoria*, in *Opere di M. Sperone Sperone degli Alvarotti*, ed. Natale dalle Laste and Marco Forcellini (Venice: Domenico Occhi, 1740), 2:269 (as model of imitation); and esp. 2:273–6.

its finality, he would have saved both himself and Speroni a great deal of effort. Bulgarini remains the principal target throughout the work, but, as the above overview has indicated, he does this in especially marked ways after the section dealing with 'laudi'. In the chain of arguments that deals with defending Dante against his detractors and their 'biasimi', Speroni provides several cross references to *particole* in Bulgarini's 1583 print *Considerazioni* (some of these references are even keyed to page numbers in this edition).[29] What is also notable in this section is the fact that the diatribe against Bulgarini, repeatedly called a 'bestia' ('beast'), is coloured by greater polemical stridency.[30]

Let us now examine the major argumentative and interpretative strategies developed in the work. According to Speroni, the ultimate aim of Dante's poem is to celebrate Beatrice in line with the promise made at the end of the *Vita nova*. Speroni openly draws upon Lenzoni's *Difesa di Dante* and its quotation of the celebrated passage at the end of the *Vita nova* where Dante relates his promise to say of Beatrice, in a future work, what has yet to be expressed about her.[31] Speroni reproduces verbatim the same passage found in Lenzoni and in Cariero (Cariero, as we have noted, is indebted to Speroni).[32] In spite of following Lenzoni when connecting the *Vita nova* and the *Commedia*, Speroni asserts that the account given in the *Difesa di Dante* did not go far enough; he, by contrast, stresses that praise of Beatrice is the principal aim of the poem.[33] Speroni also has notable things to say about the *Vita nova* itself, noting its mixture of prose and poetry, and – with real critical insight– highlighting how it had earlier influenced both Petrarch's *Rerum vulgarium fragmenta* and Bembo's *Asolani*.

---

[29] See Speroni, *Discorso*, 5:510b; 512a: 'seconda particella' = Bellisario Bulgarini, *Alcune considerazioni sopra 'l Discorso di M. Giacopo Mazzoni, fatto in difesa della Comedia di Dante* (Siena: Luca Bonetti, 1583), 18; 5:513a: 'terza particella' = Bulgarini, *Considerazioni*, 28; 5:514a: 'quinta particella'; 5:515a = 'carta 64 … carta 34' i.e. Bulgarini, *Considerazioni*, 64; 5:518: 'particola decima'. For Bulgarini as 'bestia' ('beast'), see 5:512b, 515a (four mentions in total).

[30] Simona Oberto has recently argued in a similar vein, stressing the use of Dante (including the *De vulgari eloquentia*) in the defence of the *Canace* and the intertextual elements. Similarly, Panciera, *L'officina di Speroni. Trasmissione del sapere e vita contemplativa*, 403 rightly draws attention to how Speroni's letter is more indicative of his own views.

[31] In Michele Barbi's edition this is chapter 42:1-2; in that by Guglielmo Gorni chapter 31:1-2. The place of this chapter in relation to the writing of the *Commedia* has been and remains a major locus of critical investigation in Dante Studies; see at least Albert Ascoli, *Dante and the Making of the Modern Author* (Cambridge: Cambridge University Press, 2010), 223–4; Zygmunt G. Barański, 'The "New Life" of the "Comedy": The *Commedia* and the *Vita Nuova*', *Dante Studies* 113 (1995): 1–29. In the fifteenth and sixteenth centuries, there was a relatively modest textual tradition of the *Vita nova* (the *princeps* is 1576 and is certainly used by Bulgarini in his *Antidiscorso*). On the textual tradition, see Claudio Ciociola, 'Dante', *Storia della letteratura italiana. X. La tradizione dei testi*, ed. Enrico Malato (Rome: Salerno, 2001), 144–56; Gianfranco Folena, 'La tradizione delle opere di Dante Alighieri', in *Atti del Congresso Internazionaledi Studi Danteschi (20–27 aprile 1965)*, 2 vols. (Florence: Sansoni, 1965–66), 1:1–78, pp. 14–17. On difficulties in finding copies in the Veneto in the mid-sixteenth century, and its use by Gelli and Buonanni, see Gilson, *Reading Dante*, pp. 178, 114, 139 respectively. Attention to parallelisms between the prosimetrum and the *Commedia*, with the exception of Lenzoni, Gelli and Buonanni, is relatively uncommon: Boccaccio is of course an earlier exception. We must await the romanticist rediscovery of the work for the parallels to be assessed afresh.

[32] Lenzoni, *Difesa di Dante*, 52; for Cariero, see note 22.

[33] For Lenzoni, *Difesa di Dante*, 52 'honorare la sua Beatrice' ('honouring Beatrice') is a second aim after providing utility to his readers.

In the sixteenth century, it is unusual to track the influence of the *Vita nova* on other literary works in this way. An important precedent, especially relevant to Speroni given his close connections with him, is provided by Trifone Gabriele. In his oral lessons on Dante *c.* 1525–7, for example, Trifone makes similar points about the influence of Dante's *Commedia* on Petrarch and Bembo, though not in relation to the *Vita nova*, which he does not quote.[34] Equally alert, and still more original, is Speroni's subsequent comment on how the *Vita nova* had formed part of a manuscript with other vernacular verse sent by Lorenzo de' Medici to Alfonso of Aragon. Of course, this manuscript is the lost codex prepared by Angelo Poliziano that we now know as the *Raccolta Aragonese*, and which contained the *Vita nova* in a form closely based on Boccaccio's own copies. Speroni offers this historical account of the treatise and its Dantean paternity in order that his antagonist, Bulgarini, referred to in disparaging tones as 'il Senese' ('the Sienese'; 5:504b), may not attempt to deny its authorship, as has been the case with the *De vulgari eloquentia* (ibid). This is the first of a series of ever more intemperate references to Bulgarini

Speroni goes on to consider Beatrice's role within the poem as its 'intenzione principale' ('principal aim'), and explains her intercessionary role in relation to the way Dante 'figures' himself in the narrative as 'vizioso ed abituato ne' vizii' (5:505a), that is, his construction ('figurare' is the term used by Speroni) of himself as a sinner habituated to the vices. He goes on to discuss Dante's moral and spiritual failings (there are here some overlaps with the first *Discorso*), with reference to the three beasts of *Inferno* 1 and the amorous adventures described by Boccaccio 'nella sua vita' ('in his life': ibid). Speroni also places a particular weight on references internal to the poem, providing a close reading of Dante's own catalogue of personal sins, first of all lust – mentioned in various episodes in the poem, including *Inferno* 16, *Purgatorio* 27, *Purgatorio* 30 – but also pride (*Purgatorio* 13), wrath (*Purgatorio* 16) and even potentially avarice (*Inferno* 6; 5:505a-b). Significantly, this account of Dante's failings is rooted in the concrete, literal sense of the poem, as is his explanation of the roles of Virgil and Beatrice as guides. This provides a background against which to address two charges made against Dante in the quarrel, beginning with Castravilla (who is not mentioned by name at this point), namely, the notion that the poem is no more than a dream and that Dante praises himself in a self-serving way:[35] 'Dalle cose dette si intende che la opra di Dante non fusse sogno … Si conchiude ancora delle cose dette, che Dante per lo suo andare allo 'inferno ed al Purgatorio non si loda, ma si biasima de' suoi peccati…' ('From what has been said, one can understand that Dante's work was not a dream. … One concludes from what has been said that Dante does not praise himself in his journey through Hell and Purgatory but actually castigates his own sins': 5:505b-506a).

---

[34] Trifone Gabriele, *Annotationi nel Dante fatte con M. Trifone Gabriele in Bassano*, ed. Lino Pertile (Bologna: Commissione per i testi di lingua, 1993), for *Par.* XXXIII, 1 *ad loc.* In the second *Discorso*, 5:501b Speroni refers to Trifone's conversations with him regarding the moral betterment provided by Horace's *Sermons*.
[35] On these two points, see Ridolfo Castravilla, *I discorsi di Ridolfo Castravilla contro Dante: e di Filippo Sassetti in Difesa di Dante*, ed. Mario Rossi (Città di Castello: Lapi, 1897), 21–2; Bulgarini, *Considerazioni*, 30–39, 113–14.

Speroni offers some limited allegorical reading of various kinds: the mountain in *Inferno* 1 represents moral virtues (5:505b) and is the same as Mount Purgatory (5:506a), the forest stands for his being caught up into vice (5:505b). However, careful exposition of the literal sense continues to dominate, as Speroni concentrates on Dante's moral and spiritual state in order to clarify further the role of his guides. His discussion of Virgil is alert to his limits within the narrative, and, at the same time, to the effect of Virgil's poetry upon Dante.[36] The Dante quarrel had raised doubts about the choice of Virgil as guide and about the poem's use of pagan literary authorities such as Virgil. Speroni implicitly responds to such charges within a broad consideration of Dante's narrative and imitative practices. Virgil is 'moralmente buono, cioè virtuoso' ('morally good, that is, virtuous'; 5:506b), yet he has specific jurisdictions, and does not promise to 'guidarlo più oltre, che alla cima del monte della virtù' ('guide him further than the summit of the Mount of virtue': ibid). If considered clearly, Speroni maintains, the role and place of the guides help to explain how the poem retains unity of action, and this, it is argued, is firmly anchored to the journey. Features such as the multiple invocations – again another area in which Dante had been criticized in the quarrel – do not detract in any way from the poem's unity. For Speroni, the classicizing invocations are but one indicator of Virgilian imitation. Dante, he goes on to tell us, blends tales taken from the ancients with sacred truths; the pilgrim's own *iter*, which is 'così novo' ('so new'; 5:507a), even when compared to those of Aeneas and Ulysses, is wonderous precisely because of its ability to make marvels verisimilar. Speroni further embroiders the initial parallelism between the journey of Aeneas and that of Dante, by noting various threads of Virgilian imitation in the *Commedia*. The catalogue he provides, while not entirely new, is extensive and judicious, ranging from Phlegyas, the Centaurs, the Harpies and Cacus to the two main divisions of Hell and the manner of Dante's exit from it, onto Virgilian echoes in the presentation of Cato and in the Valley of the Princes in the Antepurgatorio.[37] At the same time – and more significantly still – Speroni notes the vernacular poet's originality, and how he blends Virgil with other Greek authorities (e.g. for Pluto) and Roman poets (e.g. the Giants) and also stresses the role of ancient philosophical authorities, above all Aristotle. He also observes, again with considerable insight (this has become a *locus communis* in contemporary Dante Studies), how Dante outdoes Virgil: 'Finalmente quanto può imita Virgilio, e talora lo avanza' ('In the end, as much as he can, he imitates Virgil and on occasion surpasses him'; 5:507b).[38]

Within the opening section, Speroni also stresses Dante's own sense of the potential objections that readers might make against the poem and how he responded to these

---

[36] *Discorso secondo*, 5:506a: 'Esser guidato da Virgilio significa che poetando vuole scrivere' ('Being guided by Virgil means that he wanted to write poetry in imitation of him').
[37] Speroni, *Discorso secondo*, 5:507a. There may be hints of debts to Landino in some of these passages; see Cristoforo Landino, *Comento sopra la Comedia*, ed. Paolo Procaccioli, 4 vols. (Rome: Salerno, 2001), 3:1050, 1153 for the description of Cato and the imitation of the Elysean fields in the Valley of the Princes as based on Virgil.
[38] See also *Discorso primo*, 5:501b: 'costui leggendo Virgilio si mosse a voler descriver lo 'nferno, e Purgatorio, e Paradiso, imitando e superando Virgilio, perche meglio distinse ogni cosa di lui' ('Dante by reading Virgil was moved to want to describe Hell, Purgatory and Paradise, imitating and surpassing Virgil, because he distinguished better than him all things').

within the text. One example is the view that, instead of embarking upon a journey, Dante could have simply relied instead on the teachings of preachers, prophetic dreams and Holy Scripture (5:507b). Speroni uses passages internal to the poem to show how such objections are resolved for the reader. One consequence of such an approach (one not wholly distant from contemporary concerns with the poem's macrostructure and internal architecture) is that it stresses Dante's consciousness as an artist and his intimacy with his readership. As Speroni later comments, 'considero che non a caso, siccome si usa oggidì, ma consideratamente scrivesse; quando io trovo, che 'l principio dell'opra al mezzo e al fine per ogni loco risponde' ('I hold that he did not write in carefree manner as is the case today, but in a most considered way, for I find that the beginning of the work corresponds to its middle and end in every respect'; 5:508b). Another major issue raised by Speroni in this section, and one he will revisit, is the question of language and its inadequacy. This concern prompts him to deliver a paean to Dante's poetic prowess, as 'il primo che la innalzò' ('the first to ennoble the Italian language'; 5:507b). Approving mention is made of Dante's use of mixed language (Speroni cites *in bono* the 'libro della Volgare Eloquenzia' clearly accepting the Dantean paternity of the *De vulgari eloquentia*).[39] Speroni also tackles briefly the issue of the poem's title (5:508a), noting its accord with both Plato and Aristotle.

Rather than pursuing a minute rebuttal of his opponent's views at this stage, Speroni now offers a further closely argued section devoted to praise of Dante – the 'laudi'. Though almost entirely neglected by Weinberg, this is the most accomplished and significant section of the discourse. Speroni first notes Dante's background, his political views, above all his strong imperial leanings ('fu imperialissimo'; 'he was most imperial'),[40] and his vehement attacks on the Church's temporalism, as evoked both in the poem and 'in una opera latina chiamata Monarchia' ('in a Latin work called *Monarchia*'; 5:508a). This is itself an unusual reference at this time, given the condemnation of the work and its placement on the Index, and Bulgarini was alert to this fact in his later response.[41] Some mention is made of Dante's exile, but the reader is sent away to Boccaccio's life for further details (5:508b). Speroni returns instead to issues pertaining to what we might today call the macrostructure of Dante's text and the consistency of its internal system of references: the examples provided are the early allusion to 'Caina', which is resolved in *Inferno* 33, and the parallel treatment of the Guido and Bonconte da Montefeltro. Rather more traditional, at least initially, is the section in which Speroni lavishes praise on Dante's scientific, philosophical and theological learning (5:508b–9a). Nonetheless, Speroni soon expands and makes his own the celebration of Dante's powers of oratory by offering a very rich set of examples provided from all three *cantiche* (*Inf.* 19; *Par.* 6; *Purg.* 6; *Inf.* 5; *Purg.* 1; *Par.* 33; *Inf.* 33;

---

[39] Cf. Landino, *Comento*, 1:253: 'fu el primo che la lingua nostra patria insino a' suoi tempi roza inexercitata, et di copia et d'elegantia molto nobilitò, et fecela culta et ornata' ('Dante was the first who greatly ennobled with copiousness and elegance our home language and made it cultured and ornate: before him it had been rough and unpracticed').

[40] See Gabriele, *Annotationi, ad loc.* for *Inf.* 34.65.

[41] On the reception of *Monarchia*, see the bibliography and notes provided in Gilson, *Reading Dante*, 244–6. For Bulgarini, see *Antidiscorso*, 42: 'è stata meritatamente prohibita dalla Cattolica Romana Chiesa dal deversi leggere da' fedeli' ('it has been justifiably outlawed by the Catholic Church as a text not to be read by the faithful').

Inf. 12; *Purg.* 20). He stresses, too, the poet's capacity for variation in his descriptions (*Inf.* 1 and 20). As before, the discussion, then, remains deeply rooted in the poem, even if quarrel is not far away. One especially important passage in this respect is the discussion of how Dante handles his own character in the poem, a point to which he will return again:

> Poeta è sovranissimo nello imitare, imitando sempre o con le persone introdotte, le quali sempre fa parlare, o parlando egli stesso come poeta ed introduttore di esse persone: nelle quali parlando sempre imita, o con metafore, o con epiteti, o con comparazioni e similitudini da lui dette in tante maniere, che è una meraviglia, e dette in modi tali, che uom non si avvede che siano similitudini: il che è sommo artificio come è sommo ingegno e sapere il trovarle; perchè ciò è da uomo che molto sappia e delle scienzie e del mondo; del quale ello, come esperto d'ogni cosa moderna, e conoscitor delle storie antiche, parla benissimo: conoscitor de' costumi de' principi, delle cittadi, e delle nazioni: il che forse è cagione che [i] Senesi non ne dicano bene, per vendicarsi del male, che egli ne dice (5:509a).

> Dante is a poet who is supreme in the art of imitation, which he does either with characters that he always makes speak or speaking himself as poet as the one introducing his characters. It is a wonder how through the voices of his characters he imitates with metaphors, epithets, comparisons and similes; and he gives them voices in such ways that one is not aware of the similes. And this shows his supreme artifice as he displays supreme ingenuity and wisdom in their *inventio*. For this is a craft of someone who is steeped in sciences and the world, about which he, as an expert in all things modern and one who knows about ancient histories, speaks most fittingly. He knows too of the habits of princes and cities and nations. And this is perhaps the reason that Sienese speak ill of him so as to take revenge on him for the things he said about them.

The discussion now returns to features of Dante's Virgilian imitation that are rarely noted such as his *brevitas* and use of acrostics in *Purgatorio* 12 and 13 and *Paradiso* 19 (5:509b).[42] Once more, Speroni makes the point that Dante surpassed Virgil as a literary artist. His examples of Dante's superior stylistic and rhetorical abilities include the meetings with Pier delle Vigne and Ulysses, similes and actions that have recognizably Virgilian analogues, but are artistically superior in the *Commedia*, such as the treatment of Charon, the failed embrace and angelic 'messo'. Speroni praises Dante for the full range of his stylistic abilities, not only for his similes that are 'in stile alto e profondo' ('in a high and profound style') but also for those 'in stile basso' ('in a lowly style'; 5:510a). It is difficult not to think of implicit polemic with Bembo and others here who had targeted certain similes as demonstrating Dante's base interests and indelicate language. The theme of imitation prompts Speroni to return to the question of Dante as an object of imitation, both in prose (where both Giovanni Villani and

---

[42] Again, though not unprecedented (see Bernardino Danielo, *Annotationi, ad loc.* to *Purg.* 12:61-3), this kind of insight is rare in the earlier critical and commentary tradition.

Boccaccio are mentioned as imitators)[43] and in verse. Petrarch is, according to Speroni, the prime poetic imitator, and the discussion here takes on further polemical and anti-Bembist tones. For Speroni, Petrarch not only imitated Dante but also failed to imitate him correctly by making grammatical errors. At the close of the 'laudi' section, Speroni mentions some external authorities, in particular the praise of the poet that is conspicuous in Dante commentary. Speroni claims to have seen three or four that all praise him, but he mentions a Tuscan who claims to have seen over thirty (5:510b).

The discussion now shifts to 'biasimi', that is, the negative charges raised against Dante by his detractors. Of course, as noted, Bulgarini is the main target, but Speroni also mentions Castravilla, Capponi, Tomitano, Giovanni Della Casa and Bembo (5:510b). He prefaces his comments with a pertinent account of the local, patriotic dimensions of the dispute, stressing his own lack of parti pris: 'che Padovano essendo, e perciò non troppo in grazia di Dante, io per conscienza il difendo, non ostante che Dante dica male di Padova e di alcuni Padovani di sua età' ('though being Paduan and so amongst those whom Dante does not favour, I defend him out of conscience, even though Dante speaks ill of Padua and of some Paduans of his time'; 5:510b). Dante's concrete use of language is again his starting point. Speroni thus addresses a variety of objections made in the quarrel, noting how Dante's 'locuzioni' ('locutions') are most Tuscan, even if his lexis is not. Dante's mixed lexicon, a feature that had been such an issue for Bembo and many other writers in the period, is resolutely defended on the grounds that his own Florentine dialect was ill-suited to expressing 'così alti concetti' ('such lofty conceits'; 5:510b).[44] As a result, Dante needed to take words from Latin and from throughout Italy in a manner analogous to Homer.[45] The rich mixture of lexical items that inform Dante's style is, for Speroni, not to be explained away, but rather defended and praised as one of its defining characteristics. Similar factors help to explain the poet's highly metaphorical style ('Dante è il più metaforico poeta che mai scrivesse': 'Dante is the most metaphorical poet who ever wrote'; 5:511a), his use of neologisms and his openness to Gallicisms. In a further polemic with contemporary Petrarchists, Speroni offers lists of comparable words found in Petrarch in order to neutralize complaints about the presence of these offending lexical items in Dante. He is careful to provide a list of vocabulary that is found not only in the *Triumphi* but also 'ne sonetti e nelle canzone' ('in his sonnets and canzoni'; ibid). What is more, Speroni makes it clear that Dante's achievement is all the more notable given the tendency of his time to write primarily in Latin. Finally, Dante's mixed style is defended by means of supporting comments on linguistic admixture in classical works, including Cicero's *Paradoxes* and *Letters to Atticus*, and by the example of Lucretius.

---

[43] See also Speroni, *Dialogo della Istoria*, 2:272: 'da Dante il Boccaccio tolse la lingua delle novella' ('from Dante Boccaccio derived the language he uses in his tales').

[44] See also Speroni, *Dialogo della Istoria*, 2:269 for similar a similar point.

[45] Claudio Tolomei, *Il Cesano de la lingua Toscana*, cc. 7 and 9, ed. Ornella Castellani Pollidori (Florence: Accademia della Crusca, 1996), 39–40 and 55. Here, the Sienese Tolomei discusses *c*.1525 whether Dante's tendency to borrow from other Italian dialects, French and Spanish arises from linguistic poverty or the urge to adorn his poem in the way Homer did. For Dante as embracing all the languages of Italy as Homer did in Greece, see Pierio Valeriano, *Dialogo della volgar lingua*, in *Discussioni linguistiche del Cinquecento*, ed. Mario Pozzi (Turin: UTET, 1988), 74–5.

The remaining sections of the defence turn to a more focused rebuttal of specific charges in Bulgarini, first that Dante was impious in mixing Pagan and Christian elements (5:512a–b), then the notion that the poem is the narration of a dream (5:513a–14b), explicitly referring to *particole* 2 and 3 of the 1583 *Considerazioni*. Though concerned to overturn accusations, often with his own accumulations of learning and polemical outbursts, Speroni continues to concentrate, in illuminating ways, on the poem's narrative and mimetic properties. He praises, notably, Dante's own role as character 'in imitando se stesso in proprio nome … . È una imitazione molto più bella, che non è imitare, dipinger, medicare e conoscere altrui' ('in imitating himself in his own name … . And this is a much finer form of imitation than that which portrays, and makes known others'; 5:513b). The account begins to move through the arguments and authorities used by Bulgarini in *particola* 5 (5:514a) regarding the poem's purported lack of unity. Speroni strongly reaffirms such unity. From this section onwards, the discussion tackles specific topics and authorities mentioned by Bulgarini: the moral teaching to be found in Dante; his lack of patriotism; the view that the poem is a satire; and Giovanni Della Casa's judgement, in his *Galateo*, on the Dantean expression 'la lucerna del mondo' ('the lantern of the world'; *Par.* 1.38). Speroni stresses Dante's impartiality not only to his home city ('Che dica bene e male della sua patria, e' cosa certa'; 'It is clear that he says both good things and bad of his home city', 5:515b) and all others in Italy against which he raged but even to his guide, Virgil: 'e non [fu cortese] verso Virgilio, del quale potea dir per la sua salute quel che poi disse nel Paradiso di Rifeo Trojano' ('and he was not courteous towards Virgil, of whom he could have said with regard to his salvation that which he said in Paradise of Ripheus the Trojan'; ibid).

Linguistic and stylistic analysis of Dante's poem still forms a substantive part of the discussion, and Speroni returns yet again to questions of imitation, where he stresses and extends points he has made earlier regarding the relationship between Dante as poet and Dante-character. This is a distinction only hinted at by a few earlier commentators, but which is here given a clear and judicious formulation:[46]

> Solo dirò parlando della imitazione, che 'l poeta imita principalmente introducendo a parlare le persone, che nel poema intravengono e questa è imitazione principale, la quale usa Dante introducendo a parlare Virgilio, Stazio, Beatrice, e se stesso, dando ad ognuna di queste persone il suo proprio officio nel suo poema: onde Dante nel suo poema abbia due officii, l'uno di poeta ed imitatore, l'altro di persona ed imitato, dipintore e dipinto. (5:516b)

> All I will say is that, speaking of the art of imitation, the poet does this above all by introducing speaking characters that intervene in the poem: and this is the principal form of imitation that Dante uses when introducing the speaking characters Virgil, Statius and Beatrice and himself. In this way he gives to each of

---

[46] This is a distinction, of course, that has driven much work in twentieth-century Dante Studies; for orientation, see Giuseppe Ledda, 'Dante Alighieri, Dante Poet, Dante Character', in *A Cambridge Companion to the 'Commedia'*, ed. Zygmunt G. Barański and Simon Gilson (Cambridge: Cambridge University Press, 2019), 28–42. See also Piermario Vescovo, *Il tempo di Dante* (Rome: Salerno, 2018).

these characters their own office in the poem. And hence Dante in his poem has two offices, one as poet and imitator, and the other as character and as a person imitated, as the painter and as the one who is painted.

Speroni again discusses similes and other aspects of Dantean language; he also returns to Della Casa's discussion of the stinking oil evoked by the 'lucerna', and reverses the charge upon Bulgarini: 'come non si avvede che le sue riprensioni ci appuzzano con quello ontume...' ('how he does not see that his own criticisms stink us out with that filth'; 5:517b). His closing discussion concerns 'particola decima' on episodes, where once more he remains preoccupied not with arguing for or against Dante's conformity to Aristotle, but with close reading of the poem. Thus, he notes that the episode with Paolo and Francesca is 'bellissimo' ('most beautiful'),[47] as is the meeting with Farinata. In these concluding sections, the stress falls ever more prominently on Dante's absolute originality and the sui generis nature of his poem which is highlighted with a conscious echo of *Inferno* 4.102: 'Non è Dante poeta fatto dallo esempio, ma dalla sua propria ragione: e non pur è sesto, ma è primo fra tutti Greci e Latini' ('Dante is not a poet who follows the example of others but is one made of his own cloth: he is not the sixth but the first amongst the Greeks and the Latins'; 5:518a).[48]

As we have seen, then, Speroni's second *Discorso sopra Dante* addresses antagonists within the quarrel, above Bulgarini and to some degree Della Casa, and tackles several questions that had arisen through a renewed critical focus on Aristotle's *Poetics* – above all the question of the poem's unity and of the place of characters and episodes. He also treats issues related to the poet's alleged customs, licence, irreligiosity and lack of decorum. However, what makes Speroni's intervention most interesting and original is not the way he responds to specific charges made against Dante in the quarrel or engages with the terms of the ongoing debate. His originality as a critic, with all due respect to Weinberg, emerges from his ability to extract himself from the argumentative intricacies of the quarrel, and instead to look squarely at Dante's poem, rooting his considerations in its language, style and content, its speeches, its narrative strategies and its techniques of characterization. Speroni offers us a passionate yet carefully articulated vision of these qualities, and, by way of conclusion, we might signal again the following points of his account: the veracity and centrality of Beatrice; the unifying focus of the journey and of Dante-character within the narrative; the rich, polymorphic and unprecedented nature of Dante's language and style (including his comparisons,

---

[47] For related praise of Francesca's tale, see Speroni, *Canace e scritti in difesa*, 224–7; idem, *Dialogo della istoria*, 2:272.
[48] One notes again the connections with the *Dialogo della istoria*, 2:273: '... e sempre essendo Sovran poeta, fu sempre astrologo, sempre filosofo, sempre teologo cristiano ... fu il primo che poetasse altamente nel comun nostro romanzo, tessendo i versi in un novo modo la eccellenza della materia' ('and while always being a supreme poet, he remained an astrologer, was always a philosopher, and stayed a Christian theologian ... he was the first that wrote poetry in the high manner in our common romance language, weaving the excellence of his subject material in a new way in his verses'). See also *Discorso* 5:519: 'Rara cosa è tutto 'l poema di Dante, la disposizione dello inferno, l'invenzion del Purgatorio, l'andare in cielo' ('All of Dante's poem – the order of Hell, the invention of Purgatory, the journey through Paradise – is a rare thing'). These parallels may well merit closer study.

his mixed style, and his treatment of major episodes and dialogue); his imitation of Virgil and Petrarch's own imitation of Dante; and the poem's body of learning.

Bibliography

Andreoni, Annalisa. *La 'via della dottrina'. Le lezioni accademiche di Benedetto Varchi*. Pisa: Edizioni ETS, 2012.

Angiolillo, Giuliana. *Tra 'l vero e lo 'ntelletto. Vecchi e nuovi studi su Dante*. Naples: Liguori, 1987.

Ardissino, Erminia. 'Appunti di critica dantesca: la risposta di Vincenzio Borghini al *Discorso* del Castravilla'. *Giornale storico della letteratura italiana* 180 (2003): 56–85.

Arnaudo, Marco. *Dante barocco. L'influenza della 'Divina commedia' su letteratura e cultura del Seicento italiano*. Ravenna: Longo, 2013.

Baldassari, Guido. 'Notizie di postillati tassiani. 1. Varia'. *Studi Tassiani* 47 (1999): 117–28.

Barański, Zygmunt G. 'The "New Life" of the "Comedy": The *Commedia* and the *Vita Nuova*'. *Dante Studies* 113 (1995): 1–29.

Barbi, Michele. *Dante nel Cinquecento*. Pisa: Nistri, 1890.

Battaglia, Salvatore. 'Processo a Dante nel Cinquecento'. *Filologia & Letteratura* 13 (1967): 1–23. Reprinted in Salvatore Battaglia, *Esemplarità e antagonismo nel pensiero di Dante*, 2:52–72. 2 vols. Naples: Liguori, 1967.

Bellini, Saverio. 'Iacopo Mazzoni, Galileo e le bugie dei poeti'. In *Studi di letteratura italiana per Vitilio Masiello*, edited by Pasquale Guaragnella and Marco Santagata, 695–719. Bari: Laterza, 2006.

Bernardinello, Silvio. *Catologo dei codici della Biblioteca capitolare di Padova*. Padua: Istituto per la Storia Ecclesiastica Padovana, 2007.

Bruni, Francesco. '*Fiorentinità e Florentinitas*: Una scheda per il lessico intellettuale cinquecentesco'. *Lingua e stile* 39 (2004): 45–64.

Bruni, Francesco. 'Sperone Speroni e l'Accademia degli Infiammati'. *Filologia & Letteratura* 13 (1967): 24–71.

Brunner, Michael. *Die Illustrierung von Dantes 'Divina Commedia' in der Zeit der Dante-Debatte (1570–1600)*. München: Deutscher Kunstverlag, 1999.

Bryce, Judith. *Cosimo Bartoli (1503–72): The Career of a Florentine Polymath*. Geneva: Droz, 1983.

Bulgarini, Bellisario. *Alcune considerazioni sopra 'l Discorso di M. Giacopo Mazzoni, fatto in difesa della Comedia di Dante*. Siena: Luca Bonetti, 1583.

Bulgarini, Bellisario. *Antidiscorso. Ragioni di Bellisario Bulgarini Sanese, L'Aperto Accademico Intronato, in Risposta al primo Discorso sopra Dante scritta a penna, sotto finto nome di M. Speron Speroni*. Siena: Bonetti, 1616.

Cariero, Alessandro. *Apologia di Mons. Alessandro Cariero padovano contra le imputazioni del Sig. B. Bulgarini sanese. Palinodia del medesimo Cariero nella quale si dimostra l'eccellenza del poema di Dante*. Padua: Paolo Meietti, 1583.

Cariero, Alessandro. *Breve e ingenioso discorso contra l'opera di Dante*. Padua: Paolo Meietti, 1582.

Castravilla, Ridolfo. *I discorsi di Ridolfo Castravilla contro Dante: e di Filippo Sassetti in Difesa di Dante*. Edited by Mario Rossi. Città di Castello: Lapi, 1897.

Cerreta, Florindo. 'An Account of the Early Life of the Accademia degli Infiammati in the Letters of Alessandro Piccolomini'. *Romanic Review* 48 (1957): 249–64.

Ciociola, Claudio. 'Dante'. In *Storia della letteratura italiana. X. La tradizione dei testi*, edited by Enrico Malato, 137–99. Rome: Salerno, 2001.

Colombo, Michele, 'Bernardino Tomitano e *I Quattro libri della lingua italiana*'. In *Momenti del Petrarchismo Veneto. Cultura volgare e cultura classica tra Feltre e Belluno nei secoli XV-XVI. Atti del Convegno (Belluno-Feltre, 15–16 ottobre 2004)*, edited by Paolo Pellegrini, 111–33. Rome-Padua: Antenore, 2008.

Cosmo, Umberto. 'Le polemiche letterarie, la Crusca e Dante sullo scorcio del Cinque e durante il Seicento'. In Umberto Cosmo, *Con Dante attraverso il Seicento*, 1–91. Bari: Laterza, 1946.

Cotugno, Alessio. 'Dall'imitazione alla traduzione. Sperone Speroni fra Erasmo, Bembo e Pomponazzi'. *Lingua e stile* 2 (2017): 199–239.

Cotugno, Alessio. *La scienza della parola. Retorica e linguistica di Sperone Speroni*. Bologna: Il Mulino, 2018.

Crane, R. S. *Critics and Criticism: Ancients and Moderns*. Chicago, IL: University of Chicago Press, 1952.

Dalmas, Davide. *Dante e la crisi religiosa del Cinquecento italiano: da Trifon Gabriele a Lodovico Castelvetro*. Rome: Vecchiarelli, 2005.

Dalmas, Davide. 'Mazzoni, Jacopo'. In *Dizionario Biografico degli Italiani* 72:709–14. Rome: Istituto della Enciclopedia Italiana, 2009.

Danese, Daniele. *Cento anni di libri: La biblioteca di Bellisario Bulgarini e della sua famiglia, 1560–1660*. Pisa: Pacini, 2014.

Daniele, Antonio. 'Sperone Speroni, Bernardino Tomitano e l'Accademia degli Infiammati di Padova'. *Filologia veneta* 2 (1989): 1–55.

Davi, Maria Rosa. *Bernardino Tomitano, Filosofo, medico e letterato (1515–1576). Profilo biografico e critico*. Trieste: Lint, 1995.

Davis, Margaret Daly. 'Carlo Lenzoni's *In difesa della lingua fiorentina e Dante* and the Literary and Artistic World of the Florentine Academy'. In *Cosimo Bartoli (1503–1572). Atti del Convegno internazionale, Mantova 18–19 novembre, Firenze, 20 novembre 2001*, edited by Francesco Paolo Fiore and Daniela Lamberini, 261–82. Florence: Olschki, 2011.

Discussioni linguistiche del Cinquecento, edited by Mario Pozzi. Turin: UTET, 1988.

Fahy, Conor. Review of Bernard Weinberg, ed., *Trattati di poetica e retorica nel Cinquecento*, 3 vols. Bari: Laterza, 1970–74. In *Modern Language Review* 72, no. 4 (1977): 968.

Fano, Amelia. *Sperone Speroni (1500–1588). Saggio sulla vita e sulle opere*. Padua: Fratelli Drucker, 1909.

Feldman, Martha. *City Culture and the Madrigal*. Berkeley, Los Angeles and Oxford: University of California Press, 1995.

Folena, Gianfranco. 'La tradizione delle opere di Dante Alighieri'. In *Atti del Congresso Internazionale di Studi Danteschi*, 1:1–78, 2 vols. Florence: Sansoni, 1966.

Fournel, Jean-Louis, *Les dialogues de Sperone Speroni. Liberté de la parole et règles de l'écriture*. Marburg: Hitzeroth, 1990.

Fournel, Jean-Louis. 'Le travail de la critique dans les écrits sur Virgile de Sperone Speroni'. In *Les commentaires et la naissance de la critique littéraire. France/Italie (XIVe–XVe siècles)*, edited by Gisèle Mathieu-Castellani and Michel Plaisance, 235–42. Paris: Aux Amateurs de Livres, 1990.

Gabriele, Trifone. *Annotationi nel Dante fatte con M. Trifone Gabriele in Bassano*, edited by Lino Pertile. Bologna: Commissione per i testi di lingua, 1993.

Gigante, Claudio. *Esperienze di filologia cinquecentesca. Salviati, Mazzoni, Trissino, Costo, il Bargeo, Tasso*. Rome: Salerno, 2003.

Giglioni, Guido. 'The Matter of Imagination: The Renaissance Debate over Icastic and Fantastic Imagination'. *Camenae* 8 (2010): 1–21.

Gilson, Simon. *Reading Dante in Renaissance Italy: Florence, Venice and the 'Divine Poet'*. Cambridge: Cambridge University Press, 2018.

Girardi, Maria Teresa. 'Il ruolo delle *humanae letterae* nella riflessione di Bernardino Tomitano'. *Philosohical Readings* 8, no. 2 (2016): 79–82.

Girardi, Maria Teresa. *Il sapere e le lettere in Bernardino Tomitano*. Rome: Vita e Pensiero, 1995.

Giubilini, Roberta. 'The Place of Religion in the Academies of the Venetian Republic, 1540–1606'. Unpublished PhD dissertation, 2017. Warburg Institute, University of London.

Giubilini, Roberta. 'Reassessing the Role of the *Accademia degli Infiammati* in the Evolution of Early Modern Logic'. *Bruniana & Campanelliana* 21, no. 1 (2015): 219–24.

Grata, Giulia. 'Sopra Dante: postille di Sperone Speroni trascritte da Alessandro Tassoni'. *Rivista di Studi Danteschi* 16, no. 1 (2016): 61–104.

Grata, Giulia. 'Sperone Speroni'. In *Autografi dei letterati italiani. Il Cinquecento,* edited by Matteo Motolese, Paolo Procaccioli and Emilio Russo, 2:327–43. Rome: Salerno, 2013.

Grayson, Cecil. Review of Bernard Weinberg, *A History of Literary Criticism in the Italian Renaissance*, 2 vols. Chicago: University of Chicago Press, 1961. In *Romance Philology* 17, no. 2 (1963): 490–6.

Haugen, Kristine Louise. 'The Birth of Tragedy in the Cinquecento: Humanism and Literary History'. *Journal for the History of Ideas* 72, no. 3 (2011): 351–70.

Javitch, Daniel. 'The Emergence of Poetic Genre-Theory in the Sixteenth Century'. *Modern Language Quarterly* 59, no. 2 (1998): 139–69.

Javitch, Daniel. *Proclaiming a Classic: The Canonization of Orlando Furioso*. Princeton, NJ: Princeton University Press, 1991.

Jossa, Stefano. 'La verità della *Commedia*: I *Discorsi sopra Dante* di Sperone Speroni'. *Rivista di Studi Danteschi* 1, no. 2 (2001): 221–41.

Kantinis, Teodoro. *Sperone Speroni and the Debate over Sophistry in the Italian Renaissance*. Leiden: Brill, 2017.

Ledda, Giuseppe. 'Dante Alighieri, Dante-Poet, Dante-Character'. In *A Cambridge Companion to the 'Commedia'*, edited by Zygmunt G. Barański and Simon Gilson, 28–42. Cambridge: Cambridge University Press, 2019.

Leitch, Vincent B. *American Literary Criticism since the 1930s*. Abingdon: Routledge, 2010.

Lenzoni, Carlo and Pierfrancesco Giambullari. *In difesa della lingua fiorentina, et di Dante. Con le regole da far bella et numerosa la prosa*. Florence: Torrentino, 1556.

Lo Re, Salvatore. *Politica e cultura nella Firenze cosimiana. Studi su Benedetto Varchi*. Rome: Vecchiarelli, 2008.

Lohse, Rolf. 'The Early Reception of Aristotelian *Poetics*'. *Horizonte* N.S. 2 (2016): 38–58. Available online at http://horizonte-zeitschrift.de/de/aktuelle-ausgabe/ (accessed 10 September 2018).

Martino, Valentina. 'La *Difesa della lingua fiorentina e di Dante, con le regole da far bella et numerosa la prosa* di Carlo Lenzoni'. *Giornale storico della letteratura italiana* 189 (2012): 23–69.

Mazzoni, Jacopo. *Della difesa della Comedia distinta in sette libri nella quale si risponde alle oppositioni fatte al discorso di m. Jacopo Mazzoni e si tratta pienamente dell'arte poetica… parte prima*. Cesena: Raverij, 1587.

Mazzoni, Jacopo. *Della Difesa della Commedia di Dante: libro primo*, edited by Claudio Moreschini and Luigia Businarolo. Cesena: Società di Studi Romagnoli, 2017.

Mazzoni, Jacopo. *Della Difesa della Commedia di Dante: libro secondo*, edited by Sara Petri, Claudio Moreschini and Luigia Businarolo. Cesena: Società di Studi Romagnoli, 2018.

Moreschini, Claudio. 'Idolo, fantasia e poesia da Ficino a Mazzoni'. *Bruniana & Campanelliana* 22, no. 1 (2016): 47–60.

Oberto, Simona. 'What Happens to Aristotle in Practice? Sperone Speroni's *Canace* before the Background of the Accademia degli Infiammati and Elevati'. *Horizonte* N.S. 2 (2016). Available online at http://horizonte-zeitschrift.de/de/aktuelle-ausgabe/ (accessed 10 September 2018).

Panciera, Elena. 'Alle radici dell'Accademia degli Infiammati di Padova: i Discorsi del modo di studiare di Sperone Speroni'. *Cahiers du Celece* 6 (2013). Available online at http://cahierscelec.ish-lyon.cnrs.fr/node/64 (accessed 19 September 2018).

Panciera, Elena. *L'officina di Speroni. Trasmissione del sapere e vita contemplativa*, unpublished doctoral thesis, Université Paris 8, available online at http://octaviana.fr/document/181110210 (accessed 19 September 2018).

Procaccioli, Paolo. 'Castelvetro vs Dante: uno scenario per il Castravilla'. In *Lodovico Castelvetro. Letterati e grammatici nella crisi religiosa del Cinquecento*, edited by Massimo Firpo and Guido Mongini, 207–49. Florence: Olschki, 2008.

Quaglino, Margherita. 'Gli scritti danteschi di Bellisario Bulgarini: Vicende redazionali e cronologia'. *Rivista di Studi Danteschi* 10, no. 2 (2010): 275–317.

Quaglino, Margherita. *'Pur anco questa lingua viva, e verzica'. Bellisario Bulgarini e la questione della lingua a Siena tra la fine del Cinquecento e l'inizio del Seicento*. Florence: Accademia della Crusca, 2011.

Russo, Emilio. 'Il rifiuto della sofistica nelle postille tassiane a Jacopo Mazzoni'. *La Cultura. Rivista trimestrale di filosofia letteratura e storia* 38, no. 2 (2000): 279–318.

Samuels, Richard S. 'Benedetto Varchi, the "Accademia degli Infiammati," and the Origins of the Italian Academic Movement'. *Renaissance Quarterly* 29, no. 4 (1976): 599–633.

Scarpati, Claudio. *Dire la verità al principe. Ricerche sulla letteratura del Rinascimento*. Milan: Vita e Pensiero, 1987.

Sperone Speroni. Padua: Editoriale Programma, 1989.

Speroni, Sperone. *Apologia di Dante scritta intorno al 1575 dal Padovano Sperone Speroni*. Padua: Libreria Sacchetto Editrice, 1865.

Speroni, Sperone. *Canace e scritti in sua difesa*. Edited by Christina Roaf. Bologna: Commissione per i testi di lingua, 1982.

Speroni, Sperone. *Dialoghi*. Venice: Figliuoli di Aldo, 1542.

Speroni, Sperone. *Dialogo delle lingue. Edizione condotta sull'autografo*. Edited by Antonio Sorella. Pescara: Libreria dell'Università Editrice, 1999.

Speroni, Sperone. *Dialogo della Istoria*, In *Opere di M. Sperone Speroni degli Alvarotti*, 2:210–328. Edited by Natale dalle Laste and Marco Forcellini. Venice: Domenico Occhi, 1740.

Speroni, Sperone. *Lettere Familiari*. Edited by Maria Rosa Loi and Mario Pozzi. Alessandria: Edizioni dell'Orso, 1993–94.

Speroni, Sperone. 'Sopra Dante discorso primo' and 'Sopra Dante discorso secondo'. In *Opere di M. Sperone Speroni degli Alvarotti*, edited by Natale dalle Laste and Marco Forcellini, 5:497–504, 504–19. Venice: Domenico Occhi, 1740.

Tolomei, Claudio. *Il Cesano de la lingua Toscana*. Edited by Ornella Castellani Pollidori. Florence: Accademia della Crusca, 1996.

Tomasi, Franco. 'Le letture di poesia e il petrarchismo nell'*Accademia degli Infiammati*'. In *Il Petrarchismo. Un modello di poesia per l'Europa*, edited by Loredana Chines, Floriana Calitti and Roberto Gigliucci, 1:229–50, 2 vols. Rome: Bulzoni, 2007.

Tomitano, Bernardino. *Quattro libri della lingua Thoscana di M. Bernardino Tomitano ove si prova la philosophia esser necessaria al perfetto Oratore & Poeta con due libri nuovamente aggionti, dei precetti richiesti a lo scrivere, & parlar con eloquenza.* Padua: Marcantonio Olmo, 1570.

Tomitano, Bernardino. *Ragionamenti della lingua Toscana, dove si parla del perfetto Oratore, & poeta volgari, Dell'eccellente Medico & Philosopho Bernardin Tomitano, divisi in tre libri. ...* Venice: Giovanni de Frari & Fratelli, 1545.

Valeriano, Pierio, *Dialogo della volgar lingua*, in *Discussioni linguistiche del Cinquecento*. Edited by Mario Pozzi, 45–93. Turin: UTET, 1988.

Vallone, Aldo. *L'interpretazione di Dante nel Cinquecento. Studi e ricerche*. Florence: Olschki, 1969.

Varchi, Benedetto. *L'Hercolano*. Edited by Antonio Sorella, 2 vols. Pescara: Libreria dell'Università, 1995.

Vasoli, Cesare. 'Sperone Speroni: La filosofia e la lingua. L'"ombra" del Pomponazzi e un programma di "volgarizzamento" del sapere'. In *Il volgare come lingua di cultura dal Trecento al Cinquecento. Atti del Convegno internazionale (Mantova, 18-20 ottobre 2001)*, edited by Arturo Calzona et al., 339–59. Florence: Olschki, 2003.

Vescovo, Piermario. *Il tempo di Dante*. Rome: Salerno, 2018.

Vianello, Valerio. *Il letterato, l'Accademia, il libro: contributi sulla cultura veneta del Cinquecento*. Padua: Antenore, 1988.

Vincenzio Borghini. Filologia e invenzione nella Firenze di Cosimo I. Catalogo di mostra. Edited by Gino Belloni and Riccardo Drusi. Florence: Olschki, 2002.

Weinberg, Bernard. *A History of Literary Criticism in the Italian Renaissance*, 2 vols. Chicago: University of Chicago Press, 1961.

Weinberg, Bernard, ed. *Trattati di poetica e retorica nel Cinquecento*, 3 vols. Bari: Laterza, 1970–74.

7

Poetics in practice
How Orazio Lombardelli read his Homer

Sarah Van der Laan

How did Renaissance readers read the *Odyssey*? The question is harder to answer than it looks. The products of readings of Homer are everywhere: in treatises by philosophers and theologians and political thinkers, in literature and artwork of every genre, in emblem books and humanist compendia and in conduct manuals and operas.[1] But the readings of the *Odyssey* that underpin these varied uses of Homer's poem remain obscure. The field of sixteenth-century poetics seems a logical place to look; among the myriad translations of and commentaries on Aristotle's newly rediscovered *Poetics*, treatises on poetics, and polemics pitting Ludovico Ariosto's *Orlando furioso* against Torquato Tasso's *Gerusalemme liberata*, we might expect to find discussions of the *Odyssey* (Aristotle's paradigmatic epic) and its use by contemporary Italian poets. But the treatises that emerged from Italian academies and universities suggest at first glance that the *Odyssey*, like the other classical epics, was read for little more than its plot – if it was read at all. It appears in these texts primarily as an authoritative classical source for choices that in Cinquecento poetics were subject to heated debate: a single hero; the (more or less) successful integration of episodes into a (more or less) unified plot; and a mixture of noble and common characters. Brief, uncritical references to this handful of examples recur ad infinitum throughout the century, conveying not critical engagement with the Homeric text but the rote deployment of a few well-known commonplaces. And the more the *Odyssey* is used to defend romances as heroic

---

[1] The literature on Homer in the Renaissance is vast, and the following note represents only a sample of recent studies that attempt to trace Homeric reception across multiple authors; there is no room to acknowledge the many studies of individual creators or works. For the rich and subtle uses of Homer in Renaissance thought, see Marc Bizer, *Homer and the Politics of Authority in Renaissance France* (Oxford: Oxford University Press, 2011); Philip Ford, *De Troie à Ithaque: réception des épopées homériques à la Renaissance* (Geneva: Droz, 2007); Jessica Wolfe, *Homer and the Question of Strife from Erasmus to Hobbes* (Toronto: University of Toronto Press, 2015). For Homeric intertexts in Renaissance literature, see most recently Wolfe, and Tania Demetriou, '"Essentially Circe": Spenser, Homer, and the Homeric Tradition', *Translation and Literature* 15 (2006): 151–76. Luisa Capodieci and Philip Ford, eds, *Homère à la Renaissance: Mythe et transfigurations* (Paris: Somogy Éditions d'Art, 2011) gives a sampling of the contexts in which Homer was deployed across Renaissance literature, artwork and thought.

poems, the more unimpeachably epic it becomes. It is therefore neither a surprise nor a failing that the major studies of Renaissance poetics by Joel Spingarn and Bernard Weinberg do not seek to uncover Renaissance readings of the *Odyssey* or other classical texts.[2] The treatises themselves do not explicitly present such readings, and they give little indication that systematic – let alone interesting – readings lurk beneath their surfaces.

The newer disciplines of the histories of reading and of the book offer an alternative approach to Renaissance readings of the classics. Anthony Grafton's work on Guillaume Budé's copy of the Homeric poems reconstructs the sources of Budé's knowledge of Homer and explores the variety of interpretive practices Budé employed to arrive at readings he could subsequently use in his own treatises. Christiane Deloince-Louette's study of Jean de Sponde's commentary on Homer carefully extracts a comprehensive reading of the *Odyssey* from a series of disjunctive comments and reconstructs the intellectual, political and cultural contexts of that reading.[3] Yet the material to reconstruct individual readings of Homer – especially those of less prominent figures – remains sparse, fragmentary and elusive. And the histories of reading and the book remain separate from the history of poetics; how these readings may have shaped their authors' responses to modern poetry or poetic controversies remains mysterious.

Deep under London's Kings Cross, the vaults of the British Library hold a volume that enables us to combine the history of poetics with the history of reading: a copy of the *Odyssey* heavily annotated by the sixteenth-century Sienese academician and poetic theorist Orazio Lombardelli. Author of treatises on subjects ranging from the correct behaviour of married women to a 'defense of the correct use of the letter Z and against the abuse of the letter T', Lombardelli was also the author of the first printed judgement on Torquato Tasso's *Gerusalemme liberata*: a letter published as *Sopra il Goffredo del Signor Torqvato Tasso. Giudizio* (1582).[4] Almost immediately thereafter, furious debates arose over the merits of Tasso's epic, both in its own right and relative to the poem previously regarded as the greatest Italian heroic poem: Ludovico Ariosto's *Orlando furioso*. Within three years of the *Liberata*'s publication, these debates moved from

---

[2] Joel Elias Spingarn, *A History of Literary Criticism in the Renaissance* (New York: Columbia University Press, 1899); Bernard Weinberg, *A History of Literary Criticism in the Italian Renaissance*, 2 vols. (Chicago: University of Chicago Press, 1961).

[3] Anthony Grafton, 'How Guillaume Budé Read His Homer', in *Commerce with the Classics: Ancient Books and Renaissance Readers* (Ann Arbor: University of Michigan Press, 1997), 135–84; Christiane Deloince-Louette, *Sponde: Commentateur d'Homère* (Paris: Honoré Champion, 2001). The seminal work on Renaissance practices of reading the classics remains Lisa Jardine and Anthony Grafton, '"Studied for Action": How Gabriel Harvey Read His Livy', *Past and Present* 129 (1990): 30–78. More recently, Fred Schurink, '"Like a Hand in the Margine of a Booke:" William Blount's Marginalia and the Politics of Sidney's Arcadia', *Review of English Studies* 59 (2008): 1–24, provides a model of the analysis of marginalia to reconstruct a contemporary reading of a major Renaissance work, while the groundbreaking collaborative project *Archaeology of Reading in Early Modern Europe* (https://archaeologyofreading.org/) aims to create a systematic understanding of early modern reading practices through the digitization and analysis of a large corpus of early modern annotated texts.

[4] 'in difesa dell'buon vso del Zeta contr' all'abuso del T', Lombardelli, *Discorso*, A4v. For the primacy of Lombardelli's *Giudizio*, see Weinberg, *History*, 2:983. Weinberg offers an extensive survey of the debates over the *Liberata* and over Ariosto and Tasso, though focused on poetics rather than on the reconstruction of practices of reading either Renaissance or classical texts.

courts and academies to print, in the form of an increasingly bitter series of polemics in which defenders of each poem refuted the charges levelled against it, vindicated their chosen poem and hurled new charges against their opponents. (Tasso's own contributions to this debate included a further exchange of letters with Lombardelli, published along with his *Apologia* in 1585.) In 1586, Lombardelli returned to the fray with his *Discorso intorno a i contrasto che si fanno sopra la Gierusalemme liberata*, a treatise noteworthy both for the moderation it seeks to bring to an increasingly polemical debate and for the depth of analysis that Lombardelli applies to the *Liberata* and its classical predecessors. Lombardelli strives to establish the *Liberata* as the great Italian heroic poem on grounds that are at once Aristotelian, Horatian and indebted to classical epic – and perhaps above all to Homer.[5]

Lombardelli's *Odyssey* is thus interesting not only in its own right but also as a guide to the evolution of the understanding of classical epic that led him to defend the *Liberata* as a worthy successor to Homer and Virgil. For Lombardelli was a prolific note-taker who annotated his *Odyssey* with an impressive variety of marginalia: manicules, single and double underlinings, elaborate squiggly brackets and at least two strata of notes. From the copious traces of his readings, we can reconstruct the astonishing breadth of the concerns that one sixteenth-century reader brought to a reading of Homer's poem, and the insights he sought in it. From a comparison of those traces with his published discourses on Tasso's poem – among the more insightful and considered contributions to the debate on the *Liberata* – we can see how Lombardelli's reading of classical epic shaped his reading of its modern successor. And from this case study, fusing the histories of critical theory, literary criticism and the history of reading, we can develop new approaches to sixteenth-century poetics in theory and in practice.

The text

Lombardelli's choice of translation is itself illuminating, since it is very much an outlier among Renaissance editions of the *Odyssey*.[6] Although Homer first appeared in print in the 1474 edition of Lorenzo Valla's Latin translation of the *Iliad* (completed by Francesco Griffolini), the basic template for later editions was set by two Greek-language editions: the 1488 *editio princeps* of the Homeric corpus and the 1504 Aldine edition. In addition to a dedicatory epistle, paratexts included one or more of three ancient texts – the lives of Homer by pseudo-Plutarch and pseudo-Herodotus, and Dio Chrysostom's Oration 53 – and brief plot summaries of each book, often taken

---

[5] Orazio Lombardelli, *Discorso intorno a i contrasto che si fanno sopra la Gierusalemme liberata* (Ferrara: Vassalini, 1586). Lombardelli's moderation was not appreciated by Tasso, a prolific polemicist in his own defence; later in 1586 he published a *Risposta del S. Torq. Tasso, al Discorso del sig. Oratio Lombardelli intorno à i contrasti, che si fanno sopra la Gierusalemme liberata* (Ferrara: G. Vasalini, 1586), in which he rejects some of the grounds on which Lombardelli had defended the *Liberata*.

[6] The following paragraph draws on my examination of early editions of Homer and on Ford, *De Troie à Ithaque*.

over from the Byzantine tradition. Soon, Latin translations by Raffaele Maffei (1510, prose with a few hexameter passages), Francesco Griffolini (1510, prose) and Andrea Divo (1538, *ad verbum*) supplemented the materials of those more scholarly editions with simple paratexts adapted for the needs of readers less familiar with Homer or lacking Greek: printed marginal notes identifying speakers and addressees, similes, descriptions and plot points; indices of noteworthy events and character attributes. As the century wore on, Greek-language editions incorporated more ancient and Byzantine scholarship – the ancient scholia, the twelfth-century Byzantine archbishop Eustathius' great commentary, Porphyry's *Homeric Questions* or *On the Cave of the Nymphs* – and sometimes indices, while some bilingual editions joined Latin translations in including printed marginalia. Occasionally, an edition would include one of Melanchthon's short writings on the *Odyssey*. But the general goal appears to have been to present Homer in classical dress, with ancient and Byzantine historical and interpretive paratexts supplemented by modern 'finding aids'.

Lombardelli chose instead the one available verse translation of the *Odyssey*, replete with original modern paratexts. Translated into Latin hexameters by the Swiss humanist Simon Lemnius and published by the Basel printer Johannes Oporinus in 1549, Lemnius' *Odyssey* was presumably intended as a companion to the great neo-Latin poet Helius Eobanus Hessus's translation of the *Iliad*, first printed by the Basel-based printer Robert Winter in 1540 and reissued by Oporinus in 1549.[7] The printed marginalia of both poems are unusually wide-ranging. Marginal comments highlight plot points, similes and speaker/addressee identifications; gloss the moral and what we might even call the emotional content of the text; remind the reader of proverbs whose message agrees with the text's; refer the reader to other classical texts (from Virgil to Thucydides, Theophrastus to Pliny); and, in one notable instance, critique the infelicities of Maffei's earlier translation. Inverted double commas designate many passages as sententiae. And instead of the classical lives and essays on Homer, Oporinus offers three original prefatory poems. The cumulative effect is sharply different from any other edition on the market. The scholar or enthusiast with a command of Greek or a desire to know what the ancient world had said of Homer would have looked to a Greek or bilingual edition or to a literal translation. Lemnius' edition was designed for a reader with little or no Greek, interested in encountering Homer in modern dress and reading the *Odyssey* for pleasure as a literary work. The edition heralds the rise of a new movement in Homeric publication: the production of editions with Renaissance rather than ancient critical materials, situating the poem in modern intellectual and historical climates and using it to explore contemporary concerns.

The larger intellectual and political contexts of this edition become apparent from its three prefatory poems, which dedicate the translation to Henri II of

---

[7] Homer, *Odysseæ libri XXIIII*, ed. Simon Lemnius (Basel: Ioannis Oporini, 1549). The copy examined is BL C66.b.2; translations are my own. See Ford, *De Troie à Ithaque*, 34–5 for a brief discussion of Eobanus Hessus' *Iliad* and 126–8 for a brief discussion of Lemnius' *Odyssey*, including his speculation on the edition's role as companion to Eobanus Hessus' *Iliad*. For Lemnius' career, see Ford, *De Troie à Ithaque*, 126, and Clà Riatsch, 'Lemnius, Simon', *Dizionario storico della Svizzera* (22 February 2017): http://www.hls-dhs-dss.ch/textes/i/I9112.php.

France and address Jean-Jacques de Castion (the French ambassador to the Three Leagues, which would eventually become the Swiss canton of the Grisons) and Anne de Montmorency (Marshal of France and Constable of France). All three poems celebrate the virtues and accomplishments of their addressees in the terms of classical epic and history. In addition, the poem addressed to Montmorency presents a selection of familiar allegorizations of the *Odyssey*: Odysseus' adventures represent the triumph of virtue over the assaults of vice, while the moly that allows Odysseus to resist Circe's spells represents wisdom. The poems orient the edition towards a French and Swiss-French market, aligning it with the growing interest in France and in northern European humanist circles in using Homer to explore modern ethical and political problems.[8]

The choice of dedicatees also implies a declaration of religious allegiance. Although Lemnius studied under Melanchthon at Wittemburg, he remained a Catholic, and the choice of dedicatees suggests that the edition seeks a Catholic readership – a suggestion reinforced by the second edition. In 1581, twenty-two years after the death of Henri II and fourteen years after the death of Anne de Montmorency, Lemnius' translation was reprinted in Paris with the paratexts of the 1549 edition, including the original dedications.[9] The persistence of the dedications to the anti-Huguenot Henri II and the Catholic de Montmorency (who in the intervening years had joined with the duc de Guise and the Maréchal de Saint-André in the so-called Triumvirate at the head of the anti-Huguenot Catholic League) may have emphasized the edition's suitability for a Catholic readership. Perhaps the ownership of a classical text that declared its Catholic allegiance so strongly would have raised fewer questions in Lombardelli's (and Tasso's) post-Tridentine Italy. Certainly the extent and breadth of Lombardelli's annotations, which exceeds even that of the edition's printed marginalia, suggest a reader deeply invested in using the *Odyssey* to navigate the modern world.

The annotations

Lombardelli's *Odyssey* contains approximately 175 handwritten marginalia alongside the text of the *Odyssey*, in addition to five manicules and an extensive system of underlining and marginal brackets. These marginalia were made using various pens and inks. One stratum contains some thirty-five marginal notes, made in smaller lettering and darker ink, which consist exclusively of page numbers for cross reference within the volume and of references to works by other authors. In approximately eight of these notes – 'approximately' because it is not always clear where one note ends and another begins – a note in this lettering and ink has been supplemented by a note in larger lettering and lighter ink. The sequence of scripts suggests that this second group of marginalia, which are all in this second lettering and ink (or in a lettering and ink more closely akin to it than to the first) were made later. The marginalia, then,

---

[8] See e.g., Bizer, *Homer and the Politics of Authority*; Ford, *De Troie à Ithaque*; Wolfe, *Homer and the Question of Strife*.
[9] Confirmed by Ford, *De Troie à Ithaque*, 164.

may represent at least two if not more successive readings. However, there are enough common features in the script to ascribe both strata to a single author.

That that author was Lombardelli is clear from two ownership inscriptions, both in the larger and later of the two scripts. One, on a blank leaf at the end of the book, reads simply 'Horatii Lombardelli Senensis'.[10] The second occurs in a long footnote:

> Turpe recusare munera. sed, num deceat excipere foeminam, in dubio est; uel potius non dubium, decedere. Vide opusculum de officio mulieris nuptae; & Penelopes actum, abeuntis non actis gratijs, propende. opusculum illud scripsit Horatius Lombardellius, qui eum haec scholia.

> ('It is shameful to refuse gifts.' Yet it is doubtful if whether it befits a woman to accept gifts, or rather it is undoubtedly not appropriate. See the little work on the duties of a married woman; and note Penelope's action in departing without giving thanks. The little work was written by the same Orazio Lombardelli who is the author of these comments.)[11]

As Tania Demetriou notes, the 'opusculum' in question is Lombardelli's *Dell'uffizio della donna maritata*.[12] The note therefore provides a *terminus a quo* for this second stratum of Lombardelli's annotations – but it is difficult to date that terminus precisely. The generally accepted publication date of Lombardelli's treatise is 1583 (although the title page bears the date 1584); the published volume includes a prefatory letter from Lombardelli to his wife dated 6 October 1574 and a concluding letter to his uncle dated 14 June 1577. It is tempting to conclude that this marginal note was made after the treatise's publication in 1583, which would leave open the possibility that at least the second set of annotations were made in the hottest years of the quarrel over Ariosto and Tasso, immediately preceding the composition of Lombardelli's *Discorso*. But we can say with confidence only that the notes were made after 1574, and possibly after 1583.

Lombardelli's extensive underlinings and marginal symbols and notes make this the most comprehensively annotated copy of the *Odyssey* I have encountered in sixteen years of research, as well as one of the very few whose annotations can be attributed. What can these marginalia tell us about how Lombardelli read the *Odyssey*? And, when combined with his comments on the *Odyssey* in his discourses on Tasso, what can they tell us about how his reading of the *Odyssey* informed his reading of the *Liberata*?

---

[10] Although elsewhere I have silently modernized Lombardelli's orthography and punctuation and have expanded his abbreviations, here I note the expansion of abbreviations with italics.

[11] The direct address – 'See the little work' – raises the intriguing but unanswerable question of audience. Did Lombardelli anticipate a readership beyond himself for these notes? If so, did he imagine that the volume would circulate on its own, or that he would read it together with others, as Lisa Jardine and Anthony Grafton famously showed in 'Studied for Action' that Gabriel Harvey did?

[12] I quote the translation and refer to the discussion in Tania Demetriou, '*Periphrōn* Penelope and Her Early Modern Translations', in *The Culture of Translation in Early Modern England and France, 1500-1600*, ed. Tania Demetriou and Rowan Tomlinson (Houndmills: Palgrave Macmillan, 2015), 109n44.

How Lombardelli read the Odyssey

As one might expect from his choice of edition, Lombardelli's annotations reveal not only a deep interest in the *Odyssey* as a work of literature at the head of the long European tradition but also a profound interest in the *Odyssey*'s relevance to contemporary concerns, from religious and ethical problems to poetics and social customs. Prominent among these is an interest in the *Odyssey*'s consonance with Christian belief, reflected in notes that span Lombardelli's full range of annotating practices. Spread throughout the volume, five beautifully drawn manicules point to passages that reflect on aspects of divine justice present in both classical and Christian thought: divine omnipotence, divine rewards for good behaviour and punishment for evil-doing – the deserved fame and infamy that good and evil humans receive.[13] While the connection between these passages is readily apparent, other marginalia explicitly discuss the assimilation of classical to Christian theology. *Odyssey* 1–4 focus on the stark differences between righteous and impious humans, and on the divine justice that assists the former and stores up punishment for the latter; Lombardelli's annotations repeatedly translate these concerns into Christian terms. As Athena leaves Telemachus at the end of book 1, a suitor asks Telemachus about the strange visitor. Telemachus easily and prudently lies, and the narrator comments: 'So spoke Telemachus, but in his heart he knew the immortal goddess' (*Od*. 1.420). In a marginal comment, Lombardelli comments, 'Et nostri uix Domino credunt, iubenti, nolite cogitare, quod in illa hora, ductum satis, etc'. (And our countrymen scarcely believe in God, ordering, take no thought, for in that same hour, you will be guided sufficiently, etc.).[14] The final section of this note is a partial quotation of Mt. 10.19: 'Cum autem tradent vos, nolite cogitare quomodo, aut quid loquamini: dabitur enim vobis in illa hora, quid loquamini' (But when they deliver you up, take no thought how or what ye shall speak: for it shall be given you in that same hour what ye shall speak). For Lombardelli, a pagan epic's apparent conformity with a gospel narrative reinforces the truth of that gospel in the face of contemporary Christians' failure to understand its message; classical literature illustrates and illuminates Christian teaching for a Christian readership.[15]

Still other annotations find Lombardelli joining a three-way conversation with the text and with Lemnius' printed marginalia. In book 3, Athena reproaches Telemachus for his lack of belief in Odysseus' return, even should the gods wish it: 'Easily might a god who willed it bring a man safe home, even from afar' (*Od*. 3.321). The edition adds a printed marginal note: 'Deus undecunque iuuat, prouerb.' (God's help is everywhere) – a comment found, as many of both the printed and handwritten marginal proverbs are, in Erasmus' *Collectanea* or *Adagia* (in this case, *Adagia* 3.9.50). The proverb

---

[13] Lombardelli's interest in justice perhaps reflects the belief that Homer wrote to create just institutions, which Silvia D'Amico, 'Les *retrouvailles* d'Ulysse et Pénélope: lecture d'une scène homérique à la Renaissance', in *Homère à la Renaissance. Mythe et transfigurations*, ed. Luisa Capodieci and Philip Ford (Paris: Somogy Éditions d'Art, 2011), 193n18, traces to Heraclitus.
[14] Homer, *Odysseæ libri XXIIII*. The copy examined is BL C66.b.2; 25.
[15] For further examples of this tendency, see Wolfe, *Homer and the Question of Strife*, passim, and Sarah Van der Laan, 'Milton's Odyssean Ethics: Homeric Allusion and Arminian Thought in *Paradise Lost*', *Milton Studies* 49 (2008): 60–3.

itself, though compatible with Christian teaching, is not specifically or exclusively Christian. But Lombardelli then adds, 'Quid mirum, si et hoc sensit Euangelicus Centurio?' (What wonder if the evangelical centurion perceived this?)[16] The reference, to the story in Mt. 8.5–13 and Lk. 7.1–10 of a Roman centurion's faith in Jesus's ability to heal his servant even at a distance, again suggests that Lombardelli found in the *Odyssey* confirmation and amplification of Christian teachings. Such citations place him among the substantial group of readers, both Catholic and Protestant, who found the Homeric texts to be not only compatible with Christian faith but also a source of further insight.

Lombardelli's reactions to the *Odyssey*'s moral content extend beyond the assimilation of a classical text to Christian belief. He also finds illustrations of secular ethical precepts, filling the margins of *Od.* 15.65–89 – a passage whose comment that 'better is due measure in all things' Lemnius has already identified with printed quotation marks as a *sententia* – with four quotations on moderation from Terence, Horace and Ovid.[17] In addition to these abstract moral lessons, he draws attention to individual examples of virtuous or vicious behaviour, and extracts morals from them: 'Principibus turpe mentiri' (it is a shameful thing for a prince to lie), Lombardelli comments on Athena's assurance to Telemachus that Menelaos will not lie to him.[18] 'Casta pietas uxoris' (chaste wifely piety), he notes approvingly of Eumaios' description of Penelope's mourning for her husband – an interest in what the *Odyssey* might have to say about wifely conduct specifically that chimes with his later reference to his own treatise on married women's behaviour.[19] In Lombardelli's reading, the *Odyssey* teaches readers from many walks of life, in many situations, how to live.

Lombardelli's interest in proverbs is not limited to recasting them in Christian terms; he frequently uses them to explore the continued relevance of the *Odyssey*'s wisdom in secular terms. As Odysseus and Telemachus arm themselves to fight the suitors, Odysseus is dismayed to realize that the suitors too have a source of weapons; Telemachus takes the blame, admitting that in his haste to fetch their armour he left open the door of the storeroom where they had hidden the arms (*Od.* 22.154–9). Lombardelli comments, 'Præproperam festinationem grauissimi sæpe errores, grauissima sequuntur pericula: et nostra ferunt prouerbia, festinantem canem coecos parere catulos' (Very grave errors and very grave dangers often result from too hasty dispatch, and our proverbs relate, the hasty dog bears blind puppies).[20] Again the Latin proverb is found in Erasmus, as *Adagia* 2.2.35; Lombardelli follows the common humanist practice of transforming his reading into a commonplace.

Still other annotations reveal what might almost be called an anthropological curiosity about ancient Greek customs and their contemporary equivalents. Shipwrecked on the island of Scheria, Odysseus debates whether or not to perform the full ritual of supplication before the young princess Nausikaa; to do so would entail embracing her knees, and he is naked and covered in brine. Against Odysseus'

---

[16] Homer, *Odysseæ libri XXIIII*, 63.
[17] Ibid., 413.
[18] Ibid., 68, commenting on *Od.* 3.328.
[19] Ibid., 388, commenting on *Od.* 14.128–30.
[20] Ibid., 608.

hesitation, Lombardelli comments, 'Quod antiguitus aliena genua complecti, nunc nostra flectere est' (what in ancient times it was to grasp another's knees, now to bow is for us).[21]

This broad range of annotations – religious, moral, syncretic and anthropological – coexists with Lombardelli's extensive underlining of the allegories in the dedicatory poem to Anne de Montmorency. These traces of his reading, attuned to both classical allegory and contemporary ethics, complicate the assumption sometimes made that Catholic and Protestant readings of classical texts followed standard views of biblical hermeneutics, with Catholics more likely to accept or advance allegorical interpretations and Protestants interested primarily in ethics or rhetoric. Lombardelli's dual interests suggest that the lines were blurrier, and the overlap in hermeneutics greater, than we might think.[22] What Jessica Wolfe describes as 'a larger scholarly project of the northern Renaissance: to trace the philosophical and literary debts that early Christianity owed to Greek antiquity and to discern between those aspects of Greek antiquity that might be, or might not be, ethically or spiritually useful for Protestant culture', on Lombardelli's evidence, crossed confessional lines and the Alps, engaging Catholic readers even in a post-Tridentine era.[23]

Of even greater concern to Lombardelli, however, was the *Odyssey*'s utility for a literary culture founded on imitation and deeply invested in contemporary epic poetry's manifestations of classical categories including the verisimilar and the marvellous. The largest category of Lombardelli's annotations in both strata encompasses cross-references to an exceptionally wide range of other works. Classical Roman authors predominate; Virgil, Ovid, Horace and Cicero are among the most frequently cited, but Lucan, Pliny, Columella, Macrobius, Terence, Plautus, Sallust, Persius and Boethius also appear. Greek authors are represented by Plutarch, while Italian authors include Dante, Petrarch and Andrea Alciato. Contemporary authorities include the physician Juan Huarte, the historian Scipione Ammirato, the printer Paulus Manutius and the humanists Joachim Camerarius and Girolamo Garimberto; as discussed above, one note cites Matthew. (The choice of both Catholic and Protestant authorities again suggests an ecumenical approach to Homeric interpretation.) Citations may be as brief as an abbreviated form of the author's name and a book number, or they may include a brief quotation. Many refer to or quote passages that corroborate or amplify the moral or the perspective of the Homeric passage. At times, the quotations become complex pastiches of multiple citations, as in Lombardelli's response to the

---

[21] Ibid., 166, commenting on *Od.* 6.141–7.
[22] In recent years, scholars of early modern biblical hermeneutics have shown that these neat binaries are untenable; see e.g., Brian Cummings, 'The Problem of Protestant Culture: Biblical Literalism and Literary Biblicism', *Reformation* 17 (2012): 177–98. While Deloince-Louette, *Sponde*, 338–54 discusses Protestant rejections of certain types of allegory and the limited circumstances in which Protestant biblical or literary hermeneutics might employ allegoresis (biblical or literary), Bizer, *Homer and the Politics of Authority*, acknowledges this critical tendency on 6–8, but traces the gradual adoption of allegoresis by Huguenots – in part to contest Catholic uses of Homer on their own ground – on 137–8. Wolfe, *Homer and the Question of Strife*, argues on p. 12 and demonstrates throughout that individual readers' readings of Homeric epic and its affinities with scripture vary according to both their personal beliefs and the passage in question.
[23] Wolfe, *Homer and the Question of Strife*, 49.

hapless bard Phemios' supplication of Odysseus in the aftermath of the slaughter of the suitors. Lemnius' edition draws attention to Phemios' plea that 'I am self-taught, and the god has planted in my heart lays of all sorts, and worthy am I to sing to you as to a god; therefore do not be eager to cut my throat' through a printed marginal note: 'Laus Musicae & artis poeticæ' (praise of music and the poetic art).[24] Around this laconic marginalium, Lombardelli wraps a long handwritten comment: 'Ouid. Est Deus in nobis, sunt et commercia coeli, uel agitate calescimus illo; sunt etiam, qui nos numen habere putent' (There is a god in us, and we are in touch with heaven, or when he stirs us our bosom warms; there are those who even think we have the god within). Though attributed only to 'Ovid', the note fuses quotations from three different Ovidian texts: Est deus in nobis, et sunt commercia caeli' (There is a god in us; we are in touch with heaven) (*Ars amatoria* 3.549); 'Est deus in nobis; agitante calescimus illo' (There is a god within us. It is when he stirs us that our bosom warms) (*Fasti* 6.5); and 'sunt etiam qui nos numen habere putent' (there are those who even think we have the god within) (*Amores* 3.9.18). Such efforts to surround Homer's text with later confirmations of his thought recall the claim, made by pseudo-Plutarch in his *Essay on the Life and Poetry of Homer* and amplified by Angelo Poliziano in his *Ambra*, that the Homeric poems are the original fount of all wisdom: 'Omnia ab his et in his sunt omnia' (All things come from them and in them are all things) (481). Lombardelli appears to have shared the popular Renaissance views of Homer as a divinely inspired poet and the Homeric poems as encyclopedic texts – not only in their ethical and Christian wisdom, but also in their poetic riches.[25] But as we shall see, this interest in poetic truth also has strong implications for Lombardelli's understanding of the nature of poetry.

Many cross references identify verbal similarities between the Homeric passage and another text, offering tantalizing glimpses of a Renaissance reader's reckoning with classical intertextuality. However, it is not easy to say what Lombardelli made of these similarities, for, as Demetriou notes, Lemnius' Latin hexameters are everywhere shot through with quotations and appropriations of Latin poets.[26] To translate Penelope's conversation with the disguised Odysseus in book 19, for example, Lemnius draws heavily on Dido's conversations with Aeneas, and Lombardelli identifies two of his borrowings. The opening of Odysseus' tale of his misfortunes, 'Quanquam me tristes cogis, renouare dolores' (Although you urge me to renew harsh griefs),[27] imitates Aeneas' preface to his recounting of the fall of Troy: 'Infandum, regina, iubes renovare dolorem' (Too deep for words, O queen, is the grief you bid me renew, *Aen.* 2.3). Lombardelli's note duly cites '2° Aen.' and quotes the Virgilian passage. Later in their conversation, Penelope's lament that Odysseus left

---

[24] Homer, *Odysseæ libri XXIIII*, 618, translating *Od.* 22.347–9. All quotations and translations of classical texts are from the Loeb Classical Library unless otherwise noted.
[25] For Homer as an encyclopedic poet, see Wolfe, *Homer and the Question of Strife*, 35–42; for Homer as a divinely inspired poet, see e.g., Don Cameron Allen, *Mysteriously Meant: The Rediscovery of Pagan Syholism and Allegorical Interpretation in the Renaissance* (Baltimore: The Johns Hopkins University Press, 1970), 100–5, and Philip Ford, 'Homer in the French Renaissance', *Renaissance Quarterly* 59, no. 1 (2006): 16–17 and 22–3.
[26] Demetriou, '*Periphrōn* Penelope', 96.
[27] Homer, *Odysseæ libri XXIIII*, 533, translating *Od.* 19.167–8.

for Troy 'fatis digressus iniquis' (with an evil fate)[28] imitates Aeneas' description of his founding of Aeneadae 'fatis ingressus iniquis' (entering on the task with untoward fates, *Aen.* 3.17). Again Lombardelli cites '3º Aen.' and quotes the Virgilian passage. Lombardelli clearly read the *Odyssey* with an eye for its intertextual relationships to later Latin literature, but his understanding of those relationships remains an open question. Did Lombardelli realize what Lemnius had done? Was he identifying the sources of Lemnius' borrowings? Or did Lombardelli believe the imitation ran in the opposite direction, that he was identifying passages that later authors had quoted or adapted from Homer?

In these as in many cases, Lombardelli's annotations straightforwardly identify the Latin passage quoted. In other cases, however, Lombardelli's marginalia refer not to the source of Lemnius' imitation, but to a different passage or text. While these may be simple errors on Lombardelli's part, they may reveal his perception of more complex networks of verbal and conceptual correspondence. For example, Lemnius took his translation of the third line of the invocation from Horace's translation in the *Ars poetica* 142: 'Qui mores hominum multorum vidit et urbes' (who saw the ways and cities of many men).[29] But Lombardelli's marginal note reads 'Vide Cic. 1.2. ep.ª vi. ad Rufum, & Hor.ᵐ lib.1.ep.ª II' (aa1r.) (See Cicero, book 2 epistle 6 to Rufus, and Horace, book 1 epistle 2). Horace did also translate this passage in *Epistles* 1.2.19–20, but the translation there reads 'qui domitor Troiae multorum providus urbes / et mores hominum inspexit' (that tamer of Troy, who looked with discerning eyes upon the cities and manners of many men). Perhaps Lombardelli mixed up his Horatian epistles – or perhaps he recognized the quotation from the *Ars poetica* and, feeling it too obvious to cite, chose instead to remind himself of a similar imitation in the earlier epistle.

Other attributions suggest Lombardelli's limitations as a reader of classical literature, or those of his education.[30] Translating *Od.* 24.264–5 as 'an hospes / Ille meus quondam uesci uitalibus auris / Sustineat, nec adhuc crudelibus occubet umbris' (if that sometime friend of mine endures to feed on the breath of life, and lies not yet in the cruel shades), Lemnius combines *De rerum natura* 5.857 ('nam quaecumque vides vesci vitalibus auris' (for whatever you see feeding on the breath of life)) and *Aen.* 1.546–7 ('quem si fata virum servant, si vescitur aura aetheria neque adhuc crudelibus occubat umbris' (if fate still preserves that hero, if he feeds on the air of heaven and lies not yet in the cruel shades)). Lombardelli's marginal note reads '3º Aen.', misattributing the Virgilian quotation and missing the Lucretian quotation altogether.[31] The omission suggests that Lombardelli's classical education was (understandably) not so wide-ranging as to equip him to spot every quotation of every classical epic, but the misattribution is difficult to understand as anything other than a mistake. And it seems scarcely credible that Lombardelli would have

---

[28] Ibid., 538, translating *Od.* 19.259.
[29] My translation.
[30] On the frequent gaps between the claims of humanist educators and the reality of the schoolroom, see Anthony Grafton and Lisa Jardine, *From Humanism to the Humanities: Education and the Liberal Arts in Fifteenth and Sixteenth-Century Europe* (London: Duckworth, 1986).
[31] Homer, *Odysseæ libri XXIIII*, 661.

failed to recognize Lemnius' quotation of Mercury's famous dictum to Aeneas, 'varium et mutabile semper / femina' (A fickle and changeful thing is woman ever) (*Aen.* 4.569–70), in his translation of *Od.* 15.20, the disguised Athena's mendacious counsel to Telemachus to return to Ithaka lest Penelope marry a suitor and take some of his possessions with her. Yet Lombardelli's comment reads 'Virg. ecl.' – apparently a reference to Virgil's *Eclogues*, in which neither the phrase nor the sentiment appears. Though it could simply be an error, this last annotation also raises the possibility that Lombardelli's recollection of Virgil's *Eclogues* was filtered through Renaissance eclogues such as Mantuan's. Desire for women and women's responses to men's love are relatively infrequent in Virgil's *Eclogues* – but these are major themes, handled with scepticism and even misogyny, in Mantuan and in some of the Renaissance pastoral he inspired.[32] Lombardelli's note suggests that his reading of classical texts could be coloured by their contemporary imitators, that Menalcas' passing comment that Aegon fears Naeara prefers Menalcas to him (3.4) or the apparent competition for Galatea and Phyllis in *Eclogue* 7 may have seemed darker and weightier to Renaissance readers than they do today.

This brief survey can scarcely do justice to either the breadth of Lombardelli's reactions to the *Odyssey* or the range of reading strategies he applied to the text. His annotations hint at Renaissance reading practices that otherwise leave few traces and shed light on how Renaissance poetry could shape interpretations of the classical poetry it reworked. This is true of Lombardelli's *Discorso* as well; his treatise reveals much about how he read the *Odyssey*, and how that reading shaped his understanding of heroic poetry and his reading of the *Liberata*. And while the *Discorso*'s readings of both *Odyssey* and *Liberata* are sometimes surprising, those surprising or puzzling interpretations are illuminated by the annotations in his copy of the *Odyssey*.

From Homer to Tasso: Lombardelli's Odyssean defence of the Liberata

Like many Renaissance poetic treatises, Lombardelli's writings in defence of the *Liberata* frequently substantiate their claims about the nature of heroic or epic poetry through appeals to the *Iliad*, *Odyssey* and *Aeneid*. Lombardelli's discussions are unusual, however, both in their depth and substance and in their frequent preference for the *Odyssey* as an exemplary heroic poem. Again and again, it provides his first or even his only source for a poetic principle, especially when that principle is controversial in sixteenth-century poetics. And since Lombardelli's defence of the *Liberata* requires him both to define heroic poetry and to explain how the *Liberata*

---

[32] On Mantuan's treatment of women, see Gwenda Echard, 'The "Eclogues" of Baptista Mantuanus: A Medieval and Humanist Synthesis', *Latomus* 45, no. 4 (1986): 837–47. For an example of pastoral misogyny imported into the Virgilian tradition and inspired by Mantuan, see Helen Cooper, 'Pastoral and Georgic', in *The Oxford History of Classical Reception in English, vol. 2*, ed. Patrick Cheney and Philip Hardie (Oxford: Oxford University Press, 2015), 209.

meets those definitions, his arguments frequently imply that the *Liberata* is a heroic poem insofar as it is Odyssean.

Lombardelli's *Discorso* is structured as a point-by-point rebuttal to sixteen separate charges levelled against the *Liberata* in two major critiques: Camillo Pellegrino's *Carrafa* and Lionardo Salviati's *Difesa dell'Orlando furioso* (also known as the *Stacciata prima*). The first of these, and by far the charge on which Lombardelli spends the most time, concerns the definition of poetry itself: Pellegrino's assertion 'Che la Gierusalemme liberata è mera istoria senza favola' (that the *Gerusalemme liberata* is mere history without plot). Two further charges come to be closely implicated in this one: Salviati's claim 'Che è privo d'invenzioni maravigliose' (that it is lacking in marvellous inventions) and Pellegrino's claim 'Che nel muover gli affetti è infelice, senz'imitazione, asciutto, sforzato, freddo, invalido, inetto, e stiracchiato' (that in moving the reader's emotions it is unsuccessful, without imitation, dry, forced, cold, invalid, inept, and far-fetched).[33] In order to refute the charge that the *Liberata* lacks *favola* – which comes to be intrinsic to Lombardelli's conception of poetry and its difference from history, and to encompass not only the artful plotting of the poem but also the quality of being poetic – Lombardelli advances what he presents as an original definition of *favola*:

> La favola poetica è un raccontamento finto di cose vere in parte, e in parte false, ma pur tutte possibili ad esser' avvenute, per fin di dilettare, e tal volta di giovare ancora. La Gierusalemme è un raccontamento d'un azzion principalissima vera, e di certe altre annestate quasi tutte false, ma tutti credibili per la verisimiglianza onde son raccontate, e tutte possibili che sieno avvenute: dunque è favola poetica.[34]

> (A poetic plot is a narrative composed of things partly true and partly false, but all possible, in order to delight and sometimes to profit too. The *Gerusalemme* is a narrative of a true primary action with certain others attached, nearly all false but all believable through the verisimilitude with which they are narrated, and all possible: therefore it is a poetic plot.)

The *Liberata* exemplifies the best form of such a poem, Lombardelli claims, in that it embellishes a fundamentally true story with verisimilar elements.[35] Over the lengthy discussion that follows, Lombardelli emphasizes the importance of plausible but inventive plotting – a verisimilar *favola* – to the point that it appears to become his primary criterion for defining a poem.[36] For a model narrative that blends true and verisimilar elements, Lombardelli turns first to the *Odyssey*:

> Anco è da por mente, che, quando si dice favola di soggetto vero, e verisimile, non è necessario che tutto il soggetto con tutte le sue parti sia vero; anzi bisognia

---

[33] Lombardelli, *Discorso*, 31–3.
[34] Ibid., 37–8.
[35] Weinberg, *History*, 2:1026–7.
[36] In his combative response to Lombardelli, Tasso objects to Lombardelli's definition as un-Aristotelian and embraces instead Aristotle's definition of poetry as mimesis: 'io ridurrei il genere del Poema Epico piu tosto alla imitatione, che al raccontamento' (I would distil the genre of epic poetry rather to imitation than to narration) (*Risposta...al Discorso*, 8–9).

che la costituzion della favola sia di cosa vera, e le parti non vere, ma solamente verisimili, e così gli episodi, a voler che il poema sia perfetto e lodevole. per esempio, nell'Ulissea è vero questo, che Ulisse, finita la guerra Troiana, se ne ritorna ad Itaca, patria sua; ma il tempo che vi consumò, il viaggio che tenne, le venture ò i travagli che hebbe, che son le parti, son false in tutto ò per la più parte, ma dette con tanta sembianza del vero, nonostante il trovarvisi cose impossibili; che l'intelletto stupisce, come sieno state divisate ed acconcie.[37]

(It is also to be borne in mind that when we say a fable based on a true subject and verisimilar, it is not necessary that all the subject with all its parts should be true; in fact, it is desirable that the foundation of the fable should be true, and the parts not true, but only verisimilar, and thus the episodes, in order that the poem be perfect and praiseworthy. For example, in the *Odyssey* it is true that Odysseus, the Trojan War having ended, returns to Ithaka, his homeland; but the time that return took, the voyage he made, the accidents or the travails he encountered, which are the parts, are wholly or for the most part false, but told with such a semblance of the truth, notwithstanding that impossible things are found there, that the mind boggles at how they are orderly and appropriate.)

Lombardelli's definition of *favola* engages two central problems in sixteenth-century poetics: the role of verisimilitude in poetry and the relationship of the verisimilar to the marvellous (whose nature is also a subject of much debate). Following Aristotle's claim that 'the difference between the historian and the poet is ... that the one relates actual events, the other the kinds of things that might occur', most sixteenth-century critics agreed that 'history treats the truth and poetry treats verisimilitude'.[38] Verisimilitude encompasses plot elements that are at once invented – not Pellegrino's 'mere history' – and yet plausible; hence Aristotle's famous claim that 'things probable though impossible should be preferred to the possible but implausible'.[39] Lombardelli understands this essential term through the *Odyssey*; perhaps he also recalls his interest in the *Odyssey*'s own claims to divinely inspired truth. He defends the *Liberata*'s very nature as poetry on the grounds that it resembles Homer's poem.

It is, however, not enough for a heroic poem to construct a verisimilar fiction on a solid foundation of truth. Its *favola* must also incorporate a healthy dose of marvels. As Tasso's *Discorsi dell'arte poetica* make clear, this requirement poses significant challenges for the heroic poet:

Diversissime sono ... queste due nature, il meraviglioso e 'l verisimile ... in guisa diverse che sono quasi contrarie tra loro; nondimeno l'una e l'altra nel poema è

---

[37] Lombardelli, *Discorso*, 51–2.
[38] Aristotle, *Poetics*, 1451b; Weinberg, *History*, 1:629; see also 1:633–4. As Weinberg's discussion of Tasso's *Risposta* on 1:629–30 reveals, Tasso's position on this issue gradually evolves from his more orthodox claim in the *Discorsi dell'arte poetica* that heroic poetry requires verisimilitude in order to convince its readers of its truth to his claim in the *Risposta* that poetry requires a foundation in truth and is more perfect the more it conforms to truth – although even there it must leave some scope for the poet's invention.
[39] Aristotle, *Poetics*, 1460a25.

necessaria, ma fa mestieri che arte di eccellente poeta sia quella che insieme le accoppi; il che, se ben è stato sin ora fatto da molti, nissuno è (ch'io mi sappia) il quale insegni come si faccia.[40]

(These two qualities, the wondrous and the verisimilar, … are so different that they are nearly contrary to each other. Still, both one and the other are necessary in the epic poem. It requires, however, the skill of an excellent poet to join them together; and, though many have done so thus far, no one, to my knowledge, has taught how it is done.[41])

As a solution, Tasso proposes the incorporation of Christian miracles into heroic poetry, for miracles (he claims) are both marvellous and verisimilar. His desire for truth even in his marvels diverges sharply from much sixteenth-century practice, which followed Ariosto in embracing overtly fictitious and even implausible marvels. Lombardelli appears to share Tasso's preference for the plausible marvellous, but his sense of the marvellous differs in several respects from Tasso's. As he divides *favole* into four types, he sets the marvels of the *Odyssey*'s adventure books among the examples of episodes that are verisimilar but not true. Though inferior to true and verisimilar plots such as the main actions of the *Liberata* and the *Odyssey*, they are vital to both the missions Lombardelli ascribes to poetry ('to delight and sometimes to profit too'), 'donando al poeta gran franchezza di poter tutte le nature rappresentare, e gli affetti rassembrar più atti a indur negli animi virtù, e costumi lodevoli, ma sopra tutto diletto indicibile' (giving the poet great freedom to be able to depict all natures, and to represent the passions more apt to induce in the spirit virtue and praiseworthy customs, but above all unspeakable delight).[42] Examples from the *Odyssey* – 'le menzogne de' Lestrigoni, de' Lotofagi, delle maghe, delle tempeste, de' naufragi, delle pestilenze, delle spelonche, de' Ciclopi' (the lies of the Laestrygonians, the Lotus-eaters, sorceresses, storms, shipwrecks, plagues, caves, Cyclopses) – head the list of fictions that a masterful poet can use to move the reader's emotions as he wishes, 'che alle spese altrui si possa imparare a vivere' (so that at others' expense one may learn how to live).[43] Perhaps this emotional manipulation, which Lombardelli assimilates to the vicarious experiences induced by theatrical performance, explains one of his strangest annotations to his *Odyssey*. In book 5, Kalypso tells Odysseus that she is willing to let him leave Ogygia – a self-serving statement that omits any mention of the order from Olympos that Hermes has just delivered. Lombardelli critiques Kalypso's claim of friendship and concludes 'nec volens dimittis, guippe a Mercurio iussa' (nor willingly do you let go, for

---

[40] Torquato Tasso, *Discorsi dell'arte poetica e del poema eroico*, ed. Luigi Poma (Bari: Laterza, 1964), 6–7.
[41] Lawrence F. Rhu, *The Genesis of Tasso's Narrative Theory: English Translations of the Early Poetics and a Comparative Study of Their Significance* (Detroit: Wayne State University Press, 1993), 102–3.
[42] Lombardelli, *Discorso*, 43–4. This judgement is also reflected in his annotations of his *Odyssey*, which are concentrated in the books that take place on Ithaka and Scheria, in (or at least on the margins of) the real world. This preference again aligns Lombardelli with the humanists whose readings foreground the ethical utility of the real-world books, rather than the allegorizing readers who naturally find more grist for their mills in the adventure books. See Wolfe's extensive discussions of Erasmus' and Melanchthon's readings in *Homer and the Question of Strife*, chapters 1–2.
[43] Lombardelli, *Discorso*, 45.

in fact you were ordered by Mercury).[44] The direct address suggests that Lombardelli has become caught up in the drama of the poem, that his indignation has been aroused by Kalypso's lie of omission – that, at Odysseus' expense, he has learned a lesson in how to live.

This idea of emotional affect as marvellous extends into Lombardelli's defence of Tasso against Salviati's charge that the *Liberata* lacks marvels:[45]

> A me ... paiono invenzioni maravigliose tutte queste, cioè l'invocazion della Musa Celeste; l'episodio d'Olindo e di Sofronia; il parlamento di Plutone; più e diversi inganni d'Armida; gli avvenimenti d'Erminia; tre ò quattro guerrieri di valere invitto; le armi celesti e lo scudo di diamante in quel modo che lo finge; alcune opere d'Ismeno mago diabolico, e del Romito Astrologo, ò mago naturale; i casi di Clorinda; il bosco incantato; le tante difficultà e i tanti ostacoli moltiplicati a impedir l'acquisto; le preghiere alate; la porta cristallina onde escono i sogni; il cader della colomba in grembo a Goffredo, con alcuni movimenti di lui che tengon del miracoloso; la donzella incognita con tutt'i suoi gesti; l'augel volante che diventa cimiero dell'elmo di Rinaldo; come anco il colorarsi del suo vestire, allora ch'ei va a disfar l'incanto del bosco; e Vafrino, spia mandata al Campo d'Egitto.[46]

> (To me ... all these appear marvelous inventions: the invocation of the Celestial Muse; the episode of Olindo and Sofronia; Pluto's parliament; Armida's several deceptions; Erminia's adventures; three or four warriors of unconquered valor; the way in which the celestial arms and the diamond shield are invented; several works of the diabolical magician Ismeno, and of the hermit astrologer, or natural magician; the events that befall Clorinda; the enchanted wood; the many difficulties and the many obstacles that multiply to prevent the conquest; the winged prayers; the crystalline gate through which dreams emerge; the fall of the dove into Goffredo's lap, with several gestures that have something of the miraculous about them; the unknown damsel (Fortuna) with all her deeds; the flying bird that adorns Rinaldo's helmet, as also the coloring of his clothing when he goes to break the enchantments on the wood; and Vafrino, sent as a spy into the Egyptian camp.)

Lombardelli's mentions of 'winged prayers' and 'the miraculous' reveal his sympathy with Tasso's concept of a Christian marvellous. But while most modern readers would agree with Lombardelli's inclusion of the poem's many enchantments in his list of marvels, such episodes as Sofronia's self-sacrificing lie, Erminia's vicissitudes, or Vafrino's foray into the enemy camp do not incorporate the supernatural or rely upon magic or divine intervention. These are not Ariostan impossibilities, but marvels

---

[44] Homer, *Odysseæ libri XXIIII*, 138.
[45] Unlike Tasso, Lombardelli almost completely avoids mentioning Ariosto or the *Furioso*; he presents his discourse as a defence of the *Liberata* only, and not as a contribution to the increasingly ill-tempered argument that pitted the *Liberata* and *Furioso* against each other.
[46] Lombardelli, *Discorso*, 109–10.

of character – and, perhaps, of the emotional responses that, for Lombardelli, render fictions marvellous and excuse their incorporation into a heroic poem.

Where did Lombardelli get this expansive idea of the marvellous? Again his reading of the *Odyssey* provides clues. The one mention of verisimilitude in all the annotations appears not in books 9–12, but in book 6. Having bravely stood her ground against the shipwrecked Odysseus' terrifying appearance and provided him with food and clothing, the Phaiakian princess Nausikaa explains to Odysseus how to approach her royal parents and supplicate them for help in returning home. She offers to drive him as far as the city walls, but then, she tells him, he must descend and make his way on foot, lest the Phaiakians see them together, and gossip and grumble about this stranger who might aspire to be her husband. Against the speech in which Nausikaa imagines what her countrymen might say (*Od.* 6.276-84), Lombardelli writes 'In tota hac oratione multa sunt pulchra, et verisimilia; sed quaedam minus decora' (In all this speech many things are beautiful and verisimilar, but some are lacking in decorum).[47] The decorum of Nausikaa's conversation with Odysseus had been questioned since antiquity, and Plutarch addresses the controversy in *How the Young Man Should Study Poetry*.[48] Lemnius shares Plutarch's concern with decorum; his printed marginal quotation marks draw the reader's attention to Nausikaa's statement that she herself would condemn an unmarried woman who consorted with a man without her parents' approval. Given Lombardelli's authorship of a treatise on married women's behaviour, we might expect him too to address the decorum of Nausikaa's speech. But Lombardelli instead focuses on its verisimilitude: on the charm and conviction of the young princess's ability to imitate the rough Phaiakian sailors, while simultaneously revealing herself to be an appealing and intelligent young woman, and conveying to this handsome stranger her newfound inclination to matrimony. Verisimilitude here is a question of poetics, not ethics, and verisimilitude is prized above decorum. That Nausikaa is a convincing portrait of a smart, spunky young woman with a spine – Miss Almost-Right – matters much more than whether Nausikaa perfectly observes royal decorum.

One might defend Sofronia or Erminia on similar terms against complaints of indecorum or episodic digressiveness. Perhaps Lombardelli detected something of Nausikaa's spirit and courage and assistance to the shipwrecked Odysseus in Sofronia's courage and steadfastness, or Erminia's unexpected ability to brave adversity or succour Vafrino in the Egyptian camp; perhaps he saw Tasso's ability to emulate Homer in creating sympathetic young women of pluck and charm, and a dash of pathos, as nothing short of marvellous.

Still other marvels in Lombardelli's list, such as the description of Rinaldo's helmet or the complex plotting that delays the Christian conquest, are displays not of Aristotle's plausible impossible, but of the poet's craft in weaving together true and verisimilar elements. Lombardelli displays a sustained interest in the construction of these poetic marvels. (Had he somehow read Tasso's *Discorsi* or learned of Tasso's claim that no one had yet taught the proper combination of the verisimilar and the marvellous?) Once again, he turns to the *Odyssey* to explore this problem. Reflecting the interest

---

[47] Homer, *Odysseæ libri XXIIII*, 173.
[48] Plutarch, *How the Young Man Should Study Poetry*, 27a–b.

in Homeric intertextuality so omnipresent throughout his annotations, Lombardelli presents Tasso's intertextuality as both a source of marvels and a marvel in itself. He divides poetic marvels into two categories: those that are invented by the poet and those that,

> son prese da altri scrittori d'altre lingue; si che i lettori ignoranti di lingue morte ò straniere le hanno pur per immaginate dal poeta, che loro le mette dinanzi. Queste seconde, si come non posson recare onor d'invenzione al poeta, così non si può negar, che non sien nel medesimo grado di maraviglia appo quelli, i quali non le sanno ritrovare altrove: *e però Vergilio ne spagliò non solamente i Greci, ma anco i Latini, nobilitandole con la magnificenza dell'arte, e con l'altezza del dire; e così fece per avventura Omero:* benché (come ben dicono gli Academici) non se gli possan rivedere i conti. Non son così dunque da dispregiar le invenzioni altrui, se altri se ne sa ben valore, alterando e mutando tutte le circostanze, come il Boccaccio seppe fare in distendere alcune novelle che prima erano state scritte da Apuleio e da altri, tutto che il supremo grado della lode meriti la prima maniera.[49]

> (are taken from other writers in other languages, so that readers ignorant of dead or foreign languages take them to be imagined by the poet who sets them before them. Since this second kind cannot confer the honor of invention on the poet, it cannot be denied that they are not of the same class of marvel as those that could not be found elsewhere. *And however Virgil despoiled not solely the Greeks, but also the Latins, ennobling them with the magnificence of his art and the grandeur of his speech; and so too perhaps did Homer*, although (as the Academics say well) his books cannot be audited. The inventions of others are not therefore to be despised, if they know the merit of changing and adapting all the circumstances, as Boccacio knew to do in unfolding some tales that were originally written by Apuleius and others. However, the first method (of inventing marvels) merits the highest degree of praise.)

Lombardelli continues with a long list of marvellous elements in the *Liberata* imitated from other poets, primarily Virgil and Homer. His interest in textual imitation and intertextuality among classical poets as he read the *Odyssey*, combined with his interest in Tasso's imitations of larger units of plot and character in the *Discorso*, suggests not only that he read classical literature to help him understand modern poetic practice (and possibly vice versa) but that he also saw successful literary imitation as marvellous in its own right.

Later in the *Discorso*, the interweaving of the true and the verisimilar will itself become one of the *Odyssey*'s marvels, one emulated by the *Liberata*. Citing the *Ars poetica*, Lombardelli positions Tasso as Homer's successor:

> Dico dunque che a me pare scernere una maraviglia in questo poema perpetua .... E quale è questa perpetua maraviglia? La maravigliosa catena di tutte l'azzioni

---

[49] 104–5, emphasis added.

annestate alla principale con que'maravigliosi nodi, che pur son descritti dal medesimo per tenuti da Omero.⁵⁰

(I say therefore that I seem to discern a perpetual marvel in this poem …. And what is this perpetual marvel? The marvelous chain of all the actions attached to the principal action with those marvelous knots that are described by Horace through the writings of Homer.)

Weinberg dismisses as mere wordplay Lombardelli's characterization of these elements as marvellous, but a comparison of Lombardelli's argument with his annotations and Tasso's *Discorsi* suggests that Lombardelli was perfectly serious: Homer provides the grounds on which to consider both the fabric of Tasso's poem and its fabrication not only ideal but also marvellous.⁵¹ Lombardelli's reliance on the *Odyssey* to understand the *Liberata*'s concatenation of the marvellous and the verisimilar reveals that his reading of the *Odyssey* and its presence in the *Liberata* is not limited to individual moments of imitation or even individual characters. He perceives the fabric and the fabrication of Tasso's poem to be Homeric, and the *Liberata* to be a fundamentally Odyssean text.

Drawing together Lombardelli's annotated *Odyssey* and his defence of the *Liberata* enables us to see not only how one perceptive sixteenth-century reader read his Homer but indeed how that reading informed both his appreciation of a Renaissance epic and the development of his poetic theory. Lombardelli's *Odyssey* is a rare survival, but it is not unique. Other such volumes no doubt lurk in libraries and archives – and as this essay in combining the histories of poetics and reading has tried to suggest, the time and effort invested in discovering them can yield rich dividends indeed.

Bibliography

Allen, Don Cameron. *Mysteriously Meant: The Rediscovery of Pagan Sybolism and Allegorical Interpretation in the Renaissance*. Baltimore: The Johns Hopkins University Press, 1970.

Aristotle, Longinus, Demetrius. *Poetics. On the Sublime. On Style*. Translated by Stephen Halliwell, W. Hamilton Fyfe, Doreen C. Innes, W. Rhys Roberts. Rev. Donald A. Russell. Cambridge, MA: Harvard University Press, 1995.

Bizer, Marc. *Homer and the Politics of Authority in Renaissance France*. Oxford: Oxford University Press, 2011.

Capodieci, Luisa and Philip Ford, eds. *Homère à la Renaissance: Mythe et transfigurations*. Paris: Somogy Éditions d'Art, 2011.

Cooper, Helen. 'Pastoral and Georgic'. In *The Oxford History of Classical Reception in English*, vol. 2, edited by Patrick Cheney and Philip Hardie, 201–24. Oxford: Oxford University Press, 2015.

Cummings, Brian. 'The Problem of Protestant Culture: Biblical Literalism and Literary Biblicism'. *Reformation* 17 (2012): 177–98.

---

⁵⁰ 110–11.
⁵¹ Weinberg, *History*, 2:1028.

D'Amico, Silvia. 'Les retrouvailles d'Ulysse et Pénélope: lecture d'une scène homérique à la Renaissance'. In *Homère à la Renaissance. Mythe et transfigurations*, edited by Luisa Capodieci and Philip Ford, 175–96. Paris: Somogy Éditions d'Art, 2011.

Demetriou, Tania. '"Essentially Circe": Spenser, Homer, and the Homeric Tradition'. *Translation and Literature* 15 (2006): 151–76.

Demetriou, Tania. '*Periphrōn* Penelope and Her Early Modern Translations'. In *The Culture of Translation in Early Modern England and France, 1500–1600*, edited by Tania Demetriou and Rowan Tomlinson. Houndmills: Palgrave Macmillan, 2015.

Echard, Gwenda. 'The "Eclogues" of Baptista Mantuanus: A Medieval and Humanist Synthesis'. *Latomus* 45, no. 4 (1986): 837–47.

Ford, Philip. *De Troie à Ithaque: réception des épopées homériques à la Renaissance*. Geneva: Droz, 2007.

Ford, Philip. "Homer in the French Renaissance." *Renaissance Quarterly* 59 (1) (2006), 1–28.

Grafton, Anthony. *Commerce with the Classics: Ancient Books and Renaissance Readers*. Ann Arbor: University of Michigan Press, 1997.

Grafton, Anthony and Lisa Jardine. *From Humanism to the Humanities: Education and the Liberal Arts in Fifteenth and Sixteenth-Century Europe*. London: Duckworth, 1986.

Homer. *Odysseæ libri XXIIII*. Edited by Simon Lemnius. Basel: Ioannis Oporini, 1549.

Homer. *Odyssey*. 2 vols. Translated by A. T. Murray. Rev. George E. Dimock. Cambridge, MA: Harvard University Press, 1919, 2nd rev. edn, 1998.

Horace. *Satires, Epistles, and Ars Poetica*. Translated by H. Rushton Fairclough. Cambridge, MA: Harvard University Press, 1926.

Jardine, Lisa and Anthony Grafton. '"Studied for Action": How Gabriel Harvey Read His Livy'. *Past and Present* 129 (1990): 30–78.

Lombardelli, Orazio. *Discorso intorno a i contrasto che si fanno sopra la Gierusalemme liberata*. Ferrara: Vassalini, 1586.

Lucretius. *On the Nature of Things*. Translated by W. H. D. Rouse. Rev. Martin F. Smith. Cambridge, MA: Harvard University Press, 1924; rev. edn, 1992.

Ovid. *The Art of Love and Other Poems*. Translated by J. H. Mozley. Rev. G. P. Goold. Cambridge, MA: Harvard University Press, 1929, 2nd edn, 1979.

Ovid. *Fasti*. Translated by James George Frazer. Rev. G. P. Goold. Cambridge, MA: Harvard University Press, 1931; rev. edn, 1989.

Ovid. *Heroides. Amores*. Translated by Grant Showerman. Rev. G. P. Goold. Cambridge, MA: Harvard University Press, 1914; rev. edn, 1977.

Plutarch. *Moralia, Volume I*. Translated by Frank Cole Babbitt. Cambridge, MA: Harvard University Press, 1927.

Rhu, Lawrence F. *The Genesis of Tasso's Narrative Theory: English Translations of the Early Poetics and a Comparative Study of Their Significance*. Detroit: Wayne State University Press, 1993.

Riatsch, Clà. 'Lemnius, Simon'. *Dizionario storico della Svizzera* (22 February 2017): http://www.hls-dhs-dss.ch/textes/i/I9112.php

Schurink, Fred. '"Like a Hand in the Margine of a Booke:" William Blount's Marginalia and the Politics of Sidney's Arcadia'. *Review of English Studies* 59 (2008): 1–24.

Spingarn, Joel Elias. *A History of Literary Criticism in the Renaissance*. New York: Columbia University Press, 1899.

Tasso, Torquato. *Discorsi dell'arte poetica e del poema eroico*. Edited by Luigi Poma. Bari: Laterza, 1964.

Tasso, Torquato. *Risposta del S. Torq. Tasso, al Discorso del sig. Oratio Lombardelli intorno à i contrasti, che si fanno sopra la Gierusalemme liberata*. Ferrara: G. Vasalini, 1586.
Van der Laan, Sarah. 'Milton's Odyssean Ethics: Homeric Allusion and Arminian Thought in *Paradise Lost*'. *Milton Studies* 49 (2008): 49–76.
Virgil. *Eclogues. Georgics. Aeneid*, 2 vols. Translated by H. Rushton Fairclough. Rev. G. P. Goold. Cambridge, MA: Harvard University Press, 1916; rev. edn, 1999.
Weinberg, Bernard. *A History of Literary Criticism in the Italian Renaissance*, 2 vols. Chicago: University of Chicago Press, 1961.
Wolfe, Jessica. *Homer and the Question of Strife from Erasmus to Hobbes*. Toronto: University of Toronto Press, 2015.

Part III

New theoretical frontiers

8

Epic (in)hospitality

The case of Tasso

Jane Tylus

In a painting from 1666, Claude Lorrain depicted an episode from Tasso's epic, *Gerusalemme liberata*, that would seem to be notable mostly for its insignificance for the rest of the poem (Figure 8.1).¹ Lorrain returned over the course of his long career to what we might call the classic authors of world literature – Virgil, Homer and that most recent classic, Tasso. But amid the dashing noise of war that hallmarked these great works, the scene Lorrain chose to depict took place far from the typical setting for an epic poem, even as it represents the perceived threat of epic's invasion into a place of pastoral isolation. The Muslim princess Erminia, bereft of a kingdom, a family and even a shelter, has fled Jerusalem disguised in the armour of a woman warrior in the hopes of finding Tancredi, the Christian knight with whom she is in love. Unable to fulfil her plan of tending to him in the Christian camp, she stumbles into this lonely pastoral space where the rustic denizens are shocked (*sbigottiti*) by her martial gear, and then embrace her once they learn that she is not, in fact, a seasoned warrior bent on doing them harm but a defenceless young woman in need. Lorrain chooses to give us this potentially epic moment unravelling itself, as the warrior lifts her visor to reveal the hapless, errant young woman beneath, prompting one of the few moments in the *Liberata* of unconditional hospitality in a tiny and neglected corner of the world. Neglected, according to the elderly shepherd, either because 'sia grazie del Ciel che l'umiltade / d'innocente pastor salvi e sublime, / o che sì come il folgore non cade/ in basso piano ma su l'eccelse cime, / così il furor di peregrine spade / sol de' gran re l'altere teste opprime...' (heaven's grace saves and raises up the humility of innocent shepherds, or because just as lightning never alights on the lowly plain but on the tallest slopes, so does the furor of foreign swords strike only the proud heads of great kings; 7.9).²

---

¹ *Erminia and the Shepherds* was probably painted in or around 1666. It is now in Holkham Hall. Lorrain returned to the episode throughout his career; his earliest known execution dates to 1630, the small panel of Erminia carving the name of her beloved Tancredi into the trees, at the Metropolitan Museum in New York.

² All citations from the edition of Tasso's *Gerusalemme liberata*, ed. Fredi Chiappelli (Milan: Rusconi, 1982). Translations are my own unless otherwise indicated.

Figure 8.1 *Landscape with Erminia in Discourse with the Old Man and his Sons* (oil on canvas), Claude Lorrain (Claude Gellée) (1600–82) / By kind permission of the Earl of Leicester and the Trustees of the Holkham Estate / Bridgeman Images.

As Lorrain may have known, Erminia is similar to the poet who wove her as one of his most fascinating creations into the otherwise historical account of the First Crusade. This was a Tasso also in need of hospitality as he spent years searching for the ideal patron while writing, revising and obsessively commenting on his tortured but brilliant epic poem, donning the trappings of a warrior in search of something he may never have found.[3] Hence, perhaps, what I will maintain was his deep connection to the passage cited above. As the following pages will suggest, Tasso's lifelong efforts – beginning with his adolescent *Gerusalemme* and finishing in the revised *Gerusalemme conquistata* of 1593 – both accompanied, and precipitated, fierce debates not so much about epic's purpose, but whether it was possible to write epic at all in the still struggling, still 'unofficial' Tuscan tongue. As Bernard Weinberg systematically discussed in his seminal *History of Literary Criticism in the Italian Renaissance,* the so-called Tasso–Ariosto quarrel was at the heart of this tense conversation. The focus of Weinberg's remarks, however, was less the linguistic and stylistic dimensions of epic than the generic and structural ones: plot, characters and thought. These categories correspond to the first three divisions of Aristotle's incomplete *Poetics,* recovered and translated first into Latin in the 1530s, and then into Italian by Bernardo Segni in 1549. Yet Aristotle, of course, went on to discuss the stylistics of epic and tragedy – and

---

[3] For the most explicit analysis of the connection between Erminia and Tasso, see Walter Stephens, 'Trickster, Textor, Architect, Thief: Craft and Comedy in *Gerusalemme liberata*', in *Renaissance Transactions: Ariosto and Tasso*, ed. Valeria Fanucci (Durham: Duke University Press, 1999), 146–77. For some earlier reflections of mine on the episode of Erminia and Tasso's interest in this errant *peregrina*, see 'Parole Pellegrine: L'ospitalità linguistica nel Rinascimento', in *L'ospite del libro: Sguardi sull'ospitalità*, ed. Nicola Catelli and Giovanna Rizzarelli (Pisa: Pacini, 2015), 13–26.

in these admittedly briefer and occasionally enigmatic reflections lay much of what galvanized the quarrel.

They certainly galvanized Tasso, and those who cared most about the literary capabilities of a language which Cinzio Giraldi, waxing about Ariosto's *Orlando furioso* in 1549, called a 'favella maestosa' ('majestic tongue') despite the absence of a correspondingly majestic empire:

> Our Ariosto treated only those things which seemed to him capable of receiving light and splendor and which brought with them neither ugliness nor impropriety, such as are seen frequently in the foreign romances … . All of which he left aside as unworthy of the majesty of our language and of our nation, which now occupies among the barbarian nations that greatness which Latin once held, even though the majesty of empire is found in other hands. (che non portavano con loro ne bruttezza, ne sconvenevolezza, come se ne veggono molte ne Romanzi stranieri … . le quali egli ha tutte lasciate come indegne della maestá della nostra favella, et della nostra natione, laquale tiene hora tra le barbare quella grandezza, che la Latina gia tenne, quantunque la maestà dello impero si ritrovi in altrui mano.)[4]

'La maestà della nostra favella' vindicates Tuscan as majestic, even as the majesty of empire was in other hands. Indeed, the gap between a national language and a national political entity arguably drives Giraldi's somewhat hyperbolic statement. If the nation cannot have 'grandezza', at least its language can, and Ariosto has enabled that by perfecting the now thoroughly Italian genre of romance. Thanks to his own careful pruning of his Lombard dialect in his final and 1532 version of the *Furioso* to accommodate Pietro Bembo's rules regarding a perfect, literary, 'volgar lingua', Ariosto was seen as having enabled 'una più larga civiltà linguistica e culturale'.[5] Hence Giraldi and others championed the romance for the new language it represented – equivalent to the Latin it effectively replaced.

While Weinberg included the aforementioned citation from Giraldi in his discussion of Ariosto's reception in the first half of the sixteenth century, he tended to minimize the crucial context of poetic language – both the language particular to various genres, and the language that was coming into being as Italian.[6] At the same time, there are suggestive nuggets throughout the *History*, which, when pieced together,

---

[4] Quoted in Bernard Weinberg, *A History of Literary Criticism in the Italian Renaissance* (Chicago: University of Chicago Press, 1961), II:962.

[5] Francesco Martillotto, *La Lingua del Tasso fra polemiche e discussioni letterarie* (Arezzo: Helicon, 2014), 28.

[6] At a time when Northrop Frye was exploring the 'anatomy of criticism', Weinberg's primary interest was in the anatomy of genre – on the microscopic and macroscopic units used to put together what proved to be great Renaissance assemblages of poems: Ariosto's rambling *Furioso*, the tragicomedy that was Guarini's *Pastor fido* with which Weinberg ends his account of the era's great poetic quarrels. This was, to be sure, a great preoccupation of the sixteenth century, and the text that made such a clear-minded pursuit possible was Aristotle's less than systematic *Poetics*, finally made available to a wide reading public, in Latin and soon thereafter, Italian translation, in the 1530s. Guarini was a perfect test-case for Weinberg's study: obsessed with the *rintuzzare* or blunting of what he called the excesses of tragedy and comedy alike, and careful to balance the one with the other so as to produce

begin to create those contexts. One particularly illuminating one is an altogether too brief paragraph paraphrasing an insight by the otherwise forgotten critic Giuseppe Malatesta in his *Della nuova poesia, overo delle difese del Furioso, dialogo*, of 1581, and hence one year after Tasso's *Liberata* began to circulate, albeit without Tasso's consent, in print. After quoting a passage where Malatesta commends Ariosto for respecting the law of usage – even as he 'rebels against the laws of art' in his creation of romance – Weinberg reflects, 'In a way, this rebellion was made necessary by the very nature of the Italian language; Malatesta believes that Italian is incapable of "epic majesty" since it is a language of "harmony" rather than of "number", and since the latter is the quality required by heroic verse' (1044). Weinberg swiftly moves on to other things, but the insight is an important one. Ariosto foregoes epic not so much because it is not in keeping with modern usage – although it is also that – but because it is not in tune with a language much more suited to what Malatesta, through his *portavoce* of Speroni Sperone, calls the qualities of 'dolcezza' and 'facilità' – sweetness and ease. And in a stunning moment which Weinberg evidently missed, Malatesta has Speroni opine that it would be wonderful should God decide to send every now and then

> that very sweetness and ease of our language to that remarkable wit of Torquato Tasso by way of a kind of cross current, so that he might perhaps lose himself in a diction that would be a good deal more charming and graceful than what is demanded by the heroic style. A heroic aspect which, it is clear … is rendered impossible only by the limitations of the language itself, since what more could one desire from [Tasso's] rare intellect, or from his happy talent, his solid judgment, or his sharp ear?

> (questa istessa dolcezza, e facilità della nostra lingua, a' guisa di vento contrario [a]quel raro ingegno del Signor Torquato Tasso a' perdersi in esser forse nel suo dire assai più vago, e leggiadro di quel, che si richiede all'heroico. Il che … chiaro è, che non avien se non per l'incapacità della lingua stessa, poiche per altro, chi è, che possa desiderare in quel raro intelletto, o' felicità d'ingego [sic], o' saldezza di giuditio, o' finezza de' orecchio?)[7]

Tasso, that is, was struggling to do something that Tuscan itself is simply incapable of doing – a Tuscan that elsewhere in this animated dialogue comes up for singular criticism as the language the Florentines are trying to force on the entire peninsula.

The moment suggests a precarious relationship between the state of the Italian language in the sixteenth century and the birth of new literary forms – such as Ariosto's romance – and the rebirth of old ones – such as Tasso's epic. One might return to the literary genres that are the focus of Weinberg's remarks to ask to what

---

a perfect demonstration of how Aristotle's theories of genres might be put to use in a new age that no longer needed catharsis nor craved lewdness.

[7] *Della nuova poesia, overo delle difese del Furoso, dialogo* (Verona, 1589), ff. 63–5. Although the dialogue was written in 1581, it was not published until eight years later; see Anna Bognolo, 'Il costume di scrivere alla romanzesca: il dialogo *Della nuova poesia, overo delle difese del Furoso* (1589) di Giuseppe Bastiani Malatesta', *Historias fingidas* 6 (2018): 5–20.

extent their emergence depended on Italians' perceptions of what their language could and could not do. As in Malatesta's dialogue, written as the Accademia della Crusca of Florence was just beginning its work as arbiter of Italy's national tongue, many Italians disagreed with the proposition that Italian *was* a single language rather than a multilingual one – despite the fact that Malatesta himself approved of Ariosto's poem as accommodating itself to the limitations of Tuscan.[8] Needless to say, much work has been done since Weinberg's groundbreaking books, from much-needed studies on the social backdrops of the critical quarrels of the Cinquecento[9] to philological discussions of the development of the volgare.[10] The following remarks will hope nonetheless to add to the conversation by using the episode of Erminia as a way of illuminating Tasso's particular stake in these questions via a word used by Aristotle not only in his *Poetics* but also in the *Rhetoric,* the latter a work that Ariosto *could* have read: 'peregrino'. Already encountered in the shepherd's observation about foreign or 'peregrine spade', it was understandably a crucial term for a poem based on a Crusade of 'peregrini armati' or armed pilgrims to liberate Jerusalem from the Muslims. But Tasso also used the word as both an adjective and a noun to describe a host of other phenomena and characters: among which are Erminia and Tasso's narrator, the 'peregrino errante' who washes up in Ferrara's 'port' at the opening of the poem.[11] Perhaps most importantly, in a sonnet to the Florentine ambassador, Tasso referred to his own *style* as peregrino, the product of an itinerant life spent in southern and northern Italy, Sorrento as well as Bergamo and Ferrara.[12] Tasso's Italian, in other words, was *already* foreign. As the rest of this chapter will argue, both his theory and his poetry, most notably the episode with Erminia, reflect his interest in creating a literary form that would in turn call attention to that foreignness. But as Tasso sought to imbue his poem with all that *peregrino* implied, he found himself up against contemporaries eager to define 'Italian' as the Tuscan of Petrarch and Ariosto, a language that fit comfortably within prescribed borders and had no need of incursions from either the past or from the outside. An ethos, in other words, that believed it had no need for epic.

* * *

---

[8] See Antoine Berman's observation that 'the lettered public of the 16th century rejoiced in reading a word in its different linguistic variations' insofar as it did not (yet) 'hold the mother tongue sacred'. As the hostility to Tasso suggests, this was not quite the case, at least not in the last decades of the Cinquecento when the Crusca was indeed intent on 'sacralizing' the mother tongue as codified in works such as *Orlando furioso*. See Berman, *The Experience of the Foreign: Culture and Translation in Romantic Germany,* trans. S. Heyvaert (Albany: SUNY Press, 1992), 2–4.

[9] Déborah Blocker's work on the Accademia degli Alterati is only the most recent example; see her *Le principe de plaisir: savoirs, esthétique et politique dans la Florence des Médicis (XVIe–XVII siècles)* (Paris: Les Belles Lettres, 2019); for a discussion more focused on Tasso, see Carla Molinari, 'Tasso, i Medici e i "fiorentini ingegni"', in *Studi su Tasso* (Florence: Società Editrice Fiorentina, 2007), 99–116.

[10] As for example, Claudio Marazzini, *La Lingua italiana: Profilo storico* (Bologna: Il Mulino, 2002), 293–8, and Mario Sansone, *Da Bembo a Galiani: Il Dibattito sulla lingua in Italia* (Bari: Adriatico, 1999), 148.

[11] In I.4 the poet asks that Duke Alfonso II d'Este gather him, 'me peregrino errante' – me, a wandering stranger/pilgrim – out of the 'crags and tumultuous sea' (fra I scogli/ e fra l'onde agitato) into port.

[12] He closes the sonnet with 'may your pure taste not find displeasing this foreign style (*stile peregrino*) in which I write in solitude the virtues of magnanimous dukes' – the *Gerusalemme liberata;* Torquato Tasso, *Le Rime,* ed. Bruno Basile (Rome, 1994): sonnet 828, pp. 822–3.

Tasso's aesthetic of *pellegrinità* is perhaps best captured in the passage which Claudio Scarpati has argued was one of the most resonant moments in literary criticism from the entire Renaissance[13]: a moment from Tasso's earliest defence of his poem, his *Apologia della Gerusalemme liberata* from 1585: 'i nomi e i verbi propri fanno il parlare assai chiaro, ma l'ornamento l'è dato da gli altri. Laonde gli uomini non sono mossi altrimenti da le parole che da' peregrini: perché quel solo è venerando e degno di riverenza: e peregrino dev'esser il parlar, se dee mover maraviglia'. (Names and proper verbs make speech clear enough, but adornment is the property of other aspects of speech. Thus men are moved no less by these words than by *peregrini*: because only that alone is venerable and worthy of reverence: and thus speech should be *peregrino* if it is to move one to marvel.)[14] Conceived as a response to the virulent *Difesa dell'Orlando furioso degli Acacademia della Crusca* of Lionardo Salviati, the *Apologia* was written while Tasso was languishing in the prison where he spent seven years. It is in large part a dialogue in which a 'Forestiero' – a foreigner or stranger, and hence a word that Tasso uses frequently as a synonym for 'peregrino' – engages with a 'Segretario' and one Vincenzo Fantini to discuss, in great detail, Salviati's treatise, and to fashion a response to the Cruscante's blistering critique.[15] Tellingly, and as is the case in other dialogues, it quickly becomes clear that the Forestierio is none other than Tasso himself.

The aforementioned passage is from a long sequence that focuses primarily on questions of style. A section from Salviati's treatise has just been quoted in which Salviati maintains that 'clarity is a virtue, and its contrary is a vice, and that vice is blamed more by the learned than by the ignorant' ('La chiarezza è virtù, e 'l contrario è vizio; e 'l vizio è più biasimato de' dotti che da gli ignoranti' [117]) – prompting the Forestiero to defend the necessarily elevated discourse of epic in contrast to the general flatness of Ariosto's poetic style and its tendency to descend into the 'volgare' and generate 'disprezzo' or scorn.[16] Tasso's 'stranger' does so by quoting what is in effect a translation of a passage from Aristotle's *Rhetoric* – which itself looks back explicitly to a key moment from the *Poetics*.[17] Tasso was hardly the first to seize upon this passage, but he was certainly the first to put such an interesting spin on what would ultimately

---

[13] Claudio Scarpati, *Il vero e il falso dei poeti: Tasso, Tesauro, Pallavicino, Muratori* (Milan, 1990), 24, where he speaks of the passage as representing 'un saggio tra i più acuti dell'esegesi stilistica cinquecentesa'. For the importance of what I am calling 'pellegrinità' more generally in the late medieval and Renaissance period, see Georg Weise, *Il rinascimento e la sua eredità*, ed. P. Antonio and F. Pugliese-Carratelli (Naples: Ligouri, 1969), 397–487. Charles Klopp, who cites extensively from Weise's work and who was the first to identify the crucial role the terms 'peregrino' and 'errante' have for Tasso, in '"Peregrino" and "Errante" in the *Gerusalemme liberata*', *MLN* 94 (1979): 61–76, also cites the passage identified by Scarpati at the beginning of his essay (61). As he goes on to argue in pages important for my own work: '"peregrino" in Tasso's poem ... appears often enough and in sufficiently emotional contexts to suggest that this word and the complex concept it stood for were ... [an] important part of Tasso's emotional and poetic world as set forward in the poem'; 63.

[14] *Apologia della Gerusalemme liberata*, in Torquato Tasso, *Scritti sull'arte poetica*, ed. Ettore Mazzali (Turin: Einaudi, 1977), I:119.

[15] See, of course, Weinberg, *History*, II:954–73 on the 'Ariosto–Tasso' debate.

[16] On Tasso's theory of style, a great deal has been written; see the classic work of Fredi Chiappelli, *Studi sul linguaggio del Tasso epico* (Florence: Le Monnier, 1957), and more recently, S. Bozzola, *Purità ed ornamento di parole* (Florence: Accademia della Crusca, 1999).

[17] Curiously, Tasso does not cite his source in the *Rhetoric*, and the *Apologia*'s most recent edition does not cite it either.

become the basis for the seventeenth-century obsession with the marvellous.[18] Thus, from the *Poetics*: 'the merit of diction is to be clear and not commonplace. The clearest diction is that made up of ordinary words, but it is commonplace. An example is the poetry of Cleophon and of Sthenelus. That which employs unfamiliar words is dignified and outside the common usage. By "unfamiliar", I mean a rare word, a metaphor, a lengthening and anything beyond the ordinary use' (1458a).[19] And from the *Rhetoric*:

> Of nouns and verbs, it is the proper ones that make style perspicuous; all the others which have been spoken of in the *Poetics* elevate and make it ornate; for departure from the ordinary makes it appear more dignified. In this respect men feel the same in regard to style as in regard to foreigners and fellow-citizens. Wherefore we should give our language a 'foreign air'; for men admire what is remote, and that which excites admiration is pleasant. (1404b)[20]

At key in Aristotle's Greek are two words, necessarily linked: the *xenikoi* – translated above as both 'strange' and 'foreign' – and *semnos,* 'sacred, holy or revered', a term used of gods and in the above two English translations translated as 'dignified'. Clearly, the intent in Aristotle is that the one is productive of the other, and the sacred or holy deemed to be the essential ingredient of elevated discourse. That such elevation is as necessary to tragedy and epic as to certain aspects of oration, albeit used more sparingly in prose than in poetry, is critical for what Aristotle will call the importance of admiration and the production of the marvellous and with it, insofar as the *Rhetoric* is concerned, delight.

Several things are notable about Tasso's use of these passages. One is his firm adherence to the simile from the *Rhetoric* that compares foreigners to foreign words. Another is his interest in the elision that the simile creates between humans and language, as his choice of phrasing enables us to treat 'peregrino' as both noun and adjective. Finally, there is a question of translation. On the one hand, with respect to Aristotle's *xenikon*, he follows sixteenth-century Latin translations of the *Rhetoric*, which used *peregrinus*, and which in turn was translated in Italian versions as either *forestiero* or *peregrino.* Hence, in Antonio Riccoboni's *Aristotelis Ars Poetica* of 1579, we have: 'At grandis et immutans id, quod vulgare est, quae peregrinis utitur. Peregrinam autem voco linguam & translationem & prottactionem et quidquid preter proprium est.'[21] But the other key word noted above, *semnos,* was generally translated as 'grandior' in Latin (as again in Riccoboni's *Rhetorica*: 'Cum menim immutator, efficitur, ve grandior apparet') and in Italian, 'grandezza' – the word we have already seen in Giraldi's defence of Ariosto. It can be found as well in the 1549 translation of the *Poetics* by Bernardo Segni: 'Grandezza ha ella, e esce fuori del plebeo, usando nomi forestieri. Io chiamo nomi forestieri la Confusione della Lingua, la Metafora,

---

[18] See Joy Kenseth, 'The Age of the Marvelous: An Introduction', in *The Age of the Marvelous,* ed. Joy Kenseth (Hanover, NH: Dartmouth Museum of Art/University Press, 1991), 25–59.
[19] *The Complete Works of Aristotle: The Revised Oxford Translation,* ed. Jonathan Barnes (Princeton, 1984), II:2333.
[20] *The Complete Works of Aristotle,* ed. Jonathan Barnes, II:2239.
[21] *Aristotelis Ars Poetica ab Antonio Riccoboni latine conversa* (Venice, 1579).

l'Allungamento, e tutto qullo che si diparte dal proprio'.[22] Tasso instead returns us in a nuanced way to the notion of the sacred or godlike in the Greek to define dignity, as he characterizes the 'peregrino' as worthy of veneration. As he moves between noun and adjective, he both plays on the sense of foreigner as a religious pilgrim who is to be held in reverence and transfers that reverence to the marvel that 'parole pellegrine' should generate among their audience. And in so doing, he incorporates himself – the Forestiero who, after all, has mysteriously appeared in the midst of this dialogue to give Aristotle's simile this particular twist – into the very context of our reading, a figure to whom we should grant the dignity he deserves. Tasso thus reintroduces the sense of the sacred that is minimized in the Italian translations of *semnon* – worthy of reverence and respect, potentially godlike or divine. And what is more sacred than offering hospitality to the stranger in need – a stranger who, if welcomed within, will serve to dignify the very community of which he or she becomes a part? Just as the arrival of Erminia among the shepherds will transform the pastoral space into one that paradoxically renders the epic poem ever more marvelous, as we will shortly see.

In an article from the 1970s, Charles Klopp recognized the significance of the terms *peregrino* and *errante* in Tasso, and a decade before him, Georg Weise examined the relevance of the pilgrim for the Renaissance more generally.[23] In its Latin derivation, *peregrinus* means, quite literally, a stranger to the *urbs* that was Rome, hence someone who lived in Rome without the citizenship that would eventually be conferred on all residents in the empire after the third century. That with the advent of devotional practices in early Christianity the word would also go on to acquire the secondary meaning of a religious pilgrim is clearly relevant to Tasso's work, focused as it was on the restitution – the 'liberation' – of Jerusalem as a place for pilgrims to worship. Yet both Klopp and Weise minimize the religious dimensions of the word to focus on something more important both to Tasso and to his epoch. For as Weise exhaustively demonstrated, in the late medieval and early modern period, *pellegrino* when used as an adjective would come to take on the related but different meaning of exotic, rare or elegant: something that stands out, as would a foreigner or religious pilgrim, for its unusualness. By the sixteenth century, Weise argues, it was used almost exclusively in the context of aesthetic and poetic conditions. Thus, to have an 'ingegno pellegrino', a term one finds frequently in Italian literature of the sixteenth and seventeenth centuries, was to be a poet, open to the influence of the Muses. Indeed, the condition of *pellegrinità* would seem to be its very receptivity to something beyond or outside of it, something ennobling or uplifting. Hence Weise notes how often the 'pellegrino' is described as open to nobility or love, citing, for example, from the fifteenth-century *Isoldiano*, and arguing that 'the term *Pellegrino* refers to rare qualities of spirit, to a sublime spirit that wants to fulfill great things, to a receptivity to love and its ennobling influence' ('il termine "pellegrino" è riferito a rare qualità dello spirito, all'animo elevato, che vuole e fa compiere cose grandi, alla ricettività per l'amore e al suo influsso nobilitante') (460). And although neither Weise nor Klopp puts it in these terms, the

---

[22] Bernardo Segni, *Poetica di Aristotile tradotta di greco in lingua volgare* (Florence, 1549), f. 334.
[23] See Weise, *Il Rinascimento,* and Klopp, '"Peregrino" and "Errante" in the *Gerusalemme liberata.*'

pellegrino in turn ideally induces such receptivity in those that it – or they – encounter. The true *pellegrino* can only be realized and revealed through its effects on others.

And of course, the *pellegrino* can be a word. As we have seen, Aristotle took care to highlight the 'strange': to afford it special place, to make sure it stands out, gets noticed and is welcomed in.[24] That such elevation was achieved by letting the foreign in – and letting the foreign *remain* foreign – is exactly what got Tasso into trouble. Rare and unusual words, lengthenings and other stylistic ornaments – 'locuzioni peregrine' in the words of one of Tasso's critics – constitute much of what the Crusca would attack; at one point, Salviati even provides a list of words he dislikes, which Tasso dutifully reproduces in the *Apologia*.[25] Salviati explains that he does not reject outright Aristotle's ideas about stylistic dignity, but that Aristotle had asked for a little water, not a tempest. Tasso's Forestiero insists that Salviati chose to make his enemy not only Aristotle but also the great poet from whom Aristotle learned so much, Homer. This is in part because Salviati and, more generally, the Florentines, have neglected what Tasso – and Aristotle, and by extension, Homer – saw as the greatest component of epic poetry: its ability to generate marvel. Or as Camillo Pellegrino put it in the dialogue defending Tasso that had provoked Salviati in the first place, 'I remember having read that the beauty and excellence of locution resides primarily in moving the emotions and generating marvel and delight … in the spirit of the reader, without overdoing it' ('Mi ricordo d'aver letto che la bontà e virtù della locuzione primieramente consiste nel muover gli affetti ed in generar maraviglia e diletto … nell'animo di colui che legge, senza recargli sazietà').[26] Salviati's and the Crusca's response could not be more pointedly opposed: 'La bontà e la virtù della locuzione consiste principalmente nella chiarezza, e nella brevità, e nell'efficacia' ('the goodness and virtue of locution consists primarily in its clearness, brevity and efficacy'). But for Tasso, who uses a vibrant metaphor from painting, too much reliance on clarity is a fault, as we see in those painters who do not

---

[24] There may be, in part, a somewhat legalistic explanation for this. As Juergen Hahn has explained, since each city in Greece had its own citizenship, 'whenever one left the immediate vicinity of the city, one lived as a foreigner, exposed to all the hazards of that status'; *The Origins of the Baroque Concept of 'Peregrinatio'* (Chapel Hill: University of North Carolina Press, 1973), 20. Hence, perhaps, as Hahn goes on to demonstrate, the Greeks' preoccupation with the stranger who is 'dependent for his well-being' on foreign people's good will, as exemplified in the story of Odysseus, addressed as *xenox* by Nausikaa in Book 6 when she asks her maidens to 'give to the stranger food and drink'. All of the *Odyssey* in a certain sense becomes 'a test case of the human relationships between the stranger and his surrounding fellow man' (21) – a literary work that will go on to shape the dynamics of a work such as the *Poetics*, perhaps even with regard to Aristotle's attempt to theorize those 'human relationships' with respect to the style of the epic poem itself. But as in the *Odyssey* – or the *Poetics* – Odysseus and the uncommon word are not absorbed into their surrounding contexts. They remain distinctive, hence elevating their surroundings.

[25] The original list is from the response of Salviati to Tasso's *Apologia*, written later in 1585 and entitled *Risposta all'Apologia del Tasso dell'Infarinato* (Florence, 1585); and cited in Maurizio Vitale's invaluable lexical and stylistic study of Tasso, *L'officina linguistica del Tasso epico: la 'Gerusalemme liberata'* (Milan: LED, 2007), 43. But already in the earlier treatise by Salviati, as cited directly by Tasso himself, there is an attack on his lexical choices that 's'usano impropriamente'. *Apologia*, in *Scritti poetici*, I:132.

[26] From the work of Camillo Pellegrino, the first defence of Tasso's *Liberata* and the immediate catalyst for Lionardo Salviati's attack; *Carrafa overo dell'epica poesia* (Florence, 1584); quoted by Tasso in his *Apologia*; p. 129; as well as in Salviati's response to the *Apologia* in his *Risposta all'Apologia del Tasso dell'Infarinato*; in the edition of *Le opere del Torquato Tasso*, 395.

use or do not know how to use shade – the *oscurità* from which the stranger, or strange word, emerges. Shortly before attacking Ariosto for his 'excessive light', the Forestiero argues that poets should strike a midpoint between 'l'oscurità' and 'l'altro estremo, che non ha proprio nome' (118). Even if Ariosto's *Orlando furioso* might be welcoming of its readers, it was less so of unorthodox or 'unfamiliar' vocabulary or points of view.[27] Tasso saw Salviati and the other defenders of Ariosto attempting to limit the impact of the *Poetics* as they tried to define the *Orlando furioso* as the exemplary 'Italian' work of poetry.

Tasso's own strident defence of Aristotle – not just the Aristotle of the *Poetics,* but of pertinent passages in the *Rhetoric* and *Metaphysics* – is a fascinating testimony to this capacity of Aristotle and particularly to the recent recovery of the *Poetics* to unsettle what had been the reassuring tenets of a Roman poetics subsequently embraced by the humanists. This was the insistence on the appropriation and translation of the foreign and unfamiliar that was essentially Greece.[28] As Doreen Innes argues, the Roman writers of the first century BCE – the new rulers of the Mediterranean from a political point of view if not, at least not yet, of a cultural point of view – were particularly eager to demonstrate that Latin was capable of addressing the sophisticated philosophical and poetic issues found in their Greek predecessors, as they turned away rather decisively from 'the familiar favorites of older Roman poetry', rustic and fledgling as they were.[29] What emerges in Horace's *Ars Poetica* is an insistence on the 'propria': on saying things that are already common, but in a way that is one's own. Cicero's remarkable moment from the *Brutus*, regarding metaphors that seem natural to the place where they ended up, is telling in this context: 'You would say it had not invaded into an alien place but had migrated into its own' (274). Disguising the acts of displacement or 'migration' as these writers sought to do becomes a surer way of integrating Greek's superior literary works without explicitly calling attention to their presence – a superiority alluded to in *Aeneid 6* where Anchises famously prophesies that the Romans will be known for their rulership rather than for their science or art. Still, Virgil no doubt expected his future readers to disagree with this assessment. In making things one 'own', if even by a sleight of hand, one was fighting off the risk of being thought of as derivative or inferior. Almost 1,500 years later, Leonardo Bruni, in his *De interpretatione recta*,

---

[27] See JoAnn Cavallo's work on Ariosto's lack of interest in the otherness and difference that is so much a part of Boiardo's earlier *Orlando innamorato: The World Beyond Europe in the Epics of Boiardo and Ariosto* (Toronto: University of Toronto Presss, 2013).

[28] Weinberg divides his chapters in Volume 1 according to the influence of Horace and particularly his 'Ars Poetica' on literary criticism since the Middle Ages, and then of Aristotle, whose Poetics crashes onto the literary-critical scene in the late 1530s with Alessandro Pazzi's Latin translation (even though Valla had already translated it – a translation printed in 1498 – while the Greek edtion had come out in 1506). But as Weinberg demonstrates – a demonstration that has not gone unchallenged – it was only with Pazzi and the subsequent translation into Italian of the treatise in the late 1540s that its real force was felt. It is thus in the Aristotelian corpus an exceptional work, 'confounding the clear narrative of Aristotle's fortune in the Renaissance', as Micha Lazarus has put it, 'lacking the substantial manuscript tradition' of the rest of Aristotle's works which had centuries of scholastic commentary behind them; 'Aristotelian Criticism in Sixteenth-Century England', *Oxford Handbooks Online,* 3.

[29] Doreen Innes, 'Metaphor, Simile, and Allegory as Ornaments of Style', in *Metaphor, Allegory and the Classical Tradition*, ed. G. R. Boys-Stones (Oxford: Oxford University Press, 2003); in Oxford Scholarship Online, 2007.

the first modern treatise on the art of translation, will strongly advocate a 'Horatian' and Ciceronian stance with respect to translating from Greek into Latin, as Cicero himself had of course done. Bruni too was anxious about making a revived classical Latin hold its own vis-a-vis the Greeks, and he argues that one should never leave foreign words in one's translation: 'Don't go begging for words or borrowing them; leave nothing in Greek out of your ignorance of Latin. The translator must know with precision the exact value and efficacy of terms.'[30] Not to translate in this context is to remain a mendicant, trapped in the no-man's land between two languages and thus in exile and without a home. So does Giraldi Cinzio's point about purging a literary genre like romance of its foreign, French and Spanish origins also belong to this humanistic assessment of the importance of being vigilant about one's own language's excellence. Only this shaking-off of the foreign will enable Italian to reveal itself fully in its 'light and splendour' – 'lume, et splendore'.

Tasso's theory of translation, as it were, was instead intent on showing contemporary Tuscan's insufficiency and attempting to do something about it that would be more faithful to the differences and variety of which Italian was composed – to the point that Salviati accused him at one point of not understanding 'la nostra favella'.[31] He was nonetheless supported by at least one other Florentine, who was able to articulate in sixteenth-century terms what the mechanics of *pellegrinità* meant for a readership that was willing to take on the complexities of Italian's encounter with difference. Lorenzo Giacomini was a Florentine and member of the Accademia degli Alterati – a group that as Déborah Blocker has recently maintained, was in many ways opposed to the work of the Crusca, even welcoming Tasso into their fold for several meetings in the late 1570s. Upon Tasso's death in 1594, Giacomini would deliver an oration praising the recently departed poet as one of the four greatest poets of all time, the other three being Homer, Virgil and Dante.[32] Pointedly sidestepping Ariosto altogether, Giacomini was nonetheless careful, good Florentine that he was, to call attention to Tuscan's many virtues – even claiming that Tasso did his best to write within its strictures – while readily acknowledging its inherent limitations and difficulties. One reason, he maintains, that Tasso is at the level of Virgil and Dante is that he used his poetry to *amend* Tuscan's defects and enable it to become 'magnificent' – the same word that Giraldi used of Ariosto's style. His analysis of Tuscan's shortcomings, and Tasso's remediations, is acute:

> Egli considerando la Toscana favella come de la Latina più dolce cosi meno sonora, grandi aiuti per la magnificenza ricercare, e conoscendo la estrema chiarezza, laquale altro non è, che soprabondante agevolezza di troppo subita intelligenza

---

[30] Leonardo Bruni, *Sulla perfetta traduzione,* ed. and trans. Paolo Viti (Naples: Liguori, 2004): 'non mendicet illud aut mutuo sumat aut in greco relinquat ob ignorantam latini sermonis', 82.
[31] Salviati explains (and Tasso quotes) that 'non sono errori del Tasso, ma del suo non intender la lingua'; *Apologia,* in *Scritti poetici,* I:132.
[32] For a recent and important discussion of Giacomini's role with respect to linguistic and literary theory of the late '500', see Anna Siekiera, 'Una disputa di fine Cinquecento intorno alla questione dei forestierismi (Due lettere inedite di Lorenzo Giacomini a Scipione Bargagli)', *Studi linguistici italiani* 20 (1994): 166–95.

senza dare spazio al ascoltante d'imparare alcuna cosa da se medesimo, haver congiunta seco viltà e bassezza, e produrre dispregio e non aggradire al accorto uditore, il quale si sdegna di esser fanciullescamente trattato, con sollecito studio procacciò a suoi poemi altezza efficacia e leggiadria eccellente, ma non somma chiarezza ... [s]fugge quella soverchia sfugge quella soverchia agevolezza d'esser tosto inteso, & allontanandosi dal usitato dal humile e dal abietto, ama il nuovo il disusato linaspettato e l'ammirabile, si ne concetti se ne le parole.

(Tasso considered the 'toscana favella' sweeter and less sonorous than Latin, and thus sought intensely to give it some magnificence, knowing how extremely clear it is, conveying an abundance of knowledge much too quickly, and preventing the listener from learning anything on his own. Tuscan can produce scorn rather than pleasure for the astute listener, who feels as though he is being treated like a child! Thus Tasso sought to give his poems great efficacy and lightness of touch, but not excessive clarity ... avoiding whatever could be easily understood and distancing himself from the common, the lowly, the everyday. He was more in love with the new, the unexpected, the unusual, and the admirable, with respect to both concepts and words).[33]

Giacomini goes on to contrast a (boring) stroll on open roads ('strade pubbliche') that are flat and wide, with the challenges of hiking up a steep mountainous path. Thus, does Tasso arrive at a style that is 'nobile e pellegrino' and remote from 'un'intelligenza volgare' – far different from the plain style advocated by the Crusca and practised by Ariosto.

There is an undeniable elitism in Giacomini's words as he seeks to use Tasso's poem to illustrate what makes the perfect epic. At the same time, the sheer existence of this 'parlare pellegrino' as prescribed by Aristotle for the epic poet forces the reader to a certain kind of attentiveness.[34] If something is not immediately understood; if the encounter is not one of 'quella soverchia agevolezza', then additional time and attentiveness is required. As Alessandro Giammei has put it, 'the peculiar lexicon of the "pellegrino", difficult to grasp at the beginning, is precisely what brings us closer to the object – or the person – whom we wish, through our initial act of marveling,

---

[33] *Orationi e discorsi di Lorenzo Giacomini* (Florence, 1597), 9. Weinberg quotes only a portion of this citation, omitting the important distinction Giacomini makes between Latin and Tuscan by way of the latter's excessive 'dolcezza': hence the first part of this quote ('Egli considerando la Toscana favella come de la Latina più dolce cosi meno sonora, grandi aiuti per la magnificenza ricercare, e conoscendo la estrema chiarezza, laquale altro non è, che soprabondante agevolezza di troppo subita intelligenza senza dare spazio al ascoltante d'imparare alcuna cosa da se medesimo, haver congiunta seco viltà e bassezza, e produrre dispregio e non aggradire al accorto uditore, il quale si sdegna di esser fanciullescamente trattato'). Weinberg will pick up with 'with careful effort he obtained for his poems elevation, efficacy, and excellent beauty, but not complete clarity' – hence failing to register the qualification between languages that Giacomini is careful to make; Weinberg, *History*, II:1059.

[34] As Camillo Pellegrino puts it in his *Dialogo*, as quoted in Tasso's *Apologia*: 'Che altro, se non quel che dice Aristotele, che a l'epico poeta è solo concesso d'usar voci straniere?'; Tasso, *Scritti poetici*, I, 126.

to know'.³⁵ Or in the words of Giacomini, the excellent poem 'is nothing other than ornate wisdom that treats of God, of divine and earthly things, and of the virtues that deserve to be listed among the divine gifts; and written in the most marvelous manner possible' ('altro non è che ornata sapienza, trattante di dio e de le cose divine e dele opere create, e de le virtù, che tra beni divini meritano essere annoverate, ne la più mirabil maniera che trattare se ne possa...') (5). Dignity as something godlike, the *semnos* that is flattened out to mere *grandezza* by Giraldi and Segni, is here recaptured by Giacomini, who sees Tasso's poetics of pilgrimage as letting the potentially divine into the poem – as did Dante's. But to access that divine, one must work; and all in the service of an 'excellent story ... into which have been introduced marvelous ideas of inestimable delight' ('una favola eccellente ... in cui fanno profondamente penetrare i maravigliosi concetti di inestimabil diletto' [7–8]).

* * *

How then, does the episode with which this chapter opened prepare us for at once 'work' and 'delight'? In the midst of war – the appropriate matter of an epic poem – Tasso turns to the pastoral space and to a frightened family of shepherds, quickly calmed by Erminia's reassurance that 'non portano già guerra quest'armi / a l'opre vostre, a i vostri dolci carmi' ('these arms do not bring war to your labors, nor to your sweet songs') (*GL* 7:7). Subdued, the elderly *pastore* launches into an account of his 'povertà vile e negletta' – although he quickly qualifies the phrase by acknowledging that it is lowly and neglected only for others, not for himself, since he desires neither wealth nor power ('altrui vile e negletta, a me sí cara / che non bramo tesor né regal verga') (*GL* 7:10). These are precisely the treasures and rulership of which Erminia herself was deprived by the Crusaders when they killed her family and destroyed her home, and which she now too spurns. A parallel thus emerges between this exiled princess and the shepherd who had also once been at court: not Antioch, but the capital city of Memphis along the Nile. He abandoned a life of constant weariness to come to this place that might restore his 'perduta pace' (*GL* 7:13) – a peace that Erminia herself seeks. To their initial amazement is thus joined compassion for Erminia's story of despairing loss and love, and an offer of hospitality after she asks that they welcome her to such delightful lodging: 'me teco raccogli in così grato / albergo ch'abitar teco mi giova' (*GL* 7:15). Given rustic clothes and a shepherd's staff to lead the herds from fold to pasture, she will come to occupy herself with the domestic tasks of rural life. The shepherds, that is, have gone from terror and alarm to parental affection, and Erminia from being a wanderer to someone who has found a home, even as her rustic clothes cannot quite hide her nobility and as she continues to pine for the absent Tancredi by carving the name of her beloved on trees.³⁶

---

[35] From a paper written for a graduate class at NYU in fall 2012; my thanks to Alessandro for letting me use his citation.
[36] This is another moment from the episode that Lorrain chose to depict some three decades earlier, now in the Metropolitan Museum, and one that recalls Petrarca's lovesick narrator in the *Canzoniere*.

Erminia will quite literally disappear from Tasso's epic for twelve cantos, until we see her again, inexplicably, in the retinue accompanying the Egyptian king as he makes his way towards Jerusalem. But the old shepherd, his sons and his wife, we never see again. Like Don Quixote's goatherds, they have been left to the recesses of the narrative, marginalized in their spot alongside the Jordan river and forgotten by an epic that needs to move on elsewhere, to defeat Jerusalem and slaughter its inhabitants – in some cases, defenceless 'fugitivi' against whom Goffredo and his men turn their sword in the penultimate ottava of the poem. Tasso seems to mark the shepherds as inconsequential, as does Lorrain, other than to note their harbouring of a fugitive who fled from her own people to be with a man who was once her captor. Or in returning to the citation quoted earlier: Tasso has chosen to protect these shepherds from what he calls 'le peregrine spade', and hence from the destruction that is war. Or as the shepherd says: 'O sia grazie del Ciel che l'umiltade / d'innocente pastor salvi e sublime, / o che sì come il folgore non cade / in basso piano ma su l'eccelse cime, / così il furor di peregrine spade / sol de' gran re l'altere teste opprime...' (7.9). Tasso thus preserves his shepherds – and Erminia herself – from the violence around them by either 'raising them up' or burying them so deeply *in basso piano* that they cannot be touched or even seen.

The phrase 'peregrine spade' is not an incidental one. In addition to playing on ways that the 'foreignness' of epic would have invaded this protected, decidedly non-epic, non-elevated space, there was yet another echo. For the pairing of 'peregrine spade' would have alerted the ear of the attentive reader to the same poet whom Erminia will shortly imitate in the woods, Petrarch, and from a poem that has more to do with epic preoccupations than romantic ones: Canzone 128, 'Italia mia'. The two words come from a question that Petrarca will bitterly fling at the princes of Italy at the opening of the second stanza of Canzone 128, lines 17–20: 'Voi cui Fortuna a' posto in mano il freno / de le belle contrade / (di che nulla pietà par che vi stringa): / che fan qui tante pellegrine spade'. (You into whose hands Fortune has given the reins of these lovely regions for which no pity seems to move you: what are so many foreign swords doing here?)[37] – with particular emphasis on the *qui*. 'Italia mia' is an attempt to engage the reader of Petrarca's canzone in feeling pity for a war-torn Italy, in the desperate decade of the 1340s when Petrarca himself was in flight from unrest. But pity for Italy does not, it seems, prevent the country's lords from hiring mercenaries, mostly from Germany, to flood Italy with foreign swords. Petrarch depicts Italy as a 'bella contrada', characterized by 'nostri dolci campi'[38] or sweet fields, 'mansuete gregge' or gentle flocks and 'verde terreno', now stained with the blood of barbarians (perché 'l verde terreno / del barbarico sangue si depinga? / Why is the green earth coloured with barbarian blood?; 21–2). It is indeed a pastoral place not unlike the tranquil haven of Tasso's shepherds. In an act of foresight, nature had seemed to secure the safety of Italy by placing the Alps themselves as a 'schermo' or shield separating the country from 'la tedesca rabbia'

---

[37] *Petrarch's Lyric Poems*, trans. and ed. Robert Durling (Cambridge, MA: Harvard University Press, 1976), 256. Further translations from the Durling will be noted in the text.
[38] These are the very 'dulcia arva' that Meliboeus is forced to leave behind in Virgil's Eclogue 1:3; *The Works of Virgil*, ed. H. R. Fairclough (London: Heinemann, 1916), 2.

(the Teutonic rage; Durling 258; line 34–5) The entrance therein of these 'pellegrine spade' – the mercenaries' swords – thus appears to violate nature herself.

Written in the tradition of what has been called the 'canzone civile impegnata', Canzone 128 is very much about Italy as a place of beauty, perhaps even of pastoral innocence, betrayed by its own leaders who hire strangers to unleash their swords against the gentle flocks. Surely Tasso was aware of this when he had his shepherd invoke his own safety from the 'furor di peregrine spade'. Tasso has thus fleetingly transformed his foreign shepherds into Italians threatened by foreigners – joined by an Erminia who reveals herself not as a marauding soldier but as a woman in need of refuge; and given the Petrarchan subtext, this Muslim princess is also welcomed into the Italy of Canzone 128. But Tasso complicates this phrase with an echo from another Petrarchan canzone, exactly 100 poems earlier, and one which Gabriele Baldassari has argued is tightly linked with 128: a canzone, not insignificantly, about a crusade.[39] 'O aspettata in Ciel' was probably written in or around 1334 when Philip VI of France had declared a new Crusade to the Holy Land, and of which Petrarch will declare himself, here and elsewhere in a number of his letters, to be supportive. In this earlier canzone, the Germans ('tedeschi') are alluded to in a very different way, as Petrarch refers appreciatively to a tough people who are eager to fight and who should be recruited for the march on Jerusalem, if only they can be persuaded. 'Questa se più devota che non sòle/ col tedesco furor la spada cigne', he says – If these who have been more pious than usual might strap on their sword in Teutonic rage, then one will find out how easy it is to defeat the 'turchi Arabi et Caldi, con tutti quei che speran nelli Dei' (52–6: 'Turks, Arabs, and Chaldeans, with all those who hope in gods on this side of the sea'; Durling 76). With his own 'furor di peregrine spade', Tasso brings together these two fundamentally different versions of Teutonic rage – the one harnessed to march against Jerusalem in armed pilgrimage, the other to march against Italy as mercenary hires – to create a complex image of the nature of the precise threat against the family of shepherds that sojourn near the Jordan. For this hospitable shepherd from Egypt and his family are very much on the side of the 'Turchi Arabi et Caldi', while also dwelling in a place of protective beauty – and a place near that river symbolic for the birth of Christianity itself, the Jordan. The shepherd is hence doubly threatened, or better, doubly protected: from those who would violate his *dolci campi* and those who would march in armed pilgrimage. And, of course, these violators are one and the same: the Christian Crusaders who are the subject of Tasso's poem, the armed *peregrini* who will kill the defenceless fugitives at the poem's end.

In this reading, the Italians are both the victim and the enemy. That Petrarch is utilized for such a recrimination is telling, as though Tasso were taking two of the moments where Petrarch's vernacular output moves towards the tonalities and topics of epic in order to critique the very subject of his own poem. By the same token, in so bringing Petrarch into the *Gerusalemme*'s pastoral setting, he takes the darling of

---

[39] Gabriele Baldassari, *Unum in locum: Strategie macrotestuali nel Petrarca politico* (Milan: LED, 2006), 120.

the Cinquecento's proponents of an 'illustrious vernacular' to call attention to an Italy that was still wounded, and to the necessity of writing in a language that reflects those wounds. Tasso thus has recourse to one of his most noted precursors in the *favella toscana*, and arguably to two moments where Petrarch was most expressive about his own ambivalence regarding an Italian nation. Thus does Tasso militate against what might appear to be the *agevolezza* or ease of his predecessors and, more importantly, of a literary culture that was being progressively substituted for a non-existent empire, intolerant of the real stranger in its midst and unwilling to acknowledge the importance of *pellegrini* in the creation of that culture.

Little wonder the episode had to be removed. The revised *Conquistata* would not tolerate these small pockets of pastoral resistance, even if – or possibly, *because* – they are hidden for the rest of the poem. This pastoral oasis in which Tasso establishes a hospitable community of the estranged, momentarily 'sbigottiti' by the arrival of the marvellous stranger, will vanish in the *Conquistata*. Not only do the shepherds vanish while Erminia wanders about alone following her ill-fated flight from Jerusalem, but so does the resonance of Petrarch in the scene as well. And yet Tasso will return to the phrase 'furor di peregrine spade' – but in a much different context. It is now found in Canto 23, the penultimate canto of the *Conquistata*, which replays many of the events from what was in the *Liberata* Canto 19: the siege of Jerusalem by the soon-to-be victorious Crusaders, with Tancredi leading them on; and the duel between Tancredi and Argante resulting in the latter's death. (Significantly, Erminia will not appear when the duel is over to find Tancredi's unconscious body and heal him; she will only be seen at the close of Canto 23, back in Jerusalem, mourning Argante.) Earlier in the canto, however, Tancredi and his companions approach the temple of David where the populace has fled for safety. In an ottava new to the *Conquistata*, Tasso writes:

> La porta spazïosa apriva il passo
> incontra 'l sol quando tramonta e cade,
> l'aurea da l'orïente, e 'n vivo sasso
> lesse il nome d'Omar la nuova etade.
> Quivi da varie parti il volgo lasso
> fugge il furor di peregrine spade.
> V'è giá Tancredi intorno, e giá raccoglie
> le schiere intente a l'onorate spoglie. (23.71)[40]

(The spacious door opens a passageway toward the sun when it sets and falls, moving from east to west, and in the stone one could read the new epoch of Omar. Here from all around the tired populace had come, fleeing the fury of foreign swords. Already Tancredi is there, closing in around them, and already he has gathered his troops intent on honourable spoils.)

Vengeance is swift for the desecration of the temple, as it was in the *Liberata*, and soon the massacre will be complete: a 'misera strage atra e funeste', repeated from GL 19:38. But the image of a people fleeing to a sanctuary in the hope of saving themselves

---

[40] Tasso, *Gerusalemme conquistata*, ed. Luigi Bonfigli (Bari: Laterza, 1934).

from the 'furor di peregrine spade' is new, as Tasso takes his combination of Petrarchan phrases from the pastoral oasis of the *Liberata* and places it here: not in a secluded spot alongside the Jordan, but in the very heart of Jerusalem and in the poem's dramatic penultimate canto. And lest one opine here about the horrible fate of the 'vulgo lasso', a group that might once have included the hospitable, Muslim shepherds, Tasso now takes care to point out that it is God who is wielding justice on those who have perverted his temple. Indeed, in the ottava cited earlier, he pointedly refers to the way that the entrance into the mosque diabolically reverses that found in Christian churches, as one moves towards the west rather than towards the east. The hope for sanctuary, that is, is uttered against the backdrop of the profaned house of the Christian God.

Yet even if we are not allowed to pity these defenceless, nameless masses, the long lament sung by the new Erminia later in Canto 23 for Argante, also slain by Tancredi, shows how Tasso has shifted the balance of feeling, to a stranger and enemy who could be like us. The brave Argante, wept for, like Hector, by mother, wife and friend – Erminia/Nicea – is, as Tasso will say in his *Giudizio*, now worthy of our compassion and pity as he was not in the *Liberata*. 'E però quella pietà che si niega a la legge si può concedere a la natura ed a l'umanità' ('and so that pity denied him by [Christian] law can be granted on the basis of natural and human sentiment').[41] No longer a mere mercenary, aloof from everything but war, he is now a member of royalty, faithful to his city and his faith, even if he is of the wrong faith. One suspects that it is in some ways his very nobility that enables our pity: he was destined for greater things. Yet Argante's death should not be seen in any way as a critique of the Crusaders, or of Italy. That was the case with the pastoral moment in Book 7 of the *Liberata*, where a shepherd from Egypt tellingly if anachronistically combined lines from two Petrarchan canzoni to equate the Crusade with the foreign attacks on Italy. In the *Conquistata*, the phrase 'Il furor di peregrine spade' is uttered by the poem's narrator, who now uses the lines ironically. The divine fury of these foreign swords cannot be averted or avoided, and they are no longer violating an innocent pastoral space that may be reminiscent of Italy's sweet and pleasant lands.

If the *Conquistata* gives sanctuary to anything, it is to the possibilities of a common humanity – as when Tasso suggests that he wants to fashion the once fierce, solitary Argante into a character for whom we feel pity, 'based on natural and human sentiment'. But it is a common humanity of the nobility. So we are still well beyond the 'common world' and language that Tasso's detractors wanted to impose on him. As Tasso's epic veers towards encompassing the tragic that is at the heart of Aristotle's *Poetics*, we are clearly meant to hear the inevitable drumbeats of war – perhaps the very Ottoman/Austrian war to which Lorenzo Giacomini will rally his readers at the close of his *Oratione* several years after the *Giudizio* was published in 1595. Argante's tragedy is, moreover, inevitable, because Christianity is the superior religion, and one can only trust – as does Giacomini – in a world where God directs his anger at those who perverted the lodging place of his son. But it no longer seems capable of imagining a space where an *ingegno peregrino*, moved by marvel and another's need, might articulate resistance to those who believe they are carrying out the directives of

---

[41] *Giudicio sovra la Gerusalemme riformata,* ed. Claudio Gigante (Rome: Salerno, 2000), 164.

that angry God and hence serve to remind Tasso's Italian readers of *peregrine spade* close to home.

We also lose this: when the shepherd responds to Erminia's question about how he can live so close to war without fear, he gives her two possible answers. Either the grace of heaven preserves and elevates the innocent and humble shepherd out of danger or – just as lightning only strikes the tallest trees – so 'il furor di peregrine spade' only strikes the lofty heads of princes. The phrase in the *Conquistata* about the 'vulgo lasso' hoping to flee such furor – only then to fail a mere two stanzas later – would seem to demonstrate that the shepherd's second alternative is wrong. But the first one may then be right: heaven has reached out to save the shepherd. The language Tasso uses, moreover, is essential in identifying the nature of this salvation: it may be that heaven's grace 'salvi e sublime' 'l'humilitade/ de l'innocente pastore'. 'Sublimare' is used here in the sense of 'sollevare' – to raise up or put out of harm's way. But the suggestiveness of the term, and its juxtaposition with 'humilitade' express with admirable simplicity the work that Tasso tried to do in his *Liberata*, if not in the *Conquistata*, work one might indeed characterize using the term *pellegrinità*: a receptivity to what was not one's own, forcing one to recognize how strange indeed was what one had.

One will note a resonance here with the incarnation, echoed too in the phrase uttered about the place of Christ's birth, now turned into a mosque: 'l'alta magion ch'a Dio ne' primi tempi fu sol albergo in terra'. This juxtaposition of humility and sublimity should also remind us of the marvellous touch of Cupid in the *Aminta*, composed while Tasso was writing the *Liberata*, as he seeks to equalize 'rozzi accenti' with the distinguished lyre. Such is the 'work' of pastoral in this inaugural play in the genre, which Guarini would soon build on – to the consternation of other critics as recounted by Bernard Weinberg in his closing chapter (1074–1105), where he focuses on what is really at the heart of the *History*: questions of genre. This metamorphosis – an act of 'grazia' by a celestial being – provides a space for the humble to speak, and in ways that may be heard by those in more cultivated settings. Pastoral, in this interpretation, becomes a 'marvellous' act primarily in granting a voice to those without a voice – even if done in the context of considerable self-consciousness and even humour. But in the case of the *Liberata*, it is also a question of being moved to wonder and veneration, and hence to the force of the *pellegrino* as it was redefined and aestheticized in the Cinquecento.

'Nasce il sublime e il peregrino nell'elocuzione da le parole straniere …', Tasso had written in his youthful, 1564 *Discorsi dell'arte poetica,* and he continued: 'Umile sarà l'elocuzione, se le parole saranno proprie, non peregrine, non nove, non straniere, poche traslate; e quelle non con quell'ardire che al magnifico si conviene'. ('Elocution will be humble if the words are all common ones: not distinctive, not new, not foreign, with few metaphors, and those metaphors that are there, lack that boldness that suits a magnificent style.')[42] Only straying from the common – and the commonplace – would guarantee a language its distinctiveness. In the early seventeenth century, the Florentine Galileo Galilei would famously distinguish between his favourite poet Ariosto and

---

[42] *Discorsi dell'arte poetica, Discorso terzo,* in Torquato Tassso, *Scritti sull'arte poetica,* ed. Ettore Mazzali; I:54.

possibly his least favourite poet Tasso in his notes to the *Gerusalemme*. Ariosto, Galileo declared, was 'ricco' and 'magnifico', Tasso 'gretto' or stingy, 'miserabile', and poor.[43] These were the very binaries that Tasso spent his entire life questioning. The itinerant foreigner, the secluded shepherd, are transformed into something quietly 'magnificent' – one might even say, 'sublime' – in Canto 7. Perhaps Claude Lorrain did not so much render insignificant the little group of rustic hosts and the woman dressed as a warrior by placing them within his expansive landscape as suggest that their sublimely painted surroundings were, in fact, the perfect setting for their story. Nor would Italian viewers have failed to see the very Italian – specifically, Roman – landscape in which Lorrain, who spent much of his life in and around Latium, positioned his shepherds. So too does Tasso enable us to place them within the contexts of a linguistic and literary history that shows that Italian – and Italians – are at their most sublime when they are willing to acknowledge and even welcome the foreignness both without and within.

Bibliography

Aristotle. *Aristotelis Ars Poetica ab Antonio Riccoboni latine conversa*. Venice, 1579.
Aristotle. *The Complete Works of Aristotle: The Revised Oxford Translation*. Edited by Jonathan Barnes, 2 vols. Princeton: Princeton University Press, 1984.
Aristotle. *Poetica di Aristotile tradotta di greco in lingua volgare*. Translated by Bernardo Segni. Florence, 1549.
Baldassari, Gabriele. *Unum in locum: Strategie macrotestuali nel Petrarca politico*. Milan: LED, 2006.
Berman, Antoine. *The Experience of the Foreign: Culture and Translation in Romantic Germany*. Translated by S. Heyvaert. Albany: SUNY Press, 1992.
Blocker, Déborah. *Le principe de plaisir: savoirs, esthétique et politique dans la Florence des Médicis (XVIe–XVII siècles)*. Paris: Les Belles Lettres, 2019.
Bognolo, Anna. 'Il costume di scrivere alla romanzesca: il dialogo *Della nuova poesia, overo delle difese del Furioso* (1589) di Giuseppe Bastiani Malatesta'. *Historias fingidas* 6 (2018): 5–20.
Bozzola, S. *Purità ed ornamento di parole*. Florence: Accademia della Crusca, 1999.
Bruni, Leonardo. *Sulla Perfetta traduzione*. Edited and translated by Paolo Viti. Naples: Liguori, 2004.
Cavallo, Jo Ann. *The World Beyond Europe in the Epics of Boiardo and Ariosto*. Toronto: University of Toronto Presss, 2013.
Chiappelli, Fredi. *Studi sul linguaggio del Tasso epico*. Florence: Le Monnier, 1957.
Galileo, Galilei. 'Considerazioni al Tasso'. In *Opere*, edited by Antonio Favaro, vol. 9. Florence, 1968.
Giacomini, Lorenzo. *Orationi e discorsi di Lorenzo Giacomini*. Florence, 1597.
Hahn, Juergen. *The Origins of the Baroque Concept of 'Peregrinatio'*. Chapel Hill: University of North Carolina Press, 1973.
Innes, Doreen. 'Metaphor, Simile, and Allegory as Ornaments of Style'. In *Metaphor, Allegory and the Classical Tradition*, edited by G. R. Boys-Stones. Oxford: Oxford University Press, 2003. Accessed through Oxford Scholarship Online, 2007.

---

[43] Galilei Galileo, 'Considerazioni al Tasso', in *Opere,* ed. Antonio Favaro (Florence, 1968), 9:69.

Kenseth, Joy. 'The Age of the Marvelous: An Introduction'. In *The Age of the Marvelous*, edited by Joy Kenseth, 25–59. Hanover, NH: Hood Museum of Art/Dartmouth College, 1991.

Klopp, Charles. '"Peregrino" and "Errante" in the *Gerusalemme liberata*'. *MLN* 94 (1979): 61–76.

Lazarus, Micha. 'Aristotelian Criticism in Sixteenth-Century England', *Oxford Handbooks Online*, 3.

Malatesta, Giuseppe Bastiani. *Della nuova poesia, overo delle difese del Furoso, dialogo*. Verona, 1589.

Marazzini, Claudio. *La Lingua italiana: Profilo storico*. Bologna: Il Mulino, 2002.

Martillotto, Francesco. *La Lingua del Tasso fra polemiche e discussioni letterarie*. Arezzo: Helicon, 2014.

Molinari, Carla. 'Tasso, I Medici e I "fiorentini ingegni"'. In Carla Molinari, *Studi su Tasso*, 99–116. Florence: Società Editrice Fiorentina, 2007.

Petrarca, Francesco. *Petrarch's Lyric Poems*. Translated and edited by Robert Durling. Cambridge, MA: Harvard University Press, 1976.

Salviati, Lionardo. *Risposta all'Apologia del Tasso dell'Infarinato*. Florence, 1585. Pub. in *Le opere del Torquato Tasso*. Edited by Giuseppe Mauro, II:335–408. Venice, 1735.

Sansone, Mario. *Da Bembo a Galiani: Il Dibattito sulla lingua in Italia*. Bari: Adriatico, 1999.

Scarpati, Claudio. *Il vero e il falso dei poeti: Tasso, Tesauro, Pallavicino, Muratori*. Milan, 1990.

Siekiera, Anna. 'Una disputa di fine Cinquecento intorno alla questione dei forestierismi (Due lettere inedite di Lorenzo Giacomini a Scipione Bargagli)'. *Studi linguistici italiani* 20 (1994): 166–95.

Stephens, Walter. 'Trickster, Textor, Architect, Thief: Craft and Comedy in *Gerusalemme liberata*'. In *Renaissance Transactions: Ariosto and Tasso*, edited by Valeria Fanucci, 146–77. Durham: Duke University Press, 1999.

Tasso, Torquato. *Apologia in difesa della Gerusalemme liberata*. In *Scritti sull'arte poetica*, edited by Ettore Mazzali, I:65–39. Turin: Einaudi, 1977.

Tasso, Torquato. *Discorsi dell'arte poetica e in particolare sopra il poema eroico*. In *Scritti sull'arte poetica*, edited by Ettore Mazzali, I:3–63. Turin: Einaudi, 1977.

Tasso, Torquato. *Gerusalemme conquistata*. Edited by Luigi Bonfigli. Bari: Laterza, 1934.

Tasso, Torquato. *Gerusalemme liberata*. Edited by Fredi Chiappelli. Milan: Rusconi, 1982.

Tasso, Torquato. *Giudicio sovra la Gerusalemme riformata*. Edited by Claudio Gigante. Rome: Salerno, 2000.

Tasso, Torquato. *Le Rime*. Edited by Bruno Basile, 2 vols. Rome, 1994.

Tylus, Jane. 'Parole Pellegrine: L'ospitalità linguistica nel Rinascimento'. In *L'ospite del libro: Sguardi sull'ospitalità*, edited by Nicola Catelli and Giovanna Rizzarelli, 13–26. Pisa: Pacini, 2015.

Vergil. *The Works of Virgil*. Edited by H. R. Fairclough, 2 vols. London: Heinemann, 1916.

Vitale, Maurizio. *L'officina linguistica del Tasso epico: la 'Gerusalemme liberata'*, 2 vols. Milan: LED, 2007.

Weinberg, Bernard. *A History of Literary Criticism in the Italian Renaissance*, 2 vols. Chicago: The University of Chicago Press, 1961.

Weise, Georg. *Il rinascimento e la sua eredità*. Edited and translated by P. Antonio and F. Pugliese-Carratelli. Naples: Ligouri, 1969.

9

Soul to squeeze

Emotional history and early modern readings of Aristotle's *Poetics**

Bryan Brazeau

The reactions of spectators to performances and readers to printed texts have a long history in poetic thought. In books II and III of the *Republic*, Plato famously banishes the poets from his ideal city, as they misrepresent the gods (380b2–6) and might induce the guardians to imbibe a false reality whereby emotions can overpower strong souls (391c–5c).[1] In the *Poetics,* on the other hand, Aristotle makes a point of justifying the social benefit of tragedy through the function of catharsis as a type of purgation (1449b24–8). Similar debates with analogous features took place in late Renaissance Italy around the effects of poetry on spectators, and the civic function of tragedy – one may recall the quarrel around Battista Guarini's *Pastor Fido*. Yet most of the scholarship on such debates has tended to focus on them as hermetic intellectual exchanges rather than as an attempt to explore, consolidate and resist changing emotional norms during the period. Few scholars have suggested connecting such discussions of emotion and emotional reactions to new insights provided by the history of emotions. This chapter aims instead to suggest possible intersections between the history of emotions and early modern literary criticism. Specifically, it will interrogate how we might use certain conceptual tools developed by historians of the emotions to reframe and reconsider early modern commentaries on Aristotle's *Poetics*. On the other hand, it will also suggest that these texts may provide a wealth of source material for the history of the emotions in early modern Italy. In other words, it will ask what kinds of readings might emerge if we read poetic theory from early modern Italy – particularly sections that discuss spectators' reactions – not simply as an abstract

---

* Research leading to this publication was funded by the European Research Council under the European Union's Seventh Framework Programme (FP/2007–2013) / ERC Starting Grant 2013 – 335949 ('Aristotle in the Italian Vernacular: Rethinking Renaissance and Early-Modern Intellectual History'). Thanks are due to Simon Gilson for reading a draft of this chapter and providing helpful feedback.
[1] Plato, *Republic*, trans. Paul Shorey, in *The Collected Dialogues of Plato*, ed. Edith Hamilton and Huntington Cairns (Princeton, NJ: Princeton University Press, 1961).

academic debate or an exercise in prescriptivism, but rather as an attempt to describe contemporary reactions to new genres, texts, and performances, along with an attempt to codify changes in emotional norms. A crucial touchstone in this exploration will be the work of Lodovico Castelvetro and its profound influence on poetic theorists in late sixteenth-century Italy such as Torquato Tasso and Giason Denores. Prior to an exploration of these texts, however, the chapter will begin with a discussion of the history of emotions and their applicability to early modern Italy, along with a consideration of how Castelvetro's *Poetica d'Aristotele vulgarizzata e sposta* has often been dismissed by critics based on the ideological assumptions present in Bernard Weinberg's treatment of the text. The ultimate aim of the chapter is to outline a possible constellation of thought around emotions in late Cinquecento Italian commentaries, and to open up new avenues of critical exploration.

First, it would be helpful to define what we mean when we speak about the history of the emotions. While the delimitations of the field have been variously defined by different scholars, such as Peter and Carol Stearns, William Reddy, Barbara H. Rosenwein and others, most historians of the emotions agree on the fact that the biological explanations of emotions emerging from neurobiology, genetics, and evolutionary psychology remain guided by assumptions of universalism (that all humans experience the same basic emotions and are able to recognize them in others regardless of cultural background) and presentism (that our emotions today are the same as those of the past, and will remain so in the future).[2] These views have been challenged by a social constructionist theory of emotions emerging from evolutionary psychology and anthropology, which asserts that the experience, expression, and interpretation of emotion are all shaped by the societies in which their actors are culturally embedded. Historians of the emotions and those who espouse a social constructionist theory of emotions do not argue that emotions have no biological basis at all; rather, they argue that emotions as we understand them, name them, and interpret them are distinctively shaped by culture.

In regard to cultural studies of early modern Italy, the history of the emotions raises significant challenges. In a landmark 2002 article, Rosenwein ultimately refutes the cultural historical paradigm raised in the German sociologist Norbert Elias' 1939 book, *The Civilizing Process*.[3] This approach argued that the European Middle Ages were characterized by direct, impulsive, and explosive emotions, only becoming 'restrained' in sixteenth-century Italian court culture thanks to the 'civilizing' of impulses. The narrative that emerges, both from Elias' account – and from Johann Huizinga's characterization of medieval emotional life as childlike and naïve in his 1919

---

[2] See Peter N. Stearns and Carol Z. Stearns, 'Emotionology: Clarifying the History of Emotions and Emotional Standards', *American Historical Review* 90, no. 4 (1985): 813–36; William M. Reddy, *The Navigation of Feeling: A Framework for the History of Emotions* (Cambridge: Cambridge University Press, 2001); Barbara H. Rosenwein, *Emotional Communities in the Early Middle Ages* (Ithaca, NY: Cornell University Press, 2006). For a critical overview of the history of the field, see Peter N. Stearns, 'History of Emotions: Issues of Change and Impact', in *Handbook of Emotions*, 3rd edn, ed. Michael Lewis, Jeannette M. Haviland Jones and Lisa Feldman Barrett (New York: Guilford Press, 2008), 17–31.

[3] Barbara H. Rosenwein, 'Worrying about Emotions in History', *American Historical Review* 107, no. 3 (2002): 821–45.

The Waning of the Middle Ages on which Elias' account depended – is one whereby Renaissance court culture and absolutist rulers helped cultivate an evolution from medieval violence to modern self-control.[4] Such a paradigm relies on a 'hydraulic' or 'pneumatic' view of emotions, assuming that they behave like fluids under pressure, ready to emerge and open up at any moment, and creating a dichotomy between impulse and restraint.[5] This view, Rosenwein argues, contributes to a 'grand narrative' of the history of emotions whereby 'the history of the West is the history of increasing emotional restraint'.[6] This narrative, she points out, has guided a great deal of twentieth-century thought on the development of Western civilisation, including the works of Max Weber, Sigmund Freud and Michel Foucault.[7] Instead, what is needed, Rosenwein underlines, is a narrative that recognizes 'various emotional styles, emotional communities, emotional outlets, and emotional restraints in *every* period', underpinned by a theoretical understanding that emotions result from certain values and assessments of what things are judged are important to us.[8] The 'shift' that Elias notes in his work can thus be explained by an alternate narrative: a historical change from one emotional community to another.[9]

This leads to a concept that might be fruitfully employed by scholars of early modern literary criticism: Rosenwein's notion of 'emotional communities'. These groups are defined as

> precisely the same as social communities – families, neighbourhoods, parliaments, guilds, monasteries, parish church memberships – but the researcher looking at them seeks above all to uncover systems of feeling: what these communities (and the individuals within them) define and assess as valuable or harmful to them; the evaluations that they make about others' emotions; the nature of the affective bonds between people that they recognize; and the modes of emotional expression that they expect, encourage, tolerate, and deplore.[10]

As Déborah Blocker discusses in her chapter in this volume, the Florentine Accademia degli Alterati were a group who privileged aesthetic pleasure and a hedonistic reading of the *Poetics* in the late sixteenth and early seventeenth centuries. While these discussions might not necessarily indicate the social behaviours and emotional expressions that occurred within the academy, we might nevertheless consider their common approach to the pleasure one ought to experience from tragedy as part of a wider set of emotional norms in the period that made up the aesthetic experience.

---

[4] Ibid., 823.
[5] Ibid., 834.
[6] Ibid., 827.
[7] Ibid., 828. To this list we might equally add Stephen Greenblatt's notion of 'self-fashioning'. Stephen Greenblatt, *Renaissance Self-Fashioning: From More to Shakespeare* (Chicago: University of Chicago Press, 1980). For a rich and detailed overview of this narrative and its development, see Jan Plamper, *The History of Emotions: An Introduction*, trans. Keith Tribe (Oxford: Oxford University Press, 2012), 40–74.
[8] Rosenwein, 'Worrying about Emotions in History', 845. Emphasis in original.
[9] Rosenwein, *Emotional Communities in the Early Middle Ages*, 20–9.
[10] Rosenwein, 'Worrying about Emotions in History', 35.

Although most of Rosenwein's examples treat emotional communities who had direct contact with each other, she has recently noted that such communities may find a nucleus in Brian Stock's notion of a 'textual community', defined as a 'microsociet[y] organized around the common understanding of a script'.[11] Such a community was often centred on 'an individual, who having mastered [a written text], then utilized it for reforming a group's thought and action'.[12] While Stock's focus is primarily on the impact of literacy in eleventh- and twelfth-century monastic communities, it may very well be extended to other periods.[13] When combined with Rosenwein's notion of emotional communities, Stock's conception of a 'textual community' can allow us to see how certain groups that may not have had direct contact with each other could nevertheless construct an emotional community based on common values, emotional norms, and certain modes of emotional expression crystallized around interpretations of a certain text: namely, Aristotle's *Poetics*.

As Rosenwein has noted, despite the fact that the Italian Renaissance holds an important place in periodization, it still plays a rather limited role both in histories of theories of emotions and in histories of felt or expressed emotions.[14] Moreover, while Aristotle's *Rhetoric* has been used by historians of the emotions as one of the earliest definitions of emotions and, by some, as a typical example of how emotions were conceived in Classical Greece, the *Poetics* are rarely used for this purpose.[15] Furthermore, no scholarship to my knowledge has yet suggested that we might use commentaries and translations of the *Poetics* or of the *Rhetoric* in sixteenth-century Italy as a means for constructing a narrative of the emotional and textual community in which translators, interpreters, commentators, readers and poets actively participated. Indeed, the Alterati were not the only readers in the Cinquecento to emphasize a hedonistic interpretation of the *Poetics*. Lodovico Castelvetro embraced a similar position in his 1570 *Poetica d'Aristotele vulgarizzata e sposta*.

To consider how we might begin thinking about sixteenth-century commentaries on the *Poetics* from the perspective of the history of emotions, it is necessary to first unpack Bernard Weinberg's approach to these texts and the significant influence his

---

[11] Barbara Rosenwein, 'Problems and Methods in the History of Emotions', *Passions in Context* 1 (2010): 11–12; Brian Stock, *Listening for the Text: On the Uses of the Past* (Baltimore, MD: Johns Hopkins University Press, 1990), 23. The term is originally coined and developed in greater detail in Brian Stock, *The Implications of Literacy: Written Language and Models of Interpretation in the Eleventh and Twelfth Centuries* (Princeton, NJ: Princeton University Press, 1983), 88–240.

[12] Stock, *The Implications of Literacy*, 90.

[13] A recent example is Jane Heath's application of the concept to the study of the ancient world. See Jane Heath, '"Textual Communities": Brian Stock's Concept and Recent Scholarship on Antiquity', in *Scriptural Interpretation at the Interface between Education and Religion*, ed. Florian Wilk (Leiden and Boston: Brill, 2018), 5–35.

[14] Barbara H. Rosenwein, 'The Place of Renaissance Italy in the History of Emotions', in *Emotions, Passions, and Power in Renaissance Italy*, ed. Fabrizio Ricciardelli and Andrea Zorzi (Amsterdam: Amsterdam University Press, 2015), 15.

[15] For a recent example, see Plamper, *The History of Emotions: An Introduction*, 13–15; David Konstan takes a similar approach concerning the *Rhetoric* which may be seen as paradigmatic of ancient Greek city states, but also includes a very brief treatment of *Poetics* 1453a, where Aristotle mentions the satisfaction of our "fellow feeling" that emerges from tragedy (τὸ φιλάνθρωπον). See David Konstan, *The Emotions of the Ancient Greeks, Studies in Aristotle and Classical Literature* (Toronto: University of Toronto Press, 2006), 40, 215–16.

work continues to have on contemporary scholarship. I will limit myself to his treatment of Lodovico Castelvetro, but the following analysis could easily be adapted to a number of other commentators, translators and interpreters of the *Poetics* in sixteenth-century Italy. In his concise summary of Castelvetro's theory of poetics that was published as part of *Critics and Criticism* – the 1952 'manifesto' of the Chicago School edited by Ronald Crane – Weinberg underlines the importance of idiosyncratic approaches and intentions on the part of individual early modern commentators on the *Poetics*.[16] While someone like Francesco Robortello is characterized as approaching Aristotle's text as a 'masterpiece of clarity and logic', Castelvetro is said to begin with a 'basic scorn for the text of the *Poetics*', which he uses as a jumping-off point 'for the substitution of his own ideas for Aristotle's'.[17] While Weinberg is not incorrect in noting Castelvetro's creative departures from the Aristotelian text, his characterization of Castelvetro cast a long shadow on future criticism. Only ten years later, Baxter Hathaway would note that 'the trouble with Castelvetro was that he worried ideas as a dog worries a carcass'.[18] While on the one hand, Hathaway was attempting to dispel the oversimplifications of Henry Buckley Charlton and Joel Spingarn that Castelvetro's theory of poetry was so moral as to nearly be considered 'evangelical', he also reinforces Weinberg's idea of Castelvetro as a difficult and idiosyncratic theorist who 'did not wish to have much faith in Aristotle'.[19]

This view of Castelvetro as an idiosyncratic critic who was not afraid to reject his contemporaries' supposed 'faith in Aristotle' is present, but with a different emphasis in another 1962 text often employed for courses in the history of literary criticism – Allan H. Gilbert's anthology *Literary Criticism: Plato to Dryden*.[20] In the introduction to his selection from Castelvetro, Gilbert notes that Castelvetro was 'unnecessarily prolix, and though willing to revolt against the thought of his own age, he [was] under the authority of Aristotle'.[21] Gilbert is more charitable to Castelvetro in his brief comments than Weinberg or Hathaway, but still appears to struggle with Castelvetro's dual roles as expositor of Aristotle's text and poetic theorist in his own right. This approach to Castelvetro in Weinberg, Hathaway and Gilbert, then, seems to suggest two problematic sets of expectations. On the one hand, twentieth-century readers – in particular, the Chicago School – might expect a philological exegesis that would return to what they perceived as the 'true meaning' of the Aristotelian text, and bemoan Castelvetro's departures therefrom: a claim that Micha Lazarus richly contextualizes in his essay in this volume. On the other hand, and more broadly, such claims also suggest that there existed a 'unified' approach to Aristotelian thought in early modern Italy. Such a view has been challenged repeatedly in the

---

[16] Bernard Weinberg, 'Castelvetro's Theory of Poetics', in *Critics and Criticism: Ancient and Modern*, ed. R. S. Crane (Chicago: University of Chicago Press, 1952), 349–71, 349. Weinberg's discussion of Castelvetro in *A History of Literary Criticism in the Italian Renaissance*, 2 vols. (Chicago: University of Chicago Press: 1961), 1:502–11 is abstracted in large part from this earlier essay.
[17] Ibid., 349–51.
[18] Baxter Hathaway, *The Age of Criticism* (Ithaca, NY: Cornell University Press, 1962), 235.
[19] Ibid.
[20] Allan H. Gilbert, *Literary Criticism: Plato to Dryden* (Detroit, MI: Wayne State University Press, 1962), 304.
[21] Ibid.

past several decades. Already in 1983, Charles Schmitt's discussion of 'Renaissance Aristotelianisms' recognized the rich plurality of contemporary approaches to the Aristotelian philosophical movement in the period – a diversity of thought that applies equally to approaches to the *Poetics*.[22] In 2009, Luca Bianchi developed this insight by identifying a neglected field of enquiry in the diffusion of Aristotle's works in the period via commentaries, translations, compendia, and paraphrases in Italian.[23] This phenomenon has recently been explored in significant depth through two research projects: the 2010–13 AHRC-funded 'Vernacular Aristotelianism in Renaissance Italy' at the University of Warwick and the Warburg Institute (led by David Lines, Simon Gilson and Jill Kraye) and the 2014–2019 ERC-funded 'Aristotle in the Italian Vernacular' at the University of Ca' Foscari and the University of Warwick (led by Marco Sgarbi and David Lines).[24]

Specifically with reference to the *Poetics*, in 1998, Daniel Javitch revised Weinberg's perspective of early modern genre theory being dominated by Neo-Aristotelian conservatives, demonstrating that the unprecedented proliferation of such theory in sixteenth-century Italy was due to 'exponents of a progressive classicism ... committed to the modernization of ancient poetic kinds rather than to their mere duplication'.[25] More recently, in 2007, Claudia Rossignoli carefully examined Castelvetro's exegetical method in his *Sposizione di Lodovico Castelvetro a XXIX canti dell'Inferno dantesco*, noting how scholarship still has not been able to adequately explain the originality of his conclusions, due in part to the dominance of Weinberg's thesis 'che riduce il lavoro critico del Castelvetro all'applicazione di una radicalizzata, e quindi sterile, nozione di mimesi'.[26] Moreover, Russ Leo has recently noted the falsity of Weinberg's claim that the 1576 edition of the *Poetica* represents Castelvetro's 'final thinking on Aristotle

---

[22] Charles Schmitt, *Aristotle and the Renaissance* (Cambridge, MA: Harvard University Press, 1983), 10–33.

[23] Luca Bianchi, 'Per una storia dell'aristotelismo "volgare" nel Rinascimento: problemi e prospettive di ricerca', *Bruniana & Campanelliana* 15 (2009): 367–85.

[24] Key publications from these projects that demonstrate the rich diversity of vernacular approaches to Aristotle in early modern Italy include *Vernacular Aristotelianism in Renaissance Italy*, ed. Luca Bianchi, Simon Gilson and Jill Kraye (London: The Warburg Institute, 2016); David A. Lines, 'Beyond Latin in Renaissance Philosophy: A Plea for New Critical Perspectives', *Intellectual History Review* 25, no. 4 (2015): 373–89; *Venezia e Aristotele (ca. 1450-ca. 1600): greco, latino e italiano / Venice and Aristotle (c. 1450–c. 1600): From Greek and Latin to the Vernacular*, exhibition catalogue (Venice, Sale Monumentali della Biblioteca Nazionale Marciana, 21 April–19 May 2016), ed. Alessio Cotugno and David A. Lines (Venice: Marcianum Press, 2016); *Aristotele fatto volgare: Tradizione aristotelica e cultura volgare nel Rinascimento*, ed. David A. Lines and Eugenio Refini (Pisa: Edizioni ETS, 2014); Marco Sgarbi, 'What Does a Renaissance Aristotelian Look Like? From Petrarch to Galilei', *HOPOS. The Journal of the International Society for the History of Philosophy of Science* 7 (2017): 226–45; *I generi dell'aristotelismo volgare nel Rinascimento*, ed. Marco Sgarbi (Padua: CLEUP, 2018); *'In Other Words': Translating Philosophy in the Fifteenth and Sixteenth Centuries*, special issue of *Rivista di storia della filosofia*, ed. David A. Lines and Anna Laura Puliafito, (2019/2); Eugenio Refini, *The Vernacular Aristotle: Translation as Reception in Medieval and Renaissance Italy* (Cambridge: Cambridge University Press, 2019); and Eva del Soldato, *Early Modern Aristotle: On the Making and Unmaking of Authority* (Philadelphia, PA: University of Pennsylvania Press, forthcoming 2020).

[25] Daniel Javitch, 'The Emergence of Poetic Genre Theory in the Sixteenth Century', *Modern Language Quarterly* 59, no. 2 (June 1998): 139.

[26] Claudia Rossignoli, '"Dar Materia di Ragionamento." Strategie Interpretative Della *Sposizione*', in *Lodovico Castelvetro: filologia e ascesi*, ed. Roberto Gigliucci (Rome: Bulzoni, 2007), 93.

and on poetic theory', as Castelvetro had been dead for nearly five years upon its publication and 'it is difficult to imagine that his friends and fellow travelers would so meticulously remove references to Reformation controversies based on the final wishes of a victim of the Inquisition'.[27]

While Italian-language scholarship has begun to approach Castelvetro from a philologically-inflected approach to translation studies (as will be discussed later), English-language scholarship, despite the aforementioned revisions, continues to be dominated by Weinberg's thesis, due in part to the lack of a complete and reliable English translation of the *Poetica*, along with the accessibility of Weinberg's brief summary of Castelvetro's complex poetic theory.[28] A recent example of this phenomenon would be Andrew Ford's 2015 article, which places the blame for framing Aristotle's *Poetics* as a prescriptive text squarely at Castelvetro's feet, despite the latter's discovery of new rules far beyond Aristotle's conception 'generating such phantoms as the unity of place or the five-act rule'.[29] Moreover, Weinberg's dismissal of Castelvetro's heterodox religious views also seems to have cast a long shadow. As Leo has recently underlined, most modern scholars outside of Italy tend to ignore Castelvetro's heterodoxy and treat the *Poetica* as a 'neutral technical work' when in fact it was quite polemic and made space for the accommodation of heterodox ideas by addressing spectators and readers through the performance of tragedy: 'Castelvetro and his earliest censors recognized what many contemporary readers ignore: the extent to which tragedy is a philosophical and theological genre, the extent to which the Reformation itself is a poetic and a critical project.'[30]

On the other hand, recent scholarship in Italian on Castelvetro has been informed by the rise of translation studies as a field. Such work has led to a number of publications that have demonstrated Castelvetro's unique approach to translating not only Aristotle's *Poetics* but indeed also works by Melancthon, and potentially a lost translation of the New Testament.[31] In a sense, these studies – especially the work collected in two edited

---

[27] Russ Leo, *Tragedy as Philosophy in the Reformation World* (Oxford: Oxford University Press, 2019), 95. For recent and succinct summaries of the reception of the *Poetics* in early modern Italy, see Enrica Zanin, 'Les commentaires modernes de la *Poétique* d'Aristote', *Études littéraires* 43, no. 2 (2012): 55–83; and Daniel Javitch, 'The Assimilation of Aristotle's *Poetics* in Sixteenth-Century Italy', in *The Cambridge History of Literary Criticism: Volume 3, The Renaissance*, ed. Glyn P. Norton (Cambridge: Cambridge University Press, 1999), 53–65.

[28] An abridged translation was published in 1984. See Andrew Bongiorno, *Castelvetro on the Art of Poetry: An Abridged Translation of Lodovico Castelvetro's* Poetica d'Aristotele vulgarizzata e sposta (Binghamton, NY: Medieval and Renaissance Texts and Studies, 1984).

[29] See Andrew Ford, 'The Purpose of Aristotle's *Poetics*', *Classical Philology* 110, no. 1 (January 2015): 3.

[30] Leo, *Tragedy as Philosophy in the Reformation World*, 82–3.

[31] See, for example, Alessio Cotugno, 'Le Annotationi di Piccolomini e la *Poetica* di Castelvetro a confronto: tecnica argomentativa, vocabolario critico, dispositivi esegetici', in *Forms of Conflict and Rivalries in Renaissance Europe*, ed. David A. Lines, Marc Laureys and Jill Kraye (Göttingen: V & R Unipress for Bonn University Press, 2015), 161–206; Claudia Rossignoli, '"L'ufficio dello 'interprete'": Castelvetro Translator of Melanchthon', *Italian Studies* 68, no. 3 (2013): 317–39; Simon Gilson, 'Reading the *Convivio* from Trecento Florence to Dante's Cinquecento commentators', *Italian Studies* 64, no. 2 (2009): 266–95; Anna Siekiera, 'La *Poetica Vulgarizzata et Sposta* per Lodovico Castelvetro e le traduzioni cinquecentesche del trattato di Aristotele', in *Lodovico Castelvetro: Letterati e grammatici nella crisi religiosa del Cinquecento. Atti della XIII giornata Luigi Firpo Torino, 21-22 settembre 2006*, ed. Massimo Firpo and Guido Mongini (Florence: Leo S. Olschki, 2008),

volumes by Gigliucci and Firpo & Mongini – have served to 'rehabilitate' Castelvetro, his methodology, his heterodoxy, and his commentary for new readers. By focussing on how he translated certain texts and the adaptive strategies that he used, a new emphasis on Castelvetro's audience emerges, thus reframing his commentary on the *Poetics* from the prescriptive caricature to which it had been reduced. Building on this work, we might then take up Javitch's suggestion that commentators and theorists such as Castelvetro were attempting to adapt the *Poetics* to meet the needs of contemporary poets and audiences. Moreover, this new emphasis also opens up a space for reading Castelvetro's commentary (and others) as descriptive documents from the perspective of the history of the emotions. In order to approach commentaries such as Castelvetro's from such a perspective, we thus first need to reframe our own approach to the text keeping three key points in mind: (a) such a commentary does not simply emerge from the mind of an idiosyncratic prescriptivist, but rather from a writer who had a very unique and precise methodological approach;[32] (b) vernacular Aristotelianism in sixteenth-century Italy was a rich, complex and, at times, contradictory phenomenon, which included a number of exponents for a 'progressive classicism' that attempted to revitalize existing genres for contemporary audiences; and (c) while Weinberg's summary of many of these poetic theories may be concise and accessible, it is crucial to examine the texts themselves rather than relying on such sources and their often outdated assumptions.

Turning now to the text of the *Poetica,* Castelvetro – as part of his theory of oblique pleasure – describes at length the emotional experiences that an audience member might have.[33] Such descriptions are a departure from the Aristotelian text, but might the popularity of Castelvetro's commentary and its significant influence on early modern European poetics not suggest that many of his readers found that these descriptions echoed their own emotional reactions? Discussions of such reactions have often focused on the role of catharsis and the fraught Cinquecento debate around this topic, which I will not discuss here – both for purposes of brevity and because Castelvetro's description of the spectator's emotional reaction

---

25–45; Lorenzo Geri, 'Castelvetro traduttore di Melantone', in *Lodovico Castelvetro: filologia e ascesi*, ed. Roberto Gigliucci (Rome: Bulzoni, 2007), 241–59; Alessio Cotugno, 'Piccolomini e Castelvetro traduttori della *Poetica*', *Studi di lessicografia italiana* 23 (2006): 113–219.

[32] On Castelvetro's methodology see Alberto Roncaccia, *Il metodo critico di Ludovico Castelvetro* (Rome: Bulzoni, 2006), along with the contributions by Rossignoli, Siekiera, and Cotugno above.

[33] For a discussion of Castelvetro's oblique pleasure in dialogue with René Girard's notions of triangulated desire and sacrifice, see Pier Cesare Rivoltella, 'Il piacere obliquo statu nascenti: la riflessione estetica di Ludovico Castelvetro', in *Teatri barocchi: tragedie, commedie, pastorali nella drammaturgia europea fra '500 e '600*, ed. Silvia Carandini (Rome: Bulzoni, 2000), 15–28; and Alessandro Serpieri, 'Il piacere dell'obliquo. Note sul tragico e il tempo dai tragici greci a Shakespeare', in *Teatri barocchi: tragedie, commedie, pastorali nella drammaturgia europea fra '500 e '600*, ed. Silvia Carandini (Rome: Bulzoni, 2000), 29–63. On the relationship of Castelvetro's "piacere obliquo" to his concept of "meraviglia" see Valeria Merola, 'Il piacere obliquo e la meraviglia. Sulla poetica di Lodovico Castelvetro', in *Lodovico Castelvetro: filologia e ascesi*, ed. Roberto Gigliucci (Rome: Bulzoni, 2007), 305–17. On the textual and compositional history of Castelvetro's commentary see, in the same volume, Valentina Grohovaz, 'Per la storia del testo della *Poetica d'Aristotele vulgarizzata e sposta*', in *Lodovico Castelvetro: filologia e ascesi*, ed. Roberto Gigliucci (Rome: Bulzoni, 2007), 13–33.

departs significantly from the concept.³⁴ Nevertheless, we might note that the fierce debate on catharsis was a phenomenon particular to early modern Italian, and later European poetics. As Blocker has underlined, the very discussion of catharsis and purgation of passions – indeed, discussion of the *Poetics* itself – held little interest for medieval commentators; Averroës' middle commentary does not discuss such a form of 'purification' as moral or political justification for tragedy.³⁵ We might add that catharsis or purification is also not an important concern in Avicenna's commentary on the *Poetics*, which ascribes the differences between genres (tragedy, comedy and satire) to the differences between moral agents and the ideals they pursue.³⁶ Yet from Robortello onward, catharsis and tragic purgation are key flashpoints in poetic debates. Might such a debate have been less about the correct interpretation of Aristotle's text and more about contemporary concerns for the moral and political utility of tragedy?

In his comment on *Poetics* 1449b31–1450a14 – where Aristotle distinguishes the six parts of tragedy – Castelvetro describes in detail the emotional experiences an audience member would have when seeing certain types of plot. If a good person comes to a good end through his or her deeds, one experiences pleasure due to a type of identification with the protagonist:

> Sentiamo un piacere tacitamente nascere in noi che ci fa lieti, e per rispetto di noi e per rispetto del buono felice; percioché in noi nasce una speranza, che per essere noi simili a lui o non molto dissimili in bontà, siamo altresì per ottenere simile

---

³⁴ As Merola notes, with regard to catharsis, Castelvetro's theory of purgation retains 'solo l'aspetto della partecipazione emotiva dello spettatore' and omits all possible aspects of the purification of spectators' souls through their identification with the protagonist, as suggested in Giraldi Cinzio's *Discorso sulle commedia e sulle tragedie*. See Merola, 'Il piacere obliquo e la meraviglia', 309. The debate on catharsis in sixteenth-century poetics is quite complex. The most detailed summary (although quite dated) remains Hathaway's in *The Age of Criticism*, 203–300. For a concise and clear overview of the evolution of different positions on catharsis in Latin and vernacular texts throughout the Cinquecento see Pier Cesare Rivoltella, 'La Scena della sofferenza', *Communicazioni Sociali* 15, nos. 2–3 (1993): 101–55. For discussions on the nature of catharsis in the *Poetics* and medical implications regarding the process of purgation, see Roberto Diano, 'La catarsi tragica', in idem. *Saggezza e poetiche degli antichi* (Venice: Neri Pozza, 1968), 215–80; and, more recently, Pierre Destrée, 'Éducation Morale et Catharsis Tragique', *Les Études Philosophiques* 4 (2003): 518–35. Eugene E. Ryan has challenged such medical interpretations, particularly in the commentaries of Robortello and Vincenzo Maggi, suggesting that Maggi's renown as a medical expert and familiarity with Aristotelian medical discourse may have deterred him from discussing 'catharsis' as Aristotle's 'purging' metaphor was not intended to be associated with medical concepts of purgation. See Eugene E. Ryan, 'Robortello and Maggi on Aristotle's Theory of Catharsis', *Rinascimento* 22 (1982): 274.

³⁵ Déborah Blocker, 'Élucider et équivoquer: Francesco Robortello réinvente la "catharsis"', *Les Cahiers du Centre de recherches historiques* 28–9 (2002): 109–40.

³⁶ Due no doubt in part to a number of humanistic attacks, Avicenna's commentary on the *Poetics* does not appear to have enjoyed a wide circulation in Renaissance Italy despite the prevalence of his *Canon of Medicine* in university medical curricula. See Nancy Siraisi, *Avicenna in Renaissance Italy: The Canon and Medical Teaching in Italian Universities after 1500* (Princeton, NJ: Princeton University Press, 1987), 43–76. On Avicenna's approach to the *Poetics* see Salim Kemal, *The Philosophical Poetics of Alfarabi, Avicenna, and Averroes: The Aristotelian Reception* (Abingdon: Routledge, 2003), 170; Deborah L. Black, *Logic and Aristotle's* Rhetoric *and* Poetics *in Medieval Arabic Philosophy* (Leiden: Brill, 1991); and Ismail M. Dahiyat, *Avicenna's Commentary on the Poetics of Aristotle: A Critical Study with an Annotated Translation of the Text* (Leiden: Brill, 1974).

felicità, e nasce ancora una voglia di rallegrarci con lui della sua felicità per fargli a sapere che godiamo che abbia adempiuto il suo desiderio. [37]

(We feel the silent birth of a pleasure within us that makes us joyful, both with respect to ourselves and to the good man with a happy outcome. For this reason, within us is born a hope that since we are similar to him in goodness – or at least not very different – we will likewise obtain a similar happiness. Also, another desire is born that we should rejoice with him about his happiness in order to let him know that we are pleased that he has fulfilled his wish.)

Castelvetro's language is quite descriptive, but in this case, his 'notorious prolixity' may actually be of service. He not only speaks of pleasure but also grounds this experience within the temporality of the performance. The spectator is not said to experience pleasure directly or all at once, but rather it is the arising of this experience within the self that leads to a dual sense of happiness: the first directed towards one's own self as, understanding ourselves to be good, we expect the same happy ending to occur; the second directed towards the fictional character as a desire to celebrate his happy ending with him in order to exhibit our own joy at the achievement of his desire. As Vera Ribaudo notes, Castelvetro's approach to the spectator's reaction distinguishes two levels of emotional reaction: the first being the immediate reaction to what is represented on stage and the second being the spectator's later reflection on this reaction.[38]

Such a complex psychological depiction provides insight into how such a spectator might experience these emotions, and more importantly, the cultural contexts of selfhood in which such emotional experiences are shaped. In this particular description, we can observe that Castelvetro's spectator experiences pleasure due not only to an identification with the protagonist – already an idea present in Aristotle – but indeed also because a happy ending resulting from good works confirms the spectator's world view that good actions are rewarded. Moreover, such a spectator also seeks to communicate and socially perform this emotional experience to demonstrate his pleasure at the result. Castelvetro uses a similar formulation in the other three possible cases: 'sentiamo tacitamente un dispiacere nascere in noi' ('we feel the silent birth of a displeasure within ourselves') is used to discuss the displeasure we experience when seeing a good person come to an unhappy end, and again the duality of this displeasure is underlined – both because we fear that a similar end may await us if good persons are not spared from misfortune, and because we experience compassion for the protagonist who has fallen into such a situation.[39]

---

[37] Lodovico Castelvetro, *Poetica d'Aristotele vulgarizzata e sposta* (Vienna: Gaspar Stainhofer, 1570). For the purposes of this essay, I have used the modern edition edited by Werther Romani: L. Castelvetro, *Poetica d'Aristotele vulgarizzata e sposta*, ed. Werther Romani, 2 vols. (Rome and Bari: Laterza, 1978–79), I:167. All translations are mine unless otherwise noted.

[38] Vera Ribaudo, 'Il piacere delle lacrime: il *diletto obliquo* nella *Spositione all'Inferno* di Lodovico Castelvetro', *Philosophical Readings* VIII, no. 2 (2016): 84.

[39] Ibid., I:166.

The most interesting description from this perspective is what happens when a bad person comes to an unfortunate end:

> Ma se ci è rappresentato il reo infelice, si genera in noi un piacere, e per rispetto di noi e per rispetto del reo, percioché ci ralegriamo per la sicurtà che non averrà a noi simile aversità, non essendo simili a lui in malvagità, e ci ralegriamo che l'occhio della divina giustizia vegga le sue male operazioni e con la 'nfelicità le punisca.[40]

> (But if a bad[41] character with an unhappy end is portrayed for us, a pleasure is generated within us both with respect to ourselves and to the character. For this reason, we rejoice in the surety that similar adversity will not befall us – as we are not similar to him in wickedness – and we rejoice that the eye of divine justice observes his evil acts and punishes him with an unhappy outcome.)

In both cases when describing the emotions that we experience for a bad character ('un reo'), Castelvetro uses the reflexive verb *generarsi* instead of *tacitamente… nascere*, suggesting that such characters prompt stronger or more immediate reactions in the audience than their counterparts. Again, the duality of this pleasure is underlined; due to our lack of identification with the character we feel pleasure at the relative safety we experience from such misfortunes, and we feel pleased – yet again – by the confirmation of an ethical and religious world view whereby divine justice operates to punish those who commit evil. Such a discussion of how a plot impacts spectators' emotions and depends upon their conception of a moral universe is also present in Castelvetro's discussion of *hamartia* when glossing *Poetics* 1452b35–6, where he underlines the danger of representing holy men falling from happiness into misery. As I have discussed elsewhere, while Aristotle only mentions that that such a plot would not be poetically efficient, Castelvetro adds that such a plot would be abominable: 'sarebbe cosa che indurebbe gli uomini a credere che Dio non avesse providenza speziale de' suoi divoti e che fosse ingiusto' ('it would be something that would lead men to believe that God does not have special providence over his devotees and that he is unjust').[42] Thus, not only are the *Poetics* adapted for a Christian audience in Castelvetro's *Poetica* but the emotional impact they have also depends on the extent to which they ratify or refute the audience's world view of a moral universe.

Returning to his commentary on 1449b31–50a14, Castelvetro both anticipates and refutes a potential criticism. If two of the aforementioned plots cause displeasure

---

[40] Ibid., I:166–7.
[41] For the purposes of readability, to maintain parallelism, and in order to translate with the broadest meaning possible, I have chosen to render 'reo' with the simple term 'bad', when the actual meaning is much closer to 'guilty' or 'responsible' for an error or a transgression.
[42] Ibid., I:361. For a broader discussion of how Castelvetro's discussion of hamartia fits into sixteenth-century discussions on the topic in commentaries and translations of the *Poetics* see Bryan Brazeau, '"My Own Worst Enemy": Translating Hamartia in Sixteenth-Century Italy', *Renaissance and Reformation* 41, no. 4 (2018): 9–42.

(a good person coming to a bad end and a bad person coming to a good end), he asks, how then can pleasure be the sole end of poetry?

> Ora è da rispondere che quantunque sia dispiacere quello che sentiamo per lo male del buono e per lo bene del reo, nondimeno non dee essere considerato come dispiacere, ma più tosto è da essere giudicato piacere, poiché quel dispiacere è congiunto con un piacere che l'addolcisce e cel rende dilettevole, percioché con quel dispiacere ci riconosciamo essere buoni, conciosia cosa che ci contristiamo del male del buono e del bene del reo, e ci paia d'essere giusti; onde godiamo, per quel dispiacere, della riconoscenza della nostra giustizia: il che è diletto grandissimo e verace.[43]

> (Now, it should be answered that whatsoever be the displeasure that we feel for the evil that befalls a good man and for the good that befalls a bad one, nevertheless it ought not to be considered as displeasure. Rather, it is to be considered as pleasure since this displeasure is combined with a pleasure that sweetens it and makes it pleasurable. This is because with this displeasure we recognise ourselves to be good, insomuch as we become sorrowful about the evil that befalls a good man and the goodness that befalls a bad man, and we appear to ourselves to be just. Whence we enjoy – through this displeasure – the recognition of our own justice, which is a veritable and most great pleasure.)

Again, Castelvetro places great emphasis on the oblique pleasure the audience experiences; when seeing a tragic protagonist undeserving of their misfortune they still nevertheless also feel a type of pleasure whereby they recognize themselves to be just persons since they are displeased by the witnessing of injustice. For Weinberg, nearly all of Castelvetro's discussion of pleasure and displeasure is reducible to a tendency among commentators in the period (from Robortello onwards) to depart 'from the spirit of the *Poetics*' removing 'the principal emphasis from the poem to the audience'.[44] It is true that Castelvetro pays much greater attention to the role of the audience than other commentators, and that this emphasis leads to detailed considerations of verisimilitude as a crucial criterion for poetic efficacy;[45] nevertheless, Weinberg's assumption that Castelvetro is exclusively focused on the audience and thus articulating a kind of 'rhetorical' poetics leads him to overlook the commentator's emphasis on the possibility that such emotional reactions may actually contribute to a reification, reinforcement, or challenge of the audience members' views of the external world, the existing political and moral order, and of themselves. Indeed, in the aforementioned quotation Castelvetro's language emphasizes that it is through this very displeasure that such recognition happens, 'con quel dispiacere *ci riconosciamo essere buoni*' ('with this displeasure *we recognize ourselves* to be good') and that the pleasure the audience feels is not, as Weinberg would have it, 'a sentiment of self-

---

[43] Castelvetro, *Poetica d'Aristotele vulgarizzata e sposta*, I:167.
[44] Weinberg, 'Castelvetro's Theory of Poetics', 351. For a rich and in-depth discussion of Weinberg's own critical assumptions see the contributions by Lazarus and Brljak in this volume.
[45] Ibid., 356–7.

righteousness', but rather a joy in the '*riconoscenza* della nostra giustizia' ('*recognition of our own justice*').[46] Castelvetro also uses similar language in the very passage cited by Weinberg (commentary on 1452b25–1453b13):

> Adunque il piacere nascente della compassione e dallo spavento, che è veramente piacere, è quello che noi di sopra chiamammo piacere obliquo; e è quando noi, sentendo dispiacere della miseria altrui ingiustamente avenutagli, *ci riconosciamo essere buoni, poiché le cose ingiuste ci dispiacciono; la quale riconoscenza, per l'amore naturale che noi portiamo a noi stessi, ci è di piacere grandissimo*.[47]
>
> (Thus, the nascent pleasure of compassion and of fear – which is really pleasure – is that which we earlier called oblique pleasure; it occurs when we – feeling displeasure at the misery of another that has unjustly befallen him – *recognise ourselves to be good because unjust things displease us. Such recognition is of the greatest pleasure to us on account of the natural love that we have for ourselves*.)

Again, here, we may note Castelvetro's emphasis on the act of recognition of one's own sense of justice, and the pleasure brought by this recognition. Such an emphasis on recognition also implies a change of state from ignorance to knowledge on the part of the spectator. Indeed, only a few lines below, Castelvetro underlines the pleasure of the learning process, particularly when this process is one of self-discovery: 'l'esperienza delle cose avenute ci 'mprima più negli animi la dottrina che non fa la simplice voce del dottore, e più ci ralegriamo del poco che impariamo da noi che del molto che impariamo da altri' ('the experience of things that have occurred impress learning more deeply within our souls than does the simple voice of the learned man; we also rejoice more greatly in the small amount that we have learned on our own than in the great amount that we learn from others').[48] Castelvetro's distinction of these two levels of reaction in the spectator and his emphasis on the learning process are a natural extension of his view on Aristotle's response to Plato. An autograph manuscript of Castelvetro's critical notes in the Biblioteca Estense (alfa S.5.1) includes a section of commentary on the third book of Plato's *Republic*.[49] At the passage on imitation where Socrates underlines that the guardians should only imitate 'what is appropriate to them – men, that is, who are brave sober pious, free, and all things of that kind' and not imitate anything else, Castelvetro comments that Plato makes a fundamental error in his assumption on how poetry teaches:

> In questo luogo presuppone Platone, che la poesia non sia trovata per altro se non per insegnar per essempio, et ciò che si truova in poesia o bene o male che

---

[46] Ibid., 356. Castelvetro, *Poetica d'Aristotele vulgarizzata e sposta*, I:167.
[47] Castelvetro, *Poetica d'Aristotele vulgarizzata e sposta*, I:391. Emphases mine.
[48] Ibid. Castelvetro's emphasis on the pleasure of the learning process is underlined by Merola, 'Il piacere obliquo e la meraviglia', 312.
[49] Lodovico Castelvetro, 'Chiose intorno il terzo libro del comune di Platone', alfa.S.5.1, 124v–135r. Biblioteca Estense Universitaria, Modena. These notes were published by Lodovico Antonio Muratori, in *Opere varie critiche di Lodovico Castelvetro gentiluomo Modenese* (Lyon: Pietro Foppens, 1727), 211–28. I have consulted both the manuscript copy and the published version for this essay.

sia, altri la possa o debba seguire. Il che è falso, percioche è proposta prima che *vogliamo che insegna per materia da farvi pensamenti sopra*, et accioche habbiamo essempi d'ogni maniera e da spaventare i rei, e da consolare i buoni, e *da conoscere la natura degli huomini de delle donne*, e percio diceva Aristotele che la tragedia con le paure, et con le ingiustitie scacciava le paure e le ingiustitie dal cuore degli huomini ascoltanti riprovando quello che dice Platone in questo luogo.[50]

(In this passage Plato assumes that poetry was not invented for any other reason than to teach by example, and whatever is found in poetry – whether it be good or bad – could or should be followed by others. This is false because it is proposed earlier that *we wish that it should teach through material that prompts reflection*, and to that end we have all kinds of examples to terrify bad men, to console good men, *and to know the nature of both men and women*. For this reason, Aristotle said that tragedy – with fears and injustices – chased away fears and injustices from the hearts of spectators, thus reproaching what Plato says in this passage.)

This response to Plato further demonstrates the two levels of spectator reaction discussed above, and frames Castelvetro's own reflection on oblique pleasure as a natural extension of – what he perceives to be – Aristotle's method.

Thus, Castelvetro is not simply concerned with 'fitting pleasures into the capacities of the audience for pleasure and displeasure' as Weinberg would have it, but rather seems to be articulating the changing emotional and intellectual states that occur in a spectator when seeing certain kinds of plots represented.[51] In this regard, Hathaway's analysis of Castelvetro's orientation as 'more psychological than ethical', and of this passage in particular as evidence of Castelvetro's 'strong desire to psychologize', seems to be more consistent with Castelvetro's text.[52] Castelvetro's view of oblique pleasure, then, seems to describe two types of self-realization. On the one hand, the spectator sees his or her moral world view confirmed/refuted by the outcome of the plot and feels pleasure or displeasure; on the other hand, the spectator becomes aware of their own reaction and takes pleasure in such *self*-recognition (of themselves as a good person). As such, Castelvetro's articulation of the impact that a performance may have on the spectator naturally leads to an emphasis on verisimilitude and on the marvellous. On the one hand, the spectator identifies with the protagonist and judges the events of the plot based on his own understanding of reality – as demonstrated above.[53] On the other, as Merola notes, the process of learning and self-discovery implicitly includes the joy of the unexpected, which in tragedy manifests itself as *meraviglia*, building on Giraldi Cinzio's notion that the marvellous can help capture the spectator's attention and is thus useful for tragedy.[54]

---

[50] Castelvetro, alfa.S.5.1, 130v. The quotation from Plato is taken from *Republic*, trans. Shorey, 395c, p.640. Emphases mine.

[51] Weinberg, 'Castelvetro's Theory of Poetics', 351.

[52] Hathaway, *The Age of Criticism*, 237.

[53] Ribaudo, 'Il piacere delle lacrime', 86; on the topic of verisimilitude in Castelvetro see Giancarlo Alfano, 'Sul concetto di verosimile nei commenti cinquecenteschi alla 'Poetica' di Aristotele', *Filologia e critica* 26 (2001): 187–209.

[54] Merola, 'Il piacere obliquo e la meraviglia', 312. On Robortello's notion of the marvellous, its tragic utility and its inseparability from fear and pity, see Rivoltella, 'La Scena della sofferenza', 112–13.

Castelvetro's conception of how a spectator reacts to poetry, and his emphasis on the importance of both the marvellous and the verisimilar would have a significant impact on the poetic theories of Torquato Tasso, whose debt to Castelvetro has been recognized by modern scholarship, though few have noted the extent to which he adopts elements of Castelvetro's *Poetica* in his *Discorsi del poema eroico*.[55] Applying Castelvetro's concepts to epic poetry, Tasso claims that while other poems moved the reader to marvel in order to move them to laughter, compassion, or other affects, epic instead elicited compassion in order to move the reader to experience *meraviglia*.[56] Regarding verisimilitude, in his letter to Scipione Gonzaga, from 16 September 1575, Tasso not only cites Castelvetro but also adopts his opinion of verisimilitude with regard to the magic powers of the sorceress Armida, writing that poets should base themselves on the opinion of what the audience believes to be possible: 'gli uomini, che teologi non sono, stimano il poter de' diavoli maggior che in effetto non è, e maggior l'efficacia dell'arte maga, poterono con buona conscienza i poeti, ch'inanzi a me han scritto, in questo attenersi all'opinione vulgare' ('men who are not theologians estimate the power of demons to be stronger that it is in reality, and assume a greater efficacy for the magic arts [than is truly the case]. Poets can thus in good conscience – as those who have written before me have claimed – adhere to common opinion in this regard').[57]

We can also observe Castelvetro's impact on Tasso in the epistolary preface to the *Re Torrismondo*, a tragedy initially written in 1574 and further developed in 1586 prior to its publication the following year. In the prefatory letter, Tasso anticipates the effect that such a tragedy will have on his dedicatee, Vincenzo Gonzaga, duke of Mantova and Monferrato:

> V. Altezza leggendo, o ascoltando questa favola, troverà alcune cose da imitare, altre da schivare, altre da lodare, altre da riprendere, altre da rallegrarsi, altre da contristarsi. E potrà co'l suo gravissimo giuditio purgar in guisa l'animo et in guisa temperar le passioni, *che l'altrui dolore sia cagione del suo diletto, e l'imprudenza de gli altri, del suo avedimento; e gli infortunii, de la sua prosperità*.[58]

> (In reading or listening to this tale your highness will find some things to imitate, others to shun, some to praise, others to rebuke, some to make one rejoice, and others to make one sorrowful. With your most solemn judgment you may in this manner purge your mind and temper your passions. *May the pain of others be cause*

---

[55] Jon R. Snyder has underlined how Tasso's *Discorso dell'arte del dialogo* is a 'metacritical reading of both Castelvetro's and Sigonio's theories of dialogue', and how Tasso's interest in Castelvetro's theories was so extensive that he seems to have read works by Castelvetro that only circulated in manuscript during Tasso's lifetime. See Snyder, *Writing the Scene of Speaking: Theories of Dialogue in the Late Italian Renaissance* (Palo Alto, CA: Stanford University Press, 1989), 150 and 253n.7.

[56] Torquato Tasso, *Discorsi del poema eroico*, in idem. *Prose*, ed. Ettore Mazzali (Milan and Naples: Riccardo Ricciardi, 1959), 508. Tasso had a number of objections to Castelvetro's theory as well, most notably regarding the primacy of history over poetry. See Tasso, *Discorsi del poema eroico*, 511.

[57] Torquato Tasso, *Lettere Poetiche*, ed. Carla Molinari (Parma: Fondazione Pietro Bembo and Ugo Guanda, 1995), 268. In another letter from October 1575, to Luca Salabrino, Tasso praises Castelvetro's commentary as superior to his Latin predecessors, *Lettere Poetiche*, 200–3.

[58] Torquato Tasso, *Il re Torrismondo: Tragedia* (Cremona: Christoforo Draconi, 1587), 6–7.

for your delight, their imprudence cause for your discretion, and their misfortunes cause for your prosperity.)

Tasso's reference to finding pleasure in the pain of others, gaining discretion from witnessing imprudence and prosperity from witnessing misfortune seems to refer to Castelvetro's notion of oblique pleasure. Returning to the *Discorsi del poema eroico*, Castelvetro's influence on Tasso is most notable in the latter's description of the reaction that a reader of epic should have to the plot:

> Imperò che dice Aristotele che il rallegrarsi de la pena de gli scelerati, quantunque piaccia a gli spettatori, non è proprio de la favola tragica, ma ne l'eroica si loda senza fallo; e se talora ne' poemi eroici si vede qualche cosa orribile o compassionevole, non si cerca però l'orrore e la compassione in tutto il contesto de la favola, ne la quale ci rallegriamo de la vittoria de gli amici e de la perdita de' nemici; ma de' nemici, come sono i barbari e gl'infideli, non si dee avere egualmente misericordia.[59]

> (Therefore, Aristotle says that rejoicing in the punishment of wicked ones – although it pleases spectators – is not proper to the tragic plot, but in a heroic plot is praiseworthy and blameless. If at times some frightening or pity-inducing events are observed in heroic poems, one should not therefore search for fear and pity woven throughout the plot, in which we rejoice at the victory of friends and the loss of enemies. Yet, one ought not to have the same amount of pity and compassion for enemies, as they are barbarians and infidels.)

Much like Castelvetro, Tasso emphasizes how the audience's reaction to poetry depends upon the national and confessional community to which they belong; one ought not to have the same level of pity for enemies and infidels as one does for the crusading knights in his poem.[60] Castelvetro's theory of oblique pleasure is also poetically useful for Tasso, despite his misgivings about it. In the final lines of the sixth *Discorso*, Tasso does not mention Castelvetro directly, but his *Poetica* is certainly in the background. Tasso underlines how the pleasure of epic is not only larger, due to the size of the work, but also a truer pleasure since 'quello de la tragedia è mescolato col pianto e con le lagrime e pieno tutto d'amaritudine' ('that of tragedy is mixed with weeping and tears, and is full of bitterness throughout').[61] Indeed, Castelvetro's theory of oblique pleasure functions as a perfect antagonist for Tasso's theory of epic pleasure and for his assertion of the superiority of the epic form over the tragic:

> Ma non voglio già concedere che la tragedia meglio conseguisca il fine, anzi si move a quello *per obliqua e distorta strada*; ma l'epopeia per diritta: perciò che, essendo duo modi del giovar con l'esempio, l'uno d'incitarci a le buone operazioni mostrandoci il premio de l'eccellentissima virtù e del valor quasi divino, l'altro

[59] Tasso, *Discorsi del poema eroico*, 544.
[60] On Tasso's revisions to the *Liberata*, particularly the increase of pathos in the scene of the lament over the body of Argante, see Jane Tylus' chapter in this volume.
[61] Tasso, *Discorsi del poema eroico*, 728.

di spaventarci da le ree con la pena, il primo è proprio de l'epopeia, l'altro de la tragedia, la qual giova meno per questa cagione, e porta ancora minor diletto, perché *l'uomo non è di così fiera e scelerata natura che riponga il suo sommo piacere nel dolore e ne l'infelicità di coloro che per qualche errore umano sono caduti in miseria.*[62]

(But I do not wish to concede that tragedy better achieves its end; rather it moves towards it *through an oblique and crooked path* while epic does so on a straight one. This is because there are two ways to benefit through example: the first being for it to incite us to do good works by showing the reward of most excellent virtue and quasi-divine valour, the other to terrify us away from wicked acts by showing their punishment. The first is proper to epic, the second to tragedy. For this reason, the latter produces less benefit and contains less pleasure, because *man is not of such a wild and wicked nature that he should place his greatest pleasure in the pain and unhappiness of those who have fallen into misery on account of some mistakes.*)

The purpose of demonstrating these affinities and antagonisms between Tasso and Castelvetro's poetic theories is not simply to show the impact that Castelvetro's thought had on future theorists, but to put forward the question whether such an emphasis on the psychology of spectators and on their own sense of social identity might not have been an effect of, or indeed a response to, the emotional norms of the Counter-Reformation.[63] If we read these statements not simply as attempts to elucidate Aristotle, but indeed as part of a larger philosophical project in the period to describe, articulate, and challenge shared emotional experiences, might we not also begin to consider the outlines of emotional communities in late-sixteenth-century Italy? In the passages above, Castelvetro and Tasso suggest that spectators' reactions to poetry are not simply a matter for abstracted aesthetic debate, but indeed rely upon and may reinforce or challenge the spectator/reader's own world view, political affiliation, and self-understanding. Such theoretical texts, therefore, might be used as a springboard to investigate spectator reactions to written and performed tragedies in the period using various case studies on particular academies, community groups or even paratextual materials published within a particular geographic context.

On the other hand, the emotional reactions that spectators have to poetry and performance can also be seen to fit with what Rosenwein discusses as the 'performative' approach to Renaissance emotional life, citing Robert Solomon's analysis whereby emotions function as "'preverbal analogues of … performatives – judgments that *do* something rather than simply describe or evaluate a state of affairs … . Anger is

---

[62] Ibid., 728–9. Emphases mine.
[63] Recent scholarship has begun to examine affective experience in Counter-Reformation Italy and more widely in Early Modern Europe. See, for example, Joseph Imorde, 'Tasting God: The Sweetness of Crying in the Counter-Reformation', in *Religion and the Senses in Early Modern Europe*, 257–69, ed. Wietse De Boer and Christine Göttler (Leiden, Boston: Brill, 2013); Simone Laqua O'Donnell, 'Catholic Piety and Community', in *The Ashgate Research Companion to the Counter-Reformation*, ed. Alexandra Bamji, Geert H. Janssen and Mary Laven (Burlington, VT: Ashgate, 2013), 359–80; and, further afield, Susan Karnat-Nunn, *The Reformation of Feeling: Shaping the Religious Emotions in Early Modern Germany* (New York: Oxford University Press, 2010).

not merely a report or a "reaction" ... it *declares* that the comment is offensive" much as the marriage officiant declares two people married.'[64] Emerging from Solomon's insight is William M. Reddy's notion of 'emotives': emotions that not only constitute the world but also describe a change in emotional state within the speaker.[65] Thus, in Castelvetro's case, the audience first experiences a reaction to the plot, and then becomes aware of that reaction, taking pleasure in their own self-recognition. Such a statement of recognition, whether tacit or explicit suggests an emotion that is not simply reactionary or evaluative – i.e. this ending is displeasing to me – but rather a declaration of a particular world view and recognition of one's own selfhood – i.e. this ending displeases me because it causes me to doubt the operation of divine justice in a moral universe; such displeasure must therefore mean that I am a good person who believes in justice and a moral universe. In declaring a particular plot displeasing or upsetting, the spectator (and indeed the commentator) may be making a speech-act not only about the play but indeed about the moral world and their place within it.

Studies in the history of emotions by Guido Ruggiero and Carol Lansing suggest an approach whereby emotions in early modern Italy may also 'ratify a particular social order or challenge it to respond'.[66] Castelvetro suggests a similar idea in his commentary on *Poetics* 1452a1–2, noting that different plots will be received differently according to the social and political order in which the audience finds itself. He imagines a plot whereby a private person becomes a king and notes that such a plot would not be pleasing if it were represented to an audience in a state with a popular government 'percioché coloro che amano la libertà e la vogliono mantenere non vogliono che si propongano essempi a' cittadini di persone private che abbiano occupate le signorie' ('for this reason, those who love liberty and want to maintain it do not wish that examples of private persons who have held titles and lordships should be presented to citizens').[67] Similarly, such a plot would also not be particularly welcomed by an audience within a monarchy since the ruler would wish to retain his or her royal status, 'guardandosi da mettere avanti essempi al popolo minuto e a privati uomini che possano destare e indirizzare i loro animi a cose nuove e a mutamento di stato signorile' ('taking heed that they do not place examples before either the common people or private persons as might rouse and direct their minds to new things and to a change in the form of government').[68] While Weinberg frames such statements as simply Castelvetro's considerations on the audience, they seem to acquire a new significance in light of recent work on the history of the emotions and the roles of emotions in

---

[64] Rosenwein, 'The Place of Renaissance Italy in the History of Emotions', 22–3. The quotation from Solomon is from Robert Solomon, *The Passions* (Garden City, NY: Doubleday, 1976), 196.
[65] See Reddy, *The Navigation of Feeling*, 105–6.
[66] Rosenwein, 'The Place of Renaissance Italy in the History of Emotions', 23. See, for example, Guido Ruggiero, *The Boundaries of Eros: Sex Crime and Sexuality in Renaissance Venice* (New York: Oxford University Press, 1985); Ruggiero, *Machiavelli in Love: Sex, Self, and Society in the Italian Renaissance* (Baltimore: Johns Hopkins University Press, 2007); and Carol Lansing, *Passion and Order: Restraint of Grief in the Medieval Italian Communes* (Ithaca, NY: Cornell University Press, 2008). To this list might also be added Elisabeth Crouzet-Pavan, 'Emotions in the Heart of the City: Crime and Its Punishment in Renaissance Italy', in *Violence and Emotions in Early Modern Europe*, ed. Susan Broomhall and Sarah Finn (London: Routledge, 2016), 21–35.
[67] Castelvetro, *Poetica d'Aristotele vulgarizzata e sposta*, I:297–8.
[68] Ibid., I:298.

cultural politics. If emotions – and here we might include the complex emotional reactions described above – may permit an audience member to confirm or confound their view of a moral universe and their role within it, so too may such reactions cause them to either ratify or resist the dominant social order; the presentation of private persons as rulers can destabilize both a popular government and a monarchy. For this reason, Castelvetro concludes that tragedies should never be represented in public under monarchic rule as the common people enjoy watching the misfortune of great individuals.[69] Although such notions in Castelvetro are significant departures from his Aristotelian source, they seem to indicate a number of contemporary preoccupations in the late sixteenth century, such as the social role of poetry and its potential political and moral effects on a community.

One particular illustration of Castelvetro's insight comes from the Accademia Olimpica's famous staging of Sophocles' *Oedipus Rex* in an Italian vernacularization by Orsatto Giustinian on 3 March 1585 as the inaugural performance at the Olympic theatre in Vicenza.[70] As Stefano Mazzoni demonstrates, the performance had significant political overtones, and the calls to a former age of greatness under Pericles gave voice to imperial nostalgia among the anti-Venetian elite for the age when the city would have been occupied by Charles V during the War with the League of Cambrai.[71] One of the spectators, Filippo Pigafetta, described the performance and its effects on the spectators. The opening scene of the proem is described as one of great pleasure: 'a gran pena si potrebbe esprimere con parole, e pur né anco immaginare la grande letizia, ed il piacere smisurato che sopravenne agli spettatori per la vista del proemio' ('it would take great difficulty to express with words – indeed even to imagine – the great joy and the unbounded pleasure that came over the spectators at the sight of the proem'), and Pigafetta emphasizes the regal pomp of the protagonists and their courtiers on stage at the richly decorated theatre.[72] Moreover, he cites Aristotle's definition of the function of tragedy and the idea of catharsis to demonstrate how this particularly excellent performance 'abbia a produrre gli effetti suoi, ed annullare i dispareri della parte afflitta di questa città cortesissima, e piena di valore e d'ingegno' ('was to produce its effects and to cancel out the negative opinions from the afflicted

---

[69] Ibid.
[70] On the activities of the Accademia Olimpica and their staging of *Oedipus*, see D. J. Gordon, 'Academicians Build a Theatre and Give a Play', in *The Renaissance Imagination*, ed. Stephen Orgel (Berkeley, CA: University of California Press, 1975), 246–65; Stefano Mazzoni, 'Edipo tiranno all'*Olimpico di Vicenza* (1585)', *Dionysus ex machina* IV (2013): 280–301; and Anna Migliarisi, 'Staging Ritual all'Italiana: Edipo tiranno at Vicenza (1585)', *Italica* 90, no. 4 (2013): 532–47. On the reception and canonization of *Oedipus* in this period, see Daniel Javitch, 'La canonizzazione dell'Edipo re nell'Italia del sedicesimo secolo', in *Teatro e palcoscenico. Dall'Inghilterra all'Italia (1540-1640)*, ed. A. M. Palombi Cataldi (Rome: Bulzoni, 2001), 17–43.
[71] Mazzoni, 'Edipo tiranno all'*Olimpico di Vicenza* (1585)', 283.
[72] Pigafetta, *Lettera di Filippo Pigafetta nobile vicentino descrivva il Teatro Olimpico e la rappresentazione in esso fatta dell'Edippo di Sofocle nel MDLXXXV* (Vicenza: Picutti, 1843), 9; the manuscript is held in the Biblioteca Ambrosiana in Milan (R 123 sup. ff 322r-325r) and a transcription is available in Alberto Gallo, *La prima rappresentazione al teatro Olimpico, con i progetti e le relazioni dei contemporanei* (Milan: Il Polifilo, 1973), 53–8. I have not been able to consult either the manuscript or Gallo's transcription for this chapter, and as such have relied upon the nineteenth-century edition and the summary provided in Gordon, 'Academicians Build a Theatre and Give a Play'.

part of this most courteous city, which is filled with valour and ingenuity').[73] While Mazzoni and Migliarisi have underlined the links between the staging of this play and the civic performance of power by the Accademia Olimpica, few have reflected on Pigafetta's comment that companies of armed soldiers were placed at the doors of the theatre to guard the entrances.[74] While such soldiers might have been in the retinue of the noble audience in attendance, one might ask why the doors needed to be so heavily guarded. As Donatella Restani has recently demonstrated, one of the academy's members, Angelo Ingegnieri – a close friend of Tasso and the artistic director of the 1585 production – knew the main commentaries and translations of Aristotle's *Poetics* quite well, including Castelvetro's, which he cited extensively in his 1598 *Della poesia rappresentativa et del modo di rappresentare le favole sceniche*.[75] If Ingegnieri had read Castelvetro's *Poetica* prior to 1585, the emphasis on regal pomp and opulent surroundings might have been motivated by a similar reason for keeping a sizeable company of guards at the doors. Perhaps by restricting access in this manner, Ingegnieri ensured that the audience was primarily composed of a certain social class, and, in turn, belonged to the same emotional community – one expected to react with marvel and pleasure both at the sight of Palladio's richly decorated theatre, and at Ingegneri's strong emphasis on the royal aspect of Oedipus. Had other social classes been permitted in the theatre or were the performance to have been in a public square, the reaction may have been somewhat more mixed, as per Castelvetro's warning.

Such consideration on the political effects of tragedy would also be taken up one year after the performance at Vicenza in the first document from the debates on Guarini's *Il Pastor Fido*: Giason Denores' 1586 *Discorso intorno a quei principii, cause et accrescimenti che la comedia, la tragedia, et il poema eroico ricevono dalla filosofia morale e civile e da governatori delle republiche*. In this short treatise, Denores argues that the wisest political leaders, 'que' piu svegliati governatori delle reppubliche', propose public entertainments for their citizens, but that these should have a political goal, and contribute to conserving political stability by making citizens both desire and love their political system.[76] The genre of this entertainment is made to depend on the type of political society in which the citizens find themselves; the heroic poem represents a magnanimous prince who labours for the happiness of his subjects (monarchy); tragedy will make the audience fear tyranny (oligarchy); and comedy disposes them well to popular life (democracy).[77] Each of these genres aims to foster particular emotions and emotional norms in its audience for political and ethical ends. Yet two crucial differences between Denores' treatise and Castelvetro's discussion are the form of the 'poema eroico' – theorized by Tasso and exemplified in practice with the publication of his *Gerusalemme liberata* in 1581 – along with the performance of

---

[73] Pigafetta, *Lettera di Filippo Pigafetta nobile vicentino descrivva il Teatro*, 10.
[74] Ibid., 8.
[75] Donatella Restani, 'Theory and Musical Performance of the Chorus in Sixteenth-Century Italy. A Case Study: Vicenza 1585', *Skenè. Journal of Theatre and Drama Studies* 1 (2015): 75–100.
[76] Giason Denores, *Discorso intorno a quei principii, cause et accrescimenti che la comedia, la tragedia, et il poema eroico ricevono dalla filosofia morale e civile e da governatori delle republiche*, in *Trattati di poetica e retorica del Cinquecento*, ed. Bernard Weinberg, 4 vols. (Bari: Laterza, 1970–74), 3: 375–6.
[77] Ibid., 377.

Oedipus in Vicenza one year prior. As Denores held the chair of moral philosophy at the University of Padua from 1577 to 1590, it is possible that he might have attended the Vicenza staging of Oedipus, or at the very least have heard firsthand accounts of the production.

Denores' reflections on the link between power and emotional responses extends to his reflection on why the actions of 'great men' are often represented as horrible and filled with suffering, while those of commoners are often represented as ridiculous and pleasing:

> Coloro che sono in qualche altezza, per conservar la lor autorità, puniscono il più delle volte ogni minimo oltraggio ricevuto con gravissime atrocità; e le medesime ingiurie quegli che sono in bassa fortuna, non avendo in sé quei spiriti ardenti della iracondia né quella alterezza, sogliono vendicar con burle e con piacevolezze come ci fa vedere il Boccacio nelle sue novelle.[78]

> (In order to conserve their authority, those who are of a certain social status often punish the smallest wrong with the most severe cruelty. Those who are less fortunate – not possessing within themselves those fiery spirits of wrath nor such haughtiness – tend to avenge themselves of the very same offences with jokes and pleasant jests, as Boccaccio shows in his novelle.)

Such emotional responses from great men and from commoners thus not only serve to determine genre (tragedy or comedy) but are also seen by Denores as reflections of inherent nobility or baseness that are then modelled for the imitation of spectators. Castelvetro's comments on the political uses of tragedy are also echoed in Denores' comments on *maraviglia* in the genre:

> Chi é dunque de' spettatori che non si accenda al desiderio della vita privata, riguardando spessissime volte in queste rappresentazioni che in così breve giro di tempo ogni travaglio de' privati si rivolga in somma letizia e che non aborisca la vita tirannica de' più potenti, vedendo e considerando che ogni loro grandezza quasi in un batter d'occhio si possa rivolger in estrema ruina, in essilio, in morte, in uccisioni?[79]

> (Who is there among spectators who does not feel the kindling of a desire for private life upon seeing that – for the most part in such representations – in such a short space of time all difficulties of private men are transformed into happiness? Who is there who does not abhor the tyrannical life of the most powerful upon seeing and considering that – within the blink of an eye – all of their greatness can turn to extreme desolation, exile, death, or assassinations?)

In other words, the representation of great private citizens can not only serve to model emotional behaviours that are considered noble but also serves a civic function in

---

[78] Ibid., 387.
[79] Ibid., 391.

restraining private citizens from desiring political power and public office.[80] As such, Denores argues, poetry can serve an important civic educational purpose, teaching 'una dottrina che s'impara senza accorgersi … una filosofia morale e civile che non si apprende nelle scolle da' legenti e con istudio, ma ne' teatri da' poeti, e con sommo diletto' ('a doctrine that is learned without being aware of it … a moral and civic philosophy that is not learned in the schools from lecturers and through study, but rather in the theatres of the poets with the greatest delight').[81] Denores is building up to his rejection of pastoral tragicomedy as a monstrous hybrid form opposed to both moral and civic philosophy. Nevertheless, following in the footsteps of Castelvetro and Tasso, he seems to do so through a focus on the emotional impacts that representations can have on spectators and through a type of emotional education that will preserve the civic order. Denores is thus appealing to the shaping of spectators' emotions in order to ratify existing political systems and combining Aristotle's discussions of the effects of poetry in the *Poetics* with his distinction between different types of political orders in the *Politics*.

As such, the focus on spectator reactions and their own understanding of their place within moral, civic, and social orders is not simply a new 'focus on audience' prompted by a falling away from the study of Aristotle's *Poetics* and a return to rhetorical criticism, but rather seems to emerge from a new emphasis in Castelvetro's *Poetica* on audience psychology, and, as I have attempted to demonstrate above, from an attempt to explore spectators' emotions as more than a simple reaction, but rather as an expression of identity and deeply held convictions. The preceding analysis is fragmentary and could be significantly expanded with specific in-depth case studies on emotional norms within certain academies, such as the Alterati, within specific geographical contexts, such as Denores' Padua, or indeed within certain contexts of performances and reported reactions, such as Pigafetta's reaction to the staging of *Oedipus* at Vicenza. We might also ask whether Castelvetro's new emphasis on psychology and emotion emerges from his heterodox convictions, and whether different discussions of emotional reactions obtain in poetic treatises from Catholic and Protestant communities in the period. Another potential avenue for research would be the historicizing of certain 'emotion words' such as *diletto* or even *meraviglia*. While we might assume to know what theorists, spectators and readers meant by these terms, new case studies could be written on emotion-terms in early modern poetic theory along with their broader linguistic usage in other contexts. Finally, as this chapter has attempted to show, using tools from the history of emotions on early modern literary-critical texts might lead us to an understanding of them as not only relevant to the realm of aesthetics and poetic criticism but indeed as part of a broader cultural desire to critically reflect upon, codify, consolidate and, at times, even to resist emotional norms.

---

[80] Ibid., 411.
[81] Ibid., 405.

Bibliography

Alfano, Giancarlo. 'Sul concetto di verosimile nei commenti cinquecenteschi alla "Poetica" di Aristotele'. *Filologia e critica* 26 (2001): 187–209.

Bianchi, Luca. 'Per una storia dell'aristotelismo "volgare" nel Rinascimento: problemi e prospettive di ricerca'. *Bruniana & Campanelliana* 15 (2009): 367–85.

Bianchi, Luca, Simon Gilson and Jill Kraye, eds. *Vernacular Aristotelianism in Renaissance Italy*. London: The Warburg Institute, 2016.

Black, Deborah L. *Logic and Aristotle's* Rhetoric *and* Poetics *in Medieval Arabic Philosophy*. Leiden: Brill, 1991.

Blocker, Déborah, 'Élucider et équivoquer: Francesco Robortello réinvente la "catharsis"'. *Les Cahiers du Centre de recherches historiques* 28–9 (2002): 109–40.

Bongiorno, Andrew. *Castelvetro on the Art of Poetry: An Abridged Translation of Lodovico Castelvetro's* Poetica d'Aristotele vulgarizzata e sposta. Binghamton, NY: Medieval and Renaissance Texts and Studies, 1984.

Brazeau, Bryan. '"My Own Worst Enemy": Translating Hamartia in Sixteenth-Century Italy'. *Renaissance and Reformation* 41, no. 4 (2018): 9–42.

Castelvetro, Lodovico. 'Chiose intorno il terzo libro del commune di Platone'. MS alfa.S.5.1, 124v–135r. Biblioteca Estense Universitaria, Modena.

Castelvetro, Lodovico. *Opere varie critiche di Lodovico Castelvetro gentiluomo Modenese*. Edited by Lodovico Antonio Muratori. Lyon: Pietro Foppens, 1727.

Castelvetro, Lodovico. *Poetica d'Aristotele vulgarizzata e sposta*. Vienna: Gaspar Stainhofer, 1570.

Castelvetro, Lodovico. *Poetica d'Aristotele vulgarizzata e sposta*. Edited by Werther Romani, 2 vols. Rome and Bari: Laterza, 1978–79.

Cotugno, Alessio and David A. Lines, eds. 'Le Annotationi di Piccolomini e la *Poetica* di Castelvetro a confronto: tecnica argomentativa, vocabolario critico, dispositivi esegetici'. In *Forms of Conflict and Rivalries in Renaissance Europe*, edited by David A. Lines, Marc Laureys and Jill Kraye, 161–206. Göttingen: V & R Unipress for Bonn University Press, 2015.

Cotugno, Alessio and David A. Lines, eds. 'Piccolomini e Castelvetro traduttori della *Poetica*'. *Studi di lessicografia italiana* 23 (2006): 113–219.

Cotugno, Alessio and David A. Lines, eds. *Venezia e Aristotele (ca. 1450–ca. 1600): greco, latino e italiano / Venice and Aristotle (c. 1450–c. 1600): From Greek and Latin to the Vernacular*, exhibition catalogue (Venice, Sale Monumentali della Biblioteca Nazionale Marciana, 21 April–19 May 2016). Venice: Marcianum Press, 2016.

Crouzet-Pavan, Elisabeth. 'Emotions in the Heart of the City: Crime and Its Punishment in Renaissance Italy'. In *Violence and Emotions in Early Modern Europe*, edited by Susan Broomhall and Sarah Finn, 21–35. London: Routledge, 2016.

Dahiyat, Ismail M. *Avicenna's Commentary on the Poetics of Aristotle: A Critical Study with an Annotated Translation of the Text*. Leiden: Brill, 1974.

del Soldato, Eva. *Early Modern Aristotle: On the Making and Unmaking of Authority*. Philadelphia, PA: University of Pennsylvania Press, forthcoming 2020.

Denores, Giason. *Discorso intorno a que' principii, cause et accrescimenti che la comedia, la tragedia et il poema eroico ricevono dalla filosofia morale e civile e da' governatori delle republiche…*[1586]. In *Trattati di poetica e retorica del Cinquecento*, edited by Bernard Weinberg, 4 vols., 3:373–419. Bari: Laterza, 1970–74.

Destrée, Pierre. 'Éducation Morale et Catharsis Tragique'. *Les Études Philosophiques* 4 (2003): 518–35.

Diano, Roberto. 'La catarsi tragica'. In Roberto Diano, *Saggezza e poetiche degli antichi*, 215–80. Venice: Neri Pozza, 1968.
Ford, Andrew. 'The Purpose of Aristotle's *Poetics*'. *Classical Philology* 110, no. 1 (January 2015): 1–21.
Gallo, Alberto. *La prima rappresentazione al teatro Olimpico, con i progetti e le relazioni dei contemporanei*. Milan: Il Polifilo, 1973.
Geri, Lorenzo. 'Castelvetro traduttore di Melantone'. In *Lodovico Castelvetro: filologia e ascesi*, edited by Roberto Gigliucci, 241–59. Rome: Bulzoni, 2007.
Gilbert, Allan H. *Literary Criticism: Plato to Dryden*. Detroit, MI: Wayne State University Press, 1962.
Gilson, Simon. 'Reading the *Convivio* from Trecento Florence to Dante's Cinquecento commentators'. *Italian Studies* 64, no. 2 (2009): 266–95.
Gordon, D. J. 'Academicians Build a Theatre and Give a Play'. In *The Renaissance Imagination*, edited by Stephen Orgel, 246–65. Berkeley, CA: University of California Press, 1975.
Greenblatt, Stephen. *Renaissance Self-Fashioning: From More to Shakespeare*. Chicago: University of Chicago Press, 1980.
Grohovaz, Valentina. 'Per la storia del testo della *Poetica d'Aristotele vulgarizzata e sposta*'. In *Lodovico Castelvetro: filologia e ascesi*, edited by Roberto Gigliucci, 13–33. Rome: Bulzoni, 2007.
Hathaway, Baxter. *The Age of Criticism* Ithaca, NY: Cornell University Press, 1962.
Heath, Jane. '"Textual Communities": Brian Stock's Concept and Recent Scholarship on Antiquity'. In *Scriptual Interpretation at the Interface between Education and Religion*, edited by Florian Wilk, 5–35. Leiden and Boston: Brill, 2018.
Imorde, Joseph. 'Tasting God: The Sweetness of Crying in the Counter-Reformation'. In *Religion and the Senses in Early Modern Europe*, edited by Wietse De Boer and Christine Göttler, 257–69. Leiden and Boston: Brill, 2013.
Javitch, Daniel. 'The Assimilation of Aristotle's *Poetics* in Sixteenth-Century Italy'. In *The Cambridge History of Literary Criticism: Volume 3, The Renaissance*, edited by Glyn P. Norton, 53–65. Cambridge: Cambridge University Press, 1999.
Javitch, Daniel. 'The Emergence of Poetic Genre Theory in the Sixteenth Century'. *Modern Language Quarterly* 59, no. 2 (1998): 139–69.
Javitch, Daniel. 'La canonizzazione dell'Edipo re nell'Italia del sedicesimo secolo'. In *Teatro e palcoscenico. Dall'Inghilterra all'Italia (1540-1640)*, edited by A. M. Palombi Cataldi, 17–43. Rome: Bulzoni, 2001.
Karnat-Nunn, Susan. *The Reformation of Feeling: Shaping the Religious Emotions in Early Modern Germany*. New York: Oxford University Press, 2010.
Kemal, Salim. *The Philosophical Poetics of Alfarabi, Avicenna, and Averroes: The Aristotelian Reception*. Abingdon: Routledge, 2003.
Konstan, David. *The Emotions of the Ancient Greeks, Studies in Aristotle and Classical Literature*. Toronto: University of Toronto Press, 2006.
Lansing, Carol. *Passion and Order: Restraint of Grief in the Medieval Italian Communes*. Ithaca, NY: Cornell University Press, 2008.
Laqua O'Donnell, Simone. 'Catholic Piety and Community'. In *The Ashgate Research Companion to the Counter-Reformation*, edited by Alexandra Bamji, Geert H. Janssen and Mary Laven. Burlington, VT: Ashgate, 2013.
Leo, Russ. *Tragedy as Philosophy in the Reformation World*. Oxford: Oxford University Press, 2019.

Lines, David A. *Aristotle's Ethics in the Italian Renaissance (1300-1600): The Universities and the Problem of Moral Education*. Leiden and Boston: Brill, 2002.
Lines, David A. 'Beyond Latin in Renaissance Philosophy: A Plea for New Critical Perspectives'. *Intellectual History Review* 25, no. 4 (2015): 373-89.
Lines, David A. and Anna Laura Puliafito, eds. *'In Other Words': Translating Philosophy in the Fifteenth and Sixteenth Centuries*. Special issue of *Rivista di storia della filosofia*, fasc. 2 (2019).
Lines, David A. and Eugenio Refini, eds. *Aristotele fatto volgare: Tradizione aristotelica e cultura volgare nel Rinascimento*. Pisa: Edizioni ETS, 2014.
Mazzoni, Stefano. 'Edipo tiranno all'*Olimpico di Vicenza* (1585)'. *Dionysus ex machina* IV (2013): 280-301.
Merola, Valeria. 'Il piacere obliquo e la meraviglia. Sulla poetica di Lodovico Castelvetro'. In *Lodovico Castelvetro: filologia e ascesi*, edited by Roberto Gigliucci, 305-17. Rome: Bulzoni, 2007.
Migliarisi, Anna. 'Staging Ritual all'Italiana: Edipo tiranno at Vicenza (1585)'. *Italica* 90, no. 4 (2013): 532-47.
Pigafetta, Filippo. *Lettera di Filippo Pigafetta nobile vicentino descrivva il Teatro Olimpico e la rappresentazione in esso fatta dell'Edippo di Sofocle nel MDLXXXV*. Vicenza: Picutti, 1843.
Plamper, Jan. *The History of Emotions: An Introduction*. Translated by Keith Tribe. Oxford: Oxford University Press, 2012.
Plato. *Republic*. Translated by Paul Shorey. In *The Collected Dialogues of Plato*, edited by Edith Hamilton and Huntington Cairns, 575-844. Princeton, NJ: Princeton Unviersity Press, 1961.
Reddy, William M. *The Navigation of Feeling: A Framework for the History of Emotions*. Cambridge: Cambridge University Press, 2001.
Refini, Eugenio. *The Vernacular Aristotle: Translation as Reception in Medieval and Renaissance Italy* Cambridge: Cambridge University Press, 2019.
Restani, Donatella. 'Theory and Musical Performance of the Chorus in Sixteenth-Century Italy: A Case Study: Vicenza 1585'. *Skenè. Journal of Theatre and Drama Studies* 1 (2015): 75-100.
Ribaudo, Vera. 'Il piacere delle lacrime: il *diletto obliquo* nella *Spositione all'Inferno* di Lodovico Castelvetro'. *Philosophical Readings* VIII, no. 2 (2016): 83-8.
Rivoltella, Pier Cesare. 'Il piacere obliquo statu nascenti: la riflessione estetica di Ludovico Castelvetro'. In *Teatri barocchi: tragedie, commedie, pastorali nella drammaturgia europea fra '500 e '600*, edited by Silvia Carandini, 15-28. Rome: Bulzoni, 2000.
Rivoltella, Pier Cesare. 'La Scena della sofferenza'. *Communicazioni Sociali* 15, no. 2-3 (1993): 101-55.
Roncaccia, Alberto. *Il metodo critico di Ludovico Castelvetro*. Rome: Bulzoni, 2006.
Rosenwein, Barbara H. *Emotional Communities in the Early Middle Ages*. Ithaca, NY: Cornell University Press, 2006.
Rosenwein, Barbara H. 'The Place of Renaissance Italy in the History of Emotions'. In *Emotions, Passions, and Power in Renaissance Italy*, edited by Fabrizio Ricciardelli and Andrea Zorzi, 15-30. Amsterdam: Amsterdam University Press, 2015.
Rosenwein, Barbara H. 'Problems and Methods in the History of Emotions'. *Passions in Context* 1 (2010): 1-32.
Rosenwein, Barbara H. 'Worrying about Emotions in History'. *American Historical Review* 107, no. 3 (2002): 821-45.

Ruggiero, Guido. *The Boundaries of Eros: Sex Crime and Sexuality in Renaissance Venice*. New York: Oxford University Press, 1985.

Rossignoli, Claudia. '"Dar Materia di Ragionamento." Strategie Interpretative Della *Sposizione*'. In *Lodovico Castelvetro: filologia e ascesi*, edited by Roberto Gigliucci, 91–113. Rome: Bulzoni, 2007.

Rossignoli, Claudia. '"L'ufficio dello 'nterprete": Castelvetro Translator of Melanchthon'. *Italian Studies* 68, no. 3 (2013): 317–39.

Ruggiero, Guido. *Machiavelli in Love: Sex, Self, and Society in the Italian Renaissance*. Baltimore: Johns Hopkins University Press, 2007.

Ryan, Eugene E. 'Robortello and Maggi on Aristotle's Theory of Catharsis'. *Rinascimento* 22 (1982): 263–74.

Schmitt, Charles. *Aristotle and the Renaissance*. Cambridge, MA: Harvard University Press, 1983.

Serpieri, Alessandro. 'Il piacere dell'obliquo. Note sul tragico e il tempo dai tragici greci a Shakespeare'. In *Teatri barocchi: tragedie, commedie, pastorali nella drammaturgia europea fra '500 e '600*, edited by Silvia Carandini, 29–63. Rome: Bulzoni, 2000.

Sgarbi, Marco, ed. *I generi dell'aristotelismo volgare nel Rinascimento*. Padua: CLEUP, 2018.

Sgarbi, Marco, ed. 'What Does a Renaissance Aristotelian Look Like? From Petrarch to Galilei'. *HOPOS. The Journal of the International Society for the History of Philosophy of Science* 7 (2017): 226–45.

Siekiera, Anna. 'La *Poetica Vulgarizzata et Sposta* per Lodovico Castelvetro e le traduzioni cinquecentesche del trattato di Aristotele'. In *Lodovico Castelvetro: Letterati e grammatici nella crisi religiosa del Cinquecento. Atti della XIII giornata Luigi Firpo Torino, 21–22 settembre 2006*, edited by Massimo Firpo and Guido Mongini, 25–45. Florence: Leo S. Olschki, 2008.

Siraisi, Nancy G. *Avicenna in Renaissance Italy: The Canon and Medical Teaching in Universities after 1500*. Princeton, NJ: Princeton University Press, 1987.

Snyder, Jon R. *Writing the Scene of Speaking: Theories of Dialogue in the Late Italian Renaissance*. Palo Alto, CA: Stanford University Press, 1989.

Solomon, Robert. *The Passions*. Garden City, NY: Doubleday, 1976.

Stearns, Peter N. 'History of Emotions: Issues of Change and Impact'. In *Handbook of Emotions*, 3rd edn, edited by Michael Lewis, Jeannette M. Haviland Jones and Lisa Feldman Barrett, 17–31. New York: Guilford Press, 2008.

Stearns, Peter N. and Carol Z. Stearns. 'Emotionology: Clarifying the History of Emotions and Emotional Standards'. *American Historical Review* 90, no. 4 (1985): 813–36.

Stock, Brian. *The Implications of Literacy: Written Language and Models of Interpretation in the Eleventh and Twelfth Centuries*. Princeton, NJ: Princeton University Press, 1983.

Stock, Brian. *Listening for the Text: On the Uses of the Past*. Baltimore, MD: Johns Hopkins University Press, 1990.

Tasso, Torquato. *Discorsi del poema eroico*. In *Prose*, edited by Ettore Mazzali, 487–730. Milan and Naples: Riccardo Ricciardi, 1959.

Tasso, Torquato. *Il re Torrismondo: Tragedia*. Cremona: Christoforo Draconi, 1587.

Tasso, Torquato. *Lettere Poetiche*. Edited by Carla Molinari. Parma: Fondazione Pietro Bembo and Ugo Guanda, 1995.

Weinberg, Bernard. 'Castelvetro's Theory of Poetics'. In *Critics and Criticism: Ancient and Modern*, edited by R. S. Cranc, 349–71. Chicago: University of Chicago Press, 1952.

Weinberg, Bernard. *A History of Literary Criticism in the Italian Renaissance*, 2 vols. Chicago: The University of Chicago Press, 1961.

Zanin, Enrica. 'Les commentaires modernes de la *Poétique* d'Aristote'. *Études littéraires* 43, no. 2 (2012): 55–83.

10

Critical *imitatio*

Renaissance literary theory and its postmodern avatars

Ayesha Ramachandran

In 1997, Jacques Derrida gave a ten-hour address at the third Cerisy-la-Salle conference devoted to his work. But his lecture, which has become a foundational text in the posthumanist turn to animal studies, begins in fact with humanist imitation. 'To begin with', writes Derrida, 'I would like to entrust myself to words that, were it possible, would be naked … . I would like to choose words that are, to begin with, naked, quite simply, words from the heart.'[1] The literary play here is elegant and ironic: it leads to an expression of thanks due to a network of friends and collaborators, but it also gestures to a long rhetorical tradition, perhaps most clearly to the opening to Montaigne's *Essais*, which is soon revealed to be a crucial intertext for the lecture itself.[2] For in his opening address to the reader, Montaigne too claims that he wants 'to be seen here in my simple, natural, ordinary fashion, without straining or artifice … . I assure you I should very gladly have portrayed myself here entire and wholly naked.'[3]

This emphasis on nakedness in both Derrida and Montaigne marks a paradoxical knowingness about rhetoric and literary interpretation: we are never quite fully naked in language, which is always already mediated, and despite the yearning for transparency, we remain locked in an ongoing process of interpretation. Derrida's lecture thus knowingly begins with a commentary on Montaigne's 'Apology for Raymond Sebond', itself a text that is framed as a commentary on the *Theologia naturalis* (or *Liber naturae sive creaturarum*) of Raimond de Sabunde (Raymond Sebond), a Spanish scholar and

---

[1] Jacques Derrida, 'The Animal That Therefore I Am (More to Follow)', trans. David Wills, *Critical Inquiry* 28, no. 2 (2002): 369.
[2] The lecture turns on a question posed by Montaigne in his 'Apology for Raymond Sebond' (*Essais*, 2.12) about his relationship with his cat. On the broader significance of Derrida's evocation of Montaigne for debates on humanism and posthumanism, see my discussion in Ayesha Ramachandran, 'Humanism and Its Discontents', *Spenser Studies* 30 (2016): 3–18.
[3] 'Je veus qu'on m'y voie en ma façon simple, naturelle et ordinaire, sans contention et artifice…je t'asseure que je m'y fusse tres-volontiers peint tout entier, et tout nud'. 'Au lecteur' cited from Michel de Montaigne, *Les Essais*, ed. Pierre Villey, V. L. Saulnier and M. Conche (Paris: Quadrige/PUF, 2004), 3. Translation is from Michel de Montaigne, *The Complete Essays of Michel de Montaigne*, trans. Donald Frame (Stanford: Stanford University Press, 1958), 2.

theologian who taught at Toulouse in the early fifteenth century. But this dizzying mise-en-abyme of commentaries finally produces something powerful and new: a re-orientation in contemporary critical practice and the opening of new modes of literary criticism. It is, I will argue in this chapter, emblematic of a critical *imitatio* that connects contemporary literary critics to often-forgotten early modern forebears.

For though the literary criticism of the Renaissance is frequently and reductively characterized as Neo-Aristotelian, it was a rich, dynamic and contested field of study that remains relevant for current debates on the future of literary study. From Picolomoni and Poliziano to Castelvetro, Robortello, Trissino and Beni in Italy, to Peletier du Mans, Sébillet, de la Taille, Pinciano, Herrera, Ascham and Sidney, humanist writers across Europe produced annotations, commentaries, translations, anthologies, reviews, lectures and polemical treatises on literary texts, both ancient and contemporary, at a rapid rate. By the late sixteenth century, Michel de Montaigne would complain of over-interpretation: 'It is more of a job to interpret the interpretations than to interpret the things, and there are more books about books than about any other subject: we do nothing but write glosses about each other. The world is swarming with commentaries; of authors there is a great scarcity.'[4]

This interpretive praxis, thoroughly characteristic of humanistic modes of inquiry, might on closer examination be identified as an early modern literary criticism. Indeed, it contains the raw materials for what would soon become a robust market in Renaissance literary theory, particularly following the rediscovery of Aristotle's *Poetics* and its influential reception across Europe. But early modern literary criticism and theory was far more capacious than Aristotelianism alone. Growing from a combination of 'practical criticism', editorial commentary and forays into both prescriptive and analytical theorization, this corpus expanded to include a wide range of texts: from now-little-read manuscripts and print discussions that cluster around the reception of classical texts about literature (notably Aristotle, Longinus and Horace), readings of classic works (Homer and Vergil, but also Dante and Petrarch, for instance) and responses to contemporary literary 'events' (such as the Ariosto–Tasso quarrel or the polemics of the Pléiade in France) to the communal study of literary works and topics (as in the various academies and coteries that sprang up across the continent), early attempts at literary canon formation through the rise of edited anthologies, the emergence of new, 'modern' genres and accompanying theories about them (such as Giraldi Cinzio on the *romanzi* or Antonio Minturno on lyric) and compendious treatises on poetics (such as Scaliger's monumental *Poetices libri septem* that drew on a range of ancient and modern sources).[5] Bernard Weinberg's *History of Literary*

---

[4] 'Il y a plus affaire à interpreter les interpretations qu'à interpreter les choses, et plus de livres sur les livres que sur autre subject: nous ne faisons que nous entregloser. Tout fourmille de commentaires; d'auteurs, il en est grand cherté'. From 'On Experience', *Essais* 3.13 cited from Montaigne, *Les essais*, 1069; translation from Montaigne, *The Complete Essays*, 818.

[5] While some of these works have been collected variously in such resources as Bernard Weinberg, *Trattati di poetica e retorica del Cinquecento* (Bari: G. Laterza, 1970) and the 'Vernacular Aristotelianism in Renaissance Italy c. 1400-c. 1650' database (https://vari.warwick.ac.uk/), and while some English texts have seen new, recent editions (such as George Puttenham, *The Art of English Poesy*, ed. Frank Whigham and Wayne A. Rebhorn (Ithaca: Cornell University Press, 2007)), there have been very few modern re-printings and even fewer translations into English.

Criticism in the Italian Renaissance and the materials he assembled for the *Trattati di poetica e retorica del Cinquecento* were a seminal gathering of this corpus – one that shaped a generation's understanding of the poetics and literary-critical practices of the sixteenth century.[6] For the first time now, over half a century after the publication of Weinberg's work, a detailed catalogue of the Weinberg bequest to the Newberry Library – an archive of books and manuscripts that Weinberg collected as the basis for his scholarship – has been published (see Appendix).

There is no question that there is much, still, to learn from this important archive: scholars of the early modern period are only just beginning to explore the social, cultural and political ramifications of these texts and to revisit some of Weinberg's narratives and conclusions.[7] But the renewed interest in these materials brings with it a thorny, inevitable question: What interest – other than particular historical, antiquarian interests – do these fifteenth- and sixteenth-century debates over the right interpretation of literary texts have for us today? Why should scholars not already invested in the history of criticism and poetics turn their attention to what are often local, topical debates and polemics? What, beyond Aristotle, is there for us still to glean?

The very heterogeneity of Italian Renaissance literary criticism and its lack of systematic theorizing and self-description has made it difficult to categorize and consider as a coherent body of scholarship. Moreover, many of these texts remain untranslated and lacking in modern editions, making them less easily accessible beyond the confines of a specific national literary-historical tradition. Often, topical obscurities and seemingly pedantic minutiae make it difficult to grasp the larger interpretive vision of individual works. Given these difficulties, can contemporary literary criticism learn anything from its early modern practitioners?

This is a particularly poignant question to pose in the early twenty-first century when the heyday of literary theory in the Anglo-American academy seems to have passed and the practice of literary criticism is itself viewed with suspicion.[8] When Bruno Latour asks if critique has run out of steam and others herald a 'post-critical turn', the question about literary criticism's significance seems to apply not only to our Renaissance forebears but also to our own current condition. Two millennia after Plutarch and half a century after Montaigne, the defence of literary criticism's value, as well as the articulation of its methods and theories, has once again become a critical issue in its own right. The 'history of criticism' is now a parallel field to that of literary

---

[6] See Bernard Weinberg, *A History of Literary Criticism in the Italian Renaissance* (Chicago: University of Chicago Press, 1961) and Weinberg, *Trattati di poetica e retorica*.

[7] An important recent re-evaluation of the Weinberg corpus is to be found across the essays collected in D. Javitch, *Proclaiming a Classic: The Canonization of Orlando Furioso* (Princeton: Princeton University Press, 1991); Glyn P. Norton, *The Cambridge History of Literary Criticism*, vol. 3 (Cambridge: Cambridge University Press, 1999).

[8] See for instance the evaluation of the field in Rita Felski, *The Limits of Critique* (Chicago: The University of Chicago Press, 2015) and the essays collected in Elizabeth S. Anker and Rita Felski, eds, *Critique and Postcritique* (Durham: Duke University Press, 2017). A somewhat different account is offered by Joseph North, *Literary Criticism: A Concise Political History* (Cambridge, MA: Harvard University Press, 2017). For a provocative response see Bruce Robbins, 'Critical Correctness', *The Chronicle of Higher Education*, 12 March 2019, https://www.chronicle.com/article/The-Neoliberal-Neutering-of/245874.

history, and we are engaged in a fretful unearthing of the pasts of our profession and discipline, while simultaneously searching for its futures.

But in this, early modern literary criticism offers us a dark mirror. There are obvious analogies with our Renaissance predecessors: as they repudiated and vaulted over their immediate predecessors to seek out the greater authority of a classical past, so too are we primed to disdain twentieth-century critical trends, particularly the critical labours of the last few decades, and to go back further in time to find 'new' methods.[9] Like our own recent critical history, Renaissance criticism too is filled with jargon, seeming trivialities and personal polemic; but at the same time, both contain the seeds of important re-evaluations that would set an intellectual agenda for their descendants.

The over-abundance of interpreters that Montaigne laments signalled that the why and the how of literary study was being defended with unprecedented zeal, its battles played out in an international public sphere that stretched not only across Europe, but for the first time, across the globe. Poetics and literary study were not activities confined to universities and academies. Scholars like Lorenzo Valla and Antonio de Nebrija (to take but two examples) were well aware that philology could be the basis for revolution, that grammar could be an instrument of empire.[10] Others such as Maggi, Minturno and Castelvetro invested literary study with a moral-didactic vision, insisting on its power as a training ground for ethical judgement; still others, such as Scipione Ammirato would see poetic study as a kind of philosophical inquiry.[11] And since grammar and rhetoric remained at the heart of the revised trivium, the foundations of humanist pedagogy itself – and thus, of the modern liberal arts – were built on analytical activities that are now legible as literary criticism.

This essay consequently argues for the continuing significance of Italian Renaissance literary criticism – not merely as a historical relic or antiquarian pursuit, but rather as a still-relevant repository of methods and interpretive experiments that resonate with contemporary critical concerns. Rather than emphasizing the often-asserted claim that genealogical accounts of modern literary criticism and theory in the West begin with the Renaissance, I investigate conceptual points of encounter between early modern and contemporary critics. In doing so, I suggest how we may engage in fruitful transhistorical dialogue to make sense of our own concerns, much as the Renaissance

---

[9] See for instance the argument in Jonathan Kramnick and Anahid Nersessian, 'Form and Explanation', *Critical Inquiry* 43, no. 3 (1 March 2017): 650–69, which argues for a 'literary disciplinarity' not unlike the position of early modern commentators.

[10] I am thinking here of Valla's *De falso credita et ementita Constantini donatione declamatio* (see Lorenzo Valla, *On the Donation of Constantine*, trans. G. W. Bowersock, I Tatti Renaissance Library 24 (Cambridge, MA: Harvard University Press, 2007)) as well as his annotations on the New Testament, published by Erasmus in 1505 (see Lorenzo Valla, *In Latinam Novi Testamenti interpretationem ex collatione Graecorum exemplarium Adnotationes* (Paris: Badius, 1505). For Nebrija, see the important recent translation and introduction: Antonio de Nebrija, 'On Language and Empire: The Prologue to Grammar of the Castilian Language (1492)', trans. Magalí Armillas-Tiseyra, *PMLA* 131, no. 1 (1 January 2016): 197–208.

[11] See the classic discussion in Baxter Hathaway, *The Age of Criticism: The Late Renaissance in Italy* (Ithaca: Cornell University Press, 1962). See also Eugenio Refini, 'Aristotelian Commentaries and the Dialogue Form in Cinquecento Italy', in *Vernacular Aristotelianism in Italy from the Fourteenth to the Seventeenth Century*, ed. Luca Bianchi, Simon Gilson and Jill Kraye (London: The Warburg Institute, 2016), 93–107 and Bryan Brazeau's essay in this volume.

humanists themselves did with their classical predecessors. To talk back to Poliziano and Castelvetro, Malatesta and Strozzi is to engage in a similar critical practice – a direct engagement with a celebrated source, a return *ad fontes* – but as still-vital interlocutors whose example could help shape future debates and intellectual trajectories.

I

'Crisis in the situation of literature is a regular topos in literary texts', noted Robert Scholes in his 2004 MLA Presidential address.[12] Quoting George Steiner, he takes Milton's phrase 'Nymphs and Shepherds dance no more' (from *Arcades*) as his prime example. Already in 1630, a time when we might say 'the Muses were actually in pretty good shape', Milton laments the loss of past aesthetic greatness and appreciation, and Scholes deftly links this sentiment to the postmodern *fin de siècle* crisis in the humanities.[13] His conclusion, after a long transhistorical consideration of the most recent 'crisis' is striking: 'This means going back to ... roots that were in place before the Renaissance bent them to their own ends ... we need to start over again, from the old pre-humanistic or proto-humanistic trivium.'[14]

There are two key elements in this call to re-imagine the trivium for the twenty-first century as a 'neo-humanism': first, that it identifies the Renaissance as a pivotal moment when the humanities are 'bent' to particular ends whose long-term consequences, he argues, lie in post-1945 literary theory; and second, that we *should* go back to the cusp of humanism to recover its core elements in order to shape a new humanism for the future. In both these formulations, grappling with the legacy of the Renaissance's emphasis on literary interpretation and the place of literature within the *studia humanitatis* becomes central.

While such comparisons point to an important conjunction between the practices of Renaissance and contemporary literary criticism, we might ask just what the specific conceptual similarities or questions might in fact be. One answer – the one this essay will explore – lies in the methods of literary study. Both early modern and postmodern critics seek, uneasily, to reconcile the demands of historical analyses with the formalist-aesthetic claims of the literary text. And, in turn, to reconcile this battle of interpretive frameworks with larger questions about the political and cultural stakes of studying literature. These tensions have been sharply articulated at various historical moments, most recently perhaps since the mid-1990s, when the New Historicism tangled with the New Formalism, leading to broader meditations on literary criticism's own intellectual and political obligations.[15] While a historicist criticism privileged the sociopolitical and cultural functions, constraints and impacts of the literary text at the time of its

---

[12] Robert Scholes, 'Presidential Address 2004: The Humanities in a Posthumanist World', *PMLA* 120, no. 3 (1 May 2005): 724.
[13] Ibid.
[14] Ibid., 732.
[15] This most recent tussle mirrors, of course, the tensions between the New Criticism and the New Historicism from a previous generation. For a discussion of these critical movements see North, *Literary Criticism*.

production and dissemination, formalists insisted upon the internal arrangement of the literary text and its inherently linguistic, textual modes of making meaning apart from any local context. So powerful has this opposition seemed that it still frames Caroline Levine's important 2015 book, *Forms*, which aims to move past this impasse.[16]

Looking back at the Renaissance, however, allows us to see that this apparent conceptual binary may itself be the consequence of a methodological bifurcation in the history of criticism since the Renaissance. The emergence of a modern literary criticism in the sixteenth century was marked by the humanists' heightened perception of historical difference and emphasis on the writing of history as well as their philosophic belief in the shaping power of forms – itself a derivation from the philosophical dichotomy of form and matter. These twin commitments entailed that the period's literary criticism would be *both* formalist *and* historicist, attentive to the shape of the text and its rhetorical arrangement as well as to its social force.

For early modern students of the *bonas artes*, fascination with the rediscovery of ancient texts was matched with both curatorial zeal and the double bind of transhistorical emulation and competition. To master the classics was also to exhume, edit, analyse, comment on and interpret them. Philology and hermeneutics were twinned activities that underpinned the task of right interpretation.[17] Not only were they following in the tradition of scriptural exegesis and medieval commentary, but also in the renascent tradition of classical literary analysis. Plutarch's attention to the reading of literature, for instance, was an important touchstone for the rise of textually focused, formalist literary criticism. But, crucially, this (re)turn to formalist close reading was itself made possible by a nascent historicism: to read Plutarch on classical literature, for instance, was to learn to read the ancients as the ancients themselves had done. Moreover, Plutarch himself is conscious of the ethical charge of reading literature and confronts it as a matter for transhistorical consideration: after all, for Plutarch, a Greek writing under the Roman emperors Vespasian, Trajan and Hadrian, the question of the relationship between Greek and Roman culture from Plato onward was itself a matter of critical-historical reflection.

At the same time, Plutarch demonstrates how historical analyses themselves stand to benefit from a careful attention to form in its most ample sense.[18] In *De audiendis poetis* and other essays, Plutarch laid out an accessible moral groundwork for the importance of literature, drawing on a range of classical traditions including Plato, Aristotle, the Stoics and the Epicureans. But even more important, he did not offer a *theory* so much as a *method*: he identified particularly useful strategies and practices that could elucidate texts in specific ways usually for didactic ends. Acknowledging the various dangers of poetry, well-known from Plato onward, Plutarch outlines a method for what we might call close reading and textual editing as strategies for approaching

---

[16] Caroline Levine, *Forms: Whole, Rhythm, Hierarchy, Network* (Princeton, NJ: Princeton University Press, 2015).

[17] Teodolinda Barolini and Wayne Storey, eds, *Petrarch and the Textual Origins of Interpretation*, Columbia Studies in the Classical Tradition, v. 31 (Leiden and Boston: Brill, 2007); and Anthony Grafton and Lisa Jardine, *From Humanism to the Humanities: Education and the Liberal Arts in Fifteenth- and Sixteenth-Century Europe* (Cambridge, MA: Harvard University Press, 1986).

[18] Form for Plutarch is both a (Platonic) philosophical term and a rhetorical one.

literary texts – practices already well-established in antiquity but which gained renewed influence in the Renaissance.[19] To read in this way – with careful attention to words, rhetoric, grammatical context and intention – was to train the reader's eye and bring a new intellectual focus to the written page. But such a practice, Plutarch is quick note, is no mere rhetorical exercise – it is one with philosophical force.[20] A glance through Weinberg's *Trattati* makes clear this pervasive influence, traceable not only to Plutarch but also to a sustained engagement with classical literary criticism's focus on rhetoric and poetics.[21] It is in this twin tradition – of the humanists' emphasis on historical difference, as well as their attention to rhetoric and form – that the seeds of contemporary debates over the future of literary study lie.

Thus, moving beyond traditional classifications that tend to group early modern critical exegeses according to their classical philosophical or rhetorical frameworks, I identify some touchpoints between twenty-first-century literary-critical trends and the intellectual foci of Renaissance literary critics. Specifically, I emphasize the long histories of historicist and formalist approaches to literary study, which, I argue, find their modern form in the work of sixteenth-century interpreters. The current battle in literary criticism between partisans of formalist and historicist approaches and the efforts to enact a truce have much to gain from an engagement with Renaissance critics who also grappled with similar tensions. Not only does the contemporary battle represent the culmination of an intellectual-historical trajectory that began in the Renaissance, it rests, I argue, on a false dichotomy between history and form which is itself a product of a particular, post-Weinbergian history of criticism. To return to the humanist critics of the Renaissance is thus an invitation to write a revisionist history of criticism: one that imagines the claims of form and history as profoundly interlinked.

II

Perhaps the most obviously distinctive feature of Renaissance literary criticism from a twenty-first-century perspective is its deep formalism: its relentless attention to the 'forms' of a literary work in terms of its language, genre, rhetorical figures, its internal workings and textual effects – what Caroline Levine has described as the 'subtle arrangements of words and images'.[22] If Ernst Cassirer identified the interest in symbolic forms as a characteristic of the Renaissance itself as an intellectual movement,

---

[19] On Plutarch as a literary critic, see for instance David Konstan, '"The Birth of the Reader": Plutarch as a Literary Critic', *Scholia* 13 (2004): 3–27; Christophe Bréchet, 'Le "De audiendis poetis" de Plutarque et le procès platonicien de la poésie', *Revue de Philologie, de Littérature et d'Histoire Anciennes* 73, no. 2 (1999): 209–44; Alexei Zadorojnyi, 'Safe Drugs for the Good Boys: Platonism and Pedagogy in Plutarch's *De Audiendis Poetis*', in *Sage and Emperor: Plutarch, Greek Intellectuals, and Roman Power in the Time of Trajan (98-117 A.D.)*, ed. Philip A. Stadter and Luc Van der Stockt (Leuven: Leuven University Press, 2002), 297–314.

[20] On the links between poetry and philosophy since antiquity see Susan Stewart, 'Lyric', in *The Oxford Handbook of Philosophy and Literature*, ed. Richard Eldridge (Oxford: Oxford University Press, 2009), 45–70.

[21] See Weinberg, *Trattati di poetica e retorica*.

[22] Levine, *Forms*, ix.

that habit is evident in the period's particular ways of looking at literary texts.[23] These included the work of finding new texts and editing them; an explosion of interest in new languages, their histories and their literary traditions; and a new attention to genre as a category of analysis as well as structuralist analyses of the workings of a text – an inquiry that opened out into aesthetic ruminations on the nature of beauty, its sources and effects as well as the ethical ends of literature.

The recovery of classical texts was itself an act of formal excavation, the unearthing of the shape of complete texts from their fragments or unique manuscript exemplars. But the very encounter with these texts, and the process of editing them, transformed the forms of reading, writing and interpreting literary texts. Perhaps most famous is Petrarch's rediscovery of Cicero's letters in 1345, which as Kathy Eden writes, transformed,

> the cultural landscape of early modern Europe insofar as they reinvigorate a genre – the familiar letter – that will come to dominate the histories of education, literature, and printing, thereby changing the way the humanists and their successors read and write. As a consequence of his discovery in Verona, in other words, Petrarch bequeaths to future writers and readers not only an intimate Cicero but … a rhetoric and hermeneutics of intimacy.[24]

Petrarch records this twinning of textual recovery and generic transformation in his second letter to Cicero in the final book of the *Familiares*, a work that often veers into the domain of literary criticism and interpretation in an unconventional, autobiographical form:

> Tuorum sane, quia de his michi nunc sermo erat, quorum insignior iactura et, hec sunt nomina: reipublice, rei familiaris,rei militaris, de laude philosophie, de consolatione, de gloria, quamvis de his ultimis spes michi magis dubia, quam desperatio certa sit.

> Quin et superstitum librorum magnas partes amisimus, ut velut ingenti prelio oblivionis et ignavie superatis, duces nostros non extinctos modo sed truncos quoque vel perditos sit lugere. Hoc enim et in aliis multis, sed in tuis maxime oratoriis atque achademicorum et legum libris patimur, qui ita truncati fedatique evaserunt, ut prope melius fuerit periisse.

> (But since at present I am dealing only with yours, here are the titles of those whose loss is most to be deplored: De republica, De re familiari, De re militari, De laude philosophie, De consolatione, and De gloria, although my feeling is one of faint hope for the last ones rather than total despair. And furthermore, even of the surviving books, large portions are missing; it is as though after winning

---

[23] Ernst Cassirer, *The Individual and the Cosmos in Renaissance Philosophy*, trans. Mario Domandi (New York: Harper & Row, 1964).
[24] Kathy Eden, *The Renaissance Rediscovery of Intimacy* (Chicago: University of Chicago Press, 2012), 50.

a great battle against oblivion and sloth, we now had to mourn our leaders, and not only those who had been killed but those who had been maimed or lost. This we deplore in many of your works, but particularly in De oratore, the Academica, and De legibus, all of which have reached us in such fragmentary and mutilated condition that it would perhaps have been better for them to have perished.) (*Rerum familiarium libri,* 24.4. 13–14)[25]

Petrarch uses a favourite military metaphor here to describe the struggle against time's destructive force and the effort required by the humanist-scholar to gather remnants. The recovery of textual fragments is a victory in a costly battle, and he wonders – shockingly, perhaps – if it were not better for these 'mutilated and disfigured' (*truncati fedatique*) works simply to have vanished. Petrarch's anguish here is countered by the form of the letter itself, which mimics Ciceronian style, revivifying the classical text through modern imitation.[26]

Thus the process of textual editing that followed humanist recoveries of classical works can also be understood as a kind of form-giving: the creation of a cultural object through a careful attention to philological as well as aesthetic form. Landmark editions published by presses, such as those of Aldus, Froben or Plantin, were the end-product of a process of literary criticism that was actively engaged in reshaping a cultural tradition for the modern period. The 1501 Aldine Vergil, the first book to be set entirely in italic type and which also marked the first of a series of editions of classical authors in octavo format, was not merely a publishing novelty. It made manifest the synergy of philology and technological innovation, illustrating how new literary-critical practices of reading also affected the material form of the book itself. Even the pale blue paper ('charta caerulea') used for some Aldine editions, for instance, were not only an incidental, episodic novelty but also a formal marker of distinction and value.[27] It is worth noting too that early modern critics, collectors and editor-publishers were not just interested in classical texts: the European collecting of Oriental, foreign and indigenous texts expands significantly in the fifteenth and sixteenth centuries, as do efforts to learn and print in a range of languages and scripts.[28]

---

[25] Francesco Petrarca, *Rerum familiarum libri,* 24.4. 13-14. Citations from the *Familiares* follow Francesco Petrarca, *Epystole Familiares,* ed. Pasquale Stoppelli (Rome: Biblioteca Italiana, 1994). English translation is from Francesco Petrarca, *Letters on Familiar Matters,* trans. Aldo S Bernardo, vol. 3 (New York: Italica Press, 2005), 320–1.

[26] Eden, *Renaissance Rediscovery.*

[27] The blue Aldine editions were printed in the late summer and autumn of 1514 and then intermittently. On the use of this paper by the Aldine press, see Conor Fahy, 'Royal-Paper Copies of Aldine Editions, 1494–1550', *Studies in Bibliography* 57, no. 1 (2005): 85–113, https://doi.org/10.1353/sib.0.0010; H. George Fletcher, ed. *In Praise of Aldus Manutius: A Quincentenary Exhibition* (New York: Pierpont Morgan Library, 1995), 102–4; Antoine A. Renouard, *Annales de l'imprimerie des Alde: Ou, histoire des trois Manuce et de leurs éditions,* 3. éd (Paris: J. Renouard, 1834).

[28] Recent scholarship has begun to trace the development of Oriental manuscript collections in European libraries, but tends to focus on seventeenth century onwards: see the important work of Alexander Bevilacqua, *The Republic of Arabic Letters: Islam and the European Enlightenment* (Cambridge, MA: Harvard University Press, 2018); and the useful overview in John-Paul Ghobrial, 'The Archive of Orientalism and Its Keepers: Re-Imagining the Histories of Arabic Manuscripts in Early Modern Europe', *Past & Present* 230, no. suppl_11 (1 November 2016): 90–111. Studies of

Occluded for decades as not quite literary *criticism,* but rather something closer to linguistics, philology and editorial labour, such collecting and curation may now be legible as an important mode of formalist scholarship. The return, in our own critical moment, to lexical history and linguistic history as the building blocks for broader cultural narratives, the rise of translation studies and critical semantics as well as the renovation of comparative philology as 'new' methodologies – all evoke a Vichian inheritance whose roots lie in sixteenth-century Renaissance literary criticism.[29] Roland Greene's call for a critical semantics and Lawrence Venuti's tracing of 'genealogies of translation theory' in the work of Jerome mimic such early modern predecessors as Castelvetro and Segni, who returned to the nitty-gritty of words and their recurrence, to choices and patterns in translation and imitation.[30]

Beyond such attention to the textual production and physical form of literary texts, it is in the self-reflexive analyses of a text's internal features and effects – and its further (prescriptive) application in the making of new literature – that Renaissance literary criticism stands out. Perhaps the best and most obvious example of this kind of formalism is evident in the rediscovery of Aristotle's *Poetics,* often hailed as the defining event of early modern literary criticism, and its extensive diffusion in the space of a few decades. As the text that often demarcates a break between medieval and early modern modes of textual analysis, the critical history of the *Poetics*' reception occupies a significant part of Weinberg's *History.* His account of its dispersion and influence has for decades shaped studies of early modern poetics and literary analyses of Renaissance literature, delineating how Aristotle served as both a model and a yardstick for early modern critics.[31] Aristotle's definition of 'poetry' as mimesis established a benchmark for literary success, while his emphasis on genre as a distinctive category of analysis

---

manuscript collecting in the earlier period, i.e. before the establishment of the Medici Oriental Press in Rome in 1584, are few, but there are suggestive traces of humanist interest in the Near East. As early as the fourteenth century, Petrarch records the travels of his friend (and important collector) Giovanni Colonna to Persia, Arabia and Egypt in *Familiares* VI.3 from where he may have brought back manuscripts. See the suggestive essays of Angelo Piemontese, 'Italian Scholarship on Iran (an Outline, 1557–1987)', *Iranian Studies* 20, nos. 2–4 (January 1987): 99–130; 'Un Testo Latino-Pesiano connesso al Codex Cumanicus', *Acta Orientalia Academiae Scientiarum Hungaricae* 53, no. 1/2 (2000): 121–32; and 'Venezia e la diffusione dell'alfabeto arabo nell'Italia del Cinquecento', *Quaderni di studi arabi* 5, no. 6 (1987): 641–60; as well as Karl H. Dannenfeldt, 'The Renaissance Humanists and the Knowledge of Arabic', *Studies in the Renaissance* 2 (1955): 96–117.

[29] On Vico's method see Giuseppe Mazzotta, *The New Map of the World: The Poetic Philosophy of Giambattista Vico* (Princeton: Princeton University Press, 1999); James Robert Goetsch, *Vico's Axioms: The Geometry and the Human World* (New Haven: Yale University Press, 1995); and Paolo Rossi, *The Dark Abyss of Time: The History of the Earth & the History of Nations from Hooke to Vico* (Chicago: University of Chicago Press, 1984).

[30] Roland Greene, *Five Words: Critical Semantics in the Age of Shakespeare and Cervantes* (Chicago: University of Chicago Press, 2013); Lawrence Venuti, ed., *The Translation Studies Reader,* 3rd edn (Abingdon, Oxon and New York: Routledge, 2012); and 'Genealogies of Translation Theory: Jerome', *Boundary 2* 37, no. 3 (1 August 2010): 5–28.

[31] Several critics have noted Weinberg's emphasis on Aristotelianism at the expense of other currents; there were alternative well-developed humanist poetics that existed before the rediscovery of Aristotle, deriving from other classical sources such as Poliziano's lectures on poetics (see Dustin Mengelkoch, 'The Mutability of Poetics: Poliziano, Statius, and the Silvae', *MLN* 125, no. 1 (21 April 2010): 84–116). See the important revaluations in Javitch, *Proclaiming a Classic* and 'The Emergence of Poetic Genre Theory in the Sixteenth Century', *Modern Language Quarterly* 59, no. 2 (1998): 139–69, as well as revisionist work in Norton, eds, *The Cambridge History of Literary Criticism.*

offered a conceptual, interpretive framework for would-be literary theorists. Not only did the *Poetics* inspire a spate of commentaries and translations but it also precipitated the creation of critical compendia such as Scaliger's *Poetics,* shaping the work of early modern writers for at least two centuries.[32] They also set the terms for significant literary debates later in the century, such as the Ariosto–Tasso debate, the question of Dante and the matter of Guarini's *Il pastor fido*.[33]

This history of Aristotelian reception remains vital for critics today. Still a favourite text in university curricula, the *Poetics* commands one of the most lively areas of scholarly study today as its vernacular, European influence can now be seen as part of a broader intellectual history of modernity that is being re-examined.[34] Returning to – and revising – Weinberg's story of Renaissance literary Aristotelianism – and the formalisms it in turn engendered – therefore allows contemporary critics to reflect upon the origins of modern literary theory as a simultaneously analytical, interpretive and prescriptive instrument. Renaissance critics were already thinking about the relation of Aristotle to other classical theorists, and sought to place the *Poetics* alongside other texts in the philosopher's corpus, as was the norm with scholars of the Aristotelian *organon* in the late sixteenth century. Thus, as the humanist Ciriaco Strozzi wrote additions to the *Politics* while lecturing on the *Ethics* in Florence, his younger contemporary, Giason de Nores, wrote commentaries on the *Politics* and the *Poetics*.[35] Such interpretive work, which bubbles up in glosses, prefaces and commentaries, bears striking similarities to contemporary historical formalism, which Stephen Cohen has defined as 'a historically and ideologically sensitive formalism, one that neither denies the cultural function of form nor reduces it to a single, inherent or inevitable effect'.[36] In seeking to bridge the claims of history and form long before twentieth-century battles between the New Historicists and the New Formalists, Renaissance literary criticism reveals the joint emergence of both as well as their respective affordances.

The celebrated case of Aristotle's *Poetics* is also a reminder of the foundations of modern genre theory, since the *Poetics* along with the reception of Horace's *Ars Poetica,* precipitated the rise of genre-centric criticism in the sixteenth century. Not only did critics categorize literary works into (largely classical) generic forms, they also wrote new theoretical treatises to account for the emergence of new genres (such as romance

---

[32] There is a robust body of scholarship on Aristotelian poetics in the Renaissance in all major European languages; a useful synthetic starting point is Norton, *The Cambridge History of Literary Criticism*.

[33] For broad outlines of these debates, see Weinberg, *History;* see also the essays collected in David A. Lines and Eugenio Refini, eds, '*Aristotele fatto volgare*': *tradizione aristotelica e cultura volgare nel Rinascimento*, Biblioteca dei volgarizzamenti. Studi 2 (Pisa: Edizioni ETS, 2014).

[34] The Vernacular Aristotelianism in Renaissance Italy *c.* 1400–*c.* 1650 database is crucial step in this endeavour (https://vari.warwick.ac.uk/). A searchable catalogue of Aristotelian works written or published in Italian between 1400 and 1650, this census covers both manuscript and printed sources including over 200 printed editions, 200 manuscript works, 130 authors, 65 dedicatees and 115 printers. Lines and Refini, eds, '*Aristotele fatto volgare*' also gestures towards the broader stakes of the diffusion of Aristotle's *Poetics*.

[35] See Bryan Brazeau's essay in this volume on DeNores. Strozzi is a lesser known figure, but his wide-ranging interests are catalogued by his nephew, Zaccaria Monti in *Vita Kyriaci Strozae* (Paris: Plantin, 1604).

[36] Stephen Cohen, ed., *Shakespeare and Historical Formalism* (Aldershot: Ashgate, 2007), 14.

and lyric).[37] Daniel Javitch has rightly argued that 'far from constituting a turn against modernity ... the particular appropriation of Aristotle's *Poetics* ... enabled and justified modern versions of the ancient genres when models for them were lacking.'[38] Rather than the work of 'neo-Aristotelian conservatives who wanted to confine, even fetter, poetic creation by restricting its genres to inviolable ancient rules', the *Poetics* and the *Ars Poetica* provided a crucial template for a genre theory that sought to move away from the imitation of specific masters and towards the establishment of more general, universalizing norms.[39] Chief among such expositors is Robortello's codification of comedy, appended tellingly to his commentary on the *Poetics*, along with similar efforts to define and describe satire, epigram and elegy ('explicationes').[40]

This 'progressive classicism' was devoted to the 'modernization of ancient poetic kinds' and thus also invited reflection on the different cultural and linguistic contexts for the production of literary texts, thereby laying the foundation for a genre theory that sought to be universalizing in scope but also attentive to the particularities of local, historical contexts – a move that combines an Aristotelian formalism with the historically sensitive philological impulse of the humanists, visible perhaps most famously in Lorenzo Valla's oration on the donation of Constantine. Thus, though often couched in polemical terms as a competition for authorial supremacy – the quarrel over Dante, the Ariosto–Tasso debate or the Homer-Vergil question – Renaissance battles about literary success often cloaked substantive, future-oriented arguments about the identification and classification of specific genres. The most colourful and critically defining treatises were those that engaged in partisan sniping, for instance the famous exchange between Camillo Pellegrino, the first major champion of Tasso's *Liberata,* and Lionardo Salviati's long and energetic response in defence of Ariosto's *Furioso.*[41] But at stake in this critical flyting were the stakes and decorum of writing a modern epic in Italian: Was the chivalric romance sufficient as a form and framework for epic? Could (and should) poetry veer away from the possible into the realm of the fantastic – in other words, what was the place of verisimilitude in the modern epic? Should a text be ideologically and ethically responsible to its cultural moment or should it break free from such constraints to engage in philosophically resonant – or merely entertaining – themes?[42]

[37] Scaliger's *Poetices libri septem* (1561) is the culmination of this labour, a *summa* of known ancient and modern genres with exemplary works, key practitioners and examples. The extensive introduction to the German edition is very useful: Giulio Cesare Scaligero, *Poetices Libri Septem. Sieben Bücher Über Die Dichtkunst*, trans. Gregor Vogt-Spira, Luc Deitz and Manfred Fuhrmann (Stuttgart-Bad Cannstatt: Frommann-Holzboog, 1994).
[38] Javitch, 'Emergence of Poetic Genre Theory', 139.
[39] Ibid., especially 139, 142–3, 147–8.
[40] See Francesco Robortello, 'Explicationes de satyra, de epigrammate, de comoedia, de elegia', in Weinberg, *Trattati di poetica e retorica,* vol. 1, 493–537. See also Javitch's discussion of this text in 'Emergence of Poetic Genre Theory', 147–8.
[41] See Camillo Pellegrino, *Il Carraffa o vero della epica poesia* (1584) and Lionardo Salviati's response (in several tracts) beginning with the *Difesa dell'Orlando furioso. Contra 'l dialogo dell'epica poesia di Camillo Pellegrino* (1584). On these debates see Daniel Javitch, 'Italian Epic Theory', in *The Cambridge History of Literary Criticism*, ed. Glyn P. Norton (Cambridge: Cambridge University Press, 1999), 205–15; and *Proclaiming a Classic,* chapter six on Salviati.
[42] Even this framing of the key issues at stake owes much to Castelvetro's commentary on Aristotle's *Poetics* (*Poetica d'Aristotele Vulgarizzata e Sposta* (1570)). Also relevant here is the well-known

These questions remain at the heart of genre theory 500 years later. When *PMLA* devoted a special issue to the subject of genre in 2007, the volume's focus was on the political ramifications of genre and its manipulations of history and fiction. Though not a single essay was concerned with medieval or early modern literature, this topic would have been immediately grasped by Renaissance critics.[43] Derrida's conceptualization of genre as a 'law of purity' is preempted by Renaissance notions of generic *contaminatio*, and the French philosopher's metaphor of miscegenation finds darkly comic analogues in the famous, much-discussed opening to Horace's *Ars Poetica*:

> Humano capiti cervicem pictor equinam
> iungere si velit, et varias inducere plumas,
> undique conlatis membris, ut turpiter atrum
> desinat in piscem mulier formosa superne,
> spectatum admissi risum teneatis, amici?
> …
> scimus, et hanc veniam petimusque damusque vicissim;
> sed non ut placidis coeant inmitia, non ut
> serpentes avibus geminentur, tigribus agni.

(If a painter should wish to unite a horse's neck to a human head, and spread a variety of plumage over limbs [of different animals] taken from every part [of nature], so that what is a beautiful woman in the upper part terminates unsightly in an ugly fish below; could you, my friends, refrain from laughter, were you admitted to such a sight? … We are conscious of this, and this privilege we demand and allow in turn: but not to such a degree, that the tame should associate with the savage; nor that serpents should be coupled with birds, lambs with tigers.) Horace, *Ars Poetica*, 1–13

The invocation of (absurd) inter-species couplings to speak of generic hybridity provides the basis for Renaissance evaluations of literary texts as 'monsters' based on their generic intermixing, and looks ahead to the current literary politics of generic form, canonicity and aesthetic purity.[44] But already in his influential edition of 1500, Johannes Badius Ascensius used his rule-based commentary method to produce 'something approaching a systematic criticism': the mise-en-page balances the Horatian text with Badius's rules as though extracting an equivalence between them.[45] More eclectic and wide-ranging is Aulo Giano Parrasio (Ianus Parrhasius)

---

debate around Sperone Speroni's *Canace*: Sperone Speroni and Giambattista Giraldi Cinzio, *Canace, e scritti in sua difesa; Scritti contro la Canace*, ed. Christina Roaf, Collezione di opere inedite o rare, vol. 138 (Bologna: Commissione per i testi di lingua, 1982).

[43] *PMLA* 122: 5 (2007) special issue on 'Remapping Genre'. It is worth observing that the absence of any premodern text in the special issue demonstrates a still-prominent critical sense that pre-Enlightenment texts are of historical interest rather than active documents in transhistorical debates over genre and politics.

[44] Jacques Derrida, 'The Law of Genre', trans. Avital Ronell, *Glyph* 7 (1980): 202–32.

[45] See Paul White, *Jodocus Badius Ascensius: Commentary, Commerce and Print in the Renaissance* (Oxford: Oxford University Press, 2013), 215; and Ann Moss, 'Horace in the Sixteenth Century:

whose 1531 commentary on Horace's *Ars Poetica*, notes Ann Moss, 'touches ... on areas which were to become central to subsequent literary debate: the status of fiction, the morality of literature, the problematics of literary imitation'.[46] These early Horatian commentaries, in other words, contain the seeds of a prescriptive criticism based in rhetorical decorum – one of the conceptual building blocks of genre theory – that would come to fruition when merged with the template provided by Aristotle's *Poetics*.[47] Indeed, from the early 1540s to the mid-1550s, there are a spate of new commentaries that relate the *Ars poetica* to the *Poetics*: it is worth remembering that the Robortello (1548) and Maggi (1550) editions of the *Poetics* also include an edition of the *Ars Poetica*.

Not surprisingly, then, in his defence of the *Gerusalemme liberata*, Torquato Tasso begins by invoking precisely the Horatian metaphor of the literary work as an animal: 'L'eroica poesia, quasi animale in cui due nature si congiungono, d'imitazione e d'allegoria è composta. Con quella alletta a sè gli animi e gli orecchi degli uomini, e maravigliosamente gli diletta; con questa nella virtù o nella scienza, o nell'una e nell'altra, gli ammaestra' ('Heroic poetry, like an animal in which two separate natures are joined, is composed of Imitation and Allegory. With the former, it attracts the souls and ears of men and brings them wondrous delight, while with the latter it instructs men in virtue or knowledge or both').[48] If the spectre of a generic chimera haunts this opening to the 'Allegoria del poema', it is perhaps because, as Javitch observes, Renaissance poet-critics, such as Tasso and Giraldi Cinzio, used 'a quite unclassical generic *contaminatio*' as the source of literary innovation, expanding the Aristotelian generic system to conform to the 'generic blends' they produced.[49]

This method of producing 'self-justifying norms' in defence of aesthetic novelty anticipates the claims of contemporary critic-writers such as Salman Rushdie, who explicitly theorize 'how newness enters the world' in terms of generic hybridity.[50] Writing to defend his controversial novel, *The Satanic Verses*, from criticism and political backlash, Rushdie writes: 'Those who oppose the novel most vociferously today are of the opinion that intermingling with a different culture will inevitably weaken and ruin their own. I am of the opposite opinion. *The Satanic Verses* celebrates hybridity, impurity, intermingling, the transformation that comes of new and unexpected combinations ... it rejoices in mongrelization and fears the absolutism of the Pure.'[51] The fusion here of the aesthetic and the political – a hallmark of postmodern generic play – invokes a logic similar to that used to defend Ariosto's

---

Commentators into Critics', in *The Cambridge History of Literary Criticism*, ed. Glyn P. Norton (Cambridge: Cambridge University Press, 1999), 69-70.

[46] Moss, 'Horace in the Sixteenth Century', 69-70.
[47] On the mixing of Horatian and Aristotelian poetics see the classic work by Marvin T. Herrick, *The Fusion of Horatian and Aristotelian Literary Criticism, 1531-1555*, Illinois Studies in Language and Literature, v. 32, no. 1 (Urbana: University of Illinois Press, 1946).
[48] Torquato Tasso, 'Allegoria del poema', in *Le prose diverse*, vol. 1, ed. Cesare Guasti (Florence: Le Monnier, 1875), 297.
[49] Daniel Javitch, 'Self-Justifying Norms in the Genre Theories of Italian Renaissance Poets', *Philological Quarterly* 67, no. 2 (Spring 1988): 213.
[50] I borrow the term from Javitch, 'Self-Justifying Norms...'
[51] Salman Rushdie, *Imaginary Homelands: Essays and Criticism, 1981-1991* (London: Granta, 1991).

Orlando furioso, a hybrid epic-romance which also traffics knowingly in the interplay of politics and genre.

In a telling turn, recent genre theory has returned to the Horatian dictum, 'Singula quaeque locum teneant sortita decentem' ('Then let your style be suited to the scene,/ And its peculiar character maintain') – a statement of the integral relationship between form and content, at once functional and conceptual – to argue that genre actively generates and shapes knowledge of the world.[52] Though contemporary analyses draw from such varied sources as rhetoric, cognitive poetics and modal philosophy, they remain closely related to Horace's vision in the *Ars poetica,* and perhaps even to Aristotle's conception of poetry as an ordering, shaping force as articulated by Renaissance commentators. Following early modern critics then, we might well seek not only to identify *what genre* a text belongs to but rather to inquire *what work* a text's generic engagements does: What does it achieve? How does it work to affect our perceptions of the world? Such questions would open the polemics of literary debates to new scrutiny, while also making us newly attentive to the complex conceptual labour of genre in the period and beyond.

III

The reconsideration of the literary text as a historical object in the Renaissance brought with it a renewed appreciation for its fragility, its palimpsest-like possibilities and its iconic status as a token of exchange within various communities across time. But this perspective, which Renaissance literary critics applied so effectively to classical texts, can also be usefully brought to bear on their own work.[53] Consider, for example, Scipione Ammirato's critical dialogue, *Il Dedalione overo Del Poeta,* published in 1642 in the *Opusculi Del Signor Scipione Ammirato,* an extensive discussion of the problems of poetry in broadly Platonic terms, which emphasizes the conjunction between poetry and philosophy.[54] Drawing on a familiar analogy, Ammirato argues that the philosopher is the soul's physician who becomes a poet when he heals with sweetness: 'il filosofo in genere riguarda la sanità dell'anima, diciamo che quando egli discende à curarla con dolcezza diventa poeta à differenza dell'altre curazioni…' ('in general, the philosopher is concerned with the health of the soul, let us say that when he sets about curing it with sweetness he becomes a poet as opposed to other cures'). Thus, poetry is rightly a branch of philosophy, and its ends, following the Horatian *dulce utile,* are concerned with the treatment of the soul in order to maintain its health (understood as virtue): 'il fine della poetica è indura nell'anima

---

[52] See for instance the synthetic but wide-ranging account in John Frow, *Genre* (New York: Routledge, 2006).
[53] Such work has indeed been undertaken for literary texts across various periods – the many historicisms that have characterized early modern studies in the last half-century is an extension of humanist historicism, while the turn to the 'New Lyric Studies' with its emphasis on rooting lyric poems in specific historical context is another example.
[54] Scipione Ammirato, *Opusculi del sig. Scipione Ammirato* (Landi, 1642), Tomo III. See also the discussion in Weinberg, *History,* vol.1, 277ff.

la virtù discacciandone il vizio' ('the end of poetics is to affix firmly virtue in the soul and to discard vice from it').[55]

Such a view partakes of and extends a long classical tradition, even as it shapes a syncretic theory of poetry that grounds didactic injunctions in a broader ethical code. But beyond its critical content – which itself touches upon key topics in literary theory (the place of poets in the *polis,* the possibility of poetic knowledge, the moral-civic function of poetry) – Ammirato's dialogue opens up a further set of reflections on the social-intellectual milieu within which such criticism took shape. The manuscript of the *Il Dedalione,* preserved in the Biblioteca nazionale centrale di Firenze, contains a note that identifies the dialogue's main interlocutors as members of the Accademia dei Trasformati, founded by Ammirato in Lecce in 1558–9.[56] How did this academic exercise, written around 1560, find its way to publication eighty years later in Florence? What might the bibliographic history of this text tell us about the intellectual networks in Italy in the sixteenth century within which distinct strains of literary theory and interpretive practices arose? What social capital might particular kinds of critical claims have signalled – and how might these have connected to a broader international republic of letters?

As recent work on the Italian academies in the Renaissance has shown, there is a rich cultural history preserved in the various texts, letters and documents associated with the establishment of scholarly communities across Europe. Together, they reveal how literary criticism as a discipline was made – not merely as a history of ideas and textual transmission, but as a socio-cultural history of communities, rivalries and critical politics. The work of Déborah Blocker, Lia Markey and Jane Everson, for instance, suggests that the labour of criticism and its significance cuts beyond the critical claims made about specific texts (which themselves do not always break new ground), to offer a window into the social and cultural history of the period.[57]

Current theoretical interest in the sociology of texts and the historiography of scholarship, inspired inter alia by actor-network theory and digital humanities methods, parallels and enables this new early modern scholarship, as the Italian Academies database hosted by the British Library attests.[58] But beyond the application of a new critical trend to early modern corpora, the conceptual claim implied by such scholarship is worth unpacking, for it discloses a kinship with the humanists' poignant apprehension of their own historicity. Roger Chartier has argued that recent critical debates over the 'sociology of texts' and its transformation of the traditional field of textual bibliography has been driven by the recognition that the process of reading is not the universal act that it is often implied to be. Building on Pierre Bourdieu's insight that one of the 'illusions of the *lector*' consists in 'forgetting one's own social conditions

---

[55] Ammirato, *Opuscoli,* Tomo III, p. 386.
[56] Weinberg, *History,* 278; on the Florentine academies, see Déborah Blocker's chapter in this volume.
[57] Everson directed the important Italian Academies Project: http://italianacademies.org/. Markey's work on the contexts of the Florentine academies emerges in Lia Markey, *Imagining the Americas in Medici Florence* (University Park, PA: The Pennsylvania State University Press, 2016). See Blocker's forthcoming book, *Le Principe de plaisir: savoirs, esthétique et politique dans la Florence des Médicis (XVIe-XVIIe siècles).*
[58] See http://italianacademies.org/.

of production, and unconsciously universalizing the conditions of possibility of one's own reading', Chartier notes that

> against such an obliteration of the historicity of the reader, the history or sociology of reading shows that the meanings attributed to the texts rely on the capacities, conventions, and practices of reading proper to the communities that constitute, simultaneously or successively, their different publics ... . One of the principal tasks of the sociology of texts consists rightly in dissipating such an illusion.[59]

This repositioning of 'reader response' as a 'history of reading' that is attentive to the specificity and historicity of particular communities and their practices has important implications for the history of criticism as well.

Criticism, a situated, highly specialized reading practice, is rooted in particular times and places even as it seeks, consciously, to transcend those particularities and make universal claims. Renaissance humanist critics from Petrarch onward are sharply aware of this inherent paradox. In *Familiares* 24.12, Petrarch writes to Homer, reflecting on the historical and linguistic gulf that divides them, imagining himself, with self-conscious irony, as a Penelope yearning for Homer/ Ulysses: 'I have said many things as though you were present, but now upon emerging from these vivid flights of the imagination, I realize how far removed you are.'[60] That awareness of a temporal distance that is also a cognitive, socio-cultural distance, epitomizes what Thomas Greene called the Renaissance recognition of 'historical difference' – an early modern insight that has, finally, returned to animate contemporary critical consciousness.[61]

It is therefore no surprise that a renewed interest in the history of Italian Renaissance literary criticism has coincided with a revitalized New Bibliography – or 'critical bibliography' – and book history. From manifestos such as Virginia Jackson's call for a New Lyric Studies based on deeply historicized analyses of poetry, and innovative bibliographic work on the materiality of classical texts as well as major canonical authors such as Petrarch and Milton, to the emergence of professional organizations such as the Society for the History of Reading, Authorship and Publishing (SHARP) and a return to the teaching of book history as a discipline in its own right, our current preoccupation with the book is a striking mirror image of the Renaissance.[62] But while early modern humanist and philological practices have long been subject to study as a source for identifying nodes of cultural value, we are yet to apply that lens to our own bibliographic fascinations. Might an encounter with Renaissance literary criticism,

---

[59] Roger Chartier, 'Crossing Borders in Early Modern Europe: Sociology of Texts and Literature', trans. Maurice Elton, *Book History* 8 (2005): 39.
[60] 'Multa dixi quasi ad presentem; sed iam ab illa vehementissima imaginatione rediens, quam longe absis intelligo...' Francesco Petrarca, *Rerum libri familiares,* 24.12.43. Translation is from Petrarch, *Letters on Familiar Matters*, 350.
[61] Thomas M. Greene, *The Light in Troy: Imitation and Discovery in Renaissance Poetry* (New Haven: Yale University Press, 1982).
[62] See for instance Virginia Jackson, *Dickinson's Misery: A Theory of Lyric Reading* (Princeton, NJ: Princeton University Press, 2005); Michael F. Suarez and H. R. Woudhuysen, eds., *The Oxford Companion to the Book* (Oxford: Oxford University Press, 2010); David Finkelstein and Alistair McCleery, eds, *The Book History Reader*, 2nd edn (London and New York: Routledge, 2006).

with such long-range critical trends in mind, help us introspect on our own passion for textual materiality in an age when that materiality itself seems subject to the processes of technological obsolescence?

There is more work to be done to uncover and weave together a sociologically astute book history of the Renaissance *trattati*, even as similar histories (such as Joseph North's *Literary Criticism: A Concise Political History*) are slowly being crafted for the critical movements of our own time. Such a history would ask who the booksellers and publishers of literary criticism were, who comprised its market and what exactly was its scope and spread, not just in Italy but throughout Europe and, perhaps, the world. Markey's study of the Florentine academies' connections to the New World raises intriguing possibilities for the use of the vast corpus of early modern literary-critical texts to follow the growth of transnational literary relations long before the eighteenth century, which is too often seen as the starting point for a 'world republic of letters'.[63] If the emergence of a global world view in the sixteenth century brought with it new global circuits of production and dissemination, it is worth asking whether – and which – literary-critical texts found their way to the Americas and Asia. And in addition to a corpus of texts explicitly dedicated to literary criticism, we might also include and track the hidden circulation of literary debates – as for instance in the debate between Don Quijote and the Canon of Toledo on the nature of romance, history and fiction, which draws extensively on the debates of the sixteenth century.[64] How did early modern critics use the resources of criticism from their own European tradition (both classical and medieval) to engage with other interpretive and critical frameworks? Robust critical paradigms existed in the Arabic, Persian and South Asian traditions, and similar symbolic forms were clearly discernible in the New World as well.[65] As these materials became more widely available in Europe, how did existing European critical tools facilitate the culture's engagement with its others? How might these other paradigms, in turn, have influenced Renaissance critics?

If the emergence of a modern world view over the course of the sixteenth and seventeenth centuries brought a range of new subjects to early modern literature, as much recent scholarship has shown, it could not but have also affected the critical conversations around those texts. Did literary criticism offer tools to make sense of a shifting world? Did the vehement efforts to disambiguate poetry (and by extension its interpretation) from history and philosophy draw on a new appreciation for the work

---

[63] I am referring here to Pascale Casanova, *The World Republic of Letters* (Cambridge, MA: Harvard University Press, 2004).

[64] See the important consideration of this episode as a meditation on history and literature in Barbara Fuchs, 'Don Quijote 1 and the Forging of National History', *Modern Language Quarterly* 68, no. 3 (2007): 395–416. Frederick De Armas notes that 'the Canon's words derive from Tasso's discourses on poetry … Don Quixote's [sic] speech serves to problematize the debate between the proponents of romance and the neo-Aristotelians.' See Frederick A. De Armas, 'Cervantes and the Italian Renaissance', in *The Cambridge Companion to Cervantes* (Cambridge: Cambridge University Press, 2002), 44.

[65] Most obviously, the importance of Averroes's commentaries on Aristotle are well known: see Jill Kraye, 'The Printing History of Aristotle in the Fifteenth Century: A Bibliographical Approach to Renaissance Philosophy', *Renaissance Studies* 9, no. 2 (1995): 189–211; and more recently, the essays collected in Anna Akasoy and Guido Giglioni, eds, *Renaissance Averroism and Its Aftermath: Arabic Philosophy in Early Modern Europe* (Dordrecht: Springer, 2013).

of the speculative imagination, for the power of *poiesis* itself? When Torquato Tasso writes of the epic poem as a world-making form in his *Discorsi*, he writes as both critic and poet, recognizing not only the aesthetic labour of shaping a world but also the critical labour that makes such fashioning legible *as* labour.[66]

The continuing importance of allegorical poetics in the early modern period similarly suggests how interpretive practices could afford a distinctive vision of history.[67] Building on the long history of allegoresis, Renaissance literary critics understood allegory as multiform – it was both precise in its particular (textual) details and also abstracting and universalizing in its conceptual reach. Allegoresis, as a mode of reading the world, suggested how the heterogenous, plural globe could in fact be understood as profoundly connected through key symbolic associations. Indeed, the persistence of allegory as a fundamental critical term into the twenty-first century – witness the publication in 2010 of both a Cambridge companion and a Routledge *New Critical Idiom* volume on the topic – urges us to ask how the poetics of allegory may triangulate the seemingly competing claims of history and form.

* * *

Good readers of poetry, Plutarch tells us, must be prepared to act as physicians. In his celebrated essay, 'Quomodo adolescens poetas audire debeat', also known as *De audiendis poetis* (How a young man should study poetry), he offers a vivid description of why literary criticism and commentary is necessary:

> Just as physicians, in spite of the fact that the blister-fly is deadly, think that its feet and wings are helpful to counteract its potent effect, so in poetry if a noun or adjective or a verb by its position next to another word blunts the point which the passage, in its worse interpretation, would have, we should seize upon it and add explanation.[68]

The blister beetle is an infamous insect known since antiquity for its toxicity: it secretes cantharidin, a chemical that causes painful blistering of the skin, but which has also been used for medicinal purposes.[69] To compare the potency of a poetic text – and its right handling – to this creature suggests a knowing twist on the theme of writing as a *pharmakon,* both poison and remedy, transformative but also requiring transformation. Literary interpretation in this metaphor is both poison and medicine: venomous, dangerous and paradoxically healing.

---

[66] Torquato Tasso, *Discorsi dell'arte poetica e del poema eroico*, ed. Luigi Poma (Bari: Laterza, 1964).
[67] This is a vast subject: on early modern allegorical poetics see, most recently, the synthetic overview (though slanted towards England) in Jason Crawford, *Allegory and Enchantment: An Early Modern Poetics*, 1st edn (Oxford: Oxford University Press, 2017). See also the essay by Brjlak in this volume.
[68] Plutarch, *Moralia*, trans. Frank Cole Babbitt, vol. 1 (Cambridge, MA: Harvard University Press, 1927), 115. See the comprehensive introduction in Plutarch, *How to Study Poetry: De audiendis poetis*, ed. R. L. Hunter and D. A. Russell, Cambridge Greek and Latin classics (Cambridge: Cambridge University Press, 2011).
[69] See Plutarch, *How to Study Poetry,* 123–4.

This view is strangely familiar in the world of literary study today: from Derrida's influential reading of Plato's *pharmakon* and the so-called 'ethical turn' to debates over the New Formalism, close reading, book history and textual editing, the practices of critical analysis and commentary that Plutarch describes here continue to find modern echoes. But the return to these forms of reading – and the arguments over them – owes much to the early modern period: Plutarch's programme was a siren call to Renaissance humanists who took up the matter of literary analysis with new fervour. In an intriguing historical parallel, we might be coming full circle once more.

In a recent paper, Felski connects the crisis of direction in literary study to the humanities at large, and offers four paths as a defence of what we do (and ought to continue doing): 'curating, conveying, criticizing; composing'.[70] Central to all these is the task of curating, which Felski observes 'involves a process of caring for – the word has its origins in *caritas* – of guarding, protecting, conserving, caretaking, and looking after'. It depends on 'an ethics of preservation – on the value of the seemingly outmoded or the non-relevant'.[71] To a scholar of the early modern period, this call has an oddly familiar ring. It is the call of the Renaissance *umanisti*, those early modern curators of the *studia litterarum*, to recover, study and transmit (by teaching, publication and polemic) a distinctive tradition that gave them a new genealogy. To preserve the past, to convey it and to remake it into forms of value for their own world – these commitments find immediate resonance with Renaissance critics, whose work hinged on this tripartite technique. They forged anew the multidirectional 'transtemporal connections' that Felski and others emphasize, creating a blueprint for the modern period – an ethical claim that was already enshrined in Francis Bacon's *Advancement of Learning*. By returning to the corpus of literary criticism in Renaissance Italy to re-imagine its import and rewrite its history, we thus participate in a 'new literary humanism', a critical and constructive project that insists upon the continuing significance of the *translatio studii* and the possibilities it opens for critical conversation across different times and places.[72]

Bibliography

Akasoy, Anna and Guido Giglioni, eds. *Renaissance Averroism and Its Aftermath: Arabic Philosophy in Early Modern Europe*. Dordrecht: Springer, 2013.
Ammirato, Scipione. *Opuscoli del sig. Scipione Ammirato*. Florence: Landi, 1642.
Anker, Elizabeth S. and Rita Felski, eds. *Critique and Postcritique*. Durham: Duke University Press, 2017.

---

[70] Rita Felski, 'Introduction', *New Literary History* 47, no. 2 (20 September 2016): 215.
[71] Ibid., 216.
[72] There have been many recent efforts to revive and re-appropriate humanism for the twenty-first century – see for instance Andy Mousley, *Towards a New Literary Humanism* (Springer, 2011); and Martin Halliwell and Andy Mousley, *Critical Humanisms: Humanist/Anti-Humanist Dialogues* (Edinburgh: Edinburgh University Press, 2003). I find most compelling the non-prescriptive articulations in Edward W. Said, *Humanism and Democratic Criticism* (Columbia University Press, 2004) and Aamir Mufti, *Forget English!: Orientalisms and World Literatures* (Cambridge, MA: Harvard University Press, 2015), especially chapter 4 on Said and Auerbach.

Barolini, Teodolinda and Wayne Storey, eds. *Petrarch and the Textual Origins of Interpretation*. Leiden: Brill, 2007.
Bevilacqua, Alexander. *The Republic of Arabic Letters: Islam and the European Enlightenment*. Cambridge, MA: Harvard University Press, 2018.
Bréchet, Christophe. 'Le "De audiendis poetis" de Plutarque et le procès platonicien de la poésie'. *Revue de Philologie, de Littérature et d'Histoire Anciennes* 73, no. 2 (1999): 209–44.
Casanova, Pascale. *The World Republic of Letters*. Cambridge, MA: Harvard University Press, 2004.
Cassirer, Ernst. *The Individual and the Cosmos in Renaissance Philosophy*. Translated by Mario Domandi. New York: Harper & Row, 1964.
Chartier, Roger. 'Crossing Borders in Early Modern Europe: Sociology of Texts and Literature'. Translated by Maurice Elton. *Book History* 8 (2005): 37–50.
Cohen, Stephen, ed. *Shakespeare and Historical Formalism*. Aldershot: Ashgate, 2007.
Crawford, Jason. *Allegory and Enchantment: An Early Modern Poetics*. Oxford: Oxford University Press, 2017.
Dannenfeldt, Karl H. 'The Renaissance Humanists and the Knowledge of Arabic'. *Studies in the Renaissance* 2 (1955): 96–117.
De Armas, Frederick A. 'Cervantes and the Italian Renaissance'. In *The Cambridge Companion to Cervantes*, 32–57. Cambridge: Cambridge University Press, 2002.
Derrida, Jacques. 'The Animal That Therefore I Am (More to Follow)' Translated by David Wills. *Critical Inquiry* 28, no. 2 (2002): 369–418.
Derrida, Jacques. 'The Law of Genre'. Translated by Avital Ronell. *Glyph* 7 (1980): 202–32.
Eden, Kathy. *The Renaissance Rediscovery of Intimacy*. Chicago: University of Chicago Press, 2012.
Fahy, Conor. 'Royal-Paper Copies of Aldine Editions, 1494–1550'. *Studies in Bibliography* 57, no. 1 (2005): 85–113.
Felski, Rita. 'Introduction'. *New Literary History* 47, no. 2 (20 September 2016): 215–29.
Felski, Rita. *The Limits of Critique*. Chicago: The University of Chicago Press, 2015.
Finkelstein, David and Alistair McCleery, eds. *The Book History Reader*. New York: Routledge, 2006.
Fletcher, H. George and Aldo Manuzio. *In Praise of Aldus Manutius: A Quincentenary Exhibition*. New York : Pierpont Morgan Library, 1995.
Frow, John. *Genre*. New York: Routledge, 2006.
Fuchs, Barbara. 'Don Quijote 1 and the Forging of National History'. *Modern Language Quarterly* 68, no. 3 (1 September 2007): 395–416.
Ghobrial, John-Paul. 'The Archive of Orientalism and Its Keepers: Re-Imagining the Histories of Arabic Manuscripts in Early Modern Europe'. *Past & Present* 230, no. suppl_11 (1 November 2016): 90–111.
Goetsch, James Robert. *Vico's Axioms: The Geometry and the Human World*. New Haven: Yale University Press, 1995.
Grafton, Anthony and Lisa Jardine. *From Humanism to the Humanities: Education and the Liberal Arts in Fifteenth- and Sixteenth-Century Europe*. Cambridge, MA: Harvard University Press, 1986.
Greene, Roland. *Five Words: Critical Semantics in the Age of Shakespeare and Cervantes*. Chicago: The University of Chicago Press, 2013.
Greene, Thomas M. *The Light in Troy: Imitation and Discovery in Renaissance Poetry*. New Haven: Yale University Press, 1982.
Halliwell, Martin and Andy Mousley. *Critical Humanisms: Humanist/Anti-Humanist Dialogues*. Edinburgh: Edinburgh University Press, 2003.

Hathaway, Baxter. *The Age of Criticism: The Late Renaissance in Italy*. Ithaca: Cornell University Press, 1962.
Herrick, Marvin T. *The Fusion of Horatian and Aristotelian Literary Criticism, 1531–1555*. Urbana: University of Illinois Press, 1946.
Jackson, Virginia Walker. *Dickinson's Misery: A Theory of Lyric Reading*. Princeton: Princeton University Press, 2005.
Javitch, Daniel. 'The Emergence of Poetic Genre Theory in the Sixteenth Century'. *Modern Language Quarterly* 59, no. 2 (1998): 139–69.
Javitch, Daniel. 'Italian Epic Theory'. In *The Cambridge History of Literary Criticism*, edited by Glyn P. Norton, 205–15. Cambridge: Cambridge University Press, 1999.
Javitch, Daniel. 'Self-Justifying Norms in the Genre Theories of Italian Renaissance Poets'. *Philological Quarterly; Iowa City* 67, no. 2 (Spring 1988): 195–217.
Javitch, Daniel. *Proclaiming a Classic: The Canonization of Orlando Furioso*. Princeton: Princeton University Press, 1991.
Konstan, David. '"The Birth of the Reader:" Plutarch as a Literary Critic'. *Scholia* 13 (2004): 3–27.
Kramnick, Jonathan and Anahid Nersessian. 'Form and Explanation'. *Critical Inquiry* 43, no. 3 (1 March 2017): 650–69.
Kraye, Jill. 'The Printing History of Aristotle in the Fifteenth Century: A Bibliographical Approach to Renaissance Philosophy'. *Renaissance Studies* 9, no. 2 (1995): 189–211.
Levine, Caroline. *Forms: Whole, Rhythm, Hierarchy, Network*. Princeton: Princeton University Press, 2015.
Lines, David A. and Eugenio Refini, eds. *"Aristotele fatto volgare": tradizione aristotelica e cultura volgare nel Rinascimento*. Pisa: Edizioni ETS, 2014.
Markey, Lia. *Imagining the Americas in Medici Florence*. University Park: The Pennsylvania State University Press, 2016.
Mazzotta, Giuseppe. *The New Map of the World: The Poetic Philosophy of Giambattista Vico*. Princeton: Princeton University Press, 1999.
Mengelkoch, Dustin. 'The Mutability of Poetics: Poliziano, Statius, and the Silvae'. *MLN* 125, no. 1 (21 April 2010): 84–116.
Montaigne, Michel de. *The Complete Essays of Michel de Montaigne*. Translated by Donald Frame. Stanford: Stanford University Press, 1958.
Montaigne, Michel de. *Les Essais*. Edited by Pierre Villey, V. L. Saulnier and M. Conche. Paris: Quadrige/PUF, 2004.
Moss, Ann. 'Horace in the Sixteenth Century: Commentators into Critics'. In *The Cambridge History of Literary Criticism*, edited by Glyn P. Norton, 66–76. Cambridge: Cambridge University Press, 1999.
Mousley, A. *Towards a New Literary Humanism*. Basingstoke and New York: Springer, 2011.
Mufti, Aamir. *Forget English!: Orientalisms and World Literatures*. Cambridge, MA: Harvard University Press, 2015.
Nebrija, Antonio de. 'On Language and Empire: The Prologue to Grammar of the Castilian Language (1492)'. Translated by Magalí Armillas-Tiseyra. *PMLA* 131, no. 1 (1 January 2016): 197–208.
North, Joseph. *Literary Criticism: A Concise Political History*. Cambridge, MA: Harvard University Press, 2017.
Norton, Glyn P. *The Cambridge History of Literary Criticism*, vol. 3. Cambridge: Cambridge University Press, 1999.

Piemontese, Angelo. 'Italian Scholarship on Iran (an Outline, 1557–1987)'. *Iranian Studies* 20, no. 2–4 (January 1987): 99–130. https://doi.org/10.1080/00210868708701698.
Piemontese, Angelo. 'Un testo latino-persiano connesso al Codex Cumanicus'. *Acta Orientalia Academiae Scientiarum Hungaricae* 53, no. 1/2 (2000): 121–32.
Piemontese, Angelo. 'Venezia e la diffusione dell'alfabeto arabo nell'italia del cinquecento'. *Quaderni di studi arabi* 5, no. 6 (1987): 641–60.
Plutarch. *How to Study Poetry: De audiendis poetis*. Edited by R. L. Hunter and D. A. Russell. Cambridge Greek and Latin classics. Cambridge: Cambridge University Press, 2011.
Plutarch. *Moralia*. Translated by Frank Cole Babbitt, vol. 1. Cambridge, MA: Harvard University Press, 1927.
Puttenham, George. *The Art of English Poesy*. Edited by Frank Whigham and Wayne A. Rebhorn. Ithaca: Cornell University Press, 2007.
Ramachandran, Ayesha. 'Humanism and Its Discontents'. *Spenser Studies* 30 (2016): 3–18.
Refini, Eugenio. 'Aristotelian Commentaries and the Dialogue Form in Cinquecento Italy'. In *Vernacular Aristotelieanism in Italy from the Fourteenth to the Seventeenth Century*, edited by Luca BIanchi, Simon Gilson and Jill Kraye, 93–107. London: The Warburg Institute, 2016.
Renouard, Antoine-Augustin. *Annales de l'imprimerie des Alde: ou, histoire des trois Manuce et de leurs éditions*. Paris: J. Renouard, 1834.
Robbins, Bruce. 'Critical Correctness'. *The Chronicle of Higher Education*, 12 March 2019.
Rossi, Paolo. *The Dark Abyss of Time: The History of the Earth & the History of Nations from Hooke to Vico*. Chicago: The University of Chicago Press, 1984.
Rushdie, Salman. *Imaginary Homelands: Essays and Criticism, 1981–1991*. London: Granta, 1991.
Said, Edward W. *Humanism and Democratic Criticism*. Columbia University Press, 2004.
Scaligero, Giulio Cesare. *Poetices Libri Septem. Sieben Bücher Über Die Dichtkunst*. Translated by Gregor Vogt-Spira, Luc Deitz and Manfred Fuhrmann. Stuttgart-Bad Cannstatt: Frommann-Holzboog, 1994.
Scholes, Robert. 'Presidential Address 2004: The Humanities in a Posthumanist World'. *PMLA* 120, no. 3 (1 May 2005): 724–33.
Speroni, Sperone and Giambattista Cinzio Giraldi. *Canace, e scritti in sua difesa; Scritti contro la Canace*. Edited by Christina Roaf. Bologna: Commissione per i testi di lingua, 1982.
Stewart, Susan. 'Lyric'. In *The Oxford Handbook of Philosophy and Literature*, edited by Richard Eldridge, 45–70. Oxford: Oxford University Press, 2009.
Suarez, Michael F. and H. R. Woudhuysen, eds. *The Oxford Companion to the Book*. New York: Oxford University Press, 2010.
Tasso, Torquato. *Discorsi dell'arte poetica e del poema eroico*. Edited by Luigi Poma. Bari: Laterza, 1964.
Valla, Lorenzo. *On the Donation of Constantine*. Translated by G. W. Bowersock. Cambridge, MA: Harvard University Press, 2007.
Venuti, Lawrence. 'Genealogies of Translation Theory: Jerome'. *Boundary 2* 37, no. 3 (1 August 2010): 5–28.
Venuti, Lawrence, ed. *The Translation Studies Reader*. New York: Routledge, 2012.
Weinberg, Bernard. *A History of Literary Criticism in the Italian Renaissance*. Chicago: University of Chicago Press, 1961.
Weinberg, Bernard. *Trattati di poetica e retorica del Cinquecento*. Bari: G. Laterza, 1970.

White, Paul. *Jodocus Badius Ascensius: Commentary, Commerce and Print in the Renaissance*. Oxford: Oxford University Press, 2013.

Zadorojnyi, Alexei. 'Safe Drugs for the Good Boys: Platonism and Pedagogy in Plutarch's De Audiendis Poetis'. In *Sage and Emperor: Plutarch, Greek Intellectuals, and Roman Power in the Time of Trajan (98–117 A.D.)*, edited by Philip A. Stadter and Luc Van der Stockt, 297–314. Leuven: Leuven University Press, 2002.

Appendix

Early modern books in the library of Bernard Weinberg

Eufemia Baldassarre, Paul Gehl and Lia Markey

As demonstrated in Chapter 2 of the present volume, Bernard Weinberg was not only a pioneer in the study of Renaissance poetics but also a significant collector of books on that subject and others. His library was assembled both to support his teaching or research and with an eye to enriching publicly held collections in his hometown of Chicago. This appendix contains a short-title list of 684 pre-1800 books that we know belonged to Bernard Weinberg, the first such attempt to describe his library in detail. Given the nature of the sources, it cannot be complete; but it surely represents nearly all the early modern books he once owned.

The checklist was compiled from the two inventories described in our essay in this volume, checked as necessary and as possible against copies that are today held by the University of Chicago Library and the Newberry Library. The main entries are constructed from those two American library catalogues, and so authors' names are Anglicized following Library of Congress usage and title spellings follow those on the title pages. We have added diacritics to aid in reading. Anonymous works appear under their titles; and pseudonymous ones under the attributed author (e.g. Aelius Donatus), unless another form is authorized by the Library of Congress. LC arranges some commentaries and translations under the author commented upon (most importantly here Aristotle, Homer, Horace and Virgil); others appear under the names of the authors of the commentaries. We have also indicated translators and added cross references to aid the reader in understanding the complexity of Weinberg's personal and wide-ranging collecting of critical texts.

For the most important portion of Weinberg's library, his sixteenth-century books, we have provided references to the now standard *Censimento nazionale delle edizioni italiane del XVI secolo* (EDIT16, cited as CNCE) and to the growing *Universal Short Title Catalog* (USTC). These references clarify which of the many commentaries and variant editions of popular authors and works Weinberg owned. Similarly, for the difficult-to-identify editions of Helvétius, we cite item numbers from David Smith, *Bibliography of the Writings of Helvétius*, Perney-Voltaire, 2001.

In order to enable the reader to understand Weinberg's gift history, we have furnished all entries with one or more of the following sigla:

BW63: titles donated by Bernard Weinberg to the University of Chicago in 1963.
BW73a: titles bequeathed by Weinberg to the University in 1973 and meant to be retained by the University.
BW73b: titles from the Weinberg bequest given to the Newberry Library.
BW73c: titles from the Weinberg bequest designated for sale by the University; the present whereabouts of these copies is unknown.

Titles marked BW73b and BW73c represent books that Weinberg collected, even though they would have been available in a Chicago library, at least towards the end of his life. With respect to BW63 and BW73a, we have not been able to verify in every case that the copies of these books currently held by the University were Weinberg's. We have added an asterisk (*) to entries when the location of the Weinberg copy is now unknown or uncertain.

Weinberg did not annotate his early modern books, nor did he use a bookplate. Where we have found them, we have indicated booksellers' exlibris or sales tickets in the Weinberg copies and notes that appear to be in his hand. For early bindings and miscellaneous volumes (*Sammelbände*), we have added brief notes.

Accademici Fiorentini, *Annotationi… sopra alcuni luoghi del Decameron*, Florence, 1574.
CNCE 1950, USTC 805126   BW63

Achilles Tatius, *Dell'amor di Leucippe et di Clitophonte*, Venice, 1578.
CNCE 201, USTC 807707   BW73a

Adriani, Giovanni Battista, *Istoria de' suoi tempi*, Florence, 1583.
CNCE 293, USTC 807801   BW73a

Adriani, Giovanni Battista, *Oratio funebris*, Florence, 1563.
CNCE 285, USTC 807793   BW73a

Aelianus, Claudius, *De varia historia*, Venice, 1550.
CNCE 317, USTC 807815   BW73a
Bound with Sardi, *De moribus*

Aeschines, *Ton tes Hellados exochon*, Venice, 1549.
CNCE 324, USTC 807818   BW73a

Aesopus, *Fabellae graece et latine*, Venice, 1543.
CNCE 367, USTC 807874   BW73a

Alamanni, Luigi, *La coltivazione… e Le api di Giovanni Rucellai*, Verona, 1745.   BW73a

Alembert, Jean Lerond d', *Sur la destruction des Jésuites en France*, n.p., 1765.   BW73a

Alunno, Francesco, *Della fabrica del mondo*, Venice, 1560.
CNCE 1314, USTC 808914   BW73a

———, *La fabrica del mondo*, Venice, 1581.
CNCE 1320, USTC 808927   BW73a

———, *Le osservazioni sopra il Petrarca*, Venice, 1550.
CNCE 25767, USTC 762205   BW73b

Amaseo, Romolo Quirino: see Pausanius

Ammianus, Marcellinus, *Rerum gestarum libri XVIII*, Paris, 1544.
USTC 149244   BW73b

Ammirato, Scipione, *Discorsi... sopra Cornelio Tacito*, Florence, 1594.
CNCE 1573, USTC 809110   BW73a

Appianus of Alexandria, *Delle guerre civili de Romani*, trans. A. Braccesi, Venice, 1538.
CNCE 2204, USTC 810085   BW73a

Ariosto, Ludovico, *Sette libri di sattire*, Venice, 1563.
CNCE 2741, USTC 810732   BW73c

———, *Orlando Furioso*, Venice, 1570.
CNCE 2768, USTC 810759   BW73a

Aristophanes, *Comoediae undecim*, Venice, 1548.
CNCE 2864, USTC 810854   BW73a

Aristotle, *Poetica, per Alexandrum Paccium*, Paris, 1538.
CNCE 2904, USTC 810904   BW73a

———, *Organon*, Basel, 1545.
USTC 681725   BW73a

———, *Magentini in Aristotelis librum...*, com. G. B. Rasario, Venice, 1545.
CNCE 31697, USTC 837893   BW73a

———, *Rethoricorum... libri tres*, trans. F. Filelfo, Lyon, 1545.
USTC 149478   BW73a

———, *De arte rhetorica*, Venice, 1546.
CNCE 2919, USTC 810919   BW73a

———, *Trattato dei governi*, trans. B. Segni, Florence, 1549.
CNCE 2928, USTC 810925   BW73a

———, *De arte dicendi*, ed. P. Vettori, trans. E. Barbaro, Paris, 1549.
USTC 150205   BW73a

———, *Rettorica et poetica*, trans. B. Segni, Florence, 1549.
CNCE 2927, USTC 810924   BW73b

———, *L'Ethica d'Aristotile*, trans. B. Segni, Florence, 1550.
CNCE 2929, USTC 810926   BW73a

———, *Rhetoricorum libri III*, trans. M. Maioraggio, Milan, 1550.
CNCE 2930, USTC 810927   BW73a

———, *Rettorica et poetica*, trans. B. Segni, Venice, 1551.
CNCE 2934, USTC 810932   BW73c

———, *Omnem logicam, rhetoricam et poeticam...*, Venice, 1551.
CNCE 2936, USTC 810930   BW73b

———, *Opera omnia*, Venice, 1552 (vol. 2 only).
CNCE 2940   BW73a*

———, *Eorum quae physica sequuntur sive metaphysicorum...*, Paris, 1558.
USTC 152387 BW73a

———, *Rettorica d'Aristotile*, trans. Annibale Caro, Venice, 1570.
CNCE 2974, USTC 810976 BW63

———, *M. A. Maioragii in tres Aristoteles libros de arte rhetorica*, Venice, 1572.
CNCE 36266, USTC 839709 BW73a

———, *Poetica d'Aristotele*, trans. A. Piccolomini, Siena, 1572.
CNCE 2977, USTC 810979 BW63

———, *Annotationi di m. Alessandro Piccolomini, nel libro della poetica...*, Venice, 1575.
CNCE 40414, USTC 848279 BW63

———, *Rhetorica... libri III*, trans. M. Majoragio, Venice, 1575.
CNCE 2983, USTC 810985 BW73a

———, *Poetica d'Aristotile*, trans. and comm. Lodovico Castelvetro, Basel, 1576.
CNCE 10047, USTC 684600 BW63

———, *Petri Victorii commentarii... de arte dicendi*, Florence, 1579.
CNCE 28490, USTC 863131 BW73a

———, *Artes rhetoricae libri III etc.*, ed. Friedrich Sylburg, Frankfurt, 1584.
USTC 612984 BW73a

———, *Poetica Aristotelis*, trans. and comm. Antonio Riccobono, Padua, 1587.
CNCE 2997, USTC 811002 BW63

———, *La Rhétorique. Les deux premiers livres*, trans. R. Estienne, Paris, 1630.
USTC 6022532 BW73b

———, *La Poétique d'Aristote*, trans. and comm. André Dacier, Paris, 1692. BW73a

Aristotle: see also Batteux, Buonamici, De Nores, Lombardi, Maggi, Piccolomini, Vettori

Arnaud, Francois Thomas, *Oeuvres complètes*, Amsterdam, 1777. BW73a

Atanagi, Dionigi, *De le lettere di tredici huomini illustri libri tredici*, Rome, 1554.
CNCE 34654, USTC 800972 BW73a

———, *Lettere di xiii huomini illustri*, Venice, 1560.
CNCE 35717, USTC 804092 BW73a

———, *Lettere di xiii huomini illustri*, Venice, 1584.
CNCE 40859, USTC 805909 BW73a

Aubignac, Francois Hédelin, *La pratique du théâtre...*, Amsterdam, 1715. BW73a

Baccelli, Girolamo: see Homer

Bacon, Francis, *La politique du chevalier Bacon*, London, 1740. BW73a

Bailly, Jean Sylvain, *Lettres sur l'origine des sciences...*, London, 1777. BW73c

Baldelli, Francesco: see Vergil, Polydore

Balzac, Jean-Louis, *Socrate chrestien*, Amsterdam, 1662. BW73a

———, *Portraits sérieux, galants et critiques*, Paris, 1696. BW73a

Barba, Pompeo della, *Espositione d'un sonetto platonico*, Florence, 1549.
CNCE 16454, USTC 826222 BW73a

Barba, Simone della: see Cicero

Barbaro, Ermolao: see Aristotle

Bartoli, Cosimo, *Discorsi historici universali*, Venice, 1569.
CNCE 4302, USTC 812414 BW73a

Bastiani, Giuseppe, *Della nuova poesia overo delle difese del Furioso*, Verona, 1589.
CNCE 4608, USTC 812801 BW63

Batteux, Charles, *Les beaux arts réduits à un même principe*, Paris, 1746 (two copies).
BW73a and BW73c

———, *Parallèle de la Henriade et du Lutrin*, n.p., 1746. BW73a

———, *Principes de la littérature*, Paris, 1764. BW73a

———, *La storia delle cause primitive*, Verona, 1770. BW73a

———, *Les quatre poétiques d'Aristote, d'Horace, de Vida et de Boileau*,
Paris, 1771. BW73a

Bauduin, Domenique, *Immortalité de l'âme*, Dijon, 1781. BW73a

Bembo, Pietro, *Prose*, Venice, 1525.
CNCE 4997, USTC 813375 BW73b

———, *Prose*, Venice, 1546.
CNCE 5022, USTC 813407 BW 73a
Bound with the two following items in an early limp vellum binding with extensive notes on the front pastedown and flyleaf.

———, *Gli asolani*, Venice, 1546.
CNCE 5021, USTC 813406 BW 73a

———, *Rime*, Venice, 1547.
CNCE 5024, USTC 813409 BW73a

———, *Prose...*, [Venice, 1540].
CNCE 5011, USTC 813319 BW73a

———, *Epistolarum familiarium libri VI*, Venice, 1552.
CNCE 5041, USTC 813421 BW 73a

———, *Della historia vinitiana, libri XII*, Venice, 1552.
CNCE 5039, USTC 813419 BW73c

———, *Delle lettere... a sommi pontefici...*, Venice, 1560.
CNCE 5059, USTC 813437 BW73a

———, *Delle lettere... a sommi pontefici...*, Venice, 1587.
CNCE 5090, USTC 813476 BW73a

———, *Le prose... divise in tre libri*, Naples, 1714. BW73a

Bembo: see also Petrarca

Beni, Paolo, *Risposta alle considerationi... sopra il Pastor fido*, Padua, 1600.
CNCE 5307, USTC 813799   BW73a

Berni, Francesco, *Il secondo libro dell'opere burlesche*, Venice, 1566.
CNCE 5554, USTC 814151   BW73a

———, *Delle rime... del Berni, Casa... etc.*, Vicenza, 1609-10.   BW73a

Berosus the Chaldean, *Le antichità*, com. F. Sansovino, Venice, 1583.
CNCE 30566, USTC 844118   BW73a

Betussi, Giuseppe, *Il raverta*, Venice, 1545.
CNCE 5671, USTC 814329   BW73c

Bible, Latin, *Biblia Sacra, Vulgatae Editionis*, Venice, 1777.   BW73a

Bibliotheque italique ou histoire litteraire de l'Italie, Geneva, 1728-1734 (18 vols.).   BW73a

Boccaccio, Giovanni, *Il corbaccio*, Paris, 1569.
USTC 814871   BW73a

———, *Il filocopo*, Venice, 1575.
CNCE 6365, USTC 814878   BW73a

———, *L'amorosa fiammetta*, Venice, 1584.
CNCE 6378, USTC 814893   BW73a

Bound with the following two items in vellum over boards; purchased from Libreria Forni, Bologna.
———, *Laberinto d'amore*, Venice, 1584.
CNCE 6380, USTC 814894   BW73a

———, *Dialogo d'amore*, Venice, 1584.
CNCE 17025, USTC 805899   BW73a

———, *Della genealogia de gli dei*, Venice, 1585.
CNCE 6383, USTC 814897   BW73a

———, *Opera...monti, selve, boschi...*, trans. N. Liburnio, Florence, 1598.
CNCE 6407, USTC 814923   BW73a

Boethius, *Della consolazione della filosofia*, trans. B. Varchi, Florence, 1551.
CNCE 6564, USTC 815092   BW73a

———, *De conforti filosofici*, trans. L. Domenichi, Venice, 1562.
CNCE 6573, USTC 815100   BW73a

Boileau Déspréaux, Nicolas, *Oeuvres diverses*, Cologne, 1685.   BW73a

———, *Oeuvres diverses*, Amsterdam, 1686.   BW73a

———, *Oeuvres diverses*, Amsterdam, 1697.   BW73a

Boileau Déspréaux: see also Longinus

Bosset, J. P.: see Locke

Bossuet, Jacques Bénigne, *Discorso sopra la storia universale*, Venice, 1736.   BW73a

Bouhours, Dominique, *Les entretiens d'Ariste et d'Eugene*, Paris, 1671.   BW73a
Apparently purchased in 1961 from Lucien Dorbon, Paris; his catalog description laid in.

———, *La manière de bien penser*, Paris, 1688.   BW73a

———, *Trattenimento filosofico sopra il linguaggio delle bestie*, Roveredo, 1752.   BW73a

———, *La manière de bien penser*, Paris, 1756.   BW73a

Boulenger, Jules César, *Liber de Spoliis bellicis...*, Paris, 1601.
USTC 601489   BW73a

Boulenger de Rivery, Claude-Francois-Felix, *Apologie de l'esprit des loix*, Amsterdam, 1751.
   BW73a

Brillon, J.Ch., *Le Theophraste moderne*, Paris, 1701.   BW73a

Bruni, Leonardo Aretino, *Libro della guerra de Ghotti*, Venice, 1528.
CNCE 7677, USTC 817009   BW73a

———, *Libro della guerra de Ghotti*, Venice, 1542.
CNCE 7678, USTC 817011   BW73a

———, *La historia universale de suoi tempi*, Venice, 1561.
CNCE 7684, USTC 817005   BW73a

Bruzen de La Martinière, Antoine Augustin, *Nouveau recueil des epigrammatistes françois*, Amsterdam, 1720.   BW73a

Buchanan, George, *Poemata quae extant*, Leiden, 1628.
USTC 1028636   BW73a

Buchler, Johann, *Thesaurus phrasium poeticarum*, Amsterdam, 1665.   BW73a

Budé, Guillaume, *De contemptu rerum fortuitarum*, Strasbourg, 1529.
USTC 661120   BW73a

Buffier, Claude, *Cours de sciences... etc.*, Paris, 1732.   BW73a

Bulgarini, Belisario, *Alcune considerazioni... sopra 'l discorso di M.G. Mazzoni*, Siena, 1583.
CNCE 66026, USTC 817145   BW63

———, *Repliche alle risposte del Sig. Orazio Capponi*, Siena, 1585.
CNCE 7812, USTC 817146   BW63

———, *Risposte a' ragionamenti del Sig. Ieronimo Zoppio*, Siena, 1586.
CNCE 7813, USTC 817417   BW63

———, *Difese in risposta dell'Apologia e Palinodia*, Siena, 1588.
CNCE 7814, USTC 847148   BW63

———, *Chiose marginali sopra la prima parte della difesa...*, Siena, 1608.
USTC 4036742   BW63

Buonamici, Francesco, *Discorsi poetici... in difesa d'Aristotile*, Florence, 1597 (two copies).
CNCE 7832, USTC 817160   BW63 and BW73c

Buonanni, Vincenzo, *Discorso sopra la prima cantica di Dante*, Florence, 1572.
CNCE 7838, USTC 817165   BW63

Caesar, C. Julius, *Commentarii*, Lyon, 1538.
USTC 157213   BW73a

Cailhava d'Estandoux, Jean Francois, *De l'art de la comedie*, Paris, 1772.   BW73a

Calepino, Ambrogio, *Dictionarium*, Venice, 1570.
CNCE 8459, USTC 817814   BW73a

Camillo, Giulio, *Due trattati...*, Venice, 1544.
CNCE 8707, USTC 818092   BW73a

———, *Opere*, Venice, 1560.
CNCE 8716, USTC 818102   BW73a

———, *Tutte l'opere... ricorrette da Thomaso Porcacchi*, Venice, 1566.
CNCE 8720, USTC 818106   BW73a

———, *Tutte l'opere... ricorrette da Thomaso Porcacchi*, Venice, 1568.
CNCE 8722, USTC 818108   BW73a

Carafa, Giovanni, *Tractatus de simonia*, Rome, 1556.
CNCE 9341, USTC 818714   BW73a

Cariero, Alessandro, *Breve... discorso contra l'opera di Dante*, Padua, 1582.
CNCE 9516, USTC 818908   BW63

———, *Apologia contra le imputazioni del Bulgarini*, Padua, 1584.
CNCE 9519, USTC 818911   BW63

Caro, Annibale, *Apologia degli Academici di Banchi di Roma*, Parma, 1558.
CNCE 9646, USTC 819038   BW63

———, *Delle lettere familiari*, Padua, 1763.   BW73a

Caro: see also Aristotle, Castelvetro, Virgil

Cartaud de la Villate, Francois, *Essai historique et philosophique sur le goût*, Paris, 1736.
                                                                                                 BW73a

Casa, Cristóbal de los, *Vocabulario de las lenguas toscana y castelana*, Venice, 1587.
CNCE 9814, USTC 819220   BW73a

Casa, Giovanni della, *Rime et prose*, Florence, 1571-72.
CNCE 16480, USTC 826256   BW73b

Casaubon, Isaac, *Animadversionum in Athenaei dipnosophistas*, Lyon, 1600.
USTC 158521   BW73b

———, *De satyrica graecorum poesi et romanorum satira*, Paris, 1605.
USTC 6016805   BW73a

———, *Della satirica poesia...*, Florence, 1728.   BW73a

Casellius, Johannes: see Demetrius of Phaleron

Castelvetro, Lodovico, *Alcune cose segnate nella canzone di... Annibal Caro*, Venice, 1560.
CNCE 10040, USTC 819464   BW63

———, *Opere varie critiche*, Bern, 1727.   BW73a

Castelvetro: see also Aristotle

Castiglione, Baldassarre, *Il libro del cortigiano*, Florence, 1531.
CNCE 10061, USTC 819487   BW73a

Cattani da Diacceto, Francesco, *L'essamerone*, Florence, 1563.
CNCE 10329, USTC 819779   BW73a

Catullus, Gaius Valerius, *Catullus, Tibullus, Propertius*, Venice, 1553.
CNCE 10363, USTC 811187   BW73a

[Cavalcanti, Bartolomeo], *Giuditio sopra la tragedia di Canace e Macareo*, Lucca, 1550.
CNCE 21258, USTC 833266   BW63
Attributed by Weinberg to G. B. Giraldi Cinzio.

Cavalcanti, Bartolomeo, *La retorica*, Pesaro, 1564.
CNCE 10436, USTC 21179   BW63

———, *La retorica*, Venice, 1569.
CNCE 10437, USTC 821280   BW63

[Chapuy], *Lettres saxonnes*, Berlin, 1738.   BW73a

Chevrier, Francois Antoine de, *Le codicille...*, The Hague, 1762.   BW73a

Ceruti, Federico: see Horace

Chalvet, Matthieu de: see Seneca

Cicero, Marcus Tullius, *Rhetorica*, trans. A. Brucioli, Venice, 1538.
CNCE 38486, USTC 802856   BW73a

———, *Opera ex Petri Victorii castigationibus*, Lyon, 1540.
USTC 147862   BW73a

———, *Rhetoricorum ad Herennium libri quatuor*, Lyon, 1543.
USTC 199439   BW 73a

———, *Epistolae ad Atticum, ad M. Brutum...*, Venice, 1544.
CNCE 12257, USTC 822255   BW73a

———, *Le tusculane*, Venice, 1544.
CNCE 12261, USTC 822260   BW73a

———, *Le epistole famigliari*, Venice, 1545.
CNCE 12265, USTC 822264   BW73a

———, *Les epistres familiaires*, trans. E. Dolet, Paris, 1547.
USTC 38566   BW73a

———, *I sette libri contra Gaio Verre*, trans. G. Tramezzino, Venice, 1554.
CNCE 12325, USTC 822161   BW73a

———, *Il dialogo*, trans. L. Dolce, Venice, 1555.
CNCE 12329, USTC 822365   BW73a

———, *Insignium sententiarum... compendium*, Paris, 1556.
USTC 197975   BW73a*

———, *La topica...*, trans. S. de la Barba, Venice, 1556.
CNCE 12340, USTC 822377   BW73a

———, *Ciceronianum lexicon graecolatinum*, Paris, 1557.
USTC 450456   BW73a
Bound with the following item.

———, *In M. T. Ciceronis... Castigationes Henrici Stephani*, Paris, 1557.
USTC 450457   BW73a

———, *De oratore... scholia Pauli Manutii*, Venice, 1569.
CNCE 12407, USTC 822452   BW73a

———, *Epistolae familiares dictae scholia Pauli Manutii*, Venice, 1572.
CNCE 15751, USTC 822476   BW73a

———, *De officiis libri III*, comm. M. Nizzoli, Venice, 1579.
CNCE 12443, USTC 822494   BW73a

———, *Rhetoricum posterior*, Lyon, 1585.   BW73a
Bound with the following item.

———, *Rhetoricorum ad Herennium...*, ed. P. Vettori, Lyon, 1588.
USTC 203393   BW73a

———, *Opera*, Leiden, 1642.   BW73a

Cicero: see also Majoraggio, Manuzio, Toscanella, Vettori

Clénard, Nicolas, *Institutiones absolutissimae in graecam linguam*, Lyon, 1558.
USTC 123288   BW73a

———, *Institutiones ac meditationes in graecam linguam*, Paris, 1572.
USTC 170096   BW73a

———, *Institutiones absolutissimae in graecam linguam*, Turin, 1589.
CNCE 12707   BW73a
Bound with the following item in early limp vellum.

———, *Meditationes graecanicae in artem grammaticam*, Turin, 1589.
CNCE 12710, USTC 823293   BW73a

Columella, Lucius Junius Moderatus, *De re rustica libri XIII*, Lyon, 1537.
USTC 147232   BW73a

Comines, Philippe de, *Mémoires*, Brussels, 1723.   BW73a

Condillac, Etienne Bonnot de, *Traité des animaux*, Amsterdam/Paris, 1755.   BW73a

———, *Opere*, Venice, 1793-99.   BW73a

Conti, Natale, *Mythologiae sive explicationum fabularum...*, Venice, 1581.
CNCE 13168, USTC 823830   BW73a

Conti: see also Demetrius of Phaleron

[Corpus Juris Civilis], *Institutiones*, Venice, 1585.
CNCE 14128 BW73a

Crinito, Pietro, *De honesta disciplina*, Lyon, 1561.
USTC 153080 BW73b

Crousaz, Jean Pierre de, *Traité du beau*, Amsterdam, 1715. BW73b

Dacier, André: see Aristotle

Dacier, Anne, *Des causes de la corruption du goût*, Amsterdam, 1715. BW73b

Dacier, Anne: see also Homer

Damiens de Gomicourt, August Pierre, *Essai sur la poésie lyri-comique*, Amsterdam/Paris, 1771.
BW73a

Daniello, Bernardino, *La poetica*, Venice, 1536.
CNCE 15989, USTC 825452 BW73a

Daniello: see also Virgil

Dante Alighieri: see Buonanni, Cariero, Gelli, Lenzoni, Mazzoni, Zoppio

De Nores, Giasone, *Poetica di Iason Denores*, Padua, 1588.
CNCE 16819, USTC 825720 BW63

De Nores: see also Horace

De re poetica libellus incerti auctoris, Verona, 1588.
CNCE 16214, USTC 806330 BW63
Bound with Horace, *In Q. Horatii Flacci Carmina*, ed. Ceruti, 1585.

De Selincourt, *Apologie de la louange...*, Paris, 1717. BW73a

Del Rosso, Paolo: see Suetonius

Dell'Uva, Benedetto, *Il pensier della morte*, Florence, 1582.
CNCE 16626, USTC 826477 BW73b

———, *Parte delle rime di Benedetto dell'Uva* et al., Florence, 1584.
CNCE 16628, USTC 826479 BW73c

Demetrius of Phaleron, *De oratione, sive de modo dicendi*, com. N. Conti, Venice, 1557.
CNCE 16157, USTC 826494 BW73a

———, *De elocutione liber*, trans. J. Caselius, Rostock, 1583.
USTC 632342 BW73a

———, *Della locuzione*, trans. P. Segni, Florence, 1603. BW73a

Demetrius of Phaleron: see also Panigarola

Demosthenes, *Orationum pars tertia*, Venice, 1543.
CNCE 16735, USTC 826500 BW73a

———, *Orationes tres Olynthicae*, Florence, 1550.
CNCE 16741, USTC 826507 BW73a

———, *Orationum pars secunda*, Venice, 1554.
CNCE 16746, USTC 826512   BW73c

Desportes, Phillippes, *Les CL pseaumes de David mis en vers françois*, Paris, 1623.   BW73a

———, Phillippes, *Prières et méditations chrestiennes*, Paris, 1623.   BW73a

Destouches, Néricault, *Le philosophe marié*, Amsterdam, 1727.   BW73a

Di Falco, Benedetto, *Descrittione dei luoghi antiqui di Napoli...*, Naples, 1568.
CNCE 17173, USTC 826645   BW73a

Dictionnaire de l'Académie françoise, Nîmes, 1778.   BW73a

Diogenes Laertius, *Le vite de gli illustri filosofi*, Venice, 1545.
CNCE 17227, USTC 826961   BW73a

———, *De vita et moribus philosophorum libri X*, Lyon, 1546.
USTC 149575   BW73a

Dionysius of Halicarnassus, *De compositione*, Paris, 1547.
USTC 160159   BW73c

———, *Scripta quae extant omnia...*, Frankfurt, 1586.
USTC 637660   BW73a

Divus, Andreas: see Homer

Dolce, Lodovico, *Osservationi nella volgar lingua*, Venice, 1550.
CNCE 17340, USTC 827071   BW63

———, *Le osservationi*, Venice, 1556.
CNCE 17348, USTC 827079   BW73a

———, *Vita dell'... Imperador Carlo quinto*, Venice, 1561 (two copies).
CNCE 53534, USTC 827107   BW73a* and BW73b
Newberry copy bound in 18th-century vellum over boards.

———, *Le dignità de' consoli, e de gl'imperatori e i fatti de' Romani...*, Venice, 1561.
CNCE 17369, USTC 827103   BW73a

———, *Modi affigurati e voci scelte et eleganti della volgar lingua*, Venice, 1564.
CNCE 17383, USTC 827048   BW73c

———, *L'Achille et L'Enea*, Venice, 1572.
CNCE 17406, USTC 827141   BW73c

Dolce: see also Cicero

Dolet, Etienne: see Cicero

Domenichi, Lodovico, *Historia varia*, Venice, 1564.
CNCE 17567, USTC 827388   BW73a

Domenichi: see also Boethius, Plutarch, Xenophon

[Donatus, Aelius], *Il Donato al senno...*, Verona, [16--?].
CNCE 17791   BW73a

Dubos, Jean Baptiste, *Réflexions critiques sur la poésie et sur la peinture*, Paris, 1770.
	BW73a

Du Laurens, Henri Joseph, *Le compère Matthieu*, London, 1775.	BW73a

Duvernet, Theophile, *La vie de Voltaire*, Geneva, 1786.	BW73a

Encyclopédie..., ed. Diderot and d'Alembert, Lausanne, 1778-81. 39 vols.	BW73a

Encyclopédie portative ou science universelle... [attr. ed. Formey], Berlin, 1758.	BW73a

Entretien sur le théâtre au sujet de Judith tragédie, Paris, 1695.	BW73a

Erasmo da Valvasone: see Statius

Erasmus, Desiderius, *Vitae caesarum quarum scriptores*, Basel, 1546.
USTC 701519	BW73a

Erizzo, Sebastiano: see Plato

Estienne, Henri: see Cicero, Theocritus

Estienne, Robert: see Aristotle

L'esprit de l'encyclopédie..., ed. Joseph de Laporte, Geneva/Paris, 1768. 5 vols.	BW73a

Eustasthius Macrembolites, *Gli amori d'Ismenio*, Florence, 1550.
CNCE 18391, USTC 828522	BW73a

Fabrini, Giovanni: see Horace, Terence, Virgil

Faerno, Gabriello, *Fabulae centum*, Padua, 1718.	BW 73a
Bound with Navagero, *Orationes duae*.

Faydit, Pierre Valentin, *Nouvelles remarques sur Virgile et sur Homere*, n.p., 1710.
	BW73a

———, *La telemacomania*, Venice, 1751.	BW73a

Fénelon, François de Salignac, *Les aventures de Télémaque*, London, 1755.	BW73a

———, *Il Telemaco in ottava rima*, trans. F. Scarselli, Venice, 1748.	BW73a

Ferentilli, Agostino, *Discorso universale*, Venice, 1570.
CNCE 18737, USTC 829004	BW73a

[Ferrand, David], *Les veritez plaisantes ou le monde au naturel*, Rouen, 1702.	BW73b

Ficino, Marsilio, *Il comento... sopra il convito di Platone*, Rome, 1544.
CNCE 18941, USTC 829431	BW73a

Ficino: see also Plato

Figliucci, Felice, *De la filosofia morale*, Roma, 1551.
CNCE 18972, USTC 829477	BW73c

Filelfo, Francesco: see Aristotle

Florian, Jean Pierre Claris de, *Estelle, Pastorale*, Paris, n.d.	BW73a

Folengo, Girolamo, *Opus Merlini Cocaii poetae mantuani Macaronicorum*, Venice, 1613.
USTC 4027818   BW73a

Fontanini, Girolamo, *Biblioteca italiana, o sia notizia de libri rari nella lingua italiana*,
Venice, 1728.   BW73a

Fontanini, Guisto, *Biblioteca dell'eloquenza italiana*, Venice, 1753.   BW73c

Fontenelle, Bernard le Bovier de, *Oeuvres diverses*, London, 1710.   BW73a

———, *Entretiens sur la pluralité des mondes*, Paris, 1714.   BW73a

———, *Poésies pastorales*, The Hague, 1728.   BW73a

———, *Trattenimenti sopra la pluralità dei mondi*, Paris, 1749.   BW73a

———, *Oeuvres*, Paris, 1761-67.   BW73a

Foquelin, Antoine: see Persius

Formey, Jean-Henri-Samuel: see *Encyclopédie portative*.

Fornari, Simone, *La sposizione... sopra l'Orlando Furioso*, Florence, 1549.
CNCE 19529, USTC 830328   BW73a

Fracastoro, Girolamo, *Opera Omnia*, Venice, 1584.
CNCE 19616, USTC 830467   BW63

Franchetta, Girolamo, *Breve spositione di tutta l'opera di Lucrezio*, Venice, 1589.
CNCE 19623   BW73a

Franco, Nicolo, *Il due Petrarchisti dialoghi...*, Venice, 1623.
USTC 4007784   BW73c

Frederick II, *Oeuvres du philosophe de Sans-Souci*, Potsdam/Amsterdam, 1760.   BW73a

Gabbia, Giovanni Battista: see Sophocles

Gabrielli, Giulio: see Xenophon

Gaguin, Robert, *Rerum gallicarum annales*, Frankfurt, 1577.
USTC 691233   BW73a

Galilei, Galileo, *Considerazioni al Tasso*, Venice, 1793.   BW 73b
In publisher's yellow paper wrappers.

Gaultier, Pierre: see Horace

Gaurico, Pomponio, *Super arte poetica Horatii*, Venice, 1584.
CNCE 20540, USTC 832062   BW63

Gelli, Giovanni Battista, *Sopra un sonetto di M. F. Petrarca*, Florence, 1549.
CNCE 20575, USTC 832118   BW73a
Bound with the following item.

———, *La prima lettione... sopra un luogo di Dante*, Florence, 1549.
CNCE 20576, USTC 832119   BW73a

———, *Tutte le lettioni*, Florence, 1551.
CNCE 20583, USTC 832127   BW73b

———, *Lettioni... sopra vari luoghi di Dante e del Petrarca*, Florence, 1555.
CNCE 20586, USTC 832131   BW73a

———, *La circe*, Venice, 1589.
CNCE 20598, USTC 832145   BW73a

Gellius, Aulus, *Noctes Atticae*, Venice, 1544.
CNCE 20608, USTC 832158   BW73a

———, *Noctes Atticae,* Lyon, 1555.
USTC 151871   BW73a

Gentillet, Innocent, *Discours... contre Nicolas Machiavel florentin*, [Geneva], 1576.
USTC 1419   BW73a

Gerardo, Pietro, *Vita et gesti d'Ezzelino terzo da Romano*, Venice, 1552.
CNCE 20700, USTC 832283   BW73a

Ghini, Leonardo: see Heliodorus

Giambullari, Pier Francesco, *Origine della lingua fiorentina*, Florence, 1549.
CNCE 20911, USTC 832686   BW73a

———, *De la lingua che si parla e scrive in Firenze*, Florence, [1550].
CNCE 20912, USTC 832687   BW73c

———, *Lezzioni*, Florence, 1551.
CNCE 20913, USTC 832688   BW73c

Giannotti, Donato, *Della repubblica fiorentina libri quattro*, Venice, 1721.   BW73a

Giovio, Paolo, *Le iscrittioni poste sotto le vere imagini de gli huomini famosi*, Florence, 1552.
CNCE 21183, USTC 833184   BW73a

Giraldi Cinzio, Giovanni Battista, *Poematia*, Basel, 1540.
USTC 625835   BW63

Giraldi Cinzio: see also Cavalcanti

Giraldi, Lilio Gregorio, *Herculis vita*, Basel, 1540.
USTC 664406   BW73a
Bound with Vettori, *Castigationes.*

———, *Historiae poetarum*, Basel, 1545.
USTC 663515   BW63

Godard d'Aucourt, Claude, *La Pariseïde*, Paris, 1773.   BW73a

Gonzaga, Curzio, *Il fido amante*, Mantua, 1582.
CNCE 21437, USTC 833697   BW73a

Gori, Antonio Francesco: see Longinus

Graffigny, Francoise d'Issembourg d'Happencourt de, *Lettres d'une Péruvienne. Lettere d'una Peruviana*, Lyon, 1787.   BW73a

Grazzini, Giulio Cesare: see Horace

Gregory of Nazianzenus, *Homiliae IV... Antonello Arcimboldio interprete*, Milan, 1550.
BW73a

Grifoli, Jacopo see Cicero, Horace

Grifoni, Giovanni Andrea, *Specchio della lingua latina*, Venice, 1560.
CNCE 21792, USTC 834624 BW73a

Grizi, Pietro, *Il castiglione, overo dell'arme di nobiltà*, Mantua, 1586.
CNCE 21851, USTC 834721 BW73a

Gualdo Priorato, Galeazzo, *Historia del ministerio del cardinale Giulio Mazarino*, Cologne, 1669. BW73a

Guarini, Giovanni Battista, *Il verato secondo... in difesa del Pastor fido*, Florence, 1593.
CNCE 21973, USTC 834905 BW73a

———, *Lettere*, Venice, 1593.
CNCE 21965, USTC 834904 BW73a
Bound in early vellum over boards; purchased from Libreria Forni, Bologna.

———, *Il pastor fido*, Venice, 1601. BW73a
Bound with next item.

———, *Compendio della poesia tragicomica*, Venice, 1601.
USTC 4035354 BW73a

———, *Il pastor fido*, Venice, 1602.
USTC 4037486 BW73a

———, *Opere*, Verona, 1737-38. BW73a

———, *Il pastor fido*, Venice, 1788. BW73c

A single volume (no. 35) of Zatta's series *Parnaso italiano; ovvero, Raccolta de' poeti classici italiani*.
Guarneri, Giovanni Antonio, *De bello cyprio libri tres*, Bergamo, 1597.
CNCE 22030, USTC 835049 BW73a

Guastavini, Giulio, *Risposta all'Infarinato Academico della Crusca*, Bergamo, 1588.
CNCE 22042, USTC 835072 BW63

Guazzo, Marco, *Historie*, Venice, 1545.
CNCE 22057, USTC 835092 BW 73a
Bound with following item in early vellum over boards; ex libris of the Collegio Romano.

———, *Historie*, Venice, 1549.
CNCE 22062, USTC 835102 BW73a

Guazzo, Stefano, *La civil conversatione*, Venice, 1584.
CNCE 22078, USTC 835120 BW73a

Guevara, Antonio de, *La institutione del prencipe christiano*, Mantua, 1577.
CNCE 22273, USTC 835339 BW73a

Guicciardini, Francesco, *I quattro ultimi libri dell'historie d'Italia*, Parma, 1564.
CNCE 22312, USTC 835398 BW73b
Bound in early limp vellum with leather tackets and ties.

———, *Propositioni... in materia di cose di stato*, Venice, 1583.
CNCE 22328, USTC 835413　　　　　　　　　　　　　　　　　　BW73b
Bound in early pastepaper boards with leather tackets.

Hardion, Jacques, *Nouvelle histoire poétique...*, Paris, 1751.　　　　BW73a

Hay, Paul, *Traité de la guerre, ou politique militaire*, Amsterdam, n.d..　　BW73a

Heinsius, Daniel, *De tragoediae constitutione liber*, Leiden, 1643.　　BW73a

Heliodorus of Emesa, *Historia... delle cose ethiopiche*, trans. L. Ghini, Venice, 1556.
CNCE 22489, USTC 835607　　　　　　　　　　　　　　　　　　BW73a

Helvétius, Claude Adrien, *De l'esprit*, Amsterdam, 1761.
Smith E.16　　　　　　　　　　　　　　　　　　　　　　　　　BW73a

———, *Le bonheur*, London [i.e. Lyon], 1772.
Smith B.2　　　　　　　　　　　　　　　　　　　　　　　　　BW73a
Bound in early pasteboard.

———, *Le bonheur...*, London [i.e. Geneva], 1773.
Smith O.4　　　　　　　　　　　　　　　　　　　　　　　　　BW73a

———, *Le bonheur...*, London [i.e. Lausanne], 1773.
Smith B.5　　　　　　　　　　　　　　　　　　　　　　　　　BW73a
Bound in 18th-century full mottled calf.

———, *La felicità*, Lausanne, 1774.
Smith B.13　　　　　　　　　　　　　　　　　　　　　　　　　BW73a

———, *Oeuvres complèttes*, Paris, 1793-97. 10 vols.
Smith O.11　　　　　　　　　　　　　　　　　　　　　　　　　BW73a

Hermogenes, *Ars oratoria absolutissima et libri omnes*, Cologny, 1614.
USTC 2148939　　　　　　　　　　　　　　　　　　　　　　　BW73b
Bound in early limp vellum.

Herodotus, *Historiographi libri VIIII*, Lyon, 1551.
USTC 150923　　　　　　　　　　　　　　　　　　　　　　　　BW73a

Herodotus, *Historiographi libri VIIII*, Lyon, 1558.
USTC 152507　　　　　　　　　　　　　　　　　　　　　　　　BW73a

Holbach, Paul Henry Thiry d', *Système de la nature*, Paris, 1793.　　BW73a

Homer, *Ilias*, Venice, n.d.　　　　　　　　　　　　　　　　　　　BW73a*

———, *Odyssea... Batrachomyomachia... Hymni*, Venice, [1524?].
CNCE 22952, USTC 835806　　　　　　　　　　　　　　　　　　BW73a

———, *Odyssea*, trans. R. Maffei, Cologne, 1524.
USTC 663888　　　　　　　　　　　　　　　　　　　　　　　　BW73a

———, *Ilias*, trans. A. Divus, Venice, 1537.
CNCE 22955, USTC 835812　　　　　　　　　　　　　　　　　　BW73a

———, *Odyssea... Batrachomyomachia*, Venice, 1537.
CNCE 22957, USTC 835814　　　　　　　　　　　　　　　　　　BW73a

———, *Opera graecolatina quae quidem nunc extant omnia*, Basel, 1561.
USTC 663913   BW73a

———, *L'odissea*, trans. G. Baccelli, Florence, 1582.
CNCE 22973, USTC 835828   BW73a

———, *L'odyssée*, trans. Mme. Dacier, Amsterdam, 1731.   BW73a

———, *L'iliade*, trans. Mme. Dacier, Amsterdam, 1731.   BW73a

Homer: see also Faydit

Horace, *Omnia poemata*, Venice, 1549.
CNCE 22709, USTC 835899   BW73a

———, *De arte poetica Iacobi Grifoli... explicatus*, Florence, 1550.
CNCE 34574, USTC 834604   BW73c

———, *In epistolam... De arte poetica Iasonis de Nores... interpretatio*, Venice, 1553.
CNCE 16809, USTC 825705   BW63

———, *Opera*, ed. M. Muret, Venice, 1559.
CNCE 22716, USTC 835908   BW73a

———, *Liber de arte poetica Iacobi Grifoli... explicatus*, Venice, 1562.
CNCE 21778, USTC 834607   BW63

———, *L'opere d'Oratio... comentate da Giovanni Fabrini...*, Venice, 1566.
CNCE 22728, USTC 835917   BW63

———, *Opera*, com. Denis Lambin, Venice, 1566.
CNCE 22730, USTC 835920   BW73a

———, *Omnia poemata cum ratione carminum*, Venice, 1567.
CNCE 22732, USTC 835921   BW73a

———, *Opera*, Paris, 1567.
USTC 140489   BW73a

———, *Opera*, Antwerp, 1579.
USTC 401821   BW73a

———, *Praelectiones... Petri Gualterii Chabotii*, Basel, 1587.
USTC 686183   BW73a

———, *In Q. Horatii Flacci Carmina... paraphrasis*, ed. F. Ceruti, Verona, 1585.
CNCE 10888, USTC 821691   BW63
Bound with the following item and with *De re poetica libellus incerti auctoris*, 1588.

———, *Paraphrasis in Q. Horatii Flacci librum De arte poetica*, ed. F. Ceruti, Verona, 1588.
CNCE 10895, USTC 821699   BW63

———, *Della poetica... parafrasi di Grazzini*, Ferrara, 1698.   BW73a

———, *Opera*, London, 1749.   BW73b

———, *Ars poetica...*, London, 1753.   BW73a

Horace: see also Batteux, Gaurico, Luisini, Pigna, Pindemonte, Robortello

Huet, Pierre Daniel, *Traité de l'origine des romans*, Paris, 1711. BW73a

Isocrates, *Orationes et epistolae*, trans. H. Wolf, Paris, 1553.
USTC 154209 BW73a

Jacquin, Armand Pierre, *Entretiens sur les romans*, Paris, 1755. BW73a

Josephus, Flavius, *De antichità giudaiche*, trans. P. Lauro, Venice, 1544.
CNCE 36091, USTC 836541 BW73a

Justinus, Marcus Junianus, *Justini ex trogi pompeii historiis externis*, Lyon, 1543.
USTC 140892 BW73a

Juvenal, *Satyrae*, Lyon, 1559.
USTC 152697 BW73a*

La Chambre, Marin Cureau de, *Traité de la connaissance des animaux*, Paris, 1664.
BW73a

La Rochefoucauld, François duc de, *Mémoires de la minorité de Louis XIV*, Amsterdam, 1688.
BW73b

Lacombe, Jacques, *Dictionnaire portatif des beaux-arts*, Paris, 1755. BW73a

———, *Le spectacle des beaux arts*, Paris, 1758. BW73a

———, *Dizionario portatile delle belle arti*, Venice, 1768. BW73a

Lallement, Jacques Philippe, *Entretiens du docteur au sujet des affaires présentes par rapport à la religion*, n.p., 1738. BW73a

Lambert, Anne Thérèse de Marguenat, *Lettres sur la véritable éducation*, Amsterdam, 1729.
BW73a

Lambin, Denis: see Horace.

Lamy, Bernard, *La rhétorique ou l'art de parler*, Amsterdam, 1712. BW73a

Lancelot, Claude, *Le iardin des racines greques*, Paris, 1657. BW73a

Lascaris, Janus: see Polybius

Lauro, Pietro: see Josephus

Le Bossu, René, *Traité du poème épique*, Paris, 1693. BW73b

———, *Traité du poème épique,* Paris, 1708. BW73b

Lenzoni, Carlo, *In difesa della lingua fiorentina, et di Dante…*, Florence, 1556.
CNCE 34636, USTC 837843 BW73a

Leo Magentinus: see Aristotle

Lettere volgari di diversi nobilissimi huomini…, Venice, 1545.
CNCE 26953, USTC 803138 BW73a

Lettere volgari di diversi nobilissimi huomini…, Venice, 1558.
CNCE 52812, USTC 803929 BW73a

Lexicon graecolatinum, Basel, 1543.
USTC 671849   BW73a*

Leonico Tomeo, Niccolò, *Li tre libri... de varie historie*, Venice, 1544.
CNCE 35124, USTC 838049   BW73b

Liburnio, Niccolò, *Le tre fontane*, Venice, 1526.
CNCE 29760, USTC 838127   BW63

Lionardi, Alessandro, *Dialogi... della inventione poetica*, Venice, 1554.
CNCE 45608, USTC 838212   BW73c

Livy, *Le deche... delle historie romane*, trans. Jacopo Nardi, Venice, 1547.
CNCE 26894, USTC 838296   BW73c

———, *Exercitationes rhetoricae in orationes Titi Livii*, Padua, 1707.   BW73a

Locke, John, *Du gouvernement civil*, Geneva, 1724.   BW73a

———, *Essai philosophique concernant l'entendement humain*, Amsterdam, 1735.
                                                                            BW73a

———, *Abrégé de l'essai... sur l'entendement humain*, trans. J.P. Bosset, Geneva, 1741.
                                                                            BW73a

———, *Oeuvres diverses*, Amsterdam, 1732.   BW73a

Lollio, Alberto: see Terence

Lombardelli, Orazio, *Discorso intorno ai contrasti che si fanno sopra la Gerusalemme Liberata*, Ferrara, 1586.
CNCE 41035, USTC 838515   BW63
Bound with Tasso, *Risposta*, Mantua, 1585.

———, *Gli aforismi scolastici*, Siena, 1603.
USTC 4033020   BW73a

Lombardi, Bartolomeo: see Maggi, Vincenzo

Longinus, *De sublima genere dicendi*, ed. C. Manolessi, Bologna, 1644.
USTC 4017718   BW73a

———, *De sublimitate*, ed. Z. Pearce, Amsterdam, 1733.   BW73a

———, *De sublima dicendi genere*, com. N. Boileau Despréaux and A. F. Gori, Verona, 1733.
                                                                            BW73a

———, *L'aureo trattato...*, trans. Antonio Francesco Gori, Venice, 1782.   BW73a

Lottini, Giovanni Francesco, *Avvedimenti civili*, Florence, 1574.
CNCE 32549, USTC 838699   BW73a

Luisini, Francesco, *In librum Q. Horatii Flacci de arte poetica commentarius*, Venice, 1554.
CNCE 27191   BW63

Mably, Gabriel Bonnot de, *I dialoghi di Focione*, Venice, 1764.   BW73a

Macrobius, *In somnium Scipionis... Saturnaliorum*, Lyon, 1548.
USTC 150062   BW 73a

Magentinus, Leo: see Aristotle

Maggi, Vincenzo, and Bartolomeo Lombardi, *In Aristotelis librum De poetica...*, Venice, 1550.
CNCE 36137, USTC 839586   BW73c

Majoragio, Antonio Maria, *In dialogum... Ciceronis commentarius*, Milan, 1569.
CNCE 24347, USTC 839706   BW73b

———, *Orationes & praefationes omnes*, Venice, 1582.
CNCE 26592, USTC 839711   BW73c

———, *Commentarius in dialogum... Ciceronis*, Venice, 1587.
CNCE 28368, USTC 839713   BW73a

Manolessi, Carlo: see Longinus

Malacreta, Giovanni Pietro, *Considerazioni sopra il Pastor Fido*, Vicenza, 1600.
CNCE 46670, USTC 839725   BW73a

———, *Considerazioni sopra il Pastor Fido*, Venice, 1601.
USTC 4034825   BW63
Bound in early pasteboard.

Malebranche, Nicolas, *Réflexions sur la prémotion physique*, Paris, 1715.   BW73a

Malespini, Ricordano, *Historia antica*, Florence, 1568.
CNCE 28306, USTC 839758   BW73c

Mantova Benavides, Marco, *Annotationi brevissime sovra le rime di Petrarca*, Padua, 1566.
CNCE 32984, USTC 840248   BW73a

Manuzio, Aldo the Younger, *Eleganze... scielte*, Venice, 1558.
CNCE 28038, USTC 840343   BW73a

———, *Orthographiae ratio*, Venice, 1566.
CNCE 28262, USTC 840368   BW73a

Manuzio, Paolo, *Commentarius Pauli Manutii in epistolas Ciceronis ad Atticum*, Venice, 1561.
CNCE 28074, USTC 840480   BW73a

———, *Apophthegmatum*, Venice, 1577.
CNCE 27553, USTC 840495   BW73a

———, *Epistolarum, libri XII*, Venice, 1582.
CNCE 35431, USTC 840500   BW73a

Manuzio, Paolo: see also Cicero

Marmontel, Jean Francois, *Poétique françois*, Paris, 1763.   BW73a

———, *Contes moraux...*, The Hague, 1766.   BW73a

———, *Belisario*, Milan, 1768.   BW73a

———, *Belisario*, Venice, 1784.   BW73a

———, *Élémens de littérature*, [Paris ?], 1787. 6 vols.   BW73a

Marretti, Fabio: see Ovid

Martial, *Epigrammata*, Lyon, 1547.
USTC 149791 BW73a

Maupertuis, Pierre Louis Moreau de, *Vénus physique*, n.p., 1777. BW73a

Mazzoni, Jacopo, *Della difesa della commedia di Dante*, Cesena, 1587.
CNCE 36295, USTC 841789 BW63

———, *Della difesa della commedia di Dante*, Cesena, 1688. BW63

Ménage, Gilles, *Discours... sur l'heautontimorumenos de Terence*, Utrecht, 1690.
BW73a

Minturno, Antonio Sebastiano, *De poeta*, Venice, 1559.
CNCE 36263, USTC 842877 BW63

———, *L'arte poetica*, Venice, 1564 [1563 in colophon].
CNCE 59706, USTC 842884 BW73a
Bound in early limp vellum; apparently purchased from C.E. Rappaport, Rome, whose ticket appears on the rear paste down.

———, *L'arte poetica*, Venice, 1564.
CNCE 39536, USTC 842883 BW63

Mirandula, Octavianus, *Illustrium poetarum flores*, Lyon, 1579.
USTC 156301 BW73a

Molière, *Les oeuvres posthumes*, Lyon, 1692. BW73a

Montesquieu, Charles Louis de Secondat, *Considérations sur les causes de la grandeur des Romains et de leur décadence*, Paris, 1735. BW73a

———, *Considerazioni sopra le cagioni della grandezza de' Romani e della loro decadenza*, Venice, 1735. BW73a

———, *Dello spirito delle leggi*, Naples, 1751. BW73a

———, *Oeuvres*, London, 1767. BW73a

———, *Arsace et Ismenie*, Amsterdam, 1784. BW73a

Moreri, Louis, *Supplément aux anciennes éditions du grand dictionaire*, Amsterdam, 1716. BW73a

———, *Le grand dictionaire historique...*, Amsterdam, 1717. BW73a

———, *Supplément au grand dictionaire historique...*, Paris, 1735. BW73a

Muratori, Ludovico Antoniao, *Della poetica libri tre*, Palermo, 1734. BW73a

Muret, Marc-Antoine, *Orationes XXIII*, Venice, 1586.
CNCE 23956, USTC 843790 BW73b

———, *Orationum volumina duo*, Lyon, 1604.
USTC 6900467 BW73a

———, *Orationum volumina duo*, Venice, 1618.
USTC 4029670 BW73a

Naogeorg, Thomas: see Plutarch

Nardi, Jacopo: see Livy

Navagero, Andrea, *Orationes duae*, Padua, 1718. BW 73a
Bound with Faerno, *Fabulae centum*.

Oddi, Sforza, *L'erofilomachia*, Venice, 1582.
CNCE 29583, USTC 845246 BW73a

Oradini, Lucio, *Due lezzioni*, Florence, 1550.
CNCE 34576, USTC 845401 BW73a

Ortica della Porta, Agostino: see Sallust

Ottonelli, Giulio, *Discorso... con le difese della Gierusalemme Liberata*, Ferrara, 1586.
CNCE 41040, USTC 845618 BW63

Ovid, *Metamorphoses, libri XV*, Florence, 1522.
CNCE 28770, USTC 845721 BW73a

———, *Heroidum epistolae*, ed. and com. R. Regio, Venice, 1536.
CNCE 74260, USTC 845781 BW73a

———, *Heroides*, com. Ubertino da Crescentino and A. G. Parrasio, Venice, 1543.
CNCE 23362, USTC 762184 BW73a

———, *Le metamorphosi...*, trans. F. Marretti, Venice, 1570.
CNCE 38294, USTC 845856 BW73a

Palissot de Montenoy, Charles, *Mémoires pour servir à l'histoire de notre littérature*,
Geneva, 1775. BW73a

———, *Elogio del signor di Voltaire*, Berlin, 1779. BW73a

Panigarola, Francesco, *Dichiaratione de i salmi di David*, Venice, 1590.
CNCE 38341, USTC 846453 BW73b

———, *Compendio del comento... sopra... Demetrio Falereo*, Naples, 1730. BW73a

Parabosco, Girolamo, *Libro primo delle lettere amorose*, Venice, 1581.
CNCE 39604, USTC 846766 BW73a

Parrasio, Aulo Giano: see Ovid

Partenio, Bernardino, *Della imitatione poetica*, Venice, 1560.
CNCE 29304, USTC 846902 BW73c

Pascal, Blaise, *Les provinciales*, Cologne, 1685. BW73a

———, *Les provinciales*, Renaud, 1753. BW73a

———, *Les provinciales*, Leiden, 1761. BW73a

Pascal, Carlo, *De optimo genere elocutionis*, Rouen, 1595.
USTC 206925 BW73a

Patrizi, Francesco, *Della poetica: La deca istoriale*, Ferrara, 1586.
CNCE 30130, USTC 847047 BW63

———, *Della poetica: La deca disputata*, Ferrara, 1586.
CNCE 30129, USTC 847046   BW63

———, *Della retorica dieci dialoghi*, Venice, 1562.
CNCE 27429, USTC 847040   BW63

———, *Risposta a due opposizioni fattegli dal Sig. Giacopo Mazzoni*, Ferrara, 1587.
CNCE 30364, USTC 847052   BW63

Pausanius, *Veteris graeciae regionibus*, com. R. Amaseo, Basel, 1557.
USTC 683335   BW73a

Passi, Alessandro: see Aristotle

Pearce, Zachary: see Longinus

Pellegrino, Camillo, *Brieve discorso dell'epica poesia*, Florence, 1584.
CNCE 16628   BW63

———, *Replica... alla risposta degli Accademici della Crusca*, Vico Equense, 1585.
CNCE 23541, USTC 847368   BW63

Perotti, Niccolò: see Polybius

Persius, *Antonii Foquelini Veromandui in ... satyras commentarius*, Paris, 1555.   BW73a

Pétition adressée a l'assemblée nationale par les auteurs dramatiques, Paris, 1791.
    BW73a

[Petrarca, Francesco, pseud.], *Chronica delle vite de pontefici et imperatori Romani*, Venice, 1534.
CNCE 14532, USTC 802679   BW73a

Petrarca, Francesco, *Il Petracha*, com. G. A. Gesualdo, Venice, 1533.
CNCE 32317, USTC 847841   BW73c

———, *Sonetti e canzoni*, Venice, 1536.
CNCE 41157, USTC 847824   BW73a

———, *Il Petrarca con l'espositione d'Alessandro Vellutello*, Venice, 1538.
CNCE 47365, USTC 847843   BW73a

———, *Il Petrarca... d'Alessandro Vellutello*, Venice, 1545.
CNCE 26035, USTC 762209   BW73a

———, *Il Petrarca con dichiarazini tratte dalle... prose di monsignor Bembo*, Lyon, 1558.
CNCE 30152, USTC 847865   BW73a

———, *Il Petrarca... d'Alessandro Vellutello*, Venice, 1573.
CNCE 32846, USTC 847893   BW73a

Petrarca: see also Alunno, Gelli, Mantova Benevides, Zoppio

Petrus Lombardus, *Sententiarum, lib IIII*, Paris, 1550.
USTC 150709   BW73a

Piccolomini, Alessandro, *De la institutione di tutta la vita de l'homo nato nobile...*, Venice, 1542.
CNCE 31669, USTC 848289   BW73a

———, *L'Instrumento della filosofia*, Venice, 1560.
CNCE 35722, USTC 848326   BW73a

———, *Copiosissima parafrase... nel primo libro della Retorica d'Aristotele*, Venice, 1565.
CNCE 40356, USTC 848340   BW63

———, *Della filosofia naturale*, Venice, 1585.
CNCE 36269, USTC 848370   BW73a

Piccolomini: see also Aristotle

Pigna, Giovanni Battista, *I romanzi*, Venice, 1554.
CNCE 37633, USTC 848747   BW63

———, *Gli heroici*, Venice, 1561.
CNCE 26327, USTC 848749   BW63

———, *Poetica horatiana*, Venice, 1561.
CNCE 38125, USTC 848752   BW73a

Pindar, *Opera omnia*, trans. and com. N. Sudorius, Venice, 1582.
CNCE 24500, USTC 848780   BW73a

Pindemonte, Francesco Filippo, *Ecphrasis in Horatii Flacci artem poeticam*, Venice, 1546.
CNCE 26968, USTC 848781   BW63

Plato, *Opera*, trans. M. Ficino, Venice, 1517.
CNCE 34948, USTC 849833   BW73a

———, *I dialoghi*, trans. S. Erizzo, Venice, 1574.
CNCE 40413, USTC 849834   BW73a

Plato: see also Ficino

Plautus, Titus Maccius, *Comoediae viginti*, Lyon, 1540.
USTC 147739   BW73a

———, *Comoediae viginti*, Basel, 1568.
USTC 674265   BW73b

Pluche, Noël-Antoine, *Spectacle de la nature*, Paris, 1755-64.   BW73a

Pluquet, François André Adrien, *Examen du fatalisme*, Paris, 1757.   BW73a

Plutarch, *Alcuni opusculetti de le cose morali*, trans. M. Tramezzino, Venice, 1543.
CNCE 48447, USTC 849985   BW73a

———, *Summi philosophi libelli septem*, trans. T. Naogeorg, Basel, 1556.   BW73a

———, *Moralia opuscula*, trans. N. Secondino, Paris, 1566.   BW73a

———, *Vite...*, trans. Lodovico Domenichi, Venice, 1570.
CNCE 31138, USTC 850019   BW73a

Polybius, *De romanorum militia et castrorum*, trans. J. Lascaris, Basel, 1537.
USTC 631380   BW73a

———, *Historiographi historiarum libri quinque*, com. N. Perotti, Lyon, 1542.
USTC 140442   BW73a

———, *Historiarum libri V*, com. N. Perotti, Geneva, 1597.
USTC 451585 BW73b
Bound in early limp vellum.

Pompignan, Jean-Jacques Lefranc, *Lettre à M. Racine sur le théâtre en général*, Paris, 1773.
BW73a

Pontano, Giovanni Gioviano, *Opera*, Venice, 1533.
CNCE 27213, USTC 850320 BW73b

———, *Opera*, Basel, 1566.
USTC 698690 BW73a

———, *Librorum omnium...tomus secundus*, Basel, n.d.
USTC 604856 BW73a*

Porcacchi, Thommaso, *Il primo volume delle cagioni delle guerre antiche*, Venice, 1565.
CNCE 26471, USTC 850876 BW73b

Porta, Malatesta, *Il Rossi overo del parere sopra alcune obiettioni fatte dal Infarinato*, Rimini, 1589 (two copies).
CNCE 31588, USTC 850963 BW63 and BW73b

Questions métaphysiques, dont la solution importe à l'humanité, Amsterdam, 1793.
BW73a

Quintilian, *Institutionum oratoriarum libri XII*, Venice, 1521.
CNCE 54149, USTC 851768 BW73a

———, *Oratoris eloquentissimi de institutione oratoria*, com. P. Schade, Venice, 1567.
CNCE 32322, USTC 851773 BW73a

Rabelais, François, *The Works of Francis Rabelais*, ed. John Ozell, London, 1737.
BW73a

———, *Oeuvres*, Amsterdam, 1711. BW73b
Bound in early vellum over boards.

Rapin, René, *Les comparaisons des grands hommes de l'antiquité*, Paris, 1684. BW73a

———, *Oeuvres diverses... concernant les belles lettres*, Amsterdam, 1686. BW73a

———, *Les oeuvres*, Amsterdam, 1709. BW73b

Rasario, Giovanni Battista: see Aristotle

Regio, Raffaele: see Ovid

Restaut, Pierre, *Principes généraux... de la grammaire françoise*, Brussels, 1756.
BW73a

Ricchieri, Lodovico, *Lectionum antiquarum libri XXX*, Lyon, 1560.
USTC 152947 BW73a

Riccobono, Antonio: see Aristotle

Richelet, Pierre, *Les plus belles lettres françoises*, Paris, 1705. BW73a

Rigoley de Juvigny, Jean Antoine, *De la décadence des lettres et des moeurs*, Paris, 1705.
BW73a

Robinet, Jean Baptiste René, *Parallèle de la condition... de l'homme avec la condition... des autres animaux*, Bouillon, 1769. BW73a

Robortello, Francesco, *Paraphrasis in librum Horatii... de arte poetica*, Florence, 1548.
CNCE 34564, USTC 852746 BW73a

——, *Ephemerides patavinas*, Padua, 1562.
CNCE 47614, USTC 852752 BW73a

Romei, Annibale, *Discorsi... divisi in sette giornate*, Venice, 1594.
CNCE 23739, USTC 853196 BW63

Rossi, Bastiano de, *Lettera... nella quale si ragiona di Torquato Tasso*, Florence, 1585.
CNCE 46906, USTC 825749 BW63

——, *Lettera... nella quale si ragiona di Torquato Tasso*, Mantua, 1585.
CNCE 55508, USTC 825748 BW73a
Bound with Tasso, *Apologia*, 1585.

Rousseau, Jean-Jacques, *Discours sur l'origine et les fondements de l'inégalité parmi les hommes*, Amsterdam, 1755. BW73a

——, *[Lettre]à Mr. D'Alambert... sur son article Genève dans le VIIe volume de l'Encyclopédie*, Amsterdam, 1758. BW73a

——, *[Lettre] à D'Alambert*, Amsterdam, 1759. BW 73a

——, *Émile, ou de l'éducation*, Paris, 1762. BW73a

——, *Émile, ou de l'éducation*, Amsterdam, 1762. BW73a

——, *Lettres écrites de la Montagne*, Amsterdam, 1764. BW73a

——, *[Lettre] à Christophe de Beaumont*, Amsterdam, 1765. BW73a

——, *Dictionnaire de musique*, Paris, 1768. BW73a

——, *Lettres diverses*, Amsterdam, [1763]. BW73a

Rubbi, Andrea, *Morgante Maggiore di Messer Luigi Pulci*, Venice, 1784. BW73a

——, *Poemetti del secolo XV, XVI*, Venice, 1785. BW73a

——, *Aminta, Alceo, Ecle favole teatrali*, Venice, 1786. BW73a

——, *Ariosto, Berni, satirici e burleschi*, Venice, 1787. BW73

——, *Ariosto, Castiglione, Fracastoro, Sanazzaro, Casa, canzonieri*, Venice, 1787.
BW73a

——, *Costano, Torquato, Bernardo Tasso e poetesse del secolo XVI*, Venice, 1787.
BW73a

——, *Lirici misti del secolo XVI*, Venice, 1788. BW73a

Ruscelli, Girolamo, *Tre Discorsi*, Venice, 1553 (two copies).
CNCE 853879, USTC 853879 BW63 and BW73c

——, *Del modo di comporre in versi*, Venice, 1563.
CNCE 29885, USTC 853874 BW63

———, *De' commentarii della lingua italiana*, Venice, 1581 (two copies).
CNCE 39398, USTC 853924 BW63 and BW73a

Sabatier, Antoine de Castres, *Les trois siècles de nostre littérature*, Amsterdam/Paris, 1772.
BW73a

Sabunde, Raimundo, *De natura hominis*, Lyon, 1544.
USTC 157567 BW73a

Saint-Gelais, Mellin de, *Oeuvres poétiques*, Paris, 1719. BW73a

Saint-Lambert, Jean François, *Fables orientales*, Avignon, 1773. BW73a

Saint-Martin, Louis Claude de, *Suite des erreurs et de la vérité*, [Paris], 1784. BW73a

Saint-Pierre, Jacques-Henri Bernardin de, *Études de la nature, vol. 3*, Paris, 1784. BW73a

Sallust, *Sallustio,* trans. A. Ortica della Porta, Venice, 1518.
CNCE 53868, USTC 854244 BW73a

———, *De coniuratione Catilinae, et de bello Iugurthino historiae*, Venice, 1546.
CNCE 31719, USTC 854263 BW73a

———, *De L. Sergii Catilinae coniuratione*, Lyon, 1551.
USTC 150814 BW73a
Bound with Valerius Maximus, *Dictorum factorumque memorabilia exempla*, 1551.

Salviati, Lionardo, *Primo libro delle orationi*, Florence, 1575.
CNCE 28451, USTC 854836 BW63
Bound with following item.

———, *Cinque lezzioni...*, Florence, 1575
CNCE 47704, USTC 854375 BW63

———, *Difesa dell'Orlando Furioso*, Florence, 1584.
CNCE 67, USTC 825058 BW63

———, *Risposta all'apologia di Torquato Tasso*, Florence, 1585.
CNCE 48709, USTC 854380 BW73a

———, *Risposta all'apologia del Sig. Torquato Tasso*, Mantua, 1585.
CNCE 27538 BW 73a
Bound with Lombardelli, *Discorso*, 1586 and Tasso, *Risposta*, 1585.

———, *Considerazioni... intorno a un discorso di M. Giulio Ottonelli*, Florence, 1586.
CNCE 19154, USTC 829723 BW63

———, *Lo'nfarinato secondo*, Florence, 1588.
CNCE 27778, USTC 854385 BW63

Salvini, Antonio Maria, *Prose toscane*, Venice, 1734. BW73a

Salvini, Salvino, *Fasti consolari dell'accademia fiorentina*, Florence, 1717. BW73c

Sannazaro, Iacopo, *Arcadia*, Venice, 1548.
CNCE 58800, USTC 854641 BW73a

———, *Rime*, Venice, 1560.
CNCE 49973, USTC 854693 BW73a

Sansovino, Francesco, *Cronologia del mondo*, Venice, 1582.
CNCE 30545, USTC 854825   BW 73a and BW73b

———, *Diverse orationi... scritte da molti huomini illustri*, Venice, 1561.
CNCE 31063, USTC 854762   BW73a

———, *Propositioni, overo considerationi in materia di cose di stato*, Venice, 1588.
CNCE 22331, USTC 835416   BW73a

Sansovino: see also Berosus

Sarasin, Jean François, *Les oeuvres*, Paris, 1694.   BW73a

———, *La pompe funebre de voiture*, Paris, 1650.
USTC 6006854   BW73a

Sardi, Alessandro, *Discorsi*, Venice, 1586.
CNCE 27634, USTC 854936   BW63å

———, *De moribus ac ritibus gentium*, Venice, 1557.
CNCE 40891, USTC 854934   BW 73a
Bound with Aelianus, *De varia historia* in 17th-century pasteboard.

———, *Numinum et heroum origines*, Rome, 1775.   BW73a

Savio, Giovanni, *Apologia in difesa del Pastor Fido*, Venice, 1601.
USTC 4034241   BW63

Scaliger, Julius Caesar, *Poetices libri septem*, Geneva, 1581.
USTC 450905   BW73a

———, *Poetices libri septem*, Geneva, 1594.
USTC 451458   BW73a

———, *De causis linguae Latinae*, Geneva, 1597.
USTC 451587   BW73b

Scarron, Paul, *Le iodelet ou les maistrevalet*, Rouen, 1654.   BW73a

———, *Le romant comique*, Leiden, 1655.   BW 73a

Scarselli, Flaminio: see Fènelon

Schade, Peter: see Quintilian

Sekoundinos, Nikolaos: see Plutarch

Segni, Bernardo: see Aristotle

Segni, Piero, see Demetrius of Phaleron

Seneca, Lucius Annaeus, *De benefizii*, trans. Benedetto Varchi, Florence, 1554.
CNCE 34611, USTC 855893   BW73b

———, *Tragoediae*, Rome, 1598.
CNCE 35924, USTC 855906   BW73a

———, *Les oeuvres*, trans. M. de Chalvet, Rouen, 1618.
USTC 6812515   BW73a

[Silvain], *Nouveau traité du sublime*, Paris, 1763.   BW73a

[Smarrito, pseud.], *Prose fiorentine...* , Florence, 1716. Vol. 1 only   BW73a

Sophocles, *Tragoediae omnes*, trans. G. B. Gabbia, Venice, 1543.
CNCE 26887, USTC 857023   BW73a

Speroni, Sperone, *I dialoghi*, Venice, 1542.
CNCE 53856, USTC 857235   BW73b

———, *Dialoghi*, Venice, 1564.
CNCE 24785, USTC 857247   BW73a

———, *Dialoghi*, Venice, 1596.
CNCE 30949, USTC 857248   BW73a

———, *Orationi*, Venice, 1596.
CNCE 30951, USTC 857249   BW73a

———, *Canace*, Venice, 1597.
CNCE 23975, USTC 857250   BW73c

Statius, Publius Papinius, *La Thebaide*, trans. Erasmo de Valvasone, Venice, [1570]
CNCE 27995, USTC 857457   BW73a

Strozzi, Giovanni Battista il giovane, *Orazioni et altre prose*, Rome, 1635.
USTC 4013163   BW73a

Sudorius, Nicolaus: see Pindar

Suetonius, *Duodecim Caesares*, Lyon, 1548.
USTC 150011   BW73a

———, *Le vite dei dodici Cesari*, trans. Paolo del Rosso, Venice, 1550.
CNCE 23568, USTC 857780   BW73a

Summo, Faustino, *Due discorsi*, Vicenza, 1601.
USTC 4034326   BW73a

Summonte, Pietro: see Pontano.

Sylburg, Friedrich: see Aristotle

Tacitus, Cornelius, *Annalium libri sedecim*, Lyon, 1542.
USTC 140311   BW73a

Tacitus: see also Ammirato

Tasso, Bernardo, *Prima parte delle lettere*, Venice, 1562.
CNCE 26428, USTC 858238   BW73b

———, *Il secondo volume delle lettere*, Venice, 1575.
CNCE 26914, USTC 858245   BW73a

———, *Le lettere*, Venice, 1591.
CNCE 35452, USTC 858258   BW73a

Tasso, Torquato, *Apologia... in difesa della sua Gierusalemme liberata*, Mantua, 1585.
CNCE 27541, USTC 858348   BW 73a

Bound with Rossi, *Lettera...*, Mantua, 1585.

———, *Delle rime*, Venice, 1582.
CNCE 27617, USTC 858311   BW73a

———, *Gierusalemme liberata*, Ferrara, 1585.
CNCE 23550, USTC 858356   BW73a

———, *Risposta... al discorso del Sig. Oratio Lombardelli*, Ferrara, 1586.
CNCE 23550, USTC 858359   BW73a

———, *Risposta... alla lettera di Bastian Rossi*, Ferrara, 1585.
CNCE 30127, USTC 858358   BW73a

———, *Risposta... alla lettera di Bastian Rossi*, Mantua, 1585.
CNCE 27538, USTC 854380   BW 73a
Bound with Lombardelli, *Discorso*, 1586 and Salviati, *Risposta all'apologia del Sig. Torquato Tasso*, 1585 in early limp vellum with fragments of green silk ties. Bought from Leona Rostenberg in 1966.

———, *Discorsi dell'arte poetica*, Venice, 1587.
CNCE 41069, USTC 858376   BW63

———, *Di Gerusalemme conquistata*, Rome, 1593.
CNCE 35686, USTC 858425   BW73b

———, *Discorsi del poema heroico*, Naples, [1594].
CNCE 34266, USTC 858439   BW63

Terence, *Comoediae*, Lyon, 1546.
USTC 157608   BW73a

———, *Comedia detta gli Adelphi*, trans. A. Lollio, Venice, 1554.
CNCE 27096, USTC 858747   BW73a

———, *Comoediae*, Lyon, 1556.
USTC 151971   BW73a

———, *In omnes Terentii fabulas compendiosa commentaria*, Frankfurt, 1550.
USTC 666296   BW73a

———, *Il Terenzio latino*, trans. Giovanni Fabrini, Venice, 1575.
CNCE 48063, USTC 858792   BW73a

———, *Opera*, Venice, 1580.
CNCE 35435, USTC 858803   BW73a

———, *Comoediae sex*, Venice, 1584.
CNCE 35428, USTC 858808   BW73a

———, *Comoediae VI*, Lyon, 1643.   BW73a

Terence: see also Ménage

Theocritus, *Idyllia eiusdem epigrammata*, com. H. Estienne, Geneva, 1579.
USTC 450809   BW73b

Thucydides, *Gli otto libri delle guerre...* trans. F. Strozzi, Venice, 1545 (two copies).
CNCE 36105 USTC 859006   BW73a

One copy at the University of Chicago purchased from Libreria Forni, Bologna; second copy not located.

Tiraboschi, Girolamo, *Storia della letteratura italiana*, Venice, 1795-96.
    BW73a

Tolomei, Claudio, *De le lettere... libri sette*, Venice, 1549.
CNCE 26160, USTC 859283   BW73a

Tomitano, Bernardino, *Ragionamenti della lingua toscana*, Venice, 1545.
CNCE 39253, USTC 859345   BW73a

———, *Quattro libri della lingua Thoscana*, Padua, 1570.
CNCE 27468, USTC 859354   BW73a

Torrentinus, Hermannus, *Elucidario poetico*, trans. Horatio Toscanella, Venice, 1565.
CNCE 24051, USTC 859726   BW73a

Toscanella, Orazio, *I modi... con che ha scritto Cicerone le sue epistole*, Venice, 1559.
CNCE 38169, USTC 860702   BW73a

———, *Osservazioni... sopra l'opera di Virgilio*, Venice, 1567.
CNCE 26553, USTC 860724   BW73a

———, *Precetti necessarii*, Venice, 1567.
CNCE 29959, USTC 860725   BW73a

———, *Quadrivio*, Venice, 1567.
CNCE 30774, USTC 860726   BW 73a
Bound with Toscanella, *Libro primo*, 1568 in early limp vellum.

———, *Discorsi cinque*, Venice, 1575.
CNCE 29286, USTC 860740   BW 73a
Bound with the following item in early limp vellum; bookplate of Libreria Vinciana, Milan.

———, *Modo di studiare le epistole famigliari di... Cicerone*, Venice, 1567.
CNCE 26552, USTC 860722   BW73a

———, *Gioie historiche*, Venice, 1567.
CNCE 26550, USTC 860719   BW73a

———, *Libro primo de gli artifici osservati*, Venice, 1568.
CNCE 30187, USTC 860731   BW 73a
Bound with Toscanella, *Quadrivio*, 1567

———, *Discorsi cinque*, Venice, 1575.
CNCE 29286, USTC 860740   BW73c

Toscanella: see also Torrentinus

Toussaint, François Vincent, *Éclaircissement sur les moeurs*, Amsterdam, 1762.   BW73a

Tramezzino, Giuseppe: see Cicero
Tramezzino, Michele: see Plutarch

Trissino, Gian Giorgio, *La poetica*, Vicenza, 1529.
CNCE 25808, USTC 861242   BW73a

———, *La quinta e la sesta divisione della poetica*, Venice, 1563.
CNCE 29709, USTC 861267   BW73a

Trotti de la Chétardie, *Instructions pour un jeune seigneur*, Lyon, 1701.   BW 73a
Bound with the following item in 18th-century full calf; purchased from Libreria Forni, Bologna.

———, *Instruction pour une jeune princesse*, Lyon, 1701.   BW73a

Udine, Ercole: see Virgil

Umbertino da Cresentino: see Ovid

Uncy, Mademoiselle, *Contes moraux*, Amsterdam, 1769.   BW73a

Urrea, Jerónimo de, *Dialogo del vero honore militare*, Venice, 1569.
CNCE 30191, USCT 861630   BW73a

Valerius Maximus, *Dictorum factorumque memorabilium exempla*, Venice, 1539.
CNCE 38058, USTC 861772   BW73a

———, *Dictorum factorumque memorabilia exempla*, Lyon, 1550.
USTC 150526   BW 73a
Bound with Sallust, *De L. Sergii Catilinae coniuratione* in 17th-century decorated full calf.

Valois, Adrien de, *Valesiana ou les pensées critiques*, Paris, 1695.   BW73a

Varchi, Benedetto, *L'Hercolano*, Florence, 1570.
CNCE 28885, USTC 862032   BW73a

———, *L'Hercolano*, Venice, 1580.
CNCE 28899, USTC 862035   BW73a

———, *Lezzioni*, Florence, 1590.
CNCE 28815, USTC 862036   BW73a

———, *I sonetti*, Venice, 1555.
CNCE 34717, USTC 862022   BW73a

Varchi: see also Boethius, Seneca

Varennes, Jacques Philippe de, *Les hommes*, Paris, 1712.   BW73a

Varro, Marcus Terentius, *Pars librorum... de lingua latina*, Rome, 1557.
CNCE 35852, USTC 862065   BW73a

Vellutello, Alessandro: see Petrarca

Vergil, Polydore, *I dialoghi*, trans. Francesco Baldelli, Venice, 1550.
CNCE 26169, USTC 862664   BW73a

———, *De rerum inventoribus*, Lyon, 1561.
USTC 123365   BW73a

———, *De gli inventori delle cose*, trans. F. Baldelli, Florence, 1587.
CNCE 48251, USTC 862669   BW73a

———, *De gli inventori delle cose*, trans. F. Baldelli, Florence, 1592.
CNCE 28828, USTC 862670   BW73a

Verrius Flaccus, Marcus, *M. Verrii Flacci quae extant*, Geneva, 1575.
USTC 450694   BW73a

Vettori, Pietro, *Castigationes Petrii Victorii in M.T. Ciceronis epistolas*, Basel, 1540.
USTC 619664   BW 73a
Bound with Giraldi, *Herculis vita*, 1539.

———, *Posteriores... castigationes in epistolas... familiares*, Lyon, 1541.
USTC 122592   BW73a

———, *Explicationes suarum in Catonem, Varronem, Columellam castigationum*, Lyon, 1542.
USTC 140430   BW73a

———, *Variarum lectionum libri XXV*, Lyon, 1554.
USTC 151675   BW73c

———, *Explicationes suarum in Ciceronem castigationum*, Lyon, 1560.
USTC 152906   BW73a

———, *Variarum lectionum XIII*, Florence, 1568.
CNCE 34761, USTC 863118   BW73a

———, *Commentarii in primum librum Aristotelis de arte poetarum*, Florence, 1573 (two copies).
CNCE 28430, USTC 863124   BW73b & BW73c

Vettori: see also Aristotle, Cicero

Villani, Giovanni, *La seconda parte della cronica universale*, Florence, 1554.
CNCE 34614, USTC 863354   BW73a

[Viperano, Giovanni Antonio], *Della poetica libri tre…*, ed. Gio. Felice Palesi, Palermo, 1734.
                                                                                                 BW73a

Virgil, *La georgica*, trans. B. Daniello, Venice, 1545.
CNCE 39260, USTC 862718   BW73a

———, *La georgica*, trans. B. Daniello, Venice, 1549.
CNCE 35112, USTC 862785   BW73a

———, *L'opere... cioè la Bucolica, la Georgica, e l'Eneide*, trans. G. Fabrini et al., Venice, 1588.
CNCE 30539, USTC 862889   BW73a

———, *L'Eneide*, trans. A. Caro, Venice, 1592.
CNCE 28537, USTC 862894   BW73a

———, *L'Eneide*, trans. E. Udine, Venice, 1597.
CNCE 24245, USTC 862897   BW73a

Virgil: see also Faydit, Toscanella

Viste sull'universo, o riflessioni sul sistema del mondo, Venice, 1776.   BW73a

Vogt, Johann, *Catalogus historico-criticus librorum rariorum*, Hamburg, 1738.   BW73c

Voiture, Vincent, *Les oeuvres*, Paris, 1656.   BW73a

Voltaire, *All'assemblea nazionale*, Paris, n.d.   BW73a

———, *Oeuvres complètes... commentaires sur Corneille*, n.p., n.d.   BW73a

———, *La ligue ou Henry le grand*, Geneve, 1723.   BW73a

———, *Le temple du goust*, Briasson, 1733.   BW73a

———, *La métaphysique de Neuton*, Amsterdam, 1740.   BW73a

———, *Oeuvres*, Amsterdam, 1741.   BW73a

———, *Collection complètte des oeuvres*, n.p., 1757.   BW73a

———, *Candide*, n.p., 1759.   BW73a

———, *La pucelle d'Orléans*, n.p., 1762.   BW73a

———, *Questions sur l'encyclopédie*, n.p., 1771.   BW73a

———, *Vie de Molière*, Lausanne/London, 1771.   BW 73a
Bound with several other small works of Voltaire.

———, *Commentaire... sur les oeuvres de l'auteur de la Henriade*, Neuchatel, 1776.
                                                                                    BW73a

———, *La Henriade*, Paris, 1786.   BW73a

———, *Candide*, Lille, 1793.   BW73a

Vossius, Gerardus Joannes, *Poeticarum institutionum libri tres*, Amsterdam, 1647.
USTC 1031984   BW73b
Bound with the two following titles in 18th-century vellum over boards.

———, *De artis poeticae natura*, Amsterdam, 1647.
USTC 193194   BW73b

———, *De imitatione*, Amsterdam, 1647.
USTC 1031983   BW73b

———, *Rhetorices contractae*, Amsterdam, 1710.   BW73a

Wolf, Hieronymus: see Isocrates

Wolff, Christian, *Philosophia rationalis*, Verona, 1735.   BW73a

———, *Logica ovvero riflessioni sopra le forze dell'intelletto umano*, Venice, 1737.
                                                                                    BW 73a
———, *Logica ovvero riflessioni sopra le forze dell'intelletto umano*, Venice, 1737
[second edition].   BW 73a

Xenophon, *I sette libri... della impresa di Ciro Minore*, trans. L. Domenichi, Venice, 1558.
CNCE 26289, USTC 864006   BW73a

———, *De Cyri vita et disciplina*, trans. G. Gabrielli, Venice, 1569.
CNCE 36002, USTC 864010   BW73a

———, *Le opere*, Venice, 1588.
CNCE 35308, USTC 864015   BW73a

Young, Edwards, *Pensées angloises sur divers sujets de réligion et de la morale*,
Amsterdam, 1760. BW73a

Zinano, Gabriele, *L'amico, over del sospire*, Reggio, 1591.
CNCE 30837, USTC 864402 BW 73a
Bound with the following item in early pasteboard with leather tackets.

———, *Il sogno, overo della poesia*, Reggio, 1591.
CNCE 30819, USTC 864396 BW73a

Zonaras, Joannes, *La prima... parte dell'historie*, Venice, 1572.
CNCE 26891,USTC 864431 BW73a

Zoppio, Girolamo, *Ragionamento... in difesa di Dante et del Petrarca*, Bologna, 1583.
CNCE 48367, USTC 864440 BW73a

———, *La poetica sopra Dante*, Bologna, 1589.
CNCE 32558, USTC 864446 BW73a

Index

Accademia degli Alterati 25, 100–2, 105–7, 113, 114, 117, 121, 128, 191, 203
   importance and relevance of 123–4
   as institutional locus 124
   readings, in and around *Poetics* 130–1
Accademia degli Infiammati 138–9
Accademia degli Intronati 27
Accademia dei Trasformati 242
Accademia della Crusca of Florence 185
Accademia Olimpica 219, 220
Addison, Joseph 71
   Pleasures of the Imagination 69
Aeschylus 26
Akasoy, Anna 244 n.65
Albizzi, Antonio Degli 115
Albizzi, Giovanni Degli 135 n.3
Alciato, Andrea 165
Aldine Press 235
Alexander the Sophist
   On Figures 43
Alfano, Giancarlo 214 n.53
Alfonso of Aragon 145
allegory 65, 125, 165, 240
   identification by Weinberg with Middle Ages 82
   as litmus test of poetic premodernity 73
   as multiform 245
   non-scriptural 85
   poetic universal and 74
   Renaissance and 72–4, 76, 77, 80
   scriptural 83, 85
   suppression of 69–70, 73, 76, 81–3, 85–7
Allen, Michael J. B. 85
Alterati academy.
   See Accademia degli Alterati
Alterati of Florence.
   See Accademia degli Alterati
Ammirato, Scipione 165, 230
   Il Dedalione overo Del Poeta 241, 242

Andreoni, Annalisa 138 n.12
Angiolillo, Giuliana 135 n.3
Anker, Elizabeth S. 229 n.8
annotation 158, 159, 161–5, 167, 168, 171, 173–5
   discontinuity in 117
   of manuscripts 103, 105, 109, 112–17, 119–22
anthology, of early English criticism 67–8
Aphthonius
   Progymnasmata 43
Apsines
   Art of Rhetoric 43
   On Figured Problems 43
Aquinas, Thomas 4
Arber, Edward 69
Archivio di Stato di Firenze 122, 129
Ardissino, Erminia 135 n.3
Ariosto, Ludovico 171, 198–9
   Orlando furioso 157, 158, 172 n.45, 183, 190, 241
Aristotle 26, 228. *See also individual entries*
   Ethics 237
   Metaphysics 190
   Nicomachean Ethics 3
   On Interpretation 4
   On the Soul 3
   Poetics, rediscovery of 9, 51, 62, 74–5, 98, 137, 157, 182, 190, 228, 236
   Politics 3, 27, 237
   Rhetoric 2, 27, 44, 109, 185–7, 190, 204
Arnaudo, Marco 135 n.3
Arnold, Matthew 70
Artaud, Antonin 63
Ascham, Roger 68, 228
Ascoli, Albert 144 n.31
Atkins, J. W. H. 64, 81 n.94
autonomy 63
   aesthetic 7, 40, 48, 54, 55, 60
   of expressive work of art 51

Averroes (Ibn-Rushd) 4
Avicenna (Ibn-Sīnā) 4, 209 n.35

Bacon, Francis 62, 74, 77
  Advancement of Learning 246
Badius Ascensius, Johannes 82, 239
Baldassari, Gabriele 195
Baldassarre, Eufemia 121 n.31
Baldassarri, Guido 135 n.3
Baldwin, Charles Sears 64 n.13
Baldwin, T. W. 35 n.43
Barański, Zygmunt G. 144 n.31
Barbi, Michel 135 n.3, 144 n.31
Baron, Hans 5, 7, 19, 2–9, 31–3, 35
Battaglia, Salvatore 135 n.3
Bellay, Joachim du
  Defence and Illustration of the French Language 76
Bellini, Saverio 135 n.3
Beloe, William 67–8
Bembo, Pietro 9, 134, 137–8, 140, 145, 148, 149, 183
  Asolani 144
  Prose della volgar lingua 137
Beni, Paolo 28, 228
Benivieni, Girolamo 136 n.6
Berman, Antoine 185 n.8
Bernardinello, Silvio 141 n.17
Berni, Francesco
  Dialogo contra i poeti 28
Bessarion, Cardinal 43
Bevilacqua, Alexander 235 n.28
Bianchi, Luca 5 n.19, 206
Biblioteca Nazionale Centrale di Firenze (BNCF) 98, 122, 130, 242.
  See also Magliabechi collections
  Magl. VII 1199, codicological description of 127–9
Bionda, Simone 1 n.1
Bizer, Marc 157 n.1, 165 n.22
Black, Deborah L. 209 n.35
Black, Robert 4 n.14
Blackburn, Thomas H. 67 n.25
Blocker, Déborah 22 n.10, 26 n.17, 185 n.9, 191, 203, 209, 242
Boccaccio, Giovanni 73, 86 n.125, 144 n.31, 145, 147, 149, 174, 221
Boeckh, August 106
Boethius 165

Bognolo, Anna 184 n.7
Boileau-Despréaux, Nicolas 41, 66, 76
Bolton, Edmund 67, 77
  Hypercritica 67
Bongiorno, Andrew 207 n.28
Booth, Wayne C. 21 n.5
Borghini, Vincenzo 134, 135, 136 n.6, 138
Borinski, Karl 72 n.49
Borris, Kenneth 82
Bosanquet, Bernard
  History of Aesthetic 53
Bouhours, Dominique de 29
  Les Entretiens d'Ariste et d'Eugène 29
Bourdieu, Pierre 242
Boutier, Jean 105 n.4
Boyer, Blanche 22 n.9
Boyle, Marjorie O'Rourke 85
Bramanti, Vanni 108, 129
Brazeau, Bryan 211 n.42, 230 n.11, 237 n.35
Bréchet, Christophe 233 n.19
Brljak, Vladimir 5, 212 n.44
Brooks, Cleanth
  Literary Criticism: A Short History 52, 64
Bruni, Francesco 138 n.12, 139 nn.13–14
Bruni, Leonardo 190–1
  De interpretatione recta 190
Brunner, Michael 135 n.3
Budé, Guillaume 158
Bulgarini, Bellisario 134, 135, 141 n.19, 143, 144, 145, 147, 149, 150.
  See also Dante Quarrel
  Alcune Considerazioni sopra 'l Discorso di M. Giacopo Mazzoni 144, 150
  Antidiscorso 141
Buonanni, Vincenzo 144 n.31
Burckhardt, Jacob 73, 77
  Civilization of the Renaissance in Italy, The 71
Businarolo, Luigia 135 n.3
Butcher, John George 48 n.46
Butcher, S. H. 12, 40, 50–2, 74
  Aristotle's Theory of Poetry and Fine Art 48–9
  influence on aesthetic interpretation of *Poetics* 53
  transformative aesthetic of 51

Butler, Nicholas Murray   79 n.89

Callard, Caroline   105 n.4
Camerarius, Joachim   165
Cameron, Don   166 n.25
Campion, Thomas   67
Capodieci, Luisa   157 n.1
Capponi, Orazio   134, 149
Capriano, GiovanniPietro   82
Cariero, Alessandro   134, 141 n.19, 144
    Apologia   141–2
Caro, Annibale   109
Carroll, Mitchell   49
Carte Strozziane   129
Casanova, Pascale   244 n.63
Cassirer, Ernst   233
Castelvetro, Lodovico   10, 41, 51, 52, 103,
    113, 116, 138, 206–9, 228, 230,
    231, 238 n.42
    as idiosyncratic critic   205
    on oblique pleasure (piacere obliquo)
        208, 209–14, 216
    on Plato   213–14
    on plots   218
    *Poetica d'Aristotele vulgarizzata e
        sposta*   202, 204, 206–8, 215,
        216, 220, 222
    on spectator's reaction   210, 214,
        215, 217
    unique approach to translation   207–8
Castravilla, Ridolfo   134, 135, 145, 149
    Il discorso contro Dante   133
Catelli, Nicola   182 n.3
catharsis (*catarsi*)   117–19, 201, 208,
    209, 219
Cavallo, JoAnn   190 n.27
Cerreta, Florindo   138 n.12
Cervantes, Miguel de
    Don Quijote   194, 244
Chalmers, George   67
Charlton, Henry Buckley   205
Chartier, Roger   242–3
Chiappelli, Fredi   181 n.2
Chicago School of Criticism   20–1, 35,
    38–40, 54, 121, 134 n.2.
    See also Neo-Aristotelians
    adhering to Aristotle   39
chivalric romance   238

Chrysostom, Dio   159
Cicero   2, 26, 165, 190, 191
    Letters to Atticus   149
    Paradoxes   149
Ciociola, Claudio   144 n.31
Cochrane, Eric W.   31, 107 n.7
Cohen, Stephen   237
Coleridge, Samuel Taylor   71, 74
Columella, Lucius Junius Moderatus   165
comedy   42, 51, 183 n.6, 220, 221, 238
commonplacing   46, 47, 48
Conley, Thomas   43 n.22
Cook, Albert S.   69
Cooper, Elizabeth   68
    Muses Library   68
Cooper, Helen   168 n.32
Cooper, Lane
    Poetics of Aristotle, The   52
Corneille, Pierre   41
Cosmo, Umberto   135 n.3
Cotugno, Alessio   5 n.19, 139 n.13, 206 n.24
Counter-Reformation   3, 217
Cowley, Abraham   66
Crane, R. S.   21 n.6, 45, 48, 81, 134 n.2
    on Chicago School   39–40
    Critics and Criticism   21, 22, 38, 55, 205
Crawford, Jason   245 n.67
Croce, Benedetto   3, 51
    Aesthetic   53
Crouzet-Pavan, Elisabeth   218
Cummings, Brian   165 n.22
Curtius, Ernst Robert   83

D'Amico, Silvia   163 n.13
Dahiyat, Ismail M.   209 n.35
Dalmas, Davide   135 n.3
Danese, Daniele   135 n.3
Daniel, Samuel   67
Daniele, Antonio   138 n.12, 141 n.17
Daniello, Bernardino   2 n.8, 138
Dannenfeldt, Karl H.   236 n.28
Dante   165, 228
    Commedia   133, 137, 143, 144, 148
    De vulgari eloquentia   143, 145
    Vita nova   142, 144, 145
Dante quarrel   133–7.
    See also Bulgarini, Bellisario
    Bembo on   137–8
    Lenzoni on   139

Speroni on   140–52
Tomitano on   138–9
Davenant, William   67 n.25
Davi, Maria Rosa   139 n.14
Day, Gary   64
De' Medici, Lorenzo
    Raccolta Aragonese   145
De Armas, Frederick A.   244 n.64
De Caro, Gaspare   107 n.7
De Castion, Jean-Jacques   161
decorum, poetic significance of   173, 238, 240
De la Taille, Jean   228
Della Casa, Giovanni   149, 151
    Galateo   150
Del Nero, Tommaso   101
Deloince-Louette, Christiane   158, 165 n.22
Del Soldato, Eva   206 n.24
Dembowski, Peter F.   20, 35 n.44
Demetriou, Tania   157 n.1, 162, 166
Demetrius
    On Style   43
Demetrius of Phaleron   26
De Montmorency, Anne   161, 165
Denores, Giason   4, 5, 10, 76, 202, 221–2, 237
    Discorso intorno a quei principii…   220
Derrida, Jacques   227, 239, 246
De Sponde, Jean   158
Desportes, Philippe   31–2
Destrée, Pierre   209 n.34
Diano, Roberto   209 n.34
didactic poetry and practices of reading   43, 48, 53, 55, 232, 242
Digby, Kenelm
    Observations on the … Faery Queen   86
diletto   124, 171, 193, 222. *See also* pleasure
Diller, Aubrey   43 n.21
Dillon, Wentworth   66
Dionysius of Halicarnassus
    Art of Rhetoric   43
    On Composition   43
divine justice   143 n.26, 163, 211, 218
Divo, Andrea   160
Dorbon, Lucien   31

Dryden, John   68, 69, 71, 81
    Of Dramatick Poesie   66, 67
Du Mans, Peletier   228

Echard, Gwenda   168 n.32
Eden, Kathy   234
Elias, Norbert   203
    Civilizing Process, The   202
Eliot, Thomas   68
emotional affect, as marvellous   171–2
emotional communities   203–4
    definition of   203
emotions, history of   201–2
    catharsis and   208, 209, 219
    emotional communities and   203–4
    hydraulic/pneumatic view of emotions and   203
    oblique pleasure and   208, 212–14, 216
    performative approach to Renaissance emotional life and   217–18
    pleasure and displeasure and   209–13
    spectator's reaction and   210, 214, 215, 217
    tragedy and   201, 207, 214, 216–17, 219
emotives, notion of   218
English literary criticism, history of   66–70. *See also* allegory; modernity; Renaissance poetics and literary criticism
Enlightenment   24, 29, 63
Eobanus Hessus, Helius   160
epic poetry   165, 168, 169 n.36, 171, 181, 182, 188, 189, 192, 193, 215, 216, 245
epideictic genre   44, 45 n.28
Erasmus, Desiderius   85
    Adagia   46, 163
    De copia   46, 86 n.125
    De ratione studii   46
Euripides   26, 46, 47
    Andromeda   47
    Orestes   47
Eustathius   160
Everson, Jane   242

Fahy, Conor   133, 235 n.27
Fairclough, H. R.   194 n.38
Fantini, Vincenzo   186
Feldman, Martha   136

Felski, Rita   229 n.8, 246
fiction   9, 39, 136, 170, 171, 173, 239, 240, 244
Firpo, Massimo   208
Fletcher, H. George   235 n.27
Fletcher, Harris F.   35 n.43
Flügel, Ewald   69
Folena, Gianfranco   144 n.31
Forcellini, Marco   141 n.17
Ford, Andrew   207
Ford, Philip   157 n.1, 160 n.7, 166 n.25
foreignness   181, 183, 185–91, 194–9
formalism   11, 12, 232, 233, 236–8
Fornari, Simone   82
Foucault, Michel   63, 203
Fournel, Jean-Louis   138 n.12, 139 n.13
Fracastoro, Girolamo   51, 82
fragmentation, practice by renaissance critics   45–7, 53
Freud, Sigmund   203
Friedland, L. S.
  'Dramatic Unities in England, The'   52
Fromm, Harold   55 n.76
Frye, Northrop   183 n.6
Fuchs, Barbara   244 n.64
Fussler, Herman H.   34

Gabriele, Trifone   145
Galilei, Galileo   198
Gallo, Alberto   219 n.72
Garimberto, Girolamo   165
Gascoigne, George   68, 77
  Certayne Notes of Instruction…   67, 80
Gavin, Michael   65 n.17
Gehl, Paul F.   27 n.22, 121 n.31
Gelli, Giovanni Battista   138, 144 n.31
genre, theory of   4, 136, 183–4 n.6, 198, 206, 220, 234, 236–41
genre hybridity   239, 240
German idealism   126
Ghobrial, John-Paul   235 n.28
Giacomini, Lorenzo   109, 119, 120, 122, 128, 191–3, 197
  Oratione in lode di Torquato Tasso   197
Giambullari, Pierfrancesco   138, 139
Giammei, Alessandro   192
Gigante, Claudio   135 n.3
Giglioni, Guido   135 n.3, 244 n.65
Gigliucci, Roberto   208

Gilbert, Allan H.   53
  Literary Criticism: Plato to Dryden   205
  and H. L. Snuggs, 'On the Relation of Horace to Aristotle in Literary Criticism'   52
Gilson, Simon   5, 135 n.3, 138 n.11, 144 n.31, 147 n.41, 206
Giraldi Cinzio, Giovan Battista   183, 187, 191, 193, 209 n.34, 214, 228, 239 n.42
Girard, René   208
Girardi, Maria Teresa   139 n.14, 142
Giubilini, Robert   138 n.12
Giustinian, Orsatto   219
gnomai (maxims), Aristotle's usage of   47
Godman, Peter   3 n.11
Goethe, Johann Wolfgang von   74
  Literary Essays   79
Goetsch, James Robert   236 n.29
Gonzaga, Scipione   215
Gordon, D. J.   219
Gorni, Guglielmo   144 n.31
Gosson, Stephen
  Schoole of Abuse   86
Goulimari, Pelagia   64
Grafton, Anthony   54, 158 n.3, 162 n.11, 167 n.30
Grata, Giulia   141 n.17
Grayson, Cecil   136 n.6
Greenblatt, Stephen   203 n.7
Greene, Roland   236
Greene, Thomas   243
Greenfield, Concetta Carestia   84
  Humanist and Scholastic Poetics, 1250–1500   83
Grendler, Paul   4
Griffolini, Francesco   159, 160
Groarke, Louis   21 n.5
Grohovaz, Valentina   208 n.33
Guarini, Battista   28, 198
  Il Pastor fido   28, 183 n.6, 201, 220, 237
  Il Verrato   28
Guasti, Cesare   129
Güthenke, Constanze   106 n.5
Guyer, Paul   61

Habermas, Jürgen   63
  'antimodernist' manoeuvre (Habermas)   63

Habib, M. A. R. 64
  Modern Literary Criticism and Theory 61
Hahn, Juergen 189 n.24
Hale, John 77 n.78
Halliwell, Martin 246 n.72
Halliwell, Stephen 53, 54
hamartia 211 n.42
Hardison, O. B. 55–6
Harington, John 67, 68, 86 n.125
Harland, Richard 64
Harlfinger, Dieter 44 n.25
Harvey, Gabriel 68
Haslewood, Joseph 68, 69
  Ancient Critical Essays 67, 77
Hathaway, Baxter 3, 205, 214, 230 n.11
  Age of Criticism, The 2, 209 n.34
Heath, Jane 204 n.13
hedonism 98, 120, 125, 203, 204. *See also* diletto; pleasure
Helvétius, Claude Adrien 29–30
  De l'esprit 29
  Le bonheur 29
  Oeuvres completes 29
Henley, John 69 n.36
Hermogenes
  Rhetoric 43
heroic poetry 75 n.66, 158, 159, 168–71, 173, 216, 220, 240
Herrera, Fernando De 228
Herrick, Marvin 81, 240 n.47
  Comic Theory in the Sixteenth Century 42
  Fusion of Horatian and Aristotelian Literary Criticism, The 42, 52
Hess, Jonathan M. 126 n.36
heterogeneity, of literary criticism 1, 67, 229
historical difference, Renaissance recognition of 243
historical formalism 237
history and poetry, distinction between 118
history of the emotions. *See* emotions, history of
history of reading 9, 158, 159, 243. *See also* Accademia degli Alterati; manuscript studies and aesthetics

Hobbes, Thomas 67 n.25, 80
Hoff, James D. 55 n.76
Hoffherr, F. G. 31 n.29
Hölderlin 63
Homer 149, 228
  Iliad 159
  Odyssey 9, 157–8, 189 n.24 (see also Lombardelli, Orazio)
  Christian theology in 163–4
Horace 41, 42, 52–3, 164, 165, 228
  Ars Poetica 1, 2, 52, 81, 82, 167, 174, 190, 237–41
  Epistles 167
Hotchkiss, Valerie 35 n.43
Huarte, Juan 165
Huizinga, Johann 202
  Waning of the Middle Ages, The 203
humanism 3 n.11, 11, 25, 27, 33, 73, 76, 83–4, 98, 136, 137, 139, 190, 191, 209 n.36
  poetics in practice and 161, 164, 167 n.30, 171 n.42
  Renaissance literary theory and 227 n.2, 228, 231–5, 236 nn.28, 31, 241 n.53, 243, 246 n.72
  and scholasticism compared 83–4
Hunter, G. K. 46 n.37
Hutton, James 52

imaginative literature 60, 65, 73
imitation (mimesis), Aristotelian notion of 148–9, 150–1, 165, 169 n.36, 206, 213, 227, 235, 236, 240
Imorde, Joseph 217 n.63
Ingegnieri, Angelo
  Della poesia rappresentativa et del modo di rappresentare le favole sceniche 220
Innes, Doreen 190
intertextuality 144 n.30, 157 n.1, 166, 167, 174, 227

Jackson, Virginia 243
James VI/I 67
Janko, Richard 43 n.21
Jardine, Lisa 158 n.3, 162 n.11, 167 n.30
Javitch, Daniel 1 n.3, 11, 54, 136, 206, 207 n.27, 208, 219 n.70, 236 n.31, 238, 240

on genre theory and 'progressive
   classicism' 11, 206, 208, 238
Jeanneret, Michel   85
Johnson, Samuel   66, 68
Jonson, Ben   66–9, 71, 77, 81
Jossa, Stefano   135 n.3, 141 n.17

Kallendorf, Craig   3 n.11
Kant, Immanuel   126
Kantinis, Teodoro   139 n.13
Karnat-Nunn, Susan   217 n.63
Kemal, Salim   209 n.35
Kennedy, George A.   43 n.22, 44, 45 n.28
Ker, N. R.   127 n.37
Kindt, Tom   21 n.5
Klopp, Charles   186 n.13, 188
Konstan, David   204 n.15, 233 n.19
Kramnick, Jonathan   230 n.9
Kraye, Jill   5, 206, 244 n.65
Kristeller, Paul Oskar
   Renaissance Thought   84
Kuhn, Thomas   40

Landino, Cristoforo   146 n.37
Lansing, Carol   218
Laste, Natale dalle   141 n.17
Latour, Bruno   229
Lazarus, Micha   5, 190 n.28, 205, 212 n.44
Ledda, Giuseppe   150 n.46
Leitch, Vincent B.   134 n.2
Lemnius, Simon   160, 161, 164, 166, 167, 173
Lenzoni, Carlo   9, 138, 144. See also Dante quarrel
   Difesa di Dante   139, 142, 144
Leo, Russ   206, 207
Lesser, Zachary   46 n.37
Levine, Caroline   233
   Forms   232
Levitin, Dmitri   54 n.73
Liburnio, Niccolò   138
Lines, David A.   4 n.14, 5, 206, 237 n.33
Lisci, Leonardo Ginori   101 n.3
literary criticism   1–2, 5–13, 50, 51, 136, 159, 186, 190 n.28
   history of emotions and   201, 203, 205, 222
   modernity, allegory and   60, 61, 63–5, 67, 69–73, 75, 77, 80, 81, 84, 87

Renaissance literary theory and   228–37, 242–6
Lobel, Edgar   43 n.21
Lodge, Thomas   86
Lombardelli, Orazio   9, 158–9
   Discorso intorno a i contrasto che si fanno sopra la Gierusalemme liberata   159, 169, 174
   Odyssean defence of Tasso,
      Gerusalemme Liberata   168–75
   Odyssey of
      annotations   161–2
      reading methodology   163–8
      text, BL C66.b.2   159–61
   Sopra il Goffredo del Signor Torqvato Tasso. Giudizio   158
Lombardi, Bartolomeo   4
Longinus   228
   On the Sublime   1
Lo Re, Salvatore   138 n.12
Lorrain, Claude   181, 182, 193 n.36, 194, 199
   Landscape with Erminia in Discourse with the Old Man and His Sons   182
Lucan   165
Lucretius   149
   De rerum natura   167–8
lyric poetry   228, 238, 241 n.53, 243

Mack, Peter   46 n.37
McKeon, Richard   22, 35, 40
McManamon, John M.   45 n.28
Macrobius   165
Maffei, Raffaele   160
Maggi, Vincenzo   4, 103, 113, 209 n.34, 230
Magliabechi collections   101, 105, 103, 129. See also Biblioteca Nazionale Centrale di Firenze (BNCF)
Magliani, Mariella   141 n.17
Malacreta, Giovanni Pietro   28
Malatesta, Giuseppe   231
   Della nuova poesia, overo delle difese del Furioso, dialogo   184
Mallarmé, Stéphane   63
   Le tombeau d'Edgar Poe   20
Malone, Edmond   67, 68
Manni, Domenico Maria   107 n.7

manuscript studies and aesthetics 97–105
   and rare books, on development
      of intellectual and cultural
      history 105–26
Manutius, Paulus 165
Marazzini, Claudio 185 n.10
marchese of Forano (Giovan Battista
      Strozzi) 99, 109, 129
marginalia 116, 117, 158 n.3, 159, 161–3
   printed 160, 163, 166, 173
Marino, Adrian 63
Markey, Lia 121 n.31, 242, 244
Marmi, Anton Francesco 105 n.4
material culture 6
Mazzoni, Jacopo 135
   Della difesa di Dante 134, 141
Mazzoni, Stefano 219, 220
Mazzotta, Giuseppe 236 n.29
Melancthon 160, 161, 171 n.42, 207
Menander
   On Epideictic 43
Mengelkoch, Dustin 236 n.31
meraviglia (marvel) 10, 119, 120, 165, 173,
      175, 186–9, 208 n.33, 214, 215,
      221, 222
   categories of 174
   emotional affect as 171–2
   Lodovico Castelvetro on 208 n.33, 214
   Torquato Tasso on 170, 215
   and verisimilitude compared 170–1
Meres, Francis 68
Merola, Valeria 208 n.33, 209 n.34, 214
Michell, John 55 n.76
Middle Ages 65, 66, 70–4, 80, 86 n.125, 202
   identification of allegory with 82
Migliarisi, Anna 219 n.70, 220
Milton, John 80
mimesis. *See* imitation (mimesis),
      Aristotelian notion of
Minturno, Antonio Sebastino 25, 82,
      228, 230
Minucianus/Nicagoras
   On Arguments 43
modernity 8, 21, 61, 206, 237, 238.
         See also Renaissance poetics and
      literary criticism
   aesthetic 72–3, 75
   anti-allegorism and 69–70
   literature and 62–3

poetic 7, 64, 74
   teleology of, mapping to medieval-
      Renaissance divide 82
Molinari, Carla 185 n.9
Mongini, Guido 208
Montaigne, Michel de 228, 230
   'Apology for Raymond Sebond' 227
   Essais 227
moral criticism. *See* didactic poetry and
      practices of reading
moral universe 211, 218, 219
Moreschini, Claudio 135 n.3
Moritz, Karl Philip 126
Moss, Ann 46 n.37
Moulton, Richard Green 88 n.126
Mousley, Andy 246 n.72
Mufti, Aamir 246 n.72
Mullett, Margaret 45 n.28

Naiditch, Paul 44 n.25
Nebrija, Antonio de 230
Neo-Aristotelians 5, 11, 121 n.31, 206,
      228, 238, 244 n.64. *See also*
      Chicago School of Criticism
neo-classicism 75, 76
neo-humanism 231
Neoplatonism 2, 3, 86, 125
Nersessian, Anahid 230 n.9
Newberry Library 22, 23, 26–8, 31–4, 229
New Criticism 5, 20, 21, 51, 64, 71, 121,
      231 n.15
New Formalism 11, 231, 237, 246
New Historicism 231 n.15, 237
New Lyric Studies 241 n.53
New World 244
North, Joseph 229 n.8, 231 n.15
   *Literary Criticism: A Concise
      Political History* 244
Norton, Glyn P. 237 n.32
   *Cambridge History of Literary
      Criticism, The* 85

Oberto, Simona 139 n.13, 144 n.30
oblique pleasure.
      See Castelvetro, Lodovico
O'Donnell, Simone Laqua 217 n.63
Olson, Elder 22, 40, 134 n.2
Omont, Henri 44 n.25
Ong, Walter 46

Oporinus, Johannes 160
Ovid 164, 165

Palisca, Claude 107 n.7
Panciera, Elena 139 n.13
Paoli, Maria Pia 105 n.4
Pargellis, Stanley 32
Pariguolo, Lorenzo 82
Parrasio, Aulo Giano 82, 240
pastoral poetry 168, 181, 188, 193-8, 222
Pazzi de' Medici, Alessandro 1, 75, 82, 190 n.28
Peck, Henry Thurston 79 n.89
Pedemonte, Francesco Filippi 82
Pellegrino, Camillo 170, 189, 192 n.34, 238
   Il Carrafa 169
pellegrinità, Tasso's notion of 10, 12, 186-9, 191, 198
   peregrine spade, significance in Tasso's *Gerusalemme Liberata* 194-5, 197-8
   peregrino (foreign style), Tasso's notion of 185, 186-8
Pellisson, Paul 125
Peri, Jacopo
   Euridice 125
Persius 165
Petrarca, Francesco (Petrarch) 138, 145, 149, 165, 194-6, 228, 234-5
   Canzoniere (*Rerum vulgarium fragmenta*), 144, 193 n.36
   Familiares 234, 243
   Triumphi 149
Peyre, H. 31 n.29
Phillips, Edward 75 n.66
philology 20, 21, 26, 27, 30, 38, 45, 50, 61, 85, 106 n.5, 185, 205, 207
   Renaissance literary theory and 230, 232, 235-6, 238, 243
Phoibammon
   On Figures 43
Piccolomini, Alessandro 27, 28, 113, 115, 138, 228
Piemontese, Angelo 236 n.28
Pigafetta, Filippo 219
pilgrims. *See* pellegrinità
Pinciano, Alonso López 228
Plamper, Jan 203 n.7, 204 n.15

Plato 2, 64, 81, 85, 147, 201, 213-214, 232, 241, 246; *See also* Neoplatonism
   Republic 201, 213
Plautus 165
pleasure 10, 38, 41, 60, 83, 100, 117-120, 124-126, 160, 192, 203, 216, 219-220
   Butcher on, as end of poetry 74
   Castelvetro on 209-16
   and displeasure 210, 212
   epic 216
   ethics of 120
   role of tragic poems in producing 118-19
   Tasso on 216-217
   and utility 120
   See also diletto; hedonism
Pléiade 76, 228
Pliny 76, 165
Plochmann, George Kimball 21 n.5
plot (*favola*) 111, 116-17, 193, 211, 216, 218
   Lombardelli's definition of 169, 170
   Tasso's comparison of tragic and heroic 216
Plutarch 165, 232, 245, 246
   De audiendis poetis (*How the Young Man Should Study Poetry*) 173, 232, 245
   on historical analyses 232-3
   as literary critic 233 n.19
Poetics. See Aristotle, *Poetics*; and individual entries
Poliziano, Angelo 3 n.11, 4, 145, 228, 231
   Ambra 166
Pollard, Tanya 46
Pope, Alexander 68, 69, 71
   Essay on Criticism 66
Porphyrogenitus, Constantine 43
Porphyry
   Homeric Questions 160
   On the Cave of the Nymphs 160
practical criticism 83, 121, 228
Procaccioli, Paolo 135 n.3
progymnasmata 44, 45 n.28
pseudo-Aristides
   Art of Rhetoric 43
pseudo-Aristotelian 38, 45, 74

pseudo-Herodotus   159
pseudo-Plutarch   159
    *Essay on the Life and Poetry
        of Homer*   166
psychology   10, 202, 210, 214, 217, 222
Puliafito, Anna Laura   5 n.19, 206 n.24
Puttenham, George   68
    Arts of English Poetry   66

Quaglino, Margherita   135 n.3
Quintilian   2

Rabelais, François   20
Racine, Jean   20
Ramachandran, Ayesha   227 n.2
Rambouillet, Catherine de Vivonne   125
Reddy, William   202, 218
Refini, Eugenio   206 n.24, 230 n.11,
    237 n.33
Reinsch, Diether   44 n.25
Renaissance literary theory
    humanism and   227 n.2, 228, 231–5,
        236 nn.28, 31, 241 n.53, 243,
        246 n.72
    literary criticism and   228–37, 242–6
    philology and   230, 232, 235–6,
        238, 243
Renaissance poetics and literary
        criticism   8–10, 43, 45, 64–5,
        71–2, 121, 158
    allegory and   72–4, 76, 77, 80
    conceptual impasse and
        history of   82–3, 87
    English   76–7
    rediscovery of Aristotle's
        Poetics and   74–5
    Spingarn on   78
Renouard, Antoine A.   235 n.27
Restani, Donatella   220 n.75
Reynolds, Henry
    Mythomystes   68, 81, 86
rhetoric and rhetorical criticism   2, 4,
    10–11, 24, 27, 38, 41, 43–4,
    136–7, 165, 185–7, 204, 212, 222,
    227, 230, 233–4, 240–1; *See also*
    Aristotle, *Rhetoric*; trivium
Riatsch, Clà   160 n.7
Ribard, Dinah   106 n.5
Ribaudo, Vera   210

Riccoboni, Antonio
    Aristotelis Ars Poetica   187
Rinuccini, Ottavio and Jacopo Peri
    Euridice   125
Ritter, Franciscus   48 n.46
Rivoltella, Cesare   208 n.33, 209 n.34,
        214 n.54
Rizzarelli, Giovanna   182 n.3
Robbins, Bruce   229 n.8
Robinson, Martin   55 n.76
Robortello, Francesco   1, 2 n.9, 40, 41,
        47 n.38, 103, 113, 205, 208, 209,
        228, 238, 240
Romani, Werther   210 n.37
Romanticism   61, 69, 70, 72, 74, 75,
        78, 80
Roncaccia, Alberto   208
Rosenthal, Robert   34
Rosenwein, Barbara H.   202, 203, 217–18
Ross, B. Joyce   51 n.57, 72 n.49
Rossi, Paolo   236 n.29
Rossignoli, Claudia   206
Routh, James   81 n.94
Ruggiero, Guido   218
Ruscelli, Girolamo   25
Rushdie, Salman
    Satanic Verses, The   240
Russell, D. A.   45 n.28
Russo, Emilio   135 n.3
Ryan, Eugene E.   209 n.34
Rymer, Thomas   66

sacred, sense of   146, 187–8
Said, Edward W.   246 n.72
Saintsbury, George   7, 50, 60, 63, 78
    *History of Criticism and Literary
        Taste in Europe, A*   50, 77
    Romantic medievalism of   79–80
Salabrino, Luca   215 n.57
Sallust   26, 165
Salutati, Coluccio   86 n.125
Salviati, Lionardo   169, 172, 189,
        191, 238
    Difesa dell'Orlando furioso   169, 186
Salvini, Salvino   107 n.7
Samuels, Richard S.   138 n.12
Sandys, J. E.
    History of Classical Scholarship   52
Sansone, Mario   185 n.10

Sassetti, Filippo   107–9, 111–13, 115, 117–19, 122, 128, 129. *See also* Accademia degli Alterati
   postille of   112 n.15
Scaglione, Aldo   32
Scaliger, Julius Caesar   76, 113
   Poetices libri septem   228, 237, 238 n.37
Scapecchi, Piero   104–5
Scarpati, Claudio   135 n.3, 186
Schapira, Nicolas   106 n.5
Schelling, Felix E.   71 n.46
Schmitt, Arbogast   4 n.16
Schmitt, Charles   54, 206
   'Renaissance Aristotelianisms'   206
Schneider, Ulrike   121 n.33
scholasticism and humanism, comparison of   83–4
Scholes, Robert   55 n.76, 231
Schurink, Fred   158 n.3
Scott, Roger   45 n.28
Scudéry, Madeleine de   125
Seaton, James   88 n.126
Sébillet, Thomas   228
Sebond, Raymond
   Montaigne's apology for as commentary on *Theologia naturalis*   227
Segni, Agnolo   130 n.39
Segni, Bernardo   1, 82, 113, 130 n.39, 182, 187, 193
self-fashioning, notion of.
   See Greenblatt, Stephen
self-justifying norms   240
sententia   46–7, 160, 164
Seznec, Jean   83
Sgarbi, Marco   1 n.1, 5, 206
Sherman, William H.   46 n.37
Shrivastava, Ravindra Nath   121 n.31
Shuckburgh, Evelyn S.   69
Sidney, Philip   44, 45, 68, 71, 75, 81, 125, 228
   Defence of Poesie   66, 69, 70, 73, 77
   as modern literary critic   69
Siekiera, Anna   107 n.7, 191 n.32, 207 n.31
Siraisi, Nancy   209 n.35
Smith, David Nichol   50
Smith, G. Gregory   50, 85
   Elizabethan Critical Essays   50, 85

Snuggs, H. L.   53
   and Allan Gilbert 'On the Relation of Horace to Aristotle in Literary Criticism'   52
Snyder, Jon R.   215 n.55
Society for the History of Reading, Authorship and Publishing (SHARP)   243
Solomon, Robert   217, 218
Sophocles
   Antigone   47
   Oedipus Rex   219
Spenser, Edmund   68
   Faerie Queene   70
Speroni, Sperone   9, 134, 135, 138, 139 n.13, 184
   Canace   140, 143, 239 n.42
   on Dante quarrel   140–52
   Dialogo della istoria   143, 151
   Dialogo delle lingue   142
   second *Discorso sopra Dante*   137, 140, 151
Spingarn, Joel Elias   2, 7, 65, 72 n.49, 74 n.58, 75, 76–8, 80, 86–9, 158, 205
   conception of 'modern classicism'   78, 85
   Critical Essays of the Seventeenth Century   79
   History of Literary Criticism in the Renaissance, A   50, 51, 64, 72, 78, 79, 81, 88
   medal and involvement with NAACP   51 n.57
   'New Criticism, The'   51, 78, 79
   'Origins of Modern Criticism, The'   77
Stearns, Carol and Peter   202
Steiner, George   231
Stephens, Walter   182 n.3
Stewart, Susan   233 n.20
Stock, Brian   204
   textual community   204
Strozzi, Carlo   104, 129
Strozzi, Ciriaco   237
Strozzi, Filippo   114
Strozzi, Giovanni Battista   32, 99–100, 105, 107–9, 111–15, 122, 124, 128, 231. *See also* Accademia degli Alterati

and comments on *Aristotelis Poetica Petro Victorio Interprete* 99, 101–4, 108, 110
Strozzi, Luigi di Carlo 103, 129
Strozzi manuscripts 32
Studio Fiorentino 98, 99
Stump, Donald 69 n.36
Summo, Faustino 28
Sweeting, Elizabeth J. 81 n.94
Symonds, John Addington 73

Tasso, Torquato 4, 5, 10, 125, 135, 159, 169 n.36, 171, 184, 202, 217, 220
  Aminta 198
  Apologia della Gerusalemme liberata 159, 186, 189
  Castelvetro's impact on 215–16
  Discorsi dell'arte poetica 170, 175, 245
  Discorsi del poema eroico 215, 216
  Gerusalemme Conquistata 10, 182, 196, 197, 198
  Gerusalemme Liberata 9, 10, 157, 158, 169, 181, 196, 197, 220, 240
    defence of (*see* Lombardelli, Orazio)
  Giudizio 197
  pellegrinità aesthetic of *See* pellegrinità
  Re Torrismondo 215
  Tasso–Ariosto quarrel 136 n.7, 157, 162, 169, 170, 182–7, 190–2, 228, 237–240 (see also Giacomini, Lorenzo; Pellegrino, Camillo; Salviati, Lionardo)
  viewed as Homer's successor by Lombardelli 174–5
Tedeschi, John 31 n.29, 32
Temple, William 79
Terence 164, 165
Terry, Richard 61
Thompson, Guy Andrew 81 n.94
Tolomei, Claudio 149 n.45
Tomasi, Franco 138 n.12
Tomitano, Bernardino 9, 149
  Ragionamenti 138, 139
Trabalza, Ciro 2, 81
tragedy 111, 112, 183 n.6, 187, 201, 207, 214, 216–17, 219
  meraviglia as goal of 120
  pleasure as goal of 118–19
  political effects of 220–1

tragic purgation. *See* catharsis (*catarsi*)
Trissino, Gian Giorgio 2 n.8, 228
trivium 40, 43, 45, 53, 55, 230–1
Tuscan 10, 142 n.23, 182, 183, 185, 191–2
Tylus, Jane 10, 216 n.60

Vahlen, Johannes 48 n.46
Valeriano, Pierio 149 n.45
Valla, Giorgio 75
Valla, Lorenzo 159, 230
Vallone, Aldo 135 n.3
Van der Laan, Sarah 163 n.13
Van Deusen, Marshall 51 n.57, 72 n.49
Varchi, Benedetto 138, 142
Varro, Marcus Terentius 26
Vaughan, C. E. 71 n.46, 77
Veen, Henk van 107 n.7
Venuti, Lawrence 236
verisimilitude (*verosimile*) 3, 75, 146, 165, 169–71, 173, 212, 214, 215
  and marvel compared 170–1
'Vernacular Aristotelianism in Renaissance Italy' 5, 206, 237 n.34
versification 68, 71 n.46
Vescovo, Piermario 150 n.46
Vettori, Piero 25–7, 98–100, 105, 109, 111, 113
  Trattato di Piero Vettori delle lodi, et della coltiuatione degl'vliui 27
  Aristotelis Poetica Petro Victorio Interprete 99–101
Vianello, Valerio 138 n.12, 139 n.13
Vickers, Brian 54
  English Renaissance Literary Criticism 85
Vida, Marco Girolamo 2 n.8, 66
Viola, Corrado 105 n.4
Viperano, Giovanni Antonio 82
Virgil (Vergil) 165, 174, 228
  Aeneid 166–7, 190
  Eclogues 168
Vitale, Maurizio 189 n.25

Wadsworth, P. A. 31 n.29
Walker, Jeffrey 45 n.28
  Rhetoric and Poetics in Antiquity 54
Warton, Joseph 66, 69
Webbe, William
  Arts of English Poetry 66
Weber, Max 203

Weinberg, Bernard   2 n.8, 3, 13, 19,
    107 n.7, 158 n.4, 190 n.28,
    192 n.33, 236 n.31, 237 n.33
  on allegory   81–2
  Chicago collections of   30–5
  and Chicago School   19–22
  early modern books in library of
    252–86
  French interests of   29–30
  'From Aristotle to Pseudo-Aristotle'
    40, 45
  and Hans Baron   5, 7, 19, 26–31, 35
  *History of Literary Criticism in the
    Italian Renaissance, A*   2, 5, 7,
    20, 21, 22, 26–8, 33, 35, 40, 52,
    54, 81, 98, 121, 133, 134, 139,
    140, 182, 183, 198, 228
  letter to John Tedeschi   33
  *Trattati di poetica e retorica del
    Cinquecento*   2, 7, 22, 30, 83,
    106 n.6, 229, 233

Weise, George   186 n.13, 188
Wellek, René   61, 81 n.94
  History of Modern Criticism   64
Williams, Raymond   62
Wilson, John   71
  Specimens of the British Critics   68
Wimsatt, William K. and Cleanth Brooks
  Literary Criticism: A Short History
    52, 64
Winter, Robert   160
Wolfe, Jessica   157 n.1, 163 n.15, 165,
    166 n.25, 171 n.42
Woodberry, George   51 n.57
Wordsworth, William   71
Wylie, Laura Johnson   71, 77
  *Studies in the Evolution of
    English Criticism*   70

Zadorojnyi, Alexei   233 n.19
Zanin, Enrica   1 n.3, 207 n.27
Zoppio, Girolamo   134

www.ingramcontent.com/pod-product-compliance
Lightning Source LLC
Chambersburg PA
CBHW070017010526
44117CB00011B/1610